THE BEST TEST PREPARATION

GRE

GRADUATE

RECORD

EXAMINATION

HISTORY

Niles R. Holt, Ph.D.
Professor of History
Illinois State University
Normal, Illinois

Gary Piggrem, Ph.D.
Professor of History
DeVry Institute of Technology
Columbus, Ohio

William T. Walker, Ph.D.
Associate Professor and Chair, Humanities
Philadelphia College of Pharmacy & Science
Philadelphia, Pennsylvania

Steven E. Woodworth, Ph.D.
Assistant Professor of History
Toccoa Falls College
Toccoa, Georgia

Research and Education Association
61 Ethel Road West
Piscataway, New Jersey 08854

The Best Test Preparation for the
GRADUATE RECORD EXAMINATION
(GRE) IN HISTORY

Printed in the United States of America

Library of Congress Catalog Card Number 95-71574

International Standard Book Number 0-87891-885-X

Research & Education Association
61 Ethel Road West
Piscataway, New Jersey 08854

REA supports the effort to conserve and
protect environmental resources by
printing on recycled papers.

Contents

THREE PRACTICE GRE HISTORY TESTS.....................475

About Research and Education Association

Research and Education Association is an organization of educators, scientists, and engineers who specialize in various academic fields. REA was founded in 1959 for the purpose of disseminating the most recently developed scientific information into groups in industry, government, and universities. Since then, REA has become a successful and highly respected publisher of study aids, test preps, handbooks, career guides, and reference works.

REA's Test Preparation Series extensively prepares students and professionals for the Graduate Record Admission Test (GRE), the Graduate Management Admission Test (GMAT), The Test of English as a Foreign Language (TOEFL), the Law School Admission Test (LSAT), as well as the Scholastic Aptitude Test (SAT), and the Advanced Placement Exams.

Whereas most test preparation books present a few practice exams which bear little resemblance to actual exams, REA's test preparation books usually present up to six or more exams which accurately depict the official tests in degree of difficulty and types of questions. REA's practice exams are always based on the most recently administered tests, and include every type of question that can be expected on the actual tests.

REA's publications and educational materials are highly regarded for their significant contribution to the quest for excellence that characterizes today's educational goals. We continually receive an unprecedented amount of praise from professionals, instructors, librarians, parents, and students for our books. Our authors are as diverse as the subjects and fields represented in the books we publish. They are well-known in their respective fields and serve on the faculties of prestigious universities throughout the United States.

Acknowledgments

In addition to our authors we would like to thank the following persons for their special insight and editorial contributions: Lauren Coleman-Lochner, Alec Mento, Timothy Nolan, and Barbara Stephenson.

About the Book

This book provides an accurate and complete representation of the Graduate Record Examination in History. The three practice exams and subjects in the comprehensive U.S. and European History Reviews are based on the most recently administered GRE History Examinations. Each of the three practice tests are two hours and 50 minutes in length, and contain questions based on the most recent GRE History. An answer key is provided at the end of each test along with detailed explanations which explain why the given answer is correct and the other choices are wrong. Scoring information is provided on pages viii and ix in order to help convert your raw score to the scaled score. Extensive reviews of both European and U.S. history will aid in the preparation process. Taking the tests under timed conditions, paying careful attention to answer explanations, and studying the review chapters can effectively assess and improve your performance on the GRE History.

About the Test

The GRE History is taken by college graduates applying to graduate school to study history. The questions on the test draw on material covered in the undergraduate study of history. The test is written and designed by the Education Testing Service under the direction of the Graduate Record Examination Board, an organization which is separate from ETS and affiliated with the Association of Graduate Schools and the Council of Graduate Schools. While it would be impossible for any test to evaluate all the information available in all undergraduate history curricula, this exam is designed to measure the basic knowledge necessary for successful graduate study as determined by the Graduate Record Board, and serves both institution and students alike as an indicator for the capability and calibre of future graduate work.

The test questions are usually comprised of 60% European history and 40% United States history, and may also include required historical knowledge of other countries such as Asia, Latin America, and Africa. There are approximately 190 to 195 questions, for which you are given 170 minutes. There is only one section to the test, though questions may be put into subgroups based on a narrative, chart, drawing, graph, or cartoon. While recall of factual knowledge is necessary, the test is geared to assess your ability to use knowledge gained during your undergraduate study to follow and analyze relationships throughout history as presented on the exam.

The U.S. and European history questions are divided into categories including intellectual, social, economic, cultural, political, and diplomatic histories. These categories may be combined or tested individually in light of ancient, modern, or contemporary events. Most of the emphasis is placed on the diplomatic and political categories, while the economic and social history categories carry the least weight. The chronological breakdown is as follows:

I. European History:

1) Early History (Ancient to 1800) **(45%)**

2) Later History (1800 through the 20th Century) **(55%)**

II. United States History:

1) Exploration and Colonial (25%)

2) Nineteenth Century (45%)

3) Twentieth Century (30%)

About the Authors

The questions on the practice tests were written by authors who are well respected as educators of history. They all hold doctorates in history, and are highly regarded in colleges and universities throughout the United States. Each author has devoted considerable time and research to study the test format and style in order to provide practice questions which represent the actual GRE History. In-depth explanations discuss the facts and reasoning behind each answer choice, and help you learn what the Graduate Record Board expects from examinees.

About the Review

This book contains a comprehensive review of European and United States history, from the Ancient to the Modern World. Important figures, movements, and events are highlighted and explained, along with major literary, religious, and artistic works. The review is organized chronologically, starting with Mesopotamia and continuing onward, allowing you to follow historic themes and movements on a grand scale. The topics featured in the review cover material from undergraduate history study and the basic information needed to answer the questions on the GRE History.

Scoring the Exam

There are three scores for the GRE History: one European History raw subscore, one U.S. History raw subscore, and one combined raw score that covers all the questions. The raw score is converted into a scaled score which is based on the performance of the pool of applicants who took the test. This book presents scoring information on the total combined raw and scaled score. The chart on page ix helps to convert your response ratio into the appropriate scores.

The raw score is based on the number of correct answers; unanswered questions are not counted. Incorrect answers are worth 1/4 point. Use the following formula to compute your raw score:

RIGHT answers – WRONG answers/4 = Raw Score

(round off if necessary)

First, count the number of incorrect answers (WRONG) and divide this number by four (do not round the result). Subtract the quotient from the number of correct answers (RIGHT). Take this last result and round it to the nearest whole number, which will be your raw score.

The chart on the next page provides a conversion between possible raw scores and the corresponding scaled scores. Be aware that on the actual exam, scoring ranges vary from test to test.

TOTAL SCORE

Raw Score	Scaled Score	%	Raw Score	Scaled Score	%
190	800	99			
			62–65	490	40
185–189	790	99	58–61	480	35
181–184	780	99	54–57	470	30
177–180	770	99	50–53	460	26
173–176	760	99	46–49	450	21
169–172	750	99	42–45	440	17
165–168	740	99	38–41	430	14
161–164	730	99	34–37	420	11
157–160	720	99	30–33	410	8
153–156	710	99	25–29	400	6
149–152	700	99			
			21–24	390	4
144–148	690	98	17–20	380	2
140–143	680	98	13–16	370	1
136–139	670	97	9–12	360	1
132–135	660	96	5–8	350	0
128–131	650	95	1–4	340	0
124–127	640	94	0	330	0
120–123	630	92			
116–119	620	90			
112–115	610	88			
108–111	600	86			
103–107	590	83			
99–102	580	80			
95–98	570	77			
91–94	560	73			
87–90	550	69			
83–86	540	65			
79–82	530	60			
75–78	520	55			
71–74	510	50			
66–70	500	46			

1 THE ANCIENT AND MEDIEVAL WORLDS

THE APPEARANCE OF CIVILIZATION

The earliest civilizations appeared in the Near East between 4000 and 3000 B.C. Between 6000 and 3000 B.C., humans invented the plow, utilized the wheel, harnessed the wind, discovered how to smelt copper ores, and began to develop accurate solar calendars. Small villages gradually grew into populous cities. The invention of writing in 3500 B.C. in Mesopotamia marks the beginning of civilization and divides prehistoric and historic times.

Arnold Toynbee, the late British historian, believed that civilization rose out of a series of challenges—both natural and manmade—that provoked responses which either advanced or retarded a civilization.

MESOPOTAMIA

Sumer (4000 to 2000 B.C.) included the city of Ur. The *Gilgamesh* is an epic Sumerian poem. The Sumerians constructed dikes and reservoirs and established a loose confederation of city-states. They probably invented writing (called cuneiform because of its wedge-shaped letters). The Akkadians (2300 to 2200 B.C.) conquered Sumer and eventually merged with that culture. The Amorites, or Old Babylonians (2000 to 1550 B.C.), established a new capital at Babylon, known for its famous Hanging Gardens. King Hammurabi (reigned 1792–1750 B.C.) promulgated a legal code which unified the entire lower Tigris-Euphrates Valley. It called for retributive punishment ("an eye for an eye") and provided that one's social class determined punishment for a crime.

The Assyrians (1100–612 B.C.) conquered Syria, Palestine, and much of Mesopotamia. They controlled a brutal, militaristic empire. The Chaldeans, or New Babylonians (612–538 B.C.), conquered the Assyrian territory, including Jerusalem. In 587 B.C., King Nebuchadnezzar (reigned ca. 605–562 B.C.) ordered the Temple of Solomon destroyed and the Jews brought to Babylon as slaves. In 538 B.C., Cyrus, king of the southern Persians, defeated the Chaldeans. The Persians created a huge empire and constructed a road network. Their religion, Zoroastrianism, conceived of the universe in dualistic terms, with warrings gods of good and evil. After 538 B.C., Mesopotamia, which had no natural boundaries, was absorbed into other empires.

EGYPT

Egypt's history is divided into seven periods. During the end of the Archaic Period (5000–2685 B.C.), Menes, or Narmer, probably unified Upper and Lower Egypt around 3200 B.C. During the Old Kingdom (2685–2180 B.C.), the pharaohs came to be considered living gods. The capital moved to Memphis during the

Third Dynasty (ca. 2650 B.C.). The pyramids were built during the Fourth Dynasty (ca. 2613–2494 B.C.).

During the First Intermediate Period (2180–2040 B.C.), power reverted to regional authorities. The Middle Kingdom (2040–1785 B.C.) was one of brilliance. It was ended by the invasion of the Hyskos (Second Intermediate Period, 1785–1560 B.C.), who brought horses, chariots, and body armor to Egypt. The cult of Osiris was popular in this period. Osiris's resurrection promised the possibility of an afterlife, and funerary paintings show souls being judged on how much good or evil they had done.

The New Kingdom (1560–1085 B.C.) expanded into Nubia and invaded Palestine and Syria, enslaving the Jews. King Amenhotep IV or Akhenaton (reigned ca. 1364–1347 B.C.) promulgated the idea of a single god, Aton, and closed other temples. He instructed his people to worship Aton through himself as a living god. His successor, Tutankhamen, returned to pantheism.

In the Post-Empire Period (1085–1030 B.C.), Egypt came under the successive control of the Assyrians, the Persians, Alexander the Great, and finally, in 30 B.C., the Roman Empire. The Egyptians developed papyrus and made many medical advances. Other peoples would develop their ideas of monotheism and the notion of an afterlife.

PALESTINE

Phoenicians settled along the present-day Lebanon coast (Sidon, Tyre, Beirut, Byblos) and established colonies at Carthage and in Spain. They spread Mesopotamian culture through their trade networks. The Aramaeans lived in present-day Syria, with their capital at Damascus. Christ, like others of his day in Palestine, spoke Aramaic.

The Hebrews

Abraham, father of the Hebrews, left Ur sometime between 2000 and 1700 B.C. His grandson, Jacob, led the tribes into Palestine. The Hebrews probably moved to Egypt around 1700 B.C. and were enslaved about 1500 B.C. The Hebrews fled Egypt under Moses and around 1200 B.C. returned to Palestine. A loose confederation of 12 tribes, the Hebrews fought the Canaanites and Philistines for control of Palestine. Under King David (reigned ca. 1012–972 B.C.), the Philistines were defeated and a capital established at Jerusalem. Solomon (reigned ca. 972-932 B.C.) built huge public works projects. The tribes broke apart after his death, and Palestine divided into Israel (10 tribes) and Judah (two tribes). The 10 tribes of Israel (Lost Tribes) disappeared after Assyria conquered Israel in 722 B.C.

The poor and less attractive state of Judah continued until 586 B.C., when the Chaldeans transported the Jews to Babylon as advisors and slaves (Babylonian captivity). There they preserved their faith and even converted King Nebuchadnezzar (Book of Daniel). When the Persians conquered Babylon in 539 B.C., the Jews were allowed to return to Palestine and they were tolerated by King Cyrus. Alexander the Great conquered Palestine in 325 B.C. During the Hellenistic period (323–63 B.C.)

the Jews were allowed to govern themselves. The Romans restricted Jewish autonomy. The Jews revolted in 70 A.D. The Romans quashed the revolt and ordered the dispersion of the Jews. Under the Romans, the Jews were divided into several different sects. The Jews contributed the ideas of monotheism and humankind's convenant and responsibility to God to lead ethical lives.

GREECE

The Minoans (2600–1250 B.C.) lived on Crete. They established a vast overseas trading network and developed several written languages. Heinrich Schliemann, an amateur German archaeologist, discovered the site of ancient Troy in the late 19th century, and in 1900, Arthur Evans, an English archaeologist, discovered the Minoan capital of Knossos.

The Myceneans migrated to the Peloponnesian Peninsula before 2000 B.C. Their civilization peaked around 1400–1230 B.C. The Dorian invasion helped spark the Greek Dark Ages (1200–750 B.C.). Writing was reinvented in the 8th century.

Homer's *Iliad* and *Odyssey* featured individuals on a quest for personal excellence (arete). Hesiod's *Works and Days* summarized everyday life. His *Theogony* recounted Greek myths. Greek religion was based on their writings.

The Archaic Period (800–500 B.C.)

Greek life was organized around the polis (city-state). Oligarchs controlled most of the poleis until the end of the 6th century, when individuals holding absolute power (tyrants) replaced them. By the end of the 6th century, democratic governments replaced many tyrants.

Sparta

Sparta, however, developed into an armed camp. Sparta seized control of neighboring Messenia around 750 B.C. In 650 B.C., the Spartans crushed a revolt and enslaved the Messenians, who outnumbered them 10 to one. To prevent future rebellions, every Spartan entered lifetime military service (as hoplites) at age 7. Around 640 B.C., Lycurgus promulgated a constitution. Around 540 B.C., Sparta organized the Peloponnesian League.

Athens

Athens was the principal city of Attica. Between 1000 and 700 B.C., it was governed by monarchs (legendary kings such as Perseus and Theseus). In the 8th century, an oligarchy replaced the monarchy. Draco (ca. 621 B.C.) first codified Athenian law. His Draconian Code was known for its harshness. Solon (ca. 630–560 B.C.) reformed the laws in 594 B.C. He enfranchised the lower classes and gave the state responsibility for administering justice. The Athenian governing body was the Council of Areopagus, from which were selected archons (leaders). Growing indebtedness of small farmers and insufficient land strengthened the nobles. Peisistratus (ca. 605–527 B.C.) seized control and governed as a tyrant. In 527 B.C.,

Cleisthenes led a reform movement that established the basis of Athens's democratic government, including an annual assembly to identify and exile those considered dangerous to the state.

THE FIFTH CENTURY (CLASSICAL AGE)

This was the high point of Greek civilization. It opened with the Persian War. At Marathon (490 B.C.), the Athenians defeated Darius I's (reigned 522–486 B.C.) army. Ten years later, Darius's son Xerxes (reigned 486–465 B.C.) returned to Greece with 250,000 soldiers. The Persians burned Athens, but their fleet was defeated at the Battle of Salamis (480 B.C.) and they retreated.

After the Persian War, Athens organized the Delian League. Pericles (ca. 495–429 B.C.) used League money to rebuild Athens, including construction of the Parthenon and other Acropolis buildings. Athens's dominance spurred war with Sparta.

The Peloponnesian War between Athens and Sparta (431–404 B.C.) ended with Athens's defeat, but weakened Sparta as well. Sparta fell victim to Thebes, and the other city-states warred amongst themselves until Alexander the Great's conquest.

Culture

The Greeks pioneered a rational study of the universe (cosmology), while the Milesians sought a rational, materialistic explanation for things. The Pythagoreans searched for the key to the universe in geometric forms and numbers and pioneered the study of metaphysics.

A revolution in philosophy occurred in classical Athens. The Sophists emphasized the individual and his attainment of excellence through rhetoric, grammar, music, and mathematics. Socrates (ca. 470–399 B.C.) criticized the Sophists' emphasis on rhetoric and emphasized a process of questioning, or dialogues, with his students. Like Socrates, Plato (ca. 428–348 B.C.) emphasized ethics. His *Theory of Ideas or Forms* said that what we see is but a dim shadow of the eternal Forms or Ideas. Philosophy should seek to penetrate to the real nature of things. Plato's *Republic* described an ideal state ruled by a philosopher king.

Aristotle (ca. 384–322 B.C.) was Plato's pupil. He criticized Plato, arguing that ideas or forms did not exist outside of things. He contended that it was necessary to examine four factors in treating any object: its matter, its form, its cause of origin, and its end or purpose. Aristotle tutored Alexander the Great and later opened a school, the Lyceum, near Athens.

Greek art emphasized the individual. In architecture, the Greeks developed the Doric and Ionian forms. In poetry, Sappho (ca. 610–ca. 580 B.C.) and Pindar (ca. 522–438 B.C.) wrote lyric poems. In tragedy, Aeschylus (525–456 B.C.) examined the problem of hubris, most notably in his *Orestia* trilogy: *Agamemnon, The Libation Bearers,* and *The Eumenides.* Sophocles (ca. 496–406 B.C.) used irony to explore the fate of Oedipus in *Oedipus Rex.*

Euripides (484–406 B.C.) is often considered the most modern tragedian because he was so psychologically minded. In comedy, Aristophanes (ca. 450–388 B.C.) was a pioneer who used political themes. The New Comedy, exemplified by Menander (ca. 342–292 B.C.), concentrated on domestic and individual themes.

The Greeks were the first to develop the study of history. They were skeptical and critical and banished myth from their works. Herodotus (ca. 484–424 B.C.), called the "father of history," wrote *History of the Persian War*. Thucydides (ca. 460–400 B.C.) wrote *History of the Peloponnesian War*. The Greeks pioneered the studies of metaphysics, ethics, politics, rhetoric, and cosmology.

THE HELLENISTIC AGE

Macedonia

The Macedonians were a Greek people who were considered semibarbaric by their southern Greek relatives. They never developed a city-state system and had more territory and people than any of the poleis.

In 359 B.C. Philip II (382–336 B.C.) became king. To finance his state and secure a seaport, he conquered several city-states. In 338 B.C., Athens fell. In 336 B.C., Philip was assassinated.

Philip's son, Alexander the Great (356–323 B.C.) killed or exiled rival claimants to his father's throne. He established an empire that included Syria and Persia and extended to the Indus River Valley. His troops threatened to mutiny in 325 B.C. So he would not have to depend on the questionable loyalty of his Macedonian troops, Alexander married a Persian princess and ordered 80 of his generals to do likewise. At the time of his death, Alexander had established 70 cities and created a vast trading network.

With no succession plan, Alexander's realm was divided among three of his generals. Seleucus I established a dynasty in Persia, Mesopotamia, and Syria; Ptolemy I controlled Egypt, Palestine, and Phoenicia; and Lysimachus governed Asia Minor and Macedonia. Several Greek poleis rebelled against Macedonia and formed the Achaean and Aetolian leagues, the closest the Greeks ever came to national unity until modern times. By 30 B.C., all of the successor states had fallen to Rome.

Society and Culture

The Hellenistic Age saw inflation in Europe caused by an influx of Persian gold and a growing gap between rich and poor.

Alexandria's famous library and museum, created in the early 3rd century, sponsored scientists and inventors, and eventually held more than 300,000 papyrus scrolls.

In literature, Appolonius Rhodius wrote the *Agonautica* (ca. 295 B.C.) and Menander authored his comedies. Polybius wrote a history of the rise of Rome, based on eyewitness accounts and carefully checked sources.

Epicureanism and Stoicism were the main philosophical trends. Epicurus (ca. 341–270 B.C.) based his metaphysics on Democritus's atomic theory. He argued that people should eschew public affairs and concentrate on attaining individual happiness. Epicurus thought the greatest pleasure was found in contemplation. Zeno (ca. 335–263 B.C.) founded the Stoic school, which also emphasized the individual's importance. Zeno taught that the universe was a unified whole based on a universal order (logos, or fire). Each individual carried a spark of this logos in his reason, and at death, the spark returned to its origin. Individuals should strive to discover and abide by the natural laws of the universe.

Skeptics attacked the Epicureans and Stoics. Carneades of Cyrene (ca. 213–129 B.C.) argued that nothing could be known for certain, and that all sensory impressions were flawed, so one must doubt everything. Diogenes of Sinope (d. ca. 323 B.C.) was the most famous cynic. His goal was to prepare the individual for any disaster.

The scientific and technological accomplishments of the Hellenistic Age were not equaled until the scientific revolution of the 17th century. Euclid's (ca. 310–230 B.C.) *Elements of Geometry* provided the essentials of plane and solid geometry. Ptolemy (2nd century A.D.) systematized astronomy in his *Almagest,* which served as the basis of astronomy until the 16th century.

Archimedes (ca. 276–194 B.C.) pioneered the study of geography and devised the system of longitude and latitude. In medicine, the Dogmatic school used speculation to guide research. Galen's (129–199 A.D.) theories influenced medical practice until modern times.

Erasthosthenes (ca. 287–212 B.C.) discovered the principle of the lever, pulley, and screw, and calculated pi.

In religion, the Egyptian cult of Isis, the cult of Serapis (a hybrid of Greek and Egyptian myth), and Mithraism (a variation of Zoroastrianism) won many followers. The Hebrew Scriptures were translated into Greek.

ROME

The traditional founding date for Rome is 753 B.C. Between 800 and 500 B.C., Greek tribes colonized southern Italy, bringing their alphabet and religious practices to Roman tribes. In the 6th and 7th centuries, the Etruscans expanded southward and conquered Rome.

Late in the 6th century (the traditional date is 509 B.C.), the Romans expelled the Etruscans and established an aristocratically based republic in place of the monarchy (the rebellion was supposedly marked by the rape of Lucretia, a Roman matron, by an Etruscan).

In the early Republic, power was in the hands of the patricians (wealthy landowners). A Senate composed of patricians governed. The Senate elected two consuls to serve one-year terms. Roman executives had great power (the imperium). They were assisted by two quaestors, who managed economic affairs. The consuls' actions were supposed to be approved by the Senate and then by the Assembly, which represented all the people, but in practice, consuls in early times had near-despotic power.

Society was governed by the patriarchal family and a system of clientelism in which a client was protected by his patron, or in his trust ("fides"). The plebians resented the patrician's advantages. In 494 B.C., they won the right to elect tribunes (from tribes) to represent plebians before the patrician magistrates. In 450 B.C., the Law of the Twelve Tablets codified the people's traditional rights. In 367 B.C., a plebian consul was elected. Finally, in 287 B.C., the plebian Assembly's acts were considered binding, and not subject to the Senate's veto.

Expansion Under the Republic (509–146 B.C.)

Between 509 and 264 B.C., Rome conquered Italy through a mixture of diplomatic skill and force. It then turned its attention to Carthage, a powerful trading outpost. In the three Punic Wars (264–146 B.C.), Rome defeated Carthage to gain control of the Mediterranean.

The First Punic war (264–241 B.C.) began when Carthage tried to dominate eastern Sicily. After Carthage's defeat, it relinquished its interest and paid war reparations to Rome. The Second Punic War (218–202 B.C.) saw Carthage try to expand into Spain. Carthage's general Hannibal (247–183 B.C.) led 26,000 troops and 60 elephants across the Alps into Italy. He defeated the Romans at Cannae in 216 B.C. The Roman Publicus Scipio (died ca. 211 B.C.) defeated Carthage in a series of battles in Italy and Africa. The final Roman victory, in the Battle of Zama (202 B.C.), led to Carthage's surrender in 201 B.C. Carthage was reduced to a minor state.

Macedonia allied with Carthage in the Third Punic war (149–146 B.C.). The Macedonians' defeat brought Greek slaves, culture, and artifacts into Rome. In 146 B.C., the Romans burned Carthage and salted the earth.

Collapse of the Republic (146–30 B.C.)

Rome's expansion and contact with Greek culture disrupted the traditional agrarian basis of life. Tiberius Gracchus (163–133 B.C.) and Gaius Gracchus (153–121 B.C.) led the People's Party (or *Populares*). They called for land reform and lower grain prices to help small farmers. They were opposed by the *Optimates* (best men). Tiberius was assassinated. Gaius continued his work, assisted by the *Equestrians*. After several years of struggle, Gaius committed suicide.

Power passed into the hands of military leaders for the next 80 years. General Marius (157–86 B.C.) defeated Rome's Germanic invaders. A revolt (the Social War) broke out in 90 B.C. Sulla (138–78 B.C.), Marius's successor, restored order by granting citizenship to those who could not meet property qualifications. During the 70s and 60s, Pompey (106–48 B.C.) and Julius Caesar (100–44 B.C.) emerged as the most powerful men. In 73 B.C., Spartacus led a slave rebellion, which General Crassus suppressed.

In the 60s, Caesar helped suppress Cataline, who had led a conspiracy in the Senate. In 60 B.C., Caesar convinced Pompey and Crassus (ca. 115–53 B.C.) to form the First Triumvirate. When Crassus died, Caesar and Pompey fought for leadership. In 49 B.C., Caesar crossed the Rubicon, the stream separating his province from Italy, and a civil war followed. In 47 B.C., the Senate proclaimed Caesar as dictator, and later named him consul for life. Brutus and Cassius believed that Caesar had destroyed the Republic. They formed a conspiracy, and on March 15, 44

B.C. (the Ides of March), Caesar was assassinated in the Roman Forum. His 18-year-old nephew and adopted son succeeded him.

Caesar reformed the tax code and eased burdens on debtors. He instituted the Julian calendar, in use until 1582. The Assembly under Caesar had little power.

In literature and philosophy, Plautus (254–184 B.C.) wrote Greek-style comedy. Terence, a slave (ca. 186–159 B.C.), wrote comedies in the tradition of Menander. Catullus (87–54 B.C.) was the most famous lyric poet. Lucretius's (ca. 94–54 B.C.) *Order of Things* described Epicurean atomic metaphysics, while arguing against the immortality of the soul. Cicero (106–43 B.C.), the great orator and stylist, defended the Stoic concept of natural law. His *Orations* described Roman life. Roman religion was family centered and more civic-minded than Greek religion.

THE ROMAN EMPIRE

Octavian (63 B.C.–14 A.D.), named as Caesar's heir, did not have enough power to control the state. He formed the Second Triumvirate in 43 B.C. with Mark Anthony (Caesar's lieutenant) and Lepidus, governor of the western provinces, to run the Republic and punish Caesar's assassins. Brutus's and Cassius's armies were defeated at Philippi in 42 B.C. The triumvirs divided the state, with Anthony getting Egypt and the east, Lepidus Africa, and Octavian Rome and the western provinces. Lepidus soon lost his position, and Octavian went to war with Anthony and Cleopatra, queen of Egypt. Octavian's army triumphed at Actium, in western Greece (31 B.C.), and Anthony and Cleopatra fled to Egypt, where they committed suicide (30 B.C.).

Octavian held absolute control while maintaining the appearance of a republic. When he offered to relinquish his power in 27 B.C., the Senate gave him a vote of confidence and a new title, "Augustus." Augustus ruled for 44 years (31 B.C.–14 A.D.) He introduced many reforms, including new coinage, new tax collection, fire and police protection, and land for settlers in the provinces.

Pax Romana (27 B.C.–180 A.D.)

The first two centuries of the Empire were a time of peace and prosperity. The four emperors of the Julio-Claudian dynasty (14–60 A.D.) followed Augustus. The line ended when Nero committed suicide in 68 A.D., causing a civil war. Vespasian triumphed in 69 A.D., beginning the Flavian dynasty. The Jews in Palestine revolted during his reign. In 70 A.D., the Romans destroyed the Jewish temple and dispersed them. In 73 A.D., the Zealots, a group of Jewish fighters, committed suicide at Masada rather than surrender.

The Flavian Dynasty ended when Nerva (reigned 96–98 A.D.) murdered Domitian (reigned 81–96 A.D.) in 96 A.D. However, Nerva is considered the first of the Five Good Emperors. He introduced a public assistance program for the needy. The others were Trajan (reigned 98–117 A.D.) Hadrian (reigned 117–138 A.D.), Antoninus Pius (reigned 138–161 A.D.), and Marcus Aurelius (reigned 161–180 A.D.). The empire was at its largest under Trajan.

THE ROMAN EMPIRE (265 - 44 B.C.)

Between 14 and 180 A.D., the Empire was prosperous. A road system was constructed throughout. Women gained new rights, and Hadrian forbade the execution of slaves, who had been brutally treated during the Republic.

Culture Under the Pax Romana

Between 27 B.C. and 180 A.D., Rome's greatest cultural achievements occurred. The period between 27 B.C. and 14 A.D. is called the **Augustan Age**. Vergil (70–19 B.C.) wrote the *Aeneid,* an account of Rome's rise. Horace (65–8 B.C.) wrote the lyric *Odes.* Ovid (43 B.C.–18 A.D.) published the *Ars Amatoria,* a guide to seduction, and the *Metamorphoses,* about Greek mythology. Livy (57 B.C.–17 A.D.) wrote a narrative history of Rome based on earlier accounts.

The **Silver Age** lasted from 14–180 A.D. Writings in this period were less optimistic. Seneca (5 B.C. to 65 A.D.) espoused Stoicism in his tragedies and satires. Juvenal (50–127 A.D.) wrote satire, Plutarch's (46–120 A.D.) *Parallel Lives* portrayed Greek and Roman leaders, and Tacitus (55–120 A.D.) criticized the follies of his era in his histories.

Stoicism was the dominant philosophy of the era. Epictetus (ca. 60–120 A.D.), a slave, and Emperor Marcus Aurelius were its chief exponents. In law, Rome made a lasting contribution. It distinguished three orders of law: civil law (jus civile), which applied to Rome's citizens, law of the people (jus gentium), which merged Roman law with the laws of other peoples of the Empire, and natural law (jus naturale), governed by reason.

In science, Ptolemy, an Egyptian, and Galen worked in the provinces. Pliny the Elder's (23–79 A.D.) *National History* was widely known in the Middle Ages. In architecture, the Colosseum and Pantheon were constructed. The Romans developed the use of concrete as a building material.

Mystery religions were popular, including the cult of Mithra (whose birthday was celebrated on December 25), who had come to Earth to save mankind from evil, and whose followers would receive eternal life.

The Crisis of the Third Century

Marcus Aurelius's decision to name his son Commodus as his successor (reigned 180–192 A.D.), rather than the most talented governor, provoked vicious infighting. Commodus was ultimately strangled. Three emperors governed in the next 10 years. Civil war was nearly endemic in the 3rd century. Between 235 and 284 A.D., 26 "barracks emperors" governed, taxing the population heavily to pay for the Empire's defense.

The anxiety was reflected in the culture. Plotinus (204–270 A.D.) founded Neoplatonism, an alternative to rational philosophy. He argued that everything was an emanation from God, with matter the final emanation. Each soul was part of God, and the individual could achieve a mystical knowledge of God.

Rome's frontiers were attacked constantly by barbarians. The Sassanians, a Persian dynasty, attacked Mesopotamia in 224 A.D., and took Emperor Valerian hostage in 259 A.D. By 250 A.D., the Germanic Goths had captured Rome's Balkan provinces. In the 4th century, the Huns under Attila (ca. 406–453) swept in from central Asia, driving the Visigoths and other Germanic tribes before them. In 378 A.D., the Visigoths defeated Emperor Valens in the Battle of Adrianople. In 410 A.D., the Visigoths under Alaric (ca. 370–410) looted Rome.

Emperors Diocletian (reigned 285–305 A.D.) and Constantine (reigned 306–337 A.D.) tried to stem Rome's decline. Diocletian divided the Empire into four parts and moved the capital to Nicomedia in Asia Minor. Constantine moved the capital to Constantinople.

Historians have pondered for centuries why Rome fell. The most famous, Edward Gibbon, proposed in the 18th century that the rise of Christianity was an important factor. Recent historians have argued that the important question is not why Rome fell, but why it persisted for as long as it did.

Christianity and the Ancient World

Jesus was born around 4 B.C., and began preaching and ministering to the poor and sick at the age of 30. The Gospels provide the fullest account of his life and teachings. Saul of Tarsus, or Paul (10–67 A.D.), transformed Christianity from a small sect of Jews who believed Jesus was the Messiah into a world religion. Paul, a Hellenized Jew, had a conversion experience in 35 A.D. Paul opposed Jesus's early followers, who, led by Jesus's brother, James, considered Christianity a part of Judaism and insisted that members be circumcised. Paul won followers through his missionary work. He also shifted the focus from the early followers' belief in Jesus's imminent return to concentrate on personal salvation. His *Epistles* (letters to Christian communities) laid the basis for the religion's organization and sacraments.

The Pax Romana allowed Christians to move freely through the Empire. In the

Age of Anxiety, many Romans felt confused and alienated, and thus drawn to the new religion. And unlike other mystery religions, Christianity included women. By the 1st century, the new religion had spread throughout the Empire. Generally, the Romans tolerated other religions, including Christianity, but there were short, sporadic persecutions, reaching an apex under Diocletian.

Around 312 A.D., Emperor Constantine converted to Christianity and ordered toleration in the Edict of Milan (ca. 313 A.D.). In 391 A.D., Emperor Theodosius I (reigned 371–395 A.D.) proclaimed Christianity as the Empire's official religion.

By the 2nd century, the church hierarchy had developed. Eventually, the Bishop of Rome came to have preeminence, based on the interpretation that Jesus had chosen Peter as his successor.

Doctrinal Disputes

Bishop Arius of Alexandria claimed that Jesus was a created being, thus eliminating the concept of the Trinity. The dispute over the so-called Arian Heresy threatened to destroy the Church. At the Council of Nicaea in 325 A.D., the Arian belief was declared heretical, and a statement of the articles of the Christian faith was proclaimed (Nicene Creed).

Monasticism

This movement arose as a way to prevent the debasement of Christianity. St. Basil (ca. 329–379 A.D.) established the guidelines for Eastern monasticism, St. Benedict (ca. 480–543 A.D.) for Western. Monasteries converted many barbarians and preserved classical learning.

The Christian World View

Tertullian (ca. 160–220 A.D.) attacked secular literature. St. Jerome (ca. 347–420 A.D.) translated the Hebrew Scriptures and Greek New Testament into Latin. His Bible is called the *Vulgate*. St. Ambrose (ca. 339–397 A.D.) asserted the Church's authority over temporal leaders.

St. Augustine (354–430 A.D.), a convert to Christianity, told of his struggle in his *Confessions*, and developed a Christian view of history in his *City of God*. He argued that all earthly things were doomed to sin and corruption, but that the City of God was eternal, and only through the Church could members enter it. He rejected reason in the quest for salvation and accepted the concept of predestination.

The Byzantine Empire

Emperor Theodosius II (reigned 408–450 A.D.) divided his empire between his sons, one ruling the East, the other the West. After the Vandals sacked Rome in 455 A.D., Constantinople was the undisputed leading city of the Empire. In 476 A.D., the Ostrogoth king, Odoacer, forced the last emperor in Rome, Romulus Augustulus (reigned 475–476 A.D.), to abdicate.

In 527 A.D., Justinian I (483–565 A.D.) became emperor in the East and reigned with his controversial wife Theodora until 565 A.D. The Nika revolt broke out in 532 A.D. and demolished the city. It was crushed by General Belisarius in

537 A.D., after 30,000 had died in the uprising. Justinian's campaigns to win back the western lands failed.

Justinian I exercised supreme political and religious power. This combination is known as caesaropapism, and no western leader possessed such absolute power. Under Justinian, the church of Santa Sofia was completed. His reign also produced the *Corpus Juris Civilis* (Body of Civil Laws), which centralized power and created an efficient bureaucracy. It also served as the model for most of the European legal systems after 1100 A.D.

Justinian spoke Latin and considered himself emperor of East and West. By 610 A.D., the emperors spoke Greek and had developed a "Byzantine," or Eastern, orientation. Heraclius (ca. 545–641 A.D.), governor of Carthage, seized control of the empire in 610 A.D. and divided Asia Minor into military districts. While Constantinople was under attack, Heraclius and his army defeated the Persians near Nineveh (628 A.D.).

The empire lost Syria and Palestine after defeat in the Battle of Yarmuk in 636 A.D., and by mid-century, it had lost its richest provinces to Islam. By 700 A.D., the empire was a fraction of its former size. Leo III (reigned 717–741 A.D.) pushed the Muslims out of Asia Minor, securing a 200-year respite from Arab invasion.

In 780 A.D., Constantine VI (reigned 780–797 A.D.) became emperor, but his mother, Irene (who had her henchmen blind her son), ruled as regent until 802 A.D., when she was deposed.

Under the Macedonian dynasty (867–1056 A.D.), the empire reclaimed lost lands. But in the 11th century, crisis was renewed. Nobles questioned the government's authority, and the Venetians seized many of the empire's trading posts. In 1054 A.D., the Great Schism with the Western Church occurred. In 1071 A.D., the Seljuk army defeated the Byzantines at Manazkert in eastern Anatolia, and the Normans drove them out of southern Italy and Sicily.

The Crusaders further weakened the state. In 1204 A.D., Venice contracted to transport the Crusaders to the Near East in return for the Crusaders capturing and looting Constantinople. The Byzantines were defeated in 1204 A.D. Though they drove out the Crusaders in 1261 A.D., the empire never regained its former power. In 1453 A.D., Constantinople fell to the Ottoman Turks.

Christianity in the Byzantine Empire

The Eastern Church faced a number of heresies, as well as conflict with the West. The most important heresies were Nestorianism, which claimed that Christ was more human than divine, and Monophysitism, which claimed that Christ was wholly divine. Though the Council of Chalcedon (451 A.D.) proclaimed Christ to be both human and divine, many continued to practice the heresies.

By the 8th century, the Bishop of Rome was aggressively asserting his preeminence over the other patriarchs (the bishops of Constantinople, Jerusalem, Antioch, and Alexandria).

Emperor Leo III (reigned 717-41 A.D.) banned the worship of icons in 730 A.D., spurring iconoclasts to smash images throughout the empire. The iconoclasts thought that worship of saints bordered on idolatry. This provoked conflict with the pope, who turned toward the Frankish king.

Icons were readmitted to the Eastern Church in the fourth century. The defeat of the iconoclasts caused the Eastern Church to adopt a conservative and traditional posture, and to develop a passive, mystical form of Christianity called contemplative piety.

The Great Schism

A controversy evolved in 867 A.D. from differing interpretations of the Nicene Creed (the Photian Schism). In 1054 A.D., the Orthodox patriarch and the pope excommunicated each other. This split endures today, with the Eastern Church unwilling to accept the primacy of the pope or the doctrine of the Virgin Mary's immaculate conception.

Byzantine Civilization

The economy was strong until the 11th-century decline of the free peasantry. In education, the East developed schools to train efficient administrators, preserved the Greek and Latin learning that was lost in the West, and educated its women. The most famous female intellectual was Anne Comnena, daughter of Emperor Alexis Comnenus (reigned 1081–1118 A.D.).

An important accomplishment was the conversion of the Slavs to Christianity. In the 9th century, St. Cyril and St. Methodius traveled to Bohemia and Moldavia, developing a new alphabet (Cyrillic) and translating the Bible. In 989 A.D., Emperor Basil II sent monks into Russia to convert the Slavs there.

Islamic Civilization in the Middle Ages

Mohammed was born about 570 A.D., and received a revelation from the Angel Gabriel around 610 A.D. In 630 A.D., Mohammed marched into Mecca. The Sharia (code of law and theology) outlines five pillars of faith for Muslims to observe. First is the belief that there is one God and that Mohammed is his prophet. The faithful must pray five times a day, perform charitable acts, fast from sunrise to sunset during the holy month of Ramadan, and make a haj, or pilgrimage, to Mecca. The Koran, which consists of 114 suras (verses), contains Mohammed's teachings. Mullahs (teachers) occupy positions of authority, but Islam did not develop a hierarchical system comparable to that of Christianity.

A leadership struggle developed after Mohammed's death. His father-in-law, Abu Bakr (573–634 A.D.), succeeded as caliph (successor to the prophet) and governed for two years, until his death in 634 A.D. Omar succeeded him. Between 634 and 642 A.D., Omar established the Islamic Empire. Khalid ibn-al-walid, called the Sword of Islam, defeated the Byzantines, gaining Jerusalem in 637 A.D. and the Persians in 643 A.D. He also claimed Egypt and much of North Africa.

The Omayyad caliphs, based in Damascus, governed from 661–750 A.D. They called themselves Shiites, and believed they were Mohammed's true successors. (Most Muslims were Sunnites, from "sunna," oral traditions about the prophet.) They conquered Spain by 730 A.D. and advanced into France until they were stopped by Charles Martel (ca. 688–741 A.D.) in 732 A.D. at Poitiers and Tours.

Muslim armies penetrated India and China. They transformed Damascus into a cultural center, and were exposed to Hellenistic culture from the nearby Byzantine Empire.

The Abbasid caliphs ruled from 750–1258 A.D. They moved the capital to Baghdad and treated Arab and non-Arab Muslims as equals. Islam assumed a more Persian character under their reign. Caliph Harun-al-Rashid (reigned 786–809 A.D.) is known for the collection of stories called the *Thousand and One Arabian Nights.* Al-Maman (reigned 813–833 A.D.) was a great patron of the arts and sciences. In the late 10th century, the empire began to disintegrate. In 1055 A.D., the Seljuk Turks captured Baghdad, allowing the Abbasids to rule as figureheads. Genghis Khan (ca. 1162–1227 A.D.) and his army invaded the Abbasids. In 1258 A.D., they seized Baghdad and murdered the last caliph.

Culture and Society

The prosperous Muslim society was built on commerce and industry. Arab merchants controlled the trade routes linking Asia, Africa, and Europe. Frequent dealings with infidels encouraged tolerance, and non-Muslims were allowed to pay a tax for the privilege of practicing their faiths. The Arabs further developed the Indian numeral system and laid the foundation for modern mathematics. The poet Omar Khayyám (ca. 1048–1122 A.D.), who wrote *The Rubaiyat,* pioneered the field of analytical geometry. Arab scientists also advanced in astronomy, optics, and geography. Their greatest contribution was in medicine, and they founded hospitals throughout the world.

Arab philosophers carried on the traditions of Aristotle and Plato, after knowledge of those philosophers' work had disappeared in the West. Averroes (1126–1198 A.D.) wrote a commentary on Aristotle's work that served as a guide for Western scholars.

In art and architecture, the Muslims used geometric designs and built with horseshoe arches, twisted columns, bulbous domes, and minarets.

EUROPE IN ANTIQUITY

Between 486 and 1050 A.D., Europe acquired a distinctive identity. In antiquity, much of Europe was occupied by Germanic tribes. The northern tribes became the Vikings and Norsemen. The eastern tribes (Vandals, Burgundians, and Goths) settled east of the Elbe River. The Saxons and Lombards dominated the western tribes. In Eastern Europe and Russia, the Slavs were the dominant group.

Nomadic tribes from the central Asian steppes invaded Europe and pushed Germanic tribes into conflict with the Roman Empire. The Huns invaded in the 4th century, and led by Attila (ca. 406–453 A.D.), again in the 5th. In 410 A.D., the Visigoths sacked Rome, followed by the Vandals in 455 A.D. In 476 A.D., the Ostrogoth king forced the boy emperor Romulus Augustulus to abdicate, ending the empire in the West.

INVASIONS OF EUROPE, 600 – 1000 C.E.

The Frankish Kingdom

The Frankish Kingdom was the most important medieval Germanic state. Under Clovis I (reigned 481–511 A.D.), the Franks finished conquering France and the Gauls in 486 A.D. Clovis converted to Christianity and founded the Merovingian dynasty. The Merovingian kings were known as the "do-nothing kings," and the palace mayors began to govern. Mayor Charles Martel defeated the Muslims at Poitiers in 732 A.D. Martel's son, Pepin III (reigned 751–768 A.D.), had the pope crown him king of the Franks in gratitude for his campaign against the Lombards.

Pepin's son Charles, known as Charles the Great or Charlemagne (reigned 768–814 A.D.), founded the Carolingian dynasty. He defeated the Lombards in northern Italy, declaring himself their king, and pushed the Muslims out of northern Spain. He converted the Saxons to Christianity, and helped put down a revolt of Roman nobles in 799 A.D. In 800 A.D., Pope Leo III named Charlemagne Emperor of the Holy Roman Empire. In the Treaty of Aix-la-Chapelle (812 A.D.), the Byzantine emperor recognized Charles's authority in the West.

The Holy Roman Empire was intended to reestablish the Roman Empire in the West. Charles vested authority in 200 counts, who were each in charge of a county. The royal court was at Aix-la-Chapelle (Aachen). Charles's son, Louis the Pious (reigned 814–840 A.D.), succeeded him. On Louis's death, his three sons vied for control of the Empire. After Louis II the German (ca. 804–876 A.D.), and Charles the Bald (823–877 A.D.) had sided against Lothair I (795–855 A.D.), the three eventually signed the Treaty of Verdun in 843 A.D. This gave Charles the Western Kingdom (France), Louis the Eastern Kingdom (Germany), and Lothair the Middle Kingdom, a narrow strip of land running from the North Sea to the Mediterranean.

In the 9th and 10th centuries, Europe was threatened by attacks from the Vikings in the north, the Muslims in the south, and the Magyars in the east. The Vikings occupied England, leaving only Wessex under control of the English king Alfred (reigned 871–899 A.D.). King Alfred fought back and drove the invaders into an area called the Danelaw for which he earned the name, "the Great." Viking invasions left France divided into small principalities. Danish Vikings seized control of Normandy and Brittany at the end of the 9th century. Under the leadership of William the Conqueror (reigned 1066–1087), the Normans conquered England in 1066 A.D. (Battle of Hastings).

The Saxon king Otto I stopped the Magyar advance in the east, and made the Saxons the most powerful group in Europe. In 962 A.D., Otto was crowned Holy Roman Emperor.

Economy in the Early Middle Ages

Rome's collapse ushered in the decline of cities, a reversion to a barter economy from a money economy, and a fall in agricultural productivity with a shift to subsistence agriculture.

Manorialism and feudalism developed in this period. Manorialism refers to the economic system in which large estates, granted by the king to nobles, strove for self-sufficiency. Large manors might incorporate several villages. The lands surrounding the villages were usually divided into long strips, with common land in-between. Ownership was divided among the lord and his serfs (also called villeins). The lord's property was called the demesne.

Feudalism describes the decentralized political system of personal ties and obligations that bound vassals to their lords. Serfs were peasants who were bound to the land. They worked on the demesne three or four days a week in return for the right to work their own land. In difficult times, the nobles were supposed to provide for the serfs.

The Church

The Church was the only institution to survive the Germanic invasions intact. The power of the popes grew in this period. Gregory I (reigned 590–604 A.D.) was the first member of a monastic order to rise to the papacy. He is considered one of the four Church Fathers (along with Jerome, Ambrose, and Augustine). He advanced the ideas of penance and purgatory. He centralized Church administration and was the first pope to rule as the secular head of Rome.

Increasing tension with the Eastern Church, and the increasing importance of the Germanic tribes, led the Church to discount the Byzantine emperor's claim as leader of the Roman Empire. In 756 A.D., the Donation of Pepin granted the pope control over the Vatican state. Pope Stephen II (reigned 752–757 A.D.) based his claim as temporal ruler on the forged Donation of Constantine, which asserted that the emperor had given the pope control of Rome and the western part of the empire.

In 816 A.D., Benedict of Aniane called for reform of the monasteries, which he believed had become too involved in secular affairs, and founded the Benedictine order. A century later, a new reform movement grew out of the monastery at Cluny, France. Individual monasteries were governed by priors, who were under the direction of a single abbot. Eventually, more than 1,500 monasteries were attached to Cluny.

Culture

Literacy nearly disappeared in Western Christendom during the early Middle Ages. Monasteries preserved the few remnants of antiquity that survived the decline. Outside the monasteries, the two most important literary works of the period were *Beowulf* (ca. 700 A.D.) and the Venerable Bede's (ca. 672–735 A.D.) *History of England.*

The Carolingian kings inspired a revival in learning in the 8th and 9th centuries (Carolingian Renaissance). Charlemagne employed the English monk Alcuin (ca. 732–804 A.D.) to found a number of schools to train administrators. Manuscript illumination was the chief artistic outlet of the period. In this period, science and technology came to a standstill in the West.

The High Middle Ages (1050–1300)

By 1050 A.D., Europe was poised to emerge from five centuries of decline. Inferior to the Muslim and Byzantine empires in 1050 A.D., by 1300 A.D., the Europeans had surpassed them. Between 1000 and 1350 A.D., the population grew from 38 million to 75 million. Agricultural productivity grew, aided by new technologies, such as heavy plows, and a slight temperature rise which produced a longer growing season. Horses were introduced into agriculture in this period, and the three-field system replaced the two-field system.

As new lands came into cultivation, nobles needed an incentive to get serfs to move to them. Enfranchisement, or freeing of serfs, grew in this period, and many other serfs simply fled their manors for the new lands. Enfranchisement progressed most rapidly in England, and most slowly in Russia and Eastern Europe.

The Clergy

Most villages had a church. The Cicestercian and Carthusian orders were founded in the late 11th century. In the early 13th century, St. Francis of Assisi (ca. 1181–1226 A.D.) founded the Franciscans, who worked among the poor and homeless in cities. The pope soon afterward founded the Dominican order to fight heresy.

The Nobles

The nobility grew more prosperous. During the 11th century, knights developed as a class of professional warriors. The code of chivalry, which demanded personal virtue in addition to proficiency as a warrior and horseman, developed.

Cities and Towns

The Roman road system, destroyed in the early Middle Ages, was rebuilt in this period. Cities and towns grew and guilds were established. In Italy, the economy had reverted from barter to hard currency by the 12th century.

The Holy Roman Empire

Charlemagne's grandson, Louis the German, became Holy Roman Emperor under the Treaty of Verdun. Under the weak leadership of his descendants, the dukes in Saxony, Franconia, Swabia, Bavaria, and the Lorraine eroded Carolingian power. The last Carolingian died in 911 A.D. The German dukes elected the leader of Franconia to lead the German lands. He was replaced in 919 A.D. by the Saxon dynasty, which ruled until 1024 A.D. Otto became Holy Roman Emperor in 962 A.D. His descendants governed the Empire until 1024 A.D., when the Franconian dynasty assumed power, reigning until 1125 A.D.

A dispute over lay investiture (in which monarchs chose the high church officials in their realm) between Pope Gregory VII (pope 1073–1085 A.D.) and Emperor Henry IV (reigned 1084–1105 A.D.) came to a head in 1077 A.D., when the pope forced Henry to beg forgiveness for appointing church leaders. In revenge, Henry captured Rome in 1083 A.D. and sent the pope into exile. However, in the Concordat of Worms (1122 A.D.), the emperor received the right to grant secular, but not religious, authority to German bishops.

When the Franconian line died out in 1125 A.D., the Hohenstaufen family (Conrad III, reigned 1138–1152 A.D.) won power over a contending family. Frederick I (Barbarossa) (1123–1190 A.D.) gained control of much of Italy. Frederick II (1194–1250 A.D.) was crowned Holy Roman Emperor in 1220 A.D., but warred with the pope. Charles of Anjou (1227–1285 A.D.), brother of Louis IX of France, and the pope executed the last Hohenstaufen in 1257 A.D. The Hapsburg line gained control of the Empire in 1273 A.D.

England

The Romans abandoned their last outpost in England in the 4th century. Around 450 A.D. (the time of the legendary King Arthur), the Jutes, Angles, and Saxons occupied different parts of the country. Danes began invading in the 8th century. Alfred the Great (ca. 849–899 A.D.) defeated the Danes in 878 A.D. In 959 A.D., Edgar the Peacable (reigned 959–975 A.D.) became the first king of all England. The Danes reinvaded in the 11th century, defeating Ethelred the Unready (reigned 978–1016 A.D.) in 1013 A.D., and forced the English to pay heavy tribute. Edward the Confessor ruled from 1042 to 1066 A.D. On his death, Harold of England (reigned 1066 A.D.) and William, the duke of Normandy, contended for the throne. William killed Harold at the Battle of Hastings and became king.

William (reigned 1066–1087 A.D.) stripped the Anglo-Saxon nobility of its privileges and instituted feudalism. He ordered a survey of all property of the realm, which was recorded in the Domesday Book (1086 A.D.). His descendants, William II (reigned 1087–1100 A.D.) and Henry I (reigned 1100–1135 A.D.), continued to centralize the kingdom. Henry created the Office of the Exchequer to monitor receipt of taxes.

Nineteen years of civil war followed Henry's death. In 1154 A.D., his grandson, Henry II, was crowned king, founding the Plantagenet dynasty. Henry inherited Brittany from his mother. His reign was controversial, marked by a power struggle with the pope (during which Henry had Thomas Becket murdered) and his sons' revolt. In 1189 A.D., Richard the Lionhearted (reigned 1189–1199 A.D.) succeeded his father. He spent most of his reign fighting in the Crusades.

John I (reigned 1199–1216 A.D.) became king upon his brother's death. In 1215 A.D., the English barons forced him to sign the Magna Carta Libertatum, acknowledging their "ancient" privileges. The Magna Carta established the principle of a limited English monarchy. Henry III reigned from 1216–1272 A.D. In 1272 A.D., Edward I became king. His need for revenue led him to convene a parliament of English nobles, which would act as a check upon royal power.

France and the Capetian Dynasty

Creation of a strong national monarchy was slower in France than in England. Hugh Capet founded the dynasty in 987 A.D., but it had little power until 1108 A.D., when Louis the Fat subdued the most powerful vassals. Louis's grandson, Philip Augustus (reigned 1180–1223 A.D.), defeated King John of England (Battle of Bouvines, 1214) to win large territories in western France. Philip's son, Louis VIII, conquered most of southern France during his prosperous three-year reign. His grandson, Philip IV (1285–1314 A.D.), involved France in several wars. Philip also summoned a parliament, the Estates General, but it did not develop into a counter-weight to royal power. In 1328 A.D., the Capetian dynasty ended with the death of Charles IV (reigned 1322–1328 A.D.). The succession sparked the Hundred Years' War between England and France.

Spain

In 710 A.D., the Muslims conquered Spain from the Visigoths. Under the Muslims, Spain enjoyed stable, prosperous government. The caliphate of Córdoba became a center of scientific and intellectual activity. Internal dissent caused the collapse of Córdoba and the division of Spain into more than 20 Muslim states in 1031 A.D.

The Reconquista (1085–1340 A.D.) wrested control from the Muslims. Rodrigo Diaz de Bivar, known as El Cid (ca. 1043–1099 A.D.) was the most famous of its knights. The small Christian states of Navarre, Aragon, Castile, and Portugal organized the Reconquista. Each had a *cortes*, an assembly of nobles, clergy, and townspeople. The fall of Córdoba in 1234 A.D. completed the Reconquista, except for the small state of Granada.

Eastern Europe and Russia

Most of this region was never under Rome's control, and it was cut off from Western influence by the Germanic invasions. Poland converted to Christianity in the 10th century, and after 1025 A.D. was dependent on the Holy Roman Empire. In the 12th and 13th centuries, powerful nobles divided control of the country. After 1226 A.D., the Teutonic Knights controlled most of Poland.

In Russia, Vladimir I converted to Orthodox Christianity in 988 A.D. He established the basis of Kievian Russia. After 1054 A.D., Russia broke into competing principalities. The Mongols (Tatars) invaded in 1221 A.D., completing their conquest in 1245 A.D., and cutting Russia's contact with the West for almost a century.

The Church in the High Middle Ages

The cult of the Virgin Mary eclipsed the veneration of individual saints. By the 11th century, the Church was the largest landowner in Europe. The doctrine of transubstantiation was advanced in the 12th century. Reformers in this period (including the Clunaics) wanted to end simony and establish clerical celibacy. The power of the papacy grew in this period. Pope Leo IX (1002–1054 A.D.) asserted the pope's preeminence over the other patriarchs, bringing on the schism with the Orthodox Church (1045 A.D.).

The pope tried to end the continuous warfare among Christian states by declaring the *Pax Dei* (Peace of God) in 1040 A.D. This proclamation banned fighting more than half the week and on holy days. It was ineffective.

The Crusades

The Crusades attempted to liberate the Holy Land from infidels. There were seven major crusades between 1096 and 1300 A.D. Urban II called Christians to the **First Crusade** (1096–1099 A.D.) with the promise of a plenary indulgence (exemption from punishment in purgatory). Younger sons who would not inherit their fathers' lands were also attracted. Between 5,000–10,000 knights and 25,000–50,000 infantry enlisted. Peter the Hermit persuaded 30,000 peasants to follow him to Jerusalem. These Crusaders robbed and massacred Jews as they passed through Germany and looted Christians in Bulgaria. They were defeated easily by the Seljuk Turks, with the survivors sold into slavery.

Several months later, the organized Crusaders reached the Holy Land, capturing Jerusalem in 1099 A.D. They established four feudal states: Edessa, Antioch, Tripoli, and Jerusalem. The success of the First Crusade sparked a movement of pilgrims to the Levant, and the organization of several religious and military orders to aid the pilgrims, including the Knights of St. John (Hospitalers), the Templars, and the **Teutonic Knights**. The **Second Crusade** (1147–49 A.D.) attempted to recapture Edessa, and failed.

In 1187 A.D., the Muslim leader Saladin captured Jerusalem, sparking the **Third Crusade**, which failed to dislodge the Muslims, though Richard the Lionhearted negotiated the right of Christian pilgrims to visit shrines in Jerusalem.

In the **Fourth Crusade** (1202–1204 A.D.), the Crusaders never reached the Holy Land. They had hired the Venetians to transport them to Jerusalem, in payment for which they agreed to loot Constantinople, which fell in 1204 A.D. The Crusaders then established the Latin kingdom of Constantinople, but it was recaptured by the Byzantine emperor's troops 57 years later.

In the **Fifth Crusade** (1228–1229 A.D.), Frederick II negotiated what the Crusaders could not win by force: control of Jerusalem and Nazareth. In the **Sixth Crusade** (1248–1254 A.D.), Louis IX tried unsuccessfully to capture Egypt. In 1270 A.D., Louis IX died outside of Tunis in the **Seventh Crusade**. In 1291 A.D., Acre, the last Christian enclave in the Holy Land, fell.

The Crusades helped to renew interest in the ancient world. But thousands of Jews and Muslims were massacred as a result of the Crusades, and relations between Europe and the Byzantine Empire collapsed.

Jews in Medieval Europe

Rome granted citizenship to Jews in 212 A.D., but the early Christian emperors issued a series of decrees which deprived Jews of full citizenship. The Church prohibited Christians from lending money at interest (usury), and Jews became the Holy Roman Empire's financial agents. The First Crusade opened a period of persecution of Jews, and the first pogrom took place in this period. Jews were accused of blasphemy and ritual murder. In 1215 A.D., the Fourth Lateran Council prohibited Jews from holding office, and mandated special clothes and special areas (ghettos) for them. In 1306 A.D., Jews were expelled from France. The Black Death in 1347 A.D. unleashed a wave of pogroms. Three hundred Jewish communities were destroyed in Germany alone. The persecution of Jews reached its height in Spain between 1391 and 1492 A.D., culminating in Torquemada's expulsion of the Jews from Spain in 1492 A.D.

Education

Charlemagne mandated that bishops open schools at each cathedral, and founded a school in his palace for his court. The expansion of trade and the need for clerks and officials who could read and write spurred an 1179 A.D. requirement that each cathedral set aside enough money to support one teacher. The first universities opened in Italy at Bologna (law) and Salerno, which became a center for medical studies.

Scholasticism

Scholasticism was an effort to reconcile reason and faith and to instruct Christians on how to make sense of the pagan tradition.

St. Anselm (1033–1109 A.D.) wrote that there was no conflict between man's spiritual and rational natures—both were gifts from God.

Peter Abelard (ca. 1079–1144 A.D.) was a controversial proponent of Scholasticism, both for his love affair with Heloise, niece of the canon of Notre Dame, and for his views. In *Sic et Non* (Yes and No), Abelard collected statements in the Bible and by Church leaders that contradicted each other. Abelard believed that reason could resolve the apparent contradictions between the two authorities, but the Church judged his views as heretical.

Thomas Aquinas (ca. 1225–1274 A.D.) believed that there were two orders of truth. The lower, reason, could demonstrate propositions such as the existence of God, but on a higher level, some of God's mysteries such as the nature of the Trinity must be accepted on faith. Aquinas viewed the universe as a great chain of being, with humans midway on the chain, between the material and the spiritual. Many critics, including the Bishop of Paris, attacked Aquinas for his dependence on Aristotle, claiming that he had Christianized Aristotle.

Albertus Magnus (ca. 1200–1280 A.D.) was Aquinas's teacher in Paris. Magnus tried to join Augustine to Aristotle. He advocated the use of empirical research, guided by observation and testing.

Robert Grosseteste (ca. 1175–1253 A.D.), the chancellor of Oxford University, was one of the first Europeans to translate works directly from the Greek.

Grosseteste was an Aristotelian who tried to demonstrate that the world was round. He performed experiments on the refraction of light and trained his students to ground their speculations in observation and experiment. One student, Roger Bacon (ca. 1220–1292 A.D.), eclipsed his teacher's fame. He stressed the importance of mathematics and argued that observation should guide reason. He anticipated the invention of the telescope. Men like Grosseteste and Bacon were not scientists in the modern sense. They never questioned Scholaticism's basic assumption that faith and reason were in harmony.

In law, Scholasticism spurred the development of legal studies in the 12th and 13th centuries. Until the 11th century, law in the West had consisted of the customs of various peoples. Irnerius (1088–1125 A.D.), a scholar at Bologna, introduced Justinian's *Corpus Juris Civilis* to the West, in an attempt to universalize legal studies.

In 1140 A.D., the monk Gratian published a *Concordance of Discordant Canons,* which collected contradictory papal and biblical statements. This was the beginning of the Church's struggle to reform canon law. Peter Lombard (ca. 1095–1160 A.D.), a student of Abelard, published the *Book of Sentences,* which used reason and faith to assess each contradictory statement.

Literature and Music

Latin was the language used in universities. Groups of satirical poets called Golliards also wrote in Latin. But the most vibrant works were in the vernacular. The *chansons de geste* were long epic poems composed between 1050 and 1150 A.D. Among the most famous are the *Song of Roland,* the *Song of the Nibelungs,* the Icelandic *Eddas,* and *El Cid.*

A tradition of lyric poetry developed in 12th-century southern France. The troubadours composed in Provençal, a language related to modern French. An analogous movement occurred in Germany.

Chrétien de Troyes (1165–1190 A.D.) helped create the genre of the romance. He wrote stories of the legendary King Arthur. The *Romance of the Rose* is the most famous medieval romance; it illustrates the growing secular tendency of the vernacular tradition.

The fabliaux were short stories, many of which ridiculed the clergy. Boccaccio (1313–1375 A.D.) and Chaucer (ca. 1342–1400 A.D.) belonged to this tradition. The work of Dante (1265–1321 A.D.), the greatest medieval poet, synthesized the pagan and Christian traditions.

In this period, polyphonic (more than one melody at a time) music was introduced. In architecture, Romanesque architecture (rounded arches, thick stone walls, tiny windows) flourished between 1000 and 1150 A.D. After 1150 A.D., Gothic architecture, which emphasized the use of light, came into vogue.

2 THE RENAISSANCE, REFORMATION, AND THE WARS OF RELIGION (1300–1648)

THE LATE MIDDLE AGES

The Middle Ages ("medieval" is the French word) were chronologically between the classical world of Greece and Rome and the modern world. The papacy and monarchs, after exercising much power and influence in the high Middle Ages, were in eclipse after 1300. During the late Middle Ages (1300–1500), all of Europe suffered from the Black Death. While England and France engaged in destructive warfare in northern Europe, in Italy the Renaissance had begun.

THE CHURCH AND CRITICISMS

The church was a hierarchical or pyramidal organization. The pope was the leader, and he supervised bishops, who supervised priests. The pope also governed monks, nuns, and friars.

In the late Middle Ages, numerous criticisms were directed against individuals and church practices, but the idea of the church itself or Christian beliefs were not criticized.

Corruption was widespread, with numerous decisions within the church's bureaucracy being influenced by money, friendship, or politics. Simony—the purchase of church positions, such as a bishopric, rather than appointment to the positions based upon merit—was commonplace.

Pluralism also existed. A man could hold more than one office in the church even though he would not be able to do both jobs at once. He might hire an assistant to do one of the jobs for him, or it might be left undone. As he could not be both places, he was also open to the criticism of absenteeism.

These criticisms, and others, such as those concerning extravagance, excessive wealth, political involvement, and sexual improprieties, were part of the hostility to the clergy called anticlericalism. Those who criticized were often attacked by the church as heretics.

John Wycliffe (ca. 1330–1384), an English friar, criticized the vices of the clergy, taxes collected by the pope, transubstantiation, and the authority of the pope. As he believed the church should follow only the Scriptures, he began translating the Bible from Latin into English. Wycliffe's ideas were used by the peasants in the revolt of 1381, and his followers, Lollards, survived well into the 15th century.

John Hus (ca. 1369–1415), a Czech priest with criticisms similar to Wycliffe's, produced a national following in Bohemia which rejected the authority of the pope. Hus was burned at the stake at the Council of Constance.

Lay Piety

In the Rhine Valley of Germany, mystics sought direct knowledge of God through the realm of inner feelings rather than through church rituals.

POPES

The papacy, recognized as the leader of the Western church since at least the 13th century, encountered a series of problems in the late Middle Ages which reduced the prestige of popes and interfered with their ability to deal with the problems underlying the criticisms.

Babylonian Captivity (1309–1377)

In 1305, after a confrontation with the king of France, a new pope, Clement V, was elected. He was a Frenchman and never went to Rome, settling instead in Avignon, near the French kingdom. While not held captive by the French kings, the popes in Avignon were seen as subservient to them. Also, the atmosphere was one of luxury, and the popes concentrated on money and bureaucratic matters, not spiritual leadership. Popes resided in Avignon from 1309 to 1377.

Great Schism (1377–1417)

In 1377 Pope Gregory XI returned to Rome, but died soon afterward. Disputes over the election of his successor led to the election of two popes, one of whom stayed in Rome (Urban VI). The other (Clement VII) returned to Avignon. The existence of two popes lasted until 1417.

Conciliar Movement

An effort was initiated to have the church ruled not by the pope, but by everyone in the church, such as bishops, cardinals, theologians, abbots, and laymen. The idea gained impetus from the existence of two popes and the abuses they were not correcting. Marsilius of Padua (1280–1343), author of *The Defender of the Peace*, argued that the church was subordinate to the state and that the church should be governed by a general council.

The councils at Pisa (1409) and Constance (1414–1417) united the church under one pope (Martin V) but failed to effect any reform of abuses. Martin and his successors rejected the conciliar movement.

Renaissance Popes

After 1447 a series of popes encouraged and supported much artistic work in Rome. While their personal lives were often criticized for sexual laxness, these popes took more interest in political, military, and artistic activities than in church reform. Sixtus IV (1471–1484) started the painting of the Sistine Chapel which his nephew, Julius II (1503–1513), whom Sixtus had promoted within the church, finished with the employment of Michelangelo to paint the ceiling. Julius also successfully asserted his control over the Papal States in central Italy. These popes did not cause the Reformation, but they failed to do anything that might have averted it.

THE HUNDRED YEARS' WAR

The governments of medieval Europe did not have the control over their lands that we associate with modern governments. Toward the end of the period, monarchs began to assert their power and control. The major struggle, between England and France, was the Hundred Years' War (1337–1453).

The English king was the vassal of the French king for the duchy of Aquitaine, and the French king wanted control of the duchy; this was the event that started the fighting. The English king, Edward III, had a claim to the French throne through his mother, a princess of France.

Additionally, French nobles sought opportunities to gain power at the expense of the French king. England also exported its wool to Flanders, which was coming under control of the king of France. Finally, kings and nobles shared the values of chivalry which portrayed war as a glorious and uplifting adventure.

The war was fought in France, though the Scots (with French encouragement) invaded northern England. A few major battles occurred—Crécy (1346), Poitiers (1356), Agincourt (1415)—which the English won due to the chivalrous excesses of the French. The fighting consisted largely of sieges and raids. Eventually, the war became one of attrition; the French slowly wore down the English. Technological changes during the war included the use of English longbows and the increasingly expensive plate armor of knights.

Joan of Arc (1412–1431), an illiterate peasant girl who said she heard voices of saints, rallied the French army for several victories. Due to Joan's victories, Charles VII was crowned king at Rheims, the traditional location for enthronement. Joan was later captured by the Burgundians, allies of England, and sold to the English who tried her for heresy (witchcraft). She was burned at the stake at Rouen.

Results of the Hundred Years' War

England lost all of its Continental possessions, except Calais. French farmland was devastated, with England and France both expending great sums of money. Population, especially in France, declined.

Both countries suffered internal disruption as soldiers plundered and local officials left to fight the war. Trade everywhere was disrupted and England's wool trade with the Low Countries slumped badly. To cover these financial burdens, heavy taxation was inflicted on the peasants.

In England, the need for money led kings to summon parliaments more often, which gave the nobility and merchants more power. No taxes could be levied without parliamentary approval. Parliamentary procedures and institutions changed, giving the nobles more control over government (impeachments). Representative government gained a tradition which enabled it to survive under later challenges.

A series of factional struggles led to the deposition of Richard II in 1399. After the Hundred Years' War ended, the nobility continued fighting each other in the War of the Roses (1450–1485), choosing sides as Lancastrians or Yorkists.

In France, noble factions contended for power with the king, who refused to deal with noble assemblies. The king had certain advantages. While the duchy of Burgundy was virtually independent, there was no national assembly, only a series of provincial bodies, and the king could levy the gabelle (salt tax) and taille (national tax), which exempted the nobles and clergy. He also had a standing army, so he did not have to rely on the nobles.

In both countries, the war, fed by propaganda, led to the growth of nationalism.

Literature also came to express nationalism, as it was written in the language of the people instead of in Latin. Geoffrey Chaucer portrayed a wide spectrum of English life in the *Canterbury Tales*, while François Villon (1431–1463), in his *Grand Testament*, emphasized the ordinary life of the French with humor and emotion.

THE HOLY ROMAN EMPIRE

After prolonged struggles with the papacy in the 13th century, the Holy Roman Emperor had little power in either Germany or Italy. After 1272 the empire was usually ruled by a member of the Hapsburg family, which had turned its interest to creating possessions in Austria and Hungary. The Ottoman Turks, following the conquest of Constantinople in 1453, continually pressed on the borders of the Empire.

In 1356 the Golden Bull was issued. This constitution of the empire gave the right of naming the emperor to seven German electors, but gave the pope no role.

The Swiss cantons gradually obtained independence, helped by stories such as that of William Tell.

In Italy, city-states, or communes, dominated by wealthy merchants, continued their efforts to obtain independence from the emperor.

In many cities, the governments became stronger and were dominated by despots (Milan had the Visconti and later the Sforza; Florence came under the control of the Medici) or oligarchies (Venice was ruled by the Council of Ten). Other smaller city-states disappeared as continual wars led to larger territories dominated by one large city.

THE NEW MONARCHS

After 1450, monarchs turned to strengthening their power internally, a process which produced the "New Monarchy." However, several difficulties hindered their efforts.

The general economic stagnation of the late Middle Ages combined with the increasing expense of mercenary armies to force monarchs to seek new taxes, something traditionally requiring the consent of the nobles.

Additionally, nobles, long the chief problem for kings, faced declining incomes and rising desires to control the government of their king. If not fighting external foes, they engaged in civil war at home with their fellow nobles.

Unfortunately for the monarchs, many weak, incompetent, or insane kings hindered their efforts.

Opposition to Monarchical Power

Nobles claimed various levels of independence under feudal rules or traditions. Forming an assembly provided some sort of a meeting forum for nobles. Furthermore, the core of royal armies consisted of nobles. Many of the higher clergy of the church were noble-born.

Additionally, some towns had obtained independence during times of trouble. Church and clergy saw the pope as their leader.

Help for France's Monarchy

The defeat of the English in the Hundred Years' War and of the duchy of Burgundy in 1477 removed major military threats. Trade was expanded, fostered by the merchant Jacques Coeur (1395–1456). Louis XI (1461–1483) demonstrated ruthlessness in dealing with his nobility as individuals and collectively in the Estates General.

Help for England's Monarchy

Many nobles died in the War of the Roses. Nobles were controlled by a royal court, the Star Chamber. Standard governmental procedures of law and taxation were developed.

Help for Spain's Monarchy

The marriage of Isabella of Castile (reigned 1474–1504) and Ferdinand of Aragon (reigned 1474–1516) created a united Spain. The Moslems were defeated at Granada in 1492. Navarre was conquered in 1512.

A government organization called the Mesta encouraged sheep farming. An alliance with a group of cities and towns, the Hermandad, was formed to oppose the nobility. Finally, reform and control of the church was enacted through the Inquisition.

THE BLACK DEATH AND SOCIAL PROBLEMS

The bubonic plague ("Black Death") is a disease affecting the lymph glands. It causes death quickly. Conditions in Europe encouraged the quick spread of disease. There was no urban sanitation, and streets were filled with refuse, excrement, and dead animals. Living conditions were overcrowded, with families often sleeping in one room or one bed. Poor nutrition was rampant. There was also little personal cleanliness.

Carried by fleas on black rats, the plague was brought from Asia by merchants, and arrived in Europe in 1347. The plague affected all of Europe by 1350 and killed perhaps 25 to 40 percent of the population, with cities suffering more than the countryside.

Consequences

Some of the best clergy died because they were helping the sick; the church was left to the less competent or sincere. With fewer people, the economy declined. Additionally, Jews were killed due to a belief that they poisoned wells of Christians.

A general pessimism pervaded the survivors. Flagellants whipped and scourged themselves in penance for sins which they believed caused the plague. Literature and art reflected this attitude, including such examples as the *Dance of Death*, which depicted dancing skeletons among the living.

Population

By 1300 Europe's population had reached the limit of available food resources, and famines became common. After the population decline from the Black Plague, wages rose. Governments often responded with laws trying to set wage levels, such as England's Statute of Laborers (1351). Serfdom ended in many places. Guilds were established which limited membership, and cities limited citizenship in efforts to obtain or protect monopolies. The Hanseatic League of German cities controlled the Baltic trade in the 14th and early 15th centuries. Enclosures of open fields in England, as sheep farming increased, eliminated peasants and their villages.

Peasant Revolts

Taxation was increased due to the Hundred Years' War. Higher wages were desired after the Black Death. Rising expectations were frustrated after a period of relative prosperity. Hostility to aristocrats increased, as expressed in the words of a priest, John Ball, one of the leaders of the English Peasants' Revolt: "When Adam delved and Eve span / Who was then the gentleman?"

A number of subsequent revolts ensued. In England, the largest of these, the Peasants' Revolt of 1381, involved perhaps 100,000 people. France experienced the *Jacquerie* in 1358. Poor workers revolted in Florence in 1378.

The Low Countries, Germany, Sicily, and Spain, and at other times England and France, all experienced similar occurrences.

THE RENAISSANCE (1300–1600)

The Renaissance emphasized new learning, including the rediscovery of much classical material, and new art styles.

Italian city-states, such as Venice, Milan, Padua, Pisa, and especially Florence, were the home to many Renaissance developments, which were limited to the rich elite.

Jacob Burckhardt's *The Civilization of the Renaissance in Italy* (1860) popularized the study of the period and argued that it was a strong contrast to the Middle Ages. Subsequent historians have often found more continuity with the Middle Ages.

Definitions

Renaissance—French for "rebirth;" the word describes the reawakening of interest in the heritage of the classical past.

Classical past—Greece and Rome in the years between 500 B.C. and 400 A.D. Humanist scholars were most interested in Rome from 200 B.C. to 180 A.D.

Humanism—The reading and understanding of writings and ideals of the classical past. Rhetoric was the initial area of study, which soon widened to include poetry, history, politics, and philosophy. Civic humanism was the use of humanism in the political life of Italian city-states. Christian humanism focused on early Church writings instead of secular authors.

Individualism—Behavior or theory that emphasizes each person and is contrasted with corporate or community behavior. Renaissance individualism sought great accomplishments and looked for heroes in history.

Virtu—The essence of being a person through the showing of human abilities. This ability could be displayed in speech, art, politics, warfare, or elsewhere by seizing the opportunities available. For many, the pursuit of virtu was amoral.

Causes

While no cause can be clearly identified as the source of the Renaissance, several categories have been suggested by historians.

The first explanation is economic. Northern Italy was very wealthy as a result of serving as an intermediary between the silk- and spice-producing East and the consuming West of England, France, and Germany. Also, Italian merchants had built great wealth in the cloth industry and had often turned to international banking. This wealth gave people leisure to pursue new ideas and money to support the artists and scholars who produced the new works.

Political interactions may have also contributed. Struggles between the papacy, the Holy Roman Empire, and merchants during the Middle Ages had resulted in the independence of many small city-states in northern Italy. This fragmentation meant that no single authority had the power to stop or redirect new developments. The governments of the city-states, often in the hands of one man, competed by supporting artists and scholars.

Also, northern Italian cities were often built on the ruins of ancient Roman ones, and the citizens knew of their heritage.

Finally, the appearance of men fleeing the falling Byzantine Empire brought new ideas, including the study of Greek, to Italy. Also, during the numerous wars between the Italian city-states, contestants sought justifications for their claims in the actions of the past. Finally, the study of Roman law during disputes between the popes and the Holy Roman Emperors led to the study of other Roman writers.

LITERATURE, ART, AND SCHOLARSHIP

Literature

Humanists, as both orators and poets, were inspired by and imitated works of the classical past. The literature was more secular and wide-ranging than that of the Middle Ages.

Dante (1265–1321) was a Florentine writer who spent much of his life in exile after being on the losing side in political struggles in Florence. His *Divine Comedy*, describing a journey through hell, purgatory, and heaven, shows that reason can only take people so far and that God's grace and revelation must be used. Dealing with many other issues and with much symbolism, this work is the pinnacle of medieval poetry.

Petrarch (1304–1374), who wrote in both Latin and Italian, encouraged the study of ancient Rome, collected and preserved work of ancient writers, and produced much work in the classical literary style. He is best known for his sonnets, including many expressing his love for a married woman named Laura, and is considered the father of humanism.

Boccaccio (1313–1375) wrote *The Decameron*, a collection of short stories in Italian, which meant to amuse, not edify, the reader.

Castiglione (1478–1529) authored *The Book of the Courtier*, which specified the qualities necessary for a gentleman. Abilities in conversation, sports, arms, dance, music, Latin, and Greek, he advised, should be combined with an agreeable personal demeanor. The book was translated into many languages and greatly influenced Western ideas about correct education and behavior.

Art

Artists also broke with the medieval past, in both technique and content. Renaissance art sometimes used religious topics, but often dealt with secular themes or portraits of individuals. Oil paints, chiaroscuro, and linear perspectives produced works of energy in three dimensions.

By copying classical models and using freestanding pieces, Renaissance sculptors produced works celebrating the individualistic and nonreligious spirit of the day.

Medieval architecture included the use of pointed arches, flying buttresses, and fan vaulting to obtain great heights, while permitting light to flood the interior of the building, usually a church or cathedral. The result gave a "feeling" for God. The busy details, filling every niche, and the absence of symmetry also typify medieval work.

Renaissance architects openly copied classical, especially Roman, forms, such as the rounded arch and squared angles, when constructing town and country houses for the rich and urban buildings for cities.

Several artists became associated with the new style or art. Giotto (1266–1336) painted religious scenes using light and shadow, a technique called chiaroscuro, to create an illusion of depth and greater realism. He is considered the father of Renaissance painting. Donatello (1386–1466), the father of Renaissance sculpture, produced, in his *David*, the first statue cast in bronze since classical times. Masaccio (1401–1428) emphasized naturalism in *Expulsion of Adam and Eve* by showing real human figures, in the nude, with three-dimensions, expressing emotion. Leonardo de Vinci (1452–1519) produced numerous works, including *The Last Supper* and *Mona Lisa*, as well as many mechanical designs, though few were ever constructed. Raphael (1483–1520), a master of Renaissance grace and style, theory and technique, represented these skills in *The School of Athens*. Michelangelo (1475–1564), a universal man, produced masterpieces in architecture, sculpture (*David*), and painting (the Sistine Chapel ceiling). His work was a bridge to a new, non-Renaissance style called Mannerism.

Scholars

Renaissance scholars were more practical and secular than medieval ones. Manuscript collections enabled scholars to study the primary sources and to reject all traditions which had been built up since classical times. Also, scholars participated in the lives of their cities as active politicians.

Leonardo Bruni (1370–1444), a civic humanist, served as chancellor of Florence, where he used his rhetorical skills to rouse the citizens against external enemies. He also wrote a history of his city and was the first to use the term humanism.

Lorenzo Valla (1407–1457) authored *Elegances of the Latin Language*, the standard text in Latin philology, and also exposed as a forgery the Donation of Constantine, which had purported to give the papacy control of vast lands in Italy.

Machiavelli (1469–1527) wrote *The Prince*, which analyzed politics from the standpoint of reason, rather than faith or tradition. His work, amoral in tone, describes how a political leader could obtain and hold power by acting only in his own self-interest.

THE RENAISSANCE OUTSIDE ITALY

The Renaissance in the rest of western Europe was less classical in its emphasis and more influenced by religion, particularly Christian humanism.

In the Low Countries, artists still produced works on religious themes, but the attention to detail in the paintings of Jan van Eyck (ca. 1390–1441) typifies Renaissance ideas. Later artists include the nearly surreal Pieter Brueghel (ca. 1525–1569) and Rembrandt van Rijn (1606–1669).

In Mainz, Germany around 1450, the invention of printing with movable type, traditionally attributed to Johann Gutenberg, enabled new ideas to be spread throughout Europe more easily. Albrecht Dürer (1471–1528) gave realism and individuality to the art of the woodcut.

Many Italian artists and scholars were hired in France. The Loire Valley chateaux of the 16th century and Rabelais' (ca. 1490–1553) *Gargantua and Pantagruel* reflect Renaissance tastes.

Interest in the past and new developments did not appear in England until the 16th century. Drama, culminating in the age of Shakespeare, is the most pronounced accomplishment of the Renaissance spirit in England.

In Spain, money from the American conquests supported much building, such as the Escorial, a palace and monastery, and art, such as that by El Greco (1541–1614), who is often considered to work in the style of Mannerism.

CHRISTIAN HUMANISM (1450–1530)

Theme

Much of the Renaissance outside of Italy focused on religious matters through studying writings of the early Christian church rather than through those of the secular authors of Rome and Greece.

Elements

Although they used the techniques of the Italian humanists in the analysis of ancient writings, language, and style, Christian humanists were more interested in providing guidance on personal behavior.

The work on Christian sources, done between 1450 and 1530, emphasized education and the power of the human intellect to bring about institutional change and moral improvement. The many tracts and guides of Christian humanists were directed at reforming the church, but led many into criticisms of the church, which contributed to the Reformation. The discovery that traditional Christian texts had different versions proved unsettling to many believers.

Though many Christian humanists were not clergymen, most early reformers of the church during the Reformation had been trained as Christian humanists.

Christian humanism, with its emphasis on toleration and education, disappeared due to the increasing passions of the Reformation after 1530.

Biographies

Desiderius Erasmus (1466–1536), a Dutchman and the most notable figure of the Christian humanist movement, made new translations of the Greek and Latin versions of the New Testament in order to have "purer" editions. His book *In Praise of Folly* satirizes the ambitions of the world, and especially those of the clergy. Erasmus emphasized the virtues of tolerance, restraint, and education. Erasmus led a life of simple piety, practicing the Christian virtues, which led to complaints that he had no role for the institutional church. His criticisms of the church and clergy, though meant to lead to reforms, gave ammunition to those wishing to attack the church and, therefore, it is said "Erasmus laid the egg that Luther hatched."

Thomas More (1478–1535), an English laywer, politician, and humanist, wrote *Utopia* (a Greek word for "nowhere"). Mixing civic humanism with religious ideals, the book describes a perfect society, located on an imaginary island, in which war, poverty, religious intolerance, and other problems of the early 16th century do not exist. *Utopia* sought to show how people might live if they followed the social and political ideals of Christianity. Also, in a break with medieval thought, More portrayed government as very active in the economic life of society, education, and public health. Though a critic of the church and clergy of his day, More was executed by Henry VIII, king of England, for refusing to countenance Henry's break with the pope.

Jacques Lefevre d'Etables (1454–1536), the leading French humanist, produced five versions of the Psalms, his *Quincuplex Psalterism*, which challenged the belief in the tradition of a single, authoritative Bible.

Francesco Ximenes de Cisneros (1436–1517), leader of the Spanish church as Grand Inquisitor, founded a university and produced the *Complutensian Polyglot Bible*, which had Hebrew, Greek, and Latin versions of the Bible in parallel columns. He also reformed the Spanish clergy and church, so that most criticisms of the later reformers during the Reformation did not apply to Spain.

THE REFORMATION

The Reformation destroyed western Europe's religious unity and introduced new ideas about the relationships between God, the individual, and society. Its course was greatly influenced by politics, and led, in most areas, to the subjection of the church to the political rulers.

Earlier threats to the unity of the church had been made by the works of John Wycliffe and John Hus. The abuses of church practices and positions upset many people. Likewise, Christian humanists had been criticizing abuses.

Personal piety and mysticism, which were alternative approaches to Christianity and did not require the apparatus of the institutional church and the clergy, appeared in the late Middle Ages.

MARTIN LUTHER (1483–1546) AND THE BEGINNINGS

Martin Luther was a miner's son from Saxony in central Germany. At the urgings of his father, he studied for a career in law. He underwent a religious experience while traveling, which led him to become an Augustinian friar. Later he became a professor at the university in Wittenberg, Saxony.

Religious Problems

Luther, to his personal distress, could not reconcile the problem of the sinfulness of the individual and the justice of God. How could a sinful person attain the righteousness necessary to obtain salvation? During his studies of the Bible, especially of *Romans 1:17*, Luther came to believe that personal efforts—good works such as a Christian life and attention to the sacraments of the church—could not "earn" the sinner salvation, but that belief and faith were the only way to obtain grace. By 1515 Luther believed that "justification by faith alone" was the road to salvation.

Indulgences

Indulgences, which had originated in connection with the Crusades, involved the cancellation of the penalty given by the church to a confessed sinner. Indulgences had long been a means of raising money for church activities. In 1517 the pope was building the new cathedral of St. Peter in Rome. Also, Albrecht, archbishop of Mainz, had purchased three church positions (simony and pluralism) by borrowing money from the banking family, the Fuggers. A Dominican friar, John Tetzel, was authorized to preach and sell indulgences, with the proceeds going to build the cathedral and repay the loan. The popular belief was that "As soon as a coin in the coffer rings, the soul from purgatory springs," and Tetzel had much business. On October 31, 1517, Luther, with his belief that no such control or influence could be had over salvation, nailed 95 theses, or statements, about indulgences to the door of the Wittenberg church and challenged the practice of selling indulgences. At this time he was seeking to reform the church, not divide it.

Luther's Relations with the Pope and Governments

In 1519 Luther debated various criticisms of the church and was driven to say that only the Bible, not religious traditions or papal statements, could determine correct religious practices and beliefs. In 1521 Pope Leo X excommunicated Luther for his beliefs.

In 1521 Luther appeared in the city of Worms before a meeting (Diet) of the important figures of the Holy Roman Empire, including the Emperor, Charles V.

He was again condemned. At the Diet of Worms Luther made his famous statement about his writings and the basis for them: "Here I stand. I can do no other." After this, Luther could not go back; the break with the pope was permanent.

Frederick III of Saxony, the ruler of the territory in which Luther resided, protected Luther in Wartburg Castle for a year. Frederick never accepted Luther's beliefs but protected him because Luther was his subject. The weak political control of the Holy Roman Emperor contributed to Luther's success in avoiding the pope's and the Emperor's penalties.

Luther's Writings

An Address to the Christian Nobility of the German Nation (1520) argued that nobles, as well as clergy, were the leaders of the church and should undertake to reform it.

The *Babylonian Captivity* (1520) attacked the traditional seven sacraments, replacing them with only two.

The *Freedom of the Christian Man* (1520) explains Luther's views on faith, good works, the nature of God, and the supremacy of political authority over believers.

Against the Murderous, Thieving Hordes of the Peasants (1524), written in response to the Peasants' Revolt, stated Luther's belief that political leaders, not all people, should control both church and society.

The printing press enabled Luther's works to be distributed quickly throughout Germany. By 1534 Luther had translated the Bible into German, making it accessible to many more people, as well as greatly influencing the development of the German language. Also, his composition, "A Mighty Fortress is Our God," was the most popular hymn of the 16th century.

Subsequent Developments of Lutheranism

Increased economic burdens combined with Luther's words that a Christian is subject to no one led the peasants of Germany to revolt in 1524. The ensuing noble repression, supported by Luther, resulted in the deaths of 70,000 to 100,000 peasants.

At a meeting of the Holy Roman Empire's leading figures in 1529, a group of rulers, influenced by Luther's teachings, "protested" the decision of the majority—hence the term "Protestant." Protestant originally meant Lutheran, but eventually was applied to all Western Christians who did not maintain allegiance to the pope.

After a failure of Protestant and Catholic representatives to find a mutually acceptable statement of faith, the Augsburg Confession of 1530 was written as a comprehensive statement of Lutheran beliefs.

Led by Philip Melanchthon (1497–1560), the "Educator of Germany," Lutherans undertook much educational reform, including schools for girls.

Denmark became Lutheran in 1523 and Sweden in 1527.

Lutheran rulers, to protect themselves against the efforts of Charles V, the Holy Roman Emperor, to reestablish Catholicism in Germany, formed a defensive alliance called the Schmalkaldic League in 1531.

Wherever Lutheranism was adopted, church lands were often seized by the ruler. This made a return to Catholicism more difficult, as the lands would need to be restored to the church.

The Peace of Augsburg (1555) ended years of religious and political warfare and established the permanent religious division of Germany into Lutheran and Catholic churches. The statement "cuius regio, eius religio" ("whose region, his religion") meant that the religion of any area would be that of the ruling political authority.

OTHER REFORMERS

Many other reformers were criticizing the church by the early 1520s.

Ulrich Zwingli (1484–1531) introduced reforming ideas in Zurich, Switzerland. He rejected clerical celibacy, the worship of saints, fasting, transubstantiation, and purgatory. Rejecting ritual and ceremony, Zwingli stripped churches of decorations. In 1523, the governing council of the city accepted his beliefs. Zurich became a center for Protestantism and its spread throughout Switzerland.

Zwingli, believing in the union of church and state, established a system which required church attendance by all citizens and regulated many aspects of personal behavior—all enforced by courts and a group of informers.

Efforts to reconcile the views of Zwingli and Luther, chiefly over the issue of the Eucharist, failed during a meeting in Marburg Castle in 1529.

Switzerland, divided into many cantons, also divided into Protestant and Catholic camps. A series of civil wars, during which Zwingli was captured and executed, led to a treaty in which each canton was permitted to determine its own religion.

Anabaptists

Anabaptist (derived from a Greek word meaning to baptize again) is a name applied to people who rejected the validity of child baptism and believed that such children had to be rebaptized when they became adults.

As the Bible became available, through translation into the languages of the people, many people adopted interpretations contrary to those of Luther, Zwingli, and the Catholics.

Anabaptists sought to return to the practices of the early Christian church, which was a voluntary association of believers with no connection to the state. Perhaps the first Anabaptists appeared in Zurich in 1525 under the leadership of Conrad Grebel and were called Swiss Brethren.

In 1534 a group of Anabaptists called Melchiorites, led by Jan Matthys, gained political control of the city of Münster in Germany and forced other Protestants and Catholics to convert or leave. Most of the Anabaptists were workers and peasants, who followed Old Testament practices, including polygamy, and abolished private property. Combined armies of Protestants and Catholics captured the city and executed the leaders in 1535. Thereafter, Anabaptism and Münster became stock words among Protestants and Catholics about the dangers of letting reforming ideas influence workers and peasants.

Subsequently, Anabaptists adopted pacifism and avoided involvement with the state whenever possible. Today, the Mennonites, founded by Menno Simons (1496–1561), and the Amish are the descendants of the Anabaptists.

John Calvin

In 1536 John Calvin (1509–1564), a Frenchman, arrived in Geneva, a Swiss city-state which had adopted an anti-Catholic position. He left after his first efforts at reform failed. Upon his return in 1540, Geneva became the center of the Reformation. Calvin's *Institutes of the Christian Religion* (1536), a strictly logical analysis of Christianity, had a universal appeal.

Calvin brought knowledge of organizing a city from his stay in Strasbourg, which was being led by the reformer Martin Bucer (1491–1551). Calvin emphasized the doctrine of predestination (God knew who would obtain salvation before those people were born) and believed that church and state should be united.

As in Zurich, church and city combined to enforce Christian behavior, and Calvinism came to be seen as having a stern morality. Like Zwingli, Calvin sought a simple, unadorned church. Followers of Calvinism became the most militant and uncompromising of all Protestants.

Geneva became the home of Protestant exiles from England, Scotland, and France. Many later returned to their countries with Calvinist ideas.

Calvinism triumphed as the majority religion in Scotland, under the leadership of John Knox (ca. 1514–1572), and in the United Provinces of the Netherlands. Puritans in England and New England also accepted Calvinism.

REFORM IN ENGLAND

England underwent reforms in a pattern different from the rest of Europe. Personal and political decisions by the rulers determined much of the course of the Reformation there.

The Break with the Pope

Henry VIII (1509–1547) married Catherine of Aragon, the widow of his older brother. By 1526 Henry became convinced that he was unable to produce a legitimate son to inherit his throne because he had violated God's commandments (*Leviticus 18:16, 20:21*) by marrying his brother's widow.

Soon, Henry fell in love with Anne Boleyn and decided to annul his marriage to Catherine in order to marry Anne. Pope Clement VII, who had the authority necessary to issue such an annulment, was, after 1527, under the political control of Charles V, Catherine's nephew. Efforts by Cardinal Wolsey (ca. 1473–1530) to secure the annulment ended in failure and Wolsey's disgrace. Thomas Cranmer (1489–1556), named archbishop in 1533, dissolved Henry's marriage. Henry married Anne Boleyn in January 1533.

Henry used Parliament to threaten the pope and eventually to legislate the break with Rome by law. The Act of Annates (1532) prevented payments of money to the pope. The Act of Restraint of Appeals (1533) forbade appeals to be taken to Rome, which stopped Catherine from appealing her divorce to the pope. The Act of Supremacy (1534) declared Henry, not the pope, as the head of the English church. Subsequent acts enabled Henry to dissolve the monasteries and to seize their land, which represented perhaps 25 percent of the land of England.

In 1535 Thomas More was executed for rejecting Henry's leadership of the English church.

Protestant beliefs and practices made little headway during Henry's reign, as he accepted transubstantiation, enforced celibacy among the clergy, and otherwise made the English church conform to most medieval practices.

Protestantism

Under Henry VIII's son, Edward VI (1547–1553), who succeeded to the throne at age 10, the English church adopted Calvinism. Clergy were allowed to marry, communion by the laity expanded, and images were removed from churches. Doctrine included justification by faith, the denial of transubstantiation, and only two sacraments.

Anglicanism

Under Elizabeth I (1558–1603), who was Henry VIII's daughter and half-sister to Edward and Mary, the church in England adopted Protestant beliefs again. The Elizabethan Settlement required outward conformity to the official church, but rarely inquired about inward beliefs.

Some practices of the church, including ritual, resembled the Catholic practices. Catholicism remained, especially among the gentry, but could not be practiced openly.

Some reformers wanted to purify (hence "Puritans") the church of its remaining Catholic aspects. The resulting church, Protestant in doctrine and practice but retaining most of the physical possessions, such as buildings, and many of the powers, such as church courts, of the medieval church, was called Anglican.

REFORM ELSEWHERE IN EUROPE

The Parliament in Ireland established a Protestant church much like the one in England. The landlords and people near Dublin were the only ones who followed their monarchs into Protestantism, as the mass of the Irish people were left untouched by the Reformation. The Catholic church and its priests became the religious, and eventually, the national, leaders of the Irish people.

John Knox (ca. 1514–1572), upon his return from the Continent, led the Reformation in Scotland. Parliament, dominated by nobles, established Protestantism in 1560. The resulting church was Calvinist in doctrine.

France, near Geneva and Germany, experienced efforts at establishing Protestantism, but the kings of France had control of the church there and gave no encouragement to reformers. Calvinists, known in France as Huguenots, were especially common among the nobility, and after 1562 a series of civil wars involving religious differences resulted.

The church in Spain, controlled by the monarchy, allowed no Protestantism to take root. Similarly, Italian political authorities rejected Protestantism.

THE COUNTER REFORMATION

The Counter Reformation brought changes to the portion of the Western church which retained its allegiance to the pope. Some historians see this as a reform of the Catholic church, similar to what Protestants were doing, while others see it as a result of the criticisms of Protestants.

Efforts to reform the church included new religious orders such as Theatines (1524), Capuchins (1528), and Ursulines (1535), as well as mystics such as Teresa of Avila (1515–1582).

Ignatius of Loyola (1491–1556), a former soldier, founded the Society of Jesus in 1540 to lead the attack on Protestantism. Jesuits became the leaders of the Counter Reformation. By the 1540s Jesuits, including Francis Xavier (1506–1552), traveled to Japan as missionaries.

Popes resisted reforming efforts because of fears as to what a council of church leaders might do to papal powers. The Sack of Rome in 1527, when soldiers of the Holy Roman Emperor captured and looted Rome, was seen by many as a judgment of God against the lives of the Renaissance popes. In 1534 Paul III became pope and attacked abuses while reasserting papal leadership.

Paul III convened the Council of Trent in three sessions from 1545 to 1563. It settled many aspects of doctrine including transubstantiation, the seven sacraments, the efficacy of good works for salvation, and the role of saints and priests. It also approved the "Index of Forbidden Books."

Other reforms came into effect. The sale of church offices was curtailed. New seminaries for more and better trained clergy were created. The revitalized Catholic church, the papacy, and the Jesuits set out to reunite Western Christianity.

Individuals who adopted other views but who had less impact on large groups of people included Thomas Muntzer (d. 1525), Caspar Schwenckfeld (d. 1561), Michael Servetus (d. 1553), and Lelio Sozzini (d. 1562).

DOCTRINES

The Reformation produced much thought and writing about the beliefs of Christianity. Most of the major divisions of the Western church took differing positions on these matters of doctrine, and individual churches became increasingly rigid. Protestants emphasized the Bible, while Catholics included the traditions developed by the church during the Middle Ages, as well as papal pronouncements. Catholics retained the medieval view about the special nature and role of clergy, while Protestants emphasized the "priesthood of all believers," which meant all individuals were equal before God. Protestants sought a clergy that preached.

Church governance varied widely. Catholics retained the medieval hierarchy of believers, priests, bishops, and pope. Anglicans rejected the authority of the pope and substituted the monarch as the Supreme Governor of the church. Lutherans rejected the authority of the pope but kept bishops. Most Calvinists governed their church by ministers and a group of elders, a system called Presbyterianism. Anabaptists rejected most forms of church governance in favor of congregational democracy.

Most Protestants denied the efficacy of some or all of the sacraments of the medieval church. The issue which most divided the various churches came to be the one called by various names: the Eucharist, the mass, the Lord's supper, the communion. According to the belief of transubstantiation, the bread and wine retain their outward appearances but are transformed into the body and blood of Christ; this was a Catholic doctrine. According to the belief in consubstantiation, nothing of the bread and wine is changed, but the believer realizes the presence of Christ in the bread and wine ("a piece of iron thrust into the fire does not change its composition but still has a differing quality"); this was a Lutheran doctrine.

Other views included one that the event was symbolic. It served as a memorial to the actions of Christ, or was a thanksgiving for God's grant of salvation.

The means of obtaining salvation differed. Catholics believed in living life according to Christian beliefs and participating in the practices of the church—good works. Lutherans accepted the notion of justification by faith—salvation cannot be earned and a good life is the fruit of faith. Calvinists believed in predestination—that salvation is known only to God, but a good life can be some proof of predestined salvation.

Church-state relations also differed. Catholics and Calvinists believed in theocracy—the church should control and absorb the state. Lutheran and Anglican belief held that the state controls the church. Anabaptists held that the church ignores the state.

RESULTS

The map of Europe and its religions did not change much after 1560.

Political rulers, be they monarchs or city councils, gained power over and at the expense of the church. The state thereafter could operate as an autonomous unit.

Religious enthusiasm was rekindled. While most of the reforms came from the political and religious leadership of the societies involved, the general populace eventually gained enthusiasm—an enthusiasm lacking in religious belief since far back into the Middle Ages.

All aspects of Western Christianity undertook to remedy the abuses which had contributed to the Reformation. Simony, pluralism, immoral, or badly-educated clergy were all attacked and, by the 17th century, considerably remedied.

Protestantism, by emphasizing the individual believer's direct contact with God rather than through the intermediary of the church, contributed to the growth of individualism.

Thinkers have attempted to connect religious change with economic developments, especially the appearance of capitalism. Karl Marx, a 19th-century philosopher and social theorist, believed that capitalism, which emphasized hard work, thrift, and the use of reason rather than tradition, led to the development of Protestantism, a type of Christianity he thought was especially attractive to the middle class, who were also the capitalists.

Max Weber, a later 19th-century sociologist, reversed the argument and believed that Protestantism, especially Calvinism, with its emphasis on predestination,

RELIGIOUS SITUATION IN 1560

Legend:

- ▦ Lutheran
- ▨ Anglican
- ■ Calvinist Established Groups
- ▦ Calvinist Minority Groups
- ▤ Anabaptist
- ☐ Roman Catholic
- ═ Approximate Border Between Protestant State Churches and Roman Catholic Church
- ┄ Approximate Eastern Border of Western Christianity

led to great attention being paid to the successes and failures of this world as possible signs of future salvation. Such attention, and the attendant hard work, furthered the capitalist spirit.

Most writers today accept neither view, but believe that Protestantism and capitalism are related. However, too many other factors are involved to make the connection clear or easy.

THE WARS OF RELIGION (1560–1648)

The period from approximately 1560 to 1648 witnessed continuing warfare, primarily between Protestants and Catholics. Though religion was not the only reason for the wars—occasionally Catholics and Protestants were allies—it was the dominant cause. In the latter half of the 16th century, the fighting was along the

Atlantic seaboard between Calvinists and Catholics; after 1600 the warfare spread to Germany, where Calvinists, Lutherans, and Catholics fought.

Warfare and the Effects of Gunpowder

Cannons became effective; therefore, elaborate and expensive fortifications of cities were required. Long sieges became necessary to capture a city.

The infantry, organized in squares of 3,000 men and armed with pikes and muskets, made the cavalry charge obsolete.

Greater discipline and control of armies were required to sustain a siege or train the infantry. An army once trained would not be disbanded, due to the expense of retraining. The order of command and modern ranks appeared, as did uniforms.

Better discipline permitted commanders to attempt more actions on the battlefield, so more soldiers were necessary. Armies grew from the 40,000 of the Spanish army of 1600 to the 400,000 of the French army at the end of the 17th century.

War and Destruction

Armies, mostly made up of mercenaries, lived by pillage when not paid and often were not effectively under the control of the ruler employing them. Peasants, after having their lands devastated and being tortured to reveal their valuables, left farming and turned to banditry.

THE CATHOLIC CRUSADE

The territories of Charles V, the Holy Roman Emperor, were divided in 1556 between Ferdinand, Charles's brother, and Philip II (1556–1598), Charles's son. Ferdinand received Austria, Hungary, Bohemia, and the title of Holy Roman Emperor. Philip received Spain, Milan, Naples, the Netherlands, and the New World. Both parts of the Hapsburg family cooperated in international matters.

Philip was a man of severe personal habits, deeply religious, and a hard worker. Solemn (it is said he only laughed once in his life, when the report of the St. Bartholomew's Day Massacre reached him) and reclusive (he built the Escorial outside Madrid as a palace, monastery, and eventual tomb), he devoted his life and the wealth of Spain to making Europe Catholic. It was Philip, not the pope, who led the Catholic attack on Protestants.

Sources of the Power of Philip II

The gold and silver of the New World flowed into Spain, especially following the opening of the silver mines at Potesi in Peru.

Spain dominated the Mediterranean following a series of wars led by Philip's half-brother, Don John, against Moslem (largely Turkish) forces. Don John secured the Mediterranean for Christian merchants with a naval victory over the Turks at Lepanto off the coast of Greece in 1571.

Portugal was annexed by Spain in 1580 following the death of the king without a clear successor. This gave Philip the only other large navy of the day as well as Portuguese territories around the globe.

Nature of the Struggle

Calvinism was spreading in England, France, the Netherlands, and Germany. Calvinists supported each other, often disregarding their countries' borders.

England was ruled by two queens, Mary I (reigned 1553–1558), who married Philip II, and then Elizabeth I (reigned 1558–1603), while three successive kings of France from 1559 to 1589 were influenced by their mother, Catherine de' Medici (1519–1589). Women rulers were a novelty in European politics.

Monarchs attempted to strengthen their control and the unity of their countries, a process which nobles often resisted.

CIVIL WAR IN FRANCE

Francis I (1515–1547) obtained control of the French church when he signed the Concordat of Bologna with the pope, and therefore had no incentive to encourage Protestantism. But John Calvin was a Frenchman and Geneva was near France, so Calvinist ideas spread in France, especially among the nobility. French Calvinists were sometimes called Huguenots.

The Treaty of Cateau-Cambresis in 1559 ended the struggles of the Hapsburgs and the Valois, leaving the French with no fear of outside invasion.

When Henry II (reigned 1547–1559) died, he was succeeded, in succession, by his three sons (Francis II, reigned 1559–1560, Charles IX, reigned 1560–1574, Henry III, reigned 1574–1589), each influenced by their mother, Catherine de' Medici, and often controlled by one of the noble families. Though the monarch was always Catholic until 1589, each king was willing to work with Calvinists or Catholics if it would give him more power and independence.

The Wars

A total of nine civil wars occurred from 1562 to 1589. The wars became more brutal, as the killing of civilians supplanted military action.

The St. Bartholomew's Day Massacre on August 24, 1572, was planned by Catherine de' Medici and resulted in the deaths of 20,000 Huguenots. The pope had a medal struck commemorating the event. As a result of St. Bartholomew's Day and other killings, Protestants throughout Europe feared for their future.

Several important figures were assassinated by their religious opponents, including two kings (Henry III and Henry IV). The two leading members of the Guise family were killed at the instigation of the king, Henry III, in 1588.

Spain intervened with troops to support the Catholics in 1590.

Henry of Navarre (reigned 1589–1610)

A Calvinist and member of the Bourbon family, Henry of Navarre became king in 1589 when Henry III was assassinated. Personally popular, Henry began to unite France but was unable to conquer or control Paris, a center of Catholic strength. In 1593 he converted to Catholicism, saying "Paris is worth a mass." He was a politique, more interested in political unity than religious uniformity.

To stem religious violence, in 1598 Henry issued the Edict of Nantes, which permitted Huguenots to worship publicly, attend universities, hold office, and protect themselves in fortified towns.

THE REVOLT OF THE NETHERLANDS

The Netherlands was a group of 17 provinces clustered around the mouth of the Rhine and ruled by the king of Spain. Each province had a tradition of some independence and each elected a stadholder, a man who provided military leadership when necessary. The stadholder was often an important noble. Many cities were dominated by wealthy merchants. By 1560 the cities housed many Calvinists, including some who had fled from France.

Philip II, king of Spain, sought to impose a more centralized government on the Netherlands, as well as a stronger Catholic church. Philip's efforts provoked resistance by some nobles, led by William of Orange (1533–1584), called "the Silent." An agreement and pledge to resist, called the Compromise of 1564, led to rebellion throughout the provinces.

Philip sent the Duke of Alva (ca. 1507–1582) and 20,000 soldiers to suppress the rebellion. Alva established the Council of Troubles (called the Council of Blood by its opponents), which executed several thousand Calvinists as heretics. Alva also imposed new taxes and, most significantly, established the Inquisition.

In 1576 unpaid Spanish soldiers sacked Antwerp, destroying its commercial supremacy in the Netherlands. The Calvinist northern provinces and the Catholic southern provinces united in 1576 in the Pacification of Ghent, but were unable to cooperate. They broke into two groups: the Calvinist Union of Utrecht (approximately modern day Netherlands) and the Catholic Union of Arras (approximately modern day Belgium). The English sent troops and money to support the rebels after 1585.

The Spanish were driven out of the northern Netherlands in the 1590s and the war ended in 1609, though Spain did not recognize official independence until 1648. Thereafter, the independent northern provinces, dominated by the province of Holland, were called the United Provinces, and the southern provinces, ruled by Spain, the Spanish Netherlands.

ENGLAND AND SPAIN

Mary I (reigned 1553–1558)

The daughter of Henry VIII and Catherine of Aragon, Mary sought to make England Catholic. She executed many Protestants, earning the name "Bloody Mary" from opponents.

To escape persecution, many English went into exile on the Continent in Frankfurt, Geneva, and elsewhere, where they learned more radical Protestant ideas.

Mary married Philip II, king of Spain, and organized her foreign policy around Spanish interests. They had no children.

Elizabeth I (reigned 1558–1603)

Elizabeth, a Protestant, achieved a religious settlement between 1559 and 1563 which left England with a church governed by bishops and practicing Catholic rituals, but maintaining a Calvinist doctrine. Though suppressed by Elizabeth's government, Puritans were not condemned to death.

Catholics participated in several rebellions and plots. Mary, Queen of Scots, had fled to England from Scotland in 1568, after alienating the nobles there. In Catholic eyes, she was the legitimate queen of England. Several plots and rebellions to put Mary on the throne led to her execution in 1587. Elizabeth was formally excommunicated by the pope in 1570.

In 1588, as part of his crusade and to stop England from supporting the rebels in the Netherlands, Philip II sent the Armada, a fleet of more than 125 ships, to convey troops from the Netherlands to England as part of a plan to make England Catholic. The Armada was defeated by a combination of superior English naval tactics and a wind which made it impossible for the Spanish to accomplish their goal.

A peace treaty between Spain and England was signed in 1604, but England remained an opponent of Spain.

THE THIRTY YEARS' WAR

Calvinism was spreading throughout Germany. The Peace of Augsburg (1555), which settled the disputes between Lutherans and Catholics, had no provision for Calvinists. Lutherans gained more territories through conversions and often took control of previous church-states—a violation of the Peace of Augsburg. A Protestant alliance under the leadership of the Calvinist ruler of the Palatinate opposed a Catholic League led by the ruler of Bavaria.

The Bohemian Period (1618–1625)

The Bohemians rejected a Hapsburg as their king in favor of the Calvinist ruler of Palatinate, Frederick. They threw two Hapsburg officials out a window—the "defenestration of Prague."

Frederick's army was defeated at White Mountain in 1620, Bohemia was made Catholic, and the Spanish occupied Frederick's Palatinate.

The Danish Period (1625–1629)

The army of Ferdinand, the Holy Roman Emperor, invaded northern Germany, raising fear amongst Protestants for their religion and local rulers for their political rights. Christian IV (reigned 1588–1648), king of Denmark, led an army into Germany in defense of Protestants but was easily defeated. After defeating Christian, the Holy Roman Emperor sought to recover all church lands secularized since 1552 and establish a strong Hapsburg presence in northern Germany.

The Swedish Period (1629—1635)

Gustavus Adolphus (reigned 1611–1632), king of Sweden, who was monetarily supported by France and the United Provinces, who wanted the Hapsburgs de-

EUROPE IN 1648

feated, invaded Germany in defense of Protestantism. Sweden stopped the Hapsburg cause in the battle of Breitenfeld in 1630, but Gustavus Adolphus was killed at the battle of Lutzen in 1632.

The Swedish-French Period (1635–1648)

France, guided by Cardinal Richelieu (1585–1642), supplied troops in Germany, as the war became part of a bigger war between France and Spain.

Treaty of Westphalia (1648)

The presence of ambassadors from all of the belligerents, as well as many other countries, made settlement of nearly all disputes possible. Only the French-Spanish war continued, ending in 1659.

The principles of the Peace of Augsburg were reasserted, but with Calvinists included. The pope's rejection of the treaty was ignored.

The independence of the United Provinces from the king of Spain, and of the Swiss Confederacy from the Holy Roman Empire, was recognized. Individual German states, numbering more than 300, obtained nearly complete independence from the Holy Roman Empire.

Miscellaneous

Not all issues were ones of Protestants versus Catholics. The Lutheran ruler of Saxony joined the Catholics in the attack on Frederick at White Mountain, and the leading general for the Holy Roman Emperor, Ferdinand, was Albrecht of Wallenstein, a Protestant.

The war brought great destruction to Germany, leading to a decline in population of perhaps one-third, or more, in some areas. Germany remained divided and without a strong government until the 19th century.

Results

After 1648 warfare, though often containing religious elements, would not be executed primarily for religious goals.

The Catholic crusade to reunite Europe failed, largely due to the efforts of the Calvinists. The religious distribution of Europe has not changed significantly since 1648.

Nobles, resisting the increasing power of the state, usually dominated the struggle. France, then Germany, fell apart due to the wars. France was reunited in the 17th century.

Spain began a decline which ended its role as a great power of Europe.

THE GROWTH OF THE STATE AND THE AGE OF EXPLORATION

In the 17th century the political systems of the countries of Europe began dividing into two types, absolutist and constitutionalist. England, the United Provinces, and Sweden moved towards constitutionalism, while France was adopting absolutist ideas.

Overseas exploration, begun in the 15th century, expanded. Governments supported such activity in order to gain wealth and to preempt other countries.

Definitions

Constitutionalism meant rules, often unwritten, defining and limiting government. It sought to enhance the liberty of the individual and thus shaded into liberalism. Constitutional regimes usually had some means of group decision making, such as a parliament, but a constitutional government need not be a democracy and usually was not. Consent of the governed provided the basis for the legitimacy of the regime.

Absolutism emphasized the role of the state and its fulfillment of some specific purpose, such as nationalism, religion, or the glory of the monarch. The usual form of government of an absolutist regime was, in the 17th century, kingship, which gained its legitimacy from the notion of divine right.

Nobles and/or bourgeoisie provided the chief opposition to the increasing power of the state. In constitutionalist states, they often obtained control of the state, while in absolutist states they became servants of the state.

POLITICAL THOUGHT

The collapse of governments during the wars of religion, and the subjection of one religious group to the government of another, stimulated thought about the nature of politics and political allegiances. The increasing power of monarchs raised questions.

Both Protestants and Catholics developed theories of resistance to government. Though Luther and Calvin had disapproved of revolt against government, John Knox's *Blast of the Trumpet Against the Terrible Regiment of Women* (1558), directed against Mary, Queen of Scots, approved rebellion against a heretical ruler.

In France, Huguenot writers, stimulated by the St. Bartholomew's Day Massacre, developed the idea of a covenant between people and God and between subjects and monarch. If the monarch ceased to observe the covenant, the purpose of which was to honor God, the representatives of the people (usually the nobles or others in an assembly of some sort) could resist the monarch.

Catholic writers saw the monarch as being given authority, especially religious authority, by God. The pope could dispose of a monarch who put people's souls in jeopardy by wrong beliefs.

Jean Bodin (1530–1596) developed the theory of sovereignty in response to the chaos of France during the civil wars. He believed that in each country one power or institution must be strong enough to make everyone else obey, or chaos would result. Bodin provided the theoretical basis for absolutist states.

Resistance to the power of monarchs was based upon claims to protect local customs, "traditional liberties," and "the ancient constitution." Nobles and towns appealed to the medieval past, when sovereignty had been shared by kings, nobles, and other institutions.

The French king dispensed with all representative institutions, dominated the nobility, and ruled directly. The nobles controlled the English government through the representative institution of Parliament. In Germany various components of the Holy Roman Empire defeated the Emperor and governed themselves independently of him.

ENGLAND

Problems Facing English Monarchs

The English church was a compromise of Catholic practices and Protestant beliefs and was criticized by both groups. The monarchs, after 1620, gave leadership of the church to men with Arminian beliefs, a modified Calvinist creed that deemphasized predestination. Arminius (1560–1609), a Dutch theologian, had changed Calvinist beliefs so as to modify, slightly, the emphasis on predestination. English Arminians also sought to emphasize the role of ritual in church services and to enjoy the "beauty of holiness," which their opponents took to be too Catholic. William Laud (1573–1645), Archbishop of Canterbury, accelerated the growth of Arminianism.

Opponents to this shift in belief were called Puritans, a term that covered a wide range of beliefs and people. To escape the church in England, many Puritans began moving to the New World, especially Massachusetts. Both James I and Charles I made decisions which, to Puritans, favored Catholics too much.

In financial matters, inflation and Elizabeth's wars left the government short of money. Contemporaries blamed the shortage on the extravagance of the courts of

James I and Charles I. James I sold titles of nobility in an effort to raise money, annoying nobles with older titles. The monarchs lacked any substantial source of income and had to obtain the consent of a Parliament to levy a tax.

Parliament met only when the monarch summoned it. Though Parliaments had existed since the Middle Ages, there were long periods of time between parliamentary meetings. Parliaments consisted of nobles and gentry, and a few merchants and lawyers. The men in a Parliament usually wanted the government to remedy grievances as part of the agreement to a tax. In 1621, for the first time since the Middle Ages, the power to impeach governmental servants was used by a Parliament to eliminate men who had offended its members.

The Counties

The 40 English counties had a tradition of much local independence. The major landowners—the nobles and the gentry—controlled the counties and resented central government interference.

James I (reigned 1603–1625)

James ended the war with Spain and avoided any other entanglements. The Earl of Somerset and then the Duke of Buckingham served as favorites for the king, doing much of the work of government.

Charles I (reigned 1625–1649)

Charles I inherited both the English and Scottish thrones at the death of his father, James I. He claimed a "divine right" theory of absolute authority for himself as king and sought to rule without Parliament. That rule also meant control of the Church of England. Henrietta Maria, a sister of the king of France and a Catholic, became his queen.

Charles stumbled into wars with both Spain and France during the late 1620s. A series of efforts to raise money for the wars led to confrontations with his opponents in Parliament. A "forced loan" was collected from taxpayers with the promise it would be repaid when a tax was voted by a Parliament. Soldiers were billeted in subjects' houses during the wars. People were imprisoned for resisting these royal actions. In 1626 the Duke of Buckingham was nearly impeached. In 1628 Parliament passed the Petition of Right, which declared royal actions involving loans and billeting illegal.

Charles ruled without calling a Parliament during the 1630s. A policy of "thorough"—strict efficiency and much central government activity—was followed, which included reinstating many old forms of taxation.

Breakdown

Charles, with the help of Archbishop Laud, attempted to impose English rituals and the English prayer book on the Scottish church. The Scots revolted and invaded northern England with an army.

To pay for his own army, Charles called the Short Parliament, but was not willing to remedy any grievances or change his policies. In response, the Parliament did not vote any taxes. Charles called another Parliament, the Long Parliament, which attacked his ministers, challenged his religious policies, and refused to trust him with money.

Archbishop Laud and the Earl of Strafford, the two architects of "thorough," were driven from power. The courts of Star Chamber and High Commission, which had been used to prosecute Charles's opponents, were abolished. When the Irish revolted, Parliament would not let Charles raise an army to suppress them, as it was feared he would use the army against his English opponents. John Pym (1584–1643) emerged as a leader of the king's opponents in Parliament.

Civil War

In August 1642 Charles abandoned all hope of negotiating with his opponents and instead declared war against them. Charles's supporters were called Royalists or Cavaliers. His opponents were called Parliamentarians or Roundheads, due to many who wore their hair cut short. This struggle is called the Puritan Revolution, the English Civil War, or the Great Rebellion.

Charles was defeated. His opponents had allied with the Scots who still had an army in England. Additionally, the New Model Army, with its general Oliver Cromwell (1599–1658), was superior to Charles's army.

With the collapse of government, new religious and political groups, such as Levellers, Quakers, and Ranters, appeared. Following the defeat of Charles, his opponents attempted to negotiate a settlement with him but with that failing, he was executed on January 30, 1649, and England became a republic for the next 11 years, headed by Cromwell.

The search for a settlement continued until 1689, when the nobles, gentry, and merchants, acting through Parliament, controlled the government and the monarchy.

FRANCE

Problems Facing the French Monarchs

The regions of France had long had a large measure of independence, and local parliaments could refuse to enforce royal laws. The centralization of all government proceeded by replacing local authorities with intendants, civil servants who reported to the king.

As a result of the Edict of Nantes, the Huguenots had separate rights and powers. All efforts to unify France under one religion faced both internal resistance from the Huguenots and the difficulty of dealing with Protestant powers abroad.

By 1650 France had been ruled by only one competent adult monarch since 1559. Louis XIII came to the throne at age 9 and Louis XIV at the age of 5. The mothers of both kings, Maria de' Medici and Anne of Austria, governed until the boys were of age. Both queens relied on chief ministers to help govern: Cardinal Richelieu and Cardinal Mazarin (1602–1661).

Henry IV (reigned 1589 – 1610)

Henry relied on the duke of Sully (1560–1641), the first of a series of strong ministers in the 17th century. Sully and Henry increased the involvement of the state in the economy, acting on a theory known as mercantilism. Monopolies on the production of gunpowder and salt were developed.

Louis XIII (reigned 1610–1643)

Cardinal Richelieu became the real power in France. Foreign policy was difficult because of the problems of religion. The unique status of the Huguenots was reduced through warfare and the Peace of Alais (1629), when their separate armed cities were eliminated. The nobility was reduced in power through constant attention to the laws and the imprisonment of offenders.

Breakdown

Cardinal Mazarin governed while Louis XIV (reigned 1643–1715) was a minor. During the Fronde, from 1649 to 1652, the nobility controlled Paris, drove Louis XIV and Mazarin from the city, and attempted to run the government. Noble ineffectiveness, the memories of the chaos of the wars of religion, and the overall anarchy convinced most people that a strong king was preferable to a warring nobility. The Fronde had little impact.

Absolutism

Louis XIV saw the need to increase royal power and his own glory and dedicated his life to these goals. He steadily pursued a policy of "one king, one law, one faith."

OTHER CONSTITUTIONAL STATES

United Provinces

Each province elected a stadholder to the Estates General. Usually all of the provinces elected the same man, the head of the house of Orange.

Calvinism divided when Arminius proposed a theology that reduced the emphasis on predestination. Though the stricter Calvinism prevailed, Arminians had full political and economic rights after 1632, and Catholics and Jews were also tolerated, though with fewer rights.

The merchants dominating the Estates General supported the laxer Arminianism and wanted peace, while the house of Orange adopted the stricter Calvinism and sought a more aggressive foreign policy.

The 17th century witnessed tremendous growth in the wealth and economic power of the Dutch. Amsterdam became the financial center of Europe. The Dutch also developed the largest fleet in Europe devoted to trade rather than warfare, and became the dominant trading country.

Sweden

Gustavus Adolphus reorganized the government, giving the nobles a dominant role in both the army and the bureaucracy.

As a result of Gustavus Adolphus's military actions, Sweden became a world power. Swedish economic power resulted from dominating the copper mines, the only ones in Europe.

In both the United Provinces and Sweden, the government was dominated by rich and powerful groups who used representative institutions to limit the power of the state and produce non-absolutist regimes.

EXPLORATIONS AND CONQUESTS

Motives

Specie, spices, and new trade routes were the impetus for exploration. Religion was also a strong motivation. To engage in missionary work, Jesuits, including Francis Xavier, traveled to India, Japan, and other areas by 1550.

Results

The wealth of the new world enabled Spain to embark on its military activities. European inflation, which existed prior to the discoveries, was further fueled by the influx of gold and silver. Disease killed perhaps 25 million, or 80 percent, of the Indians of the Americas. Syphilis appeared in Europe for the first time. Many foods, such as potatoes and tomatoes, were introduced to Europe. Europeans began transporting slaves from Africa to the Americas. A large number of English settled in North America and a smaller number of Spaniards in Central and South America.

Early Explorations

Portugal. Prince Henry the Navigator (1394–1460) supported exploration of the African coastline, largely in order to seek gold. Bartholomew Dias (1450–1500) rounded the southern tip of Africa in 1487. Vasco de Gama (1460–1524) reached India in 1498 and, after some fighting, soon established trading ports at Goa and Calicut. Albuquerque (1453–1515) helped establish an empire in the Spice Islands after 1510.

Spain. Christopher Columbus (1451–1506), seeking a new route to the (East) Indies, "discovered" the Americas in 1492. Ferdinand Magellan (1480–1521) circumnavigated the globe in 1521–1522. Conquests of the Aztecs by Hernando Cortes (1485–1547), and the Incas by Francisco Pizarro (ca. 1476–1541), enabled the Spanish to send much gold and silver back to Spain.

Other Countries. In the 1490s the Cabots, John (1450–1498) and Sebastian (ca. 1483–1557), explored North America, and after 1570, various Englishmen, including Francis Drake (ca. 1540–1596), fought the Spanish around the world. Jacques Cartier (1491–1557) explored parts of North America for France in 1534.

Early Seventeenth-Century Explorations and Settlements

Samuel de Champlain (1567–1635) and the French explored the St. Lawrence River, seeking furs to trade. The Dutch established settlements at New Amsterdam and in the Hudson River Valley. The Dutch founded trading centers in the East Indies, the West Indies, and southern Africa. Swedes settled on the Delaware River in 1638.

EARLY EUROPEAN EXPLORATIONS

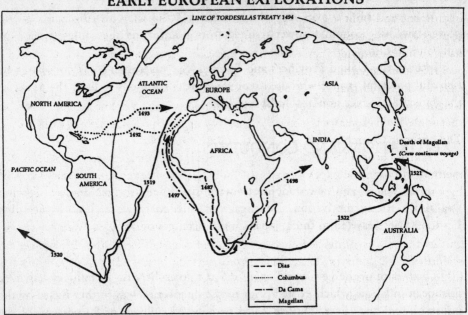

SCIENCE, LEARNING, AND SOCIETY

Beginnings of Modern Science

The scientific theories of the 16th and 17th centuries replaced religion as the explanation for the occurrences of the physical world. The approach of science relied on experiment and mathematics. Learning, including the arts, moved away from Renaissance models to emphasize the emotions and individual variations.

While the family as an institution remained unchanged, much of society was transformed through population growth, inflation, and new patterns of landholding, trade, and industry.

Scientific Revolution

Modern science had its origins in the 16th and 17th century "Scientific Revolution." "The Enlightenment" was an 18th-century movement.

Nicholas Copernicus (1473–1543) discovered that the Earth is but one of many planets revolving around the Sun, and that it turns on its own axis to make day and night. He demonstrated that the Greek mathematician, Ptolemy, was mistaken in his idea that the Earth was a stationary planet in the center of the universe.

Tycho Brahe (1546–1601), a Danish nobleman, built an expensive observatory and systematically pursued Copernicus's theories.

Johannes Kepler (1571–1630), the first great Protestant scientist and assistant to Brahe, discovered that the orbits of the planets are ellipses which complete their orbits in equal times. He explained the speed of the planets in their orbits and found that planets do not move with the Sun as focal point.

Galileo Galilei (1564–1642) was Professor of Physics and Military Engineering at the University of Padua. He was the first to use the telescope as a scientific instrument and built a powerful telescope himself. His discoveries and use of the telescope were a great aid in the voyages of discovery and had a direct effect on navigation. He provided artillery with a means of surveying distant targets for more accurate marksmanship. Galileo's discoveries in mechanics had far-reaching significance. He proved that all falling bodies descend with equal velocity, regardless of weight. He found that a long pendulum swing takes the same time as a short one, so that some force increases the speed of each swing by equal amounts in equal times. The Catholic Church forced him to recant his views.

Francis Bacon (1561–1626), Lord Chancellor of England, specified inductive method for scientific experimentation. Inductive observation, the development of hypotheses, experimentation, and organization were to be the keys to scientific inquiry.

René Descartes (1596–1650) wrote his *Discourse on Method* to build on the scientific method by using deductive analysis on scientific discoveries. He wrote that science must begin with clear and incontrovertible facts and then subdivide each problem into as many parts as necessary, following a step-by-step logical sequence in solving complex problems. Descartes was a leader in mathematics and philosophy.

LITERATURE AND THE ARTS

Literature

Cervantes's (1547–1616) *Don Quixote* (1605) satirized chivalric romances, describing a worldly-wise, skeptical peasant (Sancho Panzo) and a mentally unstable religious idealist (Don Quixote). William Shakespeare (1564–1616) mixed country, court, and Renaissance ideas of the English in the 1600s to produce tragedies, comedies, histories, and sonnets. The unique manner in which he utilized the English language permanently altered its future use. In *Paradise Lost*, John Milton (1608–1674), a Puritan, studied the motives of those who reject God. Michel de Montaigne (1533–1592) invented the essay and wrote about obtaining knowledge.

The Arts

Rejecting the balance and calm of Renaissance arts, Mannerists, who dominated painting and sculpture in the latter part of the 16th century, emphasized dramatic and emotional qualities. El Greco (1541–1614), a Greek who lived in Spain, took Mannerism to the extreme.

Seventeenth-century artists, such as Bernini (1598–1680) and Rubens (1577–1640), attempted to involve the viewer by emphasizing passion and mystery, as well as drama. Baroque, which emphasized grandeur, was connected with the Counter Reformation and monarchies, and was found primarily in Catholic countries.

Monteverdi (1567–1643) created the opera and the orchestra, and used many new instruments.

SOCIETY

Hierarchy

Hierarchical systems dominated Europe in the 16th and 17th centuries. Rural hierarchy consisted of landlords, peasants, and landless laborers. Urban hierarchy was comprised of merchants, artisans, and laborers. Clergy, lawyers, teachers, and civil servants fit somewhat awkwardly in both hierarchies. People seeking to join the aristocracy often sought education as a means of acquiring noble status and behavior. Wealth permitted an artisan to become a merchant or, after a generation or two, a rich peasant to become a noble. Higher groups were exempt from some taxes.

Demography

The population of Europe nearly doubled between 1500 and 1650. The population (very approximate) of some European countries in 1650 can be estimated as follows:

England	5.5 million
France	18.0 million
Holy Roman Empire	11.0 million
Italian peninsula	12.0 million
Spain	5.2 million
Sweden	1.5 million
United Provinces	1.5 million

Cities grew much faster than the population as a whole, as people migrated from the countryside. London grew from 50,000 in 1500 to 200,000 in 1650. Cities contained perhaps 10 to 20 percent of the total population of Europe.

The Family

The majority of households consisted of the nuclear family. A baby had a 25 percent chance of surviving to the age of 1, a 50 percent chance of surviving to the age of 20 and a 10 percent chance of reaching 60. The average age of marriage was approximately 27 for men and 25 for women, though the nobility married younger. Few people married early enough or lived long enough to see their grandchildren. The ideal of family relationships was patriarchal. Romantic love did exist, especially after marriage, but historians disagree as to whether it was the dominant element in forming marriages. Women, particularly in urban areas, shared in the work of their artisan and merchant husbands but rarely operated businesses themselves. Divorce was rare.

Witchcraft

Witch-hunting, though found in the late Middle Ages, peaked in the 16th and 17th centuries. Belief in witches was found at all levels of society. Increased concern with religion, as a result of the Reformation, focused more attention on the role of the devil in life, and may help explain the rise in witch-hunting. A charge of witchcraft could punish the nonconformist. Repression of sexuality could result in the projection of fears and hopes onto women, who then had to be punished. Though exact numbers are not possible, we know that thousands of witches were executed, with numbers varying from place to place.

The Economy

Inflation, sometimes called the price revolution, began around 1500 and continued until about the middle of the 17th century. Foodstuffs rose tenfold in price. The rise in population was the primary cause of the inflation. Another possible cause was the flow of silver from the Americas. Farmers sought to increase output as the price of food rose. Land that had been idle since the Black Death was recultivated. In England, enclosures produced larger, more efficient farms, but resulted in fewer people living on the land. In eastern Europe, landlords turned their lands into large wheat-exporting operations and began the process of converting the peasants and laborers into serfs. Trade and industry grew. The textile industry, the chief industry of Europe since the Middle Ages, underwent change. Regional specialization occurred on a large scale in textiles, Europe's chief industry. The putting-out system appeared, whereby the industry moved out of the cities into the countryside, and the process of production was divided into steps, with different workers doing each step.

3 BOURBON, BAROQUE, AND THE ENLIGHTENMENT (1648–1789)

HISTORICAL SETTING

The Thirty Years' War (1618–1648) had just ended, leaving a devastated Germany and a central Europe of some 400 semiautonomous states, referred to as "The Empire" (i.e., the Holy Roman Empire of the Middle Ages).

The Bourbon Dynasty emerged stronger than the Hapsburgs, who had dominated Europe for a century and a half.

Peace of Westphalia (1648)

The principle that "the religion of the prince is the religion of the realm" was extended to permit the Reformed faith (Calvinism) in Germany as well as Catholic and Lutheran churches.

Dutch and Swiss republics were granted formal recognition as independent powers. Additionally, Sweden, Prussia, and France gained new territory.

Treaty of the Pyrenees (1659)

The war between France and Spain continued for 11 more years until Spain finally ceded part of the Spanish Netherlands and territory in northern Spain to France. A marriage was arranged between Louis XIV, Bourbon king of France, and Maria Theresa, daughter of the Hapsburg king of Spain, Philip IV.

War of Devolution (First Dutch War), 1667–1668

After the death of his father-in-law, Philip IV, Louis XIV claimed the Spanish Netherlands (Belgium) in the name of his wife. The Law of Devolution granted inheritance to the heirs of a first marriage precedent to those of a second marriage. This law applied in private relationships to property rights, but Louis XIV applied it to political sovereignty.

France invaded the Spanish Netherlands with 50,000 troops in 1667 without a declaration of war. As a defensive measure, England, Holland, and Sweden formed the Triple Alliance.

Treaty of Aix-la-Chapelle (1668)

France received 12 fortified towns on the border of the Spanish Netherlands, but gave up Franche-Comté (Burgundy). The question of sovereignty over the Spanish Netherlands was deferred.

Second Dutch War (1672–1678)

Louis XIV sought revenge for Dutch opposition to French annexation of the Spanish Netherlands. France disputed the Triple Alliance by signing separate treaties with England (Charles II—Treaty of Dover, 1670) and with Sweden (1672).

In 1672, France invaded southern Holland with 100,000 troops. William III of Orange became head of state. At the war's end, Holland regained its lost territory.

Invasion of the Spanish Netherlands (1683)

France occupied Luxemburg and Trier and seized Lorraine while signing a 20-year truce with the Empire. The League of Augsburg was formed in 1686 to counteract the French and restore the balance of power. Members included the Empire, Holland, Spain, Sweden, the palatinate, Saxony, Bavaria, and Savoy.

War of the League of Augsburg (1688–1697)

The Glorious Revolution of 1688 brought William III of Orange and his English wife, Mary, to the throne of England, ending the possibility of another Catholic monarch.

The War of the League of Augsburg opened the long period of Anglo-French rivalry which continued until the defeat of Napoleon in 1815. France fought against the two leading naval powers of the day, Holland and England, in three theaters of war—the Rhine, the Low Countries, and Italy. Known in North America as King William's War (1689–1697), English and French colonials clashed along the New York and New England frontiers.

Treaty of Ryswick (1697)

France, England, and Holland agreed to restore captured territories. Fortresses in the Spanish Netherlands were to be garrisoned with Dutch troops as a buffer zone between France and Holland. French sovereignty over Alsace and Strasbourg was acknowledged as permanent.

War of the Spanish Succession (1702–1713)

Charles II, the last of the Hapsburg kings of Spain, died childless on November 1, 1700. The king's will named Philip of Anjou, the grandson of Louis XIV and Maria Theresa, to be king of Spain. In 1698, King Charles had named Emperor Leopold's grandson, the 7-year-old Electoral Prince Joseph Ferdinand of Bavaria, as his sole heir. The boy died a few months later in October 1700, and the king signed a new will in favor of Philip.

The Second Partition Treaty, however, signed by England, Holland, and France in May 1700, agreed that the son (later Emperor Charles VI) of the Austrian Hapsburg Emperor Leopold would become king of Spain, and Philip of Anjou would be compensated with Italian territories. (Both the mother and first wife of Leopold were daughters of Spanish kings.)

Issues involved in the War of the Spanish Succession concerned the future of the Spanish Empire. Additional primary causes concerned the possible separation of Austrian Hapsburg lands from Spain as well as the question of French/Bourbon strength in Spain.

The Grand Alliance

William III, king of England and stadtholder of Holland, did not want to see the Spanish Netherlands fall into French control. England also faced Spanish and French competition in the New World. A merger of the Spanish and French thrones would result in a coalition of Spain and France against England and Holland in the

Americas. In response, England, Holland, the Empire, and Prussia formed the Grand Alliance in September 1701.

War

France and Spain were stronger on land. England and Holland controlled the sea. The Battle of Blenheim, August 13, 1704, was a brilliant victory for England and the Duke of Marlborough, and one of the key battles of the war. It began a series of military reverses that prevented French domination of Europe. The allies invaded Spain and replaced Philip with Charles. The French and Spanish, however, rallied and drove the allies from both countries, restoring the Spanish throne to the Bourbons.

The war was known as Queen Anne's War (1702–1713) in North America. England was faced for the first time with an alliance of its two great rival empires, Spain and France.

Treaty of Utrecht (1713)

This was the most important European treaty since the Peace of Westphalia in 1648. The Spanish Empire was partitioned and a Bourbon remained on the throne of Spain. Philip V (Philip of Anjou) retained Spain and the Spanish Empire in America and renounced his claims to the French throne. The Hapsburg Empire in Central Europe acquired the Spanish Netherlands (Austrian Netherlands thereafter) and territories in Italy. England took Gibraltar, Minorca, Newfoundland, Hudson's Bay, and Nova Scotia. France retained Alsace and the city of Strasbourg. As a result, the Hapsburgs became a counterbalance to French power in western Europe, but no longer occupied the Spanish throne.

War of the Austrian Succession (1740–1748)

Charles VI died in 1740 and his daughter, 23-year-old Maria Theresa (reigned 1740–1780), inherited the Austrian Hapsburg Empire. Frederick the Great, age 28, (reigned 1740–1786) had just inherited the Prussian throne from his father, Frederick William I. In 1740 Frederick suddenly invaded the Hapsburg territory of Silesia, and England joined Austria against Prussia, Bavaria, France, and Spain.

Frederick's brilliant military tactics won many victories. His long night marches, sudden flank attacks, and surprise actions contrasted with the usual siege warfare of the time.

The war was known in North America as King George's War (1744–1748). The Treaty of Aix-la-Chapelle (1748) ended the war and Prussia emerged as one of the Great Powers. By retaining Silesia, Prussia doubled its population.

The Seven Years' War (1756–1763)

Britain and France renewed hostilities as the French and Indian War (1754–1763) began at the entrance to the Ohio Valley. At stake was control of the North American continent.

In Europe, Austria sought to regain Silesia, with its important textile industry and rich deposits of coal and iron. Maria Theresa persuaded Louis XV of France to aid Austria in a war with Prussia.

Russia, under Tsarina Elizabeth (reigned 1741–1762), joined the alliance. Great Britain provided Prussia with funds but few troops. Prussia was faced with fighting almost alone against three major powers of Europe: Austria, France, and Russia. Their combined population was 15 times that of Prussia.

In six years Prussia won eight brilliant victories and lost eight others. Berlin was twice captured and partially burned by Russian troops. Still, Prussia prevailed. In the process it emerged as one of the great powers of Europe.

William Pitt the Elder (1708–1778) led the British to victory. The Royal Navy defeated both the French Atlantic and Mediterranean squadrons in 1759. The British captured French posts near Calcutta and Madras in India, and defeated the French in Quebec and Montreal.

In 1762 Elizabeth of Russia died, and her successor, Tsar Peter III, took Russia out of the war at a historically decisive moment.

By the Treaty of Hubertsburg (1763,) Austria recognized Prussian retention of Silesia.

Treaty of Paris (1763)

France lost all possessions in North America to Britain. (In 1762 France had ceded to Spain all French claims west of the Mississippi River and New Orleans.) France retained fishing rights off the coast of Newfoundland and Martinique and Guadeloupe, sugar islands in the West Indies. Spain ceded the Floridas to Britain in exchange for the return of Cuba.

The American War for Independence as a European War (1775–1783)

France entered the French-American Alliance of 1778 in an effort to regain lost prestige in Europe and to weaken her British adversary. In 1779 Spain joined France in the war, hoping to recover Gibraltar and the Floridas. Rochambeau's (1725–1807) and Lafayette's(1757–1834) French troops aided Washington at Yorktown.

Treaty of Paris (1783)

Britain recognized the independence of the United States of America and retroceded the Floridas to Spain. Britain left France no territorial gains by signing a separate and territorially generous treaty with the United States.

ECONOMIC DEVELOPMENTS

Traditional Economic Conditions

Poverty was the norm during the Middle Ages. As late as 1700, the overall life expectancy was 30 years of age. Subsistence farming was the dominant occupation, and famine was a regular part of life. One-third of the population of Finland, for example, died in the famine of 1696–1697. France, one of the richer agricultural lands, experienced 11 general famines in the 17th century and sixteen in the 18th century. Contagious diseases decimated towns and villages: smallpox, measles, diptheria, typhoid, scarlet fever, bubonic plague, and typhus.

Political and economic freedoms associated with the Protestant Reformation and the biblical work ethic gradually began to change the economy of Europe as innovation, hard work, frugality, and entrepreneurship became the norm.

Social Institutions Necessary for Commerce and a Prosperous Economy

Innovations in business arrangements included joint-stock companies, which enabled enterprises to accumulate capital from many investors. Double-entry book-keeping provided a check on clerical accuracy, enabling managers to detect errors. Banknotes were used as a medium of exchange.

Mercantilism

There were several basic assumptions of mercantilism: 1) Wealth is measured in terms of commodities, especially gold and silver, rather than in terms of productivity and income-producing investments; 2) Economic activities should increase the power of the national government in the direction of state controls; 3) Since a favorable balance of trade was important, a nation should purchase as little as possible from nations regarded as enemies. The concept of the mutual advantage of trade was not widely accepted; 4) Colonies existed for the benefit of the mother country, not for any mutual benefit that would be gained by economic development.

The philosophy of mercantilism had mixed results in the economy of Europe. On the one hand, the state encouraged economic growth and expansion. On the other, it tended to stifle entrepreneurship, competition, and innovation through monopolies, trade restrictions, and state regulation of commerce.

Taxes were generally low enough to not discourage economic expansion. There were few administrative officials, and communication and transportation were slow. Compare France, one of the most bureaucratic states of Europe in the 18th century, with France in the 20th century. Then there was one bureaucrat for every 1,250 people. Today it is one for every 70 people.

The wars of the 17th and 18th centuries involved dynastic disputes, balance-of-power struggles, and mercantilistic competition for trade, raw materials, and colonies.

The Dutch and the English led the way toward the concept of productivity as a measure of national wealth. As a result Holland became one of the most productive countries in the 17th century, and England in the 18th and 19th centuries.

In France Jean Baptiste Colbert (1619–1683), economic adviser to Louis XIV, used the government to encourage economic productivity and aided in the prosperity of France. But his dictatorial regulations were also counterproductive. For example, he forbade the emigration of skilled French workers and specified methods of production in detail. He also believed that foreign trade was a fixed quantity rather than one that grew with demand and lower prices. France, as did most states, had high protective tariffs. The lowering of interest rates also stimulated investment and productivity.

Growth of Trade

The need for spices for food preservation, and the desire for luxury goods from the Far East and the Near East served as incentive for expanding Europe's overseas trade.

Population growth expanded domestic markets far in excess of overseas trade. European population at the beginning of the seventeenth century was 70 million. By the end of the 18th century it had doubled. Productivity and economic growth increased even faster.

Scientific and technological discoveries and inventions stimulated trade. Three-masted trading vessels lowered the costs of transportation and made trading possible over greater distances. Canal and road building also stimulated trade and productivity.

Capitalist systems of banking, insurance, and investment made possible the accumulation of capital essential for discovery and economic growth.

Urbanization was both a cause and a result of economic growth. Urbanization required and created a network of market relationships. Towns with prosperous trade increased in population, while towns which did not prosper in trade quickly stagnated. Urbanization provided the opportunity and market for commercial services such as banking, insurance, warehousing, and commodity trading, as well as medicine, law, government, and churches.

Agricultural Changes

Absentee landlords and commercial farms replaced feudal manors, especially in England. Urbanization, increased population, and improvements in trade stimulated the demand for agricultural products.

The design of farm implements improved. Drainage and reclamation of swamp land was expanded. Experiments with crops, seeds, machines, breeds of animals, and fertilizers were systematically attempted.

Improvements in Transportation

The construction of canals and roads was of fundamental importance. The major rivers of France were linked by canals during the 17th century.

Industrial Technology

Thomas Newcomen in 1706 invented an inefficient steam engine as a pump. James Watt, between 1765 and 1769, improved the design so that the expansive power of hot steam could drive a piston. Later Watt translated the motion of the piston into rotary motion.

The steam engine became one of the most significant inventions in human history. It was no longer necessary to locate factories on mountain streams where water wheels were used to supply power. Its portability meant that both steamboats and railroad engines could be built to transport goods across continents. Ocean-going vessels were no longer dependent on winds to power them.

At the same time, textile machines revolutionized that industry. John Kay introduced the flying shuttle in 1733. James Hargreaves patented the spinning jenny in 1770. Richard Arkwright perfected the spinning frame in 1769. Samuel Crompton introduced the spinning mule in 1779. Edward Cartwright invented the power loom in 1785.

Factors in Sustained Economic Growth

The development of free enterprise stimulated new ideas. This was more possible where the state was not excessively involved in the economy. In England, the Puritan Revolution of the 1640s challenged the royal right to grant monopolies and trade privileges. The English common law afterwards adopted the principle of free enterprise open to all. With free enterprise came the responsibility of risk taking.

Free movement of populations provided necessary labor resources. Many moved to England from the continent. The population of England, about 5.5 million in 1700s, was only 6 million by 1750. The economic growth during the last half of the century increased the population of England to 9 million by 1800, and to 18 million by 1850.

BOURBON FRANCE

French Foreign Policy

France was the dominant European power from 1660 to 1713. Louis XIV, however, was unable to extend French boundaries to the Rhine River—one of his chief objectives.

From 1713 to 1789 no one European power dominated international politics. Instead, the concept of the balance of power prevailed. A readjustment of power was necessary in central and eastern Europe as a result of the decline of Sweden, Poland, and the Ottoman Empire. This period was characterized by a power struggle between France and England for colonial supremacy in India and in America.

France Under Louis XIV (reigned 1643–1715)

Louis XIV was vain, arrogant, and charming. The king had hours of council meetings and endless ceremonies and entertainments. He aspired to be an absolute ruler.

The most significant challenge to royal absolutism in France in the 17th century was a series of three revolts (called *Frondes*, meaning "a child's slingshot") by some of the nobility and judges of the parlements or courts of Paris. Competition among the nobility, however, enabled the government to put down the revolts. All three of these occurred when Louis XIV was very young (from 1648 to 1653) and made a lasting impression on him; he was determined that no revolt would be successful during his reign.

The king believed in absolute, unquestioned authority. Louis XIV deliberately chose his chief ministers from the middle class in order to keep the aristocracy out of government. No members of the royal family or the high aristocracy were admitted to the daily council sessions at Versailles, where the king presided personally over the deliberations of his ministers.

Council orders were transmitted to the provinces by intendants, who supervised all phases of local administration (especially courts, police, and the collection of taxes). Additionally, Louis XIV nullified the power of French institutions which might challenge his centralized bureaucracy.

Louis XIV never called the Estates General. His intendants arrested the members of the three provincial estates who criticized royal policy, and the parlements were too intimidated by the lack of success of the *Frondes* to offer further resistance.

Control of the peasants, who comprised 95 percent of the French population, was accomplished by numerous means. Some peasants kept as little as 20 percent of their cash crops after paying the landlord, the government, and the Church. Peasants also were subject to the *corvée*, a month's forced labor on the roads. People not at work on the farm were conscripted into the French army or put into workhouses. Finally, rebels were hanged or forced to work as galley slaves.

Colbert, finance minister from 1661 to 1683, improved the economy and the condition of the royal treasury. He reduced the number of tax collectors; reduced local tolls in order to encourage domestic trade; improved France's transportation system with canals and a growing merchant marine; organized a group of French trading companies (the East India Company, the West India Company, the Levant Company, and the Company of the North); and paid bounties to shipbuilders to strengthen trade.

Palace of Versailles

Louis XIV moved his royal court from the Louvre in Paris to Versailles, 12 miles outside of Paris. In Paris the court included 600 people. At Versailles it grew to 10,000 noblemen, officials, and attendants. Sixty percent of the royal tax revenue was spent on Versailles and the upkeep of the court of Louis XIV. Extravagant amusements such as tournaments, hunts, tennis, billiards, boating parties, dinners, dances, ballets, operas, concerts, and theater were meant to occupy the aristocratic court so that they would not challenge the king. In order to celebrate the birth of his son in 1662, the king arranged a ball at the Palace of the Carousel, which was attended by 15,000 people who danced under 1,000 lights before massive mirrors.

Louis XIV's Policies Toward Christianity

The king considered himself the head of the French Catholic church and claimed that the pope had no temporal authority over the French church. Louis XIV sided with the Jesuits against the Jansenists, Catholics like Blaise Pascal (1623–1662) who reaffirmed St. Augustine's doctrine of inherent depravity, i.e., that man is born by nature a sinner and that salvation is only for the elect of God.

About a million French citizens were Protestant. Louis XIV attempted to eradicate Protestantism from France by demolishing Huguenot churches and schools, paying cash rewards to Protestants to convert to Catholicism, and billeting soldiers in the homes of those who refused to convert. In 1685 the king revoked the Edict of Nantes, thus withdrawing civil rights and religious freedom from Protestants. Protestant children were required by law to be raised as Catholics. French Protestant clergymen were exiled or sent to the galleys. As many as 200,000 Huguenots fled from France—to England, Holland, and America. Protestantism did survive in France, but was greatly weakened.

France Under Louis XV (reigned 1715–1774)

French people of all classes desired greater popular participation in government, and resented the special privileges of the aristocracy. All nobles were exempt from certain taxes. Many were subsidized with regular pensions from the government. The highest offices of government were reserved for aristocrats. Promotions were based on political connections rather than merit. Life at Versailles was wasteful, extravagant, and frivolous.

There was no uniform code of laws and little justice. The king had arbitrary powers of imprisonment. Government bureaucrats were often petty tyrants, many of them merely serving their own interests. The bureaucracy became virtually a closed class. Vestiges of the feudal and manorial systems taxed peasants excessively compared to other segments of society. The *philosophes* gave expression to these grievances and discontent grew.

When Louis XV died, he left many of the same problems he had inherited from his great-grandfather, Louis XIV. Corruption and inequity in government were even more pronounced. Ominously, crowds lined the road to St. Denis, the burial place of French kings, and cursed the king's casket just as they had his predecessor.

France Under Louis XVI (reigned 1774–1792)

Louis XVI was the grandson of Louis XV. He married Marie Antoinette (1770), daughter of the Austrian Empress Maria Theresa. Louis XVI was honest, conscientious, and sought genuine reforms, but he was indecisive and lacking in determination. He antagonized the aristocracy when he sought fiscal reforms. One of his first acts was to restore judicial powers to the French parlements. When he sought to impose new taxes on the undertaxed aristocracy, the parlements refused to register the royal decrees. In 1787 he granted toleration and civil rights to French Huguenots (Protestants).

In 1787 the king summoned the Assembly of the Notables, a group of 144 representatives of the nobility and higher clergy. Louis XVI asked them to tax all lands, without regard to privilege of family; to establish provincial assemblies; to allow free trade in grain; and to abolish forced labor on the roads. The Notables refused to accept these reforms and demanded the replacement of certain of the king's ministers.

The climax of the crisis came in 1788 when the king was no longer able to achieve either fiscal reform or new loans. He could not even pay the salaries of government officials. By this time one-half of government revenues went to pay interest on the national debt (at eight percent).

For the first time in 175 years, the king called for a meeting of the Estates General (1789). The Estates General formed itself into the National Assembly, and the French Revolution was under way.

SPAIN: HAPSBURG AND BOURBON

Spain in the Seventeenth Century

The Peace of Westphalia (1648) did not end the war between Spain and France; it continued for 11 more years. In the Treaty of the Pyrenees (1659), Spain ceded Artois in the Spanish Netherlands and territory in northern Spain to France. Marriage was arranged between Louis XIV, Bourbon king of France, and Maria Theresa, Hapsburg daughter of Philip IV, king of Spain. (Louis XIV's mother was the daughter of Philip III of Spain.)

The population of Spain in the 17th century declined as Spain continued expelling Moors. In 1550 Spain had a population of 7.5 million; by 1660 it was about 5.5 million. Formerly food-producing lands were deserted. In Castile, sheep raising took the place of food production. Food was imported from elsewhere in Europe. As production declined, inflation increased. Work was looked upon as a necessary evil, to be avoided when possible. The upper classes preferred a life of cultured ease instead of developing and caring for their estates. Patents of nobility were purchased from the crown, carrying with them many tax exemptions.

Capitalism was almost non-existent in Spain, as savings and investment were viewed as beneath the dignity of the nobility. What industry there was in Spain— silk, woolens, and leatherwork—was declining instead of growing.

Catholic orthodoxy and aristocratic exclusiveness were valued in Spanish society. In 1660 the Spanish clergy numbered 200,000, an average of one for every 30 people.

The Spanish navy had ceased to exist by 1700, and most of the soldiers in the Spanish army were foreigners.

Spain Under Charles II (reigned 1665–1700)

Charles II, the last of the Spanish Hapsburg kings, was only 4 years old when his father, Philip IV, died. His mother, Marie Anne of Austria, controlled the throne as head of the council of regency. Afflicted with many diseases and a weak constitution, the king was expected to die young. Charles's timidity and lack of willpower made him one of the worst rulers in Spanish history.

In 1680 he married Marie Louise of France, and on her death in 1689, he married Marie Anne of Bavaria. Since he had no children, Charles II's death in 1700 led to the War of the Spanish Succession.

Philip V (reigned 1683–1746)

The grandson of Louis XIV, this first Bourbon king of Spain was only 17 when he became king in 1700. The first dozen years of his reign were occupied with the War of the Spanish Succession, which ended successfully for him. He modernized the Spanish army and increased it to 40,000 men.

Philip V centralized the Spanish government by using the French intendant system. He abolished many pensions and government subsidies and restored fiscal health to the Spanish government.

Industry, agriculture, and shipbuilding were actively encouraged. The Spanish navy was revived and the fleet was substantial by the end of his reign.

Philip V married 14-year-old Marie Louise of Savoy, and when she died in 1714 he married Elizabeth Farnese of Parma. Philip V died during the War of the Austrian Succession and was succeeded by his son by Marie Louise, Ferdinand VI, who ruled for an uneventful 13 years from 1746 through 1759.

Charles III (reigned 1759–1788)

Charles III had already had political experience as duke of Parma and king of the Two Sicilies. He was an able ruler and enacted many reforms during his long reign. Moral, pious, and hardworking, Charles III was one of the most popular Spanish kings.

Charles helped stimulate the economy by eliminating laws that restricted internal trade and reducing tariffs. He encouraged new agricultural settlements and established banks for farmers. He created factories and gave them monopolies: woolens, tapestries, mirrors and glass, silks, and porcelain. Schools were established to teach trades. By the end of his reign, the population of Spain had grown to 10.5 million.

Spain was a strongly Catholic country, and Spanish intellectuals were not interested in the doctrines of the Enlightenment, and were repulsed by the irreligion of the philosophes.

AUSTRIAN HAPSBURGS AND CENTRAL EUROPE

History of the Hapsburgs

In 1273 Rudolf of Hapsburg was elected Holy Roman Emperor and gained permanent possession of Austria for the Hapsburg family. The Holy Roman Empire was still intact in the 18th century and consisted of 300 separate states, 51 free towns, and 1,500 free knights ruling tiny states with an average of 300 subjects and an annual income of $500. The largest states of the Empire were the Hapsburg Monarchy, with a population of 10 million inside the Empire and 12 million outside; Prussia, with a population of 5.5 million; Bavaria and Saxony, with a population of 2 million each; and Hanover, with a population of 900,000. The emperor also claimed authority over 75 five small principalities.

The custom was to select the ruler of Austria as the emperor because he alone had sufficient power to enforce imperial decisions. (A brief exception was Charles VII of Bavaria.) After the War of the Spanish Succession (1702–1713) and the Treaty of Utrecht (1713), the Spanish throne was occupied by a Bourbon, so Hapsburg power was concentrated in Austria. The Austrian Hapsburgs ruled the Empire: Naples, Sardinia, and Milan in Italy; the Austrian Netherlands (now Belgium); Hungary and Transylvania. Austria's lands included Germans, Hungarians, Czechs, Croats, Italians, Serbs, Rumanians, and others.

Government of the Austrian Empire

Since different parts of the Empire bore a different legal relationship to the emperor, there was no single constitutional system or administration for all parts of the realm. The emperor held a number of titles, including king of Bohemia.

Feudalism in the Hapsburg Empire

The lords of the manor had political, judicial, and economic power over the peasants. They could not marry without the lord's consent. Their children could not work or serve an apprenticeship outside the estate. The peasant could not contract a loan or sell anything without the lord's consent. Peasants were obligated to the *corvée*, or compulsory labor, for as many as 100 days a year. They were obliged to buy products supplied by the lord at the prices he set. There were tolls to pay, customs duties, duties on transactions, quitrents and other taxes.

Emperor Leopold I (reigned 1658–1705)

Leopold I was the first cousin of King Louis XIV of France and of King Charles II of Spain. He loved poetry, music, and was a patron of the arts. A devout Catholic, Leopold followed the advice of the Jesuits and sought to severely restrict his Protestant subjects.

One of Leopold's most severe tests came with the Turkish invasion of Austria, and siege of Vienna itself, in 1683. The Turks were driven back by the Poles, Austrians, and Hungarians.

Emperor Leopold I was a key figure in the War of Spanish Succession.

Emperor Charles VI (reigned 1711–1740)

Following a brief reign by his older brother, Joseph I (1705–1711), Charles VI, son of Leopold I, came to the Austrian throne. Charles VI had a keen sense of duty and lived a moral life. He was meticulous in his administration and personally involved in the details of governing.

Maria Theresa (reigned 1740–1780)

Maria Theresa was a courageous, high-minded, pious, and capable ruler. Her first reform was to increase the Austrian standing army from 30,000 to 108,000 by persuading the various estates to accept tax reforms and a tax increase. She gradually centralized the Empire and increased the power of the Austrian government.

Maria Theresa was a conservative Catholic who considered the Church and the nobility to be the foundations of her state. But she was concerned with the freedom and well-being of her subjects. Political realism was the hallmark of her reign. The two most important international events of her 40-year reign were the War of the Austrian Succession (1740–1748) and the Seven Years' War (1756–1763).

Joseph II (reigned 1765–1790)

Joseph II was co-regent with his mother for the last 15 years of her reign. He sought to be an "enlightened despot"—with emphasis on despot. He wanted to govern decisively and forcefully, but rationally with the interests of his subjects in mind—at least as he envisioned them. He sought a full treasury, economy in government, and a strong military force. He sought to emulate the achievements and style of Frederick the Great of Prussia.

Although the emperor was a devout Catholic, he expanded the state schools of Austria and granted religious toleration to both Protestants and Jews. Joseph II died at the age of 49 having suffered recent military defeats from the Turks and fearing both the growing power of Russia and revolts in the Austrian Netherlands.

PRUSSIA AND THE HOHENZOLLERNS

Brandenburg-Prussia in 1648

The Thirty Years' War had devastated Germany. Brandenburg lost half its population through death, disease, and emigration. Brandenburg's ruler was an elector of the Holy Roman Empire. Despite its central location, Brandenburg was an insignificant part of the empire. By marriage, the House of Hohenzollern had acquired widely separated parts of the Empire. In the west Hohenzollerns governed the duchy of Cleves and the counties of Mark and Ravensberg; in the east they governed the duchy of East Prussia.

The Peace of Westphalia (1648) granted the elector eastern Pomerania, three tiny bishoprics, and the archbishopric of Magdeburg. Nothing in these possessions or any of the other disparate territories showed any promise of becoming a great power of Europe. Each province had its own estates, representing the towns and the nobility. They had little in common and no common administration. The terrain had no natural frontiers for defense and was not economically significant. Its population was sparse, its soil poor and sandy. It was cut off from the sea and was not on any of the trade routes of Europe.

Frederick William (reigned 1640–1688)

During his half-century reign, the "Great Elector" established Prussia as a great power and laid the foundation for the future unification of Germany in the 19th century. He took the title "king of Prussia," since East Prussia lay outside the boundaries of the Holy Roman Empire and thus was not in the jurisdiction of the Austrian Hapsburgs.

Frederick William was the nephew of King Gustavus Adolphus of Sweden and his wife was the granddaughter of William the Silent, hero of Dutch independence. He sought to emulate the government organization of the Swedes and the economic policies of the Dutch. Frederick was well educated and spoke five languages. He was a strict Calvinist and settled 20,000 Huguenot refugees on his estates. He also granted toleration to both Catholics and Jews.

His most significant innovation was the building of a strong standing army. He was able to do this only through heavy taxes, at a rate of taxation twice as heavy as that of the French during the height of Louis XIV's power. But the Prussian nobility were not exempt from heavy taxes as were the French aristocracy.

The Elector sought to encourage industry and trade, but he was in danger of taxing them out of existence. New industries were started: woolens, cottons, linen, velvet, lace, silk, soap, paper, and iron products. The Frederick William Canal through Berlin linked the Elbe and Oder rivers and enabled canal traffic from Breslau and Hamburg to Berlin.

The central dynamic of Frederick William's life was Calvinism, through which he became convinced of direct protection and guidance from God in all he did. He valued learning highly and founded the University of Pufendorf and the Berlin Library. He was greatly alarmed at the threat to Protestantism implied in Louis XIV's revocation of the Edict of Nantes in 1685 and joined the League of Augsburg in 1686.

Frederick I (reigned 1688–1713)

The Great Elector's son (i.e., Elector Frederick III and King Frederick I) was a weak and somewhat deformed man, but he won the affection of his people as did no other Hohenzollern. He loved the splendor of the monarchy and elaborate ceremony.

Frederick I founded the University of Halle in 1694, a center for two of the great concepts of the time, Pietism and Natural Law. The king welcomed as immigrants both craftsmen and scholars. The Enlightenment philosopher Gottfried Wilhelm Leibnitz persuaded Frederick to found an academy of science.

Much of Frederick I's reign was spent at war. Prussia participated in the War of the League of Augsburg (1688–1697) and the War of the Spanish Succession (1702–1713). It did not gain territorially, but built up its military tradition. The costs of war were a heavy financial burden to the small state.

Frederick William I (reigned 1713–1740)

This king was quite different from his father. He cut the number of court officials drastically, not only for economy, but because he was impatient with ceremony.

He believed Prussia needed a strong standing army and a plentiful treasury and proceeded to acquire both. Prussia's army grew from 45,000 to 80,000 during his reign, despite a population of only 2.5 million. Military expenditures consumed 80 percent of state revenues, compared with 60 percent in France and 50 percent in Austria. On the other hand, he only spent 2 percent of tax revenues to maintain his court, compared with 6 percent in Austria under Maria Theresa. Frederick built the fourth largest army in Europe, repaid all state debts, and left his successor a surplus of 10 million thaler.

The only time he went to war was when Charles XII of Sweden occupied Stalsund. Prussia immediately attacked and forced Sweden out. In 1720 Sweden agreed to the Prussian annexation of the port of Stettin and Pomeranian territory west of the river Oder.

Prussia continued close relations with Holland and England. King George I of England was Frederick William's uncle and father-in-law.

Prussia developed the most efficient bureaucracy in Europe. Merit promotions rewarded efficiency and diligence. The civil bureaucracy as well as the military were based on the principle of absolute obedience and discipline.

The king was a ceaseless worker and expected the same from those about him, including his son, the future Frederick the Great. The king entrusted his son's early education to his old governess, who taught Frederick to speak French better than German. Frederick William also established a thousand schools for peasant children.

Frederick the Great (Frederick II, reigned 1740–1786)

Frederick the Great inherited his throne at age 28. His father left him a prosperous economy, a full treasury, an income of seven million thalers, and an army of 80,000. Unlike his father, Frederick loved French literature, poetry, and music. He played the flute and wrote poetry all his life.

Frederick's philosophy of government was that the state existed for the gratification of the ruled, not the ruled for the state. All his life Frederick pondered questions of religion, morality, and power. French literature dominated his reading.

In October 1740 the Emperor Charles VI died, and in December Frederick ordered a sudden attack on Silesia. Thus began 23 years of warfare, with the Great Powers of Europe (France, Austria, and Russia) aligned against Prussia. Their combined population was 15 times that of Prussia. Yet Prussia emerged a quarter century later with enlarged territories of rich land and nearly twice its former population. Prussia alone saw 180,000 killed and its entire society was seriously disrupted. Still, Prussia emerged as one of the Great Powers of Europe.

The remaining 23 years of the king's life were spent in rebuilding and reforming what he had nearly destroyed. Society stressed frugality, discipline, and hard work. The king provided funds to rebuild towns and villages, used reserve grain for seed-planting, and requisitioned horses for farming. He suspended taxes in some areas for six months as an economic stimulant. He started many new industries. Frederick also oversaw the reform of the judicial system. His system was one of "constitutional absolutism."

In 1772, as part of the First Partition of Poland, Prussia acquired western Prussia, thus linking most of its territories.

THE DUTCH REPUBLIC

Historical Background

The Netherlands, known today as Holland and Belgium, were governed by the Spanish Hapsburgs, but each of the 17 provinces had its own special privileges and limited autonomy within the Spanish Empire.

During the Protestant Reformation of the 16th century, large numbers of Dutch were converted to Calvinism ("Reformed" churches), especially in the north. Catholicism remained stronger in the south (now Belgium).

When Philip II, king of Spain, began demonstrating his determination to use the Spanish Inquisition to enforce laws against "heresy," the Netherlands began a revolt against Spain which continued intermittently for more than 80 years (1566–1648).

In 1578, the Duke of Parma restored many of the old privileges of self-government to the 10 southern provinces, and large numbers of Calvinists moved north. In 1581 the seven northern Dutch provinces, under the leadership of William the Silent, declared themselves independent of Spain. In 1588 the great Spanish Armada sent to attack both the English and the Dutch was partially destroyed by a storm and then defeated by the English seadogs.

In 1648 the Peace of Westphalia recognized the independence of the Republic of the United Provinces. This had already been conceded by Spain in the Treaty of Münster, January 20, 1648.

Government of the Netherlands

The Dutch republic consisted of the seven northern provinces of Zeeland,

Utrecht, Holland, Gelderland, Overijssel, Groningen, and Friesland. Holland was the wealthiest and most powerful. Each province and city was autonomous.

National problems were governed by the States General, which consisted of delegates from the provinces that could act only on the instructions of the provincial assemblies. Each province had a stadtholder, or governor, who was under the authority and instructions of the assembly. In times of crisis the provinces would sometimes choose the same stadtholder, and he thereby became the national leader.

Dutch Economy

The 17th century was the Golden Age of the Dutch. Not only was it the age of Rembrandt (1606–1669) and other great Dutch painters, but the Netherlands was the most prosperous part of Europe. It was also the freest. The Dutch did not have government controls and monopolies to impede their freedom of enterprise. As a result they became the greatest mercantile nation in Europe, with the largest merchant marine in the world.

Medium-sized cities and ports such as Leyden, Haarlem, Gouda, Delft, and Utrecht (with populations ranging from 20,000 to 40,000) were characteristic of the Netherlands. Amsterdam, with a population of 100,000, was the richest city in Europe. The quays and wharves of Dutch cities were stocked with Baltic grain, English woolens, silks and spices from India, sugar from the Caribbean, salted herring, and coal.

The Dutch had almost no natural resources, but built their economy around the carrying of trade, mercantile businesses, and other service occupations. They were skilled in finishing raw materials. Coarse linens from Germany were bleached and finished into fine textiles. The Dutch excelled at furniture making, fine woolen goods, sugar refining, tobacco cutting, brewing, pottery, glass, printing, paper making, armament manufacturing, and shipbuilding.

The Dutch taught accounting methods and provided banks and rational legal methods for settling disputes. Their low interest rate was a key to economic growth—it was 3 percent, half of the normal rate in England. The Dutch were held up as champions of free enterprise and individual rights, in contrast to state absolutism, economic nationalism, mercantilism, and protective tariffs.

The Dutch East India Company and the Dutch West India Company were organized as cooperative ventures of private enterprise and the state. The various provinces contributed part of the capital for these ventures and the companies were subject to the authority of the States General.

Dutch Art

The artistic center of the Netherlands was Amsterdam, where the Dutch school of painters was noted for their landscape and portrait painting, and especially for "genre painting" in which scenes of everyday life predominate. The Calvinist influence in Holland is reflected in their celebration, but not idealization, of God's Creation. The realistic portrait paintings show mankind as great and noble, but also flawed.

The Dutch painters were masters of light and shadow. It is interesting to contrast the equally-great Flemish contemporary school in the Spanish Netherlands, which was strongly influenced by the counter-Reformation Baroque. Peter Paul Rubens (1577–1640) from Antwerp is a good example.

Dutch Wars and Foreign Policy

After being freed from Spanish domination, the Dutch were faced with a series of wars against England over trading rights and colonial competition. Then Louis XIV's efforts to move into the Low Countries brought the Dutch into a drawn out war with France.

The accession of William and Mary to the throne of England in 1688 brought an end to the warfare with England. In the War of the Spanish Succession (1702–1713), England and Holland fought against France and Spain.

ENGLAND, SCOTLAND, AND IRELAND

The English Civil War (1642–1649)

One of the underlying issues in this conflict was the constitutional issue of the relationship between king and Parliament. Could the king govern without the consent of Parliament, or go against the wishes of Parliament? In short, the question was whether England was to have a limited constitutional monarchy, or an absolute monarchy as in France and Prussia.

The theological issue focused on the form of church government England was to have—whether it would follow the established Church of England's hierarchical, episcopal form of church government, or acquire a presbyterian form. The episcopal form meant that the king, the Archbishop of Canterbury, and the bishops of the church would determine policy, theology, and the form of worship and service. The presbyterian form of polity allowed for more freedom of conscience and dissent among church members. Each congregation would have a voice in the life of the church, and a regional group of ministers, or "presbytery," would attempt to ensure "doctrinal purity."

The political implications for representative democracy were present in both issues. That is why most Presbyterians, Puritans, and Congregationalists sided with Parliament and most Anglicans and Catholics sided with the king.

The Petition of Right (1628)

The Parliament in effect bribed the king by granting him a tax grant in exchange for his agreement to the Petition of Right. It stipulated that no one should pay any tax, gift, loan, or contribution except as provided by an act of Parliament; no one should be imprisoned or detained without due process of law; all were to have the right to the writ of *habeas corpus;* there should be no forced billeting of soldiers in the homes of private citizens; and that martial law was not to be declared in England.

The Parliament of 1629

In the midst of a stormy debate over theology, taxes, and civil liberties, the king sought to force the adjournment of Parliament. But when he sent a message to the

Speaker ordering him to adjourn, some of the more athletic members held him in his chair while the door of the House of Commons was locked to prevent the entry of other messengers from the king. That famous date was March 2, 1629. A number of resolutions passed. Concessions towards Catholicism or Arminianism were to be regarded as treason. Whoever advised any collection of taxes without consent of Parliament would be guilty of treason. Whoever should pay a tax levied without the consent of Parliament would be considered a betrayer of liberty and guilty of treason.

A royal messenger was allowed to enter the Commons and declare the Commons adjourned and a week later Charles I dissolved Parliament—for 11 years. Puritan leaders and leaders of the opposition in the House of Commons were imprisoned by the king, some for several years.

Religious Persecution

The established Church of England was the only legal church under Charles I, a Catholic. Archbishop of Canterbury William Laud (1573–1645) sought to enforce the king's policies vigorously. Arminian clergymen were to be tolerated, but Puritan clergymen silenced. Criticism was brutally suppressed. Several dissenters were executed.

National Covenant of Scotland (1638)

In 1638 Scottish representatives signed a protest against Charles, who was also king of Scotland, called the National Covenant. The covenant affirmed the loyalty of the people to the crown, but declared that the king could not reestablish the authority of the episcopate over the church. The Church of Scotland had had a presbyterian form of church government since the Reformation of the 16th century under John Knox. King Charles declared everyone who signed the National Covenant a rebel and prepared to move an army into Scotland.

War in Scotland

King Charles called out the militia of the northern counties of England and ordered the English nobility to serve as officers at their own expense. A troop of the king's horses entered Scotland only to find their way blocked by a large Scottish army. They returned south of the border without fighting.

Charles signed the Pacification of Berwick with the Scots in June 1639 by which each side would disband its forces, and a new General Assembly of the Church of Scotland and a Scottish Parliament would determine the future constitution of the government.

The Short Parliament (1640)

For the first time in 11 years, the king convened the English Parliament to vote new taxes for the war with Scotland. Instead the Commons presented a long list of grievances. In anger the king again dissolved Parliament.

The Scots Invade

The Scots invaded northern England. Charles called a Great Council of Lords, who arranged a treaty with the Scots to leave things as they were.

The Long Parliament

The king was cornered—he had no money, no army, and no popular support. He summoned the Parliament to meet in November 1640. The Commons immediately moved to impeach one of the king's principal ministers, Thomas Wentworth, Earl of Strafford (1593–1641). With mobs in the street and rumors of an army enroute to London to dissolve Parliament, a bare majority of an underattended House of Commons passed a bill of attainder to execute the earl. Fearing mob violence as well as Parliament itself, the king signed the bill and Strafford was executed in 1641. Archbishop William Laud was also arrested and eventually tried and executed in 1645.

The House of Commons passed a series of laws to strengthen its position and protect civil and religious rights. The Triennial Act (1641) provided that no more than three years should pass between Parliaments. Another act provided that the current Parliament should not be dissolved without its own consent. Various hated laws, taxes, and institutions were abolished: the Star Chamber, the High Commission, power of the Privy Council to deal with property rights. Ship money, a form of tax, was abolished, and tonnage duties were permitted only for a short time. The courts of common law were to remain supreme over the king's courts.

The Commons was ready to revoke the king's power over the Church of England, but there was disagreement over what form the state church would take: episcopal, presbyterian, or congregational. Puritans were in the majority.

The Grand Remonstrance listed 204 clauses of grievances against the king and demanded that all officers and ministers of the state be approved by Parliament.

In 1641 a rebellion began in Ireland. Irish Catholics murdered thousands of their Protestant neighbors. The Commons voted funds for an army, but it was unclear whether parliament or the king would control the army.

The English Civil War Begins

Men began identifying themselves as Cavaliers if they supported the king, or Roundheads if they supported Parliament.

The king withdrew to Hampton Court and sent the queen to France for safety. In March 1642 Charles II went to York, and the English Civil War began.

The Division of the Country

Every locality had supporters of the king and supporters of Parliament. Geographically, though, the north and west of England sided with the king, and the south and east with Parliament. The Midlands was divided.

Eighty great nobles sided with the king, 30 against him. The majority of the gentry supported the king, a large minority were for Parliament. The yeomen tended to side with the gentry of their areas.

A few London merchants were Royalists, but most businessmen in various towns sided with Parliament. London, which was strongly Presbyterian, supplied Parliament with many men and much money.

Parliament had two great advantages. The navy and merchant marine supported Parliament. Parliament also had control of the wealthier and more strategic areas, including London, and was able to secure the three principal arsenals: London, Hull, and Portsmouth.

The King Attacks London

Charles put together a sizeable force with a strong cavalry and moved on London, winning several skirmishes. He entered Oxford, but was beaten back from London. Oxford then became his headquarters for the rest of the war.

Oliver Cromwell

Oliver Cromwell (1599–1658), a gentleman farmer from Huntingdon, led the parliamentary troops to victory, first with his cavalry, which eventually numbered 1,100, and then as lieutenant general in command of the well-disciplined and well-trained New Model Army.

Early Stages of the War

The early part of the war went in favor of the king. Charles sought allies among Irish Catholics, and Parliament sought aid from Presbyterian Scotland.

In January 1644 a well-equipped Scottish army of 21,000 crossed into England, greatly upsetting the military balance. Cromwell decisively defeated the king's cavalry at the Battle of Marston Moor, July 1644. The north was now in parliamentary hands.

Parliament reconstructed and improved its army, giving Oliver Cromwell the top command. In June 1645 Charles marched into enemy territory and was crushed by Cromwell's "Ironsides" at Naseby. The king was then a fugitive and surrendered himself to the Scots in May 1646.

Controversy Between Parliament and the Army

During the Civil War, under the authority of Parliament, the Westminster Assembly convened to write a statement of faith for the Church of England that was Reformed or Presbyterian in content. Ministers and laymen from both England and Scotland participated for six years and wrote the *Westminster Confession of Faith*, still a vital part of Presbyterian theology.

When the war ended Parliament ordered the army to disband without receiving the pay due them. The army refused, and in 1647 Parliament sought to disperse them by force. The plan was to bring the Scottish army into England and use it against the men who had won the war.

The army refused to obey Parliament and arrested the king when he was brought across the border. In August the army occupied London and some of their leaders wrote an "Agreement of the People," to be presented to the House of Commons. It called for a democratic republic with a written constitution and elections every two years, equal electoral districts and universal manhood suffrage, freedom of conscience, freedom from impressment, equality before the law, and no office of king or House of Lords.

The Death of the King

On the night of November 11, 1647, the king escaped from Hampton Court and went to the Isle of Wight. He had made a secret agreement with the Scots that he would establish Presbyterianism throughout England and Scotland if they would restore him to his throne.

The Second Civil War followed in 1648, but it consisted only of scattered local uprisings and the desertion of part of the English fleet.

The Scots invaded England, but were defeated by Cromwell at Preston, Wigan, and Warrington in the northwest of England. After these victories, the English army took control. London was again occupied. The army arrested 45 Presbyterian members of Parliament, excluded the rest, and admitted only about 60 Independents, who acted as the "Rump Parliament."

The army then tried Charles Stuart, formerly king of England, and sentenced him to death for treason. The execution of the king particularly shocked the Scots, because the English had specifically promised not to take the king's life when the Scots delivered him into English hands.

The Commonwealth (1649–1653)

After the execution of the king, Parliament abolished the office of king and the House of Lords. The new form of government was to be a Commonwealth, or Free State, governed by the representatives of the people in Parliament. Many large areas of the country had no representatives in Parliament. Parliament was more powerful than ever because there was neither king nor House of Lords to act as a check.

Opposition to the Commonwealth

Royalists and Presbyterians both opposed Parliament for its lack of broad representation and for regicide. The army was greatly dissatisfied that elections were not held, as one of the promises of the Civil War was popular representation.

Surrounded by foreign enemies, the Commonwealth became a military state with a standing army of 44,000. The North American and West Indian colonies were forced to accept the government of the Commonwealth.

Ireland

In the summer of 1649 Cromwell landed in Dublin with a well-equipped army of 12,000. Drogheda was the scene of the first massacre, when Cromwell ordered the slaughter of the entire garrison of 2,800. Another massacre took place at Wexford.

By the end of 1649 the southern and eastern coast were in English hands. The lands of all Roman Catholics who had taken part in the war were confiscated and given in payment to Protestant soldiers and others. Two-thirds of the land in Ireland changed hands, coming mostly under the control of Protestant landlords.

Scotland

Scottish Presbyterians proclaimed Charles II as their king. Charles accepted the National Covenant and agreed to govern a Presbyterian realm.

On September 3, 1650, Cromwell defeated the Scots at Dunbar. The next year King Charles II led a Scottish army into England, which was annihilated at Worcester. Charles was a fugitive for six weeks before escaping to France.

The Protectorate (1653–1659)

When it became clear that Parliament intended to stay in office permanently, Cromwell agreed to serve as Lord Protector with a Council of State and a Parliament. The new government permitted religious liberty, except for Catholics and Anglicans.

England was not strongly opposed to military rule, particularly after Cromwell divided the country into 12 districts with a major general in charge of each.

Oliver Cromwell died on September 3, 1658. After his death a new Parliament was elected under the old historic franchise. Cromwell's son, Richard, succeeded as Lord Protector from 1658–1659.

The Restoration (1660–1688)

The new Parliament restored the monarchy, but the Puritan Revolution clearly showed that the English constitutional system required a limited monarchy. Parliament in 1660 was in a far stronger position in its relationship to the king than it ever had been before.

Charles II (1660–1685)

Thirty years of age at the Restoration, the new king was dissolute and intelligent. He was interested in science and trade. Because he had so little interest in religion, he was willing to be tolerant.

While still on the Continent, Charles II issued the Declaration of Breda, in which he agreed to abide by Parliament's decisions on the postwar settlement.

The Convention Parliament (1660)

Royalists whose lands had been confiscated by the Puritans were allowed to recover them through the courts. Manorialism was largely abolished.

The Clarendon Code

Of England's 9,000 parish churches, 2,000 were pastored by Presbyterian ministers, 400 by Independents, and the rest by Anglicans. The Cavalier Parliament, elected early in 1661, sought to drive out all Puritans and exclude them from public and ecclesiastical life.

The Corporation Act of 1661 excluded from local government any one who refused to swear to the unlawfulness of resistance to the king, and those who did not receive communion according to the pattern of the Church of England. The Act of Uniformity in 1662 issued a new Prayer Book and ordered ministers either to accept it or resign their positions and livelihood. Twelve hundred pastors refused and vacated their churches.

The Conventicle Acts of 1664 and 1670 imposed harsh penalties on those who attended religious services which did not follow the forms of the Anglican Church. The Five-Mile Act of 1665 prohibited ministers from coming within five miles of a parish from which they had been removed as pastor. A licensing act permitted the archbishop of Canterbury and the bishop of London to control the press and the publishing of books.

The effect of all this was to divide England into two great groups—the Anglican Church and Nonconformists. The church was purged of Puritans and regained its property. It levied tithes and controlled education at all levels. Nonconformists were excluded from the universities, from government, from many professions, and from membership in the House of Commons. Nonconformists became shopkeepers, artisans, small farmers, merchants, bankers, and manufacturers. Their diligence, thrift, and self-discipline brought prosperity.

Disasters for England

War with the Dutch cost England enormously in both ships and money. The bubonic plague hit London in 1665, killing 68,000. The Great Fire of London in 1666 destroyed 13,000 homes, 84 churches, and many public buildings, none covered by insurance.

Scotland's Independence

Scotland regained her independence at the restoration of Charles II in 1660. Some of the Scottish Presbyterian ministers reminded the king of the National Covenant of 1638 and of his own covenant-oath in 1651, pledging that Scotland be governed according to Presbyterian polity and principles.

Charles II declared himself head of the Church of Scotland and decreed that the episcopal form of hierarchical church government would be used in Scotland.

In 1661 the Scottish Parliament declared that the National Covenant was no longer binding and prohibited anyone to renew any covenant or oath without royal permission.

A dictatorship was established in Scotland to enforce episcopacy and rule by approved bishops. The government demanded absolute obedience and used illegal detention. Drastic fines were levied on hundreds of people suspected of being sympathetic to the Covenanters. Presbyterianism was outlawed and hundreds of ministers lost their positions.

By 1666 the covenanters finally took to arms against oppression and captured the commanding general at Dumfries. Perhaps as many as 18,000 ordinary people died for the cause of religious liberty in the persecution that followed. Dragoons were sent to prevent people from meeting in the files and in "unlicensed" homes for the purpose of worshipping God and studying the Bible. Others were fined for not attending the parish church.

The last two years of Charles II's reign in Scotland were known as "The Killing Times," because of the wholesale slaughter of hundreds who were shot down without trial if they refused to take the oath of objuration of the Covenant. Charles II died on February 5, 1685, in his 56th year and received Roman Catholic absolution on his deathbed.

James II (reigned 1685–1688)

The new king, 51 years of age, was the brother of Charles II. He had served as Lord Admiral and commanded an English fleet against the Dutch. James II began his reign in a strong position. The Whigs were weak and the Tories had overwhelming strength in Parliament.

James II, a strong Roman Catholic, was determined to return England to Catholicism. He appointed Catholics to many of the high positions in his government. In 1685 he created a court of Ecclesiastical Commission with power over the clergy, and suspended the bishop of London from office. Three colleges at the University of Oxford were put under Roman Catholic rule. In April 1687 King James issued a Declaration of Indulgence which declared both Catholics and Nonconformists free to worship in public and to hold office. The Nonconformists knew that the king's intent was to enable Catholics to eventually control the government.

The Glorious Revolution of 1688

The leaders of Parliament were not willing to sacrifice the constitutional gains of the English Civil War and return to absolute monarchy. Two events in 1688 goaded them to action. In May James reissued the Declaration of Indulgence with the command that it be read on two successive Sundays in every parish church. On June 10, 1688, a son was born to the king and his queen, Mary of Modena. As long as James was childless by his second wife, the throne would go to one of his Protestant daughters, Mary or Anne. The birth of a son, who would be raised Roman Catholic, changed the picture completely.

A group of Whig and Tory leaders, speaking for both houses of Parliament, invited William and Mary to assume the throne of England. William III was stadtholder of Holland and Mary was the daughter of James II by his Protestant first wife, Anne Hyde. They were both in the Stuart dynasty.

On November 5, 1688, William and his army landed at Torbay in Devon. King James offered many concessions, but it was too late. He finally fled to France. William assumed temporary control of the government and summoned a free Parliament. In February 1689 William and Mary were declared joint sovereigns, with the administration given to William.

The English Declaration of Rights (1689) declared the following:
1) The king could not be a Roman Catholic
2) A standing army in time of peace was illegal without Parliamentary approval
3) Taxation was illegal without Parliamentary consent
4) Excessive bail and cruel and unusual punishments were prohibited
5) Right to trial by jury was guaranteed
6) Free elections to Parliament would be held

The Toleration Act (1689) granted the right of public worship to Protestant Nonconformists, but did not permit them to hold office. The Act did not extend liberty to Catholics or Unitarians, but normally they were left alone. The Trials for Treason Act (1696) stated that a person accused of treason should be shown the accusations against him and should have the advice of counsel. They also could not be convicted except upon the testimony of two independent witnesses. Freedom of the press was permitted, but with very strict libel laws.

Control of finances was to be in the hands of the Commons, including military appropriations. There would no longer be uncontrolled grants to the king.

The Act of Settlement in 1701 provided that should William, or later Anne, die without children (Queen Mary had died in 1694) the throne should descend, not to the exiled Stuarts, but to Sophia, Electress Dowager of Hanover, a granddaughter of King James I, or to her Protestant heirs.

Judges were made independent of the Crown. Thus, England declared itself a limited monarchy and a Protestant nation.

Queen Anne (reigned 1702–1714)

Much of Queen Anne's reign was occupied with the War of the Spanish Succession (1702–1713). The reign of Queen Anne is also called the Augustan Age of English elegance and wealth. Anne, a devout Anglican, was a semi-invalid who ate too much and was too slow-witted to be an effective ruler. She had 16 children, none of whom survived her.

The Act of Union (1707) united Scotland and England into one kingdom. The Scots gave up their Parliament and sent members to the English House of Commons and House of Lords. Presbyterianism was retained as the national church.

Eighteenth-Century England

Following the Act of Settlement in 1701, and Queen Anne's death in 1714, the House of Hanover inherited the English throne in order to ensure that a Protestant would rule the realm.

The Hanover dynasty order of reign was as follows: George I (1714–1727); George II (1727–1760); George III (1760–1820); George IV (1820–1830); William IV (1830–1837); and Queen Victoria (1837–1901).

Because of the English Civil War, the Commonwealth, and the Glorious Revolution of 1688, the Hanovers were willing to rule as King-in-Parliament, which meant that to rule England, the king and his ministers had to have the support of a majority in Parliament. Sir Robert Walpole (1676–1745), who served 42 years in the English government, created the office of Prime Minister, a vital link between king and Parliament.

In March 1689 James II arrived in Dublin with 7,000 French troops and was joined by Irish Catholics seeking independence from England. Protestants fled to Londonderry, which withstood a siege of 105 days. In June 1690. William landed in Ireland with an army of 36,000 and at the Battle of the Boyne completely defeated James, who fled to France.

Repercussions in Ireland were harsh—no Catholic could hold office, sit in the Irish Parliament, or vote for its members. He could enter no learned profession except medicine. He was subject to discriminatory taxation.

Scotland, at this time, was the scene of Jacobin efforts to restore the Stuarts to the throne. In 1688 the Scots declared that James had "forfeited" the Scottish throne, which they offered to William and Mary with the understanding that Scotland would be Presbyterian. Some of the Highland clans, however, turned out in defense of James. They were defeated at the Battle of Killiecrankie in July 1689.

In 1715, James II's son, then 27 years old, raised an army of 10,000 Highlanders in a revolt. James Francis Edward Stuart (1688–1766), the "Old Pretender," was soundly defeated and fled to France. In 1745, James Francis Edward Stuart's son, Charles Edward (1720–1788), the "Young Pretender," then in his mid-20s, obtained two ships from the French and sought to incite an uprising in Scotland, winning lasting fame as "Bonnie Prince Charlie."

SCANDINAVIA

Sweden in the Thirty Years' War

King Gustavus Adolphus (1594–1632) drove the Imperial forces from Pomerania in 1630. Swedish troops occupied all of Bohemia, organized a new Protestant Union, and invaded Bavaria. Gustavus Adolphus was killed in 1632 in the Battle of Lützen.

In the fall of 1634, Imperial forces decisively defeated the Swedish army at Nördlingen. The Treaty of Prague (1635) restored Catholic and Protestant lands to their status as of 1627.

Catholic France allied with Protestant Sweden against the Hapsburg Empire during the last phase of the war from 1635–1648. Sweden acquired western Pomerania as part of the Peace of Westphalia (1648), ending the Thirty Years' War.

Swedish Empire

The high point of Swedish power in the Baltics was in the 1650s.

Sweden was not a large or productive country. Maintaining a strong standing army proved to be too much of a strain on the economy. Sweden sought to control the trade of the Baltic Sea with its important naval stores, but even at the height of Swedish power only 10 percent of the ships in the Baltic trade were Swedish; 65 percent were Dutch.

Swedish provinces in the Baltic and in Germany were impossible to defend against strong continental powers such as Russia, Prussia, and Austria.

Political Situation

After the death of Gustavus Adolphus in 1632, the government was effectively controlled by an oligarchy of the nobility ruling in the name of the Vasa dynasty. Christina, the daughter of Gustavus Adolphus, became queen at 6 years of age and ruled from 1632 to 1654. At age 28 she abdicated the throne to her cousin and devoted the rest of her life to the Catholic faith and to art. Charles X reigned from 1654 to 1660 during the First Northern War against Poland, Russia, and Denmark.

Poland ceded Livonia to Sweden by the Treaty of Oliva (1660). Denmark surrendered the southern part of the Scandinavian peninsula by the Treaty of Copenhagen (1660).

Charles XI (1655–1697) became king at age 4. With the help of the Lower Estates of the Riksdag, he ruled as absolute king. This was in dramatic contrast to the centuries-long struggles in Holland and England to constitutionally limit their kings.

King Charles XII (1682–1718) came to the throne at age 15 and reigned for 21 years. He spent most of his life at war and was an outstanding military leader in the Great Northern War (1700–1721).

Denmark, Saxony, Poland, and Russia formed an alliance to destroy the Swedish Empire. In February 1700 Poland attacked Swedish Livonia and Denmark invaded Holstein. The Swedish navy defeated the Danes and attacked Copenhagen, forcing Denmark to make peace. Charles then shifted his attention to Estonia and routed a Russian invasion in the Battle of Narva, inflicting heavy losses.

The next several years were spent fighting in Poland. In 1709 the Russians, outnumbering the Swedish forces two-to-one, defeated them and took the Baltic provinces of Livonia and Estonia.

Years of warfare, poor government, and high taxes led to Charles XII's alienation from his people. In 1718, he was killed by a stray bullet.

Eighteenth-Century Sweden

The loss of the empire meant a move to a more democratic, limited monarchy, and new freedom led to a sharp increase in peasant enterprises and independence. The Swedish economy prospered. By 1756 many civil liberties were established. Principal decisions of government were made by the Riksdag (Parliament).

Under Gustavus III (1746–1792), there was a temporary return to royal absolutism, until he was assassinated in 1792.

Scandinavian Relations

Finland was part of the Swedish Empire in the 17th century and Norway was part of Denmark.

Denmark

Frederick III (1648–1670) established himself as absolute ruler.

Frederick IV (1699–1730) fought in the Northern War and achieved a rough parity in the Baltic with Sweden, but accepted Swedish control in the south of the Scandinavian peninsula.

Christian VII experimented with both enlightened despotism and reforms that allowed more civil liberties and economic freedoms for the Danish people.

RUSSIA UNDER THE ROMANOVS

Ivan III (reigned 1462–1505)

In 1480, Ivan III (1440–1505), "Ivan the Great," put an end to Mongol domination over Russia. He married Sophie Paleologus in 1472, the niece of the last emperor of Constantinople. (The Byzantine Empire was conquered by the Ottoman Turks in 1453). Ivan took the title of Caesar (Tsar) as heir of the Eastern Roman Empire (Byzantine Empire). He encouraged the Eastern Orthodox Church and called Moscow the "Third Rome." Many Greek scholars, craftsmen, architects, and artists were brought to Russia.

Ivan IV (reigned 1533–1584)

Ivan IV (1530–1584), "Ivan the Terrible," grandson of Ivan III, began westernizing Russia. A contemporary of Queen Elizabeth, he welcomed both the English and Dutch and opened new trade routes to Moscow and the Caspian Sea. English merchant adventurers opened Archangel on the White Sea and provided a link with the outer world free from Polish domination.

The ruling Muscovite family died out upon Ivan's death in 1584. The following "Time of Troubles" was a period of turmoil, famine, power struggles, and invasions from Poland.

The Romanov Dynasty

The Romanov dynasty ruled Russia from 1613 to 1917. Stability returned to Russia in 1613 when the Zemsky Sobor (estates general representing the Russian Orthodox Church, landed gentry, townspeople, and a few peasants) elected Michael Romanov, who ruled as tsar from 1613 to 1645.

Russia, with a standing army of 70,000, was involved in a series of unsuccessful wars with Poland, Sweden, and Turkey. In 1654 Russia annexed the Ukraine with its rich farmlands.

Under Michael Romanov, Russia continued its expansion and extended its empire to the Pacific. Romanov continued westernization. By the end of the 17th century, 20,000 Europeans lived in Russia, developing trade and manufacturing, practicing medicine, and smoking tobacco, while Russians began trimming their beards and wearing western clothing.

Western books were translated into Russian. In 1649 three monks were appointed to translate the Bible for the first time into Russian. The Raskolniki (Old Believers) refused to accept any Western innovations or liturgy in the Russian Orthodox Church and were severely persecuted as a result. In 20 years 20,000 of them were burned at the stake, but millions still called themselves Old Believers as late as 1917.

Peter the Great (reigned 1682–1725)

Peter I was one of the most extraordinary people in Russian history. He was nearly seven feet tall, with physical strength so great that he could bend a horse shoe with his bare hands. His restless energy kept him active doing things incessantly, perpetually at work building boats, extracting teeth, dissecting corpses, shoemaking, cooking, etching, writing dispatches and instructions, sometimes for 14 hours a day. He could be cruel and vicious. He often whipped his servants, killed people who angered him, and even tortured his son to death.

Peter was born in 1672. When Peter was only 4 years old, his father died and the oldest son, Theodore, ruled until 1682, when he also died without an heir. For seven years Peter and his older half-brother ruled with the older half-sister Sophia as regent. Discovering a plot by Sophia to kill him, Peter, in 1689, banished her to a monastery and began ruling in his own right with his mother Natalia as regent. When she died in 1694, Peter, at age 22, took over the administration of the Russian government.

The driving ambitions of Peter the Great's life were to modernize Russia and to compete with the great powers of Europe on equal terms. Peter visited western Europe in disguise in order to study the techniques and culture of the West. He worked as a carpenter in shipyards, attended gunnery school, and visited hospitals and factories. He sent back large numbers of European technicians and craftsmen to train Russians and to build factories. By the end of Peter's reign Russia produced more iron than England.

Wars of Peter the Great

Peter built up the army through conscription and a 25-year term of enlistment. He gave flintlocks and bayonets to his troops instead of the old muskets and pikes. Artillery was improved and discipline enforced. By the end of his reign, Russia had a standing army of 210,000, despite a population of only 13 million. Peter also developed the Russian Navy. In 1696 Peter sailed his fleet of boats down the Don River and took Azov on the Black Sea from the Turks.

The Great Northern War (1700–1721)

In 1699 Peter allied with Poland and Denmark against Sweden. Charles XII, the 18-year-old Swedish king, defeated the Russian army of 35,000. Though the main Swedish effort was against Poland, it fought against Russia for 20 years. In 1706 Sweden again defeated Russia at Grodno, but in 1709 Peter won at Poltava.

The Treaty of Nystad (1721) ended the war. Russia returned Finland and Livonia (Latvia) and Estonia became part of the Russian Empire. Russia now had possessions on the Baltic Sea and a "window on the West."

St. Petersburg

The building of this great city out of a wilderness was one of Peter's crowning achievements. Construction, done by conscripted labor and supervised by the tsar himself, began in 1703. Peter wanted St. Petersburg to look like Amsterdam. It became a cosmopolitan city with French theater and Italian opera. St. Petersburg was built mostly of stone and brick rather than traditional Russian wood. The tsar ordered a number of noble families to move to St. Petersburg and build their houses according to his plans. At Peter's death in 1725, St. Petersburg was the largest city in northern Europe.

Reforms Under Peter the Great

The tsar ruled by decree (*ukase*). Government officials and nobles acted under government authority, but there was no representative body.

All landowners owed lifetime service to the state, either in the army, the civil service, or at court. In return for government service, they received land and serfs to work their fields.

Conscription required each village to send recruits for the Russian army. By 1709 Russia manufactured most of its own weapons and had an effective artillery.

The Russian navy, mostly on the Baltic, grew to a fleet of 850 ships, but declined sharply after Peter's death.

Taxes were heavy on trade, sales, and rent. The government also levied a head tax on every male.

State-regulated monopolies brought income to the government, but stultified trade and economic growth and in the long run were counter-productive. Half of the 200 enterprises begun during Peter's reign were state owned; the rest were heavily taxed.

Peter sought unsuccessfully to link the main rivers by canals. Thousands died in the effort, but only one of his six great canals was completed: St. Petersburg was linked to the Volga by canal in 1732.

The Russian secret police ferreted out opposition and punished it as subversion.

The Swedish model was followed in organizing the central government. Russia was divided into 12 provinces with a governor in charge of each. This decentralized many of the functions previously performed by the national government.

When the patriarch of the Russian Orthodox Church died in 1700, Peter abolished his authority and began treating the Church as a government department. He eventually gave governing authority to a Holy Synod.

Eighteenth Century Russian Tsars After Peter the Great

Catherine I, who ruled from 1725 to 1727, was the second wife of Peter the Great.

Peter II, (1727–1730), the son of Alexis and grandson of Peter the Great, died at age 15.

Anna (reigned 1730–1740) was dominated by German advisers. Under her rule the War of the Polish Succession (1733–1735) gave Russia firmer control over Polish affairs. War against the Turks (1736–1739) gave Azov to Russia once again. Russia agreed not to build a fleet on the Black Sea.

Ivan VI (reigned 1740–1741) was overthrown by a military coup.

Elizabeth (reigned 1741–1762) was the youngest daughter of Peter the Great. This was the Golden Age of the aristocracy, as they freed themselves from some of the obligations imposed on them by earlier tsars. Russia entered the Seven Years' War (1756–1763) during Elizabeth's reign.

Peter III (reigned 1762) was deposed and killed in a military revolt.

Catherine II "the Great," (reigned 1762–1796) continued the westernization process begun by Peter the Great. The three partitions of Poland, in 1772, 1793, and 1795 respectively, occurred under Catherine II's rule. Russia also annexed the Crimea and warred with Turkey during her reign.

ITALY AND THE PAPACY

The Papacy

For the first time in its long history, the papacy was of secondary importance in European diplomacy. There were a number of factors contributing to the decline of the papacy:

1) The Protestant Reformation of the 16th century and the emergence of many Protestant kingdoms throughout Europe.

2)   The emphasis on limited constitutional government adopted in the Protestant Reformation and accepted by many non-Protestants as well.

3)   The relatively few sanctions available to the pope in an international atmosphere of realpolitik.

4)   The beginnings of secularization of Europe through the growing influence of the Enlightenment.

5)   The anticlericalism associated with the Enlightenment spread a desire to reduce the power and economic holdings of the church in traditionally Catholic countries. Anti-clericalism reached a climax in the French Revolution.

6)   The lack of papal leadership in countering the above. Most of the 17th and 18th-century popes were more concerned about administering their own territories than with the wider political milieu.

Pope Innocent X (ruled 1644–1655) protested against the Peace of Westphalia (1648) because it acknowledged the rights of Lutherans and Calvinists in Germany, but the diplomats at Westphalia paid him little attention.

Quiet obscurity characterized the next three popes, Alexander VIII (1655–1667), Clement IX (1667–1669), and Clement X (1670–1676), though they did clash with King Louis XIV over the prerogatives of the Church versus the prerogatives of the Crown, particularly in the appointment of bishops.

Innocent XI (ruled 1676–1689) was scrupulous in financial matters and worked actively against the Turkish invasion of Europe. He subsidized Poland's relief of Vienna in the great campaign against the Turks in 1683.

Clement XI (ruled 1700–1721) sided with France in the War of the Spanish Succession, and in the course of the war, the Papal States were invaded by Austria. Clement renewed the condemnation of Jansenism, which had made extraordinary progress in France. (Jansenism was an Augustinian Catholic reform movement akin to Protestant Calvinism in its theology.)

Benedict XIV (ruled 1740–1758), much influenced by the Enlightenment, sought to salvage some of the Church's lost influence in absolute European states by compromising the state's influence in nationally established Catholic churches.

Clement XIV (ruled 1769–1774) ordered the Jesuit Society dissolved (July 21, 1773).

Pius VI (ruled 1775–1799) felt the full force of French radical anticlericalism, which finally led to the French invasion of the Papal States in 1796.

Seventeenth and Eighteenth-Century Italy

Italy in the 17th and 18th centuries remained merely a geographic expression divided into small kingdoms, most of which were under foreign domination. Unification of Italy into a national state did not occur until the mid-19th century.

In the 17th century Spain controlled most of the Italian peninsula. Spain owned Lombardy (or Milan), in the north and Naples, Sicily, and Sardinia in the south. Lombardy's strategic location linked Spain with Austria and, through Franche-Comté, Flanders. It served as a barrier to a French invasion of Italy.

Savoy

Savoy was the only state with a native Italian dynasty. In the early 16th century, Savoy was a battleground between the French and the Spanish. Emmanuel Philibert, Duke of Savoy (reigned 1553–1580), was rewarded by the Holy Roman Emperor with the restoration of the independence of Savoy. He built Savoy into a modern state.

Charles Emmanuel I (reigned 1580–1630) maintained his independence by playing France against Spain and vice versa.

Victor Amadeus (reigned 1630–1637) married Marie Christine, Louis XIII's sister, thus increasing French influence in Savoy. Charles Emmanuel II (reigned 1637–1675) was similarly dominated by France.

Victor Amadeus II (reigned 1675–1731) championed the Protestant Vaudois against Louis XIV. He joined William of Orange and the League of Augsburg against France. France defeated Savoy and forced Savoy to change sides. Nevertheless, the Peace of Ryswick confirmed Savoy's independence and left Savoy the leading Italian state and an important entity in the balance of power.

In 1713 Victor Amadeus was awarded Sicily. In 1720 he gave Sicily to Austria in exchange for the island of Sardinia. Henceforth, he was known as the king of Sardinia.

Charles Emmanuel III (reigned 1731–1773) joined France and Spain in the War of the Polish Succession in an unsuccessful attempt to drive Austria out of Italy. Savoy sided with Austria in the War of the Austrian Succession and received part of Milan as a reward.

THE OTTOMAN TURKISH EMPIRE IN EUROPE

Christian Europe versus Islamic Mediterranean

During the Middle Ages the Islamic Empire included Spain, North Africa, and the Middle East. Expansion of Islam into Europe was blocked by France in the West (and, after 1492, by Spain) and by the Byzantine Empire in the East. When Constantinople fell to the Ottoman Turks in 1453, eastern Europe was open for Islamic expansion.

Hungary and the Hapsburg Empire became the defenders of Europe. Under Suleiman the Magnificent (reigned 1520–1566), the Turks captured Belgrade and took over nearly half of eastern Europe. Ottoman power extended from the Euphrates River to the Danube.

Turkish Decline in the Seventeenth and Eighteenth Centuries

The sultan headed an autocratic and absolutist political system, often controlled by intrigue, murder, and arbitrary capital punishment.

Government finance was based more on spoils of war, tribute, and sale of offices than on a sound economy. The Turkish military and bureaucracy were dependent on the training and loyalty of Christian slaves, the famous Janissaries, and officials of the sultan's household.

Mohammed IV (reigned 1648–1687)

In 1683 the Turks besieged Vienna with 200,000 men for six weeks. John Sobieski, the king of Poland, went to the relief of the city with 50,000 Polish troops. The Turks massacred 30,000 Christians, but were defeated in a terrible slaughter.

Mustapha II (reigned 1695–1703)

Austrian and Polish armies defeated the Turks again, killing 26,000 in battle and drowning 10,000. The Treaty of Karlowitz (1699) recognized Austrian conquests of Hungary and Transylvania. The Ottoman Empire never recovered its former power or aggressiveness.

Ahmed III (reigned 1703–1730)

In 1711 the Turks attacked the Russians and forced Peter the Great to surrender and restore the Black Sea port of Azov.

In 1716 Austria forced the Turks out of Belgrade and overran Serbia at a cost of 20,000 lives. The Treaty of Passarowitz (1718) ceded the rest of Hungary and the great fortress of Belgrade to Austria. The sultan abdicated in the face of a rebellion.

Mahmud I (reigned 1730–1754)

Power was wielded by the chief eunuch in Mahmud's harem, Bashir, an Abyssinian slave who elevated and deposed sixteen grand viziers.

Austria and Russia coalesced to dismember the Turkish Empire. Russia regained Azov in 1737, but Austria was defeated and gave up Belgrade in 1739.

The Janissaries disintegrated as an effective military force when the sultan began selling the rank of Janissary to anyone willing to pay for it.

Provincial governors also became more independent of the sultan.

Abdul Hamid I (reigned 1774–1789)

In the Treaty of Kutchuk-Kainardji (1774), Catherine the Great forced the Turks to surrender the Crimea and to recognize Russia's right to protect Eastern Orthodox Christians in the Balkans.

Russia and Austria declared war on Turkey in 1788, and Austria recaptured Belgrade in 1789.

The Ottoman Empire was no longer an important power in Europe. Competition to take over parts of eastern Europe, especially the Balkans, was called the "Eastern Question" in European history and was a causal factor in starting World War I.

THE SCIENTIFIC REVOLUTION AND SCIENTIFIC SOCIETIES

Scientific societies were organized in many European countries in the 17th century. Italy began the first scientific societies in Naples, Rome, and Florence. The Royal Observatory was established at Greenwich in 1675 and the Royal Society in 1662; private donations and entrance fees from members financed the groups. The

French Académie des Sciences was founded in 1666. King Frederick I of Brandenburg-Prussia chartered the Berlin Academy of Sciences in 1700. Finally, Peter the Great founded the St. Petersburg Academy of Sciences in 1725.

Sir Isaac Newton (1642–1727) taught mathematics at Cambridge, was Master of the Royal Mint in London, and for 25 years was the President of the Royal Society. Most of his work was done in astronomy, the dominant science of the 17th century. He worked with magnification, prisms, and refraction. He used lenses with different curvature and different kinds of glass. Newton's greatest contribution, however, was in discovering his principle of universal gravitation, which he explained in *Philosophiae Naturalis Principia Mathematica*, published in 1687. He claimed to "subject the phenomena of nature to the laws of mathematics," and saw order and design throughout the entire cosmos.

Science and religion were not in conflict in the seventeenth and eighteenth centuries. Scientists universally believed they were studying and analyzing God's creation, not an autonomous phenomenon known as "Nature." There was no attempt, as in the 19th and 20th centuries, to secularize science. The question of the extent of the Creator's involvement in Creation was an issue of the 18th century, but there was universal agreement among scientists and philosophers as to the supernatural origin of the universe.

The Age of the Enlightenment

For the first time in human history, the 18th century saw the appearance of a secular worldview. In the past, some kind of a religious perspective had always been central to Western civilization. The philosophical starting point for the Enlightenment was the belief in the autonomy of man's intellect apart from God. The most basic assumption was faith in reason rather than faith in revelation. The "Enlightened" claimed for themselves, however, a rationality they were unwilling to concede to their opponents.

The Enlightenment believed in the existence of God as a rational explanation of the universe and its form; "God" was a deistic Creator who made the universe and then was no longer involved in its mechanistic operation. That mechanistic operation was governed by "natural law."

Rationalists

Rationalists stressed deductive reasoning or mathematical logic as the basis for their epistemology (source of knowledge). They started with "self-evident truths," or postulates, from which they constructed a coherent and logical system of thought.

René Descartes (1596–1650) sought a basis for logic and thought he found it in man's ability to think. "I think; therefore, I am" was his most famous statement. That statement cannot be denied without thinking. Therefore, it must be an absolute truth that man can think. His proof depends upon logic alone.

Benedict de Spinoza (1632–1677) developed a rational pantheism in which he equated God and nature. He denied all free will and ended up with an impersonal, mechanical universe.

Gottfried Wilhelm Leibniz (1646–1716) worked on symbolic logic and calculus, and invented a calculating machine. He, too, had a mechanistic world- and life-view and thought of God as a hypothetical abstraction rather than a persona.

Empiricists

Empiricists stressed inductive observation—the "scientific method"—as the basis for their epistemology.

John Locke (1632–1704) pioneered in the empiricist approach to knowledge and stressed the importance of environment in human development. He classified knowledge as 1) according to reason 2) contrary to reason or 3) above reason. Locke thought reason and revelation were both complementary and from God.

David Hume (1711–1776) was a Scottish historian and philosopher who began by emphasizing the limitations of human reasoning and later became a dogmatic skeptic.

The people of the Enlightenment believed in absolutes. They believed in absolute truth, absolute ethics, and absolute natural law. And they believed optimistically that these absolutes were discoverable by man's rationality. It wasn't long, of course, before one rationalist's "absolutes" clashed with another's.

The Enlightenment believed in a closed system of the universe in which the supernatural was not involved in human life, in contrast to the traditional view of an open system in which God, angels, and devils were very much a part of human life on earth.

The Philosophes

The new learning was promoted by a relatively small number of thinkers called *philosophes*—not philosophers in a traditional sense, but rather social activists for whom knowledge was something to be converted into reform. They were not always original thinkers, but popularizers of leading reformist thought. The philosophes believed their task was to do for human society what the scientists had done for the physical universe—apply reason to society for the purpose of human improvement, and in the process, discover the natural laws governing God, humans, and society.

Philosophes were men and women "of letters," such as journalists and teachers. They frequented the salons, cafes, and discussion groups in France. They were cultured, refined, genteel intellectuals who had unbounded confidence in man's ability to improve society through sophistication and rational thought. They had a habit of criticizing everything in their path—including rationalism.

Chronology

The Enlightenment varied in emphasis from country to country. Chronologically the end of the 17th and first half of the 18th century saw a reaction against "enthusiasm," or emotionalism, and sought moderation and balance in a context of ordered freedom. From the mid-18th century on, the Enlightenment moved into a skeptical, almost iconoclastic phase in which it was fashionable to deride and tear down. The last three decades of the 18th century were revolutionary, radical, and aggressively dogmatic. "Love of mankind" made it one's duty to crush those who disagreed and thus impeded "progress."

The "Counter-Enlightenment"

The "Counter-Enlightenment" is a comprehensive term encompassing diverse and disparate groups who disagreed with the fundamental assumptions of the Enlightenment and pointed out its weaknesses.

Theistic Opposition

German pietism, especially Count von Zinzendorf (1700–1760), leader of the Moravian Brethren, taught the need for a spiritual conversion and a religious experience. Methodism of the 18th century similarly taught the need for spiritual regeneration and a moral life that would demonstrate the reality of the conversion. Methodism was led by an Anglican minister, John Wesley (1703–1791).

Roman Catholic Jansenism in France argued against the idea of an uninvolved or impersonal God. Hasidism in eastern European Jewish communities, especially in the 1730s, stressed a joyous religious fervor in direct communion with God.

Philosophic Reaction

Some philosophers questioned the fundamental assumptions of rationalist philosophy.

David Hume struck at faith in natural law as well as at faith in religion. He insisted that "man can accept as true only those things for which he has the evidence of factual observation." Since the philosophes lacked indisputable evidence for their belief in the existence of natural law, Hume believed in living with a "total suspension of judgment."

Immanuel Kant (1724–1804) separated science and morality into separate branches of knowledge. He said that science could describe the natural phenomena of the material world, but could not provide a guide for morality. Kant's "categorical imperative" was an intuitive instinct implanted by God in the conscience. He thought ethical sense and aesthetic appreciation in human beings are beyond the knowledge of science, and that reason is a function of the mind and has no content in and of itself.

CULTURE OF THE BAROQUE AND ROCOCO

Age of the Baroque (1600–1750)

The Baroque emphasized grandeur, spaciousness, unity, and emotional impact. The splendor of Versailles typifies the baroque in architecture; gigantic frescoes unified around the emotional impact of a single theme is Baroque art; the glory of Bach's *Christmas Oratorio* expresses the baroque in music. Although the Baroque began in Catholic Counter-Reformation countries to teach in a concrete, emotional way, it soon spread to Protestant nations as well, and some of the greatest Baroque artists and composers were Protestant (e.g., Johann Sebastian Bach and George Frideric Handel).

Baroque Architecture

Michelangelo's (1475–1564) work provided much of the initial inspiration for Baroque architecture. A dynamic and unified treatment of all the elements of architecture combined in the Baroque. Oval or elliptical plans were often used in Baroque church design. Gian Lorenzo Bernini (1598–1680) was perhaps the leading early Baroque sculptor as well as an architect and great painter. Bernini's most famous architectural achievement was the colonnade for the piazza in front of St. Peter's Basilica in Rome. Louis XIV brought Bernini to Paris to plan a design for the completion of the palace of the Louvre, but the final design selected was that of Claude Perrault (1613–1688).

Louis XIV's magnificent palace at Versailles was particularly the work of Louis LeVau (1612–1670) and Jules-Hardouin Mansart (1646–1708). The geometric design of the palace included the gardens, which excel in symmetry and balance. The many fountains are also typical of the Baroque.

Baroque Art

Baroque art concentrated more on broad areas of light and shadow than on the linear arrangements of the High Renaissance. Color was an important element because it appealed to the senses. The baroque was not as concerned with clarity of detail as with the overall dynamic effect. It was designed to give a spontaneous personal experience.

Leaders in baroque painting were Annibale Carracci (1560–1609) from Bologna and Caravaggio (Michelangelo Merisi) (ca. 1571–1610) from near Milan. They are known for the concrete realism of their subjects. Their work is forceful and dramatic, with sharp contrasts of light and darkness (*chiaroscuro*).

The Flemish painter Peter Paul Rubens (1577–1640) is one of the most famous of baroque artists. He emphasized color and sensuality.

There existed, of course, other types of painting along with the Baroque. One example is the school of Italian genre painters known as *bamboccianti* who painted street scenes of Roman peasant life on a small scale.

Rembrandt van Rijn (1606–1669), the great Dutch painter, was so unique that he could not be considered typically Baroque. Nicolas Poussin (1594–1665) also followed a different line of reasoning. His paintings were rationally organized to give a total effect of harmony and balance; even his landscapes are orderly.

Baroque Music

A major underlying presupposition of Baroque music was that the text should dominate the music rather than the music dominating the text, as was done formerly. The idea that music can express the emotion and drama of the text was a major innovation of the baroque period. Instead of writing lyrics appropriate to a musical composition, the lyrics or libretto came first and determined the texture and structure of the composition. Dissonance was used freely to make the music conform to the emotion in the text. Devices of melody, rhythm, harmony, and texture all contributed to emotional effects.

The Baroque was a conscious effort to express a wide range of ideas and feelings vividly in music. These were intensified by the sharp contrasts in the music and a variety of moods experienced—anger, excitement, exaltation, grandeur, heroism, wonder, a contemplative mood, mystic exaltation.

Bach's (1685–1750) "St. Matthew Passion" illustrates this with a frenzied effect of cruelty and chaos obtained by a double chorus of four voices singing, "Crucify him! Crucify Him!" The jubilant Easter Oratorio reflects the triumph of the Resurrection. Violins and violas maintain a steady progression of pizzicato chords to depict the gentle knocking of Christ in the cantata, "Behold I stand at the door and knock...."

The splendor and grandeur of Baroque art and architecture was similarly expressed in Baroque music.

The concerto, involving interaction between a solo instrument and a full orchestra, was also a baroque innovation. Antonio Vivaldi (1678–1741) pioneered the concerto and standardized a cycle of three movements. The major-minor key system of tonality was also developed during the baroque period.

The baroque developed a new counterpoint, different from that of the Renaissance. There was still a blending of different melodic lines, but those melodies were subordinated to the harmonic scheme. Bach was particularly successful in balancing harmony and counterpoint and melody with polyphony. George Frideric Handel (1685–1759) was a master of Baroque grandeur, especially in his dramatic oratorios. He brought a poetic depth to his music, and his use of the chorus profoundly affected his audiences. Handel was like a painter who was at his best with gigantic frescoes that involved his audience in the whole uplifting experience.

Rococo

Rococo comes from a French word meaning shell or decorative scroll. It describes a tendency towards elegance, pleasantness, and even frivolity, in contrast to the impressive grandeur of the baroque. The effect was more sentimental than emotional.

The Rococo movement was centered in France, and François Boucher (1703–1770) was one of the most famous French Rococo painters. His paintings are elegant, delicate, innocent, and sensual all at the same time, as his paintings of Madame de Pompadour and Diana illustrate.

Characteristics of the rococo can be found in the compositions of both Franz Josef Haydn (1732–1809) and Wolfgang Amadeus Mozart (1756–1791).

4 REVOLUTION AND THE NEW EUROPEAN ORDER (1789–1848)

THE FRENCH REVOLUTION I (1789–1799)

Radical ideas about society and government were developed during the 18th century in response to the success of the "scientific" and "intellectual" revolutions of the preceding two centuries. Armed with new scientific knowledge of the physical universe, as well as new views of the human capacity to detect "truth," social critics assailed existing modes of· thought governing political, social, religious, and economic life. Ten years of upheaval in France (1789–1799) further shaped modern ideas and practices.

The ideas and institutions created by the revolutionaries would be perpetuated and extended by Napoleon Bonaparte, who conquered and converted Europe. The modern world that came of age in the 18th century was characterized by rapid, revolutionary changes which paved the way for economic modernization and political centralization throughout Europe.

IMPACT OF THE SCIENTIFIC REVOLUTION (c. 1500–1700)

Consequences

The "scientific method" involved identifying a problem or question, forming a hypothesis (unproven theory), making observations, conducting experiments, interpreting results with mathematics, and drawing conclusions.

The Scientific Revolution gave birth to the modern scientific community, whose goal was the expansion of knowledge based on modern scientific methods that rejected traditional knowledge. It likewise convinced many persons that all the complexities of the universe, including human relations, could be reduced to relatively simple mechanical laws such as those found in the physical universe.

INFLUENCE OF THE ENLIGHTENMENT (c. 1700–1800)

The Scientific Revolution gravely undermined the foundation on which the traditional social order of the 18th century rested by producing ideas which seriously challenged the status quo. The Enlightenment was a response to economic and political changes at work in European society. It heralded the coming of a new secular society.

The Philosophes: Agents of Change

While they came from virtually every country in Europe, most of the famous social activists were French, and France was the center of this intellectual revolution. François Marie Arouet (1694–1778), better known as Voltaire, was one of the most famous philosophes. He attended an upper-class Jesuit school in Paris and became well known for his unusual wit and irreverence. His sharp tongue and "subversive" poetry led to an 11-month imprisonment in the Bastille. Voltaire lived in England for several years and greatly admired the freedom of the relatively open English society. He accepted deism and believed in a finite, limited God who he thought of as the watchmaker of the universe. Characteristically, Voltaire relied on ridicule rather than reason to present his case.

Denis Diderot (1713–1784) served as editor of the *Encyclopedia*, the bible of the Enlightenment period. This 28-volume work was a compendium of all new learning.

Baron de Montesquieu (1689–1755) authored *The Spirit of the Laws* (1748), in which the separation of powers theory was found. Montesquieu believed such a separation would keep any individual (including the king) or group (including the nobles) from gaining total control of the government.

Jean Jacques Rousseau (1712–1778) wrote the *Social Contract* (1762) in an attempt to discover the origin of society, and to propose that the composition of the ideal society was based on a new kind of social contract. He lived in Geneva until he was forced to flee to England because of what the government considered radical ideas. Rousseau thought of man in a simpler state of nature as "the noble savage" and sought to throw off the restraints of civilization. Rousseau saw autonomous freedom as the ultimate good. Later in life he decided that if people did not want his utopian ideas, they would be "forced to be free," an obvious contradiction in terms. His book on education, *Emile* (1762), is still popular, despite the fact that he left his five illegitimate children in an orphanage instead of putting his educational theories to work on them.

The dissemination of Enlightenment thought was largely accomplished through philosophes touring Europe or writing and printing books and essays, the publication of the *Encyclopedia* (1751), and the discussions in the salons of the upper classes. The salons became the social setting for the exchange of ideas, and were usually presided over by prominent women.

Major Assumptions of the Enlightenment

Human progress was possible through changes in one's environment; i.e., better people, better societies, better standard of living.

Humans were free to use reason to reform the evils of society.

Material improvement would lead to moral improvement.

Natural science and human reason would discover the meaning of life.

Laws governing human society would be discovered through application of the scientific method of inquiry.

Inhuman practices and institutions would be removed from society in a spirit of humanitarianism.

Human liberty would ensue if individuals became free to choose what reason dictated was good.

The Enlightenment's Effect on Society

Religion. Deism or "natural religion" rejected traditional Christianity by promoting an impersonal God who did not interfere in the daily lives of the people. The continued discussion of the role of God led to a general skepticism associated with Pierre Bayle (1647–1706), a type of religious skepticism pronounced by David Hume (1711–1776), and a theory of atheism or materialism advocated by Baron d'Holbach (1723–1789).

Political Theory. John Locke (1632–1704) and Jean Jacques Rousseau (1712–1778) believed that people were capable of governing themselves, either through a political (Locke) or social (Rousseau) contract forming the basis of society. However, most philosophes opposed democracy, preferring a limited monarchy that shared power with the nobility.

Economic Theory. The assault on mercantilist economic theory was begun by the physiocrats in France, who proposed a "laissez-faire" (nongovernmental interference) attitude toward land usage, and culminated in the theory of economic capitalism associated with Adam Smith (1723–1790) and his slogans of free trade, free enterprise, and the law of supply and demand.

Attempting to break away from the strict control of education by the church and state, Jean Jacques Rousseau advanced the idea of progressive education, where children learn by doing and where self-expression is encouraged. This idea was carried forward by Johann Pestalozzi, Johann Basedow, and Friedrich Fröbel, and influenced a new view of childhood.

Psychological Theory. In the *Essay Concerning Human Understanding* (1690), John Locke offered the theory that all human knowledge was the result of sensory experience, without any preconceived notions. He believed that the mind at birth was a blank slate (tabula rasa) that registered the experience of the senses passively. According to Locke, since education was critical in determining human development, human progress was in the hands of society.

Gender Theory. The assertion of feminist rights evolved through the emergence of determined women who had been denied access to formal education, yet used their position in society to advance the cause of female emancipation. The Enlightenment salons of Madame de Geoffren and Louise de Warens are examples of self-educated women taking their place alongside their male counterparts. One woman fortunate enough to receive education in science was Emilie du Chatelet, an aristocrat trained as a mathematician and physicist. Her scholarship resulted in the translation of Newton's work from Latin into French. The writings of Lady Mary Montagu and Mary Wollstonecraft promoted equal political and educational rights for women. Madame Marie Roland was a heroic figure throughout the early period of the French Revolution when she attacked the evils of the Ancient Regime.

Era of "Enlightened Despotism"

Most philosophes believed that human progress and liberty would ensue as absolute rulers became "enlightened." The rulers would still be absolute, but would use their power benevolently, as reason dictated. Most of the philosophes opposed democracy. According to Voltaire, the best form of government was a monarchy in which the rulers shared the ideas of the philosophes and respected the people's rights. Such an "enlightened" monarch would rule justly and introduce reforms. Voltaire's and other philosophes' influence on Europe's monarchs produced the "enlightened despots," who nonetheless failed to bring about lasting political change. Some famous "despots" included Frederick the Great of Prussia (reigned 1740–1786), Catherine the Great of Russia (reigned1762–1796), and Joseph II of Austria (reigned 1765–1790).

Influence of the American Revolution

The American Revolution acted as a "shining beacon" to Europeans anxious for change, and helped prove that people could govern themselves without the help of monarchs and privileged classes. France, the center of Enlightenment thought, was particularly vulnerable. Eighteenth-century ideas about the "rights of man" and the "consent of the governed" were discussed widely in French salons, as well as in the rest of Europe. French reformers believed that their nation was a perfect example of everything wrong with society.

Finally, the concept of revolution was validated as a legitimate means to procure social and political change when it could not be effected through existing avenues. The American Revolution, however, was not a radical revolution, but a conservative movement: it preserved the existing social order and property rights, and led to a carefully thought-out constitutional system built on stability and continuity.

CAUSES OF THE FRENCH REVOLUTION

Cumulative Discontent with the Ancient Regime

The rising expectations of "enlightened" society were demonstrated by the increased criticism directed toward government inefficiency and corruption, and toward the privileged classes. The clergy (First Estate) and nobility (Second Estate), representing only 2 percent of the total population of 24 million, were the privileged classes and were essentially tax exempt. The remainder of the population (Third Estate) consisted of the middle class, urban workers, and the mass of peasants, who bore the entire burden of taxation and the imposition of feudal obligations. As economic conditions worsened in the 18th century, the French state became poorer, and totally dependent on the poorest and most depressed sections of the economy for support at the very time this tax base had become saturated.

The mode of absolute government practiced by the Bourbon dynasty was wed to the "Divine Right of Kings" philosophy. This in turn produced a government that was irresponsible and inefficient, with a tax system that was unjust and inequitable and without any means of redress because of the absence of any meaningful representative assembly. The legal system was chaotic, with no uniform or codified laws.

The economic environment of the 18th century produced a major challenge to the state-controlled French economy (mercantilism), as businessmen and bankers assailed the restrictive features of this system. With the growth of new industrial centers and the development of modern capitalist thought, the middle classes began to assert themselves, demanding that their political and social power be made commensurate with their economic power.

The intellectual currents of the 18th century were responsible for creating a climate of opposition based on the political theories of John Locke, Jean Jacques

Rousseau, Baron Montesquieu and other philosophes, the economic ideas of the French physiocrats, and Adam Smith and the general reform-minded direction of the century.

Immediate Cause—Financial Mismanagement

The coming of revolution seemed a paradox in a nation that was one of the largest and richest in the world. Dissatisfaction with the way France was administered reached a critical stage during the reign of King Louis XVI (1774–1792).

The deepening public debt was of grave concern and resulted from (1) the colonial wars with England (1778–1783) (2) French participation in the American War of Independence (3) maintaining large military and naval establishments, and (4) the extravagant costs of maintaining the Royal Court at Versailles. Unable to secure loans from leading banking houses in Europe (due to a poor credit rating), France edged closer to bankruptcy.

Between 1730 and the 1780s, there was an inflationary spiral which increased prices dramatically, while wages failed to adjust accordingly. Government expenses continued to outstrip tax revenues. The "solution" to the debt problem was to either increase the rates of taxation or decree new taxes. The French tax system could not produce the amount of taxes needed to save the government from bankruptcy because of the corruption and inefficiency of the system. The legal system of *parlements* (courts), controlled by the nobility, blocked tax increases as well as new taxes in order to force the king to share power with the Second Estate.

As France slid into bankruptcy, Louis XVI summoned an Assembly of Notables (1787) in the mistaken hope they would either approve his new tax program, or consent to removing their exemption from payment of taxes. They refused to agree to either proposal.

Estates General Summoned

Designed to represent the three estates of France, this ancient feudal body had only met twice, once at its creation in 1302 and again in 1614. When the French parlements insisted that any new taxes must be approved by this body, King Louis XVI reluctantly ordered it to assemble at Versailles by May 1789. Each estate was expected to elect its own representatives. As a gesture to the size of the Third Estate, the king doubled the number of its representatives. However, the Parlement of Paris decreed that voting in the Estates General would follow "custom and tradition," with each estate casting a vote as a unit. Therefore the First and Second Estates, with similar interests to protect, would control the meeting despite the increased size of the Third Estate.

Election fever swept over France for the very first time. The 1788–1789 election campaign is sometimes considered the precursor of modern politics. Each estate was expected to compile a list of suggestions and complaints called "cahier de doléances" and present them to the king. These lists of grievances emphasized the need for government reform and civil equality. Campaigning focused on debate and the written word (pamphlets). The most influential writer was the Abbé Sieyès (1748–1836), whose pamphlet, "What is the Third Estate?" answered "everything."

The election campaign took place in the midst of the worst subsistence crisis in 18th-century France, with widespread grain shortages, poor harvests, and inflated bread prices. Finally, on May 5, 1789, the Estates General met and argued over whether to vote by estate or individual. Each estate was ordered to meet separately and vote as a unit. The Third Estate refused and insisted that the entire assembly stay together.

PHASES OF REVOLUTION

The National Assembly (1789–1791)

After a six-week deadlock over voting methods, representatives of the Third Estate declared themselves the true National Assembly of France (June 17). They were immediately locked out of their meeting place by order of Louis XVI. Instead they assembled in an indoor tennis court, where they swore an oath never to disband until they had given France a constitution (Tennis Court Oath, June 20). Defections from the First and Second Estates then caused the king to recognize the National Assembly (June 27) after dissolving the Estates General. At the same time, Louis XVI ordered troops to surround Versailles.

The "Parisian" revolution began at this point. Angry because of food shortages, unemployment, high prices, and fear of military repression, the workers and tradespeople began to arm themselves. On July 14 they stormed the ancient fortress of the Bastille in search of weapons. The fall of this hated symbol of royal power gave the revolution its baptism of blood. The king recalled his troops from Versailles. Rebellion spread to the French countryside, triggered by a wave of rumor and hysteria. A feeling of fear and desperation called "The Great Fear" took hold of the people. They attacked the manor houses, symbols of upper-class wealth, in an effort to destroy the legal records of their feudal obligations. The middle class responded to this lower-class violence by forming the National Guard Militia to protect property rights. Hoping to put an end to further violence, the National Assembly voted to abolish feudalism in France and declare the equality of all classes (August 4). The assembly then issued a constitutional blueprint, the "Declaration of the Rights of Man and Citizens" (August 26), which guaranteed due process of law and the sovereignty of the people. The National Assembly then proceeded to its twin functions of governing France on a day-to-day basis and writing a constitution.

Among the achievements of the National Assembly were the following:

1) *Secularization of Religion*—Church property was confiscated to pay off the national debt. The Civil Constitution of the Clergy (1790) created a national church with 83 bishops and dioceses. All clergy were to be democratically elected by the people and have their salaries paid by the state. The practical result was to polarize the nation over the question of religion.

2) *Governmental Reform*—To make the country easier to administer, the Assembly divided the country into 83 departments (replacing the old provincial boundary lines) governed by elected officials, and 83 judicial districts.

3) *Constitutional Changes*—Despite a failed attempt by Louis XVI and his fam-

ily to escape from France (June 20, 1791) in order to avoid having to approve the 1791 Constitution, the National Assembly completed what may have been its greatest task. It transformed France into a constitutional monarchy with a unicameral Legislative Assembly. Middle-class control of the government was assured through an indirect method of voting and property qualifications.

The Legislative Assembly (1791–1792)

While the National Assembly had been rather homogeneous in its composition, the new government began to fragment into competing political factions. The most important political clubs were republican groups such as the Jacobins (radical urban) and Girondins (moderate rural), while the sans-culottes (working-class, extremely radical) were a separate faction with an economic agenda.

The focus of political activity during the 10-month life of the Legislative Assembly was the question of "war." Influenced by French nobles who had fled France beginning in 1789 (*émigrés*), the two largest continental powers, Prussia and Austria, issued the Declaration of Pillnitz (August 1791), which declared the restoration of French monarchy as their goal. With a sharply polarized nation, mounting political and economic chaos, and an unpopular monarch, republican sentiment gained strength, and war against all monarchs was promoted to solve domestic problems. Ideological fervor and anti-Austrian sentiment drove the Legislative Assembly to declare war on Austria (April 1792). Unprepared, the French revolutionary forces proved no match for the Austrian military. The Jacobins blamed their defeat on Louis XVI, believing him to be part of a conspiracy with Prussia and Austria. Mobs reacted to the threat made by the invading armies to destroy Paris if any harm came to the royal family (Brunswick Manifesto, July 25, 1792) by seizing power in Paris and imprisoning the king. The Legislative Assembly came under attack and obliged the radicals by suspending the 1791 Constitution. It ordered new elections based on universal male suffrage for the purpose of summoning a national convention to give France a republican form of government.

The National Convention (1792–1795)

Meeting for the first time in September 1792, the Convention abolished monarchy and installed republicanism. Louis XVI was charged with treason, found guilty, and executed on January 21, 1793. Later the same year, the queen, Marie Antoinette, would meet the same fate.

By the spring of 1793, the new republic was in a state of crisis. England and Spain had joined Austria and Prussia in opposing the revolution. Food shortages and counterrevolution in western France threatened the radicals' grip on the revolution. A power struggle ensued between Girondins and Jacobins until the Jacobins ousted their enemies and installed an emergency government to handle external and internal challenges to the revolution. A Committee of Public Safety, directed by Maximilien Robespierre (1758–1794), responded to the food shortages and related economic problems by decreeing a planned economy (Law of the Maximum) which would also enable France to wage total war against its external enemies. Lazare

Carnot (1753–1823), known as "The Organizer of Victory," was placed in charge of reorganizing the French army. The entire nation was conscripted into service (*levée en masse*), and war was defined as a national mission.

The most notorious event of the French Revolution was the famous "Reign of Terror" (1793–1794), the government's campaign against its internal enemies and counterrevolutionaries. Revolutionary Tribunals were created to hear the cases of accused enemies brought to "justice" under a new Law of Suspects. Approximately 25,000 people throughout France lost their lives. Execution by guillotine became a spectator sport. A new political culture began to emerge, called the "Republic of Virtue." This was Robespierre's grand scheme to de-Christianize France and inculcate revolutionary virtue. The terror spiraled out of control, consuming Jacobin leaders (Danton (1757–1794), Desmoulins (1760–1794), and Hébert (ca. 1757–1794)), until no one could feel secure in the shadow of Robespierre's dictatorship. On July 27, 1794, Robespierre was denounced in the convention, arrested, and executed the next day, along with his close associate St. Just.

The fall of Robespierre was followed by a dramatic swing to the right called the Thermidorian Reaction (1794). Tired of terror and "virtue" alike, the moderate bourgeoise politicians regained control of the National Convention. The Girondins were readmitted. A retreat from the excesses of revolution was begun. A new constitution was written in 1795 which set up a republican form of government. A new Legislative Assembly would choose a five-member executive board, the Directory, from which the new regime was to take its name. Before its rule came to an end, the convention removed all economic controls, which dealt a death blow to the Sans-culottes. Finally, the Convention decreed that the new government would reserve two-thirds of the seats in the Legislative Assembly for at least two years.

The Directory (1795–1799)

The Constitution of 1795 restricted voting and office holding to property owners. The middle class was in control. It wanted peace in order to gain more wealth and to establish a society in which money and property would become the only requirements for prestige and power. These goals confronted opposition groups such as the aristocracy, who in October 1795 attempted a royalist uprising. It might have succeeded were it not for the young Napoleon Bonaparte, who happened to be in Paris at the time, and loyally helped the government put down the rebellion. The Sans-culottes repeatedly attacked the government and its economic philosophy, but, leaderless and powerless, they were doomed to failure. Despite rising inflation and mass public dissatisfaction, the Directory government ignored a growing shift in public opinion. When elections in April 1797 produced a triumph for the royalist right, the results were annulled, and the Directory shed its last pretense of legitimacy.

But the weak and corrupt Directory government managed to hang on for two more years because of great military success. French armies annexed the Austrian Netherlands, the left bank of the Rhine, Nice, and Savoy. The Dutch republic was made a satellite state of France. The greatest military victories were won by Napoleon Bonaparte, who drove the Austrians out of northern Italy and forced them to sign the Treaty of Campo Formio (October 1797), in return for which the Directory government agreed to Bonaparte's scheme to conquer Egypt and threaten English interests in the East.

But a steady loss of support continued in the face of a government that was bankrupt, filled with corruption, and unwilling to halt an inflationary spiral that was aggravating the already-impoverished masses of French peasants.

European Reaction to the Events of 1789–1799

Liberals and radicals in Europe and America hailed the birth of liberty and freedom. Among those who defended the French Revolution were the German philosophers Immanuel Kant (1724–1804) and Johann Fichte (1762–1814), the English scientist Joseph Priestley (1733–1804), and the American pamphleteer Tom Paine (1737–1809). The romantic poet William Wordsworth (1770–1850) captured the sense of liberation and limitless hope inspired by the French Revolution:

> "Bliss it was in that dawn to be alive
>> But to be young was very heaven."

Not all reaction was favorable. Conservatives predicted that anarchy would ensue everywhere if the French revolutionaries succeeded. Friedrich Von Gentz's (1764–1832) and Edmund Burke's (1729–1797) (1790) "Reflections on the Revolution in France" remains to this day the classic statement of the conservative view of history.

Results

The first 10 years of revolution in France destroyed the old social system and replaced it with a new one based on equality, ability, and the law. It guaranteed the triumph of capitalist society, gave birth to the notion of secular democracy, laid the foundations for the establishment of the modern nation-state, and gave the great mass of the human race what it had never had before except from religion—hope.

THE FRENCH REVOLUTION II: THE ERA OF NAPOLEON (1799–1815)

The first 10 years of revolution did not prepare anyone in France for the dramatic changes that would distinguish this era. France was about to be mastered by a legendary "giant," and Europe overwhelmed by a mythical "titan."

Background of Napoleon's Life

Napoleon was born on the island of Corsica, August 15, 1769, to a prominent family of Italian descent. France had annexed Corsica in 1768. Napoleon pursued a military career while advocating Corsican independence. He associated with Jacobins, and advanced rapidly in the army when vacancies were caused by the emigration of aristocratic officers. His first marriage was to Josephine de Beauharnais (1763–1814), whom he divorced after a childless marriage. In 1810 Napoleon arranged a marriage of state with Marie Louise (1791–1847), daughter of the Austrian emperor. Their son was known as Napoleon II (1811–1832), "king of Rome."

Napoleon was a military genius whose specialty was artillery. He was also a charismatic leader with the nationalist's clarity of mind and the romantic's urge for action. Napoleon galvanized a dispirited, divided country into a unified and purposeful nation at the price of individual liberty.

Role in Directory Government (1795–1799)

In 1793 Napoleon was responsible for breaking the British siege of Toulon. He was made Commander of the Army of the Interior after saving the new Directory government from being overthrown by a Parisian mob in 1795, and selected to lead an army into Italy in the Campaign of 1796 against the First Coalition (1792–1797). There he defeated the Austrians and Sardinians and imposed the Treaty of Campo Formio (1797) on Austria, effectively ending the First Coalition and isolating England.

The election results of 1797 forced the Directory government to abandon the wishes of the country and establish a dictatorship of those favorable to the revolution ("Post-Fructidorian Terror"). After defending the government, Napoleon launched his invasion of Egypt (1798) only to have his navy destroyed by England's Lord Nelson at the Battle of the Nile. Napoleon and the French army were isolated in North Africa.

Popular indignation against the Directory government, along with financial disorder and military losses, produced a crisis atmosphere in France. Fearing a return to monarchy, a group of conspirators headed by the Abbé Sieyès decided to save the revolution by overthrowing the Directory. Napoleon was invited to furnish the armed power, and his name, to the takeover (Coup d'État Brumaire, November 9, 1799).

Consulate Period, 1799–1804 (Enlightened Reform)

The new government was installed on December 25, 1799, with a constitution which concentrated supreme power in the hands of Napoleon. Executive power was vested in three consuls, but the First Consul (Napoleon) behaved more as an enlightened despot than a revolutionary statesman. His aim was to govern France by demanding obedience, rewarding ability, and organizing everything in orderly hierarchical fashion. Napoleon's domestic reforms and policies affected every aspect of society, and had an enduring impact on French history. Among the features were the following:

1) Strong central government and administrative unity

2) Religious unity (Concordat of 1801 with the Roman Catholic Church)

3) Financial unity (Bank of France), emphasizing balanced budget and rigid government economy

4) Economic reform to stimulate the economy, provide food at low prices, increase employment, and allow peasants to keep the land they had secured during the revolution

5) Educational reforms based on a system of state-controlled public education (University of France).

The Legal Unity provided the first clear and complete codification of French law (Code Napoleon), and made permanent many of the achievements of the French Revolution. It stipulated equality before the law, freedom of conscience, property rights, abolition of serfdom, and the secular character of the state. Its major regressive provisions denied women equal status with men, and denied true political liberty. Thus, in the tradition of enlightened despotism, Napoleon repressed liberty, subverted republicanism, and restored absolutism to France.

Empire Period, 1804–1814 (War and Defeat)

After being made Consul for Life (1801), Napoleon felt that only through an empire could France retain its strong position in Europe. On December 2, 1804, Napoleon crowned himself emperor of France in Notre Dame Cathedral.

Militarism and Empire Building

Beginning in 1805 Napoleon engaged in constant warfare that placed French troops in enemy capitals from Lisbon and Madrid to Berlin and Moscow, and temporarily gave Napoleon the largest empire since Roman times. Napoleon's Grand Empire consisted of an enlarged France, satellite kingdoms, and coerced allies.

The military campaigns of the Napoleonic Years included the War of the Second Coalition (1798–1801), the War of the Third Coalition (1805–1807), the Peninsular War (1808–1814), the "War of Liberation" (1809), the Russian Campaign (1812), the War of the Fourth Coalition (1813–1814), and the Hundred Days (March 20–June 22, 1815).

French-ruled peoples viewed Napoleon as a tyrant who repressed and exploited them for France's glory and advantage. Enlightened reformers believed Napoleon had betrayed the ideals of the Revolution. The downfall of Napoleon resulted from his inability to conquer England, economic distress caused by the Continental System (boycott of British goods), the Peninsular War with Spain, the German War of Liberation, and the invasion of Russia. The actual defeat of Napoleon was the result of the Fourth Coalition and the Battle of Leipzig ("Battle of Nations"). Napoleon was exiled to the island of Elba as a sovereign with an income from France.

After learning of allied disharmony at the Vienna peace talks, Napoleon left Elba and began the Hundred Days by seizing power from the restored French king, Louis XVIII. Napoleon's gamble ended at Waterloo in June 1815. He was exiled as a prisoner of war to the South Atlantic island of St. Helena, where he died in 1821.

Evaluation

The Napoleonic era produced the first egalitarian dictatorship of modern times. Although Napoleon ruled France for only 15 years, his impact had lasting consequences on French and world history. He consolidated revolutionary institutions. He thoroughly centralized the French government. He made a lasting settlement with the Church. He also spread the positive achievements of the French Revolution

EXTENT OF NAPOLEONIC POWER, 1812

to the rest of the world. But Napoleon also repressed liberty, subverted republicanism, oppressed conquered peoples, and caused terrible suffering.

THE POST-WAR SETTLEMENT:
THE CONGRESS OF VIENNA (1814–1815)

The Congress of Vienna met in 1814 and 1815 to redraw the map of Europe after the Napoleonic era, and to provide some way of preserving the future peace of Europe. Europe was spared a general war throughout the remainder of the 19th century. But the failure of the statesmen who shaped the future in 1814–1815 to recognize the forces, such as nationalism and liberalism, unleashed by the French Revolution, only postponed the ultimate confrontation between two views of the world—change and accommodation, or maintaining the status quo.

The "Big Four"

The Vienna settlement was the work of the representatives of the four nations that had done the most to defeat Napoleon: England, Austria, Russia, and Prussia.

Prince Klemens Von Metternich (1773–1859), who represented Austria, epitomized conservative reactionism. He resisted change and was generally unfavorable to ideas of liberals and reformers because of the impact such forces would have on the multinational Hapsburg Empire.

Lord Castlereagh (1769–1822) was England's representative. His principal objective was to achieve a balance of power on the Continent by surrounding France with larger and stronger states.

Karl Von Hardenberg (1750–1822), as chancellor, represented Prussia. His goal was to recover Prussian territory lost to Napoleon in 1807, and gain additional territory in northern Germany (Saxony).

Tsar Alexander I represented Russia. He was a mercurial figure who vacillated between liberal and reactionary views. The one specific "nonnegotiable" goal he advanced was a "free" and "independent" Poland, with himself as its king.

While Charles Maurice de Talleyrand Périgord (1754–1838), the French foreign minister, was not initially included in the early deliberations, he became a mediator when the interests of Prussia and Russia clashed with those of England and Austria. He thereby brought France into the ranks of the principal powers.

The "Dancing Congress"

This European gathering was held amid much pageantry. Parties, balls, and banquets reminded the delegates what life had been like before 1789.

Principles of Settlement: Legitimacy, Compensation, Balance of Power

"Legitimacy" meant returning to power the ruling families deposed by more than two decades of revolutionary warfare. Bourbon rulers were restored in France, Spain, and Naples. Dynasties were restored in Holland, Sardinia, Tuscany, and Modena. Papal States were returned to the Pope.

"Compensation" meant territorially rewarding those states which had made considerable sacrifices to defeat Napoleon. England received far-flung naval bases (Malta, Ceylon, Cape of Good Hope). Austria recovered the Italian province of Lombardy, and was awarded adjacent Venetia as well as Galicia (from Poland) and the Illyrian Provinces along the Adriatic. Russia was given most of Poland, with the tsar as king, as well as Finland and Bessarabia. Prussia was awarded the Rhineland, three-fifths of Saxony and part of Poland. Sweden was given Norway.

"Balance of power" meant arranging the map of Europe so that never again could one state upset the international order and cause a general war. Encirclement of France was achieved through the following: strengthening the Netherlands, uniting Belgium (Austrian Netherlands) and Holland to form the Kingdom of the United Netherlands; giving Prussia Rhenish lands bordering on the eastern French frontier; giving Switzerland a guarantee of perpetual neutrality; enhancing Austrian influence over the Germanies by creating the German Confederation (Bund) of 39 states with Austria as president of the Diet (Assembly) of the Confederation; and restoring Sardinia's former territory, with the addition of Genoa.

Enforcement Provisions (Concert of Europe)

Arrangements to guarantee the enforcement of the status quo as defined by the Vienna settlement included two provisions: The "Holy Alliance" of Tsar Alexander I of Russia, an idealistic and unpractical plan, existed only on paper. No one except Alexander took it seriously. But the "Quadruple Alliance" of Russia, Prussia, Austria, and England provided for concerted action to arrest any threat to the peace or balance of power.

England defined concerted action as the great powers meeting in "congress" to

EUROPE 1815 (After the Congress of Vienna)

solve each problem as it arose, so that no state would act unilaterally and independently of the other great powers. France was always believed to be the possible violator of the Vienna settlement.

Austria believed concerted action meant the great powers defending the status quo as established at Vienna against any change or threat to the system, including liberal or nationalist agitation.

Congress System

From 1815 to 1822, European international relations were controlled by the series of meetings held by the great powers to monitor and defend the status quo: the Congress of Aix-la-Chapelle (1818), the Congress of Troppau (1820), the Congress of Laibach (1821), and the Congress of Verona (1822).

The principle of collective security required unanimity among members of the Quadruple Alliance. The history of the congress system points to the ultimate failure of this key provision in light of the serious challenges to the status quo after 1815.

Evaluation

The Congress of Vienna has been criticized for ignoring the liberal and nationalist aspirations of so many peoples. Hindsight suggests statesmen at Vienna may have been more successful in stabilizing the international system than we have been able to do in the 20th century. Not until the unification of Germany in 1870–1871 was the balance of power upset; not until World War I in 1914 did Europe have another general war. But hindsight also instructs us that the leading statesmen at Vienna underestimated the new nationalism generated by the French Revolution, and did not understand the change that citizen armies and national wars had effected among people. The men at Vienna in 1815 underestimated the growing liberalism of the age and failed to see that an industrial revolution was beginning to create a new alignment of social classes and new needs and issues.

THE INDUSTRIAL REVOLUTION

Twentieth-century English historian Arnold Toynbee began to refer to the period since 1750 as "the Industrial Revolution." The term was intended to describe a time of transition when machines began to significantly displace human and animal power in methods of producing and distributing goods, and an agricultural and commercial society converted into an industrial one.

These changes began slowly, almost imperceptibly, gaining momentum with each decade, so that by the midpoint of the 19th century, industrialism had swept across Europe west to east, from England to eastern Europe. Few countries purposely avoided industrialization, because of its promised material improvement and national wealth. The economic changes that constitute the Industrial Revolution have done more than any other movement in Western civilization to revolutionize Western life.

England Begins the Revolution in Energy and Industry

Roots of the Industrial Revolution could be found in the following: 1) the Commercial Revolution (1500–1700), which spurred the great economic growth of Europe and brought about the Age of Discovery and Exploration, which in turn helped to solidify the economic doctrines of mercantilism 2) the effect of the Scientific Revolution, which produced the first wave of mechanical inventions and technological advances 3) the increase in population in Europe from 140 million people in 1750, to 266 million people by the mid-part of the 19th century (more producers, more consumers) and 4) the political and social revolutions of the 19th century, which began the rise to power of the "middle class," and provided leadership for the economic revolution.

England began the economic transformation by employing her unique assets:

1) A supply of cheap labor as the result of the Enclosure Movement, which created unemployment among the farmers (yeomen); former agricultural laborers were now available for hire in the new industrial towns

2) A good supply of coal and iron, both indispensable for the technological and energy needs of the "revolution"

3) The availability of large supplies of capital amassed from profitable commercial activity in the preceding centuries, and ready to be invested in new enterprises

4) A class of inventive people who possessed technological skill, and whose independence and nonconformity allowed them to take risks

5) England had access to the raw materials needed for the development of many industries through its colonial and maritime ventures

6) A government which was sympathetic to industrial development, and well-established financial institutions ready to make loans available

7) After a long series of successful wars, freedom to develop its new industries, which prospered because of the economic dislocations caused by the Napoleonic Wars.

Early Progress

The revolution occurred first in the cotton and metallurgical industries, because those industries lent themselves to mechanization. A series of mechanical inventions (1733–1793) would enable the cotton industry to mass-produce quality goods. The need to replace wood as an energy source led to the use of coal, which increased coal mining, and resulted ultimately in the invention of the steam engine and the locomotive. The development of steam power allowed the cotton industry to expand and transformed the iron industry. The factory system, which had been created in response to the new energy sources and machinery, was perfected to increase manufactured goods.

A transportation revolution ensued in order to distribute the productivity of machinery and deliver raw materials to the eager factories. This led to the growth of canal systems, the construction of hard-surfaced "macadam" roads, the commercial use of the steamboat (demonstrated by Robert Fulton, 1765–1815), and the railway locomotive (made commercially successful by George Stephenson, 1781–1848).

A subsequent revolution in agriculture made it possible for fewer people to feed the population, thus freeing people to work in factories, or in the new fields of communications, distribution of goods, or services like teaching, medicine, and entertainment.

Spread of Industrialization to Europe and the World

In the wake of the Industrial Revolution, all modes of life would be challenged and transformed.

The Challenges to the Spread of Industrialism

Continental economic growth had been retarded by the wars of the Napoleonic period. Because England was so technically advanced, European countries found it difficult to compete. However, they were able to catch up by avoiding the costly mistakes of early British experiments, and by using the power of strong central governments and banking systems to promote native industry. But on the Continent there was no large labor supply in cities, and iron and coal deposits were not as concentrated as in England.

Route of Industrialization

England was the undisputed economic and industrial leader until the mid-19th century. The industrialization of the Continent occurred mostly in the latter half of the 19th century, and, in its southern and eastern regions, in the 20th century.

By 1830 industrialism had begun to spread from England to Belgium, France, and other scattered areas of Europe. These successful industrial operations were due to the exportation from England of machines, management, and capital. Germany was slower in following English methods until a tariff policy was established in 1834 (the *Zollverein*), which induced capital investment in German manufacturers.

Growth of Industrial Society

The undermining and eventual elimination of Western society's traditional social stratification model (i.e., clergy, nobility, and the masses) would result from the Industrial Revolution.

The Bourgeoisie: The New Aristocracy

The middle class were the major contributors to as well as the principal beneficiaries of early industrialism. They measured success in monetary terms, and most tended to be indifferent to the human suffering of the new wage-earning class. The industrial bourgeoisie had two levels: 1) upper bourgeoisie, i.e., great bankers, merchants, and industrialists who demanded free enterprise and high tariffs, and 2) lower bourgeoisie, i.e., small industrialists, merchants, and professional men who demanded stability and security from government.

The Factory Worker: The New Wage-Earning Class

The Industrial Revolution created a unique new category of people who were dependent on their job alone for income, a job from which they might be dismissed without cause. The factory worker had no land, no home, no source of income but his labor. During the first century of the Industrial Revolution, the factory worker was completely at the mercy of the law of supply and demand for labor. Working in the factory meant more self-discipline and less personal freedom for workers. Contemporary social critics complained that industrialism brought misery to the workers, while others claimed that life was improving. Until 1850 workers as a whole did not share in the general wealth produced by the Industrial Revolution. Conditions would improve as the century wore on, as union action combined with general prosperity and a developing social conscience to improve the working conditions, wages, and hours first of skilled labor, and later of unskilled labor.

Social Effects of Industrialization

The most important sociological result of industrialism was urbanization. The new factories acted as magnets, pulling people away from their rural roots and beginning the most massive population transfer in history. Thus, the birth of factory towns and cities that grew into large industrial centers. The role of the cities changed in the 19th century from governmental and cultural centers to industrial centers. Workers in cities became aware of their numbers and their common problems. Cities made the working class a powerful force by raising consciousness and enabling people to unite for political action and to remedy economic dissatisfaction.

In this urban setting the century's great social and political dilemmas were framed: working class injustices, gender exploitation, and standard-of-living issues.

Family structure and gender roles within the family were altered by the growth of industrialism. Families as an economic unit were no longer the chief unit of both production and consumption, but existed rather for consumption alone.

The new wage economy meant that families were less closely bound together than in the past; the economic link was broken. Productive work was taken out of the home (cottage) and placed elsewhere. As factory wages for skilled adult males rose, women and children were separated from the workplace. A new pattern of family life emerged.

Gender-determined roles in the home and domestic life emerged slowly. Married women came to be associated with domestic duties, while the male tended to be the sole wage earner, at least in the middle and upper classes.

Single women and widows had much work available, but that work commanded low wages and low skills and provided no protection from exploitation.

Marriage began to change. Women were now expected to create a nurturing environment to which the family members returned after work. Married women worked outside the home only when family needs, illness, or death of a spouse required them to do so.

Evaluation

The Industrial Revolution conquered and harnessed the forces of nature: water power, coal, oil, and electricity all provided power to replace human effort. The amount of wealth available for human consumption increased. Vast amounts of food, clothing, and energy were produced and distributed to the workers of the world. Luxuries were made commonplace, life expectancy increased, and leisure time was made more enjoyable.

But the workers would not begin to share in this dramatic increase in the standard of living until the second half of the 19th century, when all the evils associated with the factory system (low wages, poor working conditions, etc.) and early industrialism in general began to be corrected. In the first century of industrialism, the wealth created went almost exclusively to the entrepreneurs and owners of capital—the middle class.

IMPACT OF THOUGHT SYSTEMS ("ISMS") ON THE EUROPEAN WORLD

The mindset of Western civilization was being challenged in the first half of the 19th century by the appearance of numerous new thought systems. Not since the 18th-century Enlightenment had humans sought to catalog, classify, and categorize their thoughts and beliefs. Several of these systems of thought acted as agents of change throughout the 19th century, while others would continue to define the modern world into the 20th century.

Romanticism

Romanticism was a reaction against the rigid classicism, rationalism, and deism of the 18th century. Strongest between 1800 and 1850, the Romantic movement differed from country to country and from Romanticist to Romanticist. Because it emphasized change, it was considered revolutionary in all aspects of life. It was an atmosphere in which events occurred and came to affect not only the way humans thought and expressed themselves, but also the way they lived socially and politically.

Characteristics

Romanticism appealed to emotion rather than to reason (i.e., truth and virtue can be found as surely by the heart as by the head), and rejected classical emphasis on order and the observance of rules (i.e., let the imagination create new cultural forms and techniques).

It also rejected the Enlightenment view of nature as a precise, harmonious whole (i.e., viewed nature as alive, vital, changing, and filled with the divine spirit), as well as the cold impersonal religion of deism (i.e., viewed God as inspiring human nobility; deplored decline of Christianity).

Romanticism further rejected the Enlightenment's counter-progressive view of the past (i.e., viewed the world as an organism that was growing and changing with each nation having a unique history, and expressed vital optimism about life and the future.

Romantics enriched European cultural life by encouraging personal freedom and flexibility. By emphasizing feeling, humanitarian movements were created to fight slavery, poverty, and industrial evils.

Romantic Literature, Art, Music, and Philosophy

English Romantics like Wordsworth and Coleridge epitomized the romantic movement, along with Burns, Byron, Shelley, Keats, Tennyson, Browning, and Scott. The greatest German figures were Goethe, Schiller, Heine, and Herder. French romantics were Hugo, Balzac, Dumas, and Stendhal. The outstanding Russian exponents were Pushkin, Dostoyevsky, and Turgenev. Among the greatest American figures were Longfellow, Cooper, Irving, Emerson, Poe, Whitman, and Thoreau.

The leading Romantic painters in popular taste were the Frenchmen Millet and David, the Englishmen Turner and Constable, and the Spaniard Goya. The Gothic Revival Style marked the Romantic Era in architecture.

Music did not change as dramatically as did literature. Classical forms were still observed, but new ideas and innovations were increasing. Beethoven was a crossover, while straight romantics included Brahms, Schumann, Schubert, Berlioz, Chopin, and von Weber.

Romantic philosophy stimulated an interest in Idealism, the belief that reality consists of ideas, as opposed to materialism. This school of thought (Philosophical Idealism), founded by Plato, was developed through the writings of 1) Immanuel Kant whose work, *Critique of Pure Reason* (1781), advanced the theory that reality is twofold—physical and spiritual. Reason can discover what is true in the physical, but not in the spiritual, world 2) Johann Gottlieb Fichte, a disciple of Kant, and Friedrich Schelling, collaborator of Fichte, and 3) Georg Wilhelm Hegel, the greatest exponent of this school of thought. Hegel believed that an impersonal God rules the universe and guides humans along a progressive evolutionary course by means of a process called dialecticism; this is a historical process by which one thing is constantly reacting with its opposite (the thesis and antithesis), producing a result (synthesis) that automatically meets another opposite and continues the series of reactions. Hegel's philosophy exerted a great influence over Karl Marx, who turned the Hegelian dialectic upside down to demonstrate that the ultimate meaning of reality was a material end, not a higher or spiritual end, as Hegel suggested.

Impact

Romanticism destroyed the clear simplicity and unity of thought which characterized the 18th century. There was no longer one philosophy which expressed all the aims and ideals of Western civilization.

Conservatism

Conservatism arose in reaction to liberalism and became a popular alternative for those who were frightened by the violence, terror, and social disorder unleashed by the French Revolution. Early conservatism was allied to the restored monarchical governments of Austria, Russia, France, and England. Support for conservatism came from the traditional ruling classes as well as the peasants who still formed the majority of the population. Intellectual ammunition came from the pens of the Englishman Edmund Burke, the Frenchmen Joseph de Maistre and Louis de Bonald, the Austrian Friedrich Gentz, and many of the early romantics. In essence, conservatives believed in order, society, and the state; faith and tradition.

Characteristics

Conservatives believed the basis of society was organic, not contractual. Society was not a machine with replaceable parts. Stability and longevity, not progress and change, marked a good society. The only legitimate sources of political authority were God and history. The social contract theory was rejected because a contract cannot make authority legitimate.

Investing society with the theory of individualism ignored humans as social beings and undermined the concept of community, which was essential to life. Conservatives said self-interest did not lead to social harmony, but to social conflict. Conservatives argued that measuring happiness and progress in material terms ignored humans as spiritual beings. Conservatives rejected the philosophy of natural rights and believed that rights did not pertain to people everywhere, but were determined and allocated by a particular state. The conservatives denounced the philosophes and reformers, with their exaggerated emphasis on reason and intellect, for ignoring each human as an emotional being, and for underestimating the complexity of human nature. To conservatives, society was hierarchical, i.e., some humans were better able to rule and lead than those who were denied intelligence, education, wealth, and birth.

Impact

Conservatism was basically "anti-" in its propositions. It never had a feasible program of its own. The object of conservatives' hatred was a liberal society, which they claimed was antisocial and morally degrading. While their criticisms contained much justification, conservatives ignored the positive and promising features of liberal society. Conservative criticism poked holes in liberal ideology and pointed toward a new social tyranny of the aggressive middle class.

Liberalism

The theory of liberalism was the first major theory in the history of Western thought to teach that the individual is a self-sufficient being whose freedom and well-being are the sole reasons for the existence of society. Liberalism was more closely connected to the spirit and outlook of the Enlightenment than to any of the other "isms" of the early 19th century. While the general principles and attitudes associated with liberalism varied considerably from country to country, liberals tended to come from the middle class or bourgeoisie and to favor increased liberty for their class, and indirectly, for the masses of people, as long as the latter did not ask for so much freedom that they endangered the security of the middle class. Liberalism was reformist and political rather than revolutionary in character.

Characteristics

Individuals are entitled to seek their freedom in the face of arbitrary or tyrannical restrictions imposed upon them. Humans have certain natural rights and governments should protect them. These rights include the right to own property, freedom of speech, freedom from excessive punishment, freedom of worship, and freedom of assembly. These rights are best guaranteed by a written constitution with careful definition of the limits to which governmental actions may go. Examples include the American Declaration of Independence (1776) and the French Declaration of the Rights of Man (1789).

Another view of liberalism was presented by individuals who came to be known as the Utilitarians. Their founder, Jeremy Bentham (1748–1832), held the pleasure-pain principle as the key idea—that humans are ordained to avoid pain and to seek pleasure. Bentham equated pleasure with good, and pain with evil. The goodness or badness of any act, individual or public, was found by balancing the pleasure against the pain it caused. One tested the utility of any proposed law or institution by "the greatest happiness of the greatest number."

Liberals advocated economic individualism (i.e., laissez-faire capitalism), heralded by Adam Smith (1723–1790) in his 1776 economic masterpiece, *Wealth of Nations.* They regarded free enterprise as the most productive economy and the one that allowed for the greatest measure of individual choice. Economic inequality will exist and is acceptable, liberals held, because it does not detract from the individual's moral dignity, nor does it conflict with equality of opportunity and equality before the law.

Economic liberalism claimed to be based on the realities of a new industrial era. The "classical economists" (Thomas Malthus and David Ricardo) taught that there were inescapable forces at work—competition, the pressure of population growth, the iron law of wages, and the law of supply and demand—in accordance with which economic life must function. It was the duty of government to remove any obstacle to the smooth operation of these natural forces.

Internationally, liberals believed in the balance-of-power system and free trade because they allowed individual nations the opportunity to determine their own course of action. Liberals believed in a pluralistic society as long as it did not block progress. War and revolutionary change disrupted progress and enlarged the power of government. Education was an indispensable prerequisite to individual responsibility and self-government.

Early Nineteenth-Century Advocates of Liberalism

In England advocates included the political economists, the utilitarians, and individuals like Thomas Babington Macaulay and John Stuart Mill; in France, Benjamin Constant de Rebecque, Victor Cousin, Jean Baptiste Say, and Alexis de Tocqueville; in Germany, Wilhelm von Humboldt, Friedrich List, Karl von Rotteck, and Karl Theodor Welcker.

Impact

Liberalism was involved in the various revolutionary movements of the early 19th century. It found concrete expression in more than 10 constitutions secured between 1815 and 1848 in states of the German Confederation. Its power was demonstrated in the reform measures that successive British governments adopted during these same decades. It affected German student organizations and permeated Prussian life.

Alexis de Toqueville spoke for many liberals when he warned against the masses' passion for equality, and their willingness to sacrifice political liberty in order to improve their material well-being. These fears were not without foundation. In the 20th century, the masses have sometimes shown themselves willing to trade freedom for authority, order, economic security, and national power.

Nationalism

The regenerative force of liberal thought in early 19th-century Europe was dramatically revealed in the explosive force of the power of nationalism. Raising the level of consciousness of people having a common language, soil, traditions, history, culture, and experience to seek political unity around an identity of what or who constitutes the nation, nationalism was aroused and made militant during the turbulent French Revolutionary era.

Characteristics

Early nationalist sentiment was romantic, exuberant, and cosmopolitan, as compared to the more intense, hate-filled nationalism of the latter half of the 19th century.

The breakdown of society's traditional loyalties to church, dynastic state, and region began during the course of the 18th century. Impelled by French Revolutionary dogma, new loyalties were fashioned which said that people possessed the supreme power (sovereignty) of the nation and were, therefore, the true nation united by common language, culture, history, etc. Only then did people develop the sense of pride, tradition, and common purpose which would come to characterize modern nationalism.

Nationalism, as loyalty to one's nation, did not originate in the early 19th century. Men and women have been fighting for, and dying for, their respective countries for thousands of years. But it wasn't until the early 19th century that this feeling and motivation changed into something far more intense and far more demanding than it had been. The focus of the loyalty changed from dynastic self-interest to individual self-interest as part of a greater collective consciousness.

Impact

Nationalistic thinkers and writers examined the language, literature, and folkways of their people, thereby stimulating nationalist feelings. Emphasizing the history and culture of the various European peoples reinforced and glorified national sentiment.

Most early 19th-century nationalist leaders adopted the ideas of the German philosopher-historian Johann Gottfried Herder (1744–1803), who is regarded as the father of modern nationalism. Herder taught that every people is unique and possesses a distinct national character, or *Volksgeist*, which has evolved over many centuries. No one culture or people is superior to any other. All national groups are parts of that greater whole which is humanity. Herder's doctrine of the indestructible *Volksgeist* led to a belief that every nation had the right to become a sovereign state encompassing all members of the same nationality. Since most Western states contained people of many different nationalities, and few states contained all the members of any one nationality, nationalism came to imply the overthrow of almost every existing government.

Evaluation

Because of its inherently revolutionary implications, nationalism was suppressed by the established authorities. Yet it flourished in Germany, where conservative and reactionary nationalists competed with a somewhat more liberal form of nationalism associated with intellectuals like Fichte, Hegel, von Humboldt, and von Ranke. In Eastern Europe conservative nationalists stressed the value of their own unique customs, culture, and folkways, while western European nationalists demanded liberal political reforms. The influence of the Italian nationalist Mazzini and the Frenchman Michelet in stimulating nationalist feeling in the West was also key.

It should be noted that there was always a fundamental conflict between liberalism and nationalism. Liberals were rationalists who demanded objectivity in studying society and history, while nationalists relied on emotion and would do anything to exalt the nation, even subvert individual rights. By the late 19th century, nationalism was promoting competition and warfare between peoples and threatening to douse liberal ideas of reason and freedom.

Socialism

With the chief beneficiaries of industrialism being the new middle class, the increasing misery of the working classes disturbed the conscience of concerned liberal thinkers such as Bentham and Mill, who proposed a modification of the concept of laissez-faire economics. Other socially-concerned thinkers, observing the injustices and inefficiencies of capitalistic society, began to define social questions in terms of human equality and the means to be followed in order to secure this goal. As cures for the social evils of industrialism were laid out in elaborate detail, the emerging dogma came to be called socialism.

Characteristics

Since biblical times humans have been concerned with the problem of social justice, but it was not until the 19th century that it possessed a broader intellectual base and greater popular support. The difficulty with the existing system, according to social critics of the day, was that it permitted wealth to be concentrated in the hands of a small group of persons and deprived the working classes of a just share in what was rightfully theirs. A social mechanism had to be developed so a just distribution of society's wealth could be attained. The result was a variety of approaches.

The Utopian Socialists (from *Utopia*, Saint Thomas More's (1478–1535) book on a fictional ideal society) were the earliest writers to propose an equitable solution to improve the distribution of society's wealth. While they endorsed the productive capacity of industrialism, they denounced its mismanagement. Human society was to be organized as a community rather than a mixture of competing, selfish individuals. All the goods a person needed could be produced in one community.

Generally, the Utopians advocated some kind of harmonious society in the form of model communities, social workshops, or the like, where the ruthless qualities of individualistic capitalism would disappear. Utopian ideas were generally regarded as idealistic and visionary, with no practical application. With little popular support from either the political establishment or the working classes, the movement failed to produce any substantial solution to the social question. Leading Utopian thinkers included Henri de Saint-Simon (1760–1825), Charles Fourier (1772–1837), Robert Owen (1771–1858), and Louis Blanc (1811–1882).

The Anarchists rejected industrialism and the dominance of government. Auguste Blanqui (1805–1881) advocated terrorism as a means to end capitalism and the state. Pierre Joseph Proudhon (1809–1865) attacked the principle of private property because it denied justice to the common people.

Christian Socialism began in England circa 1848. Believing that the evils of industrialism would be ended by following Christian principles, the advocates of this doctrine tried to bridge the gap between the antireligious drift of socialism, and the need for Christian social justice for workers. The best known Christian Socialist was the novelist Charles Kingsley (1819–1875), whose writings exposed the social evils of industrialism.

"Scientific" Socialism, or Marxism, was the creation of Karl Marx (1818–1883), a German scholar who, with the help of Friedrich Engels (1820–1895), intended to replace utopian hopes and dreams with a militant blueprint for socialist working-class success. The principal works of this revolutionary school of socialism were *The Communist Manifesto* and *Das Kapital.*

The theory of dialectical materialism enabled Marx to explain the history of the world. By borrowing Hegel's dialectic, substituting materialism and realism in place of Hegel's idealism and inverting the methodological process, Marx was able to justify his theoretical conclusions. Marxism consisted of a number of key propositions: 1) An economic interpretation of history, i.e., all human history has been determined by economic factors (mainly who controls the means of production and distribution) 2) Class struggle, i.e., since the beginning of time there has been a class struggle between the rich and the poor or the exploiters and the exploited 3) Theory of surplus value, i.e., the true value of a product was labor, and since the worker received a small portion of his just labor price, the difference was surplus value, "stolen" from him by the capitalist and 4) Socialism was inevitable, i.e., capitalism contained the seeds of its own destruction (overproduction, unemployment, etc.); the rich would grow richer and the poor would grow poorer until the gap between each class (proletariat and bourgeoisie) is so great that the working classes would rise up in revolution and overthrow the elite bourgeoisie to install a "dictatorship of the proletariat." As modern capitalism was dismantled, the creation of a classless society guided by the principle "from each according to his abilities, to each according to his needs" would take place.

Evaluation

Ideologies ("isms") are interpretations of the world from a particular viewpoint. They are, or imply, programs of action and thrive when belief in general standards and norms has broken down. The proliferation after 1815 of so many thought systems and movements based upon them suggests that the basic division of society was between those who accepted the implications of the intellectual, economic, and political revolutions of the 18th and early 19th centuries and those who did not. A polarization in ideology was the result.

EUROPE IN CRISIS (1815–1833): REPRESSION, REFORM AND REVOLUTION

The Vienna peace settlement signaled the triumph of the conservative political and social order in Europe. The "dangerous" ideas (liberalism and nationalism) associated with the French Revolution and Napoleonic period had been "contained" by the territorial provisions of the 1815 agreement. The status quo had once again been defined. "Order" and "stability" were expected in the European state system.

Underestimating the power of ideas, the conservative leadership after 1815 was instead faced with a dramatic confrontation between those who had been converted to the "new" ideas (which required political changes), and the traditional ruling classes, who were reluctant to make any accommodation with the believers in the "new" ideas. The result of such confrontation in most states was government-sponsored repression followed by revolution. Few states chose to respond to the call for liberal reform. Only nationalist impulses in Greece and Belgium were successful, for reasons which could hardly comfort liberals. The intellectual climate of romanticism provided a volatile atmosphere in which these events unfolded.

Post-War Repression (1815–1820)

Initially the great powers followed the lead of the Austrian statesman Prince Metternich (1773–1859) in suppressing any direct or indirect expression of liberal faith. Most leaders attempted to reinstitute conservative means of governmental control in order to prevent reforms in the direction of greater participation by more people in government. The literate middle class, supported by urban workers, demanded reform and was willing to use violence to obtain it.

England

The Tory (conservative) government that defeated Napoleon was in control of England. Facing serious economic problems that had produced large numbers of industrial unemployed, the conservatives tried to follow a reactionary policy.

The Corn Laws of 1815 effectively halted the importation of cheaper foreign grains, aiding the Tory landholding aristocracy, but increasing the cost of bread and driving the poor and unemployed to protest and demand parliamentary reform.

The Coercion Acts of 1817 suspended *habeas corpus* for the first time in English history, provided for arbitrary arrest and punishment, and drastically curtailed freedom of the press and public mass meetings.

The "Peterloo Massacre" of 1819 occurred when several members of a large crowd who were listening to reformers demand liberal changes, including repeal of the Corn Laws, were killed, and hundreds of others injured, by police breaking up the meeting.

The Six Acts of Parliament (1819) in response to the "Peterloo" episode, were a series of repressive measures which attempted to remove the instruments of agitation from the hands of radical leaders and to provide the authorities with new powers.

The Cato Street Conspiracy of 1820 took place when a group of extreme radicals plotted to blow up the entire British cabinet. It provided new support for repression by the Tories, as well as discrediting the movement for parliamentary reform. By 1820 England was on the road to becoming a reactionary authoritarian state, when numerous younger Tories argued that such repressive legislation was not in the English tradition, and that the party itself might need to change its direction.

France

France emerged from the chaos of the long revolutionary period (1789–1815) as the most liberal large state on the continent. The period from 1815–1830 is always referred to as the Restoration era, signifying the return of the legitimate royal dynasty of France—the infamous Bourbon line.

Louis XVIII (reigned 1814–1824) governed France as a constitutional monarch by agreeing to observe the "charter" or constitution of the Restoration Period. This moderate document managed to limit royal power, grant legislative powers, protect civil rights, and uphold the Code Napoleon and other pre-Restoration reforms. Louis XVIII wished to unify the French populace, which was divided into those who accepted the Revolution and those who did not. The leader of those who did not was the Count of Artois, later Charles X, (1757–1836), brother of the king and leader of the Ultra Royalists.

The 1815 "White Terror" saw royalist mobs murder thousands of former revolutionaries. New elections in 1816 for the Chamber of Deputies resulted in the Ultras being rejected in favor of a moderate royalist majority dependent on middle-class support. The war indemnity was paid off, France was admitted to the Quadruple Alliance (1818), and liberal sentiment began to grow.

In February 1820 the duke of Berri, son of Artois and heir to the throne after his father, was murdered. Royalists charged that the left (liberals) was responsible and that the king's policy of moderation had encouraged the Left. Louis XVIII began to move the government more and more to the right. Changes in the electoral laws narrowed the eligible voters to the most wealthy, and censorship was imposed. Liberals were being driven out of legal political life and into near-illegal activity. The triumph of reactionism came in 1823, when French troops were authorized by the Concert of Europe to crush the Spanish Revolution and restore another Bourbon ruler, Ferdinand VII (1784–1833).

Austria and the Germanies

Throughout the first half of the 19th century, the Austrian Empire and the German Confederation were dominated by Prince Metternich, who epitomized conservative reactionism. In no other country or empire were the programs of liberalism and nationalism potentially more dangerous. Given the multiethnic composition of the Hapsburg Empire, any recognition of the political rights and aspirations of any of the national groups would mean the probable dissolution of the empire.

Napoleon had reduced more than 300 German states to 39, and the Congress of Vienna preserved this arrangement under Austrian domination. The purpose of the German Confederation (Bund) was to guarantee the independence of the member states, and by joint action, to preserve all German states from domestic disorder or revolution. Its organization of government was a Diet (Assembly), presided over by Austria as president.

The two largest states in the confederation were Austria and Prussia. Austria was ruled by the Hapsburg dynasty, and through Metternich's anti-liberal and nationalist pathology, held the line against any change in the status quo. Prussia was ruled by the Hohenzollern dynasty, a very aggressive royal family when it came to expanding the borders of this northern German state. For a short time after 1815, German liberals looked to Prussia as a leader of German liberalism because of liberal reforms in government enacted after a humiliating defeat at the hands of Napoleon. These reforms were intended to improve the efficiency of government and were not the portent of a general trend. The Prussian government and its traditional ruling class (Junkers) intended to follow the lead of Metternich in repressing all liberal-nationalist agitation.

Liberal-nationalist agitation was highly vocal and visible in and among German universities in the first half of the 19th century. Student organizations such as the Burschenschaften were openly promoting political arrangements that seemed radical and revolutionary at the time. At the Wartbug Festival (1817), students burned various symbols of authority. Russian agent Kotzebue was assassinated in 1819 by Karl Sand, a student member of the Burschenschaften.

The Carlsbad Diet (1819) was summoned by Metternich to end the seditious activity of German liberals and nationalists. The passage of a series of decrees effectively ended the activities of these reformers, and the movements were driven underground.

Russia

From 1801 to 1825, Tsar Alexander I (1717–1825) governed this traditional authoritarian state. A man of many moods, this Russian emperor thought he was called upon to lead Europe into a new age of benevolence and good will. After the

Congress of Vienna, he became increasingly reactionary and a follower of Metternich. Alexander I was torn between an intellectual attraction to the ideas of the Enlightenment and reform and a very pragmatic adherence to traditional Russian autocracy (absolutism). With the help of liberal adviser Michael Speransky (1772–1839), plans were made for a reconstruction of the Russian government due to the tsar's admiration for Napoleon's administrative genius. This and other liberal policies alienated the nobility, and Speransky was dismissed.

Alexander I came to regard the Enlightenment, the French Revolution, and Napoleon in biblical terms, seeing all three as anti-Christian. Turning to a new reactionary advisor, General Arakcheev (1769–1834), repression became the order of the day. There could be no toleration of political opposition or criticism of the regime. The early years of possible liberal reform had given way to conservative repression.

REVOLUTIONS I (1820–1829)

Nationalism, liberalism, and industrialism were all key factors in the outbreak of revolution during the first half of the 19th century. All three "isms" were opposed by conservative groups (royalists, clergy, landed aristocracy), who were rooted in the way of life before the French Revolution. Promoting the new forces of change was a younger generation, the heirs of the Enlightenment, who believed in progress. Romanticism was the atmosphere against which these events were played out.

The International System: The Concert of Europe

At the 1815 Congress of Vienna, the enforcement provisions of the settlement were designed to guarantee stability and peace in the international arena. The Quadruple Alliance (Austria, Russia, Prussia, England) that had defeated Napoleon was to continue through a new spirit of cooperation and consultation that would be referred to as the "Concert of Europe." At the suggestion of Lord Castlereagh, England's foreign minister, foreign policy issues affecting the international order would be worked out in a series of meetings or congresses, so that no one nation could act without the consent of the others. But under the leadership of Metternich, the congress system became the means to preserve the political status quo of autocracy in Europe against all revolutionary ideas. The congress system was short-lived because the continental powers could not always agree on cooperative action, and the English refused to support interference in the domestic affairs of nation-states. In the end each nation became guided by its own best interests.

The Congress System of Conferences.

The Congress of Aix-la-Chapelle (1818) arranged for the withdrawal of the allied army of occupation from France, and the admission of France into the Concert of Europe (Quintuple Alliance).

The Congress of Troppau (1820) was summoned by Metternich because of the outbreak of revolution in Spain. A policy statement (Protocol of Troppau) which would authorize armed intervention into any state that underwent revolutionary change was opposed by England.

The Congress of Laibach (1821) authorized Austrian troops to end the revolutionary changes in the kingdom of the Two Sicilies, where revolutions had spread from Spain. No decision was made concerning Spain.

The Congress of Verona (1822) was called because of the continuing Spanish Revolution and the outbreak of revolution in Greece (1821). When Russia, Prussia, and Austria agreed to support French intervention in Spain, the new English foreign minister, George Canning (1770–1827), withdrew England from the Concert of Europe. Verona marked the effective end of the congress system.

The Monroe Doctrine and the Concert of Europe

British fears that Metternich would attempt the restoration of Spain's colonies, then revolting in Latin America, prompted George Canning to suggest, and then support, the foreign policy statement of the United States of America known as the Monroe Doctrine (1823), which prohibited any further colonization and intervention by European powers in the western hemisphere.

England hoped to replace Spain by establishing her own trading monopoly with the former Spanish colonies. Throughout the 19th century, British commercial interests dominated Latin America.

Latin America in Revolution

Inspired by the French Revolution and the Napoleonic period, the rise of Latin American nationalism between 1804 and 1824 would witness the end of three centuries of Spanish colonial rule, and the emergence of new heroes such as Toussaint L'Ouverture, José San Martín, Bernardo O'Higgins, Simón Bolívar, and Miguel Hidalgo y Costilla.

The Revolutions of the 1820s

Spain (1820–1823): Beginning in January 1820, a mutiny of army troops under Colonel Rafael de Riego y Nuñez began, in opposition to the persecution of liberals by the restored monarch, King Ferdinand VII. The Congress of Verona (1822) authorized a French army to invade Spain and crush the revolutionaries.

Italy (1820–1821): Incited to revolution by the activities of secret liberal-nationalist organizations ("carbonari"), liberals revolted in Naples in July 1820, protesting the absolute rule of Ferdinand I of the kingdom of the Two Sicilies. The Congress of Laibach (1821) authorized Austria to invade and suppress the rebels. An attempted uprising in Piedmont (1821) was crushed by Austrian forces.

The Greek Revolt (1821–1830): The revolution which broke out in Greece in 1821, while primarily a nationalist uprising rather than a liberal revolution, was part of a larger problem known as "The Eastern Question." Greece was part of the Ottoman Empire, whose vast territories were gradually being reduced throughout the 18th and early 19th centuries. The weakness of the Ottoman Empire, and the political and economic ramifications of this instability for the balance of power in Europe, kept the major powers in a nervous state of tension.

Because of conflicting interests, the major powers were unable to respond in any harmonious fashion for several years. The Greek revolt was a leading political question in Europe throughout the 1820s. Occurring in the Romantic era, it touched the sensitivities of romantics in the West. A Greek appeal to Christian Europe did not move Prussia or Austria, but did fuse England, France, and Russia into a united force that defeated a combined Turco-Egyptian naval force at Navarino Bay (1827). Greek independence was recognized through the Treaty of Adrianople (1829).

Russian intervention on the side of Greek revolutionaries was based on Russian national interest, because any dimunition of Ottoman power increased Russian chances of further expansion into the Turkish empire.

Greek nationalism triumphed over the conservative Vienna settlement, and three of the five great powers had aided a movement that violated their agreement of 1815. The self-interests of the great powers demonstrated the growing power of nationalism in the international system.

The Decembrist Uprising in Russia (1825): The death of Alexander I on December 1, 1825, resulted in a crisis over the succession to the throne, and in turn produced the first significant uprising in Russian history. The expected succession of Constantine, older brother of Alexander I, who was believed somewhat more liberal than the late tsar, did not materialize. Instead, the younger brother Nicholas (1796–1855), no liberal by any measure, prepared to assume the throne that Constantine had actually renounced.

Hoping to block Nicholas' succession, a group of moderately liberal junior military officers staged a demonstration in late December, 1825, in St. Petersburg, only to see it quickly dissipated by artillery attacks ordered by Tsar Nicholas I. The Decembrists were the first upper-class opponents of the autocratic Russian system of government who called attention to the popular grievances within Russian society. The insurrection developed in Nicholas I a pathological dislike for liberal reformers.

A program called "Official Nationality," with the slogan "Autocracy, Orthodoxy, and National Unity," was designed to lead Russia back to its historic roots. Through it, Nicholas I became Europe's most reactionary monarch. Domestically, Russia became a police state with censorship and state-sponsored terrorism. There would be no representative assemblies, and education was not only limited, but university curricula were carefully monitored. A profound alienation of Russian intellectual life ensued.

In foreign affairs the same extreme conservatism was demonstrated. The Polish Revolution of 1830–1831 was crushed, and Russian troops played a key role in stamping out Hungarian nationalism in the Hapsburg Empire during the revolutionary uprisings of 1848–1849. Russia's traditional desire for expansion in the direction of the Ottoman Empire produced a confrontation between France and Russia over who was entitled to protect Christians and the holy places in the Near East. When the sultan of Turkey awarded France the honor, Nicholas I was prepared to go to war against Turkey to uphold Russia's right to speak for Slavic Christians. The result was the Crimean War (1854–1856), which Russia would lose. Nicholas I died (1855) during the course of fighting this war.

England Chooses Reform Over Revolution

The climax of repression in England was the Six Acts of Parliament (1819). Yet even as these laws were enacted, younger conservative politicians were questioning the wisdom of their party elders, such as Wellington and Castlereagh, and calling for moderation. During the 1820s a new group of younger Tories would moderate their party's unbending conservatism.

Reform was promoted by George Canning and Robert Peel, in opposition to the reactionary policies of earlier Tory leaders. With the help of liberal Whig politicians, enough votes were found to put England on the road to liberal reform. Canning inaugurated a liberal policy in foreign affairs, including abandonment of the congress system. Robert Peel reformed prisons and the outdated criminal code and established an efficient metropolitan police force ("bobbies"). Mercantile and navigation acts were liberalized, enabling British colonies to trade with nations other than England. The 1673 Test Act, which was a religious test used for barring non-Anglicans from participation in the government, was repealed. The Catholic Emancipation Act (1829) granted full civil rights to Roman Catholics.

The momentum for liberal reform would continue into the 1830s, as Britain realized that accommodation with the new merchant and financial classes was in the spirit of English history. The acid test of liberal reform, however, would come to focus on the willingness of Parliament to repeal the Corn Laws and reform itself.

REVOLUTIONS II (1830–1833)

The conservative grip on Europe following the turbulence of the 1820s was very quickly challenged when revolution broke out in France in 1830. By then the forces of liberalism and nationalism had become so strong that they constituted major threats to the security of many governments. In eastern Europe nationalism was the greater danger, while in the west the demands of middle-class liberals for various political reforms grew louder.

France: The July Revolution

The death of King Louis XVIII in 1824 brought his brother Charles, Count of Artois and leader of the Ultra Royalists, to the throne as Charles X. This set the stage for a return to the Old Regime.

Attempting to roll back the revolutionary gains, Charles X alienated the moderate forces on the Right as well as the entire Left. French voters registered their displeasure in the elections of 1827 by giving the Liberals a substantial gain in the Chamber of Deputies.

In 1829 Charles X (reigned 1824-1830) appointed a ministry led by the Prince Jules de Polignac (1780–1847), who was the personification of reactionism in France. Liberals considered this a declaration of war. Elections in 1830 produced a stunning victory for the Liberals. Charles X responded by decreeing the Four Ordinances, which would have amounted to a royal *coup d'état* if not stopped. The spark of revolt was set off by the radicals of Paris, with the workers and students raising barricades in the streets with the intention of establishing a republic. Charles X abdicated and fled France.

The Liberals in the Chamber of Deputies, under the leadership of Adolphe Thiers, preferred a constitutional monarchy without a Bourbon ruler. With the cooperation of Talleyrand and Lafayette, they agreed on Prince Louis Philippe, head of the Orleans family and cousin to Charles X.

France was now controlled by a bourgeoisie of upper-middle class bankers and businessmen. King Louis Philippe (reigned 1830–1848) was "the bourgeoisie king" who would tilt the government towards these interests. While the July Monarchy of Louis Philippe was politically more liberal than the Restoration government, socially it proved to be quite conservative.

The news of the successful July Revolution in France served as a spark ("When France sneezes, the rest of Europe catches cold") to revolutionary uprisings throughout Europe.

The Belgian Independence Movement (1830–1831)

Since being merged with Holland in 1815, the upper classes of Belgium had never reconciled themselves to rule by a country with a different language, religion, and economic life. Inspired by the news of the July Revolution in France, a revolt against Dutch rule broke out in Brussels, led by students and industrial workers. The Dutch army was defeated and forced to withdraw from Belgium by the threat of a Franco-British fleet. A national congress wrote a liberal Belgian Constitution. In 1831, Leopold of Saxe-Coburg (1831–1865) became king of the Belgians. In 1839, the Great Powers declared the neutrality of Belgium.

Poland (1830–1831)

The new tsar of Russia, Nicholas I, had the first opportunity to demonstrate his extreme conservatism in foreign policy when a military insurrection broke out late in 1830 in Warsaw. This nationalist uprising challenged the historic Russian domination of Poland. The Russian garrison was driven out of Poland, the tsar was deposed as king of Poland, and the independence of Poland was proclaimed by a revolutionary government.

Nicholas I ordered the Russian army to invade Poland; it ruthlessly proceeded to crush the nationalist rebellion. Poland became "a land of graves and crosses." The Organic Statute of 1832 declared Poland to be an integral part of the Russian Empire.

Italy (1831–1832)

Outbreaks of liberal discontent occurred in northern Italy, centering on Modena, Parma, and the Papal States. The inspiration for Italian nationalists who spoke of a unification process were (1) Guiseppe Mazzini (1805–1872) and his secret revolutionary society called Young Italy (2) the Carbonari, secret nationalist societies which advocated the use of force to achieve national unification. Still too disorganized, the Italian revolutionaries were easily crushed by Austrian troops under Metternich's enforcement of the Concert of Europe's philosophy. Still, the Italian Risorgimento (resurgence of the Italian spirit) was well under way.

Germany (1830–1833)

The Carlsbad Decrees of 1819 had effectively restricted freedom throughout Germany. At the news of France's July Revolution, German university students and professors led street demonstrations that forced temporary granting of constitutions in several minor states. These expressions of liberal sentiment and nationalistic desires for German unification were easily crushed by Metternich's domination of the German Bund and his influence over Prussia.

Great Britain: Reform Continues

The death of King George IV (reigned 1820–1830) and the accession of King William IV (reigned 1830–1837) in 1830 resulted in a general parliamentary election in which the oppositional political party, the Whigs, scored major gains with its platform calling for parliamentary reform. With the Tory party divided, the king asked the leader of the Whig party, Earl Charles Grey (1764–1845), to form a government.

Immediately a major reform bill was introduced, designed to increase the number of voters by 50 percent, and to eliminate underpopulated electoral districts ("Rotten Boroughs") and replace them with representatives from previously unrepresented manufacturing districts and cities. After a national debate, new elections, and a threat from King William IV to alter the composition of the House of Lords, the Great Reform Bill of 1832 was enacted into law. While the Reform Bill did not resolve all political inequities in British political life, it marked a new beginning. Several more notable reforms would begin to redraw the sociological landscape of British life.

Evaluation

Neither the forces of revolution nor reaction were able to maintain the upper hand between 1789 and 1848. Liberalism and nationalism, socialism and democracy, were on the march, but the forces of conservatism and reaction were still strong enough to contain them. The polarization of Europe was becoming clear—the liberal middle-class West, which advocated constitutionalism and industrial progress, and the authoritarian East, which was committed to preserving the status quo. The confrontation would continue until one side or the other won decisively.

THE REVOLUTIONARY TRADITION

The era of reaction which had followed the collapse of the Napoleonic regime and the Congress of Vienna (1815) was followed by a wave of liberal and national agitation which was manifested in the revolutions of 1820, 1825, and 1830.

The Revolutions of 1848

The year 1848 is considered the watershed of the 19th century. The revolutionary disturbances of the first half of the 19th century reached a climax in a new wave of revolutions that extended from Scandinavia to southern Italy, and from France to central Europe. Only England and Russia avoided violent upheaval.

The issues were substantially the same as they had been in 1789. What was new in 1848 was that these demands were far more widespread and irrepressible than ever. Whole classes and nations demanded to be fully included in society. The French Revolution of 1789 came at the end of a period ("Ancien Regime"), while the revolutions of 1848 signaled the beginning of a new age. Aggravated by rapid population growth and the social disruption caused by industrialism and urbanization, a massive tide of discontent swept across the western world.

Generally speaking, the 1848 upheavals shared the strong influences of Romanticism, nationalism, and liberalism, as well as a new factor of economic dislocation and instability. The increasingly radical political, economic, and social proposals advanced by the Utopian Socialists (Charles Fourier, Robert Owen), the Anarchists (Pierre Proudhon), and the Chartists in England also contributed to the revolutionary climate. Some authorities believe the absence of liberty was most responsible for the uprisings.

Specifically, a number of similar conditions existed in several countries: 1) Severe food shortages caused by poor harvests of grain and potatoes (e.g., Irish potato famine) 2) Financial crises caused by a downturn in the commercial and industrial economy 3) Business failures 4) Widespread unemployment 5) A sense of frustration and discontent among urban artisan and working classes as wages diminished 6) A system of poor relief which became overburdened 7) Living conditions, which deteriorated in the cities 8) The power of nationalism in the Germanies and Italies and in eastern Europe to inspire the overthrow of existing governments. Middle-class predominance within the unregulated economy continued to drive liberals to push for more government reform and civil liberty. They enlisted the help of the working classes to put more pressure on the government to change.

Republicanism: Victory in France and Defeat in Italy

In France, working-class discontent and liberals' unhappiness with the corrupt regime of King Louis Philippe (reigned 1830–1848)—especially his minister Guizot (1787–1874)—erupted in street riots in Paris on February 22–23, 1848. With the workers in control of Paris, King Louis Philippe abdicated on February 24, and a provisional government proclaimed the Second French Republic.

Heading the provisional government was the liberal Alphonse Lamartine (1790–1869), who favored a moderate republic and political democracy. Lamartine's bourgeois allies had little sympathy for the working poor, and did not intend to pursue a social revolution.

The working-class groups were united by their leader Louis Blanc (1811–1882), a socialist thinker who expected the provisional government to deal with the unemployed, and anticipated the power of the state being used to improve life and conditions of labor. Pressed by the demands of Blanc and his followers, the provisional government established national workshops to provide work and relief for thousands of unemployed workers.

The "June Days" revolt was provoked when the government closed the national workshop. A general election in April resulted in a National Assembly dominated by the moderate republicans and conservatives under Lamartine who regarded socialist ideas as threats to private property. The Parisian workers, feeling that their revolution had been nullified, took to the streets.

This new revolution (June 23–26) was unlike previous uprisings in France. It marked the inauguration of genuine class warfare; it was a revolt against poverty and a cry for the redistribution of property. It foreshadowed the great social revolutions of the 20th century. The revolt was extinguished after General Cavaignac was given dictatorial powers by the government. The June Days confirmed the political predominance of conservative property holders in French life.

The new Constitution of the Second French Republic provided for a unicameral legislature (with the National Assembly designating themselves as the first members), and executive power vested in a popularly-elected president of the Republic. When the election returns were counted, the government's candidate was defeated by a "dark horse" candidate, Prince Louis Napoleon Bonaparte (1808–1873), a nephew of the great emperor. On December 20, 1848, Louis Napoleon was installed as president of the Republic.

It was clear the voters turned to the name of Bonaparte as a source of stability and greatness. They expected him to prevent any further working-class disorder. However, the election of Louis Napoleon doomed the Second Republic. He was a Bonaparte, dedicated to his own fame and vanity, and not to republican institutions. In December 1852 Louis Napoleon became Emperor Napoleon III (reigned 1852–1870), and France retreated from republicanism again.

Italian nationalists and liberals wanted to end Hapsburg (Austrian), Bourbon (Naples and Sicily), and papal domination and unite these disparate Italian regions into a unified liberal nation. A revolt by liberals in Sicily in January 1848 was followed by the granting of liberal constitutions in Naples, Tuscany, Piedmont, and the Papal States. Milan and Venice expelled their Austrian rulers. In March 1848 upon hearing the news of the revolution in Vienna, a fresh outburst of revolution against Austrian rule occurred in Lombardy and Venetia, with Sardinia-Piedmont declaring war on Austria. Simultaneously, Italian patriots attacked the Papal States, forcing the pope, Pius IX (1792–1878), to flee to Naples for refuge.

The temporary nature of these initial successes was illustrated by the speed with which the conservative forces regained control. In the north Austrian Field Marshal Radetzky (1766–1858) swept aside all opposition, regaining Lombardy and Venetia and crushing Sardinia-Piedmont. In the Papal States the establishment of the Roman Republic (February 1849) under the leadership of Giuseppe Mazzini and the protection of Giuseppe Garibaldi (1807–1882), would fail when French troops took Rome in July 1849 after a heroic defense by Garibaldi. Pope Pius IX returned to Rome cured of his liberal leanings. In the south and in Sicily the revolts were suppressed by the former rulers.

Within 18 months the revolutions of 1848 had failed throughout Italy. Among the explanations for these failures were the absence of conservative, rural support for the revolutions; the divisions in aim and technique among the revolutionaries; the fear the radicals aroused among moderate groups of Italians who would be needed to guarantee the success of any revolution; and the general lack of experience and administrative ability on the part of the revolutionaries.

Nationalism Resisted in Austrian Empire

The Hapsburg Empire was vulnerable to revolutionary challenge. With its collection of subject nationalities (more non-Germans than Germans), the Empire was stirred by an acute spirit of nationalism; its government was reactionary (liberal institutions were nonexistent); and its reliance on serfdom doomed the masses of people to a life without hope. As soon as news of the "February Days" in France reached the borders of the Austrian Empire, rebellions began. The long-suppressed opponents of the government believed the time had come to introduce liberal institutions into the Empire.

Vienna

In March 1848 Hungarian criticism of Hapsburg imperial rule was initiated by Magyar nationalist leader Louis Kossuth (1802–1894), who demanded Hungarian independence. Students and workers in Vienna rushed to the streets to demonstrate on behalf of a more liberal government. The army failed to restore order and Prince Metternich, the symbol of reaction, resigned and fled the country. Emperor Ferdinand (reigned 1835–1848) granted a moderately-liberal constitution, but its shortcomings dissatisfied more radical elements and continual disorder prompted the emperor to flee from Vienna to Innsbruck, where he relied on his army commanders to restore order in the Empire. The Austrian imperial troops remained loyal to the Hapsburg crown. Prince Felix von Schwarzenberg (1800–1852) was put in charge of restoring Hapsburg control.

A people's committee ruled Vienna, where a liberal assembly gathered to write a constitution. Revolutionary outbreaks occurred in Hungary and Bohemia. The Hapsburgs issued the April Decree (1848), which pledged to eliminate the feudal services and duties imposed on the peasants. The inability of the revolutionary groups in Vienna to govern effectively made it easier for the Hapsburgs to lay siege to Vienna in October 1848. The rebels surrendered, and Emperor Ferdinand abdicated in favor of his 18-year-old nephew, Francis Joseph (reigned 1848–1916), who promptly restored royal absolutism.

The imperial government had been saved at Vienna through the loyalty of the army and the lack of ruling capacity on the part of the revolutionaries. The only thing the revolutionaries could agree on was their hatred of the Hapsburg dynasty.

Bohemia

Nationalist feeling among the Czechs, or Bohemians, had been smoldering for centuries. They demanded a constitution and autonomy within the Hapsburg Empire. A Pan-Slav Congress attempted to unite all Slavic peoples, but accomplished little because divisions were more decisive among them than was unified opposition to Hapsburg control. In June 1848 Prague submitted to a military occupation, followed by a military dictatorship in July, after all revolutionary groups had been crushed.

Hungary

The kingdom of Hungary was a state of about 12 million people under Hapsburg authority. Magyars or Hungarians, who represented about five-million subjects of the emperor, enjoyed a privileged position in the Empire. The remaining seven-million Slavic and Rumanian natives were powerless.

In March 1848 Nationalist leader Louis Kossuth took over direction of the movement and tamed a more radical Hungarian rebellion. Hungarian autonomy was declared in April, but failed to win popular support because of the tyrannical treatment of the Slavic minorities. Because the government in Vienna was distracted by revolutions everywhere in the Empire in the summer and fall of 1848, Louis Kossuth had time to organize an army to fight for Hungarian independence.

War between Austria and Hungary was declared on October 3, 1848, and Hungarian armies drove to within sight of Vienna. But desperate resistance from Slavic minorities forced the Hungarians to withdraw. Hungary was invaded by an Austrian army from the west, joined in June 1849 by a Russian army from the north. Along with Serbian resistance in the south and Rumanian resistance in the east, the combined opposition proved too much for Louis Kossuth's Hungarian Republic (proclaimed in April 1849), which was defeated. Kossuth fled into exile, while 13 of his guards were executed. Not until Austria was defeated by Prussia in 1866 would Hungary be in a position again to demand governmental equality with the Austrians.

Italy

In the Italian peninsula revolutionary activity broke out in Milan in March 1848 and was directed primarily by nationalists who were interested in expelling the Austrians from Lombardy and Venetia. King Charles Albert of Sardinia-Piedmont (reigned 1831–1849) capitalized on the revolution by declaring war on Austria, but his army was twice defeated in battle (Custozza and Novara) by the Russian general, Radetzky. In central Italy, Pope Pius IX expressed support for a unified Italian state. In the Kingdom of the Two Sicilies, an isolated revolt in Palermo, which occurred earlier than the rebellion in Paris, resulted in the granting of a liberal constitution by the reactionary King Ferdinand II (reigned 1830–1959).

Throughout Italy the revolution emphasized the cause of Italian nationalism and the reemergence of Italian pride through the Risorgimento. There was no evidence that the revolution was seriously concerned with the economic and social problems which confronted the Italian peasants.

King Charles Albert abdicated in favor of his son, Victor Emmanuel II (1820–1878), who was destined to complete the unification of Italy in the second half of the 19th century.

The revolutions of 1848 failed in Austria for several reasons. The subject nationalities sometimes hated each other more than they despised Austria. The Hapsburgs used the divisions between the ethnic groups as an effective weapon against each. The imperial army had remained loyal to its aristocratic commanders, who favored absolutism. There were too few industrial workers and an equally small number of middle class. The industrial workers could not exert any political power, and the middle class feared working-class radicalism and rallied to the government as defender of the status quo.

Liberalism Halted in the Germanies

The immediate effect of the 1848 Revolution in France was a series of liberal and nationalistic demonstrations in the German states (March 1848), with the rulers promising liberal concessions. The liberals' demand for constitutional government was coupled with another demand—some kind of union or federation of the German states. While popular demonstrations by students, workers, and the middle class produced the promise of a liberal future, the permanent success or failure of these "promises" rested on Prussian reaction.

Prussia, the Frankfurt Parliament, and German Unification

Under King Frederick William IV (reigned 1840–1861), Prussia moved from revolution to reaction. After agreeing to liberalize the Prussian government following street rioting in Berlin, the king rejected the constitution written by a specially called assembly. The liberal ministry resigned and was replaced by a conservative one. The king felt powerful enough to substitute his own constitution, which guaranteed royal control of the government, for a complicated three-class system of indirect voting that excluded all but landlords and wealthy bourgeoisie from office. This system prevailed in Prussia until 1918. Finally, the government ministry was responsible to the king, and the military services swore loyalty to the king alone.

Self-appointed liberal, romantic, and nationalist leaders called for elections to a constituent assembly from all states belonging to the German Bund, for the purpose of unifying the German states. Meeting in May 1848, the Frankfurt Parliament was mostly composed of intellectuals, professionals, lawyers, businessmen, and the middle class. After a year of deliberation over questions of (1) monarchy or republic (2) federal union or centralized state (3) boundaries (i.e., only German populated or mixed nationalities), the assembly produced a constitution.

The principal problem facing the Frankfurt Assembly was to obtain Prussian support. The smaller German states generally favored the Frankfurt Constitution, as did liberals throughout the large and middle-sized states. Austria made it clear that it was opposed to the work of the Assembly and would remain in favor of the present system.

The Assembly leaders made the decision to stake their demands for a united Germany on King Frederick William IV of Prussia. They selected him as emperor in late March 1849 only to have him reject the offer because he was a divine-right monarch not subject to popularly elected assemblies. Without Prussia there could be no success, so the Frankfurt Parliament dissolved without achieving a single accomplishment.

The Prussian King Frederick William IV had his own plans for uniting Germany. Right after refusing a "crown from the gutter," he offered his own plan to the German princes, whereby Prussia would play a prominent role along with Austria. When Austria demanded allegiance to the Bund, the Prussian king realized pushing his plan would involve him in a war with Austria and her allies (including Russia). In November 1850 Prussia agreed to forego the idea of uniting the German states at a meeting with Austria called the "Humiliation of Olmutz." Austrian domination of the German Bund was confirmed.

Great Britain and the Victorian Compromise

The Victorian Age (1837–1901) is associated with the long reign of Queen

Victoria, who succeeded her uncle King William IV at the age of 18, and married her cousin, Prince Albert. The early years of her reign coincided with the continuation of liberal reform of the British government, accomplished through an arrangement known as the "Victorian Compromise." The Compromise was a political alliance of the middle class and aristocracy to exclude the working class from political power. The middle class gained control of the House of Commons, the aristocracy controlled the government, the army, and the Church of England. This process of accommodation worked successfully.

Highlights of the "Compromise Era"

Parliamentary reforms continued after passage of the 1832 Reform Bill. Laws were enacted abolishing slavery throughout the Empire (1833). The Factory Act (1831) forbade the employment of children under the age of nine. The New Poor Law (1834) required the needy who were able and unemployed to live in workhouses. The Municipal Reform Law (1835) gave control of the cities to the middle class. The last remnants of the mercantilistic age fell with the abolition of the Corn Laws (1846) and repeal of the old navigation acts (1849).

Working-class protest arose in the wake of belief that passage of the "Great Reform Bill" of 1832 would bring prosperity. When workers found themselves no better off, they turned to collective political action. They linked the solution of their economic plight to a program of political reform known as Chartism, or the Chartist movement, from the charter of six points which they petitioned Parliament to adopt—universal male suffrage, secret ballot for voting, no property qualifications for members of Parliament, salaries for members of Parliament, annual elections for Parliament, and equal electoral districts.

During the age of Victorian Compromise these ideas were considered dangerously radical. Both the middle class and aristocracy vigorously opposed the working-class political agenda. Chartism as a national movement failed. Its ranks were split between those who favored violence and those who advocated peaceful tactics. The return of prosperity, with steady wages and lower food prices, robbed the movement of momentum. Yet the Chartist movement came to constitute the first large-scale, working-class political movement.

After 1846 England was more and more dominated by the middle class; this was one of the factors that enabled it to escape the revolutions which shook Europe in 1848. The ability of the English to make meaningful industrial reforms gave the working class hope that its goals could be achieved without violent social upheaval.

Evaluation

The revolutions of 1848 began with much promise, but all ended in defeat for a number of reasons. They were spontaneous movements which lost their popular support as people lost their enthusiasm. Initial successes by the revolutionaries were due less to their strength than to the hesitancy of governments to use their superior force. Once this hesitancy was overcome, the revolutions were smashed. They were essentially urban movements, and the conservative landowners and peasants tended, in time, to nullify the spontaneous actions of the urban classes. The middle class, who led the revolutions, came to fear the radicalism of their working-class allies.

While in favor of political reformation, the middle class drew the line at social engineering, much to the dismay of the laboring poor. Divisions among national groups, and the willingness of one nationality to deny rights to other nationalities, helped to destroy the revolutionary movements in central Europe.

In central Europe, revolutions, which had been led by the middle class, did not express any interest in addressing social and economic problems. When the workers and students demanded social and economic revolution, the middle class became alienated from the revolution which they had led earlier; they desired only political change through the establishment of a constitutional process. This breach within the revolutionary camp was detected and exploited by the old regime.

In eastern and southern Europe, the nationalist revolutions lacked organization, and above all, the military capacity to resist the professional armies of the Austrian Empire. However, the results of 1848–1849 were not entirely negative. Universal male suffrage was introduced in France; serfdom remained abolished in Austria and the German states; parliaments were established in Prussia and other German states, though dominated by princes and aristocrats; and Prussia and Sardinia-Piedmont emerged with new determination to succeed in their respective unification schemes.

The revolutions of 1848–1849 brought to a close the era of liberal revolutions that had begun in France in 1789. Reformers and revolutionists alike learned a lesson from the failures of 1848. They learned that planning and organization is necessary; that rational argument and revolution would not always assure success. With 1848, the Age of Revolution sputtered out. The Age of Romanticism was about to give way to an Age of Realism.

EPILOGUE: THE VIEW FROM MID-NINETEENTH-CENTURY EUROPE

A new age followed the revolutions of 1848–1849, as Otto von Bismarck (1815–1898), one of the dominant political figures of the second half of the 19th century, was quick to realize. If the mistake of these years was to believe that great decisions could be brought about by speeches and parliamentary majorities, the sequel showed that in an industrial era new techniques involving ruthless force were all too readily available. The period of *Realpolitik*—of realistic, iron-fisted politics and diplomacy—followed.

By 1850 all humankind was positioned to become part of a single, worldwide, interacting whole. The military technology and industrial productivity of the Europeans allowed them to impose their wills on the rest of the world.

The half-century after 1850 witnessed the political consolidation and economic expansion that paved the way for the brief global domination of Europe. The conservative monarchies of Sardinia-Piedmont and Prussia united Italy and Germany by military force, and gave birth to new power relationships on the Continent. Externalizing their rivalries produced conflict overseas in a new age of imperialism which saw Africa and Asia fall under the domination of the West.

Nationalism overtook liberalism as the dominant force in human affairs after 1850. Nationalists were romantic, but more hardheaded. The good of the nation and not the individual became the new creed. The state was deified.

After 1848–1849 the middle class ceased to be revolutionary. It became concerned with protecting its hard-earned political power and property rights against radical political and social movements. And the working classes also adopted new tactics and organizations. They turned to trade unions and political parties to achieve their political and social goals.

A great era of progress in politics, science, industry, society, and culture began to reshape the contours of the world.

5 REALISM AND MATERIALISM (1848–1914)

REALPOLITIK AND THE TRIUMPH OF NATIONALISM

Cavour and the Unification of Italy

After the collapse of the revolutionary movements of 1848, the leadership of Italian nationalism was transferred to Sardinian leaders Victor Emmanuel II (1820–1878), Camillo de Cavour (1810–1861), and Giuseppe Garibaldi (1807–1882). They replaced the earlier leaders Giuseppe Mazzini (1805–1872) of the Young Italy movement, Charles Albert (1798–1849), the once liberal Pius IX (1792–1878), and Vincenzo Gioberti (1801–1852) and the Neo-Guelf movement, which promoted a unified Italian state centered on the Papacy. The new leaders did not entertain romantic illusions about the process of transforming Sardinia into a new Italian Kingdom; they were practitioners of the politics of realism, *Realpolitik*.

Cavour was a Sardinian who served as editor of *Il Risorgimento*, a newspaper that argued that Sardinia should be the basis of a new Italy. Between 1852 and 1861, Cavour served as Victor Emmanuel II's Prime Minister. In that capacity Cavour transformed Sardinian society by implementing a series of liberal reforms designed to modernize the Sardinian state and attract the support of liberal states such as Great Britain and France. Among Cavour's reforms were the following: 1) The Law on Convents and the Siccardi Law, which were directed at curtailing the influence of the Roman Catholic Church 2) the reform of the judicial system 3) the full implementation of the Statuto, the Sardinian Constitution which was modeled on the liberal French Constitution of 1830, and 4) support for economic development projects such as port and highway construction.

In 1855, under Cavour's direction, Sardinia joined Britain and France in the Crimean War against Russia. At the Paris Peace Conference (1856), Cavour addressed the delegates on the need to eliminate the foreign (Austrian) presence in the Italian peninsula and attracted the attention and sympathy of the French Emperor, Napoleon III. Cavour and Napoleon III met at Plombières on July 20, 1858. The Plombières Agreement stated that in the event that Sardinia went to war with Austria—presumably after being attacked or provoked—France would provide military assistance to Sardinia, and with victory, Sardinia would annex Lombardy, Venetia, Parma, Modena, and a part of the Papal states. Additionally, the remainder of Italy would be organized into an Italian Confederation under the direction of the Pope, France would receive Nice and Savoy, and the alliance would be finalized by a marriage between the two royal families. The Plombières Agreement was designed to bring about a war with Austria and to assist Sardinia in developing an expanded northern Italian kingdom. The concept of an Italian confederation under the papacy was contributed by Napoleon III and demonstrates his lack of understanding about the nature of Italian political ambitions and values during this period.

After being provoked, the Austrians declared war on Sardinia in 1859. French forces intervened and the Austrians were defeated in the battles of Magenta (June 4)

THE UNIFICATION OF ITALY

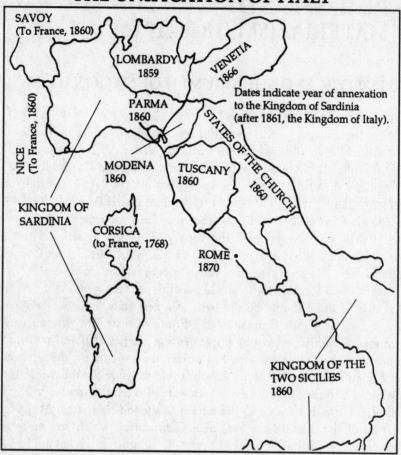

SAVOY
(To France, 1860)

LOMBARDY
1859

VENETIA
1866

Dates indicate year of annexation
to the Kingdom of Sardinia
(after 1861, the Kingdom of Italy).

PARMA
1860

NICE
(To France, 1860)

STATES OF THE CHURCH
1860

MODENA
1860

TUSCANY
1860

KINGDOM OF
SARDINIA

CORSICA
(to France, 1768)

ROME •
1870

KINGDOM OF THE
TWO SICILIES
1860

and Solferino (June 24). Napoleon III's support then wavered for four reasons: 1) Prussia mobilized and expressed sympathy for Austria 2) the outbreak of uncontrolled revolutions in several Northern Italian states 3) the forcefulness of the new Austrian military efforts, and 4) the lack of public support in France for his involvement and the mounting criticism being advanced by the French Catholic Church, which opposed the war against Catholic Austria.

Napoleon III, without consulting Cavour, signed a secret peace (The Truce of Villafranca) on July 11, 1859. Sardinia received Lombardy but not Venetia; the other terms indicated that Sardinian influence would be restricted and that Austria would remain a power in Italian politics. The terms of Villafranca were clarified and finalized with the Treaty of Zurich (1859).

In 1860, Cavour arranged the annexation of Parma, Modena, Romagna, and Tuscany into Sardinia. These actions were recognized by the Treaty of Turin between Napoleon III and Victor Emmanuel II; Nice and Savoy were transferred to France. With these acquisitions, Cavour anticipated the need for a period of tranquility to incorporate these territories into Sardinia.

Giuseppe Garibaldi and his Red Shirts landed in Sicily in May 1860 and extended the nationalist activity to the south. Within three months, Sicily was taken and by September 7th, Garibaldi was in Naples and the Kingdom of the Two Sicilies had fallen under Sardinian influence. Cavour distrusted Garibaldi, but Victor Emmanuel II encouraged him.

In February 1861, in Turin, Victor Emmanuel was declared King of Italy and presided over an Italian Parliament which represented the entire Italian peninsula with the exception of Venetia and the Patrimony of St. Peter (Rome). Cavour died in June 1861.

Venetia was incorporated into the Italian Kingdom in 1866 as a result of an alliance between Bismarck's Prussia and the Kingdom of Italy which preceded the German Civil War between Austria and Prussia. In return for opening a southern front against Austria, Prussia, upon its victory, arranged for Venetia to be transferred to Italy.

Bismarck was again instrumental in the acquisition of Rome into the Italian Kingdom in 1870. In 1870, the Franco-Prussian War broke out and the French garrison, which had been in Rome providing protection for the Pope, was withdrawn to serve on the front against Prussia. Italian troops seized Rome, and in 1871, as a result of a plebiscite, Rome became the capital of the Kingdom of Italy.

BISMARCK AND THE UNIFICATION OF GERMANY

In the period after 1815 Prussia emerged as an alternative to a Hapsburg-based Germany. During the early 19th century, Germany was politically decentralized and consisted of dozens of independent states. This multistate situation had been in place for centuries and had been sanctioned by the Peace of Westphalia in 1648. Prussia had absorbed many of the smaller states during the 18th and early 19th centuries.

Otto von Bismarck (1810–1898) entered the diplomatic service of Wilhelm I as the Revolutions of 1848 were being suppressed. By the early 1860s, Bismarck had emerged as the principal adviser and minister to the King. Bismarck was an advocate of a Prussian-based (Hohenzollern) Germany. During the 1850s and 1860s, he supported a series of military reforms which improved the Prussian army. In 1863, Bismarck joined the Russians in suppressing a Polish rebellion; this enterprise resulted in improved Russian-Prussian relations.

In 1863, the Schleswig-Holstein crisis broke. These provinces, which were occupied by Germans, were under the personal rule of Christian IX (1818–1906) of Denmark. The Danish government advanced a new constitution which specified that Schleswig and Holstein would be annexed into Denmark. German reaction was predictable and Bismarck arranged for joint Austro-Prussian military action. Denmark was defeated and agreed (Treaty of Vienna, 1864) to give up the provinces, and Schleswig and Holstein were to be jointly administered by Austria and Prussia.

Questions of jurisdiction provided the rationale for estranged relations between Austria and Prussia. In 1865, a temporary settlement was reached in the Gastein Convention, which stated that Prussia would administer Schleswig and Austria would manage Holstein. During 1865 and 1866, Bismarck made diplomatic prepa-

THE UNIFICATION OF GERMANY

rations for the forthcoming struggle with Austria. Italy, France, and Russia would not interfere, and Great Britain was not expected to involve itself in a Central European war.

The German Civil War (also known as The Seven Weeks' War) was devastating to Austria. The humiliating defeat at Königgrätz (July 4, 1866) demonstrated the ineptitude of the Austrian forces when confronted by the Prussian army led by General von Moltke. Within two months, Austria had to agree to the peace terms which were drawn up at Nikolsburg and finalized by the Peace of Prague (August 1866). There were three principal terms. Austria would not be part of any new German state. Venetia would be ceded to Italy. Austria would pay an indemnity to Prussia.

In the next year, 1867, the North German Confederation was established by Bismarck. It was designed to facilitate the move toward a unified German state and included all the German states except Baden, Württemberg, Bavaria, and Saxony; the King of Prussia served as President of the Confederation.

In 1870, deteriorating relations between France and Germany collapsed over the Ems Dispatch. Wilhelm I, while vacationing at Ems, was approached by representatives of the French government who requested a Prussian pledge not to interfere on the issue of the vacant Spanish throne. Wilhelm I refused to give such a pledge and informed Bismarck of these developments through a telegram from Ems.

Bismarck exploited the situation by initiating a propaganda campaign against the French. Subsequently, France declared war and the Franco-Prussian War (1870–1871) commenced. Prussian victories at Sedan and Metz proved decisive; Napoleon III and his leading general, Marshal Mac-Mahon, were captured. Paris continued to resist but fell to the Prussians in January 1871. The Treaty of Frankfurt (May 1871) concluded the war and resulted in France ceding Alsace-Lorraine to Germany and a German occupation until an indemnity was paid.

The German Empire was proclaimed on January 18, 1871 with Wilhelm I becoming the Emperor of Germany. Bismarck became the Imperial Chancellor. Bavaria, Baden, Württemberg, and Saxony were incorporated into the new Germany.

INTER-EUROPEAN RELATIONS (1848–1878)

Since the Napoleonic Era, the peace in Europe had been sustained because of the memories of the devastation and the disruption caused by the wars of the French Revolution and Napoleonic Age; the primary structure that maintained the peace was the Concert System. The Concert of Europe was a rather loose and ill-defined understanding among the European nations that they would join together to resolve problems which threatened the status quo; it was believed that joint action would be undertaken to prohibit any drastic alteration in the European system or balance of power. The credibility of the Concert of Europe was undermined by the failure of the powers to cooperate during the revolutions of 1848 and 1849. Between 1848 and 1878 the peace among the European powers was interrupted by the Crimean War (1854–1856) and challenged by the crisis centered on the Russo-Turkish War of 1877–1878.

THE CRIMEAN WAR

The Crimean War originated in the dispute between two differing groups of Christians and their protectors over privileges in the Holy Land. During the 19th century, Palestine was part of the Ottoman Turkish Empire. In 1852, the Turks negotiated an agreement with the French to provide enclaves in the Holy Land to Roman Catholic religious orders; this arrangement appeared to jeopardize already existing agreements which provided access to Greek Orthodox religious orders. Czar Nicholas I (reigned 1825–1855), unaware of the impact of his action, ordered Russian troops to occupy several Danubian principalities; his strategy was to withdraw from these areas once the Turks agreed to clarify and guarantee the rights of the Greek Orthodox orders. The role of Britain in this developing crisis was critical; Nicholas mistakenly was convinced that the British Prime Minister, Lord Aberdeen, would be sympathetic to the Russian policy. Aberdeen, who headed a coalition cabinet, sought to use the Concert of Europe system to settle the question. However, Lord Palmerston, the Home Secretary, supported the Turks; he was suspicious of Russian intervention in the region. Consequently, misunderstandings about Britain's policy developed. In October 1853, the Turks demanded that the Russians withdraw from the occupied principalities. The Russians failed to respond, and the Turks declared war. In February 1854, Nicholas advanced a draft for a settlement of the Russo-Turkish War; it was rejected and Great Britain and France joined the Ottoman Turks and declared war on Russia.

With the exception of some naval encounters in the Gulf of Finland off the Aaland Islands, the war was conducted on the Crimean Peninsula in the Black Sea. In September 1854, more than 50,000 British and French troops landed in the Crimea, determined to take the Russian port city of Sebastopol. While this war has been remembered for the work of Florence Nightingale (1820–1910) and the "Charge of the Light Brigade," it was a conflict in which there were more casualties from disease and the weather than from combat. In December 1854, Austria reluctantly became a co-signatory of the Four Points of Vienna, a statement of British and French war aims. The Four Points specified that 1) Russia should renounce any claims to the occupied principalities 2) the 1841 Straits Convention would be revised 3) navigation in the mouth of the Danube River (on the Black Sea) should be internationalized, and 4) Russia should withdraw any claim to having a "special" protective role for Greek Orthodox residents in the Ottoman Empire. In 1855, Piedmont joined Britain and France in the war. In March 1855, Czar Nicholas I died and was succeeded by Alexander II (reigned 1855–1881), who was opposed to continuing the war. In December 1855, the Austrians, under excessive pressure from the British, French, and Piedmontese, sent an ultimatum to Russia in which they threatened to renounce their neutrality. In response, Alexander II indicated that he would accept the Four Points.

Representatives convened in Paris between February and April 1856. The resulting Peace of Paris had the following major provisions: Russia had to acknowledge international commissions to regulate maritime traffic on the Danube, recognize Turkish control of the mouth of the Danube, renounce all claims to the Danubian Principalities of Moldavia and Wallachia (which later led to the establishment of Rumania), agree not to fortify the Aaland Islands, renounce its previously espoused position of protector of the Greek Orthodox residents of the Ottoman Empire, and return all occupied territories to the Ottoman Empire. The Straits Convention of 1841 was revised by neutralizing of the Black Sea. The Declaration of Paris specified rules to regulate commerce during periods of war. Lastly, the independence and integrity of the Ottoman Empire were recognized and guaranteed by the signatories.

THE EASTERN QUESTION AND THE CONGRESS OF BERLIN

Another challenge to the Concert of Europe developed in the 1870s with a seemingly endless number of Balkan crises. Once again, the conflict initially involved Russia and Ottoman Turks, but Britain and Russia quickly became the principal protagonists.

In 1876, Turkish forces under the leadership of Osman Pasha soundly defeated Serbian armies. Serbia requested assistance from the great powers and, as a consequence of the political pressures exercised by the great powers, the Turks agreed to participate in a conference in Constantinople. The meeting resulted in a draft agreement between the Serbs and the Turks. However, Britain quietly advised the Sultan, Abdülhamid II (reigned 1876–1909), to scuttle the agreement, which he did. In June 1877, Russia dispatched forces across the Danube. During the next month, Osman Pasha took up a defensive position in Plevna. During the period of the siege, sympathy in the west shifted toward the Turks, and Britain and Austria became alarmed over the extent of Russian influence in the region. In March 1878, the Russians and the Turks signed the Peace of San Stephano; implementation of its provisions would have resulted in Russian hegemony in the Balkans and dramatically altered the balance of power in the eastern Mediterranean. The treaty provided for the establishment of a large Bulgarian state which would be under Russian influence; the transfer of Dobrudja, Kars, Ardahan, Bayazid, and Batum to Russia; the expansion of Serbia and Montenegro; and the establishment of an autonomous Bosnia-Herzegovina which would be under Russian control.

Britain, under the leadership of Prime Minister Benjamin Disraeli (1804–1881), denounced the San Stephano Accord, dispatched a naval squadron to Turkish waters, and demanded that the San Stephano agreement be scrapped. The German Chancellor, Otto von Bismarck, intervened and offered his services as mediator.

The delegates of the major powers convened in June and July 1878 to negotiate a settlement. Prior to the meeting, Disraeli had concluded a series of secret arrangements with Austria, Russia, and Turkey. The combined impact of these accommodations was to restrict Russian expansion in the region, reaffirm the independence of Turkey, and maintain British control of the Mediterranean. The specific terms of the Treaty of Berlin resulted in the following: 1) recognition of Rumania, Serbia, and Montenegro as independent states 2) the establishment of the autonomous principality of Bulgaria 3) Austrian acquisition of Bosnia and Herzegovina and 4) the transfer of Cyprus to Great Britain.

The Russians, who had won the war against Turkey and had imposed the harsh terms of the San Stephano Treaty, found that they left the conference with very little (Kars, Batum, etc.) for their effort. Although Disraeli was the primary agent of this anti-Russian settlement, the Russians blamed Bismarck for their dismal results. Their hostility toward Germany led Bismarck (1879) to embark upon a new system of alliances which transformed European diplomacy and rendered any additional efforts of the Concert of Europe futile.

CAPITALISM AND THE EMERGENCE OF THE NEW LEFT (1848–1914)

Economic Developments: The New Industrial Order

During the 19th century, Europe experienced the full impact of the Industrial Revolution. The Industrial Revolution resulted in improving aspects of the physical lives of a greater number of Europeans; at the same time, it led to a factory system with undesirable working and living conditions and the abuses of child labor.

As the century progressed, the inequities of the system became increasingly evident. Trade-unionism and socialist political parties emerged which attempted to address these problems and improve the lives of the working class. In most of these expressions of discontent, the influences of Utopian Socialism or Marxism were evident. Socialism was steeped in economic materialism, which had emerged in the 18th century and came to dominate the 19th and 20th centuries. Economics was a component in the rise of scientism; by its very nature, it advanced the values of material culture.

Marx and Scientific Socialism

During the period from 1815 to 1848, Utopian Socialists such as Robert Owen (1771–1858), Saint Simon, and Charles Fourier advocated the establishment of a political-economic system which was based on romantic concepts of the ideal society. The failure of the Revolutions of 1848 and 1849 discredited the Utopian Socialists, and the new "Scientific Socialism" advanced by Karl Marx (1818–1883) became the primary ideology of protest and revolution. Marx, a German philosopher, developed a communist philosophic system which was founded on the inherent goodness of man; this Rousseau-influenced position argued that men were basically good but had been corrupted by the artificial institutions (states, churches, etc.) from which they had evolved. Marx stated that the history of humanity was the history of class struggle and that the process of the struggle (the dialectic) would continue until a classless society was realized. The Marxian dialectic was driven by the dynamics of materialism. Marx contended that the age of the bourgeois domination of the working class was the most severe and oppressive phase of the struggle. The proletariat, or the industrial working class, needed to be educated and led towards a violent revolution which would destroy the institutions which perpetuated the struggle and the suppression of the majority. After the revolution, the people would experience the dictatorship of the proletariat, during which the Communist Party would provide leadership. Marx advanced these concepts in a series of tracts and books including *The Communist Manifesto* (1848), *Critique of Political Economy* (1859), and *Capital* (1863–1864). In most instances, his arguments were put forth in scientific form; Marx accumulated extensive data and developed a persuasive rhetorical style. In the 1860s, Marxism was being accepted by many reformers. Marx lived most of his adult life in London, where he died in 1883.

The Anarchists

Anarchism emerged in the early 19th century as a consequence of the Industrial Revolution. Its early proponents, William Godwin (1756–1836) and Pierre Proudhon, (1809–1865) argued that anarchism, a situation where there would be no property or authority, would be attained through enlightened individualism. Proudhon, in *What is Property* (1840), stated that anarchism would be achieved through education and without violence. After the revolutions of 1848 and 1849, Mikhail Bakunin (1814–1876), a Russian, stated that violent, terrorist actions were necessary to move the people to revolt against their oppressors; anarchism has been associated with violence since Bakunin's time. A variation of anarchism, called syndicalism, was developed by Georges Sorel (1847–1922) in France. Syndicalism, sometimes referred to as anarcho-syndicalism, involved direct economic actions in order to control industries. The strike and industrial sabotage were employed frequently by the syndicalists. Syndicalist influence was restricted to France, Spain (Confederación Nacional del Trabajo, an organization of several syndicalist unions), and Italy (Filippo Corridoni and the young Benito Mussolini).

The Revisionist Movement

A reconsideration of Marxism commenced before Marx's death in 1883. In that year, a group of British leftists organized themselves into the Fabian Society and declared that while they were sympathetic to Marxism—indeed, they considered themselves Marxists—they differed from the orthodoxy on two major points. They did not accept the inevitability of revolution in order to bring about a socialist, i.e., communist society; democratic societies possessed the mechanisms which would lead to the gradual evolution of socialism. Also, they did not accept the Marxist interpretation of contemporary history. They contended that historical processes endured and were difficult to redirect and reform, while Marxists tended to accept the notion that world revolution was imminent. Sidney and Beatrice Webb, George Bernard Shaw, Keir Hardie, and several others joined in forming the Fabian Society. Later, it would split over the Boer War, but its members would serve in every Labor ministry.

In Germany, the Social Democratic Party (SDP) had been established along the lines of Marxist orthodoxy. In the 1890s, Eduard Bernstein (1850–1932), who was influenced by the Fabians, redirected the efforts and platform of the SDP toward the revisionist position. Within a few years, the SDP extended its credibility and support to acquire a dominant position in the Reichstag.

The French Socialist Jean Jaurès (1859–1914) led his group to revisionism; its moderation led to increasing its seats in the Chamber of Deputies and in developing acceptance for its criticisms and proposals during the tumultuous years of the Dreyfus Affair. While orthodox Marxists (Lenin) denounced the revisionist movement, the majority of socialists in 1914 were revisionists who were willing to use the democratic process to bring about their goals.

BRITAIN AND FRANCE

During the second half of the 19th century, Britain and France enjoyed considerable economic prosperity, experienced periods of jingoistic nationalism, and were confronted with demands for expanding democracy. Great Britain, under the leadership of Lord Palmerston, William Gladstone, and Benjamin Disraeli, represented a dichotomy of values and political agendas. On one hand, Britain led Europe into an age of revitalized imperialism and almost unbridled capitalism; on the other hand, Gladstone and the Liberal Party advocated democratic reforms, an anti-imperialist stance, and a program to eliminate or restrict unacceptable working and social conditions. In France, the evolution of a more democratic political order was slowed by the collapse of the Second French Republic and the development of the Second Empire. However, in 1871, the Third Republic was established and the French moved closer to realizing democracy.

The Age of Palmerston

During the period from 1850 to 1865, Lord Palmerston (1784–1865) was the dominant political power in Great Britain. Palmerston served in a range of positions including Foreign Secretary, Home Secretary, and Prime Minister. In foreign affairs,

Palmerston was preoccupied with colonial problems such as the Indian Mutiny of 1857, troubles in China, and British interests in the American Civil War. Palmerston expressed little interest in domestic affairs. This period witnessed the realignment of political parties within British politics. The Tory Party was transformed into the Conservative Party under Disreali, and the Whig Party became the Liberty Party, with Gladstone serving as its new leader. John Bright (1811–1889), a manufacturer, anti-corn law advocate, and leader of the Manchester School of classical economics, contributed significantly to the development of the Liberal Party.

Until the 1850s, the British East India Company managed India for the British government. During this decade a new rifle, the Enfield, was introduced. The procedure for loading the Enfield required that the covering for the cartridges be removed by the teeth prior to inserting them in the rifle. Rumors circulated that the covering was a grease made from the fat of cows and swine; these rumors alarmed the Hindu and Muslim troops. Troops mutinied in Calcutta in 1857 and within a few months more than a third of India was in the hands of rebels and Europeans were being killed. A British-led force of about 3,000 troops suppressed the mutiny, which lacked cohesion in its aims, organization, and leadership. By January 1858, Britain had reestablished its control of India; the East India Company was dissolved and replaced by the direct authority of London.

During the 1850s and 1860s, Palmerston sought to clarify British commercial access to China. In 1858, with the support of French troops, the British army took the Taka Forts on the Peiko River and, in 1860, captured Peking. As a result, China agreed to open Tientsin and other ports to the European powers.

The American Civil War (1861–1865) curtailed the supply of unprocessed cotton to British mills. The British economy was affected adversely and significant unemployment and factory closings resulted. The American war also led to a discussion within Britain on the fundamental issues of liberty, slavery, and democracy. A crisis between Britain and the United States developed over the Trent Affair, (1861) during which a British ship was boarded by American sailors. In the end, the British government and people supported the Union cause because of ideological considerations; even in the areas affected by the shortage of cotton, there was general support for the North.

Disraeli, Gladstone, and the Era of Democratic Reforms

In 1865, Palmerston died, and during the next two decades significant domestic developments occurred which expanded democracy in Great Britain. The dominant leaders of this period were William Gladstone (1809–1898) and Benjamin Disraeli (1804–1881). Gladstone, who was initially a Conservative, emerged as a severe critic of the Corn Laws and, as a budgetary expert, became Chancellor of the Exchequer under Palmerston. As the leader of the Liberal Party (until 1895), Gladstone supported Irish Home Rule, fiscal responsibility, free trade, and the extension of democratic principles. He was opposed to imperialism, the involvement of Britain in European affairs, and the further centralization of the British government. Disraeli argued for an aggressive foreign policy, the expansion of the British Empire, and, after opposing democratic reforms, the extension of the franchise.

After defeating Gladstone's effort to extend the vote in 1866, Disraeli advanced the Reform Bill of 1867. This bill, which expanded on the Reform Bill of 1832, was enacted and specified two reforms: 1) There would be a redistribution (similar to reapportionment) of seats which would provide a more equitable representation in the House of Commons; the industrial cities and boroughs gained seats at the expense of some depopulated areas in the north and west. 2) The right to vote was extended to include all adult male citizens of boroughs who paid £10 or more rent annually, and all adult male citizens of the counties who were £12 tenants or £5 leaseholders.

The consequence of this act was that almost all men over 21 years in age who resided in urban centers were granted the right to vote. In 1868, the newly-extended electorate provided the Liberals with a victory and Gladstone commenced his first of four terms as Prime Minister.

Gladstone's first ministry (1868–1874) was characterized by a wave of domestic legislation which reflected the move toward democracy. Among the measures which were enacted were five acts:

1) The Ballot Act (1872) provided for a secret ballot, and realized a major Chartist demand of the 1830s.

2) Civil Services Reform (1870) introduced a system of competitive examination for government positions.

3) The Education Act (1870) established a system of school districts throughout the country, provided assistance in the organization of school boards, and established schools in poverty-stricken regions. Free elementary education in Britain would not be realized until 1891.

4) The Land Act (1870) attempted to resolve economic and social inequities in Ireland. However, it did not succeed in providing Irish tenants with reasonable safeguards against arbitrary eviction or the imposition of drastic increases in rent.

5) The University Act (1870) eliminated the use of religious tests which provided a quota of seats in universities for members of the Anglican church.

Between 1874 and 1880, Disraeli served as Prime Minister, and while he was deeply concerned with foreign difficulties, he did succeed in developing the notion of Tory Democracy, which was directed at domestic issues. Tory Democracy represented Disraeli's views on how the Conservative Party would support necessary domestic action on behalf of the common good.

In 1875, through Disraeli's support, the following measures were passed: 1) Laws which lessened the regulation of trade unions 2) A Food and Drug Act which regulated the sale of these items 3) A Public Health Act which specified government requirements and standards for sanitation 4) The Artisan's Dwelling Act.

While a few Conservatives, such as Lord Randolph Churchill (1849–1895), attempted to extend the progress of Tory Democracy and to incorporate it permanently within the Conservative program, most of the Conservative Party abandoned this approach after Disraeli's death in 1881.

During his remaining ministries (1880–1885, 1886, and 1892–1895),

Gladstone was preoccupied with Ireland. A further extension of the franchise occurred in 1884 with the passage of the Representation of the People Act, which granted the right to vote to adult males in the counties on the same basis as in the boroughs. In 1885, another redistribution of seats in the House of Commons was approved on the ratio of one seat for every 50,000 citizens.

The Second French Republic and the Second Empire

Louis Napoleon became the President of the Second French Republic in December 1848. It was evident that he was not committed to the Republic and in May 1849, elections for the Legislative Assembly clearly indicated that the people were not bound to its continuance either. In this election, the Conservatives and Monarchists scored significant gains, and the Republicans and Radicals lost power in the Assembly. During the three-year life of the Second Republic, Louis Napoleon demonstrated his skills as a gifted politician through the manipulation of the various factions in French politics. His deployment of troops in Italy to rescue and restore Pope Pius IX was condemned by the republicans, but strongly supported by the monarchists and moderates. As a consequence of the French military intervention, a French garrison under General Oudinot was stationed in Rome until the fall of 1870, when it was recalled during the Franco-Prussian War.

Louis Napoleon minimized the importance of the Legislative Assembly, capitalized on the developing Napoleonic Legend, and courted the support of the army, the Catholic Church, and a range of conservative political groups. The Falloux Law returned control of education to the church. Further, Louis Napoleon was confronted with Article 45 of the constitution, which stipulated that the president was limited to one four-year term; he had no intention of relinquishing power. With the assistance of a core of dedicated supporters, Louis Napoleon arranged for a coup d'état on the night of December 1–2, 1851. The Second Republic fell and was soon replaced by the Second French Empire.

Louis Napoleon drafted a new constitution which resulted in a highly-centralized government. He was to have a 10-year term, power to declare war, lead the armed forces, conduct foreign policy, initiate and pronounce all laws, and control the new Legislative Assembly. On December 2, 1852, he announced that he was Napoleon III, Emperor of the French.

The domestic history of the Second Empire is divided into two periods: 1851 to 1860, during which Napoleon III's control was direct and authoritarian, and 1860 to 1870, the decade of the Liberal Empire, during which the regime was liberalized through a series of reforms. During the Second Empire, living conditions in France generally improved. The government instituted agreements and actions which stimulated the movement toward free trade (Cobden-Chevalier Treaty of 1860), improved the efficiency of the French economic system (Credit Mobilier and the Credit Focier, both established in 1852), and conducted major public works programs in French cities with the assistance of such talented leaders as Baron Haussmann (1809–1891), the prefect of the Seine. Though many artists and scholars (Victor Hugo (1802–1885), Jules Michelet (1798–1874), and Gustav Flaubert (1821–1880)) were censored and, on occasion, prosecuted for their works, the artistic and scholarly achievements of the Second Empire were impressive. Flaubert and Baudelaire (1821–1867), and in music, Jacques Offenbach (1819–1880), were most productive during these decades, and younger artists such as Renoir (1841–1919), Manet (1832–1883), and Cezanne (1839–1900) began their careers and were influenced by the culture of the Second Empire. The progressive liberalization of the government during the 1860s resulted in extending the powers of the Legislative Assembly, restricting church control over secondary education, and permitting the development of trade unions. In large part, this liberalization was designed to divert criticism from Napoleon III's unsuccessful foreign policy. French involvement in Algeria, the Crimean War, the process of Italian unification, the establishment of colonial presences in Senegal, Somaliland, and Indo-China (Laos, Cambodia, and Viet Nam), and the ill-fated Mexican adventure (the short-lived rule of Maximilian from 1864–1867), resulted in increased criticism of Napoleon III and his authority. The Second Empire collapsed after the capture of Napoleon III during the Franco-Prussian War (1870–1871). After a regrettable Parisian experience with a communist type of government, the Third French Republic was established; it would survive until 1940.

IMPERIAL RUSSIA

The autocracy of Nicholas I's (reigned 1825–1855) regime was not threatened by the revolutionary movements of 1848. The consequences of the European revolutionary experience of 1848 to 1849 reinforced the conservative ideology which was the basis of the Romanov regime. In 1848 and 1849, Russian troops suppressed disorganized Polish attempts to reassert Polish nationalism.

Russian involvement in the Crimean War met with defeat. Russian ambitions in the eastern Mediterranean had been thwarted by a coalition of western European states. In 1855 Nicholas I died and was succeeded by Alexander II (reigned 1855–1881) who feared the forces of change and introduced reforms in order to remain in power.

Fearing the transformation of Russian society from below, Alexander II instituted a series of reforms which altered the nature of the social contract in Russia. In 1861, Alexander II declared that serfdom was abolished. Further, he issued the following reforms: 1) The serf (peasant) would no longer be dependent upon the lord 2) all people were to have freedom of movement and were free to change their means of livelihood, and 3) the serf could enter into contracts and could own property.

The lives of most peasants were not affected by these reforms. Most peasants lived in local communes which regulated the lives of their members; thus, the requirements of commune life nullified the reforms of Alexander II. Another significant development was the creation of the *zemstvos*, which were assemblies which administered the local areas. Through the *zemstvos* the Russian rural nobility retained control over local politics. Alexander II also reformed the Russian judiciary system. The new judiciary was to be based upon such enlightened notions as jury trial, the abolition of arbitrary judicial processes, and the equality of all before the law. In fact, the only substantive change was the improvement in the efficiency of the Russian judiciary. However, the reforms did lead to expectations which were later realized.

The reforms of Alexander II did not resolve Russia's problems. During the 1860s and 1870s, criticism of the regime mounted. Moderates called for Russia to proceed along Western lines in addressing political and economic problems; radicals argued that the overthrow of the system was the only recourse to the problems which confronted the Russian people. Alexander II and other members of the power structure maintained that Russia would solve its own problems within the existing structure and without external intervention. The economic problems which plagued Russia were staggering. Under the three-field system utilized, one-third of Russian agricultural land was not being used. The population was increasing dramatically but food production was not keeping pace. Even with the establishment of the Peasants Land Bank (1883), most peasants were unable to take advantage of the opportunity to become property owners. During years of great hardship, the government did intervene with emergency measures which temporarily reduced, deferred, or suspended taxes and/or payments.

While Russian agriculture experienced no real growth during this period, Russian industry, particularly in textiles and metallurgy, did develop. Between 1870 and 1900, as the result of French loans, the Russian railroad network expanded significantly. In addition to constructing railroads, the government subsidized industrial development through a protective tariff and by awarding major contracts to emerging industries. From 1892 to 1903 (1849–1915) Count S. Y. Witte served as Minister of Finance. As a result of his efforts to stimulate the economy, Russian industry prospered during most of the 1890s. During this same period, the government consistently suppressed the development of organized labor. In 1899 a depression began and the gains of the 1890s were quickly reduced. The Russo-Japanese War broke out in 1904.

The last years of the reign of Alexander II witnessed increased political opposition, manifested in demands for reforms from an ever more hostile group of intellectuals, the emergence of a Russian populist movement, and attempts to assassinate the czar. Some of the demands for extending reforms came from within the government from such dedicated and talented ministers as D. A. Miliutin, a Minister of War, who reorganized the Russian military system during the 1870s. However, reactionary ministers such as Count Dimitri Tolstoy, Minister of Education, did much to discredit any progressive policies emanating from the regime; Tolstoy repudiated academic freedom and advanced anti-scientism. As the regime matured, greater importance was placed on traditional values. This attitude developed at the same time that nihilism, which rejected romantic illusions of the past in favor of a rugged realism, was being advanced by such writers as Ivan Turgenev in his *Fathers and Sons*.

The notion of the inevitability and desirability of a social and economic revolution was promoted through the Russian populist movement. Originally, the populists were interested in an agrarian utopian order. The populists had no national support. Government persecution of the populists resulted in the radicalization of the movement. In the late 1870s and early 1880s, leaders such as Andrei Zheleabov and Sophie Perovsky became obsessed with the need to assassinate Alexander II. In March 1881, the czar was killed in St. Petersburg when his carriage was bombed. He was succeeded by Alexander III, (reigned 1881–1894) who advocated a national policy based on "Orthodoxy, Autocracy, and Nationalism." Alexander III selected as his primary aides conservatives such as Count Dimitri Tolstoy, now Minister of the Interior, Count Delianov, Minister of Education, and Constantine Pobedonostev, who headed the Russian Orthodox Church. Alexander III died in 1894 and was succeeded by the last of the Romanovs to hold power, Nicholas II (reigned 1894–1917). Nicholas II displayed lack of intelligence, wit, political acumen, and the absence of a firm will throughout his reign. From his ministers to his wife, Alexandra, to Rasputin (1872–1916), Nicholas was influenced by stronger personalities.

The opposition to the Czarist government became more focused and thus, more threatening, with the emergence of the Russian Social Democrats and the Russian Social Revolutionaries. Both groups were Marxist. Vladimir Ilyich Ulyanov, also known as Lenin, became the leader of the Bolsheviks, a splinter group of the Social Democrats. Until the impact of the 1899 depression and the horrors associated with the Russo-Japanese War were realized, groups advocating revolutions commanded little support. By winter (1904–1905), the accumulated consequences of inept management of the economy and the prosecution of the Russo-Japanese War reached a critical stage. A group under the leadership of the radical priest Gapon marched on the Winter Palace in St. Petersburg (January 9, 1905) to submit a list of grievances to the czar. Troops fired on the demonstrators and many casualties resulted on this "Bloody Sunday." In response to the massacre, a general strike was called followed by a series of peasant revolts through the spring. During these same months, the Russian armed forces were being defeated by the Japanese and a lack of confidence in the regime became widespread. In June 1905, naval personnel on the battleship Potemkin mutinied while the ship was in Odessa. With this startling development, Nicholas II's government lost its nerve. In October 1905, Nicholas II issued the October Manifesto calling for the convocation of a Duma, or assembly of state, which would serve as an advisory body to the czar, extending civil liberties to include freedom of speech, assembly, and press, and announcing that Nicholas II would reorganize his government.

The leading revolutionary forces differed in their responses to the manifesto. The Octobrists indicated that they were satisfied with the arrangements; the Constitutional Democrats, also known as the Kadets, demanded a more liberal representative system. The Duma convened in 1906 and, from its outset to the outbreak of the First World War, was paralyzed by factionalism which was exploited by the Czar's ministers. By 1907, Nicholas II's ministers had recovered the real power of government. Russia experienced a general though fragile economic recovery by 1909, which lasted until the war.

THE HAPSBURGS IN DECLINE: AUSTRIA-HUNGARY

After the disruptions of the Revolutions of 1848 and 1849, the Austrian government had to address a series of major issues 1) German nationalism—the *Kleindeutsch* and the *Grossdeutsch*; 2) the rise of the national aspirations of the ethnic groups which resided in the Balkans, and 3) the management of a historically- and culturally-diverse empire.

During the 1850s the Hapsburg leadership deferred any attempt to resolve these problems, and in doing so, lost the initiative. To the north, Bismarck was developing the Prussian army in anticipation for the struggle with Austria over the future of Germany; in the Balkans, the Hungarians and Czechs, while smarting from the setbacks of 1849, were agitating for national self-determination or, at the least, for a semi-autonomous state. In 1863 and 1864 Austria became involved with Prussia in a war with Denmark. This war was a prelude for the German Civil War of 1866 between Austria and Prussia; Prussia prevailed. The impact of these developments on the Austrian government necessitated a reappraisal of its national policies. The most significant development resulting from this reappraisal was the Ausgleich, or Compromise, which transformed Austria into the Austro-Hungarian Empire. The Hungarians would have their own assembly, cabinet, and administrative system, and would support and participate in the Imperial army and Imperial government. Not only did the Ausgleich assimilate the Hungarians and nullify them as a primary opposition group, it also led to a more efficient government.

During the period from 1867 to 1914, Austria-Hungary continued to experience difficulties with subject nationalities and with adjusting to a new power structure in Central Europe in which it was secondary to Germany. At the same time, it enjoyed a cultural revival. Its scholars (Sigmund Freud, Karl Menger, and Heinrich Friedjung), painters (Hans Makart), dramatists (Hugo von Hofmannsthal), and writers (Adalbert Stifter, Stefan Zweig, and Rainer Maria Rilke) were renowned throughout the world.

THE BALKAN STATES AND THE DISINTEGRATION OF THE OTTOMAN EMPIRE

During the period from 1848 to 1914, the influence of the Ottoman Empire eroded steadily because of its internal structure and system, the ineptitude of its leaders, the lack of cohesion within the empire, the development of nationalist ambitions among many ethnic groups in the region, and the expansionist policies of Austria-Hungary and Russia in the Balkans, and of Great Britain in the eastern Mediterranean.

By 1914 Rumania, Serbia, Bulgaria, and Montenegro had been established as independent states, Austria had annexed Bosnia and Herzegovina, Britain held Cyprus, and Russia had extended its influence over the new Bulgaria.

ORIGINS, MOTIVES, AND IMPLICATIONS OF THE NEW IMPERIALISM (1870–1914)

During the first seven decades of the 19th century, the European powers did not pursue active imperial expansion. Internal European development preoccupied the powers; colonies were viewed as liabilities because of the direct costs associated with their administration. However, by the 1870s, the European industrial economies required external markets to distribute products which could not be absorbed within their domestic economies. Further, excess capital was available and foreign investment, while risky, appeared to offer high returns. Finally, the need for additional sources of raw materials served as a rationale and stimulant for imperialism. Politicians were also influenced by the numerous missionary societies which sought government protection, in extending Christianity throughout the world. (British and French missionary societies were vehemently anti-slavery.) European statesmen, were also interested in asserting their national power overseas through the acquisition of strategic (and many not so strategic) colonies. Disraeli and Salisbury (1830–1903) of England, Thiers (1797–1877) and Ferry (1832–1893) of France, and later Bismarck of Germany were influenced by yet another factor: the European cultural sentiments of the 1870s and 1880s. The writings of John Seely, Anatole Leroy-Beaulieu, and others suggested that the future status of the powers would be dependent upon the extent and significance of their imperial holdings; these thoughts were later amplified by the social and national Darwinists. Exploration and imperial policies were supported by the public throughout the era.

Unlike colonial policies of earlier centuries, the "New Imperialism" of the 1870s was comprehensive in scope and, as Benjamin Disraeli argued in 1872, a call to "greatness" where a nation could fulfill its destiny. From Disraeli to Kipling (1865–1936) to Churchill, there were few leaders who would differ sharply from this view. On the continent, the New Imperialism was opposed most vigorously by orthodox Marxists. Even the revisionist groups such as the Social Democratic Party and, during the Boer War, the English Fabian Society, supported imperial policies.

The Scramble for Colonies

The focus of most of the European imperial activities during the late 19th century was Africa. Since the 1850s, Africa had commanded the attention of European explorers such as Richard Burton, Carl Peters, David Livingstone, and many others, who were interested in charting the unknown interior of the continent, and, in particular, in locating the headwaters of the Nile. Initially, European interest in these activities was romantic. With John Hanning Speke's discovery of Lake Victoria (1858), Livingstone's surveying of the Zambezi, and Stanley's work on the Congo River, Europeans became enraptured with the greatness and novelty of Africa south of the Sahara.

Disraeli was involved in the intrigue which would result in the British acquisition of the Suez Canal (1875), and during the 1870s and 1880s Britain was involved in a Zulu War and announced the annexation of the Transvaal, which the Boers regained after their great victory of Majuba Hill (1881). At about the same time, Belgium established its interest in the Congo; France, in addition to seizing Tunisia, extended its influence into French Equitorial Africa, and Italy established small colonies in East Africa. During the 1880s Germany acquired several African colonies including German East Africa, the Cameroons, Togoland, and German South West Africa. All of these imperial activities heightened tensions among the European

EUROPEAN IMPERIALISM IN AFRICA, 1914

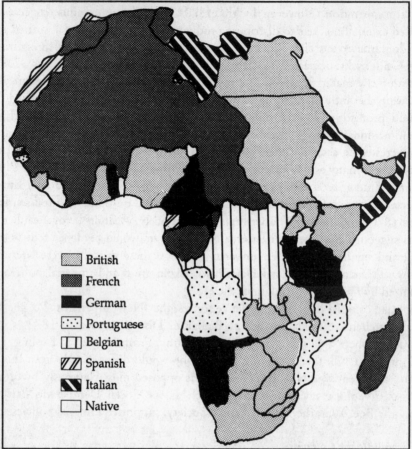

British
French
German
Portuguese
Belgian
Spanish
Italian
Native

powers. Consequently, the Berlin Conference (1884–1885) was convened. The conference resulted in an agreement which specified the following: 1) The Congo would be under the control of Belgium through an International Association 2) More liberal use of the Niger and Congo river 3) European powers could acquire African territory through first occupation and second notifying the other European states of their occupation and claim.

Between 1885 and 1914, the principal European states continued to enhance their positions in Africa. Without doubt, Britain was the most active and successful. From 1885 to 1890, Britain expanded its control over Nigeria, moved north from the Cape of Good Hope, and became further involved in East Africa. By this time, Salisbury was the leader of the Conservative Party and, when in office, he fostered imperial expansion. Gladstone was still an anti-imperialist and the leader of the Liberal Party; he found the imperialist forces so formidable that he had to compromise his position on occasion when he was Prime Minister. During the 1880s, an Islamic revolution under the Mahdi, an Islamic warrior, developed in the Sudan. In 1884 Gladstone sent General Charles Gordon to evacuate Khartoum; Gordon and the city's defenders were slaughtered by the Mahdi's forces in January 1885. The

British found themselves confronted with a continuing native insurrection in the Sudan which was not suppressed effectively until Kitchener's victory at Omdurman in 1898.

The French were also quite active during this period. They unified Senegal, the Ivory Coast and Guinea into French West Africa and extended it to Timbuktu, then moved up the Ubangui toward Lake Chad. While the British had difficulties in the Sudan, the French had to suppress a native insurrection in Madagascar which lasted until 1896.

British movement north of the Cape of Good Hope resulted in a different type of struggle—one that involved Europeans fighting one another rather than a native African force. The Boers had lived in South Africa since the beginning of the 19th century. With the discovery of gold (1882) in the Transvaal, many English Cape settlers moved into the region. The Boers, under the leadership of Paul Kruger, restricted the political and economic rights of the British settlers and developed alternative railroads through Mozambique which would lessen the Boer dependency on the Cape colony. Relations between the British and Boers steadily deteriorated; in 1895, the Jameson Raid, an ill-conceived action not approved by Britain, failed to result in restoring the status of British citizens. The crisis mounted and, in 1899, the Boer War began. Until 1902, the British and Boers fought a war which was costly to both sides. Britain prevailed and by 1909, the Transvaal, Orange Free State, Natal, and the Cape of Good Hope were united into the Union of South Africa.

Another area of increased imperialist activity was the Pacific. In 1890, the American naval Captain Alfred Mahan published *The Influence of Sea Power Upon History*; in this book he argued that history demonstrated that nations which controlled the seas prevailed. During the 1880s, and 1890s naval ships required coaling stations. While Britain, the Netherlands, and France demonstrated that they were interested in Pacific islands, the most active states in this region during the last 20 years of the 19th century were Germany and the United States. Britain's Pacific interests were motivated primarily in sustaining its control of Australia. The French were interested in Tahiti; after a dispute with France over the Samoan Islands, the islands were split with France, Germany, and the United States. The United States acquired the Philippines in 1898. Germany gained part of New Guinea, and the Marshall, Caroline, and Mariana island chains. The European powers were also interested in the Asian mainland. In 1900, the Boxer Rebellion broke in Peking; it was a native reaction against Western influence in China. An international force was organized to break the siege of the Western legations. Most powers agreed with the American Open Door Policy which recognized the independence and integrity of China and provided economic access for all the powers. Rivalry over China (Manchuria) was a principal cause for the outbreak of the Russo-Japanese War in 1904.

THE AGE OF BISMARCK (1871–1890)

The Development of the German Empire

During the period from the establishment of the German Empire in January 1871 to his dismissal as Chancellor of Germany in March 1890, Otto von Bismarck dominated European diplomacy and established an integrated political and economic structure for the new German state. Bismarck established a statist system which was reactionary in political philosophy and based upon industrialism, militarism, and innovative social legislation. German adaptation during the *Grundjahre* (the founding years of the new industrial order, 1870–1875) was staggering and remarkable increases in productivity and the expansion of industrialization took place from 1870–1890.

Until the mid-19th century, Germany consisted of numerous independent states which identified with regional rather than national concerns. This condition reflected the continuing impact of the Peace of Westphalia (1648). With the unification of Germany, a German state became a reality, but the process of integration of regional economic, social, political, and cultural interests had not yet occurred. Bismarck, with the consent and approval of Wilhelm I (1797–1888), the German Emperor, developed a constitution for the new nation which provided for the following:

1) The Emperor would be the executor of state and, as such, establish the domestic and foreign policies; he was also the commander of the armed forces. The Chancellor (similar to Prime Minister) held office at the discretion of the Emperor.

2) A bicameral legislature was established. It consisted of the *Reichstag*, a lower body which represented the people (the *Volk*); and the *Bundesrat*, an upper body which represented the various German states. During Bismarck's tenure, the *Bundesrat* identified with reactionary conservative positions and served to check any populism in the *Reichstag*.

During the 1870s and 1880s, Bismarck's domestic policies were directed at the establishment of a strong united German state which would be capable of defending itself from a French war of revenge designed to restore Alsace-Lorraine to France. Laws were enacted which unified the monetary system, established an Imperial Bank and strengthened existing banks, developed universal German civil and criminal codes, and required compulsory military service. All of these measures contributed to the integration of the German state.

The German political system was multi-party. The most significant political parties of the era were 1) the Conservatives, who represented the Junkers of Prussia 2) the Progressives, who unsuccessfully sought to extend democracy through continuing criticism of Bismarck's autocratic procedures 3) the National Liberals, who represented the German middle class, identified with German nationalism and provided support for Bismarck's policies; 4) the Center party (also known as the Catholic Party), which approved Bismarck's policy of centralization and promoted the political concept of Particularism, which advocated regional priorities 5) the Social Democratic Party (SPD), a Marxist group which advocated sweeping social legislation, the realization of genuine democracy, and the demilitarization of the German government. Bismarck was unsuccessful in stopping the influence of the Center Party through his anti-Catholic *Kulturkampf* (the May Laws) and in thwarting the growth of the Social Democrats.

In order to develop public support for the government and to minimize the threat from the left, Bismarck instituted a protective tariff, to maintain domestic production and introduced many social and economic laws to provide social security, regulate child labor, and improve working conditions for all Germans.

European Diplomacy

Bismarck's foreign policy was centered on maintaining the diplomatic isolation of France. After a few years of recovery from their defeat in the Franco-Prussian War, the French were regaining their confidence and publicly discussing the feasibility of a war of revenge to regain Alsace-Lorraine. In 1875, the War-In-Sight-Crisis occurred between the French and Germans. While war was avoided, the crisis clearly indicated the delicate state of the Franco-German relationship. In the crisis stemming from the Russo-Turkish War (1877–1878), Bismarck tried to serve as the "Honest Broker" at the Congress of Berlin (see Chapter 5). Russia did not succeed at the conference and incorrectly blamed Bismarck for its failure. Early in the next year, a cholera epidemic affected Russian cattle herds and Germany placed an embargo on the importation of Russian beef. The Russians were outraged by the German action and launched an anti-German propaganda campaign in the Russian press. Bismarck, desiring to maintain the peace and a predictable diplomatic environment, concluded a secret defensive treaty with Austria-Hungary in 1879. The Dual Alliance was very significant because it was the first "hard" diplomatic alliance of the era. A "hard" alliance involved the specific commitment of military support; traditional or "soft" alliances involved pledges of neutrality or to hold military conversations in the event of a war. The Dual Alliance, which had a five year term and was renewable, directed that one signatory would assist the other in the event that one power was attacked by two or more states.

In 1882, another agreement, the Triple Alliance, was signed between Germany, Austria-Hungary, and Italy. In the 1880s, relations between Austria-Hungary and Russia became estranged over Balkan issues. Bismarck, fearing a war, intervened and by 1887, had negotiated the secret Reinsurance Treaty with Russia. This was a "hard" defensive alliance with a three-year term, renewable. Since these were "defensive" arrangements, Bismarck was confident that through German policy, the general European peace would be maintained and the security of Germany ensured by sustaining the diplomatic isolation of France. Bismarck also acted to neutralize the role of Great Britain in European affairs through a policy which in most instances was supportive of British interests.

In 1888, Wilhelm I died and was succeeded by his son Friedrich III, who also died within a few months. Friedrich's son, Wilhelm II (reigned 1888–1918), came to power and soon found himself in conflict with Bismarck. Wilhelm II was intent upon administering the government personally and viewed Bismarck as an archaic personality. Early in 1890, two issues developed which led ultimately to Bismarck's dismissal. First, Bismarck had evolved a scheme for a fabricated attempted coup by the Social Democratic Party; his intent was to use this situation to create a national hysteria through which he could restrict the SPD through legal action. Second, Bismarck intended to renew the Reinsurance Treaty with Russia to maintain his policy of French diplomatic isolation. Wilhelm II opposed both of these plans; in

March 1890, Bismarck, who had used the threat of resignation so skillfully in the past, suggested that he would resign if Wilhelm II would not approve of these actions. Wilhelm II accepted his resignation; in fact, Bismarck was dismissed. The diplomatic developments after 1890 (see Chapter 11) radically altered the alignment of power in Europe. The position of Chancellor of Germany was filled by a series of less talented statesmen including Count von Caprivi (1890–1894), Prince Hohenlohe (1894–1900), Prince Bernhard von Bulow (1900–1909), and Chancellor Bethmann-Hollweg.

THE MOVEMENT TOWARD DEMOCRACY IN WESTERN EUROPE TO 1914

Great Britain

Even after the reform measures of 1867 and 1884 to 1885, the movement toward democratic reforms in Great Britain continued unabated. Unlike other European nations where the focus on democracy was limited to gaining the vote, British reform efforts were much more complex and sophisticated and involved social and economic reforms as well as continuing changes in the political process; participation in the system as well as representation was desired by many. During the 1880s and 1890s, new groups emerged which intended to extend the definition of democratic government to include the new social and economic philosophies of the period. From women's suffrage and the condemnation of imperialism to the redistribution of wealth and the demise of nationalism, these groups represented a broad spectrum of radical and reform ideologies. Among the most significant was the Fabian Society (1883) which advanced a mode of revisionist Marxism and whose members included Sidney (1859–1947) and Beatrice Webb (1858–1943), the Scottish politician Keir Hardie (1856–1915) (who later led the Labor Party), George Bernard Shaw (1856–1950), H. G. Wells (1866–1946), the historian G. D. H. Cole, and the young Ramsay MacDonald (1866–1937), who became the first Labor Prime Minister. The Fabians argued for evolutionary political transformation which would result in full political democracy and economic socialism. In 1884, the Social Democratic Federation was formed by H. M. Hyndman (1842–1921). In 1893, Keir Hardie established the Independent Labor Party which rapidly became a vocal third party in British politics. The Labor Party attracted trade unionists, socialists, and those who thought that the Conservative and Liberal Parties had no genuine interest in the needs of the general public.

During the early years of the 20th century, both the Conservatives and the Liberals advanced more aggressive social and economic programs. The Conservatives, through the efforts of Arthur James Balfour (1848–1930), promoted the Education Act of 1902, which they argued would provide enhanced educational opportunities for the working class. In fact, this act was criticized soundly for not providing what it claimed as its purpose. In 1905, the Liberals under Sir Henry Campbell-Bannerman (1836–1908) came to power. The government ministries were staffed by such talented leaders as Herbert Asquith (1852–1928), Sir Edward Grey (1862–1933), David Lloyd George (1863–1945), and Winston Churchill (1874–1965).

The most significant political reform of this long-lived Liberal government was the Parliament Act of 1911, which eliminated the powers of the House of Lords and resulted in the House of Commons becoming the unquestioned center of national power. All revenue bills approved by the House of Commons would automatically become law 30 days after being sent to the House of Lords. If the Lords voted favorably, the law would be enacted earlier. The Lords had no veto power.

Non-revenue bills opposed by the Lords would be enacted if passed by three consecutive sessions of the Commons. It was not difficult to transform such measures into revenue bills. Finally, the life-span of Parliament was reduced from seven to five years.

The British political climate during this period was rather volatile. Issues relating to trade unions, Ireland, and women's suffrage factionalized British politics. The Liberal Party, which was in power from 1905 to the early 1920s, came to be institutionalized and in the process to be identified as "the government."

The most recurring and serious problem which Great Britain experienced during the period from 1890 to 1914 was the "Irish Question." Gladstone, in his final ministry, argued unsuccessfully for Irish Home Rule. In Ireland opposition to British rule and the abuses of British power was advanced by the National Land League established in 1879. This organization stimulated and coordinated Irish opposition to British and Irish landlords. During the 1880s Charles Stewart Parnell led the Irish delegation to the House of Commons. Parnell, through the support of Gladstone, attained some gains for the Irish such as the Land Reform Act and the Arrears Act. In 1890 Parnell became involved in a divorce case and the scandal ruined his career; he died the next year. In 1893, Gladstone devised the Irish Home Rule bill, which was passed by the House of Commons but rejected by the House of Lords. The Irish situation became more complicated when the Protestant counties of the north started to enjoy remarkable economic growth from the mid-1890s; they were adamant in their rejection of all measures of Irish Home Rule. In 1914, an Irish Home Rule Act was passed by both the Commons and the Lords, but the Protestants refused to accept it. Implementation was deferred until after the war.

The Third French Republic

In the fall of 1870, Napoleon III's Second Empire collapsed when it was defeated by the Prussian armies. Napoleon III and his principal aides were captured; later, he abdicated and fled to England. A National Assembly (1871–1875) was created and Adolphe Thiers was recognized as its chief executive. At the same time, a more radical political entity, the Paris Commune (1870–1871), came into existence and exercised extraordinary power during the siege of Paris. After the siege and the peace agreement with Prussia, the Commune refused to recognize the authority of the National Assembly. Led by radical Marxists, anarchists, and republicans, the Paris Commune repudiated the conservative and monarchist leadership of the National Assembly. From March to May 1871, the Commune fought a bloody struggle with the troops of the National Assembly. Thousands died and when Paris surrendered, there were thousands of executions—accepted estimates place the number at 20,000 during the first week after Paris fell on May 28, 1871. France began a program of recovery which led to the formulation of the Third French Republic in 1875. The National Assembly sought to 1) put the French political house in order 2) establish a new constitutional government, 3) pay off an imposed indemnity and, in doing so, remove German troops from French territory 4) restore the honor and glory of France. In 1875 a Constitution was adopted which provided for a republican government of a president (with little power), a Senate, and a Chamber of Deputies, which was the center of political power. The overwhelming influence of the French bourgeoisie (middle class), which was intent upon establishing and sustaining a French republican government; the mounting hostility between the Catholic Church and the French government (anti-clericalism was frequently manifested in the Chamber of Deputies) the unpredictability which accompanied multi-party politics, and finally, the extreme nationalism which gripped France during these decades and resulted in continuing calls for a war of revenge against Germany in order to regain Alsace-Lorraine were the chief challenges to the new Republic.

During the early years of the Republic, Leon Gambetta (1838–1882) led the republicans. Beginning in the 1880s the Third French Republic was challenged by a series of crises which threatened its continuity. The Boulanger Crisis (1887–1889), the Panama Scandal (1894), and the Dreyfus Affair (1894–1906) were serious domestic problems; in all of these developments, the challenge to republicanism came from the right. The sustenance of republicanism through this time of troubles came primarily from 1) the able leadership of the republican government, and 2) the continuing commitment of the bourgeoisie to republicanism. Since the founding of the Third Republic, monarchists and conservatives were interested in overthrowing the regime; however, until the appointment of General Georges Boulanger (1837–1891) as Minister of War in 1886, there was no one to lead the anti-republican cause. Boulanger won over the army by improving the basic conditions of military life. His public popularity was high in 1888 and his supporters urged him to conduct a coup; he delayed and by the spring of 1889, the republicans had mounted a case against him. He was directed to appear to respond to charges of conspiracy, but fled to Belgium, and committed suicide in 1891. The Boulanger crisis resulted in renewed confidence in the Republic; but what popular gains it made were unravelled in 1892 with the Panama Scandal. The French had been involved with the engineering and the raising of capital for the Panama Canal since the 1870s. Early in the 1890s the promoters of the project resorted to the bribery of government officials and of certain members of the press who had access to information which indicated that the work on the canal was not proceeding as had been announced. In 1892 the scandal broke and for months the public indicated that it thought that the entire French government was corrupt. However, by 1893, elections to the Chamber of Deputies resulted in the socialists making notable gains. The monarchists did not attract much public support.

The most serious threat to the Republic came through the Dreyfus Affair. In 1894, Captain Alfred Dreyfus (1859–1935) was assigned to the French General Staff. A scandal broke when it was revealed that classified information had been provided to German spies. Dreyfus, a Jew, was charged, tried, and convicted. Later, it was determined that the actual spy was Commandant Marie Charles Esterhazy

(1847–1923), who was acquitted in order to save the pride and reputation of the army. The monarchists used this incident to criticize republicanism; the republicans countered when Emile Zola (1840–1902) took up Dreyfus's cause and wrote an open letter entitled *J'accuse*, which condemning the General Staff's actions and pronouncing Dreyfus's innocence. Leftists supported the Republic and in 1906, the case was closed when Dreyfus was declared innocent and returned to the ranks. Rather than lead to the collapse of the Republic, the Dreyfus Affair demonstrated the intensity of anti-Semitism in French society, the level of corruption in the French army, and the willingness of the Catholic Church and the monarchists to join in a conspiracy against an innocent man. The republicans launched an anti-clerical campaign which included the Association Act (1901) and the separation of church and state (1905).

From 1905 to 1914 the socialists under Jean Jaurès gained seats in the Chamber of Deputies. The Third French Republic endured the crises which confronted it and, in 1914, enjoyed the support of the vast majority of French citizens.

The Lesser States of Europe

In the Low Countries during the decades prior to 1914, there were differing approaches to extending democracy. An appreciation of democracy was evident in Belgium under the leadership of Leopold II (reigned 1865–1909) and Albert I (reigned 1909–1934); during their reigns the franchise was extended, social and economic reforms were introduced, and equity was the basis of the settlement between Flemish and French-speaking Belgians. To the north, the Netherlands was slow to adopt democracy. By 1896, only 14 percent of the Dutch had the vote and it would not be until 1917 that universal manhood suffrage would be enacted.

Denmark experienced a struggle between the old guard represented by Christian IX (1863–1906), who opposed parliamentary government, and the Social Democrats who advocated democratic principles. The Danish Constitution of 1915 provided a basic democratic political system. Sweden, after a decade of debilitating debate, recognized the independence of Norway in 1905; Norway moved quickly toward democracy, granting women the vote in 1907. Sweden, under Gustavus V (1907–1950), pronounced a comprehensive democratic system in 1909.

In southern Europe, advocates of democracy did not meet with any substantive success prior to 1914. In Spain, Portugal, and Italy, the monarchist establishments were preoccupied with survival. While an occasional reform was promulgated, there was no intent to move toward full democracy.

EUROPEAN CULTURAL DEVELOPMENTS (1848–1914)

The great political and economic changes of this period were accompanied by cultural achievements which included the development of a literate citizenry and substantive innovations in science, literature, art, music, and other areas of intellectual activity. In large part, these developments occurred as a reaction against the mechanistic sterility of the scientism and positivism of the age; however, some of the initial achievements, such as Darwin's theories of evolution and natural selection, resulted in extending the exaggerated claims of scientism. From Charles Darwin (1809–1882), Richard Wagner (1813–1883), Friedrich Nietzsche (1844–1900), and Sigmund Freud (1856–1939) to Claude Monet (1840–1926), Richard Strauss (1864–1949), Igor Stravinsky (1882–1971), Oscar Wilde (1854–1900), Thomas Mann (1875–1955), and James Joyce (1882–1941), intelligent Europeans of the era pursued many differing, approaches in their quest for truth and understanding. Many philosophers were critical of the movement toward democracy, which they identified with mass culture and political ineptitude.

Darwin, Wagner, Freud, and the Emergence of a New Tradition

In 1859 Charles Darwin's (1807–1882) *On the Origin of Species by Means of Natural Selection* was published; it argued the theory of evolution which had been discussed for more than a generation in Europe. Darwin's contributions to the advocacy of this theory were based 1) on the data which he provided to demonstrate the theory 2) in the formulation of a well-structured and argued defense of the theory of natural selection (survival of the fittest). The reaction to *On the Origin of Species* was diverse, thorough, and enduring; some were concerned with the implication of the theory on religion, while others were interested in applying aspects of the theory to the understanding of contemporary social problems. Within the Darwinian camp, factions emerged which supported or rejected one or more components of the theory. Samuel Butler (1835–1902) and George Bernard Shaw accepted evolution but rejected natural selection; Thomas Huxley (1825–1895) was Darwin's most consistent and loyal supporter. Herbert Spencer (1820–1903) developed a Social Darwinism which enjoyed extensive acceptance in both scholarly and general circles. One of the obvious consequences of Darwin's theory was that the doctrine of creation was challenged and thus the authenticity of prevailing religion was endangered.

In classical music, the erratic Richard Wagner (1813–1883) reflected the incongruities and the harshness of the new age. Wagner developed and imposed an aestheticism that had one fundamental element—it demanded absolute artistic integrity. Wagner shifted styles several times during his career; his *Ring* cycle was centered on German epics and advanced numerous fantasies about the history of the German people.

Sigmund Freud (1856–1939) established a new approach to understanding human behavior known as psychoanalysis. In Vienna, Freud developed his concepts that the unconscious was shaped during the formative years, that sexuality was a dominant life force, and that free will may not exist. Freud argued his theories in a formidable body of literature which included the *Origins of Psychoanalysis* and *Civilization and Its Discontents*. The establishment rejected his views as threats to religion.

New developments challenged the certainty and security of the old science. Max Planck's (1858–1947) *Quantum Physics*, Albert Einstein's *Theory of Relativity*, and the impact of the Michelson-Morley Experiment (1887; regarding the measurement of speed; conducted in the United States) led to scientists re-examining many of the assumptions of the past.

Impressionism and Symbolism: Forces of the New Art

The turbulence within European cultural life during the 50 years prior to the outbreak of the First World War can be seen most evidently in new attitudes which emerged in art and literature. Not only did the intellectuals find themselves looking for a new synthesis through which to offer new vision and hope, they were also liberated from the limitations imposed on their predecessors. The development of photography resulted in artists no longer being required to produce actual representations. Painters were now free to pursue the dictates of their imaginations. Impressionism developed in France during the 1870s; Monet, Manet, Renoir, and others pioneered the new art. Impressionism soon gave way to Post-Impressionism and later Expressionism. At the turn of the century, more radical artistic forms such as Symbolism and Cubism enjoyed notoriety if not general acceptance.

Literature was transformed through the writings of such innovators as Oscar Wilde ((1854–1900) *The Picture of Dorian Gray*), Thomas Mann ((1875–1955) *Death in Venice*), and the young James Joyce ((1882–1941) prior to 1914, *Portrait of the Artist as a Young Man* and *Dubliners*). These writers were interested in discussing themes which had great personal value and meaning. Joyce would emerge as the most seminal stylist of the 20th century.

INTERNATIONAL POLITICS AND THE COMING OF THE WAR (1890–1914)

Heightened nationalism and the cultural materialism of the period strained relations between European powers.

The Polarization of Europe

In March 1890, Bismarck was dismissed as Chancellor of Germany by the immature, impetuous, and inexperienced Kaiser William II. With Bismarck's dismissal, the continuing dominance of Germany over European affairs was questionable.

Germany failed to renew the Reinsurance Treaty with Russia and so Russia looked elsewhere to eliminate its own perceived isolation. In 1891, secret negotiations were entered into by the French and Russians. By 1894, these deliberations resulted in the Dual Entente, a comprehensive military alliance. This agreement was sustained through 1917 and allowed France to pursue a more assertive foreign policy. From the Russian perspective, fears of isolation and of the development of an anti-Russian combination were abated. Within four years of Bismarck's dismissal, the essential imperative of German foreign policy in the late 19th century—the diplomatic isolation of France—was no longer a reality.

In 1895, a new Conservative government came to power in Great Britain. Led by Lord Salisbury, who served as Prime Minister and Foreign Secretary, this government included a wide range of talented statesmen including Joseph Chamberlain (1836–1914), John Morley, Lord Landsdowne, and the young Arthur James Balfour. The Salisbury government was interested in terminating the long-standing policy of "Splendid Isolationism" which had prevailed as Britain's response to European alliances. Salisbury came to argue that the new realities of world politics and economics deemed it advisable for Britain to ally itself with a major power. While coming under general European criticism for its role in the Boer War (1899–1902) in South Africa, British representatives approached Berlin in an attempt to develop an Anglo-German alliance. Germany declined the British advances. Consequently, Britain pursued diplomatic opportunities which resulted in the Anglo-Japanese Alliance (1902), the Entente Cordiale or Anglo-French Entente (1904), and the Anglo-Russian Entente (1907).

The Anglo-Japanese Alliance of 1902 resulted in the two powers agreeing to adopt a position of benevolent neutrality in the event that the other member state was involved in war. This arrangement was sustained through the First World War.

The Entente Cordiale (1904), also known as the Dual Entente or the Anglo-French Entente, was a settlement of long-standing colonial disputes between Britain and France over North African territories. It was agreed that northeast Africa (Egypt and the Anglo-Egyptian Sudan) would be a British sphere of influence and that northwest Africa (Morocco) would be a French sphere of influence. This was a colonial settlement, not a formal alliance; neither power pledged support in the event of war.

While Anglo-French relations improved during 1904 to 1905, the historically tense Anglo-Russian relationship was aggravated further by the Russo-Japanese War (1904–1905). The Dogger Bank Incident resulted in a crisis between these powers when Russian naval ships fired on and sank several British fishing boats in the North Sea. Britain responded by deploying the Home Fleet and curtailing the activities of the Russian fleet. The crisis was resolved when Russia agreed to apologize for the incident and to pay compensation. In 1905, a Liberal government came to power in Britain, and Russia was absorbed in its own revolution which liberalized, at least temporarily, the autocratic regime. Negotiations between these powers were initiated and were facilitated by the French; in 1907 Britain and Russia reached a settlement on their outstanding colonial disputes. They agreed on three points:

1) Persia would be divided into three zones: a northern sector under Russian influence, a southern sector under British control, and a central zone which could be mutually exploited.

2) Afghanistan was recognized as a British sphere of influence.

3) Tibet was recognized as part of China and, as such, was to be free from foreign intervention.

By 1907, France, Britain, and Russia had formed a Triple Entente which effectively balanced the Triple Alliance. While Britain was not formally committed to an alliance system, Sir Edward Grey (1862–1933), British Foreign Minister from 1905, supported secret conversations between British and French military representatives. Thus Germany became isolated by 1907.

The Rise of Militarism

During the period after 1890, Europeans began to view the use of military power as not only feasible but also as desirable to bring about a resolution to the increasingly hostile political conditions in Europe. The apparent inability of diplomats to develop lasting settlements supported the further development of this perception. The notion that a major European war was inevitable became acceptable to many.

Within the structure of the European states, militarists enjoyed increased credibility and support. The General Staffs became preoccupied with planning for the anticipated struggle and their plans affected national foreign policies. The Germans, under the influence of General Count Alfred von Schlieffen, developed the Schlieffen Plan by 1905. It was predicated on the assumption that Germany would have to conduct a two front war with France and Russia.

The Arms Race

This wave of nationalistic militarism also manifested itself through a continuing arms race which resulted in several threats to the balance of power because of revolutionary technological developments. Field weapons such as mortars and cannons were improved sharply in range, accuracy, and firepower; the machine gun was perfected and produced in quantity. New weapons such as the submarine and airplanes were recognized as having the capacity to be strategic armaments.

In naval weaponry, the rivalry between the British and the Germans over capital ships not only exacerbated the deteriorating relationship between the two powers, but also led to restrictions on the national domestic expenditures during peacetime in order to pay for the increasingly-costly battleships and cruisers. In 1912, the British-sponsored Haldane Mission was sent to Berlin to negotiate an agreement; the Germans were suspicious and distrustful of the British and were not receptive to any proposal.

Imperialism as a Source of Conflict

During the late 19th century, the economically-motivated "New Imperialism" resulted in further aggravating the relations among the European powers. The Fashoda Crisis (1898–1899), the Moroccan Crisis (1905–1906), the Balkan Crisis (1908), and the Agadir Crisis (1911) demonstrated the impact of imperialism in heightening tensions among European states and in creating an environment in which conflict became more acceptable.

The Fashoda Crisis developed between France and Britain when the French, ordered Commandant Jean Baptiste Marchand (1863–1934) and a small number of French troops to march across Africa and establish a French "presence" near the headwaters of the Nile. Marchand arrived in Fashoda (now Kodok) in 1898; Fashoda was located on the White Nile, south of Khartoum in the Anglo-Egyptian Sudan. A British army under General Herbert Kitchener marched on Fashoda. In the end, the French withdrew and recognized the position of the British in the Anglo-Egyptian Sudan. However, for several months there was serious consideration of war.

The Moroccan Crisis (1905–1906) developed when William II of Germany travelled to Tangier, (March 1905) where he made a speech in support of the independence of Morocco; this position was at odds with that agreed to by the

British and the French in the Entente Cordiale. Initially, the German position prevailed because of lack of organization within the Franco-Russian alliance; however, in 1906, at the Algerciras Conference, the German effort was thwarted and the French secured their position in Morocco. Russia, Britain, and Italy, supported the French on every important issue. German diplomatic isolation—save for the Austrians—became increasingly evident.

Since the Congress of Berlin in 1878, the Austro-Hungarian Empire had administered the Balkan territories of Bosnia and Herzegovina. Austrian influence in this area was opposed by Russia, which considered the region as a natural area of Russian influence. The Russians hoped to capitalize upon the collapse of the Ottoman Turkish Empire and gain access to the Mediterranean Sea. In 1908, the decadent Ottoman Empire was experiencing domestic discord which attracted the attention of both the Austrians and the Russians. These two powers agreed that Austria would annex Bosnia and Herzegovina and Russia would be granted access to the Straits and thus the Mediterranean. Great Britain intervened and demanded that there be no change in the status quo in the Straits. Russia backed down from a confrontation, but Austria proceeded to annex Bosnia and Herzegovina. The annexation was condemned by the Pan-Slavists who looked to Russia for assistance; a crisis developed and it appeared that war between Austria and Russia was likely. However, the Russians disengaged because of their lack of preparedness for a major struggle and because there were clear indications that Germany would support Austria. The Balkan Crisis was another example of the nature of European rivalries and the rather rapid recourse to sabre-rattling on the part of great powers.

The Agadir Crisis (1911) broke when France announced that its troops would be sent to several Moroccan towns to restore order. Germany, fearing French annexation of all of Morocco, responded by sending the *Panther*, a German naval ship, to Agadir. After exchanging threats for several weeks, the French and Germans agreed to recognize Morocco as a French protectorate and to transfer two sections of the French Congo to Germany.

Diplomatic Crisis of the Summer (1914)

During the late 19th and early 20th centuries, the Ottoman Empire was disintegrating. At the same time, Austria and Russia were interested in extending their influence in the region. Furthermore, nationalism among the ethnic groups in the Balkans was rapidly developing. In addition to the Balkan Crisis of 1908, the region was involved in the Italian-Turkish War (1911) and the Inter-Balkan Wars of 1912 and 1913.

On June 28, 1914, Archduke Franz Ferdinand (1863–1914), heir to the Austro-Hungarian throne, and his wife were assassinated while on a state visit to Sarajevo, the capital of Bosnia. Their assassin was a radical Serb, Gavrilo Princip, who opposed Franz Ferdinand's plan to integrate the Slavs more fully into the government. The assassination resulted in a crisis between Austria-Hungary and Serbia. Austria, determined to respond with force as a great power, dispatched a representative, Count Alexander Hoyos, to Germany to determine the level of German support in the event of an expanded conflict. The Hoyos Mission resulted in the Blank Cheque of July 5, 1914, in which William II pledged to militarily support Austria. Serbia was accused of serving as a refuge for radical anti-Austrian groups such as the "Black Hand." On July 23rd, the Austrian Foreign Minister, Count Berchtold, sent an ultimatum to Serbia. This 10-point document was drafted purposely for rejection. On July 25th, Serbia responded that, while it was sympathetic with the Austrians on their loss, it must reject the terms of the ultimatum.

German Chancellor Bethmann–Hollweg and British Foreign Secretary Sir Edward Grey attempted to mediate the conflict. It was too late. On July 28th, Austria declared war on Serbia and by August 4th, Britain, France, and Russia (The Allies) were at war with Germany and Austria-Hungary (The Central Powers); later, other nations would join one of the two camps.

The initial military actions did not proceed as planned. The German Schlieffen Plan failed to succeed in the West as a result of German tactical adjustments and the French and British resistance in the First Battle of the Marne (September, 1914). The war of movement in the West, which was critical to the success of German strategy, was transformed into a war of trenches. In the East, the Germans scored significant victories over the numerically-superior Russians at the battles of Tannenberg and Masurian Lakes (August–September 1914).

CONCLUSION

Between 1848 and 1914, Europeans experienced revolutionary changes in their culture. Nationalism, science and technology, and the rapid expansion of the population were primary factors which contributed to these changes and to the further expansion of European culture throughout the world. The growth in the European standard of living was uneven. Western Europe developed most comprehensively; Central Europe—especially German urban centers—witnessed remarkable growth during the last decades of the period; and Southern and Eastern Europe lagged behind. Reaction to these changes varied from the development of Marxism, anarchism, and trade unionism in response to the adverse consequences of capitalism and industrialism, to the emergence of Impressionism, Expressionism, and Symbolism in reaction to the perceived intellectual sterility of mechanistic positivism. Nineteenth century Europe, which was identified with hope, progress, and rationality, gave way to the uncertainty, violence, and irrationality of the 20th century.

6 WORLD WAR I AND EUROPE IN CRISIS (1914–1935)

THE ORIGINS OF WORLD WAR I

In August 1914, most of the world's major powers became engaged in a conflict that most people welcomed romantically and felt would last only a few months. Instead, a war of world dimensions evolved that saw the clash of outdated military values with modern technological warfare. A war that no one seemed to be able to win lasted more than four years, and resulted in 12 million deaths.

The long-range roots of the origins of World War I can be traced to numerous factors, beginning with the creation of modern Germany in 1871. Achieved through a series of wars, the emergence of this new German state completely destroyed Europe's traditional balance of power, and forced its diplomatic and military planners back to their drawing boards to rethink their collective strategies. In the period between 1871 and 1914, a number of developments took place that increased tensions between the major powers.

Balance of Power and Europe's Alliance System

From 1871 to 1890, balance of power was maintained through the network of alliances created by the German Chancellor, Otto von Bismarck, and centered around his *Dreikaiserbund* (League of the Three Emperors) that isolated France, and the Dual (Germany, Austria) and Triple (Germany, Austria, Italy) Alliances. Bismarck's fall in 1890 resulted in new policies that saw Germany move closer to Austria, while England and France (Entente Cordiale, 1904), and later Russia (Triple Entente, 1907), drew closer.

Arms Buildup and Imperialism

Germany's dramatic defeat of France in 1870–1871 coupled with Kaiser William II's decision in 1890 to build up a navy comparable to that of Great Britain created a reactive arms race. This, blended with European efforts to carve out colonial empires in Africa and Asia—plus a new spirit of nationalism and the growing romanticization of war—helped create an unstable international environment in the years before the outbreak of World War I.

IMMEDIATE CAUSE OF WORLD WAR I

The Balkan Crisis

The Balkans, the area of Europe that now comprises Yugoslavia, Albania, Greece, Bulgaria, and Rumania, was Europe's most unstable area. Part of the rapidly-decaying Ottoman (Turkish) Empire, it was torn by ethnic nationalism among the various small groups that lived there, and competition between Austria-Hungary and Russia over spheres of influence in the region. Friction was intense in the region between Austria and Serbia, particularly after the former annexed Bosnia and

Herzegovina in 1908. In 1912, with Russian encouragement, a Balkan League which included Serbia, Montenegro, Greece, and Bulgaria went to war with Turkey. Serbia, which wanted a spot on the Adriatic, was rebuffed when Austria created Albania in an attempt to deter Serbia. This intensified bitterness between both countries, and prompted Russia to take a more protective attitude toward its Southern Slavic cousins.

THE OUTBREAK OF THE WORLD WAR

Assassination and Reprisals

On June 28, 1914, the Archduke Franz Ferdinand (1863–1914), heir to the Austrian throne, was assassinated by Gavrilo Princip, a young Serbian nationalist. Princip was working for the Serbian Army Intelligence in Sarajevo, then the capital of Bosnia. Austria's rulers felt the murder provided them with an opportunity to move against Serbia and end anti-Austrian unrest in the Balkans. Austria consulted with the German government on July 6 and received a "blank check" to take whatever steps necessary to punish Serbia. On July 23, 1914 the Austrian government presented Serbia with 11 threatening demands. They required Serbia to suppress and punish all forms of anti-Austrian sentiment there with the help of Austrian officials. On July 25, 1914, three hours after mobilizing its army, Serbia accepted most of Austria's terms with qualifications.

The Conflict Expands

Austria immediately broke official relations with Serbia and mobilized its army. Meanwhile, between July 18–24, Russia let the Austrians and the Germans know that it intended to fully back Serbia in the dispute. France, Russia's ally, voiced support of Russia's moves. On July 28, 1914, Austria went to war against Serbia, and began to bombard Belgrade the following day. At the same time, Russia gradually prepared for war against Austria and Germany, declaring full mobilization on July 30.

Germany and the Schlieffen Plan

German military strategy, based in part on the plan of the Chief of the General Staff Count Alfred von Schlieffen, viewed Russian mobilization as an act of war. The Schlieffen Plan was based on a two-front war with Russia and France. It was predicated on a swift, decisive blow against France while maintaining a defensive position against slowly-mobilizing Russia, which would be dealt with after France. Attacking France required the Germans to march through neutral Belgium, which would later bring England into the war as a protector of Belgian neutrality.

War Begins

Germany demanded that Russia demobilize in 12 hours, and appealed to the Russian ambassador in Berlin. Russia's offer to negotiate the matter was rejected, and Germany declared war on Russia on August 1, 1914. Germany asked France its intentions and Paris replied that it would respond according to its own interests. On August 3, Germany declared war on France. Berlin asked Belgium for permission to send its troops through its territory to attack France, which Belgium refused. On August 4, England, which agreed in 1839 to protect Belgian neutrality, declared war on Germany; Belgium followed suit. Between 1914 and 1915, the alliance of the Central Powers (Germany, Austria-Hungary, Bulgaria, and Turkey) faced the Allied Powers of England, France, Russia, Japan, and in 1917, the United States. A number of smaller countries were also part of the Allied coalition.

THE WAR IN 1914

The Western Front

After entering Belgium, the Germans attacked France on five fronts in an effort to encircle Paris rapidly. France was defeated in the Battle of the Frontier (August 14–24) in Lorraine, the Ardennes, and in the Charleroi-Mons area. However, the unexpected Russian attack in East Prussia and Galicia from August 17 to 20 forced Germany to transfer important forces eastward to halt the Russian drive.

To halt a further German advance, the French army, aided by Belgian and English forces, counterattacked. In the Battle of the Marne (September 5–9), they stopped the German drive and forced small retreats. Mutual outflanking maneuvers by France and Germany created a battlefront that would determine the demarcation of the Western Front for the next four years. It ran, in uneven fashion, from the North Sea to Belgium and from northern France to Switzerland.

The Eastern Front

Russian forces under Pavel Rennenkampf and Aleksandr Samsonov (1859–1914), invaded East Prussia and Galicia in mid-August. With only 9 of 87 divisions in the east, the German defense faltered. Generals Paul von Hindenburg (1847–1934) and Erich Ludendorff (1865–1937), aided by two corps from the Western Front, were sent on August 23 to revive the Eighth Army in East Prussia.

In the Battles of Tannenberg (August 25–31) and Mazurian Lakes (September 6–15), the Russian 2nd Army, under Samsonov, met the German 8th Army. Suffering from poor communications and Rennenkampf's refusal to send the 1st Army to aid him, Samsonov surrendered with 90,000 troops and committed suicide. Moving northward, the German 8th Army now confronted Rennenkampf's 1st Army. After an unsuccessful initial encounter against the Germans, Rennenkampf rapidly retreated, suffering significant losses.

Nikolai Ivanov's Southwest Army group enjoyed some successes against Austro-Hungarian forces in Galicia and southern Poland throughout August. By the end of 1914, they were poised to strike deeper into the area.

The Germans retreated after their assault against Warsaw in late September. Hindenburg's attack on Lodz, 10 days after he was appointed Commander-in-Chief of the Eastern Front (Nov. 1), was a more more successful venture; by the end of 1914 this important textile center was in German hands.

THE WAR IN 1915

The Western Front

With Germany concentrating on the East, France and England launched a series of small attacks throughout the year that resulted in a few gains and extremely heavy casualties. Wooed by both sides, Italy joined the Allies and declared war on the Central Powers on May 23 after signing the secret Treaty of London (April 26). This treaty gave Italy Austrian provinces in the north and some Turkish territory. Italian attacks against Austria near Trieste were unsuccessful because of difficult terrain, and failed to lessen pressure on the Russians in the East.

The Eastern Front

On January 23, 1915, Austro-German forces began a coordinated offensive in East Russia and in the Carpathians. The two-pronged German assault in the north was stopped on February 27, while Austrian efforts to relieve their besieged defensive network at Przemysl failed when it fell into Russian hands on March 22. In early March, Russian forces under Nikolai Ivanov drove deeper into the Carpathians with inadequate material support.

German forces, strengthened by troops from the Western Front under August von Mackensen, began a move on May 2 to strike at the heart of the Russian Front. They used the greatest artillery concentration of the war at that time as part of their strategy. In June, Mackensen shifted his assault towards Lublin and Brest-Litovsk, while the German XII, X, and Niemen armies moved toward Kovno in the Baltic. By August 1915, much of Russian Poland was in German hands.

In an effort to provide direct access to the Turks defending Gallipoli, Germany and Austria invaded Serbia in the early fall, aided by their new ally, Bulgaria. On October 7, the defeated Serbian army retreated to Corfu. Belated Allied efforts to ship troops from Gallipoli to help Bulgaria failed.

Command Changes

Allied frustration resulted in the appointment of Marshal Joseph Joffre (1852–1931) as French Commander-in-Chief, and Field Marshal Sir Douglas Haig (1861–1928) as British Commander in December 1915.

The Eastern Mediterranean

Turkey entered the war on the Central Power side on October 28, 1914, which prevented the shipment of Anglo-French aid to Russians through the Straits.

The Western stalemate caused Allied strategists to look to the eastern Mediterranean for a way to break the military deadlock. Winston Churchill, Britain's First Lord of the Admiralty, devised a plan to seize the Straits of the Dardanelles to open lines to Russia, take Constantinople, and isolate Turkey. These unsuccessful efforts occurred between February 19 and March 18, 1915.

On April 25, Allied forces invaded Gallipoli Peninsula in a different attempt to capture the Straits. Turkish troops offered strong resistance, and forced the Allies (after suffering 252,000 casualties) to begin a three week evacuation that began on December 20, 1915.

The Middle East, 1914–1916

In an effort to protect its petroleum interests in the Persian Gulf, an Anglo-Indian force took Al Basrals (Basra) in Southern Iraq in November 1915. The following year, British forces moved north and took Al Kut (Kut al Irnara) from Turkey on September 28. To counter failures on the Western Front, British forces then tried to take Baghdad, but were stopped by the Turks at Ctesiphon on November 22. Turkish forces besieged Al Kut on December 8, and captured it on April 29, 1916. Two-thirds of the 10,000 captured British POW's died of Turkish mistreatment.

THE WAR IN 1916

The Western Front

In order to break the stalemate on the Western Front and drain French forces in the effort, the Germans decided to attack the French fortress town of Verdun. The Battle for Verdun lasted from February 21 to December 18, 1916. From February until June, German forces, aided by closely coordinated heavy artillery barrages, assaulted the forts around Verdun. The Germans suffered 281,000 casualties while the French, under Marshal Henri Pétain (1856–1951), lost 315,000 while successfully defending their position.

To take pressure off the French, an Anglo-French force mounted three attacks on the Germans to the left of Verdun in July, September, and November. After the Battle of the Somme (July 1–November 18), German pressure was reduced, but at great loss. Anglo-French casualties totaled 600,000.

The Eastern Front

Initially, the Allies had hoped for a general coordinated attack on all fronts against the Central Powers. Now efforts centered on relieving pressure at Verdun and on the Italians at Trentino.

Orchestrated by Aleksei Brusilov (1853–1926), The Brusilov Offensive (June 4–September 20) envisioned a series of unexpected attacks along a lengthy front to confuse the enemy. By late August, he had advanced into Galicia and the Carpathians. The number of enemy troops dead, wounded, or captured numbered 1.5 million. Russian losses numbered 500,000.

Rumania entered the war on the Allied side as a result of Russian successes and the secret Treaty of Bucharest (August 17). This treaty specified that Rumania would get Translyvania, Bukovina, the Banat, and part of the Hungarian Plain if the Allies won. The ensuing Rumanian thrust into Translyvania was pushed back, and on December 6, a German-Bulgarian army occupied Bucharest as well as the bulk of Rumania.

Central Powers Propose Peace Talks

The death of Austrian Emperor Franz Joseph (reigned 1848–1916) on November 21 prompted his successor, Charles I (1887–1922), to discuss the prospect of peace terms with his allies. On December 12, the four Central Powers, strengthened by the fall of Bucharest, offered four separate peace proposals based on their recent military achievements. The Allies rejected them on December 30 because they felt them to be insincere.

War on the High Seas, 1914–1916

Britain's naval strategy in the first year of the war was disrupt German shipping world-wide with the aid of the French and the Japanese. Germany sought ways to defend itself and weaken Allied naval strength. By the end of 1914, Allied fleets had gained control of the high seas, which caused Germany to lose control of its colonial empire.

Germany's failure in 1914 to weaken British naval strength prompted German naval leaders to begin using the submarine as an offensive weapon to weaken the British. On February 4, Germany announced a war zone around the British Isles, and advised neutral powers to sail there at their own risk. On May 7, 1915 a German submarine sank the *Lusitania*, a British passenger vessel because it was secretly carrying arms. There were 1,201 casualties, including 139 Americans.

The United States protested the sinking as a violation of the Declaration of London (1909). After four months of negotiations, Germany agreed not to sink any passenger vessels without warning, and to help all passengers and crew to lifeboats. Germany shifted its U-boat activity to the Mediterranean.

The main naval battle of World War I was the Battle of Jutland/Skagerrak (May –June 1916). It pitted 28 British dreadnoughts and nine cruisers against 16 German dreadnoughts and five cruisers. In the end, the battle was a draw, with England losing 14 ships and Germany 11. It forced the German High Seas Fleet not to venture out of port for the rest of the war. Instead, they concentrated on use of the U-boat.

New Military Technology

Germany, Russia, and Great Britain all had submarines, but the German U-boats were the most effective. Designed principally for coastal protection, they increasingly used them to reduce British naval superiority through tactical and psychological means.

By the spring of 1915, British war planners finally awoke to the fact that the machine gun had become the mistress of defensive trench warfare. In a search for a weapon to counter trench defenses, the British developed tanks as an armored "land ship," and first used them on September 15, 1916, in the battle of the Somme. Their value was not immediately realized because there were too few of them to be effective, and interest in them waned. Renewed interest came in 1917.

Airplanes were initially used for observation purposes in the early months of the war. As their numbers grew, mid-air struggles using pistols and rifles took place, until the Germans devised a synchronized propeller and machine gun on its Fokker aircraft in May 1915. The Allies responded with similar equipment and new squadron tactics during the early days of the Verdun campaign in February 1916, and briefly gained control of the skies. They also began to use their aircraft for bombing raids against Zeppelin bases in Germany. Air supremacy shifted to the Germans in

1917.

During the first year of the war, the Germans began to use Zeppelin airships to bomb civilian targets in England. Though their significance was neutralized with the development of the explosive shell in 1916, Zeppelins played an important role as a psychological weapon in the first two years of the war.

In the constant search for methods to counter trench warfare, the Germans and the Allied forces experimented with various forms of internationally-outlawed gas. On October 27, 1914, the Germans tried a nose/eye irritant gas at Neuve-Chapelle, and by the spring of 1915 had developed an asphyxiating lachaymatory chlorine gas at the battle of Spres. The British countered with a similar chemical at the battles of Champagne and Loos that fall. Military strategists initially had little faith in gas since its use depended heavily on wind conditions, which could change the direction of the gas at any moment. However, as they desperately struggled to find ways to break the deadlock on the Western Front, they devised tactics and protection methods that enabled them to integrate the use of gas into their strategy.

THE RUSSIAN REVOLUTIONS OF 1917

Two events that would have a dramatic impact on the war and the world were the February and October Revolutions in 1917. The former toppled the Romanov Dynasty and spawned that country's brief flirtation with democracy under the temporary Provisional Government. It collapsed later that year as a result of the October Revolution, which brought Lenin and his Bolshevik faction to power.

Plagued for centuries by a backward autocratic government and a rural serf economy, Russia seemed on the verge of dramatic change after Tsar Alexander II (1855–1881) freed the serfs in 1861. Emancipation, coupled with other important government and social reforms, created chaos nationwide and helped stimulate a new class of violent revolutionaries bent on destroying the tsarist system. Terrorists murdered Alexander II, which prompted the country's last two rulers, Alexander III (reigned 1881–1894) and Nicholas II (reigned 1894–1917) to turn the clock backward politically.

The Russo-Japanese War and the 1905 Revolution

In February 1904, war broke out between Russia and Japan over spheres-of-influence in Korea and Manchuria. Russia's inability to adequately support its military forces in Asia, coupled with growing battlefield losses, prompted a nationwide revolution after police fired on peaceful demonstrators in January 1905. A groundswell of strikes and demonstrations swept the country and neutralized the government, which was on the verge of collapse. Nicholas II survived because he agreed in his October Manifesto (October 30, 1905) to create a constitution, share power with a legislature (Duma), and grant civil rights. This decree defused the crisis and enabled the government to survive and rebuild its political base.

Era of Reaction and Reforms (1906–1912)

Once the czar diminished the threat to his throne, he issued the Fundamental Laws (May 6, 1906), which severely limited the power of the Duma. But over the next 11 years, four increasingly conservative Dumas met, providing a tradition of constitutional government for the country. Workers' and soldiers' soviets (councils) and political parties (Kadets, Constitutional Democrats, Octobrists) emerged to challenge the government. To counter this mood, the czar appointed Peter Stolypin as Prime Minister (1906–1911) to initiate mollifying reforms for the peasants and develop a private agricultural system throughout the country. These efforts, and an industrial boom, improved Russia's economy.

Rasputin and Upheaval (1912–1914)

The death of Stolypin in 1911, coupled with a government incapable of dealing with new labor unrest brought to power a semi-illiterate holy man, Grigory Rasputin (1872–1916). He seemed to possess the power to save the czar's hemophiliac son, Alexei, and obtained tremendous influence over the royal family.

RUSSIA AT WAR: THE HOME FRONT (1914–1917)

Russia's entrance into World War I was met with broad public acceptance and support. Serious problems, however, plagued the government, the military, and the economy, and threatened to undermine a military effort most expected would win the war in a matter of months.

The Military

The draft increased Russia's armed forces from 1,350,000 to 6,500,000 during the war, though the government was only able to equip fully a small percentage of these troops. In addition, the country's military leaders differed on whether to concentrate their efforts on the Austrians or the Germans. While in the field, commanders were handicapped by inadequate communication and maps. As a result, German drives in the spring and summer of 1915 saw Russian spirit collapse as defensive efforts proved ineffective. However, by the end of that year, High Command personnel changes, aided by new industrial output, enabled the Russians to briefly turn the tide of battle.

The Government and the Bureaucracy

As the country's problems mounted, the czar responded by assuming direct command of his army on the front in September 1915, leaving the government in the hands of his wife, Alexandra, and Rasputin. Those critical of the czar's policies were dismissed, and the country lost its most effective leaders. The Duma, which was forced to assume more responsibilities, formed the Progressive Bloc, a coalition mainly of Kadets and Octobrists, in an effort to try to force the czar to appoint more competent officials. The Czar's refusal to accept this group's proposals led to increasing criticism of his policies. In November 1916, distant relatives of the czar and a Duma member secretly murdered Rasputin.

THE FEBRUARY REVOLUTION

The February Revolution, so named because the Russian calendar at the time was 13 days behind that of the West, was a spontaneous series of events that forced the collapse of the Romanov Dynasty.

Riots and Strikes

The government's handling of the war prompted a new wave of civilian unrest. Estimates are that 1,140 riots and strikes swept Russia in January and February. Military and police units ordered to move against the mobs either remained at their posts or joined them.

The Duma

Though ordered by the czar not to meet until April, Duma leaders demanded dramatic solutions to the country's problems. Though dissolved on March 11, the Duma met in special session on March 13 and created a Provisional Committee of Elders to deal with the civil war. After two days of discussions, it decided that the czar must give up his throne, and on March 15, 1917, President Michael Rodzianko and Aleksandr Ivanovich Guchkov, leader of the Octobrist Party, convinced the czar to abdicate. He agreed and turned the throne over to his brother, the Grand Duke Michael, who gave it up the following day.

THE PROVISIONAL GOVERNMENT IN POWER (MARCH–NOVEMBER, 1917)

From March through November 1917, a temporary Provisional Government ruled Russia. It tried to move the country toward democracy and keep Russia in the war as a loyal western ally.

Leadership

The principle figures in the new government were: Prince George Lvov (1861–1925), a Kadet Party and *zemstvo* leader, who served as Prime Minister and Minister of the Interior; Paul Miliukov (1849–1943), head of the Kadet Party, Foreign Minister; A.I. Guchkov, an Octobrist leader, Minister of War; and Alexander Kerensky (1881–1970), a conservative Socialist Revolutionary and Vice-Chairman of the Petrograd Soviet, Minister of Justice.

Problems

The Provisional Government was made up of middle-class and intellectual leaders, and had little contact or sympathy with the problems or concerns of the workers or peasants. Its leaders, particularly Miliukov, felt the government had to stay in the war to maintain its international credibility. Despite pressure to redistribute land, Lvov's government felt that it did not have the authority to deal with this complex issue. Instead, it left the problem to a future Constituent Assembly that would convene within a year. The Provisional Government did, however, implement a number of far-reaching reforms, including full political and religious freedom, election of local officials, an eight-hour working day, and legal and judicial changes.

THE PETROGRAD SOVIET

On the eve of Nicholas II's abdication, a "shadow government," the Petrograd Soviet, was formed from among the capital's workers, and took control of the city administration.

Creation

On March 13, delegates were elected to a Soviet of Worker's Deputies, later renamed the Soviet of Workers and Soldiers Deputies. It was made up of 1,300 representatives, and grew to 3,000 the following week with the addition of military delegates. Because of its size, the Petrograd Soviet created an Executive Committee headed by N.S. Chkeidze, a Menshevik, to make its most important decisions.

Policies

In response to an unsuccessful request to the Provisional Government to absolve soldiers from potentially treasonous actions during the March Revolution, the Petrograd Soviet issued Order No. I (March 14) that granted them amnesty and stated that officers were to be elected by their units. It later issued Order No. II for units throughout the country. These decrees, hesitatingly approved later by the Provisional Government, caused a collapse of discipline in the armed forces.

LENIN RETURNS TO RUSSIA

Vladimir Ilyich Ulyanov (Lenin, 1870–1924) became involved in revolutionary activity after the execution of his brother for an assassination plot against Alexander III. A committed Marxist, he split with the Menshevik wing of the Russian Social Democratic Party and formed his "Bolshevik" (majority) faction in 1903. Lenin felt the party should be led by a committed elite. He spent much of the period between 1905 and 1917 in exile, and was surprised by the February Revolution. However, with the aid of the Germans, he and some followers were placed in a sealed train and transported from Switzerland to Russia.

The April Theses

On April 16, Lenin arrived at Petrograd's Finland Station and went into hiding. The next day, he proposed his April Theses to the city's Bolshevik leaders, who rejected them. Lenin felt that the Bolsheviks should oppose the Provisional Government and support the theme "All Power to the Soviets." The world war should become a revolution against capitalism, with all soldiers on both sides joining the struggle. In addition, he wanted the country's land, factories, and banks to be nationalized, and the Bolshevik Party to call itself the Communist Party.

THE FIRST COALITION

Paul Miliukov's decision on May 1 to assure the Allies that his country would not sign a separate agreement with Germany and would continue to fight until a "decisive victory" was won, caused public demonstrations that forced his resignation and the Lvov government to disavow his note. The Soviet now permitted its members to join the Provisional Government. The First Coalition was formed under Prince Lvov, and included nine non-socialists and six socialist representatives.

THE JULY CRISES

Because of Allied pressure, the Provisional Government decided to mount an offensive on the Eastern Front to counter French military failures and mutinies on the Western Front. But mass desertions after a failed July attack in Galicia contributed to the army's collapse.

The Second Coalition

In the midst of the July Offensive, the First Coalition collapsed. Prince Lvov stepped down as Prime Minister over the land question and efforts to strengthen Soviet influence in the Cabinet. Alexander Kerensky became Prime Minister, and announced elections for a Constituent Assembly.

The July Days

Many top Bolsheviks went underground or fled abroad after leading demonstrations of more than 500,000 protesters. Government troops dissolved the demonstrations.

THE SECOND COALITION AND THE KORNILOV AFFAIR

The Moscow State Conference (August 26–28)

In an effort to find an alternative base of support for the Petrograd Soviet before elections to the Constituent Assembly, Kerensky convened the Moscow State Conference on August 26.

Over 2,000 delegates, representing the Duma, the military, the Soviets, the professions, and other groups, met in Moscow. The Bolsheviks opposed the meeting and responded with a general strike.

The conference accentuated the growing difference between Kerensky and the conservatives, who looked to the government's Commander-in-Chief, General Lavr Kornilov, as a leader. Kornilov represented elements who decried the collapse of military discipline and left the Moscow Conference convinced that Kerensky did not have the ability to restore order and stability to the nation and the military.

The Kornilov Affair

The mutual suspicion between Kerensky and Kornilov resulted in a series of indirect, unofficial negotiations between the two that ended in Kornilov's dismissal on September 9. Kornilov responded by ordering his Cossack and "Savage" divisions to march to Petrograd to stop a Bolshevik coup. The Petrograd Soviet rallied to save the revolution, and freed the Bolsheviks from prison to help with defense preparations. Kornilov's coup collapsed, and he surrendered on September 14. Kerensky now became Supreme Commander-in-Chief.

The Third Coalition

On September 14, Kerensky restructured his government as a temporary Directory of Five, and declared Russia a Republic. Thirteen days later, he convened a large gathering of 1,200 representatives from throughout the country to rebuild his power base. From it emerged a Third Coalition government on October 8, that consisted of Socialist Revolutionaries, Mensheviks, Kadets, and ministers without ties to any faction. The Bolsheviks and other leftists opposed these efforts, which weakened Kerensky's efforts.

THE BOLSHEVIK OCTOBER REVOLUTION

The Kornilov affair and Kerensky's failure to rebuild support for the Provisional Government convinced the Bolshevik's two leaders, Lenin and Leon Trotsky (1879–1940), that now was the time for them to attempt to seize power.

Lenin's Decision to Seize Power

On October 23–24, Lenin returned from Finland to meet with the Party's Central Committee to plan the coup. Though he met with strong resistance, the Committee agreed to create a Political Bureau (Politburo) to oversee the revolution.

Trotsky and the Military Revolutionary Committee

Leon Trotsky, head of the Petrograd Soviet and its Military Revolutionary Committee, convinced troops in Petrograd to support Bolshevik moves. While Trotsky gained control of important strategic points around the city, Kerensky, well-informed of Lenin's plans, finally decided on November 6 to move against the plotters.

The Coup of November 6–7

In response, Lenin and Trotsky ordered their supporters to seize the city's transportation and communication centers. The Winter Palace was captured later that evening, along with most of Kerensky's government.

The Second Congress of Soviets

The Second Congress opened at 11 p.m. on November 7, with Lev Kamenev (1883–1936), a member of Lenin's Politburo, as its head. Over half (390) of the 650 delegates were Bolshevik supporters, and its newly selected 22-member Presidium had 14 Bolsheviks on it. Soon after the Second Congress opened, many of the moderate socialists walked out in opposition to Lenin's coup, leaving the Bolsheviks and the Left Socialist Revolutionaries in control of the gathering. Lenin now used the rump Congress as the vehicle to announce his regime.

At the Congress, it was announced that the government's new Cabinet, officially called the Council of People's Commissars (Sovnarkom), and responsible to a Central Executive Committee, would include Lenin as Chairman or head of government, Trotsky as Foreign Commissar, and Josef Stalin as Commissar of Nationalities. The Second Congress issued two decrees on peace and land. The first called for immediate peace without any consideration of indemnities or annexations, while the second adopted the Socialist Revolutionary land program that abolished private ownership of land and decreed that a peasant could only have as much land as he could farm. Village councils would oversee distribution.

THE CONSTITUENT ASSEMBLY

The Constituent Assembly, long promised by the Provisional Government as the country's first legally-elected legislature, presented serious problems for Lenin, since he knew the Bolsheviks could not win a majority of seats in it. Regardless, Lenin allowed elections for it to be held on November 25 under universal suffrage. More than 41,000,000 Russians voted. The SR's got 58 percent of the vote, the Bolsheviks 25 percent, the Kadets and other parties, 17 percent. When the assembly convened on January 18 in the Tauride Palace, the building was surrounded by Red Guards and others. The Assembly voted down Bolshevik proposals and elected Victor Chernov, a Socialist Revolutionary, as president, and declared the country a democratic federal republic. The Bolsheviks walked out. The next day, troops dissolved the Assembly.

WORLD WAR I: THE FINAL PHASE (1917–1918)

Marshall Henri Pétain (1856–1951) became French Commander in May 1917 after a failed French offensive in Champagne (second Battle of the Aisne) resulted in large-scale mutinies. Against French wishes, Haig began a new series of unsuccessful assaults (Third Battle of Ypres from July 31 to November 4).

The Italian Front and the Battle of Caporetto

On October 24, a Central Power campaign began at Caporetto, which resulted in an Italian retreat through November 12 and the capture of 250,000 Italians. The loss convinced the Allies to form a Supreme War Council at Versailles to enhance Allied cooperation.

The Tank Battle of Cambrai

From November 20 to December 3, the largest tank battle of the war, involving 400 British tanks, took place at Cambrai. A German counteroffensive on November 30 pushed the British back.

THE MIDDLE AND NEAR EAST (1917)

Mesopotamia

The British revived their Mesopotamian campaign in 1917 and retook Al Kut on February 23. They captured Baghdad on March 11.

Palestine

British forces in Palestine unsuccessfully attacked Gaza on March 26–27, and reassaulted it with the same consequences on April 17–19. In the third offensive against Gaza from October 31 to November 7, Turkish forces retreated, which opened the way for a British attack on Jerusalem. While Col. T.E. Lawrence (Lawrence of Arabia, 1888–1935) worked to stir Arab passions against the Turks, General Sir Edmund Allenby took Jerusalem on December 9–11.

RUSSIA LEAVES THE WAR

One of the cornerstones of Bolshevik propaganda throughout 1917 was a promise to end the war after they had seized power. Once in control, Soviet authorities issued a decree that called for immediate peace "with no indemnities or annexations" at the Second Congress of Soviets on November 8, 1917.

The Armistice at Brest-Litovsk

As order collapsed among Russian units along the Eastern Front, the Soviet government began to explore cease fire talks with the Central Powers. Leon Trotsky, the Commissar of Foreign Affairs, offered general negotiations to all sides, and signed an initial armistice as a prelude to peace discussions with Germany at Brest-Litovsk on December 5, 1917.

Trotsky and Initial Peace Negotiations with Germany

Trotsky was shocked by German demands for Poland, Lithuania, and Kurland when negotiations opened on December 22, 1917. This prompted him to return to Moscow for consultations with the Bolshevik leadership.

Soviet Differences Over Peace Terms

Three different perspectives emerged over the German peace terms among the Soviet leadership. One group, led by Nikolay Bukharin (1888–1938), wanted the conflict to continue as a revolutionary war designed to spread Bolshevism. Lenin, however, felt the country needed peace for his government to survive. Western revolution would take place later. Trotsky wanted a policy of no war and no peace.

The Soviet Response and the Treaty of Brest-Litovsk

On the day the German offensive began, Lenin barely convinced Party leaders to accept Germany's earlier offer. Berlin responded with harsher ones, which the Soviets grudgingly accepted, and were integrated into the Treaty of Brest-Litovsk of March 3, 1918. According to its terms, in return for peace, Soviet Russia lost its

Baltic provinces, the Ukraine, Finland, Byelorussia, and part of Transcaucasia. The area lost totaled 1,300,000 square miles and included 62 million people.

THE AMERICAN PRESENCE: NAVAL AND ECONOMIC SUPPORT

The United States, which had originally hoped that it could simply supply the Allies with naval and economic support, made its naval presence known immediately and helped Great Britain mount an extremely effective blockade of Germany and, through a convoy system, strengthened the shipment of goods across the Atlantic.

Despite the difficulties of building a military system from scratch, the United States was slowly able to transform its peacetime army of 219,665 men and officers into a force of 2 million. An initial token group, the American Expeditionary Force under General John J. Pershing (1860–1948), arrived in France on June 25, 1917, while by the end of April 1918, 300,000 Americans a month were placed as complete divisions alongside British and French units.

The German Offensive of 1918

Emboldened by their victory over Russia, the German High Command, including General Erich Ludendorff, decided to launch an all-out offensive against the Allies in France to win the war.

Beginning on March 21, 1918, Ludendorff mounted four major attacks on the Allied forces in France: Somme (March 21–April 4), Lys (April 9–29), Aisne (May 27–June 6), and Champagne-Marne (July 15–17). The success of the assaults so concerned the Allies that they appointed the French Chief of Staff, Ferdinand Foch (1851–1929), Supreme Commander of Allied Forces on April 14. In the third attack on Aisne, the Germans came within 37 miles of Paris. However, the increasing appearance of fresh, though untried American forces, combined with irreplaceable German manpower losses, began to turn the war against the Germans. Four days after the decisive German crossing of the Marne, Foch counterattacked and began to plan for an offensive against the Germans.

The Allied Offensive of 1918 and Armistice with Germany

Stirred by the successes on the Marne, the Allies began their offensive against the Germans at Amiens on August 8, 1918. Ludendorff, who called this Germany's "dark day," soon began to think of ways to end the fighting. By September 3, the Germans retreated to the Hindenburg Line. On September 26, Foch began his final offensive, and took the Hindenburg Line the following day. Two days later, Ludendorff advised his government to seek a peace settlement. Over the next month, the French took St. Quentin (October 1), while the British occupied Cambrai, Le Cateau, and Ostend.

On September 14, Allied forces attacked in the Salonika area of Macedonia and forced Bulgaria to sue for peace on September 29. On September 19, General Allenby began an attack on Turkish forces at Megiddo in Palestine and quickly defeated them. In a rapid collapse of Turkish resistance, the British took Damascus,

Aleppo, and finally forced Turkey from the war at the end of October. On October 24, the Italians began an assault against Austria-Hungary at Vitto Veneto and forced Vienna to sign armistice terms on November 3. Kaiser William II, pressured to abdicate, fled the country on November 9, and a republic was declared. On November 11, at 11 a.m., the war ended, with Germany accepting a harsh armistice.

THE PARIS PEACE CONFERENCE OF 1919–1920

To a very great extent, the direction and thrust of the discussions at the Paris Peace Conference were determined by the destructive nature of the war itself and the political responsibilities, ideals, and personalities of the principle architects of the settlements at Paris: President Woodrow Wilson (1856–1924) of the United States, Prime Minister David Lloyd George (1863–1945) of Great Britain, Prime Minister/ Minister of War Georges Clemenceau (1841–1929) of France, and Prime Minister Vittorio Orlando (1860–1952) of Italy.

As politicians, they reflected the general mood of victorious Europe's population, who wanted the principal Central Powers, Germany and Austria-Hungary, punished severely for this inhuman calamity. Total losses are not accurately known. Consequently, high and low estimates are given in some categories:

1) France: 1,500,000/1,363,000 dead and 4,797,800/4,660,800 wounded.
2) British Empire: 1,000,000/908,000 dead and 2,282,235/2,190,235 wounded.
3) Italy: 500,000/460,000 dead and 1,737,000/1,697,000 wounded.
4) United States: 116,708/100,000 dead and 104,000/87,292 wounded.
5) Russia: 1,700,000 dead and 7,450,000 wounded.
6) Germany: 2,000,000/1,774,000 dead and 5,368,558/5,142,588 wounded.
7) Austria-Hungary: 1,250,000/1,200,000 dead and 5,820,000/5,770,000 wounded.

WOODROW WILSON AND THE FOURTEEN POINTS

Not handicapped by significant financial or territorial concerns, Wilson idealistically promoted his Fourteen Points—particularly the last, which dealt with a League of Nations—as the basis of the armistice and the peace settlement.

SECRET ALLIED AGREEMENTS CONCLUDED DURING WORLD WAR I

Throughout the war, the Allied powers had concluded a number of secret agreements designed to encourage countries to join their side or as compensation for war efforts. In March 1915, England and France had promised Russia Constantinople, the Straits, and the bordering areas as long as they were openly accessible. In April of the following year, England and France had promised one another, respectively, spheres in Mesopotamia and Palestine, as well as Syria, Adana, Cilia, and southern Kurdistan. The Sykes-Picot Treaty in May 1916 better defined both countries' Arabian spheres. Russia was to have similar rights in Armenia, portions of Kurdistan, and northeastern Anatolia. The Allies gave Italy and Rumania significant territories to encourage them in their war effort in April 1915 and August 1916, while the English promised to support Japan's desire for Germany's Asian possessions. France and Russia agreed to promote one another's claims at a future peace conference, while Arab independence and creation of a Jewish homeland were also promised to others.

PRELIMINARY DISCUSSIONS

The sudden, unexpected end of the war, combined with the growing threat of communist revolution throughout Europe created an unsettling atmosphere at the conference. The "Big Four" of Wilson (U.S.), Clemenceau (France), Lloyd-George (England), and Orlando (Italy) took over the peace discussions. Initially, the Allied Powers had hoped for a negotiated settlement with the defeated powers, which necessitated hard terms that would be negotiated down. However, the delays caused by uncertainty over direction at the beginning of the conference, Wilson's insistence that the League of Nations be included in the settlement, and fear of European-wide revolution resulted in a hastily prepared, dictated peace settlement.

THE TREATY OF VERSAILLES

Most Significant Clauses

The treaty's war guilt statements were the justification for its harsh penalties. The former German king, William II, was accused of crimes against "international morality and the sanctity of treaties," while Germany took responsibility for itself and for its allies for all losses suffered by the Allied Powers and their supporters as a result of German and Central Power aggression.

Germany had to return Alsace and Lorraine to France and Eupen-Malmedy to Belgium. France got Germany's Saar coal mines as reparations, while the Saar Basin was to be occupied by the major powers for 15 years, after which a plebiscite would decide its ultimate fate. Poland got a number of German provinces and Danzig, now a free city, as its outlet to the sea. Additionally, Germany lost all of its colonies in Asia and Africa.

The German Army was limited to 100,000 men and officers with 12 year enlistments for the former and 25 for the latter. The General Staff was also abolished. The Navy lost its submarines and most offensive naval forces, and was limited to 15,000 men and officers with the same enlistment periods as the army. Aircraft and blimps were outlawed. A Reparations Commission was created to determine Germany's war debt to the Allies, which it figured in 1921 to be $32.4 billion, to be paid over an extended period of time. In the meantime, Germany was to begin immediate payments in goods and raw materials.

German Hesitance to Sign the Treaty

The Allies presented the treaty to the Germans on May 7, 1919, but the Germans stated that its terms were too much for the German people, and that it violated the spirit of Wilson's Fourteen Points. After some minor changes were made, the Germans were told to sign the document or face an Allied advance into Germany. The treaty was signed on June 28, 1919, at Versailles.

TREATIES WITH GERMANY'S ALLIES

The Treaty of St. Germain (September 10, 1919)

The Allied treaty with Austria legitimized the breakup of the Austrian Empire in the latter days of the war and saw Austrian territory ceded to Italy and the new states of Czechoslovakia, Poland, and Yugoslavia. The agreement included military restrictions and debt payments.

Treaty of Neuilly (November 27, 1919)

Bulgaria lost territory to Yugoslavia and Greece and also had clauses on military limitations and reparations.

Treaty of Trianon (June 4, 1920)

The agreement with Hungary was delayed because of the communist revolution there in 1919 and Rumania's brief occupation of Budapest. Hungary lost two-thirds of its prewar territory in the agreement to Rumania, Yugoslavia, and Czechoslovakia, and became an almost purely Magyar nation. Reparations and military reduction terms were also in the accord.

Treaty of Sevres (August 10, 1920)

This treaty lost Turkey most of its non-Turkish territory, principally in the Middle and Near East, and saw the Straits and the surrounding area internationalized and demilitarized. The Turkish revolution of Kemal Atatürk (1881–1938) ultimately caused it to be favorably renegotiated as the Treaty of Lausanne (July 24, 1923) with Turkey gaining territory in Anatolia, Smyrna, and Thrace.

PROBLEMS OF ALLIED UNITY: JAPAN, ITALY, AND THE U.S.

During and after the meetings in Paris that resulted in the Treaty of Versailles, disputes arose among the Allies that caused friction among them later.

Japan

During the treaty talks, Japan asked for Germany's Shantung Province in China, its Pacific colonies, and a statement on racial equality in the League Covenant. Japan got what it essentially wanted on the first two requests, despite protests from China on Shantung. However, Japan's request for a racial equality clause met strong opposition from the United States and some members of the British Commonwealth, who feared the impact of the statement on immigration. The proposal was denied, principally at the instigation of President Wilson.

Italy

Italy got the Tyrol, as well as Istria and some Adriatic islands in the Treaty of Rapallo (December 12, 1920). Dalmatia, however, went to Yugoslavia, while Fiume was seized by the Italian patriot/poet Gabriele D'Annunzio, on September 12, 1919. After a 14-month occupation he departed, leaving its destiny to Italy and Yugoslavia. The Treaty of Rome (January 27, 1924) divided the city between the two, with Italy getting the lion's share of the area.

POLITICAL DEVELOPMENTS IN POST-WAR EUROPE (1918–1929)

England (1918–1922)

Like most other European powers that emerged from the First World War, England had problems unique to its status as a nation absolutely dependent on trade and commerce for its economic well-being.

With the war at an end, the Coalition government of David Lloyd George held the first parliamentary elections since 1910. Known as the "Coupon" or "Khaki" elections, the question of victory, the nature of the settlement with Germany, and the Prime Minister himself were the election's burning issues. Before it took place, the Representation of the Peoples Act granted women over 30 the right to vote. Lloyd George and his Conservative Coalition won a landslide victory (478 seats) while his opponents gained only 87 seats.

Afterwards, England enjoyed a boom fueled by government policies and economic production based on pre-war conditions. Unfortunately, government retrenchment, blended with tax increases and overproduction, resulted in a severe recession by the end of 1921. It began in 1920 with almost 700,000 unemployed by the end of that year and jumped to 2 million within months. Until the Depression, unemployment averaged 12% annually. This resulted in the passage of the Unemployment Insurance Acts (1920, 1922) for workers, and the construction of 200,000 subsidized housing units.

Triggered by the Easter Rebellion of 1916, the extremist Sinn Fein faction gained prominence in Ireland. In 1918, three quarters of its members elected to the British Parliament instead declared Irish independence in Dublin. This prompted a civil war between the Irish Republican Army and the Black and Tan, England's special occupation forces there. The Lloyd George government responded with a Home Rule division of Ireland with two legislatures, which only the northern six counties accepted. In October 1921, London created the Irish Free State, from which Ulster withdrew, as a part of the British Commonwealth.

Politics (1922–1924)

These problems caused the Conservatives to withdraw from Lloyd George's coalition. Andrew Bonar-Law replaced him as head of a new Conservative government, though ill health forced him to resign in 1923, followed briefly by Stanley Baldwin. Continued unemployment and labor problems, coupled with a decline to adopt more protectionistic trade policies resulted in a significant doctrine in support for the Conservatives in the elections of November 1923. Baldwin resigned, followed in office by Ramsay MacDonald, head of the Labour Party. His minority government only lasted nine months, and fell principally because of his efforts to establish formal ties with Russia.

England and Stanley Baldwin (1924–1929)

Baldwin entered his second Prime Ministership with a solid electoral victory (411 seats) and strong Conservative Party backing. The year 1925 marked a turn in the economic crisis, with an increase in prices and wages. The country's return to the gold standard, which made the pound worth too much, affected British trade. In May 1926, a general strike in support of miners swept the country. Baldwin refused to concede to the miners' demands, broke the strike, and in 1927 sponsored the Trade Unions Act, which outlawed such labor action. On the other hand, the government passed a number of pieces of social legislation that further allowed support for housing construction and expanded pensions through its Widows', Orphans', and Old Age Pensions Act (1925). It also passed new legislation in 1928 that gave women the same voting privileges as men. In foreign affairs, Baldwin cancelled the 1924 commercial agreement with the Soviet Union, and, as a result of Soviet espionage activities, broke formal ties with the USSR in 1927.

FRANCE

The human losses in the war deeply affected France because of a population growth slowdown that had begun in the mid-19th century. The Third Republic reflected in its political life and foreign policy a country ruled by an aging leadership that sought comfort in its rich past.

The Bloc National (1919–1924)

The election of November 1919 represented a momentary shift rightward with the moderate-conservatives winning almost two-thirds of the seats in the Chamber of Deputies. The new government, headed by Premier Alexandre Millerand (1859–1943), was a coalition known as the Bloc National. Aristide Briand (1862–1932) replaced Millerand in January 1921, but was removed a year later because of lack of firmness on the German reparations question and was succeeded by Raymond Poincaré (1860–1934).

France had borrowed heavily during the war and spent great sums afterwards to rebuild its devastated economy. Unfortunately, it relied on German reparations to fund many of these costs. Problems with these repayments created a financial crisis that saw the French public debt increase, accompanied by a steady decline in the value of the franc.

Growing Franco-German differences over Germany's willingness to meet its debt payments created friction between both countries and toppled the government of August Briand. In December 1922, Poincaré declared Germany in default on its reparations payments. In January, France and Belgium occupied the Ruhr. Efforts to obtain payments in kind via Franco-Belgium operation of the Ruhr's mines and factories failed because of passive resistance by German workers in the area. The Ruhr's occupiers gained little more financially in payments than they had through normal means, and found the cost of occupation expensive. Consequently, the French government had to raise taxes 20 percent to cover the cost of the occupation.

The Cartel des Gauches (1924–1926)

Poincaré's Ruhr occupation policy divided French voters, while tax increases helped defeat the Bloc National in the May 1924 elections, though it did gain 51 percent of the popular vote. A Radical/Socialist coalition, the Cartel des Gauches, had majority control of the Chamber. It selected Édouard Herriot (1872–1957), a Radical leader, as Premier, while Millerand continued as President, and Aristide Briand as Foreign Minister. Millerand's interference in policy questions forced his removal on June 10, 1924, with his successor, Gaston Doumergue (1863–1937) serving as President until 1931.

France's ailing economy was plagued by a declining franc and inflation. Herriot's efforts to raise direct taxes, force higher levies on the rich, and lower interest rates on government bonds met with radical opposition, which sought indirect tax increases and cuts in government expenditures. Herriot was removed from office on April 10, 1925, and replaced by Paul Painlevé (1863–1933), who served for eight months.

Briand, who dominated French foreign affairs until 1932, pursued a policy of reconciliation with Germany and better relations with Europe's other pariah, the USSR. France granted diplomatic recognition to Soviet Russia in 1924, though relations quickly worsened because of the difficulty in getting the tsarist debt question resolved and the Soviets' use of their Paris embassy for espionage activities.

The Union Nationale (1926–1928)

The most crucial domestic problem faced by the Carte des Gauches was the declining franc, which by 1926 was only worth one-tenth of its prewar value. Its fall caused a political crisis so severe that the country had six cabinets over a nine-month period. Consequently, on July 15, 1926, Briand resigned his premiership and was succeeded by Poincare, who formed a Union National cabinet that had six former premiers in it. This coalition was backed by the Radicals as well as Conservatives and centrist parties in the legislature. To resolve the franc problem, the Chamber granted Poincare special authority. Over the next two years, he dramatically raised taxes and was able to get capital that had been taken out of the country reinvested in government bonds or other areas of the economy. By 1928, the franc had risen to 20 percent of its prewar value, and Poincare was considered a financial miracle worker. Unfortunately, the political and psychological scars left by the crisis would haunt France for two more decades.

WEIMAR GERMANY (1918–1929)

The dramatic collapse of the German war effort in the second half of 1918 ultimately created a political crisis that forced the abdication of the King and the creation of a German Republic on November 9.

Provisional Government

From the outset, the Provisional Government, formed of a coalition of Majority and Independent Social Democrats Socialists, was beset by divisions from within and threats of revolution throughout Germany. The first Chancellor was Friedrich Ebert, the Majority Socialist leader. On November 22, state leaders agreed to support a temporary government until elections could be held for a nationally elected legislature, which would draw up a constitution for the new republic.

Elections for the new National Constituent Assembly, which was to be based on proportional representation, gave no party a clear majority. A coalition of the Majority Socialists, the Catholic Center Party, and the German Democratic Party (DDP) dominated the new assembly. On February 11, 1919, the assembly met in the historic town of Weimar and selected Friedrich Ebert President of Germany. Two days later, Phillip Scheidemann (1865–1939) formed the first Weimar Cabinet and became its first Chancellor.

On August 11, 1919, a new constitution was promulgated, which provided for a bicameral legislature. The upper chamber, the Reichsrat, represented the Federal states, while the lower house, the Reichstag, with 647 delegates elected by universal suffrage, supplied the country's Chancellor and Cabinet. A president was also to be elected separately for a seven-year term. As a result of Article 48 of the Constitution, he could rule through emergency decree, though the Reichstag could take this authority from him.

Problems of the Weimar Republic (1919–1920)

The new government faced a number of serious domestic problems that severely challenged or undercut its authority. Its forced acceptance of the hated Friedensdiktat ("the dictated peace") seriously undermined its prestige, while the unsuccessful, though violent Communist Spartikist Rebellion (January 5–11, 1919) in Berlin created a climate of instability. This was followed three months later by the brief communist takeover of Bavaria, and the rightist Kapp Putsch (March 13–17, 1920) in the capital the following year.

The territorial, manpower, and economic losses suffered during and after the war, coupled with a $32.4 billion reparations debt, had a severe impact on the German economy and society, and severely handicapped the new government's efforts to establish a stable governing environment.

In an effort of good faith based on hopes of future reparation payment reductions, Germany borrowed heavily and made payments in kind to fulfill its early debt obligations. The result was a spiral of inflation later promoted by the Weimar government to underline Allied insensitivity to Germany's plight, that saw the mark go from 8.4 to the dollar in 1919 to 7,000 marks to the dollar by December 1922. After the Allied Reparations Commission declared Germany in default on its debt, the French and the Belgians occupied the Ruhr on January 11, 1923.

Chancellor Wilhelm Cuno (1876–1933) encouraged the Ruhr's Germans passively to resist the occupation, and printed worthless marks which dropped from 40,000 to the dollar in January 1923 to 4.2 trillion to the dollar eleven months later. The occupation ended on September 26, and helped prompt stronger Allied sympathy to Germany's payment difficulties, though the inflationary spiral had severe economic, social, and political consequences.

Weimar Politics (1919–1923)

Germany's economic and social difficulties deeply affected its infant democracy. From February 1919 to August 1923, the country had six Chancellors. In the aftermath of the Kapp Putsch, conservative demands for new elections resulted in a June defeat for the ruling coalition that saw the Democrats (DDP) lose seats to the German National People's Party (DVP) headed by Gustav Stresemann (1878–1929), and the Majority Socialists lose seats to the more reactionary Independent socialists. Conservative Germans blamed the Weimar Coalition for the hated Versailles "Diktat" with its war guilt and reparations terms, while leftist voters felt the government had forgotten its social and revolutionary ideals.

Growing right-wing discontent with the Weimar Government resulted in the assassination of the gifted head of the Catholic Center Party, Matthias Erzberger (1875–1921), on August 29, 1921, and the murder of Foreign Minister Walter Rathenau (1867–1922) on June 24, 1922. These were two of the most serious of over 350 political murders in Germany since the end of the war.

The Policies of Gustav Stresemann

The dominant figure in German politics from 1923 to 1929 was Gustav Stresemann, the founder and leader of the DVP. Though he served as Chancellor from August 12 to November 23, 1923, his prominence derives from his role as Foreign Minister from November 1923 until his death on October 3, 1929. He received the Nobel Peace Prize for his diplomatic efforts in 1926.

As Chancellor, Stresmann felt that the only road to recovery and treaty revision lay in adherence to the Versailles settlement and positive relations with France and its allies. Consequently, on September 26, he ended passive resistance in the Ruhr and began to search for a solution to Germany's reparations payment problem with France. To restore faith in the currency, the government introduced a new one, the Rentenmark, on November 20, 1923, that was equal to 1 billion old marks, and was backed by the mortgage value of Germany's farm and industrial land.

In an effort to come up with a more reasonable debt payment plan for Germany, the Western Allies developed the Dawes Plan. According to its terms, Germany was to begin small payments of a quarter of a billion dollars annually for four years, to be increased if its economy improved. In return, the Allies agreed to help revitalize Germany's ailing economy with a $200 million American loan and withdrawal from the Ruhr.

The crowning achievement in Stresemann's efforts to restore Germany to normal status in the European community was the Locarno Pact, December 1, 1925.

Weimar Politics (1924–1928)

Reichstag elections were held twice in 1924. The May 4 contest reflected a backlash against the country's economic difficulties, and saw the Communists win 3,700,000 votes and the Nazis almost 2 million, at the expense of the moderate parties. The December 7 elections were something of a vote on the Dawes Plan and economic revival, and saw the Nazis and the Communists lose almost a million votes apiece.

Following the death of President Ebert on February 28, 1925, two ballots were held for a new president, since none of the candidates won a majority on the first vote. On the second ballot on April 26, the Reichsblock, a coalition of Conservative parties, was able to get its candidate elected. War hero Paul von Hindenburg was narrowly elected. Hindenburg, who some conservatives hoped would turn the clock back, vowed to uphold Weimar's Constitution.

The elections of May 20, 1928, saw the Social Democrats get almost one-third of the popular vote which, blended with other moderate groups, created a stable, moderate majority in the Reichstag, which chose Hermann Müller (1876–1931) as Chancellor. The Nazis, who held 14 Reichstag seats at the end of 1924, lost one, while Communist strength increased.

ITALY

Like other countries that had fought in World War I, Italy had suffered greatly and gained little. Its economy, very weak even before the war broke out, relied heavily upon small-family agriculture, which contributed 40 percent of the country's GNP in 1920. Consequently, many of the social, political, and economic problems that plagued the country after the war could not be blamed solely on the conflict itself.

Italian Politics (1918–1919)

Strengthened by universal suffrage, and new proportional representation in Parliament, the Socialists doubled the number of seats to 156 in the Chamber of Deputies in the elections of November 16, 1919. The new Catholic People's Party gained 99 positions. The former party had little faith in the current state, and longed for its downfall, while the latter mixed conservative religious ideals with a desire for political moderation. No strong majority coalition emerged in this or the Parliament elected in May 1921 that was able to deal effectively with the country's numerous problems.

Government of Giovanni Giolitti (1920–1921)

From June 9, 1920 until June 26, 1921, Italy's Premier was Giovanni Giolitti (1842–1928), a gifted musician and pre-war figure who had dominated Italian politics between 1901 and 1914. His tactics, designed to resolve Italy's international conflicts and stay aloof of its domestic conflicts, exacerbated the country's problems. The Socialists took advantage of this atmosphere and promoted a series of strikes and other labor unrest in August and September 1920 that became violent and divided the country and the Socialist movement. Giolitti let the strikes run their course, and worked successfully to lower the government's deficit by 50 percent.

Benito Mussolini and Italian Fascism

Benito Mussolini, named by his Socialist blacksmith father after the Mexican revolutionary, Benito Juarez, was born in 1883. After a brief teaching stint, he went to Switzerland to avoid military service but returned and became active in Socialist politics. In 1912, he became editor of the Party's newspaper, *Avanti*. Several months after the outbreak of the World War, he broke with the party over involvement in the war, and began to espouse nationalistic ideas that became the nucleus of his fascist movement. He then opened his own newspaper, *Il Popolo d'Italia* (The People of Italy) to voice his ideas. Mussolini was drafted into military service in 1915 and was badly wounded two years later. After recuperating, he returned to his newspaper, where he blended his feelings about socialism and nationalism with an instinct for violence.

Mussolini, capitalizing on the sympathy of unfulfilled war veterans, disaffected nationalists, and those fearful of communism, formed the Fascio Italiano di Combattimento (Union of Combat) in Milan on March 23, 1919. Initially, Mussolini's movement had few followers, and it did badly in the November 1919 elections. However, Socialist strikes and unrest enabled him to convince Italians that he alone could bring stability and prosperity to their troubled country.

Fascism's most significant growth came in the midst of the Socialist unrest in 1920. Strengthened by large contributions from wealthy industrialists, Mussolini's black-suited Squadristi attacked Socialists, Communists, and ultimately, the government itself. Mussolini's followers won 35 seats in the legislative elections in May 1921, which also toppled the Giolitti cabinet.

The center of Fascist strength was in the streets of northern Italy, which Mussolini's followers, through violence, came to control. Mussolini now transformed his movement into the Fascist Party, dropped his socialist views, and began to emphasize the predominance of Italian nationalism.

The resignation of the Bonomi Cabinet on February 9, 1922, underlined the government's inability to maintain stability. In the meantime, the Fascists seized control of Bologna in May, and Milan in August. In response, Socialist leaders called for a nationwide strike on August 1, 1922; it was stopped by Fascist street violence within 24 hours. On October 24, 1922, Mussolini told followers that if he was not given power, he would "March on Rome." Three days later, Fascists began to seize control of other cities, while 26,000 began to move towards the capital. The government responded with a declaration of martial law, which the king, Victor Emmanuel III (1869–1947), refused to approve. On October 29, the king asked Mussolini to form a new government as Premier of Italy.

Mussolini's Consolidation of Power

Using tactics similar to those D'Annunzio used to seize Fiume earlier, Mussolini built a government made up of a number of sympathetic parties. Mussolini formed a coalition cabinet that included all major parties except the Communists and the

Socialists. The Chamber of Deputies approved his government and granted him quasi-dictatorial powers for a year.

In violence-marred elections on April 6, 1924, the Fascists gained 60 percent of the popular vote and two-thirds of the Chamber's seats. In response to Fascist campaign tactics, Giacomo Matteotti, a Socialist Chamber member, attacked the Fascists for their misdeeds on May 30. Several days later, Fascist supporters kidnapped and murdered him, provoking his supporters to unwisely walk out of the Chamber in protest. Momentarily, Italy was stunned, and Mussolini was vulnerable. The opposition asked the king to dismiss Mussolini, but he refused.

Consolidation of the Dictatorship

Beginning in 1925, Mussolini arrested opponents, closed newspapers, and eliminated civil liberties in a new reign of terror. On December 24, 1925, the legislature's powers were greatly limited, while those of Mussolini were increased as the new Head of State. Throughout 1926, Mussolini intensified his control over the country with legislation that outlawed strikes and created the syndicalist corporate system. A failed assassination attempt prompted the "Law for the Defense of the State" of November 25, 1926, that created a Special Court to deal with political crimes and introduced the death penalty for threats against the king, his family, or the Head of State.

The Fascist Party

In December 1922, Mussolini created a Grand Council of Fascism made up of the Party's principle leaders. In 1928, the Grand Council became the most important organ of government in Italy. The structure of the Fascist Party did not reach final form until November 12, 1932. It was defined as a "civil militia" with the *Duce* (Mussolini) as its head. Its day-to-day affairs were run by the National Directorate headed by a Secretary, with two Vice Secretaries, an Administrative Secretary, and six other members. The Secretary of the National Directorate belonged to the Grand Council. The Party's Provincial Secretaries, appointed by Mussolini, oversaw local Party organizations, the *Fasci di Combattimento*. There were also separate Fascist youth organizations such as the *Piccole Italiane* (under 12) and the *Giovane Italiane* (over 12) for girls; the *Balilla* (8–14), the *Avanguardisti* (14–18), and the *Giovani Fascisti* (18–21) for boys. After 1927, only those who had been members of the *Balilla* and the *Avanguardisti* could be Party members.

The Syndicalist-Corporate System

On April 3, 1926, the Rocco Labor Law created syndicates or organizations for all workers and employers in Italy. It also outlawed strikes and walkouts. Later altered, it created nine syndicate corporations: four for workers and four for employers in each of the major segments of the economy and a ninth for professionals and artists.

On July 1, 1926, Corporations were created to coordinate activities between the worker-employer syndicates, while later that year a Ministry of Corporations came into existence. On February 5, 1934, a Law on Corporations created 22 such bodies that oversaw every facet of the economy, coordinated management-labor relations and economic production and shipment in every segment of the economy. Each Corporation was overseen by a Minister or other important government or Party official, who sat on the National Council of Corporations that was headed by Mussolini.

Foreign Policy

The nation's wish for post-war peace and stability saw Italy participate in all of the international developments in the 1920s aimed at securing normalcy in relations with its neighbors. Because Italy did not receive its desired portions of Dalmatia at the Paris Peace Conference, Italian nationalist Gabriele D'Annunzio seized Fiume on the Adriatic in the fall of 1919. D'Annunzio's daring gesture as well as his deep sense of Italian national pride deeply affected Mussolini. However, in the atmosphere of detente prevalent in Europe at the time, he agreed to settle the dispute with Yugoslavia in a treaty on January 27, 1924, which ceded most of the port to Italy, and the surrounding area to Yugoslavia.

In the fall of 1923, Mussolini used the assassination of Italian officials, who were working to resolve a Greek-Albanian border dispute, to seize the island of Corfu. Within a month, however, the British and the French convinced him to return the island for an indemnity.

SOVIET RUSSIA

Soon after the Bolshevik seizure of power, opposition forces began to gather throughout Russia that sought to challenge Soviet authority or use the occasion to break up the Russian Empire.

Origins of the Russian Civil War (1918)

Opposition to the Soviet takeover had begun immediately after Lenin's seizure of Petrograd. General M.V. Alexeiev (1857–1918) had formed a Volunteer Army, whose command was shared and later taken over by General Anton Denikin (1872–1947), who had fled to the Don area in early 1918. Another center of White resistance was created first by Socialist Revolutionaries at Omsk, followed later by a government there under Admiral Alexander Kolchak (1873–1920), who was backed by Czech forces and would declare himself Supreme Commander of White forces in the Civil War. In time, most of the major White Commanders would recognize Kolchak's authority.

To meet these threats, Lenin appointed Leon Trotsky as Commissar of War on March 13, 1918, with orders to build a Red Army. By the end of the year, using partial conscription, the new Soviet forces began to retake some of the areas earlier captured by the Whites.

The Russian Civil War (1919–1920)

The White forces, constantly weakened by lack of unified command and strategy, enjoyed their greatest successes in 1919, but by early 1920, White fortunes had begun to collapse. On January 4, Kolchak abdicated in favor of Denikin, and was turned over by his Czech protectors to the Soviets who executed him on February 7. In the meantime, Denikin's capital, Rostov, was taken by the Red Army and his command was taken over later by General Peter Wrangel (1878–1928), whose forces were beaten that fall. Both armies were evacuated from the Crimea.

The Polish-Soviet War (1920)

The new Polish state under Marshal Józef Pilsudski (1867–1935) sought to take advantage of the Civil War in Russia to retake territory lost to Russia during the Polish Partitions in the late 18th century. Polish forces invaded the Ukraine on April 25, and took Kiev two weeks later. A Soviet counteroffensive reached Warsaw by mid-August, but was stopped by the Poles. Both sides concluded an armistice on October 12 and signed the Treaty of Riga on March 12, 1921, that placed Poland's border east of the Curzon Line.

Domestic Policy and Upheaval (1918–1921)

In order to provide more food to Russia's cities, the Soviet government implemented a "War Communism" program that centered around forced grain seizures and class war between "Kulaks" (ill-defined middle-class peasants) and others. All major industry was also nationalized. These policies triggered rebellions against the seizures that saw the amount of land under cultivation and the total grain produced drop between 1918–1921.

The Civil War and War Communism had brought economic disaster and social upheaval throughout the country. On March 1, 1921, as the Soviet leadership met to decide on policies to guide the country in peace, a naval rebellion broke out at the Kronstadt naval base. The Soviet leadership sent Trotsky to put down the rebellion, which he did brutally by March 18.

The New Economic Policy (1921–1927)

The Kronstadt rebellion strengthened Lenin's resolve to initiate new policies approved at the X Party Congress that would end grain seizures and stimulate agricultural production. Termed the New Economic Policy (NEP), the government maintained control over the "Commanding Heights" of the economy (foreign trade, transportation, and heavy industry) while opening other sectors to limited capitalist development. It required the peasants to pay the government a fixed acreage tax, and allowed them to sell surplus for profit. Once the government had resolved the inconsistencies in agricultural and industrial output and pricing, the NEP began to near 1913 production levels. The country remained dominated by small farms and peasant communes. Industrial production also improved, though it was handicapped by outdated technology and equipment which would hinder further output or expansion beyond 1913 levels.

The Death of Lenin and the Rise of Josef Stalin

Vladimir Ilyich Lenin, the founder of the Soviet State, suffered a serious stroke on May 26, 1922 and a second in December of that year. As he faced possible forced retirement or death, he composed a secret "testament" that surveyed the strengths and weaknesses of his possible successor, Stalin, who he feared would abuse power. Unfortunately, his third stroke prevented him from removing Stalin from his position as General Secretary. Lenin died on January 21, 1924.

Iosef Vissarionovich Dzugashvili (Joseph Stalin, 1879–1953) was born in the Georgian village of Gori. He became involved in Lenin's Bolshevik movement in his 20s and became Lenin's expert on minorities. Intimidated by the Party's intellectuals, he took over numerous, and in some cases, seemingly unimportant Party organizations after the Revolution and transformed them into important bases of power. Among them were Politburo (Political Bureau), which ran the country; the Orgburo (Organizational Bureau), which Stalin headed, and which appointed people to positions in groups that implemented Politiburo decisions, the Inspectorate (Rabkrin, Commissariat of the Workers' and Peasants' Inspectorate) which tried to eliminate Party corruption, and the Secretariat, which worked with all Party organs and set the Politburo's agenda. Stalin served as the Party's General Secretary after 1921.

Leon Trotsky

Lev Davidovich Bronstein (Trotsky, 1879–1940) was a Jewish intellectual active in Menshevik revolutionary work, particularly in the 1905 Revolution. He joined Lenin's movement in 1917, and soon became his right-hand man. He was Chairman of the Petrograd Soviet, headed the early Brest-Litovsk negotiating team, served as Foreign Commissar, and was father of the Red Army. A brilliant organizer and theorist, Trotsky was also brusque and, some felt, overbearing.

The Struggle for Power (1924–1925)

The death of Lenin in 1924 intensified a struggle for control of the Party between Stalin and Trotsky and their respective supporters. Initially, the struggle, which began in 1923, appeared to be between three men: Lev Kamenev (1883–1936), head of the Moscow Soviet, Grigory Zinoviev (1883–1936), Party chief in Petrograd and head of the Comintern, and Trotsky. The former two, allied with Stalin, presented a formidable opposition group to Trotsky. Initially, the struggle centered around Trotsky's accusation that the trio was drifting away from Lenin's commitment to the revolution and "bureaucratizing" the Party. Trotsky believed in the theory of "permanent revolution" that blended an ongoing commitment to world revolution and building socialism with the development of a heavy industrial base in Russia.

Stalin responded with the concept of "Socialism in One Country," that committed the country to building up its socialist base regardless of the status of world revolution. In the fall of 1924, Trotsky attacked Zinoviev and Kamenev for the drift away from open discussion in the Party and for not supporting Lenin's initial scheme to seize power in November 1917. As a result, Trotsky was removed as Commissar of War on January 16, 1925, while two months later the Party accepted "Socialism in One Country" as its official governing doctrine.

The Struggle for Power (1925–1927)

Zinoviev and Kamenev, who agreed with the principles of "Permanent Revolution," began to fear Stalin and soon found themselves allied against him and his new

Rightist supporters, Nikolai Bukharin, Alexis Rykov, Chairman of the Council of People's Commisars (Cabinet), and Mikhail Tomsky, head of the trade unions.

The Fourteenth Party Congress rebuffed Kamenev and Zinoviev, and accepted Bukharin's economic policies. It demoted Kamenev to candidate status on the Politburo, while adding a number of Stalin's supporters to that body as well as the Central Committee. Afterwards, Kamenev and Zinoviev joined Trotsky in their dispute with Stalin. As a result, Trotsky and Kamenev lost their seats on the Politburo, while Zinoviev was removed as head of the Comintern.

In early 1927, Zinoviev and Trotsky were thrown out of the party, and Trotsky forced into exile in central Asia.

Soviet Constitutional Development

Soviet Russia adopted two constitutions in 1918 and 1924. The first reflected the ideals of the state's founders and created the Russian Soviet Federative Socialist Republic (RSFSR) as the country's central administrative unit. An All-Russian Congress of Soviets was the government's legislative authority, while a large Central Executive Committee (CEC), aided by a cabinet or Council of People's Commissars (Sovnarkom) wielded executive power. The Communist Party was not mentioned in the 1918 constitution or in the 1924 constitution. The 1924 document was similar to the earlier one, but also reflected the changes brought about by the creation of the Union of Soviet Socialist Republics (USSR) two years earlier. The CEC was divided into a Council of the Union and a Council of Nationalities, while a new Supreme Court and Procurator were added to the governmental structure. A similar political division was duplicated on lower administrative levels throughout the country. The new constitution also created a Supreme Court and a Procurator responsible to the CEC.

Foreign Policy, 1918–1929

Soviet efforts after the October Revolution to openly foment revolution throughout Europe and Asia, its refusal to pay czarist debts, and international outrage over the murder of the royal family in 1919 isolated the country. However, adoption of the NEP required more integration with the outside world to rebuild the broken economy.

Russia and Germany, Europe's post-World War I pariahs, drew closer out of necessity. By the early 1920s, Russia was receiving German technological help in weapons development while the Soviets helped train German pilots and others illegally. Soviet Russia and Germany agreed to cancel their respective war debts and to establish formal diplomatic relations.

By 1921, the British concluded a trade accord with the Soviet government and in 1924 extended formal diplomatic recognition to the USSR. Strong public reaction to this move, coupled with the publication of the "Zinoviev Letter" of unknown origin helped topple the pro-Soviet MacDonald government, because the letter encouraged subversion of the British government. Relations were formally severed in 1927 because of Communist support of a British coal mine strike, discovery of spies in a Soviet trade delegation, and Soviet claims that it hoped to use China as a means of hurting England.

The Soviets worked to consolidate their sphere-of-influence acquired earlier in Mongolia, and helped engineer the creation of an independent, though strongly pro-Soviet, People's Republic of Mongolia in 1924.

In China the Soviets helped found a young Chinese Communist Party (CCP) in 1921. However, when it became apparent that Sun Yat-sen's (1866–1925) revolutionary Kuomintang (KMT) was more mature than the infant CCP, the Soviets encouraged an alliance between its Party and this movement. Sun's successor, Chiang Kai-shek (1887–1975), was deeply suspicious of the Communists and made their destruction part of his effort to militarily unite China.

Founded in 1919, the Soviet-controlled Comintern (Third International or Communist International) sought to coordinate the revolutionary activities of communist parties abroad, though it often conflicted with Soviet diplomatic interests. It became an effectively organized body by 1924, and was completely Stalinized by 1928.

EUROPE IN CRISIS: DEPRESSION AND DICTATORSHIP (1929–1935)

England: Ramsay MacDonald and the Depression (1929–1931)

Required by law to hold elections in 1929, the May 30 contest saw the Conservatives drop to 260 seats, Labour rise to 287, and the Liberals to 59. Ramsay MacDonald formed a minority Labour government that would last until 1931. The most serious problem facing the country was the Depression, which caused unemployment to reach 1,700,000 by 1930 and over 3 million, or 25 percent of the labor force, by 1932. To meet growing budget deficits caused by heavy subsidies to the unemployed, a special government commission recommended budget cuts and tax increases. Cabinet and labor union opposition helped reduce the total for the cuts (from 78 million to 22 million), but this could not help restore confidence in the government, which fell on August 24, 1931.

The "National Government" (1931–1935)

The following day, King George VI (1895–1952) helped convince MacDonald to return to office as head of a National Coalition cabinet made up of 4 Conservatives, 4 Labourites, and 2 Liberals. The Labour Party refused to recognize the new government and ejected MacDonald and Philip Snowden (1864–1937) from the Party. MacDonald's coalition swept the November 1931 general elections winning 554 of 615 seats.

The British government abandoned the gold standard on September 21, 1931, and adopted a series of high tariffs on imports. Unemployment peaked at 3 million in 1932 and dropped to 2 million two years later.

In 1931, the British government implemented the Statute of Westminster, which created the British Commonwealth of Nations, granting its members political equality, and freedom to reject any act passed by Parliament that related to a Dominion state.

The Election of 1935

MacDonald resigned his position in June 1935 because of ill health, and was succeeded by Stanley Baldwin, whose conservative coalition won 428 seats in new elections in November.

France Under André Tardieu (1929–1932)

On July 27, 1929, Poincaré resigned as Premier because of ill health. Over the next three years, the dominant figure in French politics was André Tardieu (1876–1945), who headed or served in Moderate cabinets. Tardieu tried to initiate political changes along American or British lines in order to create a stable two-party system. He convinced the Laval government and the Chamber to accept electing its members by a plurality vote, though the Senate rejected it. In 1930, the government passed France's most important social welfare legislation, the National Workingmen's Insurance Law. It provided various forms of financial aid for illness, retirement, and death.

The Depression did not hit France until late 1931, but it took four years to begin to recover from it.

Return of the Cartel des Gauches (1932–1934)

The defeat of the Moderates and the return of the leftists in the elections of May 1, 1932, reflected growing concern over the economy and the failed efforts of the government to respond to the country's problems.

France remained plagued by differences over economic reform between the Radicals and the Socialists. The latter advocated nationalization of major factories, expanded social reforms, and public works programs for the unemployed, while the Radicals sought a reduction in government spending. This instability was also reflected in the fact that there were six Cabinets between June 1932 and February 1934.

The government's inability to deal with the country's economic and political problems saw the emergence of a number of radical groups from across the political spectrum. Some of the more prominent were the Fascist Francistes, the Solidarite Française, the "Cagoulards" (Comite Secret d'Action Révoluntionnaire), the Parti Populaire Française (PPF) and the Jeunesses Patriotes. Not as radical, though still on the right were the Croix de Feu and the Action Française. At the other extreme was the French Communist Party.

The growing influence of these groups exploded on February 6, 1934, around a scandal involving a con-man with government connections, Serge Stavisky. After his suicide on the eve of his arrest in December 1933, the scandal and his reported involvement with high government officials stimulated a growing crescendo of criticism that culminating in riots between rightist and leftist factions that resulted in 15 dead and 1,500 to 1,600 injured. The demonstrations and riots, viewed by some as a rightist effort to seize power, brought about the collapse of the Daladier government. He was immediately succeeded by ex-President Gaston Doumergue, who put together a coalition cabinet dominated by Moderates as well as Radicals and Rightists. It contained six former premiers and Marshal Pétain.

Struggle for Stability (1934–1935)

The accession of Gaston Doumergue (who had been President from 1924 to 1931) and his "National Union" cabinet, stabilized the public crisis. The new Premier (influenced by Tardieu) used radio to try to convince the public of the need to increase the power of the President, (Albert Lebrum; 1932–1940), and to enable the Premier to dissolve the legislature. Discontent with Doumergue's tactics resulted in resignations from his Cabinet and its fall in November 1934.

Between November 1934 and June 1935, France had two more governments under Pierre-Etienne Flandin and F. Bouisson. The situation stabilized somewhat with the selection of Pierre Laval as Premier, who served from June 1935 through January 1936. Laval's controversial policies, strengthened by the ability to pass laws without legislative approval, were to deflate the economy, cut government expenditures, and remain on the gold standard. Laval's government fell in early 1936.

GERMANY

The Young Plan

One of the last accomplishments of Stresemann before his death on October 3 was the Young Plan, an altered reparations proposal that required Germany to make yearly payments for 59 years that varied from 1.6 to 2.4 billion Reichsmarks. In return, the Allies removed all foreign controls on Germany's economy and agreed to leave the Rhineland the following year. Efforts by the conservative extremists to stop Reichstag adoption of the Young Plan failed miserably, while a national referendum on the reactionary bill suffered the same fate.

Germany and the Depression

The Depression had a dramatic effect on the German economy and politics. German exports, which had peaked at 13.5 billion marks in 1929, fell to 12 billion marks in 1930, and to 5.7 billion marks two years later. Imports suffered the same fate, going from 14 billion marks in 1928 to 4.7 billion marks in 1932. The country's national income dropped 20 percent during this period, while unemployment rose from 1,320,000 in 1929 to 6 million by January 1932. This meant that 43 percent of the German work force were without jobs (compared to one-quarter of the work force in the U.S.).

The Rise of Adolf Hitler and Nazism

The history of Nazism is deeply intertwined with that of its leader, Adolf Hitler. Adolf Hitler was born on April 20, 1889, in the Austrian village of Braunau am Inn. A frustrated artist, he moved to Vienna where he unsuccessfully tried to become a student in the Vienna Academy of Fine Arts. He then became an itinerant artist, living in hovels, until the advent of the World War, which he welcomed. He served four years and emerged a decorated corporal with a mission to enter politics.

In 1919, Hitler joined the German Workers Party (DAP), which he soon took over and renamed the National Socialist German Workers Party (NAZI). In 1920, the Party adopted a 25-point program that included treaty revision, anti-Semitism, economic, and other social changes. They also created a defense cadre of the *Sturm-abteilung* (SA), "Storm Troopers," or "brown shirts," which was to help the party seize power.

The Beer Hall Putsch (1923)

In the midst of the country's severe economic crisis in 1923, the Party, which now had 55,000 members, tried to seize power, first by a march on Berlin, and then, when this seemed impossible, on Munich. The march was stopped by police, and Hitler and his supporters were arrested. Their trial, which Hitler used to voice Nazi ideals, gained him a national reputation. Though sentenced to five years imprisonment, he was released after eight months. While incarcerated, he dictated *Mein Kampf* to Rudolf Hess.

The Nazi Movement (1924–1929)

Hitler's failed coup and imprisonment convinced him to seek power through legitimate political channels, which would require transforming the Nazi Party. To do this, he reasserted singular control over the movement from 1924 to 1926. Party districts were set up throughout Germany, overseen by *gauleiters* personally appointed by Hitler.

They were subdivided into Kreise (districts), and then Ortsgruppen (local chapters). A court system, the *Uschla*, oversaw the Party structure. The Party grew from 27,000 in 1925 to 108,000 in 1929. A number of new leaders emerged at this time, including Joseph Goebbels (1897–1945), who became Party Chief in Berlin and later Hitler's propaganda chief, and Heinrich Himmler (1900–1945), who became head of Hitler's private body guard, the SS (*Schutzstaffel*), in 1929.

Weimar Politics (1930–1933)

Germany's economic woes and the government's seeming inability to deal with them underlined the weaknesses of the country's political system and provided the Nazis with new opportunities.

Reichstag Elections of September 14, 1930

The September 14 elections surprised everyone. In new elections in September 1930, the Nazis saw their 1928 vote jump from 800,000 to 6.5 million (18.3 percent of the vote), which gave them 107 Reichstag seats, second only to the Social Democrats, who fell from 152 to 143 seats. Heinrich Brüenig (1885–1970), however, continued to serve as Chancellor of a weak coalition with the support of Hindenburg and rule by presidential decree. His policies failed to resolve the country's growing economic dilemmas.

Presidential Elections of 1932

Hindenburg's seven-year presidential term expired in 1932, and he was convinced to run for reelection to stop Hitler from becoming president in the first ballot of March 13. Hitler got only 30 percent of the vote (11.3 million) to Hindenburg's 49.45 percent (18.6 million).

The von Papen Chancellorship

On June 1, Bruenig was replaced by Franz von Papen (1879–1969), who formed a government made up of aristocratic conservatives and others that he and Hindenburg hoped would keep Hitler from power. He held new elections on July 31 that saw the Nazis win 230 Reichstag seats with 37 percent of the vote (13.7 million), and the Communists 89 seats. Offered the Vice-Chancellorship and an opportunity to join a coalition government, Hitler refused. Von Papen, paralyzed politically, ruled by presidential decree. Von Papen dissolved the Reichstag on September 12, and held new elections on November 6. The Nazis only got 30 percent of the vote and 196 Reichstag seats, while the Communists made substantial gains (120 seats from 89). Von Papen resigned the chancellorship in favor of Kurt von Schleicher (1882–1934), one of the president's closest advisers.

Hitler Becomes Chancellor

Von Papen joined with Hitler to undermine Schleicher, and convinced Hindenburg to appoint Hitler as Chancellor and head of a new coalition cabinet with three seats for the Nazis. Hitler dissolved the Reichstag and called for new elections on March 5. Using Presidential decree powers, he initiated a violent anti-communist campaign that included the lifting of certain press and civil freedoms. On February 27, the Reichstag burned, which enabled Hitler to get Hindenburg to issue the "Ordinances for the Protection of the German State and Nation," that removed all civil and press liberties as part of a "revolution" against Communism. In the Reichstag elections of March 5, the Nazis only got 43.9 percent of the vote and 288 Reichstag seats but, through an alliance with the Nationalists, got majority control of the legislature.

Hitler now intensified his campaign against his political and other opponents, placing many of them in newly-opened concentration camps. He also convinced Hindenburg to issue the Enabling Act on March 21 that allowed his Cabinet to pass laws and treaties without legislative backing for four years. The Reichstag gave him its full legal approval two days later, since many felt it was the only way legally to maintain some influence over his government.

Once Hitler had full legislative power, he began a policy of *gleichschaltung* (coordination) to bring all independent organizations and agencies throughout Germany under his control. All political parties were outlawed or forced to dissolve, and on July 14, 1933, the Nazi Party became the only legal party in Germany. In addition, German state authority was reduced and placed under Nazi-appointed *Statthallter* (governors), while the Party throughout Germany was divided into *Gaue* (districts) under a Nazi-selected *Gauleiter*. In addition, non-Aryans and Nazi opponents were removed from the civil service, the court system, and higher education. On May 2, 1933, the government declared strikes illegal, abolished labor unions, and later forced all workers to join the German Labor Front (DAF) under Robert Ley. In 1934 the Reichsrat was abolished and a special People's Court was created to handle cases of treason. Finally, the secret police or Gestapo (*Geheime Staatspolizei*) was created on April 24, 1933 under Hermann Göring to deal with opponents and operate concentration camps. The Party had its own security branch, the SD (*Sicherheitsdienst*) under Reinhard Heydrich.

Hitler Consolidates Power

A growing conflict over the direction of the Nazi "revolution" and the power of the SA *vis a vis* the SS and the German army had been brewing since Hitler took power. Ernst Röhm (1887–1934), head of the SA, wanted his forces to become the nucleus of a new German army headed by himself, while the military, Hitler, and the SS sought ways to contain his growing arrogance and independence. The solution was the violent Röhm purge on the night of June 30, 1934 ("The Night of the Long Knives"), coordinated by the Gestapo and the SS, that resulted in the arrest and murder of Röhm plus 84 SA leaders, as well as scores of other opponents that Hitler decided to eliminate under the cloud of his purge.

The final barrier to Hitler's full consolidation of power in Germany was overcome with the death of Hindenburg on August 2, 1934. Hitler now combined the offices of President and Chancellor, and required all civil servants and workers to take a personal oath to him as the "Führer of the German Reich and people."

Religion and Anti-Semitism

A state Protestant church of "German Christians" under a Bishop of the Reich, Ludwig Muller, was created in 1934. An underground opposition "Confessing Church" was formed under Martin Niemöller that suffered from severe persecution. On July 8, 1933, the government signed a concordat with the Vatican that promised to allow traditional Catholic rights to continue in Germany. Unfortunately, the Nazis severely restricted Catholic religious practice, which created growing friction with the Vatican.

From the inception of the Nazi state in 1933, anti-Semitism was a constant theme and practice in all *Gleichschaltung* and nazification efforts. Illegal intimidation and harassment of Jews was coupled with rigid enforcement of civil service regulations that forbade employment of non-Aryans. This first wave of anti-Semitic activity culminated with the passage of the Nuremburg Laws on September 15, 1935, that deprived Jews of German citizenship and outlawed sexual or marital relations between Jews and other Germans, thus effectively isolating them from the mainstream of German society.

International Affairs

Hitler's international policies were closely linked to his rebuilding efforts to give him a strong economic and military base for an active, aggressive, independent foreign policy. On October 14, 1933, Hitler had his delegates walk out of the Disarmament Conference because he felt the Allied powers had reneged on an earlier promise to grant Germany arms equality. The Reich simultaneously quit the League of Nations. On January 26, 1934, Germany signed a non-aggression pact with Poland, which ended Germany's traditional anti-Polish foreign policy and broke France's encirclement of Germany via the Little Entente. This was followed by the Saarland's overwhelming decision to return to Germany. The culmination of Hitler's foreign policy moves, though, came with his March 15, 1935, announcement that Germany would no longer be bound by the military restrictions of the Treaty of Versailles, that it had already created an air force (Luftwaffe), and that the Reich would institute a draft to create an army of 500,000 men. Allied opposition to this move was compromised by England's decision to conclude a naval pact with Hitler on June 18, 1935, that restricted German naval tonnage (excluding submarines) to 35 percent of that for England.

ITALY

Fascist Economic Reforms

Increased economic well-being and growth were the promised results of Mussolini's restructuring of the economic system, while the general goals of the regime were to increase production through more efficient methods and land reclamation, with less dependency upon outside resources.

Efforts to increase land under cultivation through reclamation projects were handicapped by Mussolini's emphasis on model propaganda projects, though the government had reclaimed 12 million acres by 1938. In fact, the small farmer suffered under these policies, because of Mussolini's quiet support of the larger landowner. Regardless, grain products did increase from 4,479 metric tons in 1924 to 8,184 metric tons in 1938, which enabled the government to cut grain imports by 75 percent. On the other hand, land needed to produce other agricultural products was used to increase wheat and grain output.

To aid firms affected by the Depression, the government created the I.R.I. (*Instituto per la ricostruzione industriale*) which helped most big companies while smaller unsuccessful ones failed. The result was that the vast majority of Italy's major industry came under some form of government oversight. Italian production figures are unimpressive during this period. The overall impact of Mussolini's economic programs saw the country's national income rise 15 percent from 1925 to 1935, with only a 10 percent per capita increase during this period.

Church and State

Until Mussolini's accession to power, the pope had considered himself a prisoner in the Vatican. In 1926, Mussolini's government began talks to resolve this issue, which resulted in the Lateran Accords of February 11, 1929. Italy recognized the Vatican as an independent state, with the pope as its head, while the papacy recognized Italian independence. Catholicism was made the official state religion of Italy, and religious teaching was required in all secondary schools. Church marriages were now fully legal, while the state could veto papal appointments of bishops. In addition, the clergy would declare loyalty to the Italian state. Additionally, the government agreed to pay the Church a financial settlement of 1.75 billion lira for the seizure of Church territory in 1860–1870.

A conflict soon broke out over youth education and in May 1931 Mussolini dissolved the Catholic Action's youth groups. The pope responded with an encyclical, *Non abbiano bisogno*, which defended these groups, and criticized the Fascist deification of the state. Mussolini agreed later that year to allow Catholic Action to resume limited youth work.

Foreign Policy

Since the late 1920s, Mussolini began to support German claims for revision of the Treaty of Versailles to strengthen ties with that country and to counterbalance France, a nation he strongly disliked. These goals were current in his Four Power Pact proposal of March 1933 that envisioned a concert of powers—England, France, Italy, and Germany—that included arms parity for the Reich. French opposition to arms equality and treaty revision, plus concerns that the new consortium would replace the League of Nations, saw an extremely weakened agreement signed in June that was ultimately accepted only by Italy and Germany.

In an effort to counter the significance of France's Little Entente with Czechoslovakia, Yugoslavia, and Rumania, Mussolini concluded the Rome Protocols with Austria and Hungary which created a protective bond of friendship between the three countries. The first test of the new alliance between Italy and Austria came in July 1934, when German-directed Nazis tried to seize control of the Austrian government. Mussolini, opposed to any German Anschluss with Austria, mobilized Italian forces along the northern Renner Pass as a warning to Hitler. The coup collapsed from lack of direct German aid.

In response to Hitler's announcement of German rearmament in violation of the Treaty of Versailles on March 16, 1935, France, England, and Italy met at Stresa in northern Italy on April 11–14, and concluded agreements that pledged joint military collaboration if Germany moved against Austria or along the Rhine. The three states criticized Germany's recent decision to remilitarize and appealed to the Council of the League of Nations on the matter.

Ethiopia (Abyssinia) became an area of strong Italian interest in the 1880s. The coastal region was slowly brought under Italian control until the Italian defeat at Ethiopian hands at Adowa in 1894. In 1906, the country's autonomy was recognized and in 1923 it joined the League of Nations. Mussolini, driven by a strong patriotic desire to avenge the humiliation at Adowa and to create an empire to thwart domestic concerns over the country's economic problems, searched for the proper moment to seize the country. Acquisition of Ethiopia would enable him to join Italy's two colonies of Eritrea and Somalia, which could become a new area of Italian colonization.

Mussolini, who had been preparing for war with Ethiopia since 1932, established a military base at Wal Wal in Ethiopian territory. Beginning in December 1934, a series of minor conflicts took place between the two countries, which gave Mussolini an excuse to plan for the full takeover of the country in the near future.

Mussolini refused to accept arbitration over Ethiopia, and used Europe's growing concern over Hitler's moves there to cover his own secret designs. On October 2, 1935, Italy invaded Ethiopia, while the League of Nations, which had received four appeals from Ethiopia since January about Italian territorial transgressions, finally voted to adopt economic sanctions against Mussolini. Mussolini was convinced he could act with impunity when he realized the League was reluctant to do more than make verbal objections to Italian actions. Unfortunately, the League failed to stop shipments of oil to Italy and continued to allow it to use the Suez

Canal. On May 9, 1936, Italy formally annexed the country and joined it to Somalia and Eritrea, which now became known as Italian East Africa.

SOVIET RUSSIA

The period from 1929 to 1935 was a time of tremendous upheaval for the USSR as Stalin tried to initiate major programs of collectivization of agriculture and massive industrial development.

Collectivization of Soviet Agriculture

At the end of 1927, Stalin, concerned over problems of grain supply, ordered the gradual consolidation of the country's 25 million small farms, on which 80 percent of the population lived, into state-run collective farms.

According to the First Five Year Plan's goals (1928–1932), agricultural output was to rise 150 percent over five years, and 20 percent of the country's private farms were to be transformed into collectives.

In an effort to link agricultural efficiency with heavy industrial development, Stalin decided by the end of 1929 to rapidly collectivize the country's entire agriculture system. Because of earlier resistance from peasants between 1927 and 1929, Stalin ordered war against the kulak or "middle class" peasant class. Some sources claim that as many as 5 million ill-defined kulaks were internally deported during this period.

The above, combined with forced grain seizures, triggered massive, bloody resistance in the countryside. Though half of the nation's peasants were forced onto collectives during this period, they destroyed a great deal of Russia's livestock in the process. In the spring of 1930, Stalin called a momentary halt to the process, which prompted many peasants to leave the state farms.

Over the next seven years, the entire Soviet system was collectivized, and all peasants forced onto state farms. The two major types of farms were the *sovkhoz*, where peasants were paid for their labor, and the *kovkhoz*, or collective farm, where the peasants gave the government a percentage of their crops and kept the surplus.

Direct and indirect deaths from Stalin's collectivization efforts totaled 14.5 million. Grain production levels did not reach 1928 levels until 1935. Collectivization broke the back of rural peasant independence and created a totalitarian network of control throughout the countryside. It also undercut Stalin's base of political support within the Party.

Industrialization

Stalin, concerned that Russia would fall irreparably behind the West industrially, hoped to achieve industrial parity with the West in a decade. To stimulate workers, labor unions lost their autonomy and workers, including impressed peasants, were forced to work at locations and under conditions determined by the state. A special "Turnover" tax was placed on all goods throughout the country to help pay for industrialization.

The industrialization goals of the First Five Year Plan, were to increase total industrial production by 236 percent, heavy industry by 330 percent, coal, 200 percent, electrical output, 400 percent, and pig-iron production, 300 percent. Workers were to increase their efforts over 100 percent. Efficiency was also a hallmark of this program, and production costs were to drop by over a third, and prices by a quarter.

In most instances, the Plan's unrealistic goals were hard to meet. Regardless, steel production doubled, though it fell short of the Plan's goals, as did oil and hard coal output. Total industrial production, however, did barely surpass the Plan's expectations.

The Second Five Year Plan (1933–1937) was adopted by the Seventeenth Party Congress in early 1934. Its economic and production targets were less severe than the first Plan, and thus more was achieved. By the end of the Second Plan, Soviet Russia had emerged as a leading world industrial power, though at great costs. It gave up quality for quantity, and created tremendous social and economic discord that still affects the USSR. The tactics used by Stalin to institute his economic reforms formed the nucleus of his totalitarian system, while reaction to them within the Party led to the Purges.

Party Politics and the Origin of the Purges

The tremendous upheaval caused by forced collectivization, blended with the remnants of the Rightist conflict with Stalin, prompted the Soviet leader to initiate one of the country's periodic purges of the Party. Approved by the top leadership, suspected opponents were driven from Party ranks, while Zinoviev and Kamenev were briefly exiled to Siberia. Continued uncertainty over the best policies to follow after the initiation of the Second Five Year Plan ended with the murder at the end of 1934 of Sergei Kirov, Stalin's supposed heir, and Leningrad party chief. Though the reasons for Kirov's murder are still unclear, his more liberal tendencies, plus his growing popularity, made him a threat to the Soviet leader. In the spring of 1935, the recently renamed and organized secret police, the NKVD, oversaw the beginnings of a new, violent Purge that eradicated 70 percent of the 1934 Central Committee, and a large percentage of the upper military ranks. Stalin sent between 8 and 9 million to camps and prisons, and caused untold deaths before the Purges ended in 1938.

Foreign Policy (1929–1935)

The period from 1929 to 1933 saw the USSR retreat inward as the bulk of its energies were put into domestic economic growth. Regardless, Stalin remained sensitive to growing aggression and ideological threats abroad such as the Japanese invasion of Manchuria in 1931 and Hitler's appointment as Chancellor in 1933. As a result, Russia left its cocoon in 1934, joined the League of Nations, and became an advocate of "collective security" while the Comintern adopted Popular Front tactics, allying with other parties against fascism, to strengthen the USSR's international posture. Diplomatically, in addition to League membership, the Soviet Union completed a military pact with France.

INTERNATIONAL DEVELOPMENTS (1918–1935)

The League of Nations

Efforts to create an international body to arbitrate international conflicts gained credence with the creation of a Permanent Court of International Justice to handle such matters at the First Hague Conference (1899). But no major efforts towards this goal were initiated until 1915, when pro-League of Nations organizations arose in the United States and Great Britain. Support for such a body grew as the war lengthened, and creation of such an organization became the cornerstone of President Woodrow Wilson's post-war policy, enunciated in his "Fourteen Points" speech before Congress on January 8, 1918.

The Preamble of the League's Covenant

This statement defined the League's purposes, which were to work for international friendship, peace, and security. To attain this, its members agreed to avoid war, maintain peaceful relations with other countries, and honor international law and accords.

The Organization of the League of Nations

Headquartered in Geneva, the League came into existence as the result of an Allied resolution on January 25, 1919, and the signing of the Treaty of Versailles on June 28, 1919. The League's Council originally consisted of five permanent members (France, Italy, England, Japan, and the U.S.), though the U.S. seat was left vacant because the U.S. Senate refused to ratify the Treaty of Versailles. Germany filled the vacancy in 1926. It also had four one-year rotating seats (increased to six in 1922, and raised to nine seats in 1926). The Council, with each member having one vote, could discuss any matter that threatened international stability, and could recommend action to member states. It also had the right, according to Article 8 of the League Covenant, to seek ways to reduce arms strength, while Articles 10 through 17 gave it the authority to search for means to stop war. It could recommend through a unanimous vote ways to stop aggression, and could suggest economic sanctions and other tactics to enforce its decisions, though its military ability to enforce its decisions was vague. It met four times a year from 1923 to 1929, and then three times annually afterwards.

The League's legislative body had similar debating and discussion authority, though it had no legislative powers. It initially had 43 members, which rose to 49 by the mid-1930s, though six others, including Italy, Germany, and Japan, withdrew their membership during the same period. The USSR, which joined in 1934, was expelled six years later.

The League's judicial responsibilities were handled by the "World Court" that was located at The Hague in The Netherlands. Created in 1921 and opened the following year, it would consider and advise on any case from any nation or the League, acting as an arbiter to prevent international conflict. The court's decisions were not binding: it relied on voluntary submission to its decisions.

The day-to-day affairs of the League were administered by the General Secretary and bureaucracy, the Secretariat, which was composed of an international collection of League civil servants. Lesser-known functions of the League dealt with the efforts of its International Labor Organization, (I.L.O.) which tried to find ways to reduce labor-management and class tensions; and the Mandates Commission, which oversaw territories taken from the Central Powers and were administered—as a prelude to independence—under mandate from League members. In addition, the League tried to provide medical, economic, and social welfare aid to depressed parts of the world.

THE WASHINGTON CONFERENCE (1921–1922)

The first post-war effort to deal with problems of disarmament was the Washington Conference (November 1921–February 1922). Its participants, which included the major powers in Europe and Asia plus the meeting's sponsor, the United States, discussed a number of problems that resulted in three separate agreements:

The Washington Naval Treaty (Five Power Treaty)

France, Italy, England, the United States, and Japan agreed to halt battleship construction for 10 years, while limiting or reducing capital shipping levels.

The Four Power Treaty

The United States, England, France, and Japan agreed not to seek further Pacific expansion or increased naval strength there and to respect the Pacific holdings of the other signatory powers.

The Nine Power Treaty

An agreement was signed by Japan (after Japan's agreement to return Kiachow to China), the Netherlands, Portugal, Belgium, Italy, France, England, the U.S., and China, guaranteeing China's independence and territorial autonomy.

THE GENEVA PROTOCOL (1924)

In 1923, a League Commission produced a Draft Treaty on Mutual Disarmament to aid countries who were attacked, but most countries rejected it. The Protocol for the Pacific Settlement of International Disputes, or the Geneva Protocol stated that the nation that refused to submit to arbitration by the World Court, the League Council, or special arbitrators, would be termed the aggressor. The agreement was tied to a further disarmament conference and a network of regional security pacts. Approved by the Assembly in October 1924, France and its Little Entente allies backed it quickly. England, however, backed by Commonwealth members, disapproved because of the broad commitments involved, which sank any prospect of final approval of the Protocol.

THE LOCARNO PACT (1925)

Failure of the European powers to create some type of international system to prevent aggression was followed by regional efforts prompted by Germany's visionary Foreign Minister, Gustav Stresemann, who in early 1925 approached England and France about an accord whereby Germany would accept its western borders in return for early Allied withdrawal from the demilitarized Rhine area. Stresemann also wanted League membership for his country. While England responded with guarded regional interest, France hesitated. Six months after consultation with its eastern allies, Paris countered with a proposal that would include similar provisions for Germany's eastern borders, secured by a mutual assistance pact between Italy, Great Britain, and France. These countries, along with Belgium, Czechoslovakia, and Poland, met for two months in Locarno, Switzerland, and concluded a number of separate agreements.

Treaty of Mutual Guarantees (Rhineland Pact)

Signed on October 16, 1925, by England, France, Italy, Germany, and Belgium, they guaranteed Germany's western boundaries and accepted the Versailles settlement's demilitarized zones. Italy and Great Britain agreed militarily to defend these lines if flagrantly violated.

Arbitration Settlements

In the same spirit, Germany signed arbitration dispute accords that mirrored the Geneva Protocol with France, Belgium, Poland, and Czechoslovakia, and required acceptance of League-determined settlements.

Eastern Accords

Since Germany would only agree to arbitration and not finalize its eastern border, France separately signed guarantees with Poland and Czechoslovakia to defend their frontiers.

Germany Joins the League

The Locarno Pact went into force when Germany joined the League on September 10, 1926, acquiring, after some dispute, the U.S.'s permanent seat on the Council. France and Belgium began to withdraw from the Rhineland, though they left a token force there until 1930.

THE PACT OF PARIS (KELLOGG-BRIAND PACT)

The Locarno Pact heralded a new period in European relations known as the "Era of Locarno" that marked the end of post-war conflict and the beginning of a more normal period of diplomatic friendship and cooperation. It reached its peak, idealistically, with the Franco-American effort in 1928 to seek an international statement to outlaw war. In December 1927, Frank Kellogg, the American Secretary of State, proposed that this policy be offered to all nations in the form of a treaty. On August 27, 1928, 15 countries, including the U.S., Germany, France, Italy, and

Japan, signed this accord with some minor limitations, which renounced war as a means of solving differences and as a tool of national policy. Within five years, 50 other countries signed the agreement. Unfortunately, without something more than idealism to back it up, the Kellogg-Briand Pact had little practical meaning.

THE WANING SEARCH FOR DISARMAMENT

London Naval Disarmament Treaty

In March 1930, Great Britain and the United States sought to expand the naval limitation terms of the Five Power Treaty of 1922. France and Italy could not agree on terms, while the U.S., England, and Japan accepted mild reductions in cruiser and destroyer strength.

World Disarmament Conference

Attended by 60 countries, the conference opened in 1932. Germany withdrew in 1933 after Hitler took power, and the conference closed in failure in 1934.

LEAGUE AND ALLIED RESPONSE TO AGGRESSION

By 1931, international attention increasingly turned to growing acts or threats of aggression in Europe and Asia, and transformed Europe from a world that hoped for eternal peace to a continent searching desperately for ways to contain growing aggression.

The League's Lytton Report and Manchuria

On September 19, 1931, the Japanese Kwantung Army, acting independently of the government in Tokyo, began the gradual conquest of Manchuria after fabricating an incident at Mukden to justify their actions. Ultimately, they created a puppet state, Manchukuo, under the last Chinese emperor, Henry P'u-i. China's League protest resulted in the creation of an investigatory commission under the Earl of Lytton that criticized Japan's actions and recommended a negotiated settlement that would have allowed Japan to retain most of its conquest. Japan responded by resigning from the League on January 24, 1933.

The Stresa Front

Hitler's announcement on March 15, 1935, of Germany's decisions to rearm and to introduce conscription in violation of the Treaty of Versailles prompted the leaders of England, France, and Italy to meet in Stresa, Italy (April 11–14). They condemned Germany's actions, underlined their commitment to the Locarno Pact, and re-affirmed the support they collectively gave for Austria's independence in early 1934. The League Council also rebuked Germany, and created an investigatory committee to search for economic means to punish the Reich. Great Britain's decision, however, to separately protect its naval strength vis-à-vis a German buildup in the Anglo-German Naval Treaty of June 18, 1935, effectively compromised the significance of the Stresa Front.

7 FROM WORLD WAR II TO THE DEMISE OF COMMUNISM (1935–1991)

THE AUTHORITARIAN STATES

The Soviet Union (U.S.S.R.) and Stalin

The U.S.S.R.'s 1936 Constitution was a recognition of the success of socialism. It gave the people civil rights, such as freedom of speech, customary in democracies. In addition it guaranteed a right to work, rest, leisure, and economic security. In fact, these rights were largely ignored by Stalin's government, or they existed only within the limits set by the ruling Communist Party of which Stalin was General Secretary.

Stalin's absolute dictatorship and inability to tolerate any opposition or dissent was revealed to the world by the Great Purge Trials (1936–1938). In 1936, 16 old Bolsheviks—including Gregory Zinoviev (first head of the Communist International) and Lev Kamenev—were placed on trial, publicly confessed to charges of plotting with foreign powers, and were executed. In 1937 Marshal Michael Tukhachevski and a group of the highest-ranking generals were accused of plotting with the Germans and Japanese and executed after a secret court martial. Other purges and trials followed, including the 1938 trial of Nicolai Bukharin, Alexei Rykov, and other prominent Bolsheviks charged with Trotskyite plots and wanting to restore capitalism.

These events discredited Russia as a reliable factor in international affairs, and partly explains the reluctance of British and French leaders to rely on the U.S.S.R. to help resist Germany's and Italy's acts of aggression. By the late 1930s the U.S.S.R. presented two images to the world: one a regime of absolute dictatorship and repression exemplified by the Great Purges and the other of undeniable economic progress during a period of world depression. Industrial production increased an average of 14 percent per annum in the 1930s, and Russia went from fifteenth to third in production of electricity. The Bolshevik model was, however, one of progress imposed from above at great cost to those below.

Events in Nazi Germany

The Nazi state (Third Reich) was a brutal dictatorship established with Hitler's appointment as Chancellor in 1933. By 1936, Hitler had destroyed the government of the Weimar Republic (established in 1919 at the end of the First World War), suppressed all political parties except the Nazi Party, and consolidated the government of Germany under his control as Führer (leader). Mass organizations such as the Nazi Labor Front and the Hitler Youth were established. The Nazis instituted propaganda campaigns and a regime of terror against political opponents and Jews who were made scapegoats for Germany's problems. Germany was a police state by 1936. In 1938, the Nazis used the assassination of a German diplomat by a Jewish youth as the excuse for extensive pogroms. Scores were murdered and much Jewish property was destroyed or damaged by gangs of Nazi hoodlums. Persecution of the

Jews increased in intensity, culminating in the horrors of the wartime concentration camps and the mass murder of millions.

Final control over the armed forces and the foreign office was achieved by Hitler in 1937–1938. The Nazi regime enjoyed success in part because it was able to reduce unemployment from 6,000,000 in 1932 to 164,000 by 1938 through so-called four-year plans aimed at rearming Germany and making its economy self-sufficient and free of dependence on any foreign power. The improving economic condition of many, together with Hitler's successes in foreign affairs, gave him a substantial hold over the German people. By the beginning of World War II, Germany had been transformed into a disciplined war machine with all dissent stifled.

Fascist Italy: The Corporate State

The pattern of Mussolini's dictatorship was that of the "Corporate State." Political parties and electoral districts were abolished. Workers and employers alike were organized into corporations according to the nature of their business. Twenty-two such corporations were established, presided over by a minister of corporations. The corporations and the government (with the balance heavily favoring the employers and the government) generally determined wages, hours, conditions of work, prices, and industrial polices. The structure was completed in 1938 with the abolition of the Chamber of Deputies in the Parliament and its replacement by a Chamber of Fasces and Corporations representing the Fascist party and the corporations.

Fascism provided a certain excitement and superficial grandeur but no solution to Italy's economic problems. Italian labor was kept under strict control. No strikes were allowed and by 1939 real wages were below those of 1922. Emphasis on foreign adventures and propaganda concerning a new Roman Empire were used to maintain a regime of force and brutality.

Other Authoritarian Regimes

The democratic hopes of those who established independent states in eastern and central Europe following World War I remained unfulfilled in the 1930s. Authoritarian monarchies—military regimes or governments on the fascist model—were established everywhere: Hungary by 1939 was under a military regime established by Admiral Miklos Horthy de Nagybánya, Greece by General Ioannis Metaxas. Yugoslavia, Rumania, and Bulgaria were ruled by authoritarian monarchies. In Spain, General Francisco Franco (1892–1975) established a fascist dictatorship after the Civil War (1936–1939). In Austria, the clerical-fascist regime of Kurt von Schuschnigg (1897–1977) ruled until the *Anschluss* (annexation by Germany) in 1938 and in Portugal, Antonio de Oliveira Salazar (1889–1970) ruled as dictator.

THE DEMOCRACIES

Great Britain

In Great Britain the Labour party emerged as the second party in British politics along with the Conservatives. The first Labour government under Ramsay

MacDonald governed from January to November, 1924. A second MacDonald cabinet was formed in 1931 but resigned in August because of financial crisis and disagreement over remedies. A national coalition government under Ramsey MacDonald governed from October 1931 to June 1935 when Stanley Baldwin formed a Conservative cabinet. Baldwin was succeeded by Neville Chamberlain (1937–1940) whose government dealt with the problem of German and Italian aggression by a policy of appeasement.

France: The Popular Front

In France a coalition of Radical Socialists, Socialists, and Communists campaigned in 1936 on a pledge to save the country from fascism and solve problems of the depression by instituting economic reforms. The Popular Front government, under Socialist Léon Blum (1872–1950), lasted just over a year. Much reform legislation was enacted, including a 40-hour work week, vacations with pay, collective bargaining, compulsory arbitration of labor disputes, support for agricultural prices, reorganization of the Bank of France, and nationalization of armaments and aircraft industries. Blum was attacked by conservatives and fascists as a radical and a Jew. ("Better Hitler than Leon Blum.") The Popular Front government was defeated by the Senate, which refused to vote the government emergency financial powers. Edouard Daladier then formed a conservative government which began to devote its attention to foreign affairs, collaborating with Chamberlain in the appeasement policy. Democracy was preserved from the fascist attacks of the early 1930s, but the Popular Front was not as successful in making permanent changes as might have been hoped, and it was a demoralized and dispirited France that had to meet the German attack on Poland in 1939.

Other Democratic States

Czechoslovakia was the one state of Eastern Europe that maintained a democratic, parliamentary regime. It came under heavy attack from Nazi Germany following the annexation of Austria and was ultimately deserted by its allies, France and Britain, whose leaders forced Czech compliance with the terms of the Munich Agreement of 1938. Switzerland maintained a precarious neutrality throughout the 1930s and World War II with the help of the League of Nations, which freed Switzerland of any obligation to support even sanctions against an aggressor. Sweden also maintained its democratic existence by a firm policy of neutrality. Denmark and Norway were seized by the Germans early in 1940 and remained under German control during World War II. All of the Scandinavian countries were models of liberal democratic government.

CULTURE IN THE LATE 1930s: ENGAGEMENT

The 20th century generally has been one in which there has been a feeling of fragmentation and uncertainty in European thought and the arts. Much of this was due to the discoveries of Freud and Einstein: one emphasizing that much of human behavior is irrational and the other undermining in his theories of relativity the long-held certainties of Newtonian science. The Dutch historian Johan Huizinga (1872–1945) noted in 1936 "almost all things which once seemed sacred and immutable have now become unsettled.... The sense of living in the midst of a violent crisis of civilization, threatening complete collapse, has spread far and wide." (Huizinga, *In the Shadow of Tomorrow,* London, 1936). Intellectuals came increasingly to see the world as an irrational place in which old values and truths had little relevance. Some intellectuals became "engaged" in resistance to fascism and Nazism. Some like Arthur Koestler (1905–1983) flirted with communism but broke with Stalin after the Great Purges. Koestler's *Darkness at Noon* (1941) is an attempt to understand the events surrounding those trials. German intellectuals such as Ernst Cassirer (1874–1945) and Erich Fromm (1900–1980) escaped Nazi Germany and worked in exile. Cassirer, in his *The Myth of the State* (1946), noted that the Nazis manufactured myths of race, leader, party, etc., that disoriented reason and intellect. Fromm published *Escape from Freedom* in 1941, which maintained that modern man had escaped *to* freedom from the orderly, structured world of medieval society but was now trying to escape *from* this freedom and looking for security once again.

Existentialism is the philosophy that best exemplified European feelings in the era of the World Wars. Three 19th-century figures greatly influenced this movement: Kierkegaard, Dostoyevski, and Nietzsche. Martin Heidegger (1889–1976) (though he rejected the term), Karl Jaspers (1883–1969), Jean-Paul Sartre (1905–1980), and Simone de Beauvoir (1908–1986) are four noted figures in 20th-century existentialism, which sought to come to grip with life's central experiences and the traumas of war, death, and evil.

INTERNATIONAL RELATIONS: THE ROAD TO WAR

Germany, Italy, Japan, and the U.S.S.R. were not satisfied with the peace settlement of 1919. They used force to achieve change, from the Japanese invasion of Manchuria in 1931 to the outbreak of war in 1939 over Poland. Hitler, bit by bit, dismantled the Versailles Treaty in central and eastern Europe.

The U.S.S.R. was a revisionist power profoundly distrustful of Germany, Italy, and Japan. It pursued a policy of collective security through the League of Nations (which they joined in 1934). Only after evidence of Anglo-French weakness did Stalin in 1939 enter an agreement with Hitler. This event, like the Great Purges, only heightened suspicion of Soviet motives and was later to become the subject of debate and recrimination in the Cold War that followed World War II.

Finally, Neville Chamberlain's policy of appeasement was not based on any liking for Hitler, whom he considered "half-crazed," but on a genuine desire to remove causes of discontent inherent in the Versailles settlement and thus create conditions where peace could be maintained. His error lay in his belief that Hitler was open to reason, preferred peace to war, and would respect agreements.

Britain and France, as well as other democratic states, were influenced in their policy by a profound pacifism based on their experience with the loss of life and devastation in World War I and by a dislike of the Stalinist regime in Russia.

THE COURSE OF EVENTS

Using a Franco-Soviet agreement of the preceding year as an excuse, Hitler, on March 7, 1936, repudiated the Locarno agreements and reoccupied the Rhineland (an area demilitarized by the Versailles Treaty). Neither France (which possessed military superiority at the time) nor Britain was willing to oppose these moves.

The Spanish Civil War (1936–1939) is usually seen as a rehearsal for World War II because of outside intervention. The government of the Spanish Republic (established in 1931) caused resentment among conservatives by its programs, including land reform and anti-clerical legislation aimed at the Catholic Church. Labor discontent led to disturbances in industrial Barcelona and the surrounding province of Catalonia. Following an election victory by a popular front of republican and radical parties, right-wing generals in July began a military insurrection. Francisco Franco, stationed at the time in Spanish Morocco, emerged as the leader of this revolt, which became a devastating civil war lasting nearly three years.

The democracies, including the United States, followed a course of neutrality. Nazi Germany, Italy, and the U.S.S.R. did intervene despite non-intervention agreements negotiated by Britain and France. German air force units were sent to aid the fascist forces of Franco and participated in bombardments of Madrid, Barcelona, and Guernica (the latter incident being the inspiration for Picasso's famous painting which became an anti-fascist symbol known far beyond the world of art). Italy sent troops, tanks, and other material. The U.S.S.R. sent advisers and recruited soldiers from among anti-fascists in the United States and other countries to fight in the international brigades with the republican forces. Spain became a battlefield for fascist and anti-fascist forces with Franco winning by 1939 in what was seen as a serious defeat for anti-fascist forces everywhere.

The Spanish Civil War was a factor in bringing together Mussolini and Hitler in a Rome-Berlin Axis. Already Germany and Japan had signed the Anti-Comintern Pact in 1936. Ostensibly directed against international communism, this was the basis for a diplomatic alliance between those countries, and Italy soon adhered to this agreement, becoming Germany's ally in World War II.

In 1937 there was Nazi-inspired agitation in the Baltic port of Danzig, a city basically German in its population, but which had been made a free city under the terms of the Versailles Treaty.

In 1938 Hitler pressured the Austrian chancellor to make concessions and when this did not work, German troops annexed Austria (the *Anschluss*). Again Britain and France took no effective action, and about six million Austrians were added to Germany.

Hitler turned next to Czechoslovakia. Three million persons of German origin lived in the Sudetenland, a borderland between Germany and Czechoslovakia given to Czechoslovakia in order to provide it with a more defensible boundary. These ethnic Germans (and other minorities of Poles, Ruthenians, and Hungarians) agitated against the democratic government (the only one in eastern Europe in 1938) despite its enlightened minority policy. Hitler used the Sudeten Nazi Party to deliberately provoke a crisis by making demands for a degree of independence unacceptable to the Czech authorities. He then claimed to interfere as the protector of a persecuted minority. In May 1938, rumors of invasion led to warnings from Britain and France followed by assurances from Hitler. Nevertheless, in the fall, the crisis came to a head with renewed demands from Hitler. Chamberlain twice flew to Germany in person to get German terms. The second time, Hitler's increased demands led to mobilization and other measures towards war. At the last minute a four-power conference was held in Munich with Hitler, Mussolini, Chamberlain, and Daladier in attendance. At Munich, Hitler's terms were accepted in the Munich Agreement. Neither Czechoslovakia nor the U.S.S.R. was in attendance. Britain and France, despite the French alliance with Czechoslovakia, put pressure on the Czech government to force it to comply with German demands. Hitler signed a treaty agreeing to this settlement as the limit of his ambitions. At the same time the Poles seized control of Teschen, and Hungary (with the support of Italy and Germany and over the protests of the British and French) seized 7,500 square miles of Slovakia. By the concessions forced on her at Munich, Czechoslovakia lost its frontier defenses and was totally unprotected against any further German encroachments.

In March 1939, Hitler annexed most of the rump Czech state while Hungary conquered Ruthenia. At almost the same time Germany annexed Memel from Lithuania. In April, Mussolini, taking advantage of distractions created by Germany, landed an army in Albania and seized that Balkan state in a campaign lasting about one week.

Disillusioned by these continued aggressions, Britain and France made military preparations. Guarantees were given to Poland, Rumania, and Greece. The two democracies also opened negotiations with the U.S.S.R. for an arrangement to obtain that country's aid against further German aggression. Hitler, with Poland next on his timetable, also began a cautious rapprochement with the U.S.S.R. Probably Russian suspicion that the Western powers wanted the U.S.S.R. to bear the brunt of any German attack led Stalin to respond to Hitler's overtures. Negotiations which began very quietly in the spring of 1939 were continued with increasing urgency as summer approached and with it, the time of Hitler's planned attack on Poland. On August 23, 1939, the world was stunned by the announcement of a Nazi-Soviet treaty of friendship. A secret protocol provided that in the event of a "territorial rearrangement" in eastern Europe the two powers would divide Poland. In addition, Russia would have the Baltic states (Latvia, Lithuania, and Estonia) and Bessarabia (lost to Rumania in 1918) as part of her sphere. Stalin agreed to remain neutral in any German war with Britain or France. World War II began with the German invasion of Poland on September 1, 1939, followed by British and French declarations of war against Germany on September 3.

WORLD WAR II

The Polish Campaign and the "Phony War"
The German attack (known as the "blitzkrieg" or "lightning war") overwhelmed the poorly equipped Polish army, which could not resist German tanks and airplanes. The outcome was clear after the first few days of fighting, and organized resistance ceased within a month.

In accordance with the secret provisions of the Nazi-Soviet Treaty of August 1939, Russia and Germany shared the Polish spoils. On September 17 the Russian armies attacked the Poles from the east. They met the Germans two days later. Stalin's share of Poland extended approximately to the Curzon Line. Russia also made demands on Finland. Later, in June 1940, while Germany was attacking France, Stalin occupied the Baltic states of Latvia, Lithuania, and Estonia.

Nazi Germany formally annexed the port of Danzig and the Polish Corridor and some territory along the western Polish border. Central Poland was turned into a German protectorate called the Government-General.

Following the successful completion of the Polish campaign, the war settled into a period of inaction on the part of both the Germans and the British and French known as the "phony war" or "sitzkrieg." The British and French prepared for a German attack on France and Belgium.

The "Winter War" Between Russia and Finland

The only military action of any consequence during the winter of 1939–1940 resulted from Russian demands made on Finland, especially for territory adjacent to Leningrad (then only 20 miles from the border). Finnish refusal led to a Russian attack in November 1939. The Finns resisted with considerable vigor, receiving some supplies from Sweden, Britain, and France, but eventually by March they had to give in to the superior Russian forces. Finland was forced to cede the Karelian Isthmus, Viipuri, and a naval base at Hangoe. Britain and France prepared forces to aid the Finns, but by the time they were ready to act the Finns had been defeated.

The German Attack on Denmark and Norway

The period of inactivity in the war in the west suddenly came to an end. On April 9, Denmark and Norway were simultaneously attacked. Denmark was quickly occupied. The British and French responded by sending naval and military forces to Narvik and Trondheim in an effort to assist the Norwegians and to capture some bases before the Germans could overrun the entire country. They were too slow and showed little initiative, and within a few weeks the forces were withdrawn, taking the Norwegian government with them into exile in London.

The Battle of France

On May 10, the main German offensive was launched against France. Belgium and the Netherlands were simultaneously attacked. According to plan, British and French forces advanced to aid the Belgians. At this point the Germans departed from the World War I strategy by launching a surprise armored attack through Luxembourg and the Ardennes Forest (considered by the British and French to be impassable for tanks). As these forces moved towards the Channel coast, they divided the Allied armies leaving the Belgians, the British Expeditionary Force, and some French forces virtually encircled. The Dutch could offer no real resistance and collapsed in four days after the May 13 German bombing of Rotterdam—one of the first raids intended to terrorize civilians. Queen Wilhemina and her government fled to London. The Belgians, who had made little effort to coordinate plans with the

British and French, surrendered May 25th, leaving the British and French in serious danger from the Germans who were advancing to the Channel coast; however, Hitler concentrated on occupying Paris. This provided just enough time for the British to affect an emergency evacuation of some 230,000 of their own men as well as about 120,000 French from the port of Dunkirk and the adjacent coast. This remarkable evacuation saved the lives of the soldiers, but all supplies and equipment were lost including vehicles, tanks, and artillery—a very severe blow to the British Army.

Churchill Becomes British Prime Minister

Even before the offensive against France, on May 7 and 8 an attack was launched in the House of Commons on Prime Minister Chamberlain. Chamberlain, a man of peace who had never properly mobilized the British war effort or developed an effective plan of action, fell from power. A government was formed under Winston Churchill, whose warnings of the German danger and the need for British rearmament all during the 1930s made him Chamberlain's logical successor. The opposition Labour Party agreed to join in a coalition, with Clement Attlee (1883–1967) becoming deputy prime minister. Several other Laborites followed his lead by accepting cabinet posts. This gave Britain a government which eventually led the nation to final victory but which could do little in 1940 to prevent the defeat of France.

France Makes Peace

Paris fell to the Germans in mid-June. In this crisis Paul Reynaud (1878–1966) succeeded Edouard Daladier as premier but was unable to deal with the defeatism of some of his cabinet. On June 16th Reynaud resigned in favor of a government headed by aged Marshal Pétain, one of the heroes of World War I. The Pétain government quickly made peace with Hitler, who added to French humiliation by dictating the terms of the armistice to the French at Compiégne in the same railroad car used by Marshal Foch when he gave terms to the Germans at the end of the First World War. The complete collapse of France quickly came as a tremendous shock to the British and Americans.

Mussolini declared war on both France and Britain on June 10th. He gained little by this action, and Hitler largely ignored the Italian dictator in making peace with France. Hitler's forces remained in occupation of the northern part of France, including Paris. He allowed the French to keep their fleet and overseas territories probably in the hope of making them reliable allies. Pétain and his chief minister Pierre Laval established their capital at Vichy and followed a policy of collaboration with their former enemies. A few Frenchmen, however, joined the Free French movement started in London by the then relatively unknown General Charles de Gaulle (1890–1970).

FROM THE FRENCH DEFEAT TO THE INVASION OF RUSSIA

Germany's "New Order" in Europe

By mid-summer 1940, Germany, together with its Italian ally, dominated most of western and central Europe. Germany began with no real plans for a long war, but continued resistance by the British made necessary the belated mobilization of German resources. Hitler's policy included exploiting areas Germany conquered. Collaborators were used to establish governments subservient to German policy. These received the name "Quislings" after the Norwegian traitor Vidkun Quisling (1887–1945), who was made premier of Norway during the German occupation. Germany began the policy of forcibly transporting large numbers of conquered Europeans to work in German war industries. Jews especially were forced into slave labor for the German war effort, and increasingly large numbers were rounded up and sent to concentration camps, where they were systematically murdered as the Nazis carried out Hitler's "final solution" of genocide against European Jewry. Although much was known about this during the war, the full horror of these atrocities was not revealed until Allied troops entered Germany in 1945.

The Battle of Britain

With the fall of France, Britain remained the only power of consequence at war with the Axis. Hitler began preparations for invading Britain (Operation "Sea Lion"). Air control over the Channel was vital if an invasion force was to be transported safely to the English Coast. The German Air Force (Luftwaffe) under Herman Göring began its air offensive against the British in the summer of 1940. The British, however, had used the year between Munich and the outbreak of war to good advantage, increasing their production of aircraft to 600 per month, almost equal to German production. Their Spitfire and Hurricane fighters proved superior. The British had also developed the first radar just in time to be used to give early warning of German attacks. British intelligence was also effective in deciphering German military communications and in providing ways to interfere with the navigational devices used by the German bombers. The Germans concentrated first on British air defenses, then on ports and shipping, and finally in early September they began the attack on London. The Battle of Britain was eventually a defeat for the Germans, who were unable to gain decisive superiority over the British, although they inflicted great damage on both British air defenses and major cities such as London. Despite the damage and loss of life, British morale remained high and necessary war production continued. German losses determined that bombing alone could not defeat Britain. "Operation Sea Lion" was postponed October 12th and never seriously taken up again, although the British did not know this and had to continue for some time to give priority to their coastal and air defenses.

Germany Turns East

During the winter of 1940–1941, having given up "Operation Sea Lion," Hitler began to shift his forces to the east for an invasion of Russia ("Operation Barbarossa"). The alliance of August 1939 was never harmonious, and German fears were aroused by Russia's annexation of the three Baltic states in June 1940, by the attack on Finland, and by Russian seizure of the province of Bessarabia from Rumania. Russian expansion towards the Balkans dismayed the Germans, who hoped for more influence there themselves. In addition, on October 28, 1940, Mussolini began an ill-advised invasion of Greece from Italian bases in Albania. Within a few weeks, the Greeks repulsed the Italians and drove them back into Albania.

The Balkan Campaign

These events prompted Hitler to make demands early in 1941 on Rumania, Bulgaria, and Hungary which led these powers to become German allies accepting occupation by German forces. Yugoslavia resisted and the Germans attacked on April 6th, occupying the state despite considerable resistance. They then advanced to the aid of the Italians in their attack on Greece. Greece was quickly overrun despite aid from the British forces in the Middle East. The Greek government took refuge on Crete but that island was captured from its British garrison. At the end of May, Crete was evacuated by the British, with the Greek government also going into exile in London.

Barbarossa—The Attack on Russia

The German invasion of Russia began June 22, 1941. The invasion force of three million included Finnish, Rumanian, Hungarian, and Italian contingents along with the Germans and advanced on a broad front of about 2,000 miles. In this first season of fighting the Germans seized White Russia and most of the Ukraine, advancing to the Crimean Peninsula in the south. They surrounded the city of Leningrad (although they never managed to actually capture it), and came within about 25 miles of Moscow. In November the enemy actually entered the suburbs, but then the long supply lines, early winter, and Russian resistance (strong despite heavy losses) brought the invasion to a halt. During the winter a Russian counterattack pushed the Germans back from Moscow and saved the capital.

The Far Eastern Crisis

With the coming of the Great Depression and severe economic difficulties, Japanese militarists gained more and more influence over the civilian government. On September 18, 1931, the Japanese occupied all of Manchuria. On July 7, 1937, a full-scale Sino-Japanese war began with a clash between Japanese and Chinese at the Marco Polo Bridge in Peking (now Beijing). An indication of ultimate Japanese aims came on November 3, 1938, when Prince Fumimaro Konoye's (1891–1946) government issued a statement on "A New Order in East Asia." This statement envisaged the integration of Japan, Manchuria (now the puppet state of Manchukuo), and China into one "Greater East Asia Co-Prosperity Sphere" under Japanese leadership. In July 1940, the Konoye government was re-formed with General Hideki Tojo (1884–1948) (Japan's principal leader in World War I) as minister of war. Japan's policy of friendship with Nazi Germany and Fascist Italy was consolidated with the signing of a formal alliance in September 1940. The war in Europe gave Japan further opportunities for expansion. Concessions were obtained from the Vichy government in French Indochina and Japanese bases were established there.

All of these events led to worsening relations between Japan and the two states in a position to oppose her expansion—the Soviet Union and the United States. Despite border clashes with the Russians, Japan avoided any conflict with that state, and Stalin wanted no war with Japan after he became fully occupied with the German invasion. In the few weeks after attacking the U.S. at Pearl Harbor, Japanese forces were able to occupy strategically-important islands (including the Philippines and Dutch East Indies) and territory on the Asian mainland (Malaya, with the British naval base at Singapore, and all of Burma to the border of India).

The Japanese attack brought the United States not only into war in the Pacific, but resulted in German and Italian declarations of war which meant the total involvement of the United States in World War II.

The "Turning of the Tide"

U.S. strategists decided—with British concurrence—that priority should be given to the war in Europe (a "Germany first" policy), because the danger to both Britain and the U.S.S.R. seemed more immediate than the threat from Japan. As it turned out, the United States mobilized such great resources that sufficient forces were available to go over to the offensive in the Pacific, while at the same time European theater requirements were being met and the war against Japan ended only a few weeks after the German surrender.

American involvement in the war was ultimately decisive, for it meant that the greatest industrial power of that time was now arrayed against the Axis powers. The United States became, as President Roosevelt put it, "the arsenal of democracy." American aid was crucial to the immense effort of the Soviet Union. Lend-Lease aid was extended to Russia. By 1943 supplies and equipment were reaching Russia in considerable quantities.

The Second German Offensive in Russia: Stalingrad

The German forces launched a second offensive in the summer of 1942. This attack concentrated on the southern part of the front, aiming at the Caucasus and vital oil fields around the Caspian Sea. At Stalingrad on the Volga River the Germans were stopped. There were weeks of bitter fighting in the streets of the city itself. With the onset of winter, Hitler refused to allow the strategic retreat urged by his generals. As a result, the Russian forces crossed the river north and south of the city and surrounded 22 German divisions. On January 31, 1943, following the failure of relief efforts, the German commander Friedrich Paulus (1890–1957) surrendered the remnants of his army. From then on the Russians were almost always on the offensive.

The North African Campaigns

After entering the war in 1940, the Italians invaded British-held Egypt. In December 1940, the British General Archibald Wavell (1883–1950) launched a surprise attack. The Italian forces were driven back about 500 miles and 130,000 were captured. Then Hitler intervened, sending General Erwin Rommel with a small German force (the Afrika Korps) to reinforce the Italians. Rommel took command and launched a counter-offensive which put his forces on the border of Egypt. By mid-1942 Rommel had driven to El Alamein, only 70 miles from Alexandria.

A change in the British high command now placed General Harold Alexander (1891–1969) in charge of Middle Eastern forces, with General Bernard Montgomery (1887–1976) in immediate command of the British Eighth Army. Montgomery attacked at El Alamein, breaking Rommel's lines and starting a British advance which was not stopped until the armies reached the border of Tunisia.

Meanwhile the British and American leaders decided that they could launch a second offensive in North Africa ("Operation Torch") which would clear the enemy from the entire coast and make the Mediterranean once again safe for Allied shipping. To avoid fighting the French forces which garrisoned the main landing areas (at Casablanca, Oran, and Algiers), the Allied command under the American General Dwight Eisenhower (1890–1969) made an agreement with the French commander Admiral Jean Darlan (1881–1942). There was a loud public outcry in Britain and the U.S. at this alliance with a person who condoned fascism. Darlan was assassinated in December, leading to a struggle for leadership among the French in North Africa, de Gaulle's Free French, the French Resistance, and other factions. Roosevelt and Churchill supported senior French officer General Henri Giraud, who had just escaped from imprisonment by the Germans, against the independent and imperious de Gaulle, who was especially disliked by Roosevelt and was not kept informed of the North African operation or allowed to participate. De Gaulle proved his political as well as military talent by completely outmaneuvering Giraud, and within a year he was the undisputed leader of all the French elements.

The landings resulted in little conflict with the French and the French forces soon joined the war against the Axis. It was only a matter of time before German troops were forced into northern Tunisia and surrendered. American forces, unused to combat, suffered some reverses at the Battle of the Kasserine Pass, but gained valuable experience. The final victory came in May 1943, about the same time as the Russian victory at Stalingrad.

Winning the Battle of the Atlantic

Relatively safe shipping routes across the North Atlantic to Britain were essential to the survival of Britain and absolutely necessary if a force was to be assembled to invade France and strike at Germany proper. New types of aircraft, small aircraft carriers, more numerous and better-equipped escort vessels, new radar and sonar (for underwater detection), extremely efficient radio direction finding, decipherment of German signals plus the building of more ships turned the balance against the Germans despite their development of improved submarines by early 1943, and the Atlantic became increasingly dangerous for German submarines.

A Turning Point

Success in these three campaigns—Stalingrad, North Africa, and the Battle of the Atlantic—gave new hope to the Allied cause and made certain that eventually victory would be won. Together with the beginning of an offensive in late 1942 in the Solomon Islands against the Japanese, they made 1943 the turning point of the war.

Allied Victory

At their conference at Casablanca in January 1943, Roosevelt and Churchill developed a detailed strategy for the further conduct of the war. Sicily was to be invaded, then Italy proper. Historians differ as to the significance of the Casablanca decisions. The Italian campaign did knock Italy out of the war and cause Hitler to send forces to Italy that might otherwise have opposed the 1944 landing in Normandy, and it did bring about the downfall of Mussolini and Italian surrender. It also ensured, by using up limited resources such as landing craft, that no second front in France could be opened in 1943—a fact most unpalatable to Stalin, whose Russian armies were fighting desperately against the bulk of the German army and air force. But the drawing off of forces from Italy to ensure a successful landing in France made it extremely difficult to achieve decisive victory in Italy and meant a long and costly campaign against skillful and stubborn resistance by the Germans under Marshal Albert Kesselring (1885–1960). Rome was not captured by the Allied forces until June 4, 1944. With a new Italian government now supporting the Allied cause, Italian resistance movements in Northern Italy became a major force in helping to liberate that area from the Germans.

The Second Front in Normandy

At the Teheran Conference, held in November 1943 and attended by all three major Allied leaders, the final decision reached by Roosevelt and Churchill some six months earlier to invade France in May 1944 was communicated to the Russians. Stalin promised to open a simultaneous Russian offensive.

Despite the claims of General George Marshall (1880–1959) and General Sir Alan Brooke (1883–1963) (the American and British chiefs of staff, respectively) Roosevelt and Churchill decided on General Dwight Eisenhower, their North African commander, to be supreme commander of the coming invasion. Eisenhower arrived in London to establish Supreme Headquarters Allied Expeditionary Forces (SHAEF). He proved extremely adept at getting soldiers of several nations to work together harmoniously. Included in the invasion army were American, British, Canadian, Polish, and French contingents.

The Normandy invasion (Operation "Overlord") was the largest amphibious operation in history. Plans included an air offensive with a force of 10,000 aircraft of all types, a large naval contingent and pre-invasion naval bombardment of the very strong German defenses, a transport force of some 4,000 ships, artificial harbors to receive supplies after the initial landings, and several divisions of airborne troops to be landed behind enemy coastal defenses the night preceding the sea-borne invasion. The landings actually took place beginning June 6, 1944. The first day, 130,000 men were successfully landed. Strong German resistance hemmed in the Allied forces for about a month. Then the Allies, now numbering about 1,000,000, managed a spectacular breakthrough. By the end of 1944, all of France had been seized.

A second invasion force landed on the Mediterranean coast in August, freed southern France, and linked up with Eisenhower's forces. By the end of 1944, the Allied armies stood on the borders of Germany ready to invade from both east and west.

The Eastern Front: Poland

Russian successes brought their forces to the border of Poland by July 1944. Russian relations with the Polish government in exile in London, however, had by that time been broken off after the Poles had voiced their suspicions that the Russians and not the Germans might have caused the mass executions of a large number of Polish officers in the Katyn Forest early in the war.

Stalin's armies crossed into Poland July 23, 1944, and three days later the Russian dictator officially recognized a group of Polish Communists (the so-called Lublin Committee) as the government of Poland. As the Russian armies drew near the eastern suburbs of Warsaw, the London Poles, a resistance group, launched an attack. Stalin's forces waited outside the city while the Germans brought in reinforcements and slowly wiped out the Polish underground army in several weeks of heavy street fighting. The offensive then resumed and the city was liberated by the Red Army, but the influence of the London Poles was now virtually nil. Needless to say, this incident aroused considerable suspicion concerning Stalin's motives and led both Churchill and Roosevelt to begin to think through the political implications of their alliance with Stalin.

Greece, Yugoslavia, and the Balkans

By late summer of 1944, the German position in the Balkans began to collapse. The Red Army crossed the border into Rumania leading King Michael (1921–   ) to seize the opportunity to take his country out of its alliance with Germany and to open the way to the advancing Russians. German troops were forced to make a hasty retreat. At this point Bulgaria changed sides. The German forces in Greece withdrew in October.

From October 9–18, Winston Churchill visited Moscow to try to work out a political arrangement regarding the Balkans and Eastern Europe. (Roosevelt was busy with his campaign for election to a fourth term.) In Moscow, Churchill worked out the famous agreement which he describes in his book on World War II. Dealing from a position of weakness, he simply wrote out some figures on a sheet of paper: Russia to have the preponderance of influence in countries like Bulgaria and Rumania, Britain to have the major say in Greece, and a fifty-fifty division in Yugoslavia and Hungary. Stalin agreed. The Americans refused to have anything to do with this "spheres of influence" arrangement.

In Greece, Stalin maintained a hands-off policy when the British used military force to suppress the Communist resistance movement and install a regent for the exiled government.

The German Resistance and the 1944 Attempt to Assassinate Hitler

It was obvious even before the Normandy invasion that Germany was losing the war. Some German officers and civilians had formed a resistance movement. As long as Hitler's policy was successful the movement had little chance of succeeding. Four years of aerial bombardment, however, had reduced German cities to rubble by early 1944 and virtually destroyed the Luftwaffe. The Russians were on the offensive and many German officials did not like to think, after what had happened in Russia, what the Russian army might do if it reached German soil. Hitler was in direct control of German forces and disregarded professional advice which might have provided a better, less costly defense. Knowing the war was lost after the success of the Normandy invasion, the Resistance plotted to assassinate Hitler. The leaders were retired General Ludwig Beck, Carl Goerdeler (former Mayor of Leipzig), and Count Claus Philip Shenck von Stauffenberg—a much-decorated young staff officer who undertook the dangerous task of actually planting the bomb in Hitler's headquarters on July 20, 1944. Hitler miraculously survived the explosion and launched a reign of terror in reprisal which resulted in imprisonment, torture, and death for anyone even suspected of a connection with the plot. His survival ensured that the war would be fought out on German soil to the bitter end.

Final Questions of Strategy

In General Eisenhower's headquarters there was some dispute over the best way to invade Germany and end the war. Before any final attack could be made, however, the Germans launched an offensive of their own beginning December 16. Hitler gathered his last reserves to attack the Allies in the Ardennes forest region with the goal of breaking through between the Allied forces and driving to the Channel coast. The offensive became known as the Battle of the Bulge. Bad weather for some days made impossible the effective use of Allied air power. The Allied lines held, however, and by the end of the first week of January 1945, the German offensive had been broken and the lines restored.

The End of the War in Europe

In early spring of 1945 the Allied armies crossed the Rhine. As the Americans and British and other Allied forces advanced into Germany, the Russians attacked from the east. While the Russian armies were fighting their way into Berlin, Hitler committed suicide in the ruins of the bunker where he had spent the last days of the war. Power was handed over to a government headed by Admiral Karl Dönitz (1891–1980). On May 7th, General Alfred Jodl (1890–1946), acting for the German government, made the final unconditional surrender at General Eisenhower's headquarters near Reims.

The Yalta and Potsdam Conferences

The future treatment of Germany, and Europe in general, was determined by decisions of the "Big Three" (Churchill, Stalin, and Roosevelt). There were two summit meetings attended by all three leaders. Even before the first of these was held at Teheran, Churchill and Roosevelt had met at Casablanca and laid down a basic policy of demanding the unconditional surrender of their enemies. Stalin was agreeable to this.

The first major conference convened at Teheran on November 28, 1943, and lasted until December 1st. Here the two Western allies told Stalin of the May 1944 date for the planned invasion of Normandy. In turn, Stalin confirmed a pledge made earlier that Russia would enter the war against Japan after the war with Germany was concluded. Political questions were barely touched upon. Roosevelt reflected the views of his military leaders who were concerned with the quickest ending to the war. Hence he was willing to postpone political decisions on the Balkans and Eastern Europe and concentrate on a second front in France and the shortest road to Berlin. This was agreeable to Stalin since any postponement would only better his position by allowing time for the Red Army to take control of the areas in question. Churchill seems to have had in mind political questions far more than his American colleague (hence his October 1944 visit to Moscow and "spheres of influence" agreement with Stalin referred to above), but as the American participation in the war grew in magnitude, British influence declined, and he had to defer to the wishes of the Americans. It was not softness on communism, as charged by some critics of wartime diplomacy, but rather a desire for a quick military decision, that prompted Roosevelt to cooperate as he did with Stalin despite the fears of Churchill.

The Yalta Conference was the second attended personally by Stalin, Churchill, and Roosevelt. It lasted from the 4th to the 11th of February 1945. A plan to divide Germany into zones of occupation, which had been devised in 1943 by a committee under British Deputy Prime Minister Clement Attlee, was formally accepted with the addition of a fourth zone taken from the British and American zones for the French to occupy. Berlin, which lay within the Russian Zone, was divided into four zones of occupation also.

Such lack of precision was characteristic of other parts of the Yalta agreements, such as those governing borders and reparations leading to future disputes and recriminations between the Western powers and the Russians. A Declaration on Liberated Europe promised to assist liberated nations in solving problems through elections and by "democratic" means.

In Poland, Churchill and Roosevelt had to allow Stalin to do what he pleased. It was agreed that the nucleus of the post-war Polish government would be Stalin's Lublin Committee. The only concession was an agreement to add a number of "democratic leaders" (London Poles), but these, as it turned out, were powerless to affect the course of events and prevent an eventual total takeover of Polish government by the Communists.

In the Far East, in return for his agreement to enter the war against Japan after Germany's defeat, Stalin was promised the southern part of Sakhalin Island, the Kurile Islands, a lease on the naval base at Port Arthur, a pre-eminent position in control of the commercial port of Dairen, and the use of Manchurian railroads.

The third summit meeting of the Big Three took place at Potsdam outside Berlin after the end of the European war but while the Pacific war was still going on. The conference began July 17, 1945, with Stalin, Churchill, and the new American President Harry Truman attending. (Roosevelt had died suddenly, shortly after the conclusion of the Yalta meeting.) While the conference was in session, the results of the British general election became known: Churchill was defeated, his place taken by his wartime deputy prime minister, the Labour leader Clement Attlee. The meeting confirmed, in detail, arrangements regarding Germany. A Potsdam Declaration, aimed at Japan, called for immediate Japanese surrender and hinted at the consequences that would ensue if it were not forthcoming. While at the conference, American leaders received the news of the successful testing of the first atomic bomb in the New Mexico desert, but the Japanese were given no clear warning that such a destructive weapon might be used against them.

The Atomic Bomb and the Defeat of Japan

Development of an atomic bomb became a theoretical possibility following the first splitting of uranium atoms by Otto Strassmann and Otto Hahn at the Kaiser Wilhelm Institute in Berlin just before the war. The news spread quickly and both the British and Americans became concerned that the Germans might develop a weapon based on this principle, and therefore began an effort to build an atomic bomb first. In Britain, a research project known as Tube Alloys was begun, and valuable work had been done by the time the United States entered the war. At that point the decision was made to concentrate the work in the United States because its vastly greater resources of power and industrial capacity. The Manhattan Engineering District under Major General Leslie Groves was established to manage the immense research, development, and production effort needed to develop an atomic weapon. By early 1945, it appeared that a weapon would soon be available for testing, and in July the successful test was completed.

President Truman established a committee of prominent scientists and leaders to determine how best to utilize the bomb. They advised the president that they could not devise any practical way of demonstrating the bomb. If it was to be used, it had to be dropped on Japan, and President Truman then made the decision to do this. On August 6, 1945, the bomb was dropped by a single plane on Hiroshima and an entire city disappeared, with the instantaneous loss of 70,000 lives. In time many other persons died from radiation poisoning and other effects. Since no surrender was received, a second bomb was dropped on Nagasaki, obliterating that city. Even the most fanatical of the Japanese leaders saw what was happening and surrender came quickly. The only departure from unconditional surrender was to allow the Japanese to retain their emperor (Hirohito, 1901–1989), but only with the proviso that he would be subject in every respect to the orders of the occupation commander. The formal surrender took place September 2, 1945, in Tokyo Bay on the deck of the battleship *Missouri*, and the occupation of Japan began under the immediate control of the American commander General Douglas MacArthur (1880–1964).

EUROPE AFTER WORLD WAR II: 1945 TO 1953

General Nature of the Peace Settlement

After World War II there was no clear-cut settlement in treaty form as there was after World War I. Planning had been done at the major wartime conferences and in the years immediately following the German surrender, a series of de facto arrangements were made, shaped by the course of events during the occupation of Germany and the opening years of the so-called Cold War which followed the breakdown of the wartime alliance between the Western powers (Britain, France, and the U.S.) and the Soviet Union.

The Atlantic Charter

Anglo-American ideas about what the postwar world should be like were expressed by Roosevelt and Churchill at their meeting off the coast of Newfoundland in August 1941. This was a general statement of goals: restoration of the sovereignty and self-government of nations conquered by Hitler, free access to world trade and resources, cooperation to improve living standards and economic security, and a peace that would ensure freedom from fear and want and stop the use of force and aggression as instruments of national policy, what Roosevelt had earlier called "The Four Freedoms."

Postwar Planning During World War II

At the Casablanca Conference, the policy of requiring unconditional surrender by the Axis powers was announced. This ensured that at the end of the war, all responsibility for government of the defeated nations would fall on the victors, and they would have a free hand in rebuilding government in those countries. No real planning was done in detail before the time arrived to meet this responsibility. It was done for the most part as the need arose.

At Teheran, the Big Three did discuss in a general way the occupation and demilitarization of Germany. They also laid the foundation for a post-war organization—the United Nations Organization—which like the earlier League of Nations was supposed to help regulate international relations and keep the peace and ensure friendly cooperation between the nations of the world.

One possible postwar plan for Germany was initially accepted by Roosevelt and Churchill in September 1944 and then discarded when its impracticality became apparent to all. This was the Morgenthau Plan, named after U.S. Secretary of the Treasury Henry Morgenthau, Jr., who was instrumental in proposing it. This harsh scheme would have largely destroyed Germany as an industrial power and returned it to an agricultural/pastoral economy. British and Americans realized that the resources of German heavy industry would be necessary to the recovery and vitality of the rest of Europe.

At Potsdam, agreement was reached to sign peace treaties as soon as possible with former German allies. A Council of Foreign Ministers was established to draft the treaties. Several meetings were held in 1946 and 1947 and treaties were signed with Italy, Rumania, Hungary, Bulgaria, and Finland. These states paid reparations and agreed to some territorial readjustments as a price for peace. No agreement could be reached on Japan or Germany. In 1951, the Western powers led by the U.S. concluded a treaty with Japan without Russian participation. The latter made their own treaty in 1956. A final meeting of the Council of Foreign Ministers broke up in 1947 over Germany, and no peace treaty was ever signed with that country. The division of Germany for purposes of occupation and military government became permanent, with the three Western zones joining and eventually becoming the

Federal Republic of Germany and the Russian zone becoming the German Demo-cratic Republic.

Arrangements for the United Nations were confirmed at the Yalta Conference: the large powers would predominate in a Security Council, where they would have permanent seats together with several other powers elected from time to time from among the other members of the U.N. Consent of all the permanent members was necessary for any action to be taken by the Security Council (thus giving the large powers a veto). The General Assembly was to include all members.

EASTERN EUROPE: 1945–1953

The Soviet Union

Much of European Russia had been devastated, and about 25 million people made homeless. Recovery was achieved using the same drastic, dictatorial methods used by the Communists during the 1930s. Stalin's dictatorship became more firmly entrenched than ever. Any potential opposition was purged. In March 1946 a fourth five-year plan was adopted by the Supreme Soviet intended to increase industrial output to a level 50 percent higher than before the war. A bad harvest and food shortage in 1946 had been relieved by a good harvest in 1947, and in December 1947, the government announced the end of food rationing. At the same time a drastic currency devaluation was put through, which brought immediate hardship to many people but strengthened the Soviet economy in the long run. As a result of these and other forceful and energetic measures, the Soviet Union was able within a few years to make good most of the wartime damage and to surpass pre-war levels of production. While this was being done at home, Stalin pursued an aggressive foreign policy and established a series of Soviet satellite states in Eastern Europe.

The Communization of Eastern Europe

The fate of Eastern Europe (including Poland, Hungary, Rumania, Bulgaria, Czechoslovakia, and the Russian zone of Germany) from 1945 on was determined by the presence of Russian armies in that area. Stalin undoubtedly wanted a group of friendly nations on his western border from which invasion had come twice during his lifetime. The Russian Communists were also determined to support the advance of a communist system similar to that developed in Russia into the countries of Eastern Europe.

Communization of Eastern Europe and the establishment of regimes in the satellite areas of the Soviet Union occurred in stages over a three-year period follow-ing the end of the war. The timetable of events varied in each country.

Poland: A Test Case

As agreed at Yalta, the Lublin Committee was expanded into a provisional government by the inclusion of Stanislas Mikolajczyk (1901–1967) and other lead-ers from the London Polish government in exile. Communists occupied ministries controlling police, internal affairs, and the military, ensuring that power eventually remained in their control. The Polish Workers (Communist) Party knew it had very little backing among the Polish people who were strongly Catholic and anti-Russian, and they maintained tight control over them from the beginning. Elections agreed to at Yalta were finally held in 1947, but under conditions that made the victory of the Communists inevitable. Mikolajczyk, frustrated in his efforts to influence the government, resigned, went into opposition, and then finally fled the country later in 1947.

Hungary

Toward the end of the war, with German control weakened by defeats at the hands of the Russians, the Hungarian government changed hands and a new regime concluded an armistice on January 20, 1945. Hungary then changed sides and joined the United Nations in the war against Germany. In November 1945 a general election gave victory to the anti-Communist Smallholders Party, whose leader, Zoltan Tildy (1889–1961), formed a coalition government. The government found itself in increasing economic difficulties, and by 1947 the Communists—with Soviet support—began a purge and takeover of the government. A new constitution was promulgated on August 7, 1949. The Communist regime was now firmly established and began a program of nationalization of industry followed by a five-year plan of development on the Russian model.

The refusal of the Roman Catholic Church in Hungary to make concessions to the government led to the arrest and trial of Josef Cardinal Mindszenty (1892–1975), who was sentenced in February 1949 to life imprisonment. Other bishops continued their opposition to the government for about two years before they finally took an oath of allegiance to the people's republic in July 1951.

Bulgaria

The Red Army invaded Bulgaria in 1944. The Soviet-sponsored government established in September contained only a few Communists, but they occupied key positions of power. Bulgaria formally capitulated on October 28, 1944, and remained under occupation by the Red Army. In 1946, the Communists made a sweeping purge of the government, executing or removing some 1,500 high-ranking officials of the old regime and many more lesser government officials. A referendum in September formally rejected any restoration of the pre-war monarchy, and later that same month Bulgaria was declared a people's republic.

Veteran Communist Georgi Dimitrov (1882–1949) returned from Moscow to become premier in February 1947. In that year, a Bulgarian Peace Treaty was signed at Paris requiring Bulgaria to pay indemnities and limiting the size of its armed forces. During 1947 the government began a program of nationalization by taking over banks and industries. In December, Soviet forces ended their occupation, leaving behind a firmly entrenched Communist regime which signed a treaty of friendship with the Soviet Union the following year.

Rumania

During the war, Rumania was governed by a pro-fascist regime which allied the country with the Axis. With Russian armies invading the country, King Michael dismissed the government and accepted armistice terms from the United Nations. The Russians occupied the capital of Bucharest in August 1944. As in other areas of Eastern Europe, a coalition government was first formed with Communists participating along with other parties, but from the beginning the Communists held the real power. At the end of 1947, King Michael abdicated under Communist pressure. Following elections in 1948, a new constitution was adopted patterned after the Russian model. By the end of 1949, Rumania had become completely Communist and a satellite of the Soviet Union.

East Germany

During the Nazi period, a number of German Communists fled to Moscow. When the Red Army invaded Germany, these exiles returned under the leadership of Wilhelm Pieck and Otto Grotewohl. As relations broke down between the four occupying powers, the Soviet authorities gradually created a Communist state in their zone. On October 7, 1948, a German Democratic Republic was established. Pieck became president and Grotewohl head of a predominantly Communist cabinet. In June 1950, an agreement with Poland granted formal recognition of the Oder-Neisse Line as the boundary between the two states. Economic progress was unsatisfactory for most of the population, and on June 16–17, 1953, riots occurred in East Berlin which were suppressed by Soviet forces using tanks. In East Germany, a program of economic reform was announced which eventually brought some improvement.

Special Cases

Czechoslovakia tried to remain relatively free and democratic while attempting to peacefully coexist with the Soviet Union. The government in exile in London under President Eduard Benes (1884–1948) maintained good relations with Moscow during the war. In April 1945 Benes appointed a national front government which was a genuine coalition of parties. The government moved to Prague May 10, 1945. A sweeping purge of those who had collaborated with the Germans was carried out. In addition, ethnic Germans were deprived of their citizenship and eventually expelled. On July 7, 1947, the Czech government decided to accept Marshall Plan aid and to participate in the carrying-out of the plan. At this point Soviet pressure caused the Czech government to break off this policy and withdraw.

The period of genuine coalition government lasted about three years in Czechoslovakia. But here as elsewhere in Eastern Europe, the Communists seized total control of the government, eliminating other political elements. The Communist coup was carried out February 26, 1948. With Russian support they then put pressure on President Benes to agree to a cabinet under Klement Gottwald (1896–1953) which would be primarily Communist. On March 10, a major obstacle to communization was removed when Foreign Minister Jan Masaryk (son of Thomas Masaryk, founder of the Czech Republic) was killed in a fall from his office window which the authorities reported as suicide. A far-reaching purge in the next several months transformed a democratic Czechoslovakia into a "people's democracy" with a single party government. President Benes resigned June 7 because of ill health and died shortly after on September 3. On June 14, Klement Gottwald became the new president and on January 1, 1949, a Soviet-style five-year plan of industrial development began with the aim of making the country independent of the West.

In June 1949 a campaign began against the Roman Catholic Church which as elsewhere in Eastern Europe proved to be a source of opposition to the Communist program. The government formed its own Catholic Action Committee to take control of the local church from Archbishop Joseph Beran and the Catholic hierarchy. On October 14, the government assumed full control of all Catholic affairs. The Catholic clergy were required to swear a loyalty oath to the Communist state.

Czech politics followed a course of increasingly repressive measures paralleling that of Stalin during his last years in the Soviet Union. A series of purges were carried out against enemies of the government, including some of its own members who were accused of anti-Soviet, pro-Western activities.

In Yugoslavia, Marshal Tito (1892–1980) and his Communist partisan movement emerged from the war in a strong position because of their effective campaign against the German occupation. Tito was able to establish a Communist government despite considerable pressure from Stalin, and pursue a course independent of the Soviet Union unique among the countries of Eastern Europe.

Elections held November 11, 1945 gave victory to Tito's Communist-dominated National Front. A few days later the Yugoslav monarchy was abolished and the country declared to be the Federal People's Republic of Yugoslavia.

In 1947, Yugoslavia appeared to follow the lead of the other Eastern European states when it concluded treaties of friendship and alliance with a number of these states and became a founding member of the Communist Information Agency (Cominform)—an organization created to take the place of the old Communist International. But Tito's independence caused Stalin to recall Soviety advisors and break off relations. On June 28, 1948, the Cominform formally expelled Yugoslavia.

In 1949, the satellites of Eastern Europe broke off economic relations with Yugoslavia. In September the Soviet Union denounced its Treaty of Friendship with Tito's regime. Tito's position was shown to be secure, however, when elections in March 1950 gave overwhelming victory to his People's Front candidates. Tito followed a policy of informal rapprochement with the West. In July 1952, the United States agreed to supply tanks, artillery, and jet aircraft to the Yugoslavs despite the fact that Tito—while retaining independence of Stalin—remained staunchly Communist in his government of Yugoslavia.

WESTERN EUROPE: 1945–1953

Italy

In Italy, following the end of hostilities with Germany, the leaders of the Resistance in the north ousted Premier Ivan Bonomi and placed one of their own top leaders, Ferruccio Parri, in power. Parri was the leader of a faction—the Party of Action—which was socialist in its program. Although he was a man of great moral stature, he was a poor administrator and did not appeal to the public. He was left politically isolated when the Socialist leader Pietro Nenni (1890–1980) made an alliance with the Communists. Meanwhile, more conservative forces had been gathering strength, and in November 1945, Parri was forced to resign.

The monarchy which had governed Italy since the time of unification in the mid-19th century was now discarded in favor of a republic. King Victor Emmanual III (1869–1947), compromised by his association with Mussolini, resigned in favor of his son, but a referendum in June 1946 established a republic. In simultaneous elections for a constituent assembly, three parties predominated: the Social Democrats, the Communists, and the Christian Democrats. Under the new regime Enrico de Nicola was chosen president and Alcide de Gasperi (1881–1954) formed a new coalition cabinet.

The Christian Democrats and their leader Alcide de Gasperi dominated Italian politics for the next several years. On February 10, 1947, a peace treaty was signed at Paris. Italy paid $350 million in reparations and suffered some minor losses of territory. Trieste, which was in dispute between Italy and Yugoslavia, became a free territory. De Gasperi's government followed a policy of cooperation with the West and kept Italy non-Communist. In April 1948 in the first elections under the new constitution, the Christian Democrats won an absolute majority of seats in the Italian parliament. The issue of communism remained very much alive, and there was considerable Communist-inspired unrest, especially after an attempt was made on the life of the Communist leader Palmiro Togliatti (1893–1964). The Marshall Plan helped stabilize the situation. In 1948, Italy received $601 million in aid. On April 4, 1949, Italy signed the North Atlantic Treaty and became a member of NATO, firmly allied to the West. The de Gasperi era came to an end in 1953. He won a narrow electoral victory as the head of a coalition in June and resigned July 28 after a vote of no confidence. He died a year later, August 19, 1954.

France

In the last two years of the war, France recovered sufficiently under the leadership of General Charles de Gaulle to begin playing a significant military and political role once again. In July 1944, the United States recognized de Gaulle's Committee of National Liberation as the de facto government of areas liberated from the German occupation. As the war ended, this provisional government purged collaborators, including Marshal Pétain and Pierre Laval, who had headed the Vichy regime during the war.

In October 1945 elections for a constituent assembly showed the strength of left-wing forces; de Gaulle, after a period in which he tried to work with the more radical forces, finally resigned in January 1947 and went into retirement. A revised constitution was adopted in October 1946 establishing a Fourth Republic, with a weak executive dominated by a strong legislature. This situation resulted in cabinet instability and a series of governments over the next several years.

Meanwhile, General de Gaulle had assumed control of a nationwide *Rassemblement du Peuple Français* (RPF) intended to unify non-Communist elements and reform the system of government. For a time the RPF grew in strength at both the local and national level although de Gaulle himself remained out of office. Then, with the lessening of the Communist danger and improvements in the economy, moderates began to oppose what they perceived to be de Gaulle's authoritarian tendencies. By 1953, the RPF had faded from the scene, and de Gaulle returned to retirement.

Economically, France became a welfare state. De Gaulle, during his provisional government, inaugurated this to associate the working classes with a new spirit of national unity and to deprive the Communists of their propaganda advantage. During the year and a half following de Gaulle's retirement, the three parties (Socialist, Communist, and MRP, or Popular Republican Movement) which dominated politics during that period agreed on a program building on reforms begun during the Popular Front of the 1930s. This program, included nationalization of coal mines, banking, insurance, gas, and electricity as well as allowances for dependent children, and began a comprehensive system of social security legislation which eventually came to cover more than 50 percent of the French people.

These changes were accepted by all subsequent regimes as a fait accompli. Although excessively bureaucratic and regulatory, the welfare state did provide a cushion of security for the French population during the period of inflation and economic hardship in the immediate postwar years prior to the advent of the Marshall Plan. The establishment of a national planning office was a significant achievement that provided the French government with a framework for guiding economic development, which Italy and West Germany lacked. This was important in directing French resources effectively when production began to rise during the prosperous years of the 1950s.

In foreign affairs, France occupied Germany. In addition, the Fourth Republic was faced with two major problems abroad when it attempted to assert its authority over Indochina and Algeria. The Indochina situation resulted in a long and costly war against nationalists and Communists under Ho Chi Minh (1890–1969). French involvement ended with the Geneva accords of 1954 and French withdrawal. The Algerian struggle reached a crisis in 1958 resulting in General de Gaulle's return to power and the creation of a new Fifth Republic.

Germany

In May 1945, when Germany surrendered unconditionally, the country lay in ruins. About three-quarters of city houses had been gutted by air raids, industry was in a shambles, and the country was divided into zones of occupation ruled by foreign military governors. Economic chaos was the rule, currency was virtually worthless, food was in short supply, and the black market flourished for those who could afford to buy in it. By the Potsdam agreements, Germany lost about one-quarter of its pre-war territory. In addition, some 12 million people of German origin driven from their homes in countries like Poland and Czechoslovakia had to be fed, housed, and clothed along with the indigenous population.

Demilitarization, denazification, and democratization were the initial goals of the occupation forces. All four wartime allies agreed on the trial of leading Nazis for a variety of war crimes and "crimes against humanity." An International Military Tribunal was established at Nuremburg to try 22 major war criminals, and lesser courts tried many others. Most of the defendants were executed, although a few like Rudolf Hess were given life imprisonment.

The denazification program met with indifferent success. It started out as an effort to investigate everyone who had any connection to the Nazi Party. This included so many that the proceedings became bogged down. It became apparent after a time that not all could be investigated because of the sheer magnitude of the task. Some important Nazi officials were found and punished. Often it was easier to prosecute those less involved, and some important offenders escaped. There was quiet sabotage and a conspiracy of silence by a cynical population. Eventually wider amnesties were granted. The process never officially ended but simply faded away.

The reestablishment of German government in the Western zones met with more success. As relations between the three Western powers and the Soviets gradually broke down in Germany, East and West became separate states. In the West, the British and American zones were fused into one in 1946, with the French joining in 1948. Political parties were gradually re-established.

During 1947 there were two meetings of the Council of Foreign Ministers to work out a peace treaty for Germany. Both failed and the occupying powers began to go their own ways in their own zones—the Russians to create a Communist satellite state in East Germany and the British, Americans, and French to create a West German Federal Republic.

In February 1948, a charter granted further powers of government to the Germans in the American and British zones. Later that year, the Russians and East Germans, in an effort to force the Western powers out of their zones in Berlin, began a blockade of the city which was located within the Russian zone. The response was an allied airlift to supply the city, and eventually, after some months, the blockade was called off.

Meanwhile reconstruction in western Germany proceeded. On June 1, 1948, a six-power agreement of the three Western powers and Belgium, the Netherlands, and Luxembourg was reached, calling for international control of the Ruhr industrial area, German representation in the European Recovery Program (Marshall Plan), and the drafting of a federal constitution for a western Germany.

In April 1949, the three Western powers agreed on an Occupation Statute for Western Germany which gave the Germans considerable autonomy at the national level while reserving wide powers of intervention to the occupying powers. In May, a parliamentary council representing the state governments adopted a Basic Law for a Federal Republic of Germany with its capital at Bonn. Elections in August gave the Christian Democrats a slight lead over the Social Democrats, and the next month Konrad Adenauer (1876–1967) (Christian Democrat) became Chancellor of the new West German government. Theodore Heuss (1884–1963) (Free Democrat) was elected president. For the next 14 years, Adenauer (who was 73 at the start) and the Christian Democrats remained in power.

West German economic recovery made it the strongest industrial power of Western Europe. Wartime damage to German industry was less than appeared on the surface, and despite early taking of industrial assets as reparations, recovery was rapid once the Marshall Plan came into being. Even the expellees from the east were an asset, as they provided extra labor, sometimes skilled. A program of industrial expansion with careful planning and investments, aided by the willingness of the population to accept relatively modest living standards and to work hard, paid dividends. There was little labor strife and for several years no need to provide for military expenditures. By 1950, industrial production surpassed prewar production. West German rearmament was felt by the Western powers to be necessary to the defense of Western Europe.

The possibility of West German rearmament aroused strong protests from the Soviet Union and opposition within West Germany itself from the Social Democrats. Nevertheless, in March 1954, President Heuss signed a constitutional amendment allowing German rearmament. By the end of the year, Germany and France had worked out their disagreements over the Saar, and France joined the other Western powers in agreeing to German membership in the Western alliance. In May 1955, West Germany gained sovereign status and joined NATO and the division of Germany into two separate states was complete.

Postwar Great Britain

A program of restoring the balance of trade, directing investment of resources to ensure efficiency, and a vast new outlay for social services was agreed on by the parties even before the war ended. As early as 1942, a report known for its author, Sir William Beveridge (1879–1963), proposed "full employment in a free society" and social security "from the cradle to the grave."

As the war ended in May 1945, elections were held that returned a Labour government under Clement Attlee in July. The new government enacted an extensive program increasing unemployment insurance and providing insurance for old age. A comprehensive medical and health service for the entire population was established. Educational facilities were extended, and new planned housing projects built. Efforts were made to rehabilitate depressed areas.

In addition, Labour nationalized the Bank of England, the coal mines, transportation, iron and steel, and utilities (including electricity, gas, and communications). The Conservatives accepted much of this program but centered criticism on Labor's program of nationalizing the "commanding heights" of the economy—especially the iron and steel industry.

In 1951 a Conservative majority was returned, and Winston Churchill became prime minister again. The new regime immediately reversed the nationalization of iron and steel. Other measures survived, however, especially the universal health care program which proved to be one of the most popular parts of the Labour achievement. In April 1955, Churchill resigned for reasons of age and health and turned over the prime minister's office to Anthony Eden (1897–1977).

THE MARSHALL PLAN

European recovery from the effects of the war was slow for the first two or three years after 1945. The European Recovery Program (Marshall Plan, named after the secretary of state and World War II army chief of staff) began in 1948 and showed substantial results in all the Western European countries that took part. The most remarkable gains were in West Germany. The country soon experienced gains so great as to constitute what many called an "economic miracle." During the first two

POLITICAL ALIGNMENT OF EUROPE

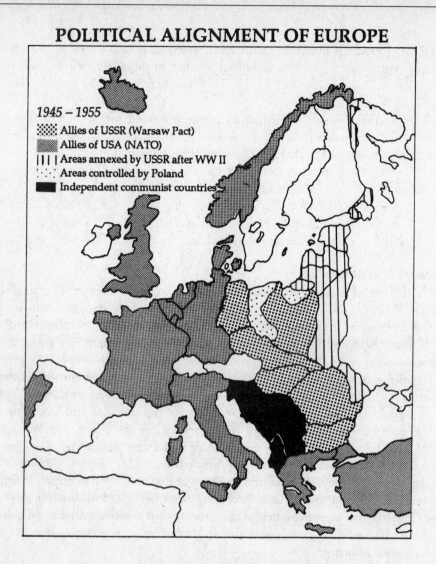

1945 – 1955

- ⬚ Allies of USSR (Warsaw Pact)
- ▨ Allies of USA (NATO)
- ||| Areas annexed by USSR after WW II
- ⬚ Areas controlled by Poland
- ■ Independent communist countries

years of the Marshall Plan about $8 billion of American aid is estimated to have resulted in an overall expansion of some $30 billion annual output of goods and services. The Plan aimed to strengthen Western Europe's resistance to Communism.

THE MOVEMENT TOWARD WEST EUROPEAN ECONOMIC UNITY

In May 1951, French Foreign Minister Robert Schuman (1886–1963) came forward with the Schuman Plan for a European Coal and Steel Community. This called for a pooling of resources in heavy industry and the elimination of tariffs throughout Western Europe (including France, West Germany, Italy, Belgium, the Netherlands, and Luxembourg). By April 1951 a treaty was signed incorporating the proposals of the Schuman Plan and creating the community from which other steps toward European unity grew (Common Market, General Agreement on Trade and Tariffs, etc.).

THE COLD WAR

World War II was an exception to the rule of general hostility between capitalism and communism. It turned out, however, to be an alliance of expediency only. It therefore broke down when the common enemy was no longer a threat.

STRENGTHENING OF NATO

One result of the Korean War was the strengthening of the NATO alliance begun in 1949. A mood approaching panic set in after the North Korean invasion began. The U.S. expressed its fear that NATO would be too weak to resist a possible Russian attack which might come while American forces were engaged in the Far East. The U.S. insisted on a policy of rearming West Germany. Eventually Western European nations accepted West German rearmament but only after agreement to make German forces part of a European defense under NATO control. This policy of military buildup changed the emphasis of foreign aid under the Marshall Plan. In the first two years the aid was primarily economic, with few strings attached. Later it became increasingly military aid.

LOSS OF EUROPEAN OVERSEAS EMPIRES

World War II created disruptions that resulted in irresistible pressures for independence in overseas European colonies. British, Dutch, French, Portuguese, and Belgian empires in Asia and Africa virtually disappeared in the space of about 15 years following the war. In some instances, withdrawal was accomplished by a relatively peaceful transfer of power (as with the British withdrawal from India in 1947), but in other cases the colonial power resisted separation and long, bitter military conflicts resulted.

BRITISH OVERSEAS WITHDRAWAL

Palestine, Israel, and the Arab-Israeli Conflict

Britain received a mandate from the League of Nations following World War I to govern Palestine. Britain indicated in the Balfour Declaration of November 2, 1917, that it favored the creation of a Jewish "national home" in Palestine. The British position there was complicated by its involvement in the creation of Arab states such as Saudi Arabia and Transjordan, which were adamantly opposed to any Jewish state in Palestine.

Creation of Israel

Following World War II, there was a considerable migration of Jews who had survived the Nazi Holocaust to Palestine to join Jews who had settled there earlier. Conflicts broke out with the Arabs. The British occupying forces tried to suppress the violence and to negotiate a settlement between the factions. In 1948, after negotiations failed, the British, feeling they could no longer support the cost of occupation, announced their withdrawal. Zionist leaders then proclaimed the independent state of Israel and took up arms to fight the armies of Egypt, Syria, and other Arab states which invaded the Jewish-held area. The new Israeli state quickly proved its technological and military superiority by defeating the invaders. Over 500,000 Arabs were displaced from their homes by the establishment of Israel. Efforts to permanently relocate them failed, and they became a factor in the continued violence in the Middle East.

The Jews of Israel created a modern parliamentary state on the European model with an economy and technology superior to their Arab neighbors. The new state was thought by many Arabs to be simply another manifestation of European imperialism made worse by religious antagonisms.

Further Arab-Israeli Wars

In 1956, the Israelis chose the opportunity created by the ill-fated Anglo-French attempt to retake the Suez Canal to launch their own attack on Egypt. Public opinion eventually forced the withdrawal of the British and French, and although the Israelis had achieved military successes, they found themselves barred from use of the Canal by Egypt, which was now in control.

In 1967, Israel defeated Egypt, Syria and Jordan in a six-day war, and the Israelis occupied additional territory including the Jordanian sector of the city of Jerusalem. An additional million Arabs came under Israeli rule as a result of this campaign.

The Palestine Liberation Organization

Although defeated, the Arabs refused to sign any treaty or to come to terms with Israel. Palestinian refugees living in camps in states bordering Israel created grave problems. A Palestine Liberation Organization (PLO) was formed to fight for the establishment of an Arab Palestinian state on territory taken from Israel on the west bank of the Jordan River. The PLO resorted to terrorist tactics both against Israel and other states in support of their cause.

In October 1973, the Egyptians and Syrians launched an attack on Israel known as the Yom Kippur War. With some difficulty the attacks were repulsed. A settlement was mediated by American Secretary of State Henry Kissinger. The situation has remained unstable, however, with both sides resorting to border raids and other forms of violence short of full-scale war.

The Egyptian Revolution

The British exercised control over Egypt from the end of the 19th century and declared it a British protectorate in December 1914. In 1922 Egypt became nominally independent.

The government under King Farouk I (1920–1965) did little to alleviate the overriding problem of poverty after the war. In 1952, a group of army officers, including Gamal Abdel Nasser (1918–1970) and Anwar Sadat (1918–1981), plotted against the government, and on July 23 the king was overthrown. Colonel Nasser became premier in April 1954. A treaty with Britain later that year resulted in the withdrawal of all British troops from the Canal Zone.

The Suez Canal Crisis

The United States had agreed to lend money to Egypt, under the leadership of Colonel Gamal Abdul Nasser, to build the Aswan Dam, but refused to give arms. Nasser then drifted toward the Soviet Union and in 1956 established diplomatic relations with the People's Republic of China. In July 1956 the U.S. withdrew its loan to Egypt. In response, Nasser nationalized the Suez Canal. France, Great Britain, and Israel then attacked Egypt but Eisenhower demanded that they pull out. On November 6, a cease fire was announced.

India and Pakistan

British rule in India, the largest and most populous of the colonial areas ruled by Europeans, came to an end in 1947 with a relatively peaceful transfer of power. Complications ensued when Muslim leaders, representing some 100 million Muslims, did not want to live in a state dominated by Hindus and the Congress Party and insisted on a state of their own.

Partition

The British decided to partition the subcontinent into two separate states: India—predominantly Hindu with a population of 350 million, and Pakistan—predominantly Muslim with a population of 75 million. About 40 million Muslims remained within Indian borders. Independence resulted in bloody rioting between the religious factions, mass expulsions, and the emigration of millions of people. Perhaps a million people lost their lives before the rioting eventually died out. The territory of Kashmir remained in dispute but finally was joined to India in 1975.

India

India under Jawaharlal Nehru (1889–1964) and the Congress Party became a parliamentary democracy. Nehru died in 1964. His daughter, Indira Gandhi (1917–1984), became prime minister from 1966 on. The country made economic progress, but gains were largely negated by a population increase to 600 million from 350 million. In 1975, Indira Gandhi was found guilty of electoral fraud. She resorted to force to keep herself in power. When elections were permitted in 1977 she was ousted by the opposition. Eventually her son, Rajiv Ghandi (1944–1991), became prime minister.

Pakistan

Pakistan retained the trappings of democracy with a written constitution and parliamentary form of government, but became in reality a military dictatorship. The country was divided into East and West Pakistan, separated by 1,000 miles of Indian territory. The two areas had the same religion but different traditions, resulting in a quarrel that led East Pakistan in 1971 to declare itself the independent state of Bangladesh. The Pakistan government in Karachi sent military forces to the east to regain control and bloody fighting ensued. India then intervened militarily, and after defeating the Pakistani army, forced the recognition of an independent Bangladesh.

Malaya, Burma, and Ceylon

Malaya, Burma, and Ceylon were other British colonies that gained independence. All three became members of the British Commonwealth. Malaya suffered nine years of internal strife which delayed independence until 1957, when the Federation of Malaya was created.

THE FRENCH IN INDOCHINA AND ALGERIA

Indochina

Following World War II, the French returned to Indochina and attempted to restore their rule there. The opposition nationalist movement was led by the veteran Communist Ho Chi Minh. War broke out between the nationalists and the French forces. Despite aid from the U.S., the French were unable to maintain their position in the north of Vietnam. In 1954 their army was surrounded at Dienbienphu and forced to surrender. This military disaster prompted a change of government in France.

The 1954 Geneva Conference: French Withdrawal

This new government under Premier Pierre Mendès-France (1907–1982) negotiated French withdrawal at a conference held at Geneva, Switzerland in 1954. Cambodia and Laos became independent and Vietnam was partitioned at the 17th parallel. The North, with its capital at Hanoi, became a Communist state under Ho Chi Minh. The South remained non-Communist. Under the Geneva Accords, elections were to be held in the South to determine the fate of that area. However, the United States chose to intervene and support the regime of Ngo Dinh Diem (1901–1963), and elections were never held. Eventually a second Vietnamese war resulted, with the United States playing the role earlier played by France.

Algeria

Following World War II, there was nationalist agitation in Algeria, Tunisia, and Morocco. The French government granted independence to Tunisia and Morocco, but Algeria was considered to be different. It was legally part of metropolitan France. Government there was heavily weighted in favor of the French minority (about 10 percent of the total population), and the Arab majority had few rights. In 1954 a large-scale revolt of Arab nationalists broke out. The French government began a campaign of suppression lasting over seven years and involving as many as 500,000 troops. Military casualties totaled at least 100,000 Arabs and 10,000 French killed, with thousands more civilian casualties. The savage campaign led to torture and other atrocities on both sides.

Army Revolt and the Return of General de Gaulle

Egypt and other Arab states gave aid to the Algerian Liberation Front. Algerian terrorists spread the violence as far as Paris itself. The rebellion led to the downfall of the Fourth Republic and the return to power of General de Gaulle, who established the Fifth Republic with himself as a strong president.

Algerian Independence

In a referendum, on January 8, 1961, the French people approved of eventual Algerian self-determination. In July 1962 French rule ended in Algeria. There was a mass exodus of Europeans from Algeria, but most Frenchmen were grateful to de Gaulle for ending the long Algerian conflict.

THE DUTCH AND INDONESIA

During World War II, the Japanese conquered the Dutch East Indies. At the end of the war, they recognized the independence of the area as Indonesia. When the Dutch attempted to return, four years of bloody fighting ensued against the nationalist forces of Achmed Sukarno (1901–1970). In 1949, the Dutch recognized Indonesian independence. In 1954, the Indonesians dissolved all ties with the Netherlands. Sukarno's regime became one of increasing dictatorship. In 1966, Sukarno was overthrown and replaced by a more stable administration under General Suharto.

THE COLD WAR AFTER THE DEATH OF STALIN

Following Stalin's death, Russian leaders—while maintaining an atmosphere first of tension and then of relaxation in international affairs—appeared more willing than Stalin to be conciliatory and to consider peaceful coexistence.

Eisenhower and the 1955 Geneva Summit

In the U.S. the atmosphere also changed with the election of President Dwight Eisenhower; and despite the belligerent rhetoric of Secretary of State John Foster Dulles (1888–1959), conciliatory gestures were not always automatically considered appeasement of the Communists. In 1955 a summit conference of Eisenhower, the British and French leaders, and Khrushchev (1894–1971) met at Geneva in an atmosphere more cordial than any since World War II. The "spirit of Geneva" did not last long, however.

THE CHANGING BALANCE OF POWER

De Gaulle as the Leader of an Independent Europe

After his return to power in France in 1958, General de Gaulle endeavored to make France a leader in European affairs with himself as spokesman for a Europe that he hoped would be a counter to the "dual hegemony" of the U.S. and U.S.S.R. His policies at times were anti-British or anti-American. He vetoed British entry into the Common Market, developed an independent French nuclear force, and tried to bridge the gap between East and West Europe. Despite his prestige as the last great wartime leader, he did not have great success. Nevertheless, Western Europe came into its own as a factor in international affairs.

Nuclear Weapons and the Arms Race

Nuclear weapons were a growing concern in the U.S., the Soviet Union, and other countries—especially those of Western Europe. The war in Korea and the rearmament of West Germany within NATO prevented any serious disarmament negotiations. Europe was divided into separate armed camps: NATO, and the Warsaw Pact led by the Soviet Union. In the next several years, the world moved into the age of rocketry, nuclear-powered submarines, and other military products of so-called "high technology." Russia tested its first bomb in 1949. By 1952 the British had tested an atomic bomb. The U.S. successfully developed and tested a thermo-nuclear weapon (H-bomb) in 1952. In 1953 the Russians exploded a similar weapon. In 1961 the Soviet Union exploded a 60-megaton H-bomb. The French joined the nuclear powers in February 1960. They tested an H-bomb in August 1968. China also became a nuclear power, exploding its first nuclear device in 1964. It fired its first rocket with a nuclear warhead in October 1966 and tested an H-bomb in June 1967. Even Israel and India built reactors with the potential for producing weapons.

The International Arms Trade and Military Expenditures

Between 1960 and 1975, the world's annual military expenditures nearly doubled. The U.S. and U.S.S.R. accounted for about 60 percent. In less affluent Afro-Asian nations, spending on weapons expanded and helped contribute to political instability and mistrust. Before World War II, military expenditures are estimated to have been less than 1 percent of the total world gross national product. In 1983 the figure had risen to 6 percent. But the overthrow of Communist regimes in Eastern Europe and changes in the former Soviet Union have led to substantial cutbacks in defense.

A NEW EUROPE

Russia after Stalin

Joseph Stalin died in March 1953. His ruthlessness and paranoid suspicions grew worse towards the end of his life. Postwar economic reconstruction was accompanied by ideological intolerance and a regime of terror and persecution with overtones of anti-Semitism. There were indications of a new series of purges coming when Stalin died.

A so-called "troika" consisting of Georgy Malenkov (1902–1988) (Chairman of the Council of Ministers), Lavrenti Beria (1899–1953) (Stalin's chief of police), and Vyacheslav Molotov (1890–1986) (foreign minister) took over government. A power struggle took place in which the first event was the secret trial and execution of Beria. Eventually a little-known party functionary, Nikita Khrushchev, became Communist Party General Secretary in 1954. Malenkov and Molotov were demoted to lesser positions and eventually disappeared from public view.

Khrushchev's Secret Speech and the Anti-Stalin Campaign

Khrushchev in 1956 delivered a "secret speech" to the 20th Congress of the

Communist Party of the Soviet Union. It soon became public knowledge that he had accused Stalin of wholesale "violations of socialist legality" and of creating a "cult of personality." Khrushchev's policy of relaxing the regime of terror and oppression of the Stalin years became known as "The Thaw," after the title of a novel by Ilya Ehrenburg (1891–1967).

Change occurred in foreign affairs also. Khrushchev visited Belgrade and reestablished relations with Tito, admitting that there was more than one road to socialism. He also visited the United States, met with President Eisenhower, and toured the country. Later, relations became more tense after the U-2 spy plane incident.

Following the loss of face sustained by Russia as a result of the Cuban Missile Crisis and the failure of Khrushchev's domestic agricultural policies, he was forced out of the party leadership and lived in retirement in Moscow until his death in 1971.

Khrushchev's Successors: Brezhnev, Andropov, and Gorbachev

After Khrushchev's ouster, the leadership in the Central Committee divided power, making Leonid Brezhnev (1906–1982) party secretary and Aleksei Kosygin chairman of the council of ministers, or premier. Brezhnev's party position ensured his dominance by the 1970s. In 1977, he presided over the adoption of a new constitution which altered the structure of the regime very little. The same year he was elected president by the Supreme Soviet.

Stalin's successors rehabilitated many of Stalin's victims. They also permitted somewhat greater freedom in literary and artistic matters and even allowed some political criticism. Controls were maintained, however, and sometimes were tightened. Anti-Semitism was also still present, and Soviet Jews were long denied permission to emigrate to Israel. American pressure may have helped to relax this policy in the 1970s, when about 150,000 Jews were allowed to leave Russia. Other evidences of continued tight control were the 1974 arrest for treason and forcible deportation of the writer Alexander Solzhenitsyn and the arrest and internal exile for many years of the physicist Andrei Sakharov, who was an outspoken critic of the regime and its violations of human rights.

Brezhnev occupied the top position of power until his death in 1982. He was briefly succeeded by Yuri Andropov (1914–1984) (a former secret police chief) and then by Mikhail Gorbachev, who carried out a further relaxation of the internal regime. Gorbachev pushed disarmament and detente in foreign relations, and attempted a wide range of internal reforms known as *perestroika* ("restructuring").

CHANGE IN EASTERN EUROPE

Poland

Khrushchev's speech denouncing Stalin was followed almost immediately by revolts in Poland and Hungary, apparently encouraged by what was happening in Russia. In Poland, Wladyslaw Gomulka (1905–1982), previously discredited and imprisoned for "nationalist deviationism," emerged to take over the government.

Khrushchev and the Russians decided to tolerate Gomulka, who had wide support. His regime proceeded to halt collectivization of agriculture and curb the use of political terror.

The Solidarity Movement

In the 1980s, the trade union movement known as Solidarity and its leader, Lech Walesa, emerged as a political force, organizing mass protests in 1980–1981 and maintaining almost continuous pressure on the government headed by General Wojciech Jaruzelski. Despite government efforts to maintain strong central control and suppress the opposition, the ruling Communists were forced to recognize the opposition and make concessions.

Hungary

In Hungary in 1956, rioting against the Communist regime broke out and brought Imre Nagy to power. Khrushchev intervened forcibly, sending in Russian troops and tanks to replace Nagy (ca. 1895–1958) with a regime subservient to Moscow under Janos Kadar. But Soviet rule in Hungary was less restrictive than elsewhere. The outbreak of the Suez Canal crisis at this time distracted the Western powers from events in Hungary.

Intervention in Czechoslovakia (1968): The Brezhnev Doctrine

Early in 1968, Alexander Dubcek became leader of the Czechoslovakian Communist Party and began a process of liberalization. On August 23, Soviet troops (together with East Germany, Hungary, Poland, and Bulgaria) established a military occupation. In April 1969, Dubcek was forced out of power and a new regime established under Gustav Husák. Nevertheless, a few changes remained, such as the federalization of the country to give equality to the Slovaks.

Continued Change in Eastern Europe

Despite the political limits imposed by the Soviet Union on their East European satellites, economic developments took place during the 1970s and 1980s which eventually led to further liberalization and change in Eastern European countries. The U.S.S.R., short of capital for development, could not supply the needs of East European states, and these began to turn to Western banks. With increasing economic ties and more East-West trade, the political situation changed. The Czechs, despite the 1968 intervention, voiced criticism of Soviet missiles on their territory. The Bulgarian government called for making East Europe a nuclear-free zone.

In Rumania, too, change occurred when the government insisted with some success on greater independence in foreign affairs. The Rumanians also resisted Soviet pressure for closer economic ties and greater dependence on the Soviet Union.

CHANGE IN WESTERN EUROPE

The Common Market

In March 1957, inspired chiefly by Belgian Foreign Minister Paul-Henri Spaak, two treaties were signed in Rome creating a European Atomic Energy Commission (Euratom) and a European Economic Community (the Common Market)—which eventually absorbed Euratom. The EEC was to be a customs union creating a free market area with a common external tariff for member nations. Toward the outside world, the EEC acted as a single bargaining agent for its members in commercial transactions, and it reached a number of agreements with other European and Third World states.

In 1976, the original six were joined by three new members: Britain, Ireland, and Denmark. The name was changed to "European Community." In 1979, there were three more applicants: Spain, Portugal, and Greece. These latter states were less well off and created problems of cheap labor, agricultural products, etc., which delayed their reception as members until 1986. The EC plans to abolish the last internal barriers and become a true common market for 320 million people by 1992. It is the largest single trading area, with one-fifth of the world's trade.

Great Britain Since 1951

After the postwar Labour government under Clement Attlee had achieved its major reforms, transforming Britain into a welfare state, it was succeeded by Conservative governments from 1951 to 1964 under Winston Churchill, Anthony Eden, and finally Harold Macmillan.

Labour returned to power under Sir Harold Wilson from 1964 to 1970. Public housing and slum clearance were again emphasized, the educational system was democratized, free medical services were restored, and social security pensions were increased. A Conservative regime under Edward Heath governed from 1970 to 1974, only to be ousted by Labour once again. Harold Wilson served as Labor prime minister from 1974 to 1976 when he retired to be succeeded by James Callaghan. In 1979, the Conservatives returned under the leadership of the first woman prime minister in British history, Margaret Thatcher, whose success in male-dominated politics earned her the name "the Iron Lady."

Britain's major postwar problems have been economic. Some $40 billion in foreign investments were liquidated to pay for the British war effort. Thus, investment income was lost after the war, making necessary a considerable expansion of exports to pay for needed imports. There was difficulty in competing for foreign markets. Labor was low in productivity and was outstripped by both West Germany and Japan. Demands for austerity and sacrifice from labor unions to control inflationary pressures resulted in a nationwide coal strike and prolonged work stoppage in 1972. Inflationary pressure increased with the Arab oil embargo and the drastic increase in oil prices during the winter of 1973–1974.

After 1974, Labour changed its policies and sought to cut public expenditures, use public funds for private investment, and limit wage increases. Priority was given to industrial expansion in several key industries with the most promise of growth. Labor for the first time in decades favored the private sector. The pound sterling was devalued from about $4 in 1945 to $1.60 in 1976 to provide more favorable trade conditions. British industry continued to be plagued by poor management and frequent strikes. Imports and pressures for higher wages and welfare benefits continued to fuel inflation.

Relations with Northern Ireland proved a burden to successive British governments. The 1922 settlement had left Northern Ireland as a self-governing part of the United Kingdom. Of 1.5 million inhabitants, one-third were Roman Catholic and two-thirds were Protestant. Catholics claimed they were discriminated against and pressed for annexation by the Republic of Ireland. Activity by the Irish Republican Army brought retaliation by Protestant extremists. From 1969 on, there was considerable violence, causing the British to bring in troops to maintain order. Over 1,500 were killed in the next several years in sporadic outbreaks of violence.

In 1976 Welsh and Scottish regional assemblies were established with jurisdiction over housing, health, education, and other areas of local concern.

Under Prime Minister Thatcher in the 1980s, the British economy improved somewhat. London regained some of its former power as a financial center. In recent years, an influx of people from former colonies in Asia, Africa, and the West Indies has caused some racial tensions.

Prime Minister Thatcher has been a partisan of free enterprise. She fought inflation with austerity and let economic problems spur British employers and unions to change for greater efficiency. She received a boost in popularity when Britain fought a brief war with Argentina over the Falkland islands and emerged victorious. She stressed close ties with the Republican administration of Ronald Reagan in the U.S. A Conservative victory in the 1987 elections made Thatcher the longest-serving prime minister in modern British history.

France Under the Fifth Republic

Under de Gaulle, a new constitution was drafted and approved establishing the Fifth Republic with a much strengthened executive in the form of a president with power to dissolve the legislature and call for elections, to submit important questions to popular referendum, and if necessary to assume emergency powers. De Gaulle used all these powers in his 11 years as president.

In domestic politics, de Gaulle strengthened the power of the president by often using the referendum and bypassing the Assembly. De Gaulle was re-elected in 1965, but people became restless with what amounted to a republican monarch. Labor became restive over inflation and housing while students objected to expenditures on nuclear forces rather than education. In May 1968, student grievances over conditions in the universities caused hundreds of thousands to revolt. They were soon joined by some 10 million workers, who paralyzed the economy. De Gaulle survived by promising educational reform and wage increases. New elections were held June 1968, and de Gaulle was returned to power. Promised reforms were begun, but in April 1969, he resigned and died about a year later.

De Gaulle's immediate successors were Georges Pompidou (1969–1974) and Valéry Giscard d'Estaing (1974–1981). Both provided France with firm leadership, and continued to follow an independent foreign policy.

In 1981 François Mitterand succeeded Giscard d'Estaing. He inherited a troubled economy. During his first year Mitterand tried to revitalize economic growth, granted wage hikes, reduced the work week, expanded paid vacations, and nationalized 11 large private companies and banks. The aim was to stimulate the economy by expanding worker purchasing power and confiscating the profits of large corporations for public investment. Loans were made abroad to finance this program. When results were poor, these foreign investors were reluctant to grant more credit. Mitterand then reversed his policy and began to cut taxes and social expenditures. By 1984, this had brought down inflation but increased unemployment.

Germany After Adenauer: Erhard as Chancellor

The Christian Democrats remained in power after West German independence for two main reasons: 1) prosperity which by the mid-1950s was reaching all classes of Germans, and 2) the unique personality of Chancellor Konrad Adenauer, who kept the country firmly allied with NATO and the West. Christian Democratic victories in 1953 and 1957 showed the public's approval of the laissez-faire policy of Adenauer's economics minister, Ludwig Erhard (1897–1977). Adenauer's long tenure made him the key figure, lessened the importance of parliament, and resulted in much government bureaucracy.

In April 1963, the Christian Democrats finally named Erhard to succeed Adenauer. Erhard had quite a different style—treating ministers and department heads as colleagues and equals.

In November 1966, the Christian Democrats formed a so-called "great coalition" with the Social Democrats under Willy Brandt. Kurt Georg Kiesinger (1904–1988) became chancellor, and Brandt the Socialist took over as foreign minister. Brandt announced his intention to work step by step for better relations with East Germany, but found that in a coalition of two very dissimilar parties he could make no substantial progress.

In domestic affairs, pressure for change in the German universities led to outbreaks of student violence just before the similar outbreaks among students in France. Early in 1969, Gustav Heinemann (1899–1976) (SD) was elected president. An active campaign won the Socialists a gain in the Bundestag elections later in 1969. The Socialists were joined by the Free Democrats and obtained the majority necessary to make Willy Brandt chancellor in October 1969.

Brandt, the former mayor of West Berlin, was Germany's first Socialist chancellor in almost 40 years. In foreign affairs, he opened the way for British entry into the Common Market. The German mark was revalued at a higher rate, emphasizing German's true economic strength. Brandt was now able also to move for improved relations with the East (the policy of *Ostpolitik*). In the summer of 1970 he negotiated a treaty with the U.S.S.R. in which both parties renounced the use of force in European affairs. Later that year an agreement was made with Poland recognizing the Oder-Neisse line as the legal border between Poland and Germany. In 1972, Brandt signed a treaty with East Germany to normalize relations and improve communications. Both states entered the United Nations.

Elections in November 1972 gave Brandt's coalition a clear victory. But there were problems for the chancellor, who had concentrated too much on foreign affairs. There was criticism also of his sometimes over-emotional approach to foreign policy, as in relations with Israel. The discovery of a spy in his immediate office was an excuse for replacing him. Brandt put up little resistance, and Helmut Schmidt (SD) became chancellor in the spring of 1974.

Problems with the economy and the environment brought an end to Schmidt's chancellorship and the rule of the Socialists in 1982. An organization called the Greens, which was a loosely-organized coalition of environmentalists alienated from society, detracted from Socialist power. In 1982, the German voters turned to the more conservative Christian Democrats again, and Helmut Kohl became chancellor. The new leadership followed a policy of using German influence to reduce U.S.-U.S.S.R. tension.

Italy

The Christian Democrats, who were closely allied with the Roman Catholic Church, dominated the national scene. Their organization, though plagued by corruption, did provide some unity to Italian politics by supplying the prime ministers for numerous coalitions.

Italy advanced economically. Natural gas and some oil was discovered in the north and the Po valley area especially benefited. Unfortunately business efficiency found no parallel in the government or civil service. Italy suffered from terrorism, kidnappings, and assassinations by extreme radical groups such as the Red Brigades. These agitators hoped to create conditions favorable to the overthrow of the democratic constitution. The most notorious terrorist act was the assassination in 1978 of Aldo Moro (1916–1978), a respected Christian Democratic leader.

In 1983, Bettino Craxi (Socialist) became prime minister at the head of an uneasy coalition which lasted four years—the longest single government in postwar Italian history.

Spain and Portugal

In Portugal, Europe's longest right-wing dictatorship came to an end in September 1968, when a stroke incapacitated Antonio Salazar, who died two years later. A former collaborator, Marcelo Caetano (1906–1980), became prime minister, and an era of change began. Censorship was relaxed and some freedom was given to political parties.

In April 1974, the Caetano regime was overthrown and a "junta of national salvation" took over, headed by General Spinola, who later retired and went into exile. Portugal went through a succession of governments. Its African colonies of Mozambique and Angola were finally granted independence in 1975. Portugal joined the Common Market in 1986.

Franco, who had been ruler of a fascist regime since the end of the Civil War in 1939, held on until he was close to 70. He then designated the Bourbon prince, Juan Carlos, to be his successor. In 1975, Franco relinquished power and died three weeks later. Juan Carlos proved a popular and able leader and over the next several years took the country from dictatorship to constitutional monarchy. Basque and Catalan separatist movements, which had caused trouble for so long, were appeased by the granting of local autonomy. Spain also entered the Common Market in 1986.

CULTURAL AND SOCIAL DEVELOPMENTS

Science and Technology

In 1900, there were about 15,000 trained scientists engaged in research and teaching—most in Europe. In the postwar years the figure reached 500,000, and in addition to Central and Western Europe, the Soviet Union, the U.S., and Japan were heavily involved in scientific research and in developing technologies that would apply scientific advances to everyday life.

Rapid advances were made in medicine with the development of sulfa drugs, penicillin, cortisone, and antibiotics to cure formerly crippling infections. Vaccines were developed for poliomyelitis (1955) and other diseases. Smallpox all but disappeared worldwide after 1975. Remarkable developments in surgery included transplantation of vital organs.

Several European countries, especially France and West Germany, made extensive use of nuclear reactors for production of electric power. The accident at the Russian power reactor at Chernobyl caused many Europeans to rethink the whole matter of nuclear reactors and public safety, and by the late 1980s nuclear power did not seem to hold the promise it did in the years after World War II.

Another technological development of incalculable influence was television. In 1980, there were 33 television sets for every 100 West Germans and 29 for every 100 persons in France. Not the least disturbing thing about television for Europeans was the influx of programs from the U.S.: some 20 percent of British television and 50 percent of French television was imported by the 1980s, mainly from the U.S..

Religion

In 1948, the World Council of Churches was founded at Geneva, Switzerland. The election of Pope John XXIII (1881–1963) in 1958 gave a boost to the ecumenical movement. The Catholic Church now established better communications with other branches of Christianity. The encyclical *Pacem in Terris* (1963) was a papal plea for reason and humane sentiments and harmonious coexistence of all faiths and social systems. This work was carried on by Paul VI (1897–1978) and the Second Vatican Council (1963–1965).

Literature and Art

In literature, the Englishman George Orwell (1903–1950) achieved fame for his frightening portrayal of a future totalitarian society in his novel *1984* (published 1949). Despite the breakup of the old colonial empires, there were those, especially among the young, who voiced concern for the enormous inequities between the privileged economic status of Europe and the United States and the underdeveloped nations of the so-called Third World. This was reflected in a number of anti-imperialist tracts such as Frantz Fanon's *The Wretched of the Earth* (published in French in 1961). The French writer Jean-Paul Sartre also contributed some passionately anti-colonialist passages in his *Critique of Dialectical Reason*.

German writers of the older generation such as Carl Zuckmayer (1896–1977) and Bertholt Brecht (1898–1956), as well as younger writers such as Wolfgang Borchert, Gunter Grass, and Heinrich Böll, produced notable work. Zuckmayer's play, *The Devil's General*, although written in America at the end of the war, gave a remarkable picture of Germany at that time. Grass's novel *The Tin Drum* (1959) was also set in Nazi Germany and became a best seller in many languages.

In the Soviet Union, government censorship continued, but failed to stifle creativity and criticism. Boris Pasternak's (1890–1960) *Doctor Zhivago* was an epic covering the period before, during, and after the Revolution. Its author was awarded the Nobel Prize, but was not allowed to leave Russia to accept it in person. Alexander Solzhenitsyn also ran afoul of the government. His novel, *One Day in the Life of Ivan Denisovich*, won critical acclaim. A later work, *The Gulag Archipelago*, was a detailed description and indictment of forced labor camps run by the secret police during the Stalin era. The author was arrested for treason and forced into foreign exile in 1974.

In film, the work of the Swedish director Ingmar Bergman (*The Seventh Seal, Wild Strawberries*) and the Italians Roberto Rosselini (*Open City*) and Vittorio de Sica (*Bicycle Thief*) attracted attention and won critical acclaim. In art, the greatest figure was Pablo Picasso, who began work before the First World War and whose productivity in many styles lasted until his death in 1973.

THE FALL OF COMMUNISM

Poland

Occupied with domestic economic concerns, Gorbachev de-emphasized Soviet concerns in eastern Europe. This was first felt in Poland which, because of Solidarity, already had an effective opposition movement. After years of effort by Solidarity, Poland became the first eastern European nation to shift from Communism to democracy through free elections held in June 1989. With the election of Tadeuiz Mazowiecki in August 1990, the Communists lost their last bastion of power.

Hungary

In August 1989, Hungary opened its borders with Austria and the following October the Communists reorganized under the Socialist banner. Hungary then proclaimed itself a "free republic."

East Germany

With Hungary opening its border with Austria, a route to the West was also opened for thousands of East Germans to cross into Hungary. The resulting destabilization forced Erich Honnecker to step down as head of state in October 1989. On November 1, the government opened the border with Czechoslovakia and eight days later, on November 9, 1989, the Berlin Wall fell. On December 6, a non-

Communist was elected head of state; on December 11, large demonstrations demanded reunification; by October 1990, Germany was reunified.

Czechoslovakia

When a crackdown on pro-democracy demonstrations in October 1989, proved futile, the pro-Soviet government was replaced by reform-minded Communists, who, on December 8, relinquished power to a freely-elected Parliament. This Parliament elected Vaclav Havel, a playwright and anti-Communist leader, president on December 29.

Rumania

As the dominos continued to fall in the Communist regimes, antigovernment demonstrations began in Rumania in December 1989. However, unlike in the other former Soviet satellite states, here the demonstrators were met by force. Hundreds were killed; as a result the military began joining the opposition and eventually forced dictator Nicolae Ceausescu from power. Ceausescu, along with his wife Elena, was captured by the military; both were executed on Christmas Day, 1989. In May 1990, the National Salvation Front won parliamentary elections.

Bulgaria and Albania

In January 1990, the Bulgarian National Assembly repealed dominance of the Communist party. By December a multi-party coalition took power. Meanwhile, Albania opened its borders with Greece and legalized religious worship in January 1990. In July, hardliners were ousted from government.

Yugoslavia

Things did not go as smoothly in Yugoslavia. From World War II until his death in 1981 dictator Josip Broz Tito had kept ethnic feuding between Serbians and Croatians in check. However, with the fall of Communists in surrounding states, the hard-line government that succeeded Tito was forced to concede power to the democrats in early 1990. While this opened the door to civil liberties, it also reopened ancient ethnic feuds. This split escalated by May, with the Croatian National Guard fighting for a sovereign Croatian state. The central Yugoslavian government, dominated by Serbs and answering pleas by Serbs living in Croatia, responded by attacking the Croatians. Attempts by the European Community to end the fighting proved fruitless; 14 cease-fires were attempted by the end of 1991 all failed. A fifteenth cease-fire brokered by the UN, went into effect January 3, 1992.

THE FALL OF THE SOVIET UNION

The End of the Cold War

With the Warsaw Pact in shambles, relations with the United States and NATO thawing, and Communist regimes in eastern Europe no longer a concern, the pressure for domestic reform grew on Gorbachev. He was forced, however, to temper perestroika to appease hard-liners. This infuriated the populace, led by Boris Yeltsin, a former Communist and opposition leader who had been elected President of the Russian Republic. As a result of Yeltsin's pressures, Gorbachev was forced to make more and more concessions to the reformers, particularly the freedom-hungry Baltic states of Latvia, Estonia, and Lithuania. In the summer of 1991 Gorbachev approved the Union Treaty, giving limited autonomy to the republics and greatly reducing the once vast powers of the central government.

Communist Coup d'État

Fearing Gorbachev had given too much to the reformers, and fearful they were losing power, the hard-line Communists in the Kremlin placed Gorbachev under house arrest at his vacation home in the Crimea on August 3, 1991. The six plotters, led by Interior Minister Boris Pugo, told the world that Gorbachev was ill and "unable to perform his duties as President" and that Gennadi Yanayev, another hard-liner, was acting president.

However, the hard-liners' coup was doomed almost from the start. First, the support of the army and the KGB was never solidified, despite the cooperation of the Defense Minister and the head of the KGB. Second, they underestimated the level of mistrust of the government felt by the Russian people, and third, they failed to neutralize the vastly popular opposition leader Yeltsin.

With Yeltsin rallying the populace and the rank-and-file members of the army, the plotters' power base soon crumbled. When the plotters didn't have enough authority to order tank columns to storm Yeltsin's headquarters, the tide turned against them. By August 6, Pugo had committed suicide, Gorbachev was released, and the other plotters were arrested and imprisoned.

The Fall of Gorbachev

Gorbachev returned to the Kremlin after the coup, but his own power had been badly eroded by Yeltsin's saving the nation from the plotters. Yeltsin had long championed total autonomy for the republics, and with the Baltics declaring their independence, Gorbachev began to appear more and more like a figurehead. In early December Yeltsin announced that Russia had formed a Commonwealth of Independent States with former republics Belarus (formerly Byelorussia) and Ukraine. By mid-December twelve other republics had joined the Commonwealth, and as the Soviet Union broke up, Gorbachev was left without a country to govern. He resigned what power he had left on Christmas Day 1991, the same day the red flag of the Soviet Union was lowered for the last time over the Kremlin.

CHANGES IN GREAT BRITAIN AND AMERICA

Major Replaces Thatcher

Although the Tories retained their hold on Parliament, by mid-1990 Thatcher had fallen out of step with her own party over Great Britain's participation in the European Community. The Tories backed the EC's doctrine of one currency for the continent, while Thatcher staunchly opposed giving up the pound sterling. Thatcher's Tory rival Michael Hesseltine, a young, brash member of Parliament, called for a vote of confidence, in which Thatcher finished third to Hesseltine and her own Chancellor of the Exchequer, John Major. Without the backing of the Tories, Thatcher resigned from the race rather than call for elections which could have turned power over to the Labor party. The Tories then voted Major as Prime Minister after Hesseltine withdrew from the race when no clear majority emerged. Although he favored the EEC, Major was viewed as a "Thatcherite," and subsequently continued most of Thatcher's domestic policies.

8 THE COLONIAL PERIOD (1500–1763)

THE AGE OF EXPLORATION

The Treaty of Tordesillas

The Treaty of Tordesillas (1493) drew a line dividing the land in the New World between Spain and Portugal. Lands east of the line were Portuguese. As a result, Brazil eventually became a Portuguese colony, while Spain maintained claims to the rest of the Americas. As other European nations joined the hunt for colonies, they tended to ignore the Treaty of Tordesillas.

The Spanish Conquistadores

To conquer the Americas, the Spanish monarchs used their powerful army, led by independent Spanish adventurers known as conquistadores. The European diseases they unwittingly carried with them devastated the local Native American populations, who had no immunities against such diseases.

In 1513, Vasco Núñez de Balboa crossed the isthmus of Panama and became the first European to see the Pacific Ocean. The same year, Juan Ponce de León explored Florida in search of gold and a fabled fountain of youth. He found neither, but claimed Florida for Spain. In 1519, Hernando (Hernán) Cortes led his dramatic expedition against the Aztecs of Mexico. Aided by the fact that the Aztecs at first mistook him for a god, as well as by firearms, armor, horses, and (unknown to him) smallpox germs, all previously unknown in America, Cortes destroyed the Aztec Empire and won enormous riches. By the 1550s, other such fortune seekers had conquered much of South America.

Hernando de Soto (ca. 1496–1542) led 600 men (1539–1541) through what is now the southeastern United States, penetrating as far west as Oklahoma and encountering the Mississippi River, on whose banks de Soto was buried. Francisco Vasquez de Coronado led an expedition (1540–1542) from Mexico north across the Rio Grande and through New Mexico, Arizona, Texas, Oklahoma, and Kansas. Some of Coronado's men were the first Europeans to see the Grand Canyon.

New Spain

Spain administered its new holdings as an autocratic, rigidly controlled empire in which everything was to benefit the parent country. The Spaniards developed a system of large manors or estates (encomiendas), with Indian slaves ruthlessly managed for the benefit of the conquistadores. The encomienda system was later replaced by the similar but somewhat milder hacienda system. As the Indian population died from overwork and European diseases, Spaniards began importing African slaves to supply their labor needs.

English and French Beginnings

In 1497, the Italian John Cabot (Giovanni Caboto, ca. 1450–1499), sailing under the sponsorship of the king of England in search of a Northwest Passage (a water route to the Orient through or around the North American continent), became the first European since the Vikings more than four centuries earlier to reach the mainland of North America, which he claimed for England.

In 1524, the king of France authorized another Italian, Giovanni da Verrazzano (ca. 1485–1528), to undertake a mission similar to Cabot's. Endeavoring to duplicate the achievement of the Spaniard Ferdinand Magellan, who had five years earlier found a way around the southern tip of South America, Verrazzano followed the American coast from present-day North Carolina to Maine.

Beginning in 1534, Jacques Cartier (1491–1557), also authorized by the king of France, mounted three expeditions to the area of the St. Lawrence River, which he believed might be the hoped for Northwest Passage. He explored up the river as far as the site of Montreal.

When the English finally began colonization, commercial capitalism in England had advanced to the point that the English efforts were supported by private rather than government funds, allowing English colonists to enjoy greater freedom from government interference.

Fearing encroachment from Huguenot settlers, the Spaniards built a fort at St. Augustine, the oldest city in North America.

Francis Drake (ca. 1540–1596), an Englishman, sailed around South America and raided the Spanish settlements on the Pacific coast of Central America before continuing on to California, which he claimed for England and named Nova Albion. Drake then returned to England by sailing around the world.

Gilbert, Raleigh, and the First English Attempts

English nobleman Sir Humphrey Gilbert (1537–1583) believed England should found colonies and find a Northwest Passage. In 1576, he sent English sea captain Martin Frobisher (ca. 1535–1594) to look for such a passage. Gilbert's attempts to found a colony in Newfoundland failed, and while pursuing these endeavors he was lost at sea.

Gilbert's half-brother, Sir Walter Raleigh (1554–1618), turned his attention to a more southerly portion of the North American coastline, which he named Virginia, in honor of England's unmarried queen. He selected as a site for the first settlement Roanoke Island, just off the coast of present-day North Carolina.

After one abortive attempt, a group of 114 settlers—men, women, and children—were landed in July 1587. Shortly thereafter, Virginia Dare became the first English child born in America. Later that year the expedition's leader, John White, returned to England to secure additional supplies. Delayed by the war with Spain, he did not return until 1590, when he found the colony deserted. It is not known what became of the Roanoke settlers. After this failure, Raleigh was forced by financial constraints to abandon his attempts to colonize Virginia. Hampered by unrealistic expectations, inadequate financial resources, and the ongoing war with Spain, English interest in American colonization was submerged for 15 years.

THE BEGINNINGS OF COLONIZATION

Virginia

Two groups of merchants gained charters from James I, Queen Elizabeth's successor. One group of merchants was based in London and received a charter to North America between what are now the Hudson and the Cape Fear rivers. The other was based in Plymouth and was granted the right to colonize in North America from the Potomac to the northern border of present-day Maine. They were called the Virginia Company of London and the Virginia Company of Plymouth, respectively. They were joint-stock companies that raised their capital by the sale of shares of stock. Companies of this sort had already been used to finance and carry on English trade with Russia, Africa, and the Middle East.

The Plymouth Company, in 1607, attempted to plant a colony in Maine, but after one winter the colonists became discouraged and returned to Britain. Thereafter, the Plymouth Company folded.

The Virginia Company of London settled Jamestown in 1607. It became the first permanent English settlement in North America. During the early years of Jamestown, the majority of the settlers died of starvation, various diseases, or hostile actions by Native Americans. The colony's survival remained in doubt for a number of years.

There were several reasons for these difficulties. The entire colony was owned by the company, and all members shared the profits regardless of how much or how little they worked; thus, there was a lack of incentive. Many of the settlers were gentlemen, who considered themselves too good to work at growing the food the colony needed to survive. Others had come with the expectation of finding gold or other quick and easy riches and wasted much time looking for these while they should have been providing for their survival.

The low and swampy location proved to be a breeding ground for all sorts of diseases, and relations with Powhatan, the local Native American chief, were hostile.

In 1608 and 1609, the dynamic and ruthless leadership of John Smith (ca. 1580–1631) kept the colony from collapsing. Smith's rule was, "He who works not, eats not." After Smith returned to England in late 1609, the condition of the colony again became critical.

In 1612, a Virginia resident named John Rolfe (1585–1622) discovered that a superior strain of tobacco, native to the West Indies, could be grown in Virginia. Rolfe's discovery gave Virginia a major cash crop.

To secure more settlers and boost Virginia's shrinking labor force, the company moved to make immigration possible for Britain's poor, who were without economic opportunity at home or financial means to procure transportation to America. This was achieved by means of the indenture system, by which a poor worker's passage to America was paid by an American planter (or the company itself); in exchange the worker was indentured to the planter (or the company) for a specified number of years. The system was open to abuse and often resulted in the mistreatment of the indentured servants.

For such reasons, Virginia continued to attract inadequate numbers of immigrants. To solve this, a reform-minded faction within the company proposed a new approach. Colonists were promised the same rights they had in England. A representative assembly, the House of Burgesses, was founded in 1619—the first in America. Additionally, private ownership of land was instituted.

The first Africans were brought to Virginia in 1619, but were treated as indentured servants rather than slaves.

Virginia's relations with the Native Americans remained difficult. In 1622, a Native American massacre took the lives of 347 settlers. In 1644, the Native Americans struck again, massacring some 300 more. Shortly thereafter, the coastal Native Americans were subdued.

Impressed by the potential profits from tobacco growing, King James I determined to have Virginia for himself. In 1624, he revoked the London Company's charter and made Virginia a royal colony. This pattern was followed throughout colonial history; both company colonies and proprietary colonies tended eventually to become royal colonies. Upon taking over Virginia, James revoked all political rights and the representative assembly (15 years later his son, Charles I, was forced, by constant pressure from the Virginians and the continuing need to attract more settlers, to restore these rights).

New France

The French opened a lucrative trade in fur with the Native Americans. In 1608, Samuel de Champlain established a trading post in Quebec, from which the rest of what became New France eventually spread.

French exploration and settlement spread through the Great Lakes region and the valleys of the Mississippi and Ohio rivers. In 1673, Jacques Marquette explored the Mississippi Valley, and in 1682, Sieur de la Salle followed the river to its mouth. French settlements in the Midwest were generally forts and trading posts serving the fur trade.

Throughout its history, New France was handicapped by an inadequate population and a lack of support by the parent country.

New Netherlands

In 1609, Holland sent an Englishman named Henry Hudson (d. 1611), to search for a Northwest Passage. In this endeavor, Hudson discovered the river that bears his name.

Arrangements were made to trade with the Iroquois for furs. In 1624, Dutch trading outposts were established on Manhattan Island (New Amsterdam) and at the site of present-day Albany (Fort Orange). A profitable fur trade was carried on and became the main source of revenue for the Dutch West India Company, the joint-stock company that ran the colony.

To encourage enough farming to keep the colony supplied with food, the Dutch instituted the patroon system, by which large landed estates would be given to wealthy men who transported at least fifty families to New Netherlands. These families would then become tenant farmers on the estate of the patroon who had transported them. As Holland's home economy was healthy, few Dutch felt desperate enough to take up such unattractive terms.

New Netherlands was weak and poorly governed. Its population was a mixture of people from all over Europe, as well as many African slaves.

The Pilgrims at Plymouth

Many Englishmen came from England for religious reasons. For the most part, these fell into two groups, Puritans and Separatists. Though similar in many respects to the Puritans, the Separatists believed the Church of England was beyond saving and so felt they must separate from it.

One group of Separatists, suffering government harassment, fled to Holland. Dissatisfied there, they went to America and later became the famous Pilgrims.

Led by William Bradford (1590–1657), they departed in 1620, having obtained from the London Company a charter to settle just south of the Hudson River. Driven by storms, their ship, the *Mayflower*, made landfall at Cape Cod in Massachusetts. They decided it was God's will for them to settle in that area. This, however, put them outside the jurisdiction of any established government; and so before going ashore they drew up and signed the Mayflower Compact, establishing a foundation for orderly government based on the consent of the governed. After a difficult first winter that saw many die, the Pilgrims went on to establish a quiet and modestly prosperous colony. After a number of years of hard work, they were able to buy out the investors who had originally financed their voyage, and thus gain greater autonomy.

The Massachusetts Bay Colony

The Puritans were far more numerous than the Separatists. Charles I determined in 1629 to persecute the Puritans aggressively and to rule without the Puritan-dominated Parliament.

In 1629, they chartered a joint-stock company called the Massachusetts Bay Company. The charter neglected to specify where the company's headquarters should be located. Taking advantage of this unusual omission, the Puritans determined to make their headquarters in the colony itself, 3,000 miles from meddlesome royal officials.

Under the leadership of John Winthrop (1588–1649), who taught that a new colony should provide the whole world with a model of what a Christian society ought to be, the Puritans carefully organized their venture, and upon arriving in Massachusetts in 1630, did not undergo the "starving time" that had often plagued other first-year colonies.

The government of Massachusetts developed to include a governor and a representative assembly (called the General Court) selected by the "freemen"—adult male church members. As Massachusetts's population increased (20,000 Puritans had come by 1642 in what came to be called the Great Migration), new towns were chartered. As in European villages, these towns consisted of a number of houses clustered around the church house and the village green. In each new town, the elect—those who testified of having experienced saving grace—covenanted together as a church.

Rhode Island, Connecticut, and New Hampshire

Puritans saw their colony not as a place to do whatever might strike one's fancy, but as a place to serve God and build His kingdom. Dissidents would only be tolerated insofar as they did not interfere with the colony's mission.

One such dissident was Roger Williams (ca. 1603–1683). When his activities became disruptive he was asked to leave the colony. He fled to the wilderness around Narragansett Bay, bought land from the Indians, and founded the settlement of Providence (1636). It was soon populated by his many followers.

Another dissident was Anne Hutchinson (1591–1643), who openly taught things contrary to Puritan doctrine. She was banished from the colony. She also migrated to the area around Narragansett Bay and with her followers founded Portsmouth (1638). She later migrated still farther west and was killed by Indians.

In 1644, Roger Williams secured from Parliament a charter combining Providence, Portsmouth, and other settlements in the area into the colony of Rhode Island. Through Williams's influence, the colony granted complete religious toleration. It suffered constant political turmoil.

Connecticut was founded by Puritans who had slight religious disagreements with the leadership of Massachusetts. In 1636, Thomas Hooker (ca. 1586–1647) led a group of settlers westward to found Hartford. In 1639, the Fundamental Orders of Connecticut, the first written constitution in America, were drawn up, providing for representative government.

In 1637, a group of Puritans led by John Davenport (1597–1670) founded the neighboring colony of New Haven. Davenport and his followers felt that Winthrop was not strict enough. In 1662, a new charter combined both New Haven and Connecticut into the officially recognized colony of Connecticut.

New Hampshire was settled as an overflow from Massachusetts. In 1677, King Charles II chartered the separate royal colony of New Hampshire. It remained economically dependent on Massachusetts.

Maryland

By the 1630s, the English crown was taking a more direct interest in exercising control over the colonies. It turned away from granting charters to joint-stock companies and towards granting them to single individuals or groups of individuals known as proprietors. The proprietors would actually own the colony and be directly responsible for it to the king, in an arrangement similar to the feudalism of medieval Europe. In practice, proprietary colonies turned out much like the company colonies because settlers insisted on self-government.

The first proprietary colony was Maryland, granted in 1632 to George Calvert, Lord Baltimore (ca. 1580–1632), as a reward for Calvert's loyal service to the king, and as a refuge for English Catholics, of which Calvert was one. George Calvert died before the colony could be planted, but the venture was carried forward by his oldest son Cecilius (ca. 1605–1675, and another son, Leonard (1606–1647), who was the colony's first governor.

From the start, more Protestants than Catholics came. To protect the Catholic minority, Cecilius approved an Act of Religious Toleration (1649), guaranteeing political rights to Christians of all persuasions. Calvert also allowed a representative assembly.

The Carolinas

In 1663, Charles II, having recently been restored to the throne after a 20-year Puritan revolution which had seen his father beheaded, moved to reward eight of the noblemen who had helped him regain the crown by granting them a charter for all the lands lying south of Virginia and north of Spanish Florida.

The new colony was called Carolina, after the king. In hopes of attracting settlers, the proprietors came up with an elaborate plan for a hierarchical, almost feudal, society. Not surprisingly this proved unworkable, and despite offers of generous land grants to settlers, the Carolinas grew slowly.

The area of North Carolina developed as an overflow from Virginia with similar economic and cultural features. South Carolina was settled by English planters from the island of Barbados, who founded Charles Town (Charleston) in 1670. These planters brought with them their black slaves. Thus, unlike the Chesapeake colonies of Virginia and Maryland, South Carolina had slavery as a fully developed institution from the outset.

New York and New Jersey

In 1664, Charles gave his brother James, Duke of York, title to all the Dutch lands in America, provided James conquered them first. To do this, James sent an invasion fleet under the command of Colonel Richard Nicols. New Amsterdam fell almost without a shot and became New York.

To add to the confusion in the newly renamed colony, James granted a part of his newly acquired domain to John Lord Berkeley and Sir George Carteret (1690–1763) (two of the Carolina proprietors), who named their new proprietorship New Jersey. James neglected to tell Colonel Nicols of this, with the result that both Nicols, on the one hand, and Carteret and Berkeley, on the other, were granting title to the same land to different settlers. Conflicting claims of land ownership plagued New Jersey for decades, and were used by the crown in 1702 as a pretext to take over New Jersey as a royal colony.

THE COLONIAL WORLD

Life in the Colonies

New England enjoyed a much more stable and well-ordered society than did the Chesapeake colonies. Puritans placed great importance on the family, which in their society was highly patriarchal. Puritans also placed great importance on the ability to read, since they believed everyone should be able to read the Bible. As a result, New England was ahead of the other colonies educationally and enjoyed extremely widespread literacy. Since New England's climate and soil were unsuited to large-scale farming, the region developed a prosperous economy based on small farming, home industry, fishing, and especially trade and a large shipbuilding industry. Boston became a major international port.

The typical Chesapeake colonist lived a shorter, less healthy life than his New England counterpart and was survived by fewer children. As a result, the Chesapeake's population steadily declined despite a constant influx of settlers. Nor was Chesapeake society as stable as that of New England. Most Chesapeake settlers came as indentured servants; and since planters desired primarily male servants for work in the tobacco fields, men largely outnumbered women in Virginia and Maryland. This hindered the development of family life.

The system of indentured servitude was open to serious abuse, with masters sometimes treating their servants brutally or contriving through some technicality to lengthen their terms of indenture. In any case, 40 percent of Chesapeake region indentured servants failed to survive long enough to gain their freedom.

By the late 17th century, life in the Chesapeake was beginning to stabilize, with death rates declining and life expectancies rising. As society stabilized, an elite group of wealthy families such as the Byrds, Carters, Fitzhughs, Lees, and Randolphs began to dominate the social and political life of the region.

On the bottom rung of Southern society were the black slaves. During the first half of the 17th century, blacks in the Chesapeake made up only a small percentage of the population, and were treated more or less as indentured servants. Between 1640 and 1670 this gradually changed, and blacks came to be seen and treated as life-long chattel slaves whose status would be inherited by their children. By 1750, they composed 30 to 40 percent of the Chesapeake population.

While North Carolina tended to follow Virginia in its economic and social development (although with fewer great planters and more small farmers), South Carolina developed a society even more dominated by large plantations and chattel slavery. By the early decades of the 18th century, blacks had come to outnumber whites in that colony. South Carolina's economy remained dependent on the cultivation of its two staple crops—rice and, to a lesser extent, indigo.

Mercantilism and the Navigation Acts

Beginning around 1650, British authorities began to take more interest in regulating American trade for the benefit of the mother country. A key idea that underlay this policy was the concept of mercantilism. Each nation's goal was to export more than it imported (i.e., to have a "favorable balance of trade"). The difference would be made up in gold and silver. To achieve their goals, mercantilists believed economic activity should be regulated by the government. Colonies could fit into England's mercantilist scheme by providing staple crops, such as rice, tobacco, sugar, and indigo, and raw materials, such as timber, that England would otherwise have been forced to import from other countries.

Parliament passed a series of Navigation Acts (1651, 1660, 1663, and 1673). The Navigation Acts stipulated that trade with the colonies was to be carried on only in ships made in Britain or America, that had at least 75 percent British or American crews. Additionally, when certain "enumerated" goods were shipped from an American port, they were to go only to Britain or to another American port. Finally, almost nothing could be imported to the colonies without going through Britain first.

While mercantilism boosted the prosperity of New Englanders, who engaged in large-scale shipbuilding, it hurt the residents of the Chesapeake by driving down the price of tobacco. On the whole, the Navigation Acts, as intended, transferred wealth from America to Britain by increasing the prices Americans had to pay for British goods and lowering the prices Americans received for the goods they produced.

Charles II and his advisors worked to tighten up the administration of colonies, particularly the enforcement of the Navigation Acts. In Virginia, tempers grew short as tobacco prices plunged.

In 1676, Bacon's Rebellion occurred when a nobleman's followers burned Jamestown because of disagreement over policy toward Native Americans. The British removed the governor, who Virginians felt was running the colony for his friends' benefit, and thenceforth Virginia's royal governors had strict instructions to run the colony for the benefit of the mother country. In response, Virginia's gentry, who had been divided over Bacon's Rebellion, united to face this new threat to their local autonomy. By political means they consistently obstructed the governors' efforts to increase royal control.

The Half-Way Covenant

By the latter half of the 17th century, many Puritans were coming to fear that New England was drifting away from its religious purpose. In 1662 some clergy proposed the "Half-Way Covenant," providing a sort of half-way church membership for the children of members, even though those children, having reached adulthood, did not profess saving grace as was normally required for Puritan church membership. Those who embraced the Half-Way Covenant felt that in an increasingly materialistic society it would at least keep church membership rolls full, and might preserve some of the church's influence in society.

Some communities rejected the Half-Way Covenant as an improper compromise, but in general, the shift toward secular values continued slowly. Many Puritan ministers strongly denounced this trend in sermons that have come to be referred to as "jeremiads."

King Philip's War

Puritans endeavored to convert Native Americans to Christianity. By 1650, although converts numbered more than 1,000, most Native Americans remained unconverted.

In 1675, a Wampanoag chief named King Philip (Metacomet, ca. 1639–1676) led a war to exterminate the whites. Some 2,000 settlers lost their lives before King Philip was killed and his tribe subdued. New England continued to experience conflicts with Native Americans from time to time, though not as severe as those suffered by Virginia.

The Dominion of New England

The trend toward increasing imperial control of the colonies continued. In 1684, the Massachusetts charter was revoked in retaliation for that colony's large-scale evasion of the restrictions of the Navigation Acts.

The following year, Charles II died and was succeeded by his brother, James II. James favored the establishment of a unified government for all of New England, New York, and New Jersey, to be called the Dominion of New England. It would abolish representative assemblies and facilitate the imposition of the Church of England on Congregationalist (Puritan) New England.

To head the dominion, James sent the obnoxious and dictatorial Sir Edmund Andros (1637–1714). Arriving in Boston in 1686, Andros quickly alienated the New Englanders. When news reached America of England's 1688 Glorious Revolution, which replaced the Catholic James with his Protestant daughter Mary and her husband William of Orange, New Englanders cheerfully shipped Andros back to England.

Similar uprisings occurred in New York and Maryland. William and Mary's new government generally accepted these actions, though Jacob Leisler, leader of Leisler's Rebellion in New York, was executed for hesitating to turn over power to the new royal governor. This unfortunate incident poisoned the political climate of New York for many years.

The charter of Massachusetts, now including Plymouth, was restored in 1691, this time as a royal colony, though not as tightly controlled as others of that type.

The Salem Witch Trials

In 1692, several young girls in Salem Village (now Danvers) claimed to be tormented by the occult activities of certain of their neighbors. Before the resulting Salem witch trials could be stopped by the intervention of Puritan ministers such as Cotton Mather (1663–1728), some 20 persons had been executed.

Pennsylvania and Delaware

Pennsylvania was founded as a refuge for Quakers. One of a number of radical religious sects that had sprung up about the time of the English Civil War, the Quakers held many controversial beliefs. They believed all persons had an "inner light" which allowed them to commune directly with God, and therefore they placed little importance on the Bible. They were also pacifists and declined to show customary deference to those who were considered to be their social superiors.

William Penn (1644–1718), a member of a prominent British family, converted to Quakerism as a young man. Desiring to found a colony as a refuge for Quakers, in 1681 he sought and received from Charles II a grant of land in America as payment of a large debt the king had owed Penn's late father.

Penn guaranteed a representative assembly and full religious freedom. He personally laid out the city of Philadelphia, and succeeded in maintaining peaceful relations with the Native Americans. Settlers flocked to Pennsylvania from all over Europe. The fertile colony became a large exporter of grain.

Delaware, though at first part of Pennsylvania, was granted a separate legislature by Penn, but until the American Revolution, Pennsylvania's proprietary governors also functioned as governors of Delaware.

THE EIGHTEENTH CENTURY

Economy and Population

America's population continued to grow rapidly, both from natural increases due to prosperity and a healthy environment and from large-scale immigration, not only of English but also of other groups such as Scots-Irish and Germans.

The Germans were prompted to migrate by wars, poverty, and religious persecution in their homeland. They found Pennsylvania especially attractive and settled fairly close to the frontier, where land was more readily available. They eventually came to be called the "Pennsylvania Dutch."

The Scots-Irish, Scottish Presbyterians who had been living in northern Ireland for several generations, settled on or beyond the frontier in the Appalachians and spread southward into the mountain valleys of Virginia and North Carolina.

The Early Wars of the Empire

Between 1689 and 1763, Britain and its American colonies fought a series of four wars with Spain, France, and France's Native American allies, in part to determine who would dominate North America.

Though the first war (1689–1697), known in America as King William's War but in Europe as the War of the League of Augsburg, was a limited conflict involving no major battles in America. It did bring a number of bloody and terrifying border raids by Native Americans. It was ended by the Treaty of Ryswick, which made no major territorial changes.

The Treaty of Utrecht ended the war known in America as Queen Anne's War (1702–1713) and gave Britain major territorial gains and trade advantages.

In 1739, war once again broke out with France and Spain. Known in America as King George's War, it was called the War of Jenkin's Ear in Europe and later the War of the Austrian Succession. American troops played an active role, accompanying the British on several important expeditions and suffering thousands of casualties.

Georgia

It was decided to found a colony as a buffer between South Carolina and Spanish-held Florida. In 1732, a group of British philanthropists, led by General James Oglethorpe (1696–1785), obtained a charter for such a colony, to be located between the Savannah and Altamaha rivers, and to be populated by such poor as could not manage to make a living in Great Britain.

The philanthropist trustees, who were to control the colony for 21 years before it reverted to royal authority, made elaborate and detailed rules to mold the new colony's society. Relatively few settlers came. By 1752, Oglethorpe and his colleagues were ready to acknowledge their efforts a failure. Thereafter, Georgia came to resemble South Carolina, though with more small farmers.

The Enlightenment

As the 18th century progressed, Americans came to be influenced by European ways of thought, culture, and society. Some Americans embraced the European intellectual movement known as the "Enlightenment."

A major English political philosopher of the Enlightenment was John Locke. He strove to find in the social and political world the sort of natural laws Isaac Newton had recently discovered in the physical realm. He held that such natural laws included the rights of life, liberty, and property; that to secure these rights people submit to governments; and that governments which abuse these rights may justly be overthrown. His writings were enormously influential in America, though usually indirectly.

The most notable Enlightenment man in America was Benjamin Franklin (1706–1790). His renown spread to Europe both for the wit and wisdom of his *Poor Richard's Almanack* and for his scientific experiments.

The Great Awakening

The Great Awakening consisted of a series of religious revivals occurring throughout the colonies from the 1720s to the 1740s. Preachers such as the Dutch Reformed Theodore Frelinghuysen (1817–1885), the Presbyterians William (1673–1745) and Gilbert (1703–1764) Tennent, and the Congregationalist Jonathan Edwards (1703–1758) proclaimed a message of personal repentance and faith in Jesus Christ for salvation from an otherwise certain eternity in hell. The most dynamic preacher of the Great Awakening was the Englishman George Whitefield (1714–1770), who traveled through the colonies several times.

America's religious community came to be divided between the "Old Lights," who rejected the Great Awakening, and the "New Lights," who accepted it—and sometimes suffered persecution because of their fervor. A number of colleges were founded for the purpose of training New Light ministers. The Great Awakening also fostered a greater readiness to reject the claims of established authority.

The French and Indian War

England and France continued on a collision course, as France determined to take complete control of the Ohio Valley and western Pennsylvania.

British authorities ordered colonial governors to resist this; and Virginia's Robert Dinwiddie, already involved in speculation on the Ohio Valley lands, was eager to comply. George Washington (1732–1799), a young major of the Virginia militia, was sent to western Pennsylvania to request the French to leave. When the French declined in 1754, Washington was sent with 200 Virginia militiamen to expel them. After success in a small skirmish, Washington was forced by superior numbers to fall back on his hastily built Fort Necessity and then to surrender.

While Washington skirmished with the French in western Pennsylvania, delegates of seven colonies met in Albany, New York, to discuss common plans for defense. Delegate Benjamin Franklin proposed a plan for an intercolonial government. While the other colonies showed no support for the idea, it was an important precedent for the concept of uniting in the face of a common enemy.

The British dispatched Major General Edward Braddock (1695–1755) with several regiments of British regular troops. Braddock marched overland toward the

French outpost of Fort Duquesne, which was at the place where the Monongahela and Allegheny rivers join to form the Ohio. About eight miles short of his goal, he was ambushed by a small force of French and Indians. Two-thirds of the British regulars, including Braddock himself, were killed. However, under the leadership of its capable and energetic prime minister, William Pitt, by 1760 England had taken Quebec and Montreal and virtually liquidated the French empire in North America.

By the Treaty of Paris of 1763, Britain gained all of Canada and all of what is now the United States east of the Mississippi River. France lost all of its North American holdings.

9 THE AMERICAN REVOLUTION (1763–1787)

THE COMING OF THE AMERICAN REVOLUTION

A drive to gain new authority over the colonies, beginning in 1763, led directly to American independence.

Grenville and the Stamp Act

In 1763, George Grenville (1712–1770) became prime minister and set out to solve some of the empire's more pressing problems. Chief among these was the large national debt incurred in the recent war.

Of related concern was the cost of defending the American frontier, recently the scene of a bloody Native American uprising led by an Ottowa chief named Pontiac (ca. 1720–1769). Goaded by French traders, Pontiac had aimed to drive the entire white population into the sea. While failing in that endeavor, he had succeeded in killing a large number of settlers along the frontier.

Grenville created a comprehensive program to deal with these problems and moved energetically to put it into effect. He sent the Royal Navy to suppress American smuggling and vigorously enforce the Navigation Acts. He also issued the Proclamation of 1763, forbidding white settlement west of the crest of the Appalachians, in hopes of keeping the Native Americans happy and the settlers close to the coast, where they would be easier to control.

In 1764, Grenville pushed through Parliament the Sugar Act (also known as the Revenue Act), which aimed at raising revenue by taxing goods imported by the Americans. It was stringently enforced, with accused violators facing trial in admiralty courts without benefit of jury or the normal protections of due process.

Grenville secured passage of the Quartering Act, which required the colonies in which British troops were stationed to pay for their maintenance. Americans had never before been required to support a standing army in their midst.

Grenville also saw the passage of his Currency Act of 1764, which forbade once and for all any colonial attempts to issue currency not redeemable in gold or silver, and made it more difficult for Americans to avoid the constant drain of money that Britain's mercantilist policies were designed to create in the colonies.

The Stamp Act (1765) imposed a direct tax on Americans for the first time. It required Americans to purchase revenue stamps on everything from newspapers to legal documents, and would have created an impossible drain on hard currency in the colonies.

Americans reacted first with restrained and respectful petitions and pamphlets in which they pointed out that "taxation without representation is tyranny." From there, resistance progressed to stronger protests that eventually became violent.

Resistance was particularly intense in Massachusetts, where it was led first by James Otis (1725–1783) and then by Samuel Adams (1722–1803), who formed the organization known as the Sons of Liberty. In Virginia, a young Burgess named

Patrick Henry (1736–1799) introduced seven resolutions denouncing the Stamp Act.

In October 1765, delegates from nine colonies met as the Stamp Act Congress. Called by the Massachusetts legislature at the instigation of James Otis, the Stamp Act Congress passed moderate resolutions against the act, asserting that Americans could not be taxed without the consent of their representatives. They pointed out that Americans were not represented in Parliament, and called for the repeal of both the Stamp and Sugar Acts. The Stamp Act Congress showed that representatives of the colonies could work together, and gave political leaders in the various colonies a chance to become acquainted with each other.

Colonial merchants' boycott of British goods spread throughout the colonies and had a powerful effect on British merchants and manufacturers, who began clamoring for the act's repeal.

Meanwhile, the fickle King George III had dismissed Grenville over an unrelated disagreement and replaced him with a cabinet headed by Charles Lord Rockingham (1730–1782). In March 1766, under the leadership of the new ministry, Parliament repealed the Stamp Act. At the same time, however, it passed the Declaratory Act, which claimed the power to tax or make laws for the Americans "in all cases whatsoever."

Though the Declaratory Act denied the exact principle they had just been at such pains to assert—that of no taxation without representation—the Americans generally ignored it in their exuberant celebration of the repeal of the Stamp Act. Americans eagerly proclaimed their loyalty to Great Britain.

The Townshend Acts

The Rockingham ministry was replaced with a cabinet dominated by Chancellor of the Exchequer Charles Townshend (1725–1767). In 1766, Parliament passed his program of taxes on items imported into the colonies. These taxes came to be known as the Townshend duties. Townshend mistakenly believed the Americans would accept this method, while rejecting the use of direct internal taxes.

The Townshend Acts also included the use of admiralty courts to try those accused of violations, the use of writs of assistance, and the paying of customs officials out of the fines they levied. Townshend also had the New York legislature suspended for noncompliance with the Quartering Act.

American reaction was at first slow. Philadelphia lawyer John Dickinson (1732–1808) wrote an anonymous pamphlet entitled "Letters from a Farmer in Pennsylvania" in which he pointed out in moderate terms that the Townshend Acts violated the principle of no taxation without representation, and that if Parliament could suspend the New York legislature it could do the same to others. At the same time, he urged a restrained response on the part of his fellow Americans.

In February 1768, the Massachusetts legislature, at the urging of Samuel Adams, passed the Massachusetts Circular Letter, reiterating Dickinson's mild arguments and urging other colonial legislatures to pass petitions calling on Parliament to repeal the acts. Had the British government done nothing, the matter might have passed quietly.

Instead, British authorities acted. They ordered that if the letter was not withdrawn, the Massachusetts legislature would be dissolved and new elections held. They forbade the other colonial legislatures to take up the matter, and they also sent four regiments of troops to Boston to prevent intimidation of royal officials. They intended to intimidate the populace instead.

The last of these actions was in response to the repeated pleas of the Boston customs agents. Corrupt agents had used technicalities of the confusing and poorly written Sugar and Townshend Acts to entrap innocent merchants and line their own pockets. Mob violence had been threatened when agentshad seized the ship *Liberty*, belonging to Boston merchant John Hancock (1737–1793). Such incidents prompted the call for troops.

The sending of troops, along with the British authority's repressive response to the Massachusetts Circular Letter, aroused the Americans to resistance. Nonimportation was again instituted, and soon British merchants were calling on Parliament to repeal the acts. In March 1770, Parliament, under the new prime minister, Frederick Lord North (1737–1792), repealed all of the taxes except that on tea, which was retained to prove Parliament had the right to tax the colonies if it so desired.

By the time of the repeal, however, friction between British soldiers and Boston citizens had led to an incident in which five Bostonians were killed. Although the British soldiers had acted more or less in self-defense, Samuel Adams labeled the incident the "Boston Massacre" and publicized it widely. At their trial, the British soldiers were defended by prominent Massachusetts lawyer John Adams (1735–1826), and were acquitted on the charge of murder.

In the years that followed, American orators desiring to stir up anti-British feeling often alluded to the Boston Massacre. Following the repeal of the Townshend duties, a period of relative peace set in.

The Tea Act

The relative peace was brought to an end by the Tea Act of 1773. In desperate financial condition—partially because the Americans were buying smuggled Dutch tea rather than the taxed British product—the British East India Company sought and obtained from Parliament concessions that allowed it to ship tea directly to the colonies rather than only by way of Britain. The result would be that East India Company tea, even with the tax, would be cheaper than smuggled Dutch tea. The colonists would thus, it was hoped, buy the tea, tax and all. The East India Company would be saved, and the Americans would be tacitly accepting Parliament's right to tax them.

The Americans, however, proved resistant to this approach; rather than seem to admit Parliament's right to tax, they vigorously resisted the cheaper tea. Various methods, including tar and feathers, were used to prevent the collection of the tax on tea. In most ports, Americans did not allow the tea to be landed.

In Boston, however, pro-British Governor Thomas Hutchinson (1711–1780) forced a confrontation by ordering Royal Navy vessels to prevent the tea ships from leaving the harbor. After 20 days, this would, by law, result in the cargoes being sold at auction and the tax paid. The night before the time was to expire, December 16,

1773, Bostonians thinly disguised as Native Americans boarded the ships and threw the tea into the harbor. Many Americans felt this was going too far, but the reaction of Lord North and Parliament quickly united Americans in support of Boston and in opposition to Britain.

The Intolerable Acts

The British responded with four acts collectively titled the Coercive Acts. First, the Boston Port Act closed the port of Boston to all trade until local citizens would agree to pay for the lost tea (they would not). Secondly, the Massachusetts Government Act greatly increased the power of Massachusetts's royal governor at the expense of the legislature. Thirdly, the Administration of Justice Act provided that royal officials accused of crimes in Massachusetts could be tried elsewhere, where chances of acquittal might be greater. Finally, a strengthened Quartering Act allowed the new governor, General Thomas Gage (1721–1787), to quarter his troops anywhere, including unoccupied private homes.

A further act of Parliament also angered and alarmed Americans. The Quebec Act, which extended the province of Quebec to the Ohio River, established Roman Catholicism as Quebec's official religion and set up for Quebec a government without a representative assembly. For Americans, this was a denial of the hopes and expectations of westward expansion for which they had fought the French and Indian War. New Englanders especially saw it as a threat. It meant that in their colonies, too, Parliament could establish autocratic government and the hated Church of England. Americans lumped the Quebec Act together with the Coercive Acts and referred to them all as the Intolerable Acts.

In response to the Coercive Acts, the First Continental Congress was called and met in Philadelphia in September 1774. It once again petitioned Parliament for relief, but also passed the Suffolk Resolves (so called because they were first passed in Suffolk County, Massachusetts), which denounced the Intolerable Acts and called for strict nonimportation and rigorous preparation of local militia companies in case the British should resort to military force.

The Congress then narrowly rejected a plan, submitted by Joseph Galloway of Pennsylvania, calling for a union of the colonies within the empire and a rearrangement of relations with Parliament. Most of the delegates felt matters had already gone too far for such a mild measure. Finally, before adjournment, it was agreed that there should be a Second Continental Congress in May of the following year if the colonies' grievances had not been righted by then.

THE WAR FOR INDEPENDENCE

Lexington and Concord

The British government paid little attention to the First Continental Congress, having decided to teach the Americans a military lesson. More troops were sent to Massachusetts, which was officially declared to be in a state of rebellion. Orders were sent to General Gage to arrest the leaders of the resistance, or failing that, to provoke any sort of confrontation that would allow him to turn British military might loose on the Americans.

Gage decided on a reconnaissance-in-force to find and destroy a reported stockpile of colonial arms and ammunition at Concord. Seven hundred British troops set out on this mission on the night of April 18, 1775. Their movement was detected by American surveillance, and news was spread throughout the countryside by dispatch riders Paul Revere (1735–1818) and William Dawes (1745–1799).

At the little village of Lexington, Captain John Parker and some 70 Minutemen (militiamen trained to respond at a moment's notice) awaited the British on the village green. As the British approached, a British officer shouted at the Minutemen to lay down their arms and disperse. The Minutemen did not lay down their arms, but did turn to file off the green. A shot was fired, and then the British opened fire and charged. Eight Americans were killed and several others wounded, most shot in the back.

The British continued to Concord only to find that nearly all of the military supplies they had expected to find had already been moved. Attacked by growing numbers of Minutemen, they began to retreat toward Boston. As the British retreated, Minutemen swarmed from every village for miles around and fired on the column from behind rocks, trees, and stone fences. Only a relief force of additional British troops saved the first column from destruction.

Open warfare had begun, and the myth of British invincibility was destroyed. Militia came in large numbers from all the New England colonies to join the force besieging Gage and his army in Boston.

Bunker Hill

In May 1775, three more British generals, William Howe (1729–1814), Henry Clinton (1738–1795), and John Burgoyne (1722–1792), arrived in Boston. The following month the Americans tightened the noose around Boston by fortifying Breed's Hill (a spur of Bunker Hill).

The British determined to remove them by a frontal attack. Twice the British were thrown back, but they finally succeeded when the Americans ran out of ammunition. Over a thousand British soldiers were killed or wounded in what turned out to be the bloodiest battle of the war (June 17, 1775). Yet the British had gained very little and remained bottled up in Boston.

Meanwhile in May 1775, American forces under Ethan Allen (1738–1789) and Benedict Arnold (1741–1801) took Fort Ticonderoga on Lake Champlain.

Congress, hoping Canada would join in resistance against Britain, authorized two expeditions into Quebec. One, under General Richard Montgomery (1736–1775), took Montreal and then turned toward the city of Quebec. It was met there by the second expedition under Benedict Arnold. The attack on Quebec (December 31, 1775) failed; Montgomery was killed, Arnold wounded, and American hopes for Canada ended.

The Second Continental Congress

While these events were taking place in New England and Canada, the Second

Continental Congress met in Philadelphia in May 1775. Congress was divided into two main factions. One was composed mostly of New Englanders and leaned toward declaring independence from Britain. The other drew its strength primarily from the Middle Colonies and was not yet ready to go that far. It was led by John Dickinson of Pennsylvania.

Congress put George Washington in command of the army, called for more troops, and adopted the "Olive Branch Petition," which pleaded with King George III to intercede with Parliament to restore peace. But the king gave his approval to the Prohibitory Act, declaring the colonies in rebellion and no longer under his protection. Preparations were made for full-scale war against America.

Throughout 1775, Americans remained deeply loyal to Britain and King George III despite the king's proclamations declaring them to be in revolt. In Congress, moderates still resisted independence.

In January 1776, Thomas Paine (1737–1809) published a pamphlet entitled *Common Sense*, calling for immediate independence. It sold widely and may have had much influence in favor of independence. Continued evidence of Britain's intention to carry on the war throughout the colonies also weakened the moderates' resistance to independence.

On June 7, 1776, Richard Henry Lee (1732–1794) of Virginia introduced a series of formal resolutions in Congress calling for independence and a national government. Accepting these ideas, Congress named two committees. One, headed by John Dickinson, was to work out a framework for a national government. The other was to draft a statement of the reasons for declaring independence. This statement, the Declaration of Independence, was primarily the work of Thomas Jefferson (1743–1826) of Virginia. It was a restatement of political ideas by then commonplace in America and showed why the former colonists felt justified in separating from Great Britain. It was formally adopted by Congress on July 4, 1776.

Washington Takes Command

Britain meanwhile was preparing a massive effort to conquer the United States. Gage was removed for being too timid, and top command went to Howe. To supplement the British army, large numbers of troops were hired from various German principalities. Since many of these Germans came from the state of Hesse-Cassel, Americans referred to all such troops as Hessians.

The British landed that summer at New York City, where they hoped to find many loyalists. Washington anticipated the move and was waiting at New York. However, the undertrained, underequipped, and badly outnumbered American army was no match for the powerful forces under General Howe and his brother, Admiral Lord Richard Howe (1726–1799). Defeated at the Battle of Long Island (August 27, 1776), Washington narrowly avoided being trapped there (an escape partially due to the Howes' slowness). Defeated again at the Battle of Washington Heights (August 29–30, 1776) in Manhattan, Washington was forced to retreat across New Jersey with the aggressive British General Lord Charles Cornwallis (1738–1805) in pursuit. By December, what was left of Washington's army had made it into Pennsylvania.

With his victory almost complete, General Howe decided to wait till spring to finish annihilating Washington's army. Scattering his troops in small detachments so as to hold all of New Jersey, he went into winter quarters.

Washington, with his small army melting away as demoralized soldiers deserted, decided on a bold stroke. On Christmas night 1776, his army crossed the Delaware River and struck the Hessians at Trenton. The Hessians, still groggy from their hard-drinking Christmas party, were easily defeated. A few days later, Washington defeated a British force at Princeton (January 3, 1777). Much of New Jersey was regained, and Washington's army was saved from disintegration.

Hoping to weaken Britain, France began making covert shipments of arms to the Americans early in the war. Shipments from France were vital for the Americans.

Saratoga and Valley Forge

For the summer of 1777, the British home authorities adopted an elaborate plan of campaign urged on them by General Burgoyne. According to the plan, Burgoyne would lead an army southward from Canada along the Lake Champlain corridor, while another army under Howe moved up the Hudson River to join Burgoyne at Albany. This, it was hoped, would cut off New England, which they considered the hotbed of the "rebellion."

Howe had other ideas and shipped his army by sea to Chesapeake Bay, hoping to capture the American capital, Philadelphia, and destroy Washington's army at the same time. At Brandywine Creek (September 11, 1777), Washington tried but failed to stop Howe's advance. Yet the American army, though badly beaten, remained intact. Howe occupied Philadelphia, while the Congress fled westward to York, Pennsylvania.

In early October, Washington attempted to drive Howe out of Philadelphia; but his attack at Germantown, though at first successful, failed at least partially due to thick fog and the still imperfect level of training in the American army, which contributed to confusion among the troops. Thereafter, Howe settled down to comfortable winter quarters in Philadelphia, and Washington and his army went to very uncomfortable ones at nearby Valley Forge. Meanwhile, far to the north, the British strategy that Howe had ignored was going badly awry.

In mid-August, a detachment of Burgoyne's force was defeated by New England militia under General John Stark near Bennington in what is now Vermont. By autumn, Burgoyne found his way blocked by an American army: continentals (American regular troops such as those that made up most of Washington's army, paid, in theory at least, by Congress) and New England militia under General Horatio Gates (ca. 1728–1806), at Saratoga, about 30 miles north of Albany. Burgoyne's two attempts to break through (September 19 and October 7, 1777) were turned back by the Americans under the brilliant battlefield leadership of Benedict Arnold. On October 17, 1777, Burgoyne surrendered to Gates.

The American victory at Saratoga convinced the French to join openly in the war against England. Eventually the Spanish (1779) and the Dutch (1780) joined as well.

The British Move South

The new circumstances brought a change in British strategy. With fewer troops available for service in America, the British would have to depend more on loyalists, and since they imagined that larger numbers of these existed in the South than elsewhere, it was there they turned their attention.

Howe was replaced by General Henry Clinton (1738–1795), who was ordered to abandon Philadelphia and march to New York. In doing so, he narrowly avoided defeat at the hands of Washington's army—much improved after a winter's drilling at Valley Forge under the direction of phony Prussian nobleman Baron von Stuben—at the Battle of Monmouth, New Jersey (June 28, 1778).

Clinton maintained New York as Britain's main base. In November 1778, the British easily conquered Georgia. Late the following year, Clinton moved on South Carolina and in May 1780 Charleston surrendered. Clinton then returned to New York, leaving Cornwallis to continue the Southern campaign.

Congress, alarmed at the British successes, sent General Horatio Gates to lead the forces opposing Cornwallis. Gates was soundly defeated at the Battle of Camden in South Carolina (August 16, 1780).

The outlook seemed bad for America. Washington's officers grumbled about not getting paid. The army was understrength and then suffered successive mutinies among the Pennsylvania and New Jersey troops. Benedict Arnold went over to the British.

In the west, George Rogers Clark (1752–1818), led an expedition down the Ohio River and into the area of present-day Illinois and Indiana, defeating a British force at Vincennes, Indiana, and securing the area north of the Ohio River for the United States.

In the south, Cornwallis began to move northward toward North Carolina, but on October 7, 1780, a detachment of his force under Major Patrick Ferguson (1744–1780), the inventor of the breech-loading rifle, was defeated by American frontiersmen at the Battle of Kings Mountain in northern South Carolina. Cornwallis unwisely moved north without bothering to secure South Carolina first. The result was that the British would no sooner leave an area than American militia or guerilla bands, such as that under Francis Marion "the Swamp Fox" (ca. 1732–1795), were once again in control.

American commander Nathaniel Greene's (1742–1786) brilliant southern strategy led to a crushing victory at Cowpens, South Carolina (January 17, 1781), by troops under Greene's subordinate, General Daniel Morgan (1736–1802) of Virginia. It also led to a near victory by Greene's own force at Guilford Court House, North Carolina (March 15, 1781).

Yorktown

The frustrated and impetuous Cornwallis now abandoned the southern strategy and moved north into Virginia, taking a defensive position at Yorktown. With the aid of a French fleet which took control of Chesapeake Bay and a French army which joined him in sealing off the land approaches to Yorktown, Washington succeeded in trapping Cornwallis. After three weeks of siege, Cornwallis surrendered (October 17, 1781).

The War at Sea

Ships of the small but daring United States Navy, as well as privateers, preyed on the British merchant marine. John Paul Jones (1747–1792), the most famous of American naval leaders, captured ships and carried out raids along the coast of Britain itself. French and Spanish naval forces also struck various outposts of the British Empire.

The Treaty of Paris (1783)

News of the debacle at Yorktown brought the collapse of Lord North's ministry, and the new cabinet opened peace negotiations. The American negotiating team was composed of Benjamin Franklin, John Adams, and John Jay (1745–1829). The negotiations continued for some time, delayed by French and Spanish maneuvering. When it became apparent that France and Spain were planning to achieve an agreement unfavorable to the United States, the American envoys negotiated a separate treaty with Britain.

The final agreement became known as the Treaty of Paris of 1783. Its terms stipulated the following: 1) The United States was recognized as an independent nation by the major European powers, including Britain 2) Its western boundary was set at the Mississippi River 3) Its southern boundary was set at 31° north latitude (the northern boundary of Florida) 4) Britain retained Canada, but had to surrender Florida to Spain 5) Private British creditors would be free to collect any debts owed by United States citizens and 6) Congress was to recommend that the states restore confiscated loyalist property.

THE CREATION OF NEW GOVERNMENTS

The State Constitutions

After the collapse of British authority in 1775, it became necessary to form new state governments. By the end of 1777, 10 new state constitutions had been formed. Most state constitutions included bills of rights—lists of things the government was not supposed to do to the people.

The Articles of Confederation

In the summer of 1776, Congress appointed a committee to begin devising a framework for a national government. John Dickinson, who had played a leading role in writing the articles, felt a strong national government was needed; but by the time Congress finished revising them, the articles went to the opposite extreme of preserving the sovereignty of the states and creating a very weak national government.

The Articles of Confederation provided for a unicameral Congress in which each state would have one vote, as had been the case in the Continental Congress. Executive authority under the articles would be vested in a committee of 13, with one member from each state. In order to amend the articles, the unanimous consent of all the states was required.

The Articles of Confederation government was empowered to make war, make treaties, determine the amount of troops and money each state should contribute to the war effort, settle disputes between states, admit new states to the Union, and borrow money. But it was not empowered to levy taxes, raise troops, or regulate commerce.

Ratification of the Articles of Confederation was delayed by disagreements over the future status of the lands that lay to the west of the original 13 states. Some states, notably Virginia, held extensive claims to these lands based on their original colonial charters. Maryland, which had no such claim, withheld ratification until, in 1781, Virginia agreed to surrender its western claims to the new national government.

Meanwhile, the country was on its way to deep financial trouble. Unable to tax, Congress resorted to printing large amounts of paper money to finance the war; but these inflated "Continentals" were soon worthless. Other financial schemes fell through, and only grants and loans from France and the Netherlands staved off complete financial collapse. A plan to amend the articles to give Congress the power to tax was stopped by the lone opposition of Rhode Island. The army, whose pay was far in arrears, threatened mutiny. Some of those who favored a stronger national government welcomed this development, and in what became known as the Newburgh Conspiracy (1783), they consulted with army second-in-command Horatio Gates about the possibility of using the army to force the states to surrender more power to the national government. This movement was stopped by an appeal to the officers by Washington himself.

The Trans-Appalachian West and the Northwest Ordinance

For many Americans, the enormous trans-Appalachian frontier represented an opportunity to escape the economic hard times that followed the end of the war. In 1775, Daniel Boone (1734–1820) opened the "Wilderness Road," which ran through the Cumberland Gap and on to the "Bluegrass" region of Kentucky. Others scouted down the Ohio River from Pittsburgh. By 1790, over 100,000 had settled in Kentucky and Tennessee, despite the risk of violent death at the hands of Native Americans.

The Land Ordinance of 1784 provided for territorial government and an orderly system by which each territory could progress to full statehood (this ordinance is sometimes considered part of the Land Ordinance of 1785).

The Land Ordinance of 1785 provided for the orderly surveying and distribution of land in townships six miles square, each composed of thirty-six one-square-mile (640 acre) sections, of which one should be set aside for the support of education. (This ordinance is sometimes referred to as the "Northwest Ordinance of 1785.") The Northwest Ordinance of 1787 provided a bill of rights for settlers and forbade slavery north of the Ohio River. These ordinances were probably the most important legislation of the Articles of Confederation government.

The Jay-Gardoqui Negotiations

Economic depression followed the end of the war because the United States remained locked into the disadvantageous commercial system of the British Empire after the trade advantages that system had provided were gone.

One man who thought he saw a way out of the economic quagmire that followed the war was Congress's secretary of foreign affairs, John Jay. In 1784, Jay began negotiating with Spanish minister Gardoqui a treaty that would have granted lucrative commercial privileges—benefiting large east-coast merchants such as Jay—in exchange for United States acceptance of Spain's closure of the Mississippi River as an outlet for the agricultural goods of the rapidly growing settlements in Kentucky and Tennessee.

When Jay reported this to Congress in the summer of 1786, the west and south were outraged. Negotiations were broken off. Some, angered that Jay could show so little concern for the other sections of the country, talked of dissolving the Union; this helped spur to action those who desired not the dissolution but the strengthening of the Union.

Shays' Rebellion (1786)

Economic hard times, coupled with high taxes intended to pay off the state's war debt, drove western Massachusetts farmers to desperation. Led by war veteran Daniel Shays (ca. 1747–1825), they shut down courts to prevent judges from seizing property or condemning people to debtors' prison.

The citizens of Boston panicked and subscribed money to raise an army to suppress the rebels. The success of this army, together with timely tax relief, caused the "rebellion" to fizzle out fairly quickly.

Amid the panic caused by the news of the uprising, many came to feel that a stronger government was needed to control such violent public outbursts.

10 THE UNITED STATES CONSTITUTION (1787–1789)

DEVELOPMENT AND RATIFICATION

Toward a New Constitution

As time went on, the inadequacy of the Articles of Confederation became increasingly apparent. Congress could not compel the states to comply with the terms of the Treaty of Paris of 1783 in regard to debts and loyalists' property. The British used this as an excuse for not evacuating their northwestern posts, hoping to be on hand to make the most of the situation when, as they not unreasonably expected, the new government fell to pieces. In any case, Congress could do nothing to force them out of the posts, nor to solve any of the nation's other increasingly pressing problems.

In these dismal straits, some called for disunion, others for monarchy. Still others felt that republican government could still work if given a better constitution, and they made it their goal to achieve this.

The Annapolis Convention met in September 1786 to discuss a new constitution, but only five states were represented. With so few states represented, it was decided instead to call for a convention of all the states to meet the following summer in Philadelphia for the purpose of revising the Articles of Confederation.

The Constitutional Convention

The men who met in Philadelphia in 1787 were remarkably able, highly educated, and exceptionally accomplished. For the most part they were lawyers, merchants, and planters. Though representing individual states, most thought in national terms. Prominent among them were James Madison (1751–1836), Alexander Hamilton (1755–1804), Gouverneur Morris (1752–1816), Robert Morris (1734–1806), John Dickinson, and Benjamin Franklin.

George Washington was unanimously elected to preside, and the enormous respect that he commanded helped hold the convention together through difficult times.

The delegates shared a basic belief in the innate selfishness of man, which must somehow be kept from abusing the power of government. For this purpose, the document that they finally produced contained many checks and balances, designed to prevent the government, or any one branch of the government, from gaining too much power.

Madison, who has been called the "father of the Constitution," devised a plan of national government and persuaded fellow Virginian Edmund Randolph (1753–1813), who was more skilled at public speaking, to introduce it. Known as the "Virginia Plan," it called for an executive branch and two houses of Congress, each based on population.

Smaller states, who would thus have seen their influence decreased, objected and countered with William Paterson's (1745–1806) "New Jersey Plan," which called for the continuation of a unicameral legislature with equal representation for the states as well as sharply increased powers for the national government.

Benjamin Franklin played an important role in reconciling the often heated delegates and in making various suggestions that eventually helped the convention arrive at the "Great Compromise," proposed by Rober Sherman (1721–1793) and Oliver Ellsworth (1745–1807). The Great (or Connecticut) Compromise provided for a presidency, a Senate with all states represented equally (by two senators each), and a House of Representatives with representation according to population.

Another crisis involved North-South disagreement over the issue of slavery. Here also a compromise was reached. Slavery was neither endorsed nor condemned by the Constitution. Each slave was to count as three-fifths of a person for purposes of apportioning representation and direct taxation on the states (the Three-Fifths Compromise). The federal government was prohibited from stopping the importation of slaves prior to 1808.

The third major area of compromise was the nature of the presidency. This was made easier by the virtual certainty that George Washington would be the first president, and the universal trust that he would not abuse the powers of the office or set a bad example for his successors. The result was a strong presidency with control of foreign policy and the power to veto Congress's legislation. Should the president commit an actual crime, Congress would have the power to impeach him. Otherwise, the president would serve for a term of four years and be reelectable without limit. As a check to the possible excesses of democracy, the president was to be elected by an electoral college, in which each state would have the same number of electors as it did senators and representatives combined. The person with the second highest total in the electoral college would be vice-president. If no one gained a majority in the electoral college, the president would be chosen by the House of Representatives.

The new Constitution was to take effect when nine states, through special state conventions, had ratified it.

The Struggle for Ratification

As the struggle over ratification got under way, those favoring the Constitution astutely named themselves Federalists (i.e., advocates of centralized power) and labeled their opponents Antifederalists. The Federalists were effective in explaining the convention and the document it had produced. The *Federalist Papers*, written as a series of 85 newspaper articles by Alexander Hamilton, James Madison, and John Jay, brilliantly expounded the Constitution and demonstrated how it was designed to prevent the abuse of power. These essays are considered to be the best commentary on the Constitution by those who helped write it.

At first, ratification progressed smoothly, with five states approving in quick succession. In Massachusetts, however, a tough fight developed. By skillful maneuvering, the Federalists were able to win over to their side such popular opponents of the Constitution as Samuel Adams and John Hancock. Others were won over by the promise that a bill of rights would be added to the Constitution, limiting the federal government just as state governments were limited by their bills of rights. With such promises, Massachusetts ratified by a narrow margin.

By June 21, 1788, the required nine states had ratified, but the crucial states of New York and Virginia still held out. In Virginia, where George Mason (1725–1792) and Patrick Henry opposed the Constitution, the influence of George Washington and the promise of a bill of rights finally prevailed and ratification was achieved. In New York, where Alexander Hamilton led the fight for ratification, *The Federalist Papers*, the promise of a bill of rights, and the news of Virginia's ratification were enough to carry the day.

Only North Carolina and Rhode Island still held out, but they both ratified within the next 15 months. In March 1789, George Washington was inaugurated as the nation's first president.

OUTLINE OF THE UNITED STATES CONSTITUTION

Articles of the Constitution

Preamble

"We the People of the United States, in order to form a more perfect Union, establish justice, insure domestic tranquility, provide for the common defense, promote the general welfare, and secure the blessings of liberty to ourselves and our posterity, do ordain and establish this Constitution for the United States of America."

Article I—Legislature

The legislature is divided into two parts—the House of Representatives (435 members currently; determined by proportional representation of the population) and the Senate (100 members currently; two from each state).

The House of Representatives may bring impeachment charges. All bills which concern money must originate in the House. Because of the size of the body, debate is limited except in special cases, where all representatives may meet as the Committee of the Whole. The Speaker of the House presides over the proceedings. Elected terms of representatives are two years, reelectable without limit, to persons who are at least 25 years of age.

The Senate, originally elected by state legislatures but now by direct election (Seventeenth Amendment), approves or rejects presidential nominations and treaties, and serves as the court and jury in impeachment proceedings. Debate within the Senate is unlimited. The president pro tempore usually presides, but the vice-president of the United States is the presiding officer, and may vote to break a tie. Senate elected terms are for six years, reelectable without limit, to persons who are at least 30 years of age.

Article II—Executive

The president of the United States is elected for a four-year term, originally electable without limit (the Twenty-Second Amendment limits election to two terms), and must be at least 35 years old.

Responsibilities for the president outlined in the Constitution include acting as chief of state, chief executive, commander-in-chief of the armed forces, chief diplomat, and chief legislator.

Article III—Judiciary

While the Constitution describes the Supreme Court in Article III, the actual construction of the court system was accomplished by the Judiciary Act of 1789. The Supreme Court has jurisdiction for federal courts and appellate cases on appeal from lower courts.

Article IV—Interstate Relations

This article guarantees that court decisions and other legal actions (marriage, incorporation, etc.) valid in one state are valid in another. Expedition of criminals (and, originally, runaway slaves), and the exchange of citizenship benefits are likewise guaranteed. Article IV also provides for the admission of new states.

Article V—Amendment Process

Amendments are proposed by a two-thirds vote of each House of Congress, or by a special convention called by Congress upon the request of two-thirds of the state legislatures. Amendments are ratified by three-fourths of the state legislatures or state conventions.

Article VI—Supremacy Clause

Article VI sets up the hierarchy of laws in the United States. The Constitution is the "supreme law of the land," and supersedes treaties. Treaties supersede federal laws, federal laws (later to include federal regulatory agency directives) supersede state constitutions, state laws, and local laws, respectively. All federal and state officials, including judges, must take an oath to support and defend the Constitution.

Article VII—Ratification

This article specified the ratification process necessary for the Constitution to take effect. Nine of the original 13 states had to ratify the Constitution before it became operative.

Amendments to the Constitution

The amendments to the Constitution guarantee certain individual rights and amend original dictates of the Constitution. The first 10 amendments are known as the Bill of Rights.

1— freedom of religion, speech, press, assembly, and government petition (1791)

2— right to bear arms in a regulated militia (on a state basis; it was not intended to guarantee an individual's rights) (1791)

3— troops will not be quartered (housed) in private citizens' homes (1791)

4— protects against unreasonable search and seizure (need for search warrant) (1791)

5— protects the rights of the accused, including required indictments, double jeopardy, self-incrimination, due process, and just compensation (1791)

6— guarantees a speedy and public trial, the confrontation of witnesses, and the right to call witnesses on one's own behalf (1791)

7— guarantees a jury trial (1791)

8— protects against excessive bail and cruel and unusual punishment (1791)

9— states that all rights not enumerated are nonetheless retained by the people (1791)

10— states that all powers not specifically delegated to the federal government are retained by the states (1791)

11— states may not be sued by individuals (1798)

12— dictates that electors will cast separate ballots for president and vice-president; in the event of no clear winner, the House will select the president and the Senate the vice-president (1804)

13— abolished slavery (1865)

14— extended citizenship to all persons; made Confederate debt void and Confederate leaders ineligible for public office; states which denied voting rights to qualified citizens (blacks) would have their representation in Congress reduced; conferred "dual" citizenship (both of the United States and of a specific state) on all citizens (1868)

15— extended voting rights to blacks (1870)

16— legalized the income tax (1913)

17— provided for the direct election of senators (1913)

18— prohibited the general manufacture, sale, and use of alcoholic beverages (1919)

19— extended voting rights to women (1920)

20— changed inauguration date from March 4 to January 20; eliminated the "lame-duck" session of Congress (after the November elections) (1933)

21— repealed the Eighteenth Amendment (1933)

22— limited presidents to two terms (1951)

23— gave presidential electoral votes to the District of Columbia (1961)

24— prohibited poll taxes (1964)

25— changed the order of the presidential line of succession and provided guidelines for presidential disability (1967)

26— extended voting rights to 18-year-olds (1971)

SEPARATION AND LIMITATION OF POWERS

Powers Reserved for the Federal Government Only
- Foreign commerce regulation
- Interstate commerce regulation
- Mint money
- Create and establish post offices
- Regulate naturalization and immigration
- Grant copyrights and patents
- Declare and wage war, declare peace
- Admit new states
- Fix standards for weights and measures
- Raise and maintain an army and navy
- Govern the federal city (Washington, D.C.)
- Conduct relations with foreign powers
- Universalize bankruptcy laws

Powers Reserved for the State Governments Only
- Conduct and monitor elections
- Establish voter qualifications
- Provide for local governments
- Ratify proposed amendments to the Constitution
- Regulate contracts and wills
- Regulate intrastate commerce
- Provide education for its citizens
- Levy direct taxes (the 16th Amendment permits the federal government to levy direct taxes)
- Maintain police power over public health, safety, and morals
- Maintain integrity of state borders

Powers Shared by Federal and State Governments
- Taxing, borrowing, and spending money
- Controlling the militia
- Acting directly on individuals

Restrictions on the Federal Government
- No ex post facto laws
- No bills of attainder
- Two-year limit on appropriation for the military

- No suspension of habeus corpus (except in a crisis)
- One port may not be favored over another
- All guarantees as stated in the Bill of Rights

Restrictions on State Governments

- Treaties, alliances, or confederations may not be entered into
- Letters of marque and reprisal may not be granted
- Contracts may not be impaired
- Money may not be printed or bills of credit emitted
- No import or export taxes
- May not wage war (unless invaded)

Required Percentages of Voting

Actions which require a simple majority include raising taxes, requesting appropriations, declaring war, increasing the national debt, instituting a draft, and introducing impeachment charge (House).

Actions which require a two-thirds majority include overriding a presidential veto, proposing amendments to the Constitution, expelling a member of Congress (in the individual house only), ratifying treaties (Senate), acting as a jury for impeachment (Senate), ratifying presidential appointments (Senate).

Approving a proposed constitutional amendment requires a three-fourths majority of states.

11 THE NEW NATION (1789–1824)

THE FEDERALIST ERA

Few Antifederalists were elected to Congress, and many of the new legislators had served as delegates to the Philadelphia Convention two years before.

The New Executive

George Washington received virtually all the votes of the presidential electors, and John Adams received the next highest number, thus becoming the vice-president. After a triumphal journey from Mount Vernon, Washington was inaugurated in New York City, the temporary seat of government (April 30, 1789).

Congress Erects the Structure of Government

Ten amendments were ratified by the states by the end of 1791 and became the Bill of Rights. The first nine spelled out specific guarantees of personal freedoms, and the Tenth Amendment reserved to the states all those powers not specifically withheld or granted to the federal government. This last was a concession to those who feared the potential of the central government to usurp the sovereignty of the individual states.

The Establishment of the Federal Court System

The Judiciary Act of 1789 provided for a Supreme Court with six justices, and invested it with the power to rule on the constitutional validity of state laws. It was to be the interpreter of the "supreme law of the land." A system of district courts was set up to serve as courts of original jurisdiction, and three courts of appeal were established.

THE ESTABLISHMENT OF THE EXECUTIVE DEPARTMENTS

Congress established three departments of the executive branch—state, treasury, and war—as well as the offices of attorney general and postmaster general. President Washington immediately appointed Thomas Jefferson, Alexander Hamilton, and Henry Knox (1750–1806), respectively, to fill the executive posts, and Edmund Randolph became attorney general.

WASHINGTON'S ADMINISTRATION (1789–1797)

Hamilton's Financial Program

Treasury Secretary Alexander Hamilton, in his "Report on the Public Credit," proposed the funding of the national debt at face value, federal assumption of state debts, and the establishment of a national bank. In his "Report on Manufactures,"

Hamilton proposed an extensive program for federal stimulation of industrial development through subsidies and tax incentives. The money needed to fund these programs would come from an excise tax on distillers and from tariffs on imports.

Opposition to Hamilton's Program

Jefferson and others objected to the funding proposal because it would benefit speculators who had bought up state and confederation obligations at depressed prices, and would profit handsomely by their redemption at face value. They opposed the tax program because it would fall primarily on the small farmers. They saw Hamilton's entire program as enriching a small elite group at the expense of the more worthy common citizen.

The Appearance of Political Parties

The Constitution omitted mention of political parties, which were seen as a detrimental force by the founding fathers. But differences in philosophy very quickly began to drive the leaders of government into opposing camps—the Federalists and the Republicans.

Alexander Hamilton and the Federalists

Hamilton interpreted the Constitution as having vested extensive powers in the federal government. This "implied powers" stance claimed that the government was given all powers that were not expressly denied to it. This is the "broad" interpretation.

Thomas Jefferson and the Republicans

Jefferson and Madison held the view that any action not specifically permitted in the Constitution was thereby prohibited. This is the "strict" interpretation, and the Republicans opposed the establishment of Hamilton's national bank based on this view of government. The Jeffersonian supporters, primarily under the guidance of James Madison, began to organize political groups in opposition to the Federalist program. They called themselves Republicans.

Sources of Partisan Support

The Federalists received their strongest support from the business and financial groups in the commercial centers of the Northeast and from the port cities of the South. The strength of the Republicans lay primarily in the rural and frontier areas of the South and West.

FOREIGN AND FRONTIER AFFAIRS

The French Revolution

The U.S. proclaimed neutrality when France went to war with Europe in 1792, and American merchants traded with both sides. In retaliation, the British began to seize American merchant ships and force their crews into service with the British navy.

Jay's Treaty with Britain (1794)

John Jay negotiated a treaty with the British that attempted to settle the conflict at sea, as well as to curtail English agitation of their Native American allies on the western borders. The agreement actually settled few of the issues and merely bought time for the new nation in the worsening international conflict. Jay was severely criticized for his efforts.

The Treaty with Spain (1795)

In the Pinckney Treaty, ratified by the Senate in 1796, the Spanish opened the Mississippi River to American traffic and recognized the 31st parallel as the northern boundary of Florida.

Frontier Problems

Native American tribes on the Northwest and Southwest borders increasingly resisted the encroachments on their lands by the American settlers. British authorities in Canada were encouraging the Native Americans in their depredations against frontier settlements.

In 1794, General Anthony Wayne (1745–1796) decisively defeated the Native Americans at the Battle of Fallen Timbers, and the resulting Treaty of Greenville cleared the Ohio territory of Native American tribes.

INTERNAL PROBLEMS

The Whiskey Rebellion (1794)

Western farmers refused to pay the excise tax on whiskey which formed the backbone of Hamilton's revenue program. When a group of Pennsylvania farmers terrorized the tax collectors, President Washington sent out a federalized militia force of some 15,000 men and the rebellion evaporated, thus strengthening the credibility of the young government.

Land Policy

New states were organized and admitted to the Union, thus strengthening the ties of the western farmers to the central government (Vermont, 1791; Kentucky, 1792; and Tennessee, 1796).

JOHN ADAMS' ADMINISTRATION (1797–1801)

The Election of 1796

John Adams was the Federalist candidate, and Thomas Jefferson the Republican. Jefferson received the second highest number of electoral votes and became vice president. Adams was a brilliant lawyer and statesman, but too dogmatic and uncompromising to be an effective politician; he endured a very frustrating and unproductive term in office.

The XYZ Affair

A three-man delegation was sent to France in 1798 to persuade the French to stop harassing American shipping. When they were solicited for a bribe, by three subordinates of the French Minister Talleyrand, they indignantly refused. Their report of this insult produced outrage at home. The cry "millions for defense, but not one cent for tribute" was raised, and public feelings against the French ran high. Since Talleyrand's officials were unnamed in the dispatches, the incident became known as the "XYZ affair."

Quasi War (1798–1799)

Adams suspended all trade with France, and American ship captains were authorized to attack and capture armed French vessels. Congress created a Department of the Navy, and war seemed imminent. In 1800, the French government, now under Napoleon, signed a new treaty and peace was restored.

REPRESSION AND PROTEST

The Alien and Sedition Acts

The elections in 1798 increased the Federalist's majorities in both houses of Congress and they used their "mandate" to enact legislation to stifle foreign influences. The Alien Act raised new hurdles in the path of immigrants trying to obtain citizenship, and the Sedition Act widened the powers of the Adams administration to muzzle its newspaper critics. Both bills were aimed at actual or potential Republican opposition, and a number of editors were actually jailed for printing critical editorials.

The Kentucky and Virginia Resolves

Republican leaders were convinced that the Alien and Sedition Acts were unconstitutional, but the process of deciding on the constitutionality of federal laws was as yet undefined. Jefferson and Madison decided that state legislatures should have that power, and they drew up a series of resolutions which were presented to the Kentucky and Virginia legislatures. They proposed that state bodies could "nullify" federal laws within those states. These resolutions were adopted only in these two states, and so the issue died, but the principle of states' rights would have great force in later years.

THE REVOLUTION OF 1800

The Election

Thomas Jefferson and Aaron Burr (1756–1836) ran on the Republican ticket against John Adams and Charles Pinckney (1746–1825) for the Federalists. The Republican candidates won handily, but both received the same number of electoral votes, thus throwing the selection of the president into the House of Representatives. After a lengthy deadlock, Alexander Hamilton threw his support to Jefferson and Burr had to accept the vice-presidency, the result obviously intended by the electorate. This increased the ill-will between Hamilton and Burr and contributed to their famous duel in 1804. Jefferson appointed James Madison as secretary of state and Albert Gallatin (1761–1849) to the treasury.

Packing the Judiciary

The Federalist Congress passed a new Judiciary Act early in 1801, and President Adams filled the newly created vacancies with party supporters, many of them with last-minute commissions. John Marshall (1755–1835) was then appointed chief justice of the United States Supreme Court, thus guaranteeing continuation of Federalist policies from the bench of the high court.

THE JEFFERSONIAN ERA

Thomas Jefferson and his Republican followers envisioned a nation of independent farmers living under a central government that exercised a minimum of control and served merely to protect the individual liberties guaranteed by the Constitution. This agrarian paradise would be free from the industrial smoke and urban blight of Europe, and would serve as a beacon light of Enlightenment rationalism to a world searching for direction. But Jefferson presided over a nation that was growing more industrialized and urban, and which seemed to need an ever-stronger president.

The New Federal City

The city of Washington was designed by Pierre-Charles L'Enfant (1754–1825), and was briefly occupied by the Adams administration. Most of its inhabitants moved out when Congress was not in session.

CONFLICT WITH THE JUDGES

Marbury vs. Madison

Judge William Marbury, one of Adams' last-minute appointments, sued Madison to force delivery of his commission as a justice of the peace in the federal district. Chief Justice John Marshall ruled that the law giving the Supreme Court jurisdiction of the case was unconstitutional, and thus asserted the power of judicial review over federal legislation, a power which has become the foundation of the Supreme Court's check on the other two branches of government.

DOMESTIC AFFAIRS

Enforcement of the Alien and Sedition Acts was immediately suspended, and the men convicted under those laws were released.

The 12th Amendment was adopted and ratified in 1804, ensuring that a tie vote between candidates of the same party could not again cause the confusion of the Jefferson-Burr affair.

Following the Constitutional mandate, the importation of slaves was stopped by law in 1808.

The Louisiana Purchase

An American delegation purchased the trans-Mississippi territory from Napoleon for $15 million in April 1803, even though they had no authority to buy more than the city of New Orleans.

The Constitutional Dilemma

Jefferson's stand on the strict interpretation of the Constitution would not permit him to purchase land without congressional approval. But he accepted his advisors' counsel that his treaty-making powers included the authority to buy the land. Congress concurred, after the fact, and the purchase price was appropriated, thus doubling the territory of the nation overnight.

Exploring the West

Meriwether Lewis (1774–1809) and William Clark's (1770–1838) group left St. Louis in 1804 and returned two years later with a wealth of scientific and anthropological information. At the same time, Zebulon Pike and others had been traversing the middle parts of Louisiana and mapping the land.

The Essex Junto (1804)

Some New England Federalists saw the western expansion as a threat to their position in the Union and they tried to organize a secessionist movement. They courted Aaron Burr's support by offering to back him in a bid for the governorship of New York. Hamilton led the opposition to that campaign, and when Burr lost the election he challenged Hamilton to a duel that resulted in Hamilton's death.

The Burr Conspiracy

Burr became involved in a scheme to take Mexico from Spain and establish a new nation in the West.

In the fall of 1806, he led a group of armed men down the Mississippi River toward New Orleans. He was arrested in Natchez and tried for treason in Richmond, Virginia. Judge John Marshall's decision for acquittal helped to narrow the legal definition of treason.

INTERNATIONAL INVOLVEMENT

The Barbary War

In 1801, Jefferson sent a naval force to the Mediterranean to break the practice of the North African Muslim rulers of exacting tribute from Western merchant ships. Intermittent, undeclared war dragged on until 1805, with no decisive settlement.

The Chesapeake-Leopard Affair (1807)

American ships were seized by both sides in the Napoleonic Wars and American soldiers were "impressed" into the British navy. The British ship H.M.S. *Leopard* stopped the U.S.S. *Chesapeake* off the Chesapeake Bay and four alleged British deserters were taken off. Public outcry for war followed, and Jefferson was hard pressed to remain neutral.

The Embargo of 1807

Jefferson's response to the cry for war was to draft a law prohibiting American ships from leaving port for any foreign destination, thus avoiding contact with vessels of either belligerent. The result was economic depression, particularly in the heavily-commercial Northeast.

MADISON'S ADMINISTRATION (1809–1817)

The Election of 1808

Republican James Madison won the election over Federalist Charles Pinckney, but the Federalists gained seats in both houses of the Congress.

The War of 1812

Congress passed a modified embargo just before Madison's inauguration, known as the Non-Intercourse Act, which opened trade to all nations except France and Britain. When it expired in 1810, it was replaced by Macon's Bill No. 2, which gave the president power to prohibit trade with any nation when they violated United States neutrality.

The Native American tribes of the Northwest and the Mississippi Valley were resentful of the government's policy of pressured removal to the West, and the British authorities in Canada exploited their discontent by encouraging border raids against the American settlements.

The Shawnee chief Tecumseh (1768–1813) set out to unite the Mississippi Valley tribes and reestablish Native American dominance in the old Northwest. On November 11, 1811, General William Henry Harrison (1773–1841) destroyed Tecumseh's village on Tippecanoe Creek and dashed his hopes for an North American confederacy.

The Congress in 1811 contained a strong prowar group called the War Hawks led by Henry Clay (1777–1852) and John C. Calhoun (1782–1850). They gained control of both houses and began agitating for war with the British. On June 1, 1812, President Madison asked for a declaration of war and Congress complied.

A three-pronged invasion of Canada met with disaster on all three fronts, and the Americans fell back to their own borders. At sea, American privateers and frigates, including "Old Ironsides," (the U.S.S. *Constitution*) scored early victories over British warships, but were soon driven back into their home ports and blockaded by the powerful British ships-of-the-line.

On September 10, 1813, Admiral Oliver Hazard Perry (1785–1819) defeated a

British force at Put-in-Bay on Lake Erie. His flagship flew the banner, "Don't Give Up the Ship." This victory opened the way for William Henry Harrison to invade Canada in October and defeat a combination British and Native American forces at the Battle of the Thames.

The War in the Southwest

Andrew Jackson (1767–1845) led a force of frontier militia into Alabama in pursuit of Creek Native Americans who had massacred the white inhabitants of Fort Mims. On March 27, 1814, he crushed the Native Americans at Horseshoe Bend, and seized the Spanish garrison at Pensacola.

British Strategy Changes (1814)

A British force came down Lake Champlain and met defeat at Plattsburgh, New York, in September. A British armada sailed up the Chesapeake Bay and sacked and burned Washington, D.C. They then proceeded up the bay toward Baltimore, which was guarded by Fort McHenry. That fort held firm through the British bombardment, inspiring Francis Scott Key's (1779–1843) "Star Spangled Banner."

The Battle of New Orleans

A powerful British invasion force was sent to New Orleans to close the mouth of the Mississippi River, but Andrew Jackson decisively defeated it. The battle was fought on January 8, 1815, two weeks after a peace treaty had been signed at the city of Ghent in Belgium.

The Treaty of Ghent (Christmas Eve 1814)

The treaty provided for the acceptance of the status quo that had existed at the beginning of hostilities, and both sides restored their wartime conquests to the other.

The Hartford Convention (December 1814)

The Federalists had increasingly become a minority party. They vehemently opposed the war, and Daniel Webster (1782–1852) and other New England congressmen consistently blocked the Administration's efforts to prosecute the war effort. On December 15, 1814, delegates from the New England states met in Hartford, Connecticut, and drafted a set of resolutions suggesting nullification—and even secession—if their interests were not protected against the growing influence of the South and the West.

Soon after the convention adjourned, the news of the victory at New Orleans was announced and their actions were discredited. The Federalist party ceased to be a political force from this point on.

POSTWAR DEVELOPMENTS

Protective Tariff (1816)

The first protective tariff in the nation's history was passed in 1816 to slow the flood of cheap British manufactures into the country.

Rush-Bagot Treaty (1817)

An agreement was reached in 1817 between Britain and the United States to stop maintaining armed fleets on the Great Lakes. This first "disarmament" agreement is still in effect.

Native American Policy

The government began to systematically pressure all the Native American tribes remaining in the East to cede their lands and accept new homes west of the Mississippi. Most declined the offer.

The Barbary Wars (1815)

In response to continued piracy and extortion in the Mediterranean, Congress declared war on the Muslim state of Algiers in 1815 and dispatched a naval force to the area under Stephen Decatur (1779–1820). He quickly defeated the North African pirates and forced them to pay indemnities. This action gained the United States free access to the Mediterranean basin.

The Adams-Onis Treaty (1819)

Spain had decided to sell the remainder of the Florida territory to the Americans before they took it anyway. Under this agreement, the Spanish surrendered all their claims to Florida. The United States agreed to assume $5 million in debts owed to American merchants.

The Monroe Doctrine

Around 1810, national revolutions had begun in Latin America, as the colonial populations there refused to accept the rule of the new Napoleonic governments in Europe. Leaders like San Martín and Bolívar declared independence for their countries and after Napoleon's fall in 1814, were in defiance of the restored Hapsburg and Bourbon rulers of Europe.

British and American leaders feared that the new European governments would try to restore the former New World colonies to their erstwhile royal owners.

In December 1823, President James Monroe (1758–1831) included in his annual message to Congress a statement that the peoples of the American hemisphere were "henceforth not to be considered as subjects for future colonization by any European powers." Thus began a 30-year period of freedom from serious foreign involvement for the United States.

INTERNAL DEVELOPMENT (1820–1830)

The years following the War of 1812 were years of rapid economic and social development, followed by a severe depression in 1819. But this slump was temporary, and it became obvious that the country was moving rapidly from its agrarian origins toward an industrial, urban future. Westward expansion accelerated, and the mood of the people became very positive. In fact, these years were referred to as the "Era of Good Feelings."

BOUNDARIES ESTABLISHED
BY TREATIES

The Monroe Presidency (1817–1823)

James Monroe, the last of the "Virginia dynasty," had been handpicked by the retiring Madison and he was elected with only one electoral vote opposed—a symbol of national unity.

Postwar Boom

The years following the war were characterized by a high foreign demand for American cotton, grain, and tobacco—commerce flourished. The Second National Bank, through its overly liberal credit policies, proved to be an inflationary influence, and the price level rose rapidly.

THE MARSHALL COURT

John Marshall delivered the majority opinions in a number of critical decisions in these formative years, all of which served to strengthen the power of the federal government and restrict the powers of state governments.

Marbury vs. Madison (1803)

This case established the precedent of the Supreme Court's power to rule on the constitutionality of federal laws.

Fletcher vs. Peck (1810)

This was the first time a state law was voided on the grounds that it violated a principle of the United States Constitution.

Dartmouth College vs. Woodward (1819)

This decision was to severely limit the power of state governments to control corporations, the emerging form of business organization.

McCulloch vs. Maryland (1819)

The state of Maryland had tried to levy a tax on the Baltimore branch of the Bank of the United States and so protect the competitive position of its own state banks. Marshall's ruling declared that no state has the right to control an agency of the federal government. Since "the power to tax is the power to destroy," such state action violated Congress's "implied powers" to establish and operate a national bank.

Gibbons vs. Ogden (1824)

In a case involving competing steamboat companies, Marshall ruled that commerce included navigation, and that only Congress has the right to regulate commerce among states. Thus the state-granted monopoly was voided.

The Missouri Compromise (1820)

The Missouri Territory, the first to be organized from the Louisiana Purchase, applied for statehood in 1819. Since the Senate membership was evenly divided between slaveholding and free states at that time, the admission of a new state would give the voting advantage either to the North or to the South. Slavery was already well-established in the new territory, so the southern states were confident in their advantage, until Representative Tallmadge of New York proposed an amendment to the bill which would prohibit slavery in Missouri. The southern outcry was immediate, and the ensuing debate grew hot.

Henry Clay's Compromise Solution

As the debate dragged on, the northern territory of Massachusetts applied for admission as the state of Maine. This offered a way out of the dilemma, and House Speaker Clay formulated a package that both sides could accept. The two admission bills were combined, with Maine coming in free and Missouri coming in as a slave state. To make the package palatable for the House, a provision was added that prohibited slavery in the remainder of the Louisiana Territory north of the southern boundary of Missouri (latitude 36 degrees 30').

THE EXPANDING ECONOMY

The Growing Population

Population continued to double every 25 years. The migration of people to the West increased, and by 1840 more than one-third of all Americans lived west of the Alleghenies. Immigration from abroad was not significant until 1820; then it began to increase rapidly, mostly from the British Isles.

The Cotton Kingdom

The new lands in the Southwest, then made up by Alabama, Mississippi, Louisiana, and Texas, proved ideal for the production of short-staple cotton. Eli Whitney's (1765–1825) invention of the cotton "gin" solved the problem of separating the seeds from the fibers.

The growing market for food and work animals in the cotton South provided the opportunity for the new western farmers to specialize in those items, and further stimulated the westward movement.

Fishing

New England and Chesapeake fishing proved very profitable. Deep-sea whaling became a significant enterprise, particularly from the Massachusetts and Rhode Island ports.

Lumbering

The expanding population created a need for building materials, and timber remained a profitable export item. Shipbuilding thrived in a number of eastern seaboard and Gulf Coast ports.

Fur Trade

John Jacob Astor (1763–1848) and others opened up business all the way to the Northwest coast. "Mountain men" probed deeper and deeper into the Rocky Mountain ranges in search of the beaver.

Trade with the Spanish

The Santa Fe Trail, which ran from New Mexico northeast to Independence, Missouri, became an active trading corridor, opening up the Spanish territories to American migration and influence, and also providing the basis for future territorial claims.

THE TRANSPORTATION REVOLUTION

The first half of the 19th century witnessed an extraordinary sequence of inventions and innovations which produced a true revolution in transport and communications.

River Traffic

The steamboats built by Robert Fulton (1765–1815), the *Clermont* in 1807 and the *New Orleans* in 1811, transformed river transport. As shipment times and freight rates both plummeted, regular steam service was established on all the major river systems.

Roadbuilding

By 1818, the National Road, which was built with federal funds, had been completed from Cumberland, Maryland, to Wheeling, Virginia, linking the Potomac with the Ohio River. A network of privately owned toll roads (turnpikes) began to reach out from every sizable city.

The Canal Era

The Erie Canal, linking the Hudson River at Albany, New York, with Lake Erie, was completed in 1825. It was followed by a rash of construction, until canals linked every major waterway system east of the Mississippi River.

Canals were the first development projects to receive large amounts of public funding. They ran east-west and so tied the new West to the old East.

The Rise of New York City

Its location as a transport hub, coupled with innovations in business practices, boosted New York City into a primary trade center. It was America's largest city by 1830. One such innovation was the packet boat, which operated on a guaranteed schedule and helped to rationalize commerce, both internal and international.

New York soon dominated the domestic market for cotton, a situation which progressively reduced the South to the status of an economic colony.

INDUSTRIALIZATION

The Rise of the Factory System

Samuel Slater (1768–1835), who had apprenticed under British inventor Richard Arkwright, built the first successful cotton-spinning mill in this country.

Eli Whitney's development and application of the principle of interchangeable parts, first used in his firearms factories, helped to speed the growth of mass-production operations.

The Corporation

The corporate form, with its limited liability and its potential for raising and utilizing large amounts of capital, became the typical type of business organization. By the 1830s, most states had enacted general laws for incorporating.

The Labor Supply

In the early days, the "Lowell System" became a popular way to staff the New England factories. Young women were hired from the surrounding countryside and housed in dormitories in the mill towns. They were paid low wages for hard work under poor conditions, but they only worked for a short time, either to earn a dowry or to help out with the family income, and they soon went back home. This "rotating labor supply" was ideal for the owners, since the girls were not motivated to agitate for better wages and conditions.

Labor was always in short supply, so the system depended on technology to increase production. This situation always placed a premium on innovation in machinery and technique.

The Growth of Unions

Although the first organized strike took place in 1828, in Paterson, New Jersey, by child workers, periodic economic downturns helped keep workers relatively dependent and passive until the 1850s.

A major goal of early unions was the 10-hour day, and this effort sparked a period of growth in organized labor which was later effectively quashed by the depression of 1837.

EDUCATIONAL DEVELOPMENT

The Growth of Public Schools

Before 1815, schools were primarily sponsored by private institutions—corporate academies in the Northeast and religious institutions in the South and mid-Atlantic states. Most were aristocratic in orientation, training the nation's leaders, and few had any interest in schooling the children of the poor.

Women were likewise considered unfit for academic training; female schools concentrated on homemaking skills and the fine arts, which would make "ornaments" of the young ladies enrolled.

Higher Education

Although the numbers of institutions of higher learning increased sharply in the early years of the 19th century, none was truly public. All relied upon high tuition rates for survival, so less than one in ten young men, and no women, ever attended a college or university.

The training these schools provided was very limited as well. The only professional training was in theology, and only a scattering of colleges offered brief courses of study in law or medicine. The University of Pennsylvania, for example, offered one year of medical schooling, after which a person could obtain a license to practice the healing arts.

The Growth of Cultural Nationalism

Jeffersonian Americans tried to demonstrate their newly won independence by championing a strong sense of cultural nationalism, a feeling that their young republic represented the "final stage" of civilization, the "last great hope of mankind."

Significant American Authors

Washington Irving (1783–1859) was by far the best known American writer. He excelled in the telling of folk tales and local color stories, and is best remembered for his portraits of Hudson River characters.

Early schoolbooks, like Noah Webster's (1758–1843) "Blue Backed Speller," as well as his dictionary of the "American" language, reflected the intense desire to promote patriotism and a feeling of national identity.

DEVELOPMENTS IN RELIGIOUS LIFE

The Post-Revolution Years

The Revolutionary War weakened the position of the traditional, established churches. The doctrines of the Enlightenment became very popular, and its religious expression, deism, gained a considerable following among the educated classes. Rationalism, Unitarianism, and Universalism all saw a period of popularity.

The Second Great Awakening

The reaction to the trend toward rationalism, the decline in church membership, and the lack of piety was a renewal of personal, heartfelt evangelicalism. It began in 1801 at Cane Ridge, Kentucky, in the first "camp meeting."

As the revival spread, its characteristics became more uniform—an emphasis on personal salvation, an emotional response to God's grace, and individualistic faith. Women took a major part in the movement. Blacks were also heavily involved, and the individualistic emphasis created unrest among their ranks, particularly in the slaveholding South.

The revival produced strong nationalistic overtones, and the Protestant ideas of a "called nation" were to flourish later in some of the Manifest Destiny doctrines of expansionism. The social overtones of this religious renewal were to spark the great reform movements of the 1830s and 1840s.

12 JACKSONIAN DEMOCRACY AND WESTWARD EXPANSION (1824–1850)

JACKSONIAN DEMOCRACY (1829–1841)

The "Age of Jackson" marked a transformation in the political life of the nation which attracted the notice of European travelers and observers. Alexis de Tocqueville observed an "equality of condition" here that existed nowhere else in the world, and an egalitarian spirit among the people that was unique.

THE ELECTION OF 1824

The Expansion of the Electorate

Most states had already eliminated the property qualifications for voting before the campaigns for this election began. The movement for reform was much slower in the southern states. Free blacks were excluded from the polls across the South, and in most of the northern states.

National elections never attracted much enthusiasm until 1824. Legislative caucuses had made the presidential nominations and kept the ruling cliques in power by excluding the voters from the process. But this year the system failed, and the caucuses were bypassed.

The members of the electoral college were now being almost universally elected by the people, rather than by the state legislatures as in the early days.

The Candidates

Secretary of the Treasury William H. Crawford of Georgia was the pick of the congressional caucus. Secretary of State John Quincy Adams (1767–1848) held the job that traditionally had been the stepping-stone to the executive office. Speaker of the House Henry Clay presented the only coherent program to the voters, the "American System," which provided a high tariff on imports to finance an extensive internal improvement package. Andrew Jackson of Tennessee presented himself as a war hero from the 1812 conflict. All four candidates claimed to be Republicans.

The Election

Jackson won 43 percent of the popular vote, but the four-way split meant that he only received 38 percent of the electoral votes. Under the provisions of the 12th Amendment, the top three candidates were voted on by the House of Representatives. This left Henry Clay out of the running, and he threw his support to Adams. The votes had no sooner been counted, when the new president, Adams, appointed Henry Clay his secretary of state.

Andrew Jackson and his supporters immediately cried "foul!" and accused Clay of making a deal for his vote. The rallying cry of "corrupt bargain" became the impetus for their immediate initiation of the campaign for the 1828 election.

The Adams Administration

The new president pushed for an active federal government in areas like internal improvements and Natve American affairs. These policies proved unpopular in an age of increasing sectional jealousies and conflicts over states' rights.

Adams was frustrated at every turn by his Jacksonian opposition, and his unwillingness, or inability, to compromise further antagonized his political enemies.

John C. Calhoun and Nullification

In 1828, Congress passed a new tariff bill which included higher import duties for many goods which were bought by southern planters. Southerners bitterly denounced the law as the "Tariff of Abominations."

John Calhoun, who was Adams's vice-president, anonymously published the "South Carolina Exposition and Protest," which outlined his theory of the "concurrent majority": a federal law which was deemed harmful to the interests of an individual state could be declared null and void within that state by a convention of the people. Thus, a state holding a minority position could ignore a law enacted by the majority which they considered unconstitutional.

The Election of 1828

Adams's supporters now called themselves the National Republicans, and Jackson's party ran as the Democratic Republicans.

It was a dirty campaign. Adams's people accused Jackson of adultery and of the murder of several militiamen who had been executed for desertion during the War of 1812. Jackson's followers accused Adams of extravagance with public funds.

When the votes were counted, Jackson had won 56 percent of the popular vote and swept 178 of the 261 electoral votes. John Calhoun was elected vice-president.

Andrew Jackson as President

Jackson was popular with the common man. He seemed to be the prototype of the self-made westerner: rough-hewn, violent, vindictive, with few ideas but strong convictions. He ignored his appointed cabinet officers and relied instead on the counsel of his "Kitchen Cabinet," a group of partisan supporters.

Jackson expressed the conviction that government operations could be performed by untrained, common folk, and he threatened to dismiss large numbers of government employees and replace them with his supporters. Actually, he talked more about this "spoils system" than he acted on it.

He exercised his veto power more than any other president before him.

Jacksonian Native American Policy

Jackson supported the removal of all Native American tribes to west of the Mississippi River. The Indian Removal Act in 1830 provided for federal enforcement of that process.

The portion of the Cherokee Nation which occupied northern Georgia claimed to be a sovereign political entity within the boundaries of that state. The Supreme Court supported that claim in its decision *Worcester vs. Georgia* (1832), but President Jackson refused to enforce the court's decision.

The result of this policy was the Trail of Tears, the forced march under United States Army escort, of thousands of Cherokees to the West. A quarter or more of the Native Americans, mostly women and children, perished on the journey.

THE WEBSTER-HAYNE DEBATE (1830)

Federal Land Policy

The method of disposing of government land raised sectional differences. Westerners wanted cheap lands available to the masses. Northeasterners opposed this policy because it would lure away their labor supply and drive up wages. Southerners supported the West, hoping to weaken the ties between East and West.

The Senate Confrontation

Senator Robert Hayne of South Carolina made a speech in support of cheap land, and he used Calhoun's antitariff arguments to support his position. In his remarks, he referred to the possibility of nullification.

Daniel Webster's famous replies to this argument moved the debate from the issue of land policy to the nature of the Union and states' rights within it. Webster argued for the Union as indissoluble and sovereign over the individual states. His concluding statements have become a part of our rhetorical heritage: "It is, Sir, the people's Constitution, the people's government, made for the people, made by the people, and answerable to the people. . . . Liberty and Union, now and for ever, one and inseparable!"

The Second Nullification Crisis

The final split between Andrew Jackson and his vice-president, John C. Calhoun, came over the new Tariff of 1832, and over Mrs. Calhoun's snub of Peggy Eaton, the wife of Secretary of War John Eaton.

Jackson was a defender of states' rights, but within the context of a dominant Union. When he supported the higher rates of the new tariff, Calhoun resigned his office in a huff and went home to South Carolina. There he composed an Ordinance of Nullification, which was duly approved by a special convention, and the customs officials were ordered to stop collecting the duties at the port of Charleston.

Jackson's response was immediate and decisive. He obtained a Force Bill from Congress (1833), which empowered him to use federal troops to enforce the collection of the taxes. He also suggested the possibility of hanging Calhoun. At the same time, he offered a gradual reduction in the levels of the duties. Calhoun backed down, both sides claimed victory, and the crisis was averted.

THE WAR ON THE BANK

The Controversy

The Bank of the United States had operated under the direction of Nicholas Biddle (1786–1844) since 1823. He was a cautious man, and his conservative economic policy enforced conservatism among the state and private banks—which many bankers resented. Many of the Bank's enemies opposed it simply because it was big and powerful. Many still disputed its constitutionality.

The Election of 1832

Andrew Jackson freely voiced his antagonism toward the Bank and his intention to destroy it. Jackson soundly defeated Henry Clay in the presidential race, and he considered his victory a mandate from the people to destroy the Bank. His first move was to remove the federal government's deposits from Biddle's vaults and distribute the funds to various state and local banks. Biddle responded by tightening up on credit and calling in loans, hoping to embarrass the government and force Jackson to back down. Jackson stood firm and the result was a financial recession.

The Panic of 1837

The Depression lasted through the 1840s. Though global factors contributed to the recession, most Americans blamed everyone in power, including Jackson, and United States institutions and business practices. This disillusionment helped to initiate and intensify the reform movement that so occupied this nation in the 19th century's second quarter.

The Election of 1836

Jackson had handpicked his Democratic successor, Martin Van Buren (1782–1862) of New York. The Whigs ran three regional candidates in hopes of upsetting the Jacksonians. The Whig party had emerged from the ruins of the National Republicans and other groups who opposed Jackson's policies. The name was taken from the British Whig tradition, which simply refers to the "opposition."

Van Buren's Presidency

Van Buren, known as Old Kinderhook (O.K.), inherited all the problems and resentments generated by his mentor. He spent most of his term in office dealing with the financial chaos left by the death of the Second Bank. The best he could do was to eventually persuade Congress to establish an Independent Treasury to handle government funds. It began functioning in 1840.

THE ELECTION OF 1840

The Candidates

The Whigs nominated William Henry Harrison, "Old Tippecanoe," a western fighter against the Native Americans. Their choice for vice-president was John Tyler (1790–1862), a former Democrat from Virginia. The Democrats put up Van Buren again, but they could not agree on a vice-presidential candidate, so they ran no one.

Harrison won a narrow popular victory, but swept 80 percent of the electoral vote. Unfortunately for the Whigs, President Harrison died only a month after the inauguration, having served the shortest term in presidential history.

THE MEANING OF JACKSONIAN POLITICS

The Party System

The Age of Jackson was the beginning of the modern two-party system. Popular politics, based on emotional appeal, became the accepted style. The practice of meeting in mass conventions to nominate national candidates for office was established during these years.

The Strong Executive

Jackson, more than any president before him, used his office to dominate his party and the government. He did so to such an extent that he was called "King Andrew" by his critics.

The Changing Emphasis Toward States' Rights

The Supreme Court reflected a shift toward states' rights in its decision on the Charles River Bridge case in 1837, delivered by Jackson's new chief justice, Roger Taney (1777–1864). He ruled that a state could abrogate a grant of monopoly if that original grant had ceased to be in the best interests of the community. This was clearly a reversal of the Dartmouth College principle of the sanctity of contracts.

Party Philosophies

The Democrats opposed big government and the requirements of modernization: urbanization and industrialization. Their support came from the working classes, small merchants, and small farmers.

The Whigs promoted government participation in commercial and industrial development, the encouragement of banking and corporations, and a cautious approach to westward expansion. Their support came largely from northern business and manufacturing interests and large southern planters. Calhoun, Clay, and Webster dominated the Whig party during the early decades of the 19th century.

ANTEBELLUM CULTURE: AN AGE OF REFORM

The American people in 1840 found themselves living in an era of transition and instability. The responses to this uncertainty were twofold: a movement toward reform and a rising desire for order and control. Both of these major streams of reform activity were centered in the Northeast, especially in New England.

The Reform Impulse: Major Sources of Reform

Romanticism held a belief in the innate goodness of man, and thus in his improvability. This movement had its roots in turn-of-the-century Europe, and it emphasized emotions and feelings over rationality. It appeared as a reaction against the excesses of the Enlightenment, which had emphasized reason to the exclusion of feelings.

There was a also growing need perceived for stability and control over the social order and the forces that were threatening the traditional values.

THE FLOWERING OF LITERATURE

James Fenimore Cooper's (1789–1851) *Leatherstocking Tales* emphasized the independence of the individual, and also the importance of a stable social order.

Walt Whitman's (1819–1892) *Leaves of Grass* likewise celebrated the importance of individualism.

Henry Wadsworth Longfellow's (1807–1882) epic poems *Evangeline* and *Hiawatha* spoke of the value of tradition and the impact of the past on the present.

Herman Melville's (1819–1891) classic stories—*Typee, Billy Budd, Moby Dick*—all lashed out at the popular optimism of his day. He believed in the Puritan doctrine of original sin, and his characters spoke of the mystery of life.

A writer of romances and tales, Nathaniel Hawthorne (1804–1864) is best remembered for his criticism of Puritan bigotry in *The Scarlet Letter*.

Author of "The Raven," "Tamerlane," and many tales of terror and darkness, Edgar Allan Poe (1809–1849) explored the world of the spirit and the emotions.

THE FINE ARTS

The Hudson River School was a group of landscape painters who portrayed the grandeur of nature in America, the new world. John James Audubon (1785–1851) painted a wide array of American birds and animals.

THE TRANSCENDENTALISTS

Major Themes

This movement had its origins in Concord, Massachusetts. These thinkers wished to transcend the bounds of the intellect, to strive for emotional understanding, and to attain unity with God without the help of the institutional church, which they saw as reactionary and stifling to self-expression.

Major Writers

Ralph Waldo Emerson (1803–1882), essayist and lecturer, authored "Nature" and "Self-Reliance." Henry David Thoreau (1817–1862), best known for his *Walden*, repudiated the repression of society and preached civil disobedience to protest unjust laws.

THE UTOPIANS

Their Purpose

The cooperative community was the utopians attempt to improve the life of the common man in the face of increasing impersonal industrialism.

The Utopian Communities

Brook Farm, in Massachusetts, was the earliest commune in America, and it was short-lived. Nathaniel Hawthorne was a short-term resident, and his *Blithedale Ro-*

mance was drawn from that experience. This work and *The Scarlet Letter* were both condemnations of the life of social isolation.

New Harmony, Indiana, was founded by Robert Owen, of the New Lanark experiment in Wales, but it failed after two years. He attacked religion, marriage, and the institution of private property, so he encountered resistance from neighboring communities.

Nashoba, near Memphis, Tennessee, was established by the free-thinking Englishwoman Frances Wright as a communal haven for freed slaves. Her community experiment encountered fierce opposition from her slaveholding neighbors and survived only briefly.

Oneida Community in New York was based on free love and open marriages.

The Shakers were directed by Mother Ann Lee (1736–1784). The communities were socialistic experiments which practiced celibacy, sexual equality, and social discipline. The name was given to them by onlookers at their community dancing sessions.

Amana Community, in Iowa, was another socialist experiment, with a rigidly ordered society.

THE MORMONS

The Mormons were the most successful of the communal experiments. They established a highly organized, centrally controlled system, which provided security and order for the faithful. They held a strong belief in human perfectability, and so were in the mainstream of romantic utopians.

Joseph Smith (1805–1844) received the "sacred" writings in New York state in 1830, and organized the Church of Jesus Christ of Latter Day Saints. They were not popular with their neighbors, primarily because of their practice of polygamy, and so were forced to move about, first to Missouri, then to Nauvoo, Illinois. There Smith was killed by a mob, and the community was led to the Great Salt Lake by their new leader, Brigham Young (1801–1877).

REMAKING SOCIETY: ORGANIZED REFORM

Sources of Inspiration

Protestant revivalism was a powerful force for the improvement of society. A strong sectarian spirit split the Protestant movement into many groups. A strong anti-Catholic element was strengthened by the new waves of immigration from Catholic Ireland and southern Germany after 1830.

Temperance

The American Society for Promotion of Temperance was organized in 1826. It was strongly supported by Protestants, but just as strongly opposed by the new Catholic immigrants.

Public Schools

The motivations for the free-school crusade were mixed. Some wanted to provide opportunity for all children to learn the skills needed for self-fulfillment and success in a republic. Others wanted to use schools as agencies for social control—to Americanize the new immigrant children as well as to Protestantize the Catholics and defuse the growing problems of urbanization. The stated purpose of the public schools was to instill social values: thrift, order, discipline, and democracy.

Public apathy and even opposition met the early reformers, Horace Mann (1796–1859), the first secretary of the Massachusetts Board of Education, and Henry Barnard (1811–1900), his counterpart in Connecticut and Rhode Island.

The movement picked up momentum in the 1830s. Few public schools were available in the West, fewer still for southern whites, and none at all for southern blacks.

Higher Education

In 1839, the first state-supported school for women, Troy Female Seminary, was founded in Troy, New York. Oberlin College in Ohio was the nation's first coeducational college. The Perkins School for the Blind in Boston was the first of its kind in the United States.

Asylums for the Mentally Ill

Dorothea Dix (1802–1887) led the fight for these institutions, advocating more humane treatment for the mentally incompetent.

Prison Reform

The purpose of the new penitentiaries was not just to punish, but to rehabilitate. The first was built in Auburn, New York, in 1821.

Feminism

The Seneca Falls, New York, meeting in 1848, and its "Declaration of Sentiments and Resolutions," was the beginning of the modern feminist movement. The Grimké sisters, Angelina (1805–1879) and Sarah (1792–1873), Elizabeth Cady Stanton (1815–1902), and Harriet Beecher Stowe (1811–1896) were active in these early days. The movement was linked with that of the abolitionists, but suffered because it was considered to be of secondary importance.

The Abolitionist Movement

The early antislavery movement advocated only the purchase and colonization of slaves. The American Colonization Society was organized in 1817, and established the colony of Liberia in 1830, but by that time the movement had reached a dead end.

In 1831, William Lloyd Garrison (1805–1879) started his paper, *The Liberator*, and began to advocate total and immediate emancipation. He founded the New England Anti-slavery Society in 1832 and the American Anti-slavery Society in 1833. Theodore Weld (1803–1895) pursued the same goals, but advocated more gradual means.

Frederick Douglass (1817–1895) escaped from his Maryland owner and became a fiery orator for the movement. He published his own newspaper, the *North Star*.

There were frequent outbursts of antiabolition violence in the 1830s. Abolitionist editor Elijah Lovejoy (1802–1837) was killed by a mob in Illinois.

The movement split into two wings: Garrison's radical followers, and the moderates who favored "moral suasion" and petitions to Congress. In 1840, the Liberty party, the first national antislavery party, fielded a presidential candidate on the platform of "free soil" (nonexpansion of slavery into the new western territories).

The literary crusade continued, with Harriet Beecher Stowe's *Uncle Tom's Cabin* being the most influential among the many books that presented the abolitionist message.

DIVERGING SOCIETIES—LIFE IN THE NORTH

As the 19th century progressed, the states seemed to polarize more into the two sections we call the North and the South, with the expanding West becoming ever more identified with the North.

Population Growth (1790-1860)

The new West was the fastest growing area of the country. From four million in 1790, population had reached 32 million in 1860, with one-half living in states and territories which did not even exist during Washington's administration.

Natural Increase

Birth rates began to drop after 1800, more rapidly in the cities than in the rural areas. The population aged, with the median age rising from 16 to 20 years.

Immigration

The influx of immigrants had slowed during the conflicts with France and England, but the flow increased between 1815 and 1837. Then the economic downturn again sharply reduced their numbers. Thus, the overall rise in population during these years was due more to incoming foreigners than to natural increase. Most of the newcomers were from Britain, Germany, and southern Ireland. Discrimination was common in the job market, and was primarily directed against the Catholics. "Irish Need Not Apply" signs were common. However, the persistent labor shortage prevented the natives from totally excluding the foreign elements.

Growth of the Cities

In 1790, 5 percent of the United States population lived in cities of 2,500 or more. By 1860, that figure had risen to 25 percent. This rapid urbanization created an array of problems.

Social Unrest

Rapid growth helped to produce a wave of violence in the cities. In New York City in 1834, the Democrats fought the Whigs with such vigor that the state militia had to be called in. New York and Philadelphia witnessed race riots in the mid-

1830s, and a New York mob sacked a Catholic convent in 1834. Street crime was common in all the major cities.

THE ROLE OF MINORITIES

Women

Women were treated as minors by the law. In most states, the woman's property became her husband's with marriage. Political activity was limited to the formation of associations in support of various pious causes such as abolition. Professional employment was largely limited to schoolteaching. The women's rights movement focused on social and legal discrimination, and women like Lucretia Mott (1793–1880) and Sojourner Truth (ca. 1797–1883) became well-known figures on the speakers' circuit.

Blacks

By 1850, 200,000 free blacks lived in the North and West. Their lives were restricted everywhere by prejudice, and "Jim Crow" laws separated the races. Black citizens organized separate churches and fraternal orders. The African Methodist Episcopal Church, for example, had been organized in 1794 in Philadelphia and flourished in the major Northern cities. Black Masonic and Odd Fellows lodges were likewise established. The economic security of the free blacks was constantly threatened by the newly arrived immigrants, who were willing to work at the least desirable jobs for lower wages. Racial violence was a daily threat.

The Growth of Industry

By 1850, the value of industrial output had surpassed that of agricultural production. The Northeast produced more than two-thirds of the manufactured goods.

Inventions and Technology

Between 1830 and 1850, the number of patents issued for industrial inventions almost doubled. Charles Goodyear's (1800–1860) process of vulcanizing rubber was put to 500 different uses and formed the basis for an entire new industry. Elias Howe's (1819–1867) sewing machine was to revolutionize the clothing industry. The mass production of iron created an array of businesses, of which the new railroad industry was the largest consumer. Samuel B. Morse's (1791–1872) electric telegraph was first used in 1840 to transmit business news and information.

The Rise of Unions

In 1835, Boston construction craftsmen struck for seven months to win a 10-hour work day, and Paterson, New Jersey, textile workers became the first factory workers to strike for shorter hours. The federal government's introduction of the 10-hour day for federal projects, in 1840, helped to speed the acceptance of this goal. The influx of immigrants who were willing to work for low wages helped to spur the drive for unions. Their numbers also helped to weaken the bargaining position of union members.

The Revolution in Agriculture

As in industry, specialization and mechanization became the rule in agriculture.

Inventions and Technology

Large-scale farming on the prairies spurred critical inventions. Cyrus McCormick's (1809–1884) mechanical reaper, patented in 1834, enabled a crew of six men to harvest in one day as much wheat as 15 men using older methods. John Deere's (1804–1886) steel plow, patented in 1837, provided a more durable tool to break the heavy prairie sod. Jerome Case's threshing machine multiplied the bushels of grain that could be separated from the stalk in a day's time.

The New Market Economy

These developments not only made large-scale production possible, they also shifted the major emphasis from corn to small grain production and made farming for the international market feasible, which in turn made the western farmer dependent on economic forces over which he had no control.

In the East, the trend was toward truck farming for the nearby burgeoning urban areas, and the production of milk, fruits, and berries.

DIVERGING SOCIETIES—LIFE IN THE SOUTH

The southern states experienced dramatic growth in the second quarter of the 19th century. The economy grew more productive and more prosperous, but still the section called the South was basically agrarian, with few important cities and only scattered industry. The plantation system, with its cash-crop production driven by the use of slave labor, remained the dominant institution. And so the South grew more unlike the North and became more defensive of its distinctive way of life.

The Cotton Kingdom

The most important economic phenomenon of the early decades of the 19th century was the shift in population and production from the old "upper South" of Virginia and the Carolinas to the "lower South" of the newly opened Gulf states of Alabama, Mississippi, and Louisiana. This shift was the direct result of the increasing importance of cotton. In the older Atlantic states, tobacco retained its importance, but shifted westward to the Piedmont. It was replaced in the East by food grains. The southern Atlantic coast continued to produce rice, and southern Louisiana and east Texas retained their emphasis on sugar cane. But the rich black soil of the new Gulf states proved ideal for the production of short-staple cotton, especially after the invention of the "gin." Cotton soon became the center of the southern economy.

By 1860, cotton was to account for two-thirds of the value of United States exports. In the words of a Southern legislator of that era, "Cotton is King!"

CLASSES IN THE SOUTH

The Planter Class

Owners of large farms who also owned 50 or more slaves actually formed a small minority of the southern population. Three-fourths of southern whites owned no slaves at all, almost half of the slave-owning families owned fewer than six, and 12 percent owned 20 or more. But this minority of large slave owners exercised political and economic power far beyond their numbers. They became a class to which all others paid deference, and they dominated the political and social life of their region.

The Yeoman Farmers

The largest group of southern whites were the independent small farmers who worked their land with their family, sometimes side-by-side with one or two slaves, to produce their own food, with sometimes enough surplus to sell for a little extra cash. These people were generally poorer than their northern counterparts.

The Poor Whites

Perhaps a half-million white southerners lived on the edge of the agrarian economy, in varying degrees of poverty. These "crackers" or "sandhillers" occupied the barren soils of the red hills or sandy bottoms, where they lived in squalor. They formed a true underclass.

Slavery as a Labor System

The utilization of slave labor varied according to the region and the size of the growing unit. The large plantations growing cotton, sugar, or tobacco used the gang system, in which white overseers directed black drivers who supervised large groups of workers in the fields, all performing the same operation. In the culture of rice, and on the smaller farms, slaves were assigned specific tasks, and when those tasks were finished, the worker had the remainder of the day to himself.

House servants usually were considered the most favored since they were spared the hardest physical labor and enjoyed the most intimate relationship with the owner's family. This could be considered a drawback, as they were frequently deprived of the social communion of the other slaves, enjoyed less privacy, and were more likely to suffer the direct wrath of a dissatisfied mistress.

Violent reaction to repression was not uncommon. Gabriel Prosser in Richmond (1800), Denmark Vesey (ca. 1767–1822) in Charleston (1822), and Nat Turner (1800–1831) in coastal Virginia (1831) all plotted or led uprisings of blacks against their white masters. Rumors of such uprisings kept whites in a state of constant apprehension.

Urban Slavery in the Southern City

A sizable number of black slaves worked in the towns, serving as factory hands, domestics, artisans, and construction workers. They lived fairly independent lives and a good number purchased their freedom with their savings. As the 19th century progressed, urban slavery practically disappeared.

The Slave Trade

The most significant demographic shift in these decades was the movement of blacks from the Old South to the new Southwest. Traders shipped servants by the thousands to the newly opened cotton lands of the Gulf states. A prime field hand fetched an average price of $800 (as high as $1,500 in peak years). Families were frequently split apart by this miserable traffic. Planters freely engaged in this trade, but assigned very low status to the traders who carried it out.

Although the importation of slaves from abroad had been outlawed by Congress since 1808, they continued to be smuggled in until the 1850s. The import ban kept the price up and encouraged the continuation of the internal trade.

Many slaves tried to run away, some successfully, especially those from the states bordering the North. An ever-increasing number fled to freedom with the aid of the "underground railroad" and smugglers such as Harriet Tubman (ca. 1820–1913), who led more than 300 of her family and friends to freedom after she herself had escaped.

Most of those in bondage, however, were forced to simply adapt, which they did. In the face of incredible odds, the slaves developed a distinctive network of tradition and interdependence, and they survived.

COMMERCE AND INDUSTRY

The lack of manufacturing and business development has frequently been blamed for the South's losing its bid for independence in 1861–1865. Actually, the South was highly industrialized for its day and compared favorably with most European nations in the development of manufacturing capacity. However, it trailed far behind the North, so much so that when war erupted in 1861, the northern states owned 81 percent of the factory capacity in the United States.

Manufacturing

The southern states saw considerable development in the 1820s and 1830s in textiles and iron production and in flour milling. Even so, most of the goods manufactured in these plants were for plantation consumption rather than for export, and they never exceeded two percent of the value of the cotton crop.

Voices for Change

There were those who saw their native South sinking ever more into the position of dependency upon northern bankers and businessmen, and they cried out for reform. James B. D. DeBow's *Review* advocated commercial development and agricultural diversification, but his cries largely fell on deaf ears.

Since most of the planter's capital was tied up in land and slaves, there was little left to invest in commerce or manufacturing. Most important, perhaps, was the value system of the southern people, who put great store in traditional rural ideals:

chivalry, leisure, and genteel elegance. Even the yeoman farmer held these values and hoped some day to attain the position the planters held.

Southern Response to the Antislavery Movement

As the crusade for abolition intensified in the North, the South assumed an ever more defensive position. Biblical texts were used to justify the enslavement of an "inferior race." Scientific arguments were advanced to prove the inherent inferiority of the black African. Southern postal authorities refused to deliver any mail that contained information antagonistic to the slave system. Any kind of dissent was brutally suppressed, and the South became more and more a closed society. Literature and scholarship shriveled.

Beginning in 1837, regular conventions were held across the South to discuss ways to escape northern economic and political hegemony.

As the 1840s opened, the two sections were becoming more and more estranged, and the channels of compromise more and more poisoned by the emotional responses to black slavery. The development which contributed most to keeping the sore festering was westward expansion.

MANIFEST DESTINY AND WESTWARD EXPANSION

Although the term "Manifest Destiny" was not actually coined until 1844, the belief that the American nation was destined to eventually expand all the way to the Pacific Ocean, and to possibly embrace Canada and Mexico, had been voiced for years by many who believed that American liberty and ideals should be shared with everyone possible, by force if necessary. The rising sense of nationalism which followed the War of 1812 was fed by the rapidly expanding population, the reform impulse of the 1830s, and the desire to acquire new markets and resources for the burgeoning economy of "Young America."

Louisiana and the Far West Fur Trade

A variety of adventurers explored the newly acquired territory of Louisiana and the lands beyond. John Jacob Astor established a fur post at the mouth of the Columbia River, which he named Astoria. This challenged the British claim to the northwest. Though he was forced to sell out his establishment to the British, he lobbied Congress to pass trade restrictions against British furs, and eventually became the first American millionaire from the profits of the American Fur Company. The growing trade with the Orient in furs and other specialty goods was sharpening the desire of many businessmen for American ports on the Pacific coast.

The Oregon Country

The Adams-Onis Treaty of 1819 had set the northern boundary of Spanish possessions near the present northern border of California. The territory north of that line and west of the vague boundaries of the Louisiana Territory had been claimed over the years by Spain, England, Russia, France, and the United States. By the 1820s, all these claims had been yielded to Britain and the United States. The Hudson's Bay Company had established a fur trading station at Fort Vancouver, and claimed control south to the Columbia. The United States claimed all the way north to the 54°40' parallel. Unable to settle the dispute, they had agreed on a joint occupation of the disputed land.

In the 1830s, American missionaries followed the traders and trappers to the Oregon country. They began to publicize the richness and beauty of the land, sending back official reports on their work, which were published in the new inexpensive "penny press" papers. The result was the "Oregon Fever" of the 1840s, as thousands of settlers trekked across the Great Plains and the Rocky Mountains to settle the new Shangri-la.

The Texas Question (1836–1845)

Texas had been a state in the Republic of Mexico since 1822, following the Mexican revolution against Spanish control. The United States had offered to buy the territory at the time, since it had renounced its claim to the area in the Adams-Onis agreement of 1819. The new Mexican government refused to sell, but invited immigration from the north by offering land grants to Stephen Austin (1793–1836) and other Americans. They wanted to increase the population of the area and to produce revenue for their infant government. By 1835, approximately 35,000 "gringos" were homesteading on Texas land.

The Mexican officials saw their power base eroding as the foreigners flooded in, so they moved to tighten control through restrictions on immigration and through tax increases. The Texans responded in 1836 by proclaiming independence and establishing a new republic. The ensuing war was short-lived. The Mexican dictator, Antonia López de Santa Anna (1794–1876), advanced north and annihilated the Texan garrisons at the Alamo and at Goliad. On April 23, 1836, Sam Houston (1793–1863) defeated him at San Jacinto, and the Mexicans were forced to let Texas go its way.

Houston immediately asked the American government for recognition and annexation, but President Andrew Jackson feared the revival of the slavery issue, as the new state would come in on the slaveholding side of the political balance. He also feared war with Mexico and so did nothing. When Van Buren followed suit, the new republic sought foreign recognition and support, which the European nations eagerly provided, hoping thereby to create a counterbalance to rising American power and influence in the Southwest. France and England both quickly concluded trade agreements with the Texans.

New Mexico and California

The district of New Mexico had, like Texas, encouraged American immigration. Soon that state was more American than Mexican. The Santa Fe Trail, running from Independence, Missouri, to the town of Santa Fe, created a prosperous trade in mules, gold, silver, and furs, which moved north in exchange for manufactured goods. American settlements sprung up all along the route.

Though the Mexican officials in California had not encouraged it, American immigration nevertheless had been substantial. Since the Missouri Compromise had established the northern limits for slavery at the 36°30' parallel, most of this Mexican territory lay in the potential slaveholding domain, and many of the settlers carried their bondsmen with them.

Manifest Destiny and Sectional Stress

The Democrats generally favored the use of force, if necessary, to extend American borders. The Whigs favored more peaceful means like diplomacy. Some Whigs, like Henry Clay, feared expansion under any circumstances, because of its potential for aggravating the slavery issue.

TYLER, POLK, AND CONTINUED WESTWARD EXPANSION

Tyler and the Whigs

When William Henry Harrison became president, he immediately began to rely on Whig leader Henry Clay for advice and direction. He appointed to his cabinet those whom Clay suggested, and at Clay's behest he called a special session of Congress to vote the Whig legislative program into action. To the Whigs' dismay, Harrison died of pneumonia just one month into his term and was replaced by Vice-President John Tyler.

A states' rights southerner and a strict constitutionalist who had been placed on the Whig ticket to draw Southern votes, Tyler rejected the entire Whig program of a national bank, high protective tariffs, and federally funded internal improvements (roads, canals, etc.). In the resulting legislative confrontations, Tyler vetoed a number of Whig-sponsored bills.

The Whigs were furious. Every cabinet member but one resigned in protest. Tyler was officially expelled from the party and made the target of the first serious impeachment attempt. (It failed.) In opposition to Tyler over the next few years, the Whigs, under the leadership of Clay, transformed themselves from a loose grouping of diverse factions to a coherent political party with an elaborate organization.

One piece of important legislation that did get passed during Tyler's administration was the Preemption Act (1841), which allowed settlers who had squatted on unsurveyed federal lands first chance to buy the land (up to 160 acres at low prices) once it was put on the market.

The Webster-Ashburton Treaty

The member of Tyler's cabinet who did not immediately resign in protest was Secretary of State Daniel Webster. He stayed on to negotiate the Webster-Ashburton Treaty with Great Britain.

There were at this time several causes of tension between the United States and Great Britain:

1) The Canada-Maine boundary in the area of the Aroostook Valley was disputed. British efforts to build a military road through the disputed area led to reaction by Maine militia in a bloodless confrontation known as the "Aroostook War" (1838).

2) The Caroline Affair (1837) involved an American ship, the *Caroline*, that had been carrying supplies to Canadian rebels. It was burned by Canadian loyalists who crossed the United States border.

3) In the Creole Incident, Britain declined to return escaped slaves who had taken over a United States merchant ship, the *Creole*, and sailed to the British-owned Bahamas.

4) British naval vessels, patrolling the African coast to suppress slave smuggling, sometimes stopped and searched American ships.

The Webster-Ashburton Treaty (1842) dealt with these problems in a spirit of mutual concession and forebearance:

1) Conflicting claims along the Canada-Maine boundary were resolved.

2) The British expressed regret for the destruction of the *Caroline*.

3) The British promised to avoid "officious interference" in freeing slaves in cases such as that of the *Creole*.

4) Both countries agreed to cooperate in patrolling the African coast to prevent slave-smuggling.

The Webster-Ashburton Treaty also helped create an atmosphere of compromise in United States-British relations.

After negotiating the treaty, Webster also resigned from Tyler's cabinet.

The Texas Issue

Rejected by the Whigs and without ties to the Democrats, Tyler was a politician without a party. Hoping to gather a political following of his own, he sought an issue with powerful appeal and believed he had found it in the question of Texas annexation.

Texas President Sam Houston made much show of negotiating for closer relations with Great Britain. Southerners feared that Britain, which opposed slavery, might bring about its abolition in Texas and then use Texas as a base to undermine slavery in the American South. Other Americans were disturbed at the possibility of a British presence in Texas because of the obstacle it would present to what many Americans were coming to believe was, in the words of New York journalist John L. O'Sullivan, America's "manifest destiny to overspread the continent."

Tyler's new secretary of state, John C. Calhoun, negotiated an annexation treaty with Texas. Calhoun's identification with extreme proslavery forces and his insertion in the treaty of proslavery statements caused the treaty's rejection by the Senate (1844).

The Election of 1844

Democratic front-runner Martin Van Buren and Whig front-runner Henry Clay agreed privately that neither would endorse Texas annexation, and that it would not become a campaign issue, but expansionists at the Democratic convention succeeded in dumping Van Buren in favor of James K. Polk (1795–1849). Polk, called "Young Hickory" by his supporters, was a staunch Jacksonian who opposed protective tariffs and a national bank, but favored territorial expansion, including not only annexation of Texas but also occupation of all the Oregon country (up to latitude 54° 40') hitherto jointly occupied by the United States and

Britain. The latter claim was expressed in his campaign slogan, "Fifty-four forty or fight."

Tyler, despite his introduction of the issue that was to decide that year's presidential campaign, was unable to build a party of his own and withdrew from the race.

The Whigs nominated Clay, who continued to oppose Texas annexation. Later, sensing the mood of the country was against him, he began to equivocate.

The antislavery Liberty party nominated James G. Birney. Apparently because of Clay's wavering on the Texas issue, Birney was able to take enough votes away from Clay in New York to give that state, and thus the election, to Polk.

Tyler, as a lame-duck president, made one more attempt to achieve Texas annexation before leaving office. By means of a joint resolution, which unlike a treaty required only a simple majority rather than a two-thirds vote, he was successful in getting the measure through Congress. Texas was finally admitted to the Union in 1845.

Polk as President

Though a relatively unknown "dark horse" at the time of his nomination for the presidency, Polk had considerable political experience both within his home state of Tennessee and as Speaker of the House. He was an adept politician and he turned out to be a skillful and effective president.

As a good Jacksonian, Polk favored a low, revenue-only tariff rather than a high, protective tariff. This he obtained in the Walker Tariff (1846). He also opposed a national debt and a national bank and reestablished Van Buren's Independent Sub-Treasury system, which remained in effect until 1920.

The Settlement of Oregon

A major issue in the election campaign of 1844, Oregon at this time comprised all the land bounded on the east by the Rockies, the west by the Pacific, the south by latitude 42°, and the north by the boundary of Russian-held Alaska at 54° 40'.

The area had been under the joint occupation of the United States and Great Britain since 1818, but Democrats in the election of 1844 had called for United States ownership of all of Oregon. Though this stand had helped him win the election, Polk had little desire to fight the British for land he considered unsuitable for agriculture and unavailable for slavery, which he favored. And trouble seemed to be brewing with Mexico over territory Polk considered far more desirable.

The British hoped to obtain the area north of the Columbia River, including the natural harbor of Puget Sound (one of only three on the Pacific coast), with its adjoining Strait of Juan de Fuca.

By the terms of the Oregon Treaty (1846), a compromise solution was reached. The current United States-Canada boundary east of the Rockies (49°) was extended westward to the Pacific, thus securing Puget Sound and shared use of the Strait of Juan de Fuca for the United States. Some northern Democrats were angered and felt betrayed by Polk's failure to insist on all of Oregon, but the Senate readily accepted the treaty.

The Mormon Migration

After Joseph Smith was killed by a crowd of hostile non-Mormons, the Mormons decided to migrate to the Far West, preferably, someplace outside United States jurisdiction. Under the leadership of new church leader Brigham Young, some 85,000 Mormons trekked overland in 1846 to settle near the Great Salt Lake in what is now Utah (but was then owned by Mexico). Young founded the Mormon republic of Deseret and openly preached and practiced polygamy.

After Deseret's annexation by the United States as part of the Mexican Cession, Young was made territorial governor of Utah. Nevertheless, friction developed with the federal government. By 1857, public outrage over polygamy prompted then President James Buchanan (1791–1868) to replace Young with a non-Mormon governor. Threats of Mormon defiance led Buchanan to send 2,500 army troops to compel Mormon obedience to federal law. Young responded by calling out the Mormon militia and blocking the passes through which the army would have to advance. This standoff, known as the "Mormon War," was resolved in 1858, with the Mormons accepting the new governor and Buchanan issuing a general pardon.

The Coming of War with Mexico

Though Mexico broke diplomatic relations with the United States immediately upon Texas's admission to the Union, there was still hope of a peaceful settlement. In the fall of 1845, Polk sent John Slidell (1793–1871) to Mexico City with a proposal for a peaceful settlement. Slidell was empowered to cancel the damage claims and pay $5,000,000 for the disputed land in southern Texas. He was also authorized to offer $25,000,000 for California and $5,000,000 for other Mexican territory in the Far West. Polk was especially anxious to obtain California because he feared the British would snatch it from Mexico's extremely weak grasp.

Nothing came of these attempts at negotiation. Racked by coup and counter-coup, the Mexican government refused even to receive Slidell.

Polk thereupon sent United States troops into the disputed territory in southern Texas. A force under General Zachary Taylor (1784–1850) (who was nicknamed "Old Rough and Ready") took up a position just north of the Rio Grande. Eight days later, April 5, 1846, Mexican troops attacked an American patrol. When news of the clash reached Washington, Polk sought and received from Congress a declaration of war against Mexico on May 13, 1846.

Some criticized the war, among them Henry David Thoreau, who, to display his protest, went to live at Walden Pond and refused to pay his taxes. Jailed for this, he wrote "Civil Disobedience."

The Mexican War

Americans were sharply divided about the war. Some favored it because they felt Mexico had provoked the war, or because they felt it was the destiny of America to spread the blessings of freedom to oppressed peoples. Others, generally northern abolitionists, saw in the war the work of a vast conspiracy of southern slaveholders greedy for more slave territory.

In planning military strategy, Polk showed genuine skill. American strategy consisted originally of a three-pronged attack: a land movement westward through New Mexico into California, a sea movement against California, and a land movement southward into Mexico.

General Stephen W. Kearny's (1794–1848) force easily secured New Mexico, entering Santa Fe on August 16, 1846, before continuing west to California. There American settlers, aided by an Army exploring party under John C. Frémont (1813–1890), had already revolted against Mexico's weak rule in what was called the Bear Flag Revolt.

Naval forces under Commodore John D. Sloat seized Monterey and declared California to be part of the United States. Forces put ashore by Commodore Robert Stockton joined with Kearny's troops to defeat the Mexicans at the Battle of San Gabriel on January 1847. This completed the conquest of California.

The third prong of the American strategy, an advance southward into Mexico, was itself divided into two parts:

1) Troops under Colonel Alexander W. Doniphan defeated Mexicans at El Brazito (December 25–28, 1846) to take El Paso, and then proceeded southward, winning the Battle of Sacramento (February 28, 1847) to take the city of Chihuahua, capital of the Mexican province of that name.

2) The main southward thrust was made by a much larger American army under General Zachary Taylor. After badly defeating larger Mexican forces at the battles of Palo Alto (May 7, 1846) and Resaca de la Palma (May 8, 1846), Taylor advanced into Mexico and defeated an even-larger Mexican force at the Battle of Monterey (September 20–24, 1846). He successfully withstood, though badly outnumbered, an attack by a Mexican force under Santa Anna at the Battle of Buena Vista, February 22–23, 1847.

Despite the Americans' success, the Mexicans refused to negotiate. Polk therefore ordered United States forces under General Winfield Scott (1786–1866) to land on the east coast of Mexico, march inland, and take Mexico City.

Scott landed at Veracruz on March 9, 1847, and by March 27 had captured the city with the loss of only 20 American lives. He advanced from there, being careful to maintain good discipline and avoid atrocities in the countryside. At Cerro Gordo (April 18, 1847), in what has been called "the most important single battle of the war," Scott outflanked and soundly defeated a superior enemy force in a seemingly impregnable position. After beating another Mexican army at Churubusco (August 19–20, 1847), Scott paused outside Mexico City to offer the Mexicans another chance to negotiate. When they declined, United States forces stormed the fortress of Chapultepec (September 13, 1847) and the next day entered Mexico City. Still, Mexico refused to negotiate a peace, and instead carried on guerilla warfare.

Negotiated peace finally came about when the State Department clerk Nicholas Trist, though his authority had been revoked and he had been ordered back to Washington two months earlier, negotiated and signed the Treaty of Guadalupe-Hidalgo (February 2, 1848), ending the Mexican War. Under the terms of the treaty, Mexico ceded to the United States the territory Polk had originally sought to buy, this time in exchange for a payment of $15,000,000 and the assumption of $3,250,000 in American citizens' claims against the Mexican government. This territory, the Mexican Cession, included the natural harbors at San Francisco and San Diego, thus giving the United States all three of the major west coast natural harbors.

Many, including Polk, felt the treaty was far too generous. There had been talk of annexing all of Mexico or of forcing Mexico to pay an indemnity for the cost of the war. Still, Polk felt compelled to accept the treaty as it was, and the Senate subsequently ratified it.

Although the Mexican War increased the nation's territory by one-third, it also brought to the surface serious political issues that threatened to divide the country, particularly the question of slavery in the new territories.

13 SECTIONAL CONFLICT AND THE CAUSES OF THE CIVIL WAR (1850–1860)

THE CRISIS OF 1850 AND AMERICA AT MIDCENTURY

The Wilmot Proviso

The Mexican War had no more than started when, on August 8, 1846, freshman Democratic Congressman David Wilmot (1814–1868) of Pennsylvania introduced his Wilmot Proviso as a proposed amendment to a war appropriations bill. It stipulated that "neither slavery nor involuntary servitude shall ever exist" in any territory to be acquired from Mexico. It was passed by the House, and though rejected by the Senate it was reintroduced again and again amid increasingly acrimonious debate.

The Wilmot Proviso aroused intense sectional feelings. Southerners, who had supported the war enthusiastically, felt they were being treated unfairly. There came to be four views regarding the status of slavery in the newly acquired territories.

The southern position was expressed by John C. Calhoun, now serving as senator from South Carolina. He argued that the territories were the property not of the United States federal government, but of all the states together, and therefore Congress had no right to prohibit in any territory any type of "property" (by which he meant slaves) that was legal in any of the states.

Antislavery northerners, pointing to the Northwest Ordinance of 1787 and the Missouri Compromise of 1820 as precedents, argued that Congress had the right to make what laws it saw fit for the territories, including, if it so chose, laws prohibiting slavery.

A compromise proposal favored by President Polk and many moderate southerners called for the extension of the 36° 30' line of the Missouri Compromise westward through the Mexican Cession to the Pacific, with territory north of the line to be closed to slavery.

Another compromise solution, favored by northern Democrats such as Lewis Cass (1782–1866) of Michigan and Stephen A. Douglas (1813–1861) of Illinois, was known as "squatter sovereignty" and later as "popular sovereignty." It held that the residents of each territory should be permitted to decide for themselves whether to allow slavery.

The Election of 1848

The Democrats nominated Lewis Cass, and their platform endorsed his middle-of-the-road popular sovereignty position with regard to slavery in the territories.

The Whigs dodged the issue even more effectively by nominating General Zachary Taylor, whose fame in the Mexican War made him a strong candidate. Taylor knew nothing of politics, had never voted, and liked to think of himself as above politics. He took no position at all with respect to slavery in the territories.

Some antislavery northern Whigs and Democrats, disgusted with their parties' failure to take a clear stand against the spread of slavery, deserted the party ranks to form an antislavery third party. Their party was called the Free Soil party, since it stood for keeping the soil of new western territories free of slavery. Its candidate was Martin Van Buren.

The election excited relatively little public interest. Taylor won a narrow victory.

Gold in California

The question of slavery's status in the western territories was made more immediate when, on January 24, 1848, gold was discovered at Sutter's Mill, not far from Sacramento, California. The next year, gold seekers from the eastern United States and from many foreign countries swelled California's population from 14,000 to 100,000.

California was a wild and lawless place. No territorial government had been organized since the United States had received the land as part of the Mexican Cession, and all that existed was an inadequate military government. In September 1849, having more than the requisite population and being in need of better government, California petitioned for admission to the Union as a state.

Since few slaveholders had chosen to risk their valuable investments in human property in the turbulent atmosphere of California, the people of the area sought admission as a free state, touching off a serious sectional crisis back East.

The Compromise of 1850

President Zachary Taylor, though himself a Louisiana slaveholder, opposed the further spread of slavery. Hoping to sidestep the dangerously divisive issue of slavery in the territories, he encouraged California as well as the rest of the Mexican Cession to organize and seek admission directly as states, thus completely bypassing the territorial stage.

Southerners were furious. Long outnumbered in the House of Representatives, the South would now find itself, should California be admitted as a free state, also outvoted in the Senate.

Other matters created friction between North and South. A large tract of land was disputed between Texas, a slave state, and the as yet unorganized New Mexico Territory, where slavery's future was at best uncertain. Southerners were angered by the small-scale but much talked of efforts of northern abolitionists' "underground railroad" to aid escaped slaves in reaching permanent freedom in Canada. Northerners were disgusted by the presence of slave pens and slave markets in the nation's capital. Radical southerners talked of secession and scheduled an all-southern convention to meet in Nashville in June 1850 to propose ways of protecting southern interests, inside or outside the Union.

At this point, the aged Henry Clay attempted to compromise the various matters of contention between North and South. He proposed an eight-part package. For the North, California would be admitted as a free state; the land in dispute between Texas and New Mexico would go to New Mexico; the New Mexico and Utah territories (all of the Mexican Cession outside of California) would not be specifically reserved for slavery, the status there would be decided by popular sovereignty; and the slave trade would be abolished in the District of Columbia.

For the South, a tougher Fugitive Slave Law would be enacted; the federal government would pay Texas's $10,000,000 preannexation debt; Congress would declare that it did not have jurisdiction over the interstate slave trade and would promise not to abolish slavery itself in the District of Columbia.

In the following eight months of intense debate, Clay, Calhoun, and Daniel Webster, the three great figures of Congress during the first half of the 19th century—all three aged and none of them with more than two years to live—made some of their greatest speeches. Clay called for compromise and "mutual forbearance." Calhoun gravely warned that the only way to save the Union was for the North to grant all the South's demands and keep quiet on the issue of slavery. Webster abandoned his previous opposition to the spread of slavery (as well as most of his popularity back in his home state of Massachusetts) to support the Compromise in an eloquent speech.

The opponents of the Compromise were many and powerful and ranged from President Taylor, who demanded admission of California without reference to slavery, to northern extremists such as Senator William Seward (1801–1872) of New York, who spoke of a "higher law" than the Constitution which forbade the spread of slavery, to southern extremists such as Calhoun or Senator Jefferson Davis (1808–1889) of Mississippi. By midsummer all seemed lost for the Compromise, and Clay left Washington exhausted and discouraged.

Then the situation changed dramatically. President Taylor died (apparently of gastroenteritis) on July 9, 1850, and was succeeded by Vice-President Millard Fillmore (1800–1874), a quiet but efficient politician, and a strong supporter of compromise. In Congress, the fight for the Compromise was taken up by Senator Stephen A. Douglas of Illinois. Called the "Little Giant" for his small stature but large political skills, Douglas broke Clay's proposal into its component parts so that he could use varying coalitions to push each part through Congress. The Compromise was adopted.

The Compromise of 1850 was received with joy by most of the nation. The issue of slavery in the territories seemed to have been permanently settled.

The Election of 1852

The 1852 Democratic convention deadlocked between Cass and Douglas and so settled on dark horse Franklin Pierce (1804–1869) of New Hampshire. The Whigs chose General Winfield Scott, a war hero of no political background.

The result was an easy victory for Pierce, largely because the Whig party, badly divided along North-South lines as a result of the battle over the Compromise of 1850, was beginning to come apart. The Free Soil party's candidate, John P. Hale of New Hampshire, fared poorly, demonstrating the electorate's weariness with the slavery issue.

Pierce and "Young America"

President Pierce expressed the nation's hope that a new era of sectional peace was beginning. He sought to distract the nation's attention from the slavery issue to an aggressive program of foreign economic and territorial expansion known as "Young America."

EXPANSION OF THE UNITED STATES

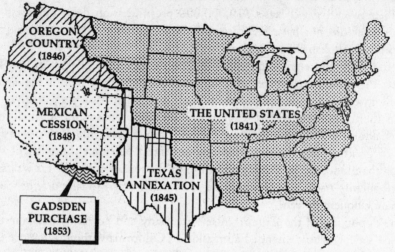

In 1853, Commodore Matthew Perry (1794–1858) led a United States naval force into Tokyo Bay on a peaceful mission to open Japan—previously closed to the outside world—to American diplomacy and commerce.

By means of the Reciprocity Treaty (1854), Pierce succeeded in opening Canada to greater United States trade. He also sought to annex Hawaii, increase United States interest in Central America, and acquire territories from Mexico and Spain.

From Mexico he acquired in 1853 the Gadsden Purchase, a strip of land in what is now southern New Mexico and Arizona along the Gila River. The purpose of this purchase was to provide a good route for a transcontinental railroad across the southern part of the country.

Pierce sought to buy Cuba from Spain. When Spain declined, three of Pierce's diplomats, meeting in Ostend, Belgium, sent him the Ostend Manifesto urging military seizure of Cuba should Spain remain intransigent.

Pierce was the first "doughface" president—"a northern man with southern principles"—and his expansionist goals aroused suspicion and hostility in anti-slavery northerners. Pierce's administration appeared to be dominated by southerners, such as Secretary of War Jefferson Davis, and seemed to be working for the good of the South.

Economic Growth

The chief factor in the economic transformation of America during the 1840s and 1850s was the dynamic rise of the railroads. They helped link the Midwest to the Northeast rather than just the South, as would have been the case had only water transportation been available.

The 1850s was the heyday of the steamboat on inland rivers, and the clipper ship on the high seas. The period also saw rapid and sustained industrial growth. The factory system began in the textile industry, with Elias Howe's invention of the sewing machine (1846). Isaac Singer's improved model (1851) aided the process of mechanization, which spread to other industries.

In the North, the main centers of agricultural production shifted from the Mid-Atlantic states to the more fertile lands of the Midwest. Unlike the South, where 3,500,000 slaves provided abundant labor, the North faced incentives to introduce labor-saving machines. Mechanical reapers and threshers came into wide use.

Decline of the Two-Party System

America's second two-party system, which had developed during the 1830s, was in the process of breaking down. The Whig party was now in the process of complete disintegration. This was partially the result of the slavery issue, which divided the party along North-South lines, and partially the result of the nativist movement.

The nativist movement and its political party, the American, or, as it was called, the Know-Nothing party, grew out of alarm on the part of native-born Americans at the rising tide of German and Irish immigration during the late 1840s and early 1850s. The Know-Nothing party, so called because its members were told to answer "I know nothing" when asked about its secret proceedings, was anti-foreign, and since many of the foreigners were Catholic, also anti-Catholic. It surged briefly to become the country's second largest party by 1855, but faded even more quickly due to the ineptness of its leaders and the growing urgency of the slavery question, which, though ignored by the Know-Nothing party, was rapidly coming to overshadow all other issues.

The collapse of a viable two-party system made it much more difficult for the nation's political process to contain the explosive issue of slavery.

THE RETURN OF SECTIONAL CONFLICT

Continuing Sources of Tension

The strengthened Fugitive Slave Law enraged northerners. Under its provisions, blacks living in the North who were claimed by slave catchers were denied trial by jury and many of the other protections of due process. Even more distasteful to antislavery northerners was the provision that required all United States citizens to aid, when called upon, in the capture and return of alleged fugitives. So violent was northern feeling against the law that several riots erupted as a result of attempts to enforce it. Some northern states passed personal liberty laws in an attempt to prevent the enforcement of the Fugitive Slave Law.

Many northerners who had not previously taken an interest in the slavery issue now became opponents of slavery as a result of having its injustices forcibly brought home to them by the Fugitive Slave Law.

Publishing of Uncle Tom's Cabin

One northerner who was outraged by the Fugitive Slave Act was Harriet Beecher Stowe. She wrote *Uncle Tom's Cabin*, a fictional book depicting what she perceived as the evils of slavery. Furiously denounced in the South, the book became an overnight bestseller in the North, where it turned many toward active opposition to slavery.

The Kansas-Nebraska Act

All illusion of sectional peace ended abruptly in 1854 when Senator Stephen A. Douglas of Illinois introduced a bill in Congress to organize the area west of Missouri and Iowa as the territories of Kansas and Nebraska.

Though he sought to avoid directly addressing the touchy issue of slavery, Douglas was compelled by pressure from southern senators such as David Atchison of Missouri to include in the bill an explicit repeal of the Missouri Compromise (which banned slavery in the areas in question) and a provision that the status of slavery in the newly organized territories be decided by popular sovereignty.

The bill was opposed by most northern Democrats and a majority of the remaining Whigs, but with the support of the southern-dominated Pierce administration it was passed and signed into law.

The Republican Party

The Kansas-Nebraska Act aroused a storm of outrage in the North, where the repeal of the Missouri Compromise was seen as the breaking of a solemn agreement. It hastened the disintegration of the Whig party and divided the Democratic party along North-South lines.

In the North, many Democrats left the party and were joined by former Whigs and Know-Nothings in the newly created Republican party. Springing to life almost overnight as a result of northern fury at the Kansas-Nebraska Act, the Republican party included diverse elements whose sole unifying principle was the firm belief that slavery should be banned from all the nation's territories, confined to the states where it already existed, and allowed to spread no further.

Though its popularity was confined almost entirely to the North, the Republican party quickly became a major power in national politics.

Bleeding Kansas

With the status of Kansas (Nebraska was never in much doubt) to be decided by the voters there, North and South began competing to see which could send the greatest number. Northerners formed the New England Emigrant Aid Company to promote the settling of antislavery men in Kansas, and southerners responded in kind. The majority of Kansas settlers were opposed to the spread of slavery. But large-scale election fraud, especially on the part of heavily armed Missouri "border ruffians" who crossed into Kansas on election day to vote their proslavery principles early and often, led to the creation of a virulently proslavery territorial government. When the presidentially appointed territorial governor protested this gross fraud, Pierce removed him from office.

Free-soil Kansans responded by denouncing the pro-slavery government as illegitimate and forming their own free-soil government in an election which the proslavery faction boycotted. Kansas now had two rival governments, each claiming to be the only lawful one.

Both sides began arming themselves, and soon the territory was being referred to in the northern press as "Bleeding Kansas" because full-scale guerilla war erupted. In May 1856, Missouri border ruffians sacked the free-soil town of Lawrence, killing two, and destroying homes, businesses, and printing presses. Two days later, a small band of antislavery zealots under the leadership of fanatical abolitionist John Brown (1800–1859) retaliated by killing and mutilating five unarmed men and boys at a proslavery settlement on Pottawatomie Creek. In all, some 200 died in the months of guerilla fighting that followed.

The Election of 1856

The election of 1856 was a three-way contest that pitted Democrats, Know-Nothings, and Republicans against each other.

The Democrats dropped Pierce and passed over Douglas to nominate James Buchanan (1791–1868) of Pennsylvania. Though a veteran of 40 years of politics, Buchanan was a weak and vacillating man whose chief qualification for the nomination was that during the slavery squabbles of the past few years he had been out of the country as American minister to Great Britain and therefore had not been forced to take public positions on the controversial issues.

The Know-Nothings, including the remnant of the Whigs, nominated Millard Fillmore. However, choice of a southerner for the nomination of vice-president so alienated northern Know-Nothings that many shifted their support to the Republican candidate.

The Republicans nominated John C. Frémont of California. A former officer in the army's Corps of Topographical Engineers, Frémont was known as "the Pathfinder" for his explorations in the Rockies and the Far West. The Republican platform called for high tariffs, free western homesteads for settlers, and most important, no further spread of slavery. Their slogan was "Free Soil, Free Men, and Frémont." Southerners denounced the Republican party as an abolitionist organization and threatened secession should it win the election.

Against divided opposition, Buchanan won with apparent ease. However, his victory was largely based on the support of the South, since Frémont carried most of the northern states.

The Dred Scott Case (1857)

In *Dred Scott vs. Sanford*, the Supreme Court attempted to finally settle the slavery question. The case involved a Missouri slave, Dred Scott (ca. 1795–1858), who had been encouraged by abolitionists to sue for his freedom on the basis that his owner had taken him for several years to a free state, Illinois, and then to a free territory, Wisconsin.

Under the domination of aging pro-southern Chief Justice Roger B. Taney of Maryland, the Court attempted to read the extreme southern position on slavery into the Constitution, ruling not only that Scott had no standing to sue in federal court, but also that temporary residence in a free state, even for several years, did not make a slave free, and that the Missouri Compromise (already a dead letter by that time) had been unconstitutional all along because Congress did not have the authority to exclude slavery from a territory. Nor did territorial governments have the right to prohibit slavery. Far from settling the sectional controversy, the Dred Scott case only made it worse.

Buchanan and Kansas

Later in 1857, the proslavery government in Kansas, through largely fraudulent means, arranged for a heavily proslavery constitutional convention to meet at the town of Lecompton. The result was a state constitution that allowed slavery. To obtain a pretense of popular approval for this constitution, the convention provided for a referendum in which the voters were to be given a choice only to prohibit the entry of additional slaves into the state.

Disgusted free-soilers boycotted the referendum, and the result was a constitution that put no restrictions at all on slavery. Touting this Lecompton constitution, the proslavery territorial government petitioned Congress for admission to the Union as a slave state. Meanwhile, the free-soilers drafted a constitution of their own and submitted it to Congress as the legitimate one for the prospective state of Kansas.

Eager to appease the South, which had started talking of secession again, and equally eager to suppress antislavery agitation in the North, Buchanan vigorously backed the Lecompton constitution. Douglas, appalled at this travesty of popular sovereignty, broke with the administration to oppose it. He and Buchanan became bitter political enemies, with the president determined to use all the power of the Democratic organization to crush Douglas politically.

After extremely bitter debate, the Senate approved the Lecompton constitution, but the House insisted that Kansans be given a chance to vote on the entire document. Southern congressmen pressured Kansas voters by adding the stipulation that should the Lecompton constitution be approved, Kansas would receive a generous grant of federal land, but should it be voted down, Kansas would remain a territory.

Nevertheless, Kansas voters, when given a chance to express themselves in a fair election, turned down the Lecompton constitution by an overwhelming margin, choosing to remain a territory rather than become a slave state. Kansas was finally admitted as a free state in 1861.

The Panic of 1857

In 1857, the country was struck by a short but severe depression. There were three basic causes for this "Panic of 1857": several years of overspeculation in railroads and lands, faulty banking practices, and an interruption in the flow of European capital into American investments as a result of the Crimean War. The North blamed the panic on low tariffs, while the South, which had suffered much less than the industrial North, saw the panic as proof of the superiority of the southern economy in general and slavery in particular.

The Lincoln-Douglas Debates

The 1858 Illinois senatorial campaign produced a series of debates that got to the heart of the issues that were threatening to divide the nation. Incumbent Democratic senator and front-runner for the 1860 presidential nomination Stephen A. Douglas was opposed by a Springfield lawyer, little known outside the state, by the name of Abraham Lincoln.

Though Douglas had been hailed in some free-soil circles for his opposition to the Lecompton constitution, Lincoln, in a series of seven debates that the candidates agreed to hold during the course of the campaign, stressed that Douglas's doctrine of popular sovereignty failed to recognize slavery for the moral wrong it was.

Douglas, for his part, maintained that his guiding principle was democracy, not any moral standard of right or wrong with respect to slavery. The people could, as far as he was concerned, "vote it up or vote it down." At the same time, he strove to depict Lincoln as a radical and an abolitionist who believed in racial equality and race mixing.

At the debate held in Freeport, Illinois, Lincoln pressed Douglas to reconcile the principle of popular sovereignty to the Supreme Court's decision in the Dred Scott case. How could the people "vote it up or vote it down," if, as the Supreme Court alleged, no territorial government could prohibit slavery? Douglas, in what came to be called his "Freeport Doctrine," replied that the people of any territory could exclude slavery simply by declining to pass any of the special laws that slave jurisdictions usually passed for their protection.

Douglas's answer was good enough to win him reelection to the Senate, although by the narrowest of margins, but hurt him in the coming presidential campaign. His Freeport Doctrine hardened the opposition of southerners already angered by his anti-Lecompton stand.

For Lincoln, despite the failure to win the Senate seat, the debates were a major success, propelling him into the national spotlight, and strengthening the resolve of the Republican party to resist compromise on the free-soil issue.

THE COMING OF THE CIVIL WAR

John Brown's Raid

On the night of October 16, 1859, John Brown, the Pottawatomie Creek murderer, led 18 followers in seizing the federal arsenal at Harpers Ferry, Virginia (now West Virginia), taking hostages, and endeavoring to incite a slave uprising. Brown, supported and bankrolled by several prominent northern abolitionists (later referred to as "the Secret Six"), planned to arm local slaves and then spread his uprising across the South. His scheme was ill conceived and had little chance of success. Quickly cornered by Virginia militia, he was eventually captured by a force of United States Marines under the command of army Colonel Robert E. Lee (1807–1870). Ten of Brown's eighteen men were killed in the fight, and Brown himself was wounded.

Charged under Virginia law with treason and various other crimes, Brown was quickly tried, convicted, sentenced, and on December 2, 1859, hanged. His death was marked in the North by signs of public mourning. Many northerners looked upon Brown as a martyr.

Though responsible northerners such as Lincoln denounced Brown's raid as a criminal act which deserved to be punished by death, many southerners became convinced that the entire northern public approved of Brown's action and that the only safety for the South lay in a separate southern confederacy. This was all the more so because Brown, in threatening to create a slave revolt, had touched on the foremost fear of white southerners.

Hinton Rowan Helper's Book

The second greatest fear of southern slaveholders was that southern whites who did not own slaves, by far the majority of the southern population, would come to see the continuation of slavery as not being in their best interest. This fear was touched on by a book, *The Impending Crisis in the South*, by a North Carolinian named Hinton Rowan Helper (1829–1909). Helper argued that slavery was economically harmful to the South and that it enriched the large planter at the expense of the yeoman farmer.

The Republicans reissued a condensed version of the book as campaign literature. When the new House of Representatives met in December 1859 for the first time since the 1858 elections, angry southerners determined that no Republican who had endorsed the book should be elected Speaker.

A fight over the election of the new Speaker of the House of Representatives in 1859 brought the House to a standstill and sectional rivalries to the boiling point. Secession was talked of openly by southerners, and as tensions rose, congressmen came to the sessions carrying revolvers and Bowie knives.

The Election of 1860

In this mood, the country approached the election of 1860, a campaign that eventually became a four-man contest.

Two Democratic conventions failed to reach consensus, and the sundered halves of the party nominated separate candidates. The southern wing of the party nominated Buchanan's vice-president, John C. Breckinridge of Kentucky, on a platform calling for a federal slave code in all the territories. What was left of the national Democratic party nominated Douglas on a platform of popular sovereignty.

A third presidential candidate was added by the Constitutional Union party, a collection of aging former Whigs and Know-Nothings from the southern and border states, plus a handful of moderate southern Democrats. It nominated John Bell of Tennessee on a platform that sidestepped the issues and called simply for the Constitution, the Union, and the enforcement of the laws.

The Republicans met in Chicago, confident of victory and determined to do nothing to jeopardize their favorable position. Accordingly, they rejected as too radical front-running New York Senator William H. Seward in favor of Illinois favorite son Abraham Lincoln. The platform called for federal support of a transcontinental railroad and for the containment of slavery.

Douglas, believing only his victory could reconcile North and South, became the first United States presidential candidate to make a vigorous nationwide speaking tour.

On election day, the voting went along strictly sectional lines. Breckinridge carried the Deep South; Bell, the border states; and Lincoln, the North. Douglas,

FREE AND SLAVE AREAS, 1861

Free states

Slave states and territories
open to slavery
(all territories opened to slavery by Dred Scott Decision, 1857)

although second in popular votes, carried only a single state and part of another. Lincoln led in popular votes, and though he was short of a majority in that category, he did have the needed majority in electoral votes and was elected.

The Secession Crisis

Lincoln had declared he had no intention of disturbing slavery where it already existed, but many southerners thought otherwise. They also feared further raids of the sort John Brown had attempted, and felt their pride injured by the election of a president for whom no southerner had voted.

On December 20, 1860, South Carolina, by vote of a special convention, declared itself out of the Union. By February 1, 1861, six more states (Alabama, Georgia, Florida, Mississippi, Louisiana, and Texas) had followed suit.

Representatives of the seceded states met in Montgomery, Alabama, in February 1861 and declared themselves to be the Confederate States of America. They elected former Secretary of War and United States senator Jefferson Davis of Mississippi as president, and Alexander Stephens (1812–1883) of Georgia as vice-president. They also adopted a constitution for the Confederate states which, while similar to the United States Constitution in many ways, contained several important differences:

1) Slavery was specifically recognized, and the right to move slaves from one state to another was guaranteed.
2) Protective tariffs were prohibited.
3) The president was to serve for a single nonrenewable six-year term.
4) The president was given the right to veto individual items within an appropriations bill.
5) State sovereignty was specifically recognized.

In the North, reaction was mixed. President Buchanan, now a lame duck, declared secession to be unconstitutional, but at the same time stated his belief that it was unconstitutional for the federal government to do anything to stop states from seceding. Taking his own advice, he did nothing.

Others, led by Senator John J. Crittenden of Kentucky, strove for a compromise that would preserve the Union. As the southern states one by one declared their secession, Crittenden worked desperately with a congressional compromise committee in hopes of working out some form of agreement.

The compromise proposals centered on the passage of a constitutional amendment forever prohibiting federal meddling with slavery in the states where it existed, as well as the extension of the Missouri Compromise line (36° 30') to the Pacific, with slavery specifically protected in all the territories south of it.

Some congressional Republicans were inclined to accept this compromise, but President-elect Lincoln urged them to stand firm for no further spread of slavery. Southerners would consider no compromise that did not provide for the spread of slavery, and talks broke down.

14 THE CIVIL WAR AND RECONSTRUCTION (1860–1877)

HOSTILITIES BEGIN

Fort Sumter

Lincoln did his best to avoid angering the slave states that had not yet seceded. In his inaugural address, he urged southerners to reconsider their actions, but warned that the Union was perpetual, that states could not secede, and that he would therefore hold the federal forts and installations in the South.

Only two remained in federal hands: Fort Pickens, off Pensacola, Florida; and Fort Sumter, in the harbor of Charleston, South Carolina. Lincoln soon received word from Major Robert Anderson, commander of the small garrison at Sumter, that supplies were running low. Desiring to send in the needed supplies, Lincoln informed the governor of South Carolina of his intention, but promised that no attempt would be made to send arms, ammunition, or reinforcements unless southerners initiated hostilities.

Not satisfied, southerners determined to take the fort. Confederate General P.G.T. Beauregard (1818–1893), acting on orders from President Davis, demanded Anderson's surrender. Anderson said he would surrender if not resupplied. Knowing supplies were on the way, the Confederates opened fire at 4:30 a.m. on April 12, 1861. The next day, the fort surrendered.

The day following Sumter's surrender, Lincoln declared an insurrection and called for the states to provide 75,000 volunteers to put it down. In response to this, Virginia, Tennessee, North Carolina, and Arkansas declared their secession.

The remaining slave states, Delaware, Kentucky, Maryland, and Missouri, wavered, but stayed with the Union. Delaware, which had few slaves, gave little serious consideration to the idea of secession. Kentucky declared itself neutral, and then sided with the North when the South failed to respect this neutrality. Maryland's incipient secession movement was crushed by Lincoln's timely imposition of martial law. Missouri was saved for the Union by the quick and decisive use of federal troops, as well as the sizable population of pro-Union, antislavery German immigrants living in St. Louis.

Relative Strengths at the Outset

The North enjoyed at least five major advantages over the South. It had overwhelming preponderance in wealth and was vastly superior in industry.

The North also had an advantage of almost three to one in manpower; and over one-third of the South's population was composed of slaves, whom Southerners would not use as soldiers. Unlike the South, the North received large numbers of immigrants during the war. The North retained control of the United States Navy, and thus would command the sea and be able to blockade the South. Finally, the North enjoyed a much superior system of railroads.

The South did, however, have several advantages. It was vast in size, making it difficult to conquer. Its troops would be fighting on their own ground, a fact that would give them the advantage of familiarity with the terrain, as well as the added motivation of defending their homes and families. Its armies would often have the opportunity of fighting on the defensive, a major advantage in the warfare of that day.

At the outset of the war, the South drew a number of highly qualified senior officers, men like Robert E. Lee, Joseph E. Johnston (1807–1891), and Albert Sidney Johnston (1803–1862), from the U.S. Army. By contrast, the Union command structure was already set when the war began, with the aged Winfield Scott, of Mexican War fame, at the top. It took young and talented officers such as Ulysses S. Grant (1822–1885) and William T. Sherman (1820–1891) time to work up to high rank. Meanwhile, Union armies were often led by inferior commanders as Lincoln experimented in search of good generals.

Though Jefferson Davis had extensive military and political experience, Lincoln was much superior to Davis as a war leader, showing firmness, flexibility, mental toughness, great political skill, and, eventually an excellent grasp of strategy.

Opposing Strategies

Both sides were full of enthusiasm for the war. In the North, the battle cry was "On to Richmond," the new Confederate capital established after the secession of Virginia. In the South, it was "On to Washington." Yielding to popular demand, Lincoln ordered General Irvin McDowell to advance on Richmond with his army. At a creek called Bull Run near the town of Manassas Junction, Virginia, just southwest of Washington, D.C., they met a Confederate force under generals P.G.T. Beauregard and Joseph E. Johnston, July 21, 1861. In the First Battle of Bull Run (called First Manassas in the South), the Union army was forced to retreat in confusion back to Washington.

Bull Run demonstrated the unpreparedness and inexperience of both sides. It also demonstrated that the war would be long and hard. Lincoln would need an overall strategy. To supply this, Winfield Scott suggested his Anaconda plan, which included a naval blockade to shut out supplies from Europe, a campaign to take the Mississippi River, splitting the South in two, and then waiting for pro-Union sentiment in the South to overthrow the secessionists. Lincoln liked the first two points of Scott's strategy, but considered the third point unrealistic.

He ordered a naval blockade, an overwhelming task considering the South's long coastline. Yet, under Secretary of the Navy Gideon Welles (1802–1878), the navy was expanded enormously and the blockade became increasingly effective.

Lincoln also ordered a campaign to take the Mississippi River. In April 1862, Captain David G. Farragut (1801–1870) took New Orleans.

Rather than waiting for pro-Unionists in the South to gain control, Lincoln hoped to raise huge armies and apply overwhelming pressure from all sides until the Confederacy collapsed. The strategy was good; the problem was finding capable generals to carry it out.

THE UNION PRESERVED

Lincoln Tries McClellan

To replace the discredited McDowell, Lincoln chose General George B. McClellan (1826–1885). McClellan was a good trainer and organizer and was loved by the troops, but he was unable to effectively use the powerful army (now called the Army of the Potomac) he had built up.

Finally, in the spring of 1862, he took the Army of the Potomac by water down Chesapeake Bay to land between the York and James rivers in Virginia. His plan was to advance up the peninsula formed by these rivers directly to Richmond.

The operations that followed were known as the Peninsula Campaign. McClellan advanced slowly and cautiously toward Richmond, while his equally cautious Confederate opponent, General Joseph E. Johnston, drew back to the outskirts of the city before turning to fight at the Battle of Seven Pines. In this inconclusive battle, Johnston was wounded. To replace him, Jefferson Davis appointed his military advisor, General Robert E. Lee.

Lee summoned General Thomas J. "Stonewall" Jackson (1824–1863) and his army from the Shenandoah Valley (where Jackson had just finished defeating several superior federal forces), and with the combined forces attacked McClellan.

After two days of bloody but inconclusive fighting, McClellan lost his nerve and began to retreat. In the remainder of what came to be called the Battle of the Seven Days, Lee continued to attack McClellan, forcing him back to his base, though at great cost in lives. McClellan's army was loaded back onto its ships and taken back to Washington.

Before McClellan's army could reach Washington, Lee took the opportunity to thrash Union General John Pope (1822–1892), who was in northern Virginia with another northern army, at the Second Battle of Bull Run.

Union Victories in the West

West of the Appalachian Mountains, matters were proceeding differently. The northern commanders there, Henry W. Halleck (1815–1872) and Don Carlos Buell (1818–1898), were no more enterprising than McClellan, but Halleck's subordinate, Ulysses S. Grant, was.

With permission from Halleck, Grant mounted a combined operation—army troops and navy gunboats—against two vital Confederate strongholds, forts Henry and Donelson, which guarded the Tennessee and Cumberland rivers in northern Tennessee. When Grant captured the forts in February 1862, Johnston was forced to retreat to Corinth in northern Mississippi.

Grant pursued, but ordered by Halleck to wait until all was in readiness before proceeding, halted his troops at Pittsburg Landing on the Tennessee River, 25 miles north of Corinth. On April 6, 1862 General Albert Sidney Johnston, who had received reinforcements and been joined by General P.G.T. Beauregard, surprised Grant there, but in the two-day battle that followed (Shiloh) failed to defeat him. Johnston was among the many killed in what was, up to this point, the bloodiest battle in American history.

Grant was severely criticized in the North for having been taken by surprise. Yet with other Union victories and Farragut's capture of New Orleans, the North had taken all of the Mississippi River except for a 110-mile stretch between the Confederate fortresses of Vicksburg, Mississippi, and Port Hudson, Louisiana.

The Success of Northern Diplomacy

Many southerners believed Britain and France would rejoice in seeing a divided and weakened America. They also believed the two countries would likewise be driven by the need of their factories for cotton and thus intervene on the Confederacy's behalf. So strongly was this view held that during the early days of the war, when the Union blockade was still too weak to be very effective, the Confederate government itself prohibited the export of cotton in order to hasten British and French intervention.

This view proved mistaken. Britain already had a large supply of cotton, and had other sources besides the U.S. British leaders may also have weighed their country's need to import wheat from the northern United States against its desire for cotton from the southern states. Finally, British public opinion opposed slavery.

Skillful northern diplomacy had a great impact. In this, Lincoln had the extremely able assistance of Secretary of State William Seward, who took a hard line in warning Europeans not to interfere, and of ambassador to Great Britain Charles Francis Adams (1807–1886). Britain remained neutral, and other European countries, including France followed its lead.

One incident nevertheless came close to fulfilling southern hopes for British intervention. In November 1861, Captain Charles Wilkes of the U.S.S. *San Jacinto* stopped the British mail and passenger ship *Trent* and forcibly removed Confederate emissaries James M. Mason and John Slidell. News of Wilkes's action brought great rejoicing in the North but outrage in Great Britain, where it was viewed as a violation of Britain's rights on the high seas. Lincoln and Seward, faced with British threats of war at a time the North could ill afford it, wisely chose to release the envoys and smooth things over with Britain.

The Confederacy was able to obtain some loans and to purchase small amounts of arms, ammunition, and even commerce-raiding ships like the highly successful C.S.S. *Alabama*. However, Union naval superiority kept such supplies to a minimum.

The War at Sea

The Confederacy's major bid to challenge the Union's naval superiority was based on a technological innovation—the ironclad ship. The first and most successful of the Confederate ironclads was the C.S.S. *Virginia*. Built on the hull of the abandoned Union frigate *Merrimac*, the *Virginia* was protected from cannon fire by iron plates bolted over her sloping wooden sides. In May 1862, she destroyed two wooden warships of the Union naval force at Hampton Roads, Virginia, and was seriously threatening to destroy the rest of the squadron before being met and fought to a standstill by the Union ironclad U.S.S. *Monitor*.

The Home Front

Congress in 1862 passed two highly-important acts dealing with domestic affairs in the North. The Homestead Act granted 160 acres of government land free of charge to any person who would farm it for at least five years. Much of the West was eventually settled under the provisions of this act. The Morrill Land Grant Act offered large amounts of the federal government's land to states that would establish "agricultural and mechanical" colleges. Many of the nation's large state universities were later founded under the provisions of this act.

Keeping morale high was made more difficult by the necessity, apparent by 1863, of imposing conscription in order to obtain adequate manpower for the huge armies that would be needed to crush the South. Especially hated by many working-class northerners was the provision of the conscription act that allowed a drafted individual to avoid service by hiring a substitute or paying $300. Resistance to the draft led to riots in New York City in which hundreds were killed.

The Confederacy, with its much smaller manpower pool on which to draw, had instituted conscription in 1862. Here, too, it did not always meet with cooperation. Some southern governors objected to it on doctrinaire states' rights grounds, doing all they could to obstruct its operation. A provision of the southern conscription act, allowing one man to stay home as overseer for every 20 slaves, led the non-slaveholding whites who made up most of the southern population to grumble that it was a "rich man's war and a poor man's fight." Draft-dodging and desertion became epidemic in the South by the latter part of the war.

Scarcity of food and other consumer goods in the South, as well as high prices, led to further desertion as soldiers left the ranks to care for their starving families.

High tariffs and an income tax weren't enough to finance the North's war drive. The Treasury Department, under Secretary of the Treasury Salmon P. Chase (1808–1873), issued "greenbacks," an unbacked fiat currency. To facilitate financing of the war through credit expansion, the National Banking Act was passed in 1863.

The South found it all but impossible to cope with the expense of war. The southern Congress issued paper money in such quantities that it became virtually worthless. That, and the scarcity of almost everything, led to skyrocketing prices.

The Confederate government seized goods, or set a payment schedule for purchasing them but paid in worthless paper currency.

To quell the threat of secession in Maryland, Lincoln suspended the writ of *habeas corpus* and imprisoned numerous suspected secessionists without charges or trial, ignoring the insistence of pro-southern Chief Justice Roger B. Taney in *ex parte Merryman* (1861) that such action was unconstitutional.

"Copperheads," northerners who opposed the war, denounced Lincoln as a tyrant and would-be dictator, but remained a minority.

Davis encountered obstructionism from various state governors, the Confederate Congress, and even his own vice-president, who denounced him as a tyrant for assuming too much power and failing to respect states' rights.

The Emancipation Proclamation

By mid-1862, Lincoln, under pressure from radical elements of his own party and hoping to create a favorable impression on foreign public opinion, determined to issue the Emancipation Proclamation, which declared free all slaves in areas still in rebellion as of January 1, 1863. At Seward's recommendation, Lincoln waited to announce the proclamation until the North should win some sort of victory. This was provided by the Battle of Antietam (September 17, 1863).

Though the Radical Republicans, prewar abolitionists for the most part, had for some time been urging Lincoln to take such a step, northern public opinion as a whole was less enthusiastic. The Republicans suffered major losses in the November 1862 congressional elections.

The Turning Point in the East

After his victory at the Second Battle of Bull Run, Lee moved north and crossed into Maryland, where he hoped to win a decisive victory that would force the North to recognize southern independence.

McClellan got hold of Lee's plans, but by extreme caution and slowness, threw away this incomparable chance to annihilate Lee and win—or at least shorten—the war.

The armies finally met along Antietam Creek, just east of the town of Sharpsburg in western Maryland. In a bloody but inconclusive day-long battle, known as Antietam in the North and Sharpsburg in the South, McClellan's timidity led him to miss another excellent chance to destroy Lee's cornered and badly out-numbered army. After the battle, Lee retreated to Virginia, and Lincoln removed McClellan from command.

To replace him, Lincoln chose General Ambrose E. Burnside (1824–1881), who promptly demonstrated his unfitness by blundering into a lopsided defeat at Fredericksburg, Virginia (December 13, 1862).

Lincoln then replaced Burnside with General Joseph "Fighting Joe" Hooker (1814–1879). Handsome and hard-drinking, Hooker had bragged of what he would do to "Bobby Lee" when he got at him; but when he took his army south, "Fighting Joe" quickly lost his nerve. He was soundly beaten at the Battle of Chancellorsville (May 5–6, 1863). At this battle, the brilliant Southern general "Stonewall" Jackson was accidentally shot by his own men and died several days later.

Lee received permission from President Davis to invade Pennsylvania. He was pursued by the Army of the Potomac, now under the command of General George G. Meade (1815–1872), who had replaced the discredited Hooker. They met at Gettysburg in a three-day battle (July 1–3, 1863) that was the bloodiest of the war. Lee, who sorely missed the services of Jackson and whose cavalry leader, the nor-mally reliable J.E.B. Stuart (1833–1864), failed to provide him with timely recon-naissance, was defeated. However, he was allowed by the victorious Meade to retreat to Virginia with his army intact if battered, much to Lincoln's disgust. Still, Lee would never again have the strength to mount such an invasion.

Lincoln Finds Grant

Meanwhile, Grant moved on Vicksburg, one of the two last Confederate bastions on the Mississippi River. In a brilliant campaign, he bottled up the Confederate forces of General John C. Pemberton (1814–1881) inside the city and placed them under siege. After six weeks, the defenders surrendered on July 4, 1863. Five days later, Port Hudson surrendered, giving the Union complete control of the Mississippi.

After Union forces under General William Rosecrans (1819–1898) suffered an embarrassing defeat at the Battle of Chickamauga in northwestern Georgia (September 19–20, 1863), Lincoln named Grant overall commander of Union forces in the West.

Grant went to Chattanooga, Tennessee, where Confederate forces under General Braxton Bragg (1817–1876) were virtually besieging Rosecrans, and immediately took control of the situation. Gathering Union forces from other portions of the western theater and combining them with reinforcements from the East, Grant won a resounding victory at the Battle of Chattanooga (November 23–25, 1863), in which federal forces stormed seemingly impregnable Confederate positions on Lookout Mountain and Missionary Ridge. This victory put Union forces in position for a drive into Georgia, which began the following spring.

Early in 1864, Lincoln made Grant commander of all Union armies. Grant devised a coordinated plan for constant pressure on the Confederacy. General William T. Sherman would lead a drive toward Atlanta, Georgia, with the goal of destroying the Confederate army under General Joseph E. Johnston (who had replaced Bragg). Grant would accompany Meade and the Army of the Potomac in advancing toward Richmond with the goal of destroying Lee's Confederate army.

In a series of bloody battles (the Wilderness, Spotsylvania, Cold Harbor) in May and June of 1864, Grant drove Lee to the outskirts of Richmond. Still unable to take the city or get Lee at a disadvantage, Grant circled around, attacking Petersburg, Virginia, an important railroad junction just south of Richmond and the key to that city's—and Lee's—supply lines. Once again turned back by entrenched Confederate troops, Grant settled down to besiege Petersburg and Richmond in a stalemate that lasted some nine months.

Sherman had been advancing simultaneously in Georgia. He maneuvered Johnston back to the outskirts of Atlanta with relatively little fighting. At that point, Confederate President Davis lost patience with Johnston and replaced him with the aggressive General John B. Hood (1831–1879). Hood and Sherman fought three fierce but inconclusive battles around Atlanta in late July, and then settled down to a siege of their own during the month of August.

The Election of 1864 and Northern Victory

In the North, discontentment grew with the long casualty lists and seeming lack of results. Yet, the South could stand the grinding war even less. By late 1864, Jefferson Davis had reached the point of calling for the use of blacks in the Confederate armies, though the war ended before black troops could fight for the Confederacy. The South's best hope was that northern war-weariness would bring the defeat of Lincoln and the victory of a peace candidate in the election of 1864.

Lincoln ran on the ticket of the National Union party, essentially the Republican party with loyal or "War" Democrats. His vice-presidential candidate was Andrew Johnson (1808–1875), a loyal Democrat from Tennessee.

The Democratic party's presidential candidate was General George B. McClellan, who, with some misgivings, ran on a platform labeling the war a failure, and calling for a negotiated peace settlement even if that meant southern independence.

Even Lincoln believed that he would be defeated. Then in September 1864, word came that Sherman had taken Atlanta. The capture of this vital southern rail and manufacturing center brought an enormous boost to northern morale. Along with other northern victories that summer and fall, it ensured a resounding election victory for Lincoln and the continuation of the war to complete victory for the North.

To speed that victory, Sherman marched through Georgia from Atlanta to the sea, arriving at Savannah in December 1864 and turning north into the Carolinas, leaving behind a 60-mile-wide swath of destruction. His goal was to impress on southerners that continuation of the war could only mean ruin for all of them. He and Grant planned that his army should press on through the Carolinas and into Virginia to join Grant in finishing off Lee.

Before Sherman's troops could arrive, Lee abandoned Richmond (April 3, 1865) and attempted to escape with what was left of his army. Pursued by Grant, he was cornered and forced to surrender at Appomattox, Virginia (April 9, 1865). Other Confederate armies still holding out in various parts of the South surrendered over the next few weeks.

Lincoln did not live to receive news of the final surrenders. On April 14, 1865, he was shot in the back of the head while watching a play in Ford's Theater in Washington. His assassin, pro-southern actor John Wilkes Booth (1838–1865), injured his ankle in making his escape. Hunted down by Union cavalry several days later, he died of a gunshot wound, apparently self-inflicted. Several other individuals were tried, convicted, and hanged by a military tribunal for participating with Booth in a conspiracy to assassinate not only Lincoln, but also Vice-President Johnson and Secretary of State Seward.

THE ORDEAL OF RECONSTRUCTION

Lincoln's Plan of Reconstruction

Reconstruction began well before the fighting of the Civil War came to an end. It brought a time of difficult adjustments in the South.

Among those who faced such adjustments were the recently freed slaves, who flocked into Union lines or followed advancing Union armies or whose plantations were part of the growing area of the South that came under Union military control. Some slaves had left their plantations, and thus their only means of livelihood, in order to obtain freedom within Union lines.

To ease the adjustment for these recently freed slaves, Congress in 1865 created the Freedman's Bureau to provide food, clothing, and education, and generally look after the interests of former slaves.

To restore legal governments in the seceded states, Lincoln's policy, known as the Ten Percent Plan, stipulated that southerners, except for high-ranking rebel officials, could take an oath promising future loyalty to the Union and acceptance of the end of slavery. When the number of those who had taken this oath within any one state reached 10 percent of the number who had been registered to vote in that state in 1860, a loyal state government could be formed. Only those who had taken the oath could vote or participate in the new government.

Tennessee, Arkansas, and Louisiana met the requirements and formed loyal governments, but were refused recognition by a Congress dominated by Radical Republicans.

Radical Republicans such as Thaddeus Stevens (1792–1868) of Pennsylvania believed Lincoln's plan did not adequately punish the South, restructure southern society, or boost the political prospects of the Republican party. The loyal southern states were denied representation in Congress and electoral votes in the election of 1864.

Instead, the radicals in Congress drew up the Wade-Davis Bill. Under its stringent terms, a majority of the number who had been alive and registered to vote in 1860 would have to swear an "ironclad" oath stating that they were now loyal and had never been disloyal. This was obviously impossible in any former Confederate state unless blacks were given the vote, something Radical Republicans desired but Southerners definitely did not. Unless the requisite number swore the "ironclad" oath, Congress would not allow the state to have a government.

Lincoln killed the Wade-Davis bill with a "pocket veto," and the radicals were furious. When Lincoln was assassinated the radicals rejoiced, believing Vice-President Andrew Johnson would be less generous to the South, or at least easier to control.

Johnson's Attempt at Reconstruction

To the dismay of the radicals, Johnson followed Lincoln's policies very closely, making them only slightly more stringent by requiring ratification of the 13th Amendment (officially abolishing slavery), repudiation of Confederate debts, and renunciation of secession. He also recommended the vote be given to blacks.

Southern states proved reluctant to accept these conditions, some declining to repudiate Confederate debts or ratify the 13th Amendment (it nevertheless received the ratification of the necessary number of states and was declared part of the Constitution in December 1865). No southern state extended the vote to blacks (at this time no northern state did, either). Instead, the southern states promulgated Black Codes, imposing various restrictions on the freedom of the former slaves.

Foreign Policy Under Johnson

On coming into office, Johnson had inherited a foreign policy problem involving Mexico and France. The French emperor, Napoleon III, had made Mexico the target of one of his many grandiose foreign adventures. In 1862, while the United

States was occupied with the Civil War and therefore unable to prevent this violation of the Monroe Doctrine, Napoleon III, with the support of French troops, had Archduke Maximilian of Austria installed as a puppet emperor of Mexico. The United States had protested, but for the time being could do nothing.

With the war over, Johnson and Secretary of State Seward were able to take more vigorous steps. General Philip Sheridan (1831–1888) was sent to the Rio Grande with a military force. At the same time, Mexican revolutionary leader Benito Juárez (1806–1872) was given the tacit recognition of the United States government. Johnson and Seward continued to invoke the Monroe Doctrine, and to place quiet pressure on Napoleon III to withdraw his troops. In May 1866, facing difficulties of his own in Europe, the French emperor did so, leaving the unfortunate Maximilian to face a Mexican firing squad.

Johnson's and Seward's course of action in preventing the extension of the French Empire into the Western Hemisphere strengthened America's commitment to and the rest of the world's respect for the Monroe Doctrine.

In 1866, the Russian minister approached Seward with an offer to sell Alaska to the United States. Seward, who was an ardent expansionist, pushed hard for the purchase of Alaska, known as "Seward's Folly" by its critics. In 1867, the sale went through and Alaska was purchased for $7,200,000.

Congressional Reconstruction

Determined to reconstruct the South as it saw fit, Congress passed a Civil Rights Act and extended the authority of the Freedman's Bureau, giving it both quasi-judicial and quasi-executive powers.

Johnson vetoed both bills, claiming they were unconstitutional; but Congress overrode the vetoes. Fearing that the Supreme Court would agree with Johnson and overturn the laws, Congress approved and sent on to the states for ratification (June 1866) the 14th Amendment, making constitutional the laws Congress had just passed. The 14th Amendment defined citizenship and forbade states to deny various rights to citizens, reduced the representation in Congress of states that did not allow blacks to vote, forbade the paying of the Confederate debt, and made former Confederates ineligible to hold public office.

With only one southern state, Tennessee, ratifying, the amendment failed to receive the necessary approval of three-fourths of the states. But the radicals in Congress were not finished. Strengthened by victory in the 1866 elections, they passed, over Johnson's veto, the Military Reconstruction Act, which divided the South into five military districts to be ruled by military governors with almost dictatorial powers. Tennessee, having ratified the 14th Amendment, was spared the wrath of the Radicals. The rest of the southern states were ordered to produce constitutions giving the vote to blacks and to ratify the 14th Amendment before they could be "readmitted." In this manner, the 14th Amendment was ratified.

Realizing the unprecedented nature of these actions, Congress moved to prevent any check or balance from the other two branches of government. Steps were taken toward limiting the jurisdiction of the Supreme Court so that it could not review cases pertaining to congressional Reconstruction policies.

To control the president, Congress passed the Army Act, reducing the president's control over the army. In obtaining the cooperation of the army, the Radicals had the aid of General Grant, who already had his eye on the 1868 Republican presidential nomination. Congress also passed the Tenure of Office Act, forbidding Johnson to dismiss cabinet members without the Senate's permission. In passing the latter act, Congress was especially thinking of radical Secretary of War Edwin M. Stanton (1814–1869), a Lincoln holdover whom Johnson desired to dismiss.

Johnson obeyed the letter but not the spirit of the Reconstruction acts, and Congress, angry at his refusal to cooperate, sought in vain for grounds to impeach him, until in August 1867 Johnson violated the Tenure of Office Act (by dismissing Stanton) in order to test its constitutionality. The matter was not tested in the courts, however, but in Congress, where Johnson was impeached by the House of Representatives and came within one vote of being removed by the Senate. For the remaining months of his term, he offered little resistance to the radicals.

The Election of 1868 and the 15th Amendment

In 1868, the Republican convention, dominated by the radicals, drew up a platform endorsing Radical Reconstruction. For president, the Republicans nominated Ulysses S. Grant, who had no political record and whose views—if any—on national issues were unknown. The vice-presidential nominee was Schuyler Colfax.

Though the Democratic nomination was sought by Andrew Johnson, the party knew he could not win and instead nominated former Governor Horatio Seymour of New York for president and Francis P. Blair Jr. of Missouri for vice-president. Both had been Union generals during the war.

Grant, despite his enormous popularity as a war hero, won by only a narrow margin, drawing only 300,000 more popular votes than Seymour. Some 700,000 blacks had voted in the southern states under the auspices of army occupation, and since all of these had almost certainly voted for Grant, it was clear that he had not received a majority of the white vote.

The narrow victory of even such a strong candidate as Grant prompted Republican leaders to decide that it would be politically expedient to give the vote to all blacks, North as well as South. For this purpose, the 15th Amendment was drawn up and submitted to the states. Ironically, the idea was so unpopular in the North that it won the necessary three-fourths approval only with its ratification by southern states required to do so by Congress.

Postwar Life in the South

During the war, approximately one in 10 southern men was killed. Those who returned from the war found destruction and poverty. Property of the Confederate government was confiscated by the federal government, and dishonest treasury agents confiscated private property as well. Capital invested in slaves or in Confederate war bonds was lost. Property values fell to one-tenth of their prewar level. The economic results of the war stayed with the South for decades.

The political results were less long-lived but more immediately disturbing to southerners. Southerners complained of widespread corruption in governments sustained by federal troops and composed of "carpetbaggers," "scalawags" (the southern names for northerners who came to the South to participate in Reconstruction governments and southerners who supported the Reconstruction regimes, respectively), and recently freed blacks.

Under the Reconstruction governments, social programs were greatly expanded, leading to higher taxes and growing state debts. Some of the financial problems were due to corruption, a problem in both North and South. Political machines, such as William Marcy "Boss" Tweed's (1823–1878) Tammany Hall machine in New York, dominated many northern city governments and grew rich.

Southern whites sometimes responded to Reconstruction governments with violence, carried out by groups such as the Ku Klux Klan, aimed at intimidating blacks and white Republicans out of voting. The activities of these organizations were sometimes a response to those of the Union League, an organization used by southern Republicans to control the black vote. The goal of southerners not allied with the Reconstruction governments was "redemption" (i.e., the end of the Reconstruction governments).

By 1876, southern whites had been successful, by legal means or otherwise, in "redeeming" all but three southern states. The following year, the federal government ended its policy of Reconstruction and the troops were withdrawn, leading to a return to power of white southerners in the remaining states.

Reconstruction ended primarily because the North lost interest, and diehard radicals such as Thaddeus Stevens and Charles Sumner (1811–1874) were dead.

Corruption Under Grant

Though personally of unquestioned integrity, Grant naively placed his faith in a number of thoroughly dishonest men. His administration was rocked by one scandalous revelation of government corruption after another.

The "Black Friday" Scandal

In the "Black Friday" scandal, two unscrupulous businessmen, James Fisk (1834–1872) and Jay Gould (1836–1892), schemed to corner the gold market. To further their designs, they got Grant's brother-in-law to convince the president that stopping government gold sales would be good for farmers. Grant naively complied, and many businessmen were ruined as the price of gold was bid up furiously on "Black Friday."

Officials of the Union Pacific Railroad used a dummy construction company called Credit Mobilier to skim off millions of dollars of the subsidies the government was paying the Union Pacific for building a transcontinental railroad, and bribed many members of Congress lavishly. Though much of this took place before Grant came into office, its revelation in an 1872 congressional investigation created a general scandal.

In the "Salary Grab Act" of 1873, Congress voted a 100 percent pay raise for the president and a 50 percent increase for itself, and made both retroactive two years back. Public outrage led to a Democratic victory in the next congressional election, and the law was repealed.

In the Sanborn Contract fraud, a politician named Sanborn was given a contract to collect $427,000 in unpaid taxes for a 50 percent commission. The commission found its way into Republican campaign funds.

In the Whiskey Ring fraud, distillers and treasury officials conspired to defraud the government of large amounts of money from the excise tax on whiskey. Grant's personal secretary was in on the plot, and Grant himself naively accepted gifts of a questionable nature. When the matter came under investigation, Grant endeavored to shield his secretary.

Grant's secretary of war, W.W. Belknap, accepted bribes from corrupt agents involved in his department's administration of Native American affairs. When the matter came out, he resigned to escape impeachment.

The Liberal Republicans

A faction of the Republican party separated and called itself the Liberal Republicans. Besides opposing corruption and favoring sectional harmony, the Liberal Republicans favored hard money and a laissez-faire approach to economic issues. For the election of 1872, they nominated *New York Tribune* editor Horace Greeley (1811–1872) for president. Greeley was easily defeated by Grant, who was again the nominee of the radicals.

Economic Issues Under Grant

Many of the economic difficulties the country faced during Grant's administration were caused by the necessary readjustments from a wartime economy back to a peacetime economy. The central economic question was deflation versus inflation, or more specifically, whether to retire the unbacked paper money, greenbacks, printed to meet the wartime emergency, or to print more.

Economic conservatives, creditors, and business interests usually favored retirement of the greenbacks and an early return to the gold standard.

Early in Grant's second term, the country was hit by an economic depression known as the Panic of 1873. Brought on by the overexpansive tendencies of railroad builders and businessmen during the immediate postwar boom, the Panic was triggered by economic downturns in Europe, and more immediately, by the failure of Jay Cooke and Company, a major American financial firm.

The Panic led to clamor for the printing of more greenbacks. In 1874, Congress authorized a small new issue of greenbacks, but it was vetoed by Grant. Pro-inflation forces were further enraged when Congress in 1873 demonetized silver, going to a straight gold standard. Silver was becoming more plentiful due to western mining, and was seen by some as a potential source of inflation. Pro-inflation forces referred to the demonetization of silver as the "Crime of '73."

In 1875, Congress took a further step toward retirement of the greenbacks and return to a working gold standard when, under the leadership of John Sherman, it passed the Specie Resumption Act, calling for the resumption of specie payments (i.e., the redeemability of the nation's paper money in gold) by January 1, 1879.

Disgruntled proponents of inflation formed the Greenback Party and nominated Peter Cooper (1791–1883) for president in 1876. However, they gained only an insignificant number of votes.

The Disputed Election of 1876

In the election of 1876, the Democrats campaigned against corruption and nominated New York Governor Samuel J. Tilden (1814–1886), who had broken the Tweed political machine of New York City.

The Republicans passed over Grant and turned to Governor Rutherford B. Hayes (1822–1893) of Ohio. Like Tilden, Hayes was decent, honest, in favor of hard money and civil service reform, and opposed to government regulation of the economy.

Tilden won the popular vote and led in the electoral vote 184 to 165. However, 185 electoral votes were needed for election, and 20 votes, from the three Southern states still occupied by federal troops and run by Republican governments, were disputed.

Though there had been extensive fraud on both sides, Tilden undoubtedly deserved at least the one vote he needed to win. Congress created a special commission to decide the matter. It was to be composed of five members each from the Senate, the House, and the Supreme Court. Of these, seven were to be Republicans, seven Democrats, and one an independent. The Republicans arranged, however, for the independent justice's state legislature to elect him to the Senate. When the justice resigned to take his Senate seat, it left all the remaining Supreme Court justices Republican. One of them was chosen, and in a series of eight-to-seven votes along straight party lines, the commission voted to give all 20 disputed votes—and the election—to Hayes.

When outraged congressional Democrats threatened to reject these obviously fraudulent results, a compromise was worked out. In the Compromise of 1877, Hayes promised to show consideration for southern interests, end Reconstruction, and withdraw the remaining federal troops from the South in exchange for Democratic acquiescence in his election.

Reconstruction would probably have ended anyway, since the North had already lost interest in it.

15 INDUSTRIALISM, WAR, AND THE PROGRESSIVE ERA (1877–1912)

THE NEW INDUSTRIAL ERA (1877–1882)

Between the 1870s and 1890s, "Gilded Age" America emerged as the world's leading industrial and agricultural producer.

POLITICS OF THE PERIOD (1877–1882)

The presidencies of Abraham Lincoln and Theodore Roosevelt (1858–1919) mark the boundaries of a half century of relatively weak executive leadership and legislative domination by Congress and the Republican party.

With the withdrawal of Union troops from the South, the country was at last reunified as a modern nation-state led by corporate and industrial interests.

Republican Factions

"Stalwarts," led by New York senator Roscoe Conkling (1829–1888) favored the old spoils system of political patronage. "Half-Breeds," headed by Maine senator James G. Blaine (1830–1893), pushed for civil service reform and merit appointments to government posts.

Election of 1880

James A. Garfield (1831–1881) of Ohio, a Half-Breed, and his vice presidential running mate Chester A. Arthur (1829–1886) of New York, a Stalwart, defeated the Democratic candidate, General Winfield S. Hancock (1824–1886) of Pennsylvania and former Indiana congressman William English. Tragically the president was assassinated in 1881 by a mentally disturbed patronage seeker, Charles Guiteau. Arthur had the courage to endorse reform of the political spoils system by supporting passage of the Pendleton Act (1883), which established open competitive examinations for civil-service positions.

The Greenback-Labor Party

This third party polled more than one million votes in 1878, and elected 14 members to Congress in an effort to promote inflation of farm prices and the cooperative marketing of agricultural produce. In 1880, the party's presidential candidate, James Weaver of Iowa, advocated public control and regulation of private enterprises such as railroads in the common interest of more equitable competition. Weaver polled only 3 percent of the vote.

THE ECONOMY (1877–1882)

Between 1860 and 1894, the United States moved from the fourth largest manufacturing nation to the world's leader through capital accumulation, natural resources, especially in iron, oil, and coal, an abundance of labor helped by massive immigration, railway transportation, and communications (the telephone was introduced by Alexander Graham Bell (1847–1922) in 1876), and major technical innovations such as the development of the modern steel industry by Andrew Carnegie (1835–1919), and electrical energy by Thomas Edison (1847–1931). In the petroleum industry, John D. Rockefeller (1839–1937) controlled 95 percent of U.S. oil refineries by 1877.

The New South

By 1880, northern capital erected the modern textile industry in the New South by bringing factories to the cotton fields. Birmingham, Alabama, emerged as the South's leading steel producer, and the introduction of machine-made cigarettes propelled the Duke family to prominence as tobacco producers.

Standard of Living

Throughout the United States the standard of living rose sharply, but the distribution of wealth was very uneven. An elite of about 10 percent of the population controlled 90 percent of the nation's wealth.

Social Darwinism

Many industrial leaders used the doctrines associated with the "Gospel of Wealth" to justify the unequal distribution of national wealth, based on the notion that God had granted wealth to a select few. These few, according to William Graham Sumner (1840–1910), relied heavily on the survival-of-the-fittest philosophy associated with Charles Darwin.

Labor Unrest and Unions

When capital overexpansion and overspeculation led to the economic panic of 1873, massive labor disorders spread through the country, leading to the paralyzing railroad strike of 1877. Unemployment and salary reductions caused major class conflict. President Hayes used federal troops to restore order after dozens of workers were killed.

The depression of the 1870s undermined national labor organizations. The National Labor Union (1866) had a membership of 600,000, but failed to withstand the impact of economic adversity. Likewise with the Knights of Labor (1869), which opened its doors to immigrants, women, and African Americans. It claimed one million members, but eventually went under in 1886 in the wake of the bloody Haymarket Riot in Chicago.

Agricultural Militancy

Agrarian discontent, expressed through the activities of the National Grange and the Farmers' Alliances in the West and South, showed greater lasting power. During the Civil War, many farmers had overexpanded their operations, purchased more land and machinery, and gone heavily into debt. Although not very successful in the 1870s, farmer militancy continued to be a powerful political and economic force in the decades of the 1880s and 1890s.

SOCIAL AND CULTURAL DEVELOPMENTS (1877–1882)

Urbanization was the primary social and cultural phenomenon of the period. Both internal and external migrations contributed to an industrial urban state which grew from 40 million people in 1870 to almost 80 million in 1900. New York, Chicago, and Philadelphia emerged as cities of more than one million people.

Skyscrapers and Immigrants

The skyscraper made its appearance after the introduction of the mechanical elevator by Elisha Otis (1811–1861). The city grew into various business, industrial, and residential sectors, usually segregated by ethnic group, social class, and race. Slums and tenements sprang up within walking distance of department stores and townhouses. Two million immigrants from northern Europe poured into the United States during the 1870s. In the 1880s, another five million entered the country, this time from southern and eastern Europe.

There were few programs to deal with the vast influx of humanity other than the prohibition of the criminal and the insane. City governments soon developed the primary responsibility for immigrants—often trading employment, housing, and social services for political support.

In time, advocates of the "social gospel" such as Jane Addams (1860–1939) and Washington Gladden (1836–1918) urged the creation of settlement houses and better health and education services to accommodate the new immigrants. New religions also appeared, including the Salvation Army and Mary Baker Eddy's (1821–1910) Church of Christian Science in 1879.

African-American Leaders

In 1881, Booker T. Washington (1856–1915) became president of Tuskegee Institute in Alabama, a school devoted to teaching and vocational education for African Americans. Among those educated there was George Washington Carver (1864–1943) an agricultural chemist who did much to find industrial applications for agricultural products.

Feminism

Millions of women worked outside the home, and continued to demand voting rights. Many women became active in social reform movements such as the prohibitionist Women's Christian Temperance Movement, planned parenthood, humane societies, antiprostitution crusades, and equal rights for all.

Literature

Important books appeared such as Henry George's (1839–1897) *Progress and Poverty* (1879), a three-million-copy seller that advocated one single tax on land as the means to redistribute wealth for greater social and economic justice. In fiction, Lewis Wallace's (1827–1905) *Ben Hur* (1880), and the many Horatio Alger (1832–1899) stories promoting hard work, honesty, and a touch of good fortune, sold many millions of copies. Other famous works of the era included Mark Twain's (1835–1910) *The Gilded Age* (1873) and *The Adventures of Tom Sawyer* (1876), Bret

Harte's (1836–1902) stories of the old West, William Dean Howell's (1837–1920) social commentaries, Henry James's (1843–1916) *Daisy Miller* (1879) and *The Portrait of a Lady* (1881).

FOREIGN RELATIONS (1877–1882)

Unlike European territorial colonialism, the United States preferred market expansion without the political liability of military occupation.

Latin America

President Hayes recognized the government of dictator Porfirio Díaz in Mexico and thus encouraged U.S. investment in railroads, mines, agriculture, and oil.

In 1881, Secretary of State James G. Blaine (1830–1893) advocated the creation of an International Bureau of American Republics to promote a customs union of trade and political stability for the Western Hemisphere. The assassination of President Garfield kept Blaine from forming this organization until 1889. The bureau subsequently evolved into the Pan American Union in 1910, and the Organization of American States in 1948.

The United States promoted the peaceful resolution of several border conflicts: in 1876 between Argentina and Paraguay; in 1880 between Colombia and Chile; in 1881 between Mexico and Guatemala, Argentina and Chile, and Peru and Chile. The United States also worked to bring an end to the War of the Pacific (1879–1884), fought between Chile and the alliance of Peru and Bolivia.

Canal Project

In 1876, the Interoceanic Canal Commission recommended a Nicaraguan route for a canal to link the Atlantic and Pacific oceans. In the 1880s, the United States officially took a hostile position against the French Panama Canal project.

The Pacific

In 1878, the United States ratified a treaty with Samoa giving it trading rights and a naval base at Pago Pago. The same year, the United States was the first country to negotiate a treaty granting tariff autonomy to Japan, and set a precedent for ending the practice by Western nations of controlling customs house collections in Asian states.

Commodore Shufeldt opened trade and diplomatic relations with Korea in 1882. The United States promoted the principles of equal opportunity of trade and the sovereignty of Korea (later known as open-door policies).

Native Americans

Westward expansion and the discovery of gold in South Dakota in the early 1870s led to the Sioux War (1876–1877), and George A. Custer's (1839–1876) "last stand." In 1877, the Nez Perce War in Idaho resulted from similar causes. The Apache in Arizona and New Mexico fought as well.

The Native American tribes were eventually vanquished and compelled to live on isolated reservations. In addition to superior U.S. military force, disease, railway construction, alcoholism, and the virtual extermination of the bison contributed to their defeat. In 1881, Helen Hunt Jackson's (1830–1885) *A Century of Dishonor* chronicled the tragic policy pursued against the Native Americans.

THE REACTION TO CORPORATE INDUSTRIALISM (1882–1887)

The rise of big business and monopoly capitalism—especially in banking, railroads, mining, and the oil and steel industries—generated new labor organizations and collective political action. Most Americans, however, were not opposed to free-enterprise economics; they simply wanted an opportunity to share in the profits.

POLITICS OF THE PERIOD (1882–1887)

The only Democrat elected president in the half century after the Civil War was Grover Cleveland (1837–1908).

Election of 1884

The Republicans nominated James G. Blaine (Maine) for president and John Logan (Illinois) for vice president. The Democrats chose New York governor Grover Cleveland and Thomas A. Hendricks (Indiana). The defection of Independent Republicans supporting civil-service reforms, known as "Mugwumps" (such as E. L. Godkin and Carl Schurz (1829–1906)), to the Cleveland camp cost Blaine, the former Speaker of the House, the election. The Democrats held control of the House, and the Republicans controlled the Senate.

President Cleveland insisted that executive appointments and removals were the prerogative of the executive and not the Senate. This was the first time since Andrew Johnson that a president had strengthened the independence of his office.

THE ECONOMY (1882–1887)

Captains of industry, or robber barons, such as John D. Rockefeller in oil, J. P. Morgan (1837–1919) in banking, Gustavus Swift (1839–1903) in meat processing, Andrew Carnegie in steel, and E. H. Harriman (1848–1909) in railroads, put together major industrial empires.

The concentration of wealth and power in the hands of a relatively small number of giant firms led to a monopoly capitalism that minimized competition. This led to a demand by smaller businessmen, farmers, and laborers for government regulation of the economy in order to promote competition.

The Interstate Commerce Act (1887)

Popular resentment of railroad abuses such as price-fixing, kickbacks, and discriminatory freight rates created demands for state regulation of the railway industry. When the Supreme Court ruled individual state laws unconstitutional (*Wabash, St. Louis and Pacific Railroad Company* vs. *Illinois* (1886)) because only Congress had the right to control interstate commerce, the Interstate Commerce Act was passed providing that a commission be established to oversee fair and just railway rates, prohibit rebates, end discriminatory practices, and require annual reports and financial statements. The Supreme Court, however, remained a friend of special interests, and often undermined the work of the I.C.C.

American Federation of Labor (1886)

Samuel Gompers (1850–1924) and Adolph Strasser put together a combination of national craft unions to represent labor's concerns with wages, hours, and safety conditions. The A.F. of L. philosophy was pragmatic and not directly influenced by the dogmatic Marxism of some European labor movements. Although militant in its use of the strike, and in its demand for collective bargaining in labor contracts with large corporations, it did not promote violence or radicalism.

Scientific Management

After graduating from Stevens Institute of Technology in 1883, Frederick W. Taylor (1856–1915), the father of scientific management, introduced modern concepts of industrial engineering, plant management, time and motion studies, efficiency experts, and a separate class of managers in industrial manufacturing.

SOCIAL AND CULTURAL DEVELOPMENTS (1882–1887)

Newspapers and Magazines

The linotype machine (1886), invented by Ottmar Mergenthaler (1854–1899), cut printing costs dramatically. Publishing became big business. In 1884, Joseph Pulitzer, a Hungarian-born immigrant, was the first publisher to reach a mass audience, selling 100,000 copies of the *New York World*. New magazines such as *Forum* (1886) emphasized investigatory journalism and controversial subjects.

Higher Education

Colleges and universities expanded and introduced more modern curriculums. Graduate study emphasized meticulous research and the seminar method as pioneered in the United States at Johns Hopkins University. A complex society required a more professional and specialized education.

Bryn Mawr (1885) was established and soon found a place among such schools as Vassar, Wellesley, and Mount Holyoke in advancing education for women.

Natural Science

Albert Michelson (1852–1931), working on the speed of light, contributed in the 1880s to theories that helped prepare the way for Einstein's theory of relativity. In 1907, Michelson was the first American to win a Nobel Prize.

The New Social Science

Richard T. Ely studied the ethical implications of economic problems. Henry C. Adams and Simon Patten put forth theories to justify government regulation and planning in the economy. In sociology, Lester Frank Ward's *Dynamic Sociology*

(1883) stressed intelligent planning and decision making over genetic determinism as promoted by Social Darwinists such as William Graham Sumner. Woodrow Wilson's (1856–1924) *Congressional Government* was a critique of the committee system in Congress, and called for a better working relationship between the executive and legislative branches of government. After winning the presidency in 1912, Wilson would be in a position to put his ideas into practice.

Realism

Romanticism declined in favor of a more realistic approach to literature. Novelists explored social problems such as crime and political corruption, urban ghetto life, class conflict, evolution, and the environment. Mark Twain's masterpiece *Huckleberry Finn* appeared in 1884. In 1885, William Dean Howell's *The Rise of Silas Lapham* presented the theme of business ethics in a competitive society. *The Bostonians* (1886) by Henry James attempted a complex psychological study of female behavior.

Realism could also be seen in the artistic works of Thomas Eakins (1844–1916), Mary Cassatt (1845–1926), Winslow Homer (1836–1910), and James Whistler (1834–1903). Museums and art schools expanded. Wealthy patrons spent fortunes on personal art collections. Immigrant artists attracted enthusiastic crowds to settlement house exhibits.

FOREIGN RELATIONS (1882–1887)

Contrary to popular belief, the United States was not an isolationist nation in the 1880s. Trade expansion and the protection of markets were primary concerns.

Modern Navy

In 1883, Congress authorized the construction of new steel ships that would take the United States Navy in a 20-year period from twelfth to third in world naval ranking. In 1884, the U.S. Naval War College was established in Newport, Rhode Island—the first of its kind.

Europe

Problems existed with Britain over violence in Ireland and England. In 1886, the United States refused to extradite an Irish national accused of terrorist activity in London.

Diseased meat products in the European market led to British and German bans against uninspected American meat exports. Congress soon provided for government regulation and inspection of meat for export. This action would set a precedent for systematic food and drug inspection in later years.

Africa

The United States participated in the Berlin Conference (1884) concerning trade in the Congo. The United States also took part in the Third International Red Cross Conference.

Asia and the Pacific

In 1882, Congress passed a law suspending Chinese immigration to the United States for 10 years. The act reflected racist attitudes and created friction with China.

In 1886, the United States obtained the Pearl Harbor Naval Base by treaty with Hawaii.

Missionaries

American Christian missionaries were active in the Pacific, Asia, Africa, Latin America, and the Middle East. Missionaries not only brought religion but also Western education, exposure to science and technology, and commercial ventures. Some missionaries also brought racist concepts of white supremacy.

Latin America

In 1884, the United States signed a short-lived pact with Nicaragua for joint ownership of an isthmian canal in Central America.

THE EMERGENCE OF REGIONAL EMPIRE (1887–1892)

Despite a protective tariff policy, the United States became increasingly international as it sought to export surplus manufactured and agricultural goods. Foreign markets were viewed as a safety valve for labor employment problems and agrarian unrest. The return of Secretary of State James G. Blaine in 1889 marked a major attempt by the United States to promote a regional empire in the Western Hemisphere and reciprocal trade programs.

POLITICS OF THE PERIOD (1887–1892)

National politics became more controversial and turbulent in this era.

Election of 1888

Although the Democrat Grover Cleveland won the popular vote by about 100,000 over the Republican Benjamin Harrison (1833–1901), Harrison carried the electoral college 233–168 and was declared president after waging a vigorous campaign to protect American industrial interests with a high protective tariff. In Congress, Republicans won control of both the House and Senate.

Department of Agriculture

The Department of Agriculture (1889) was raised to cabinet status with Norman Coleman as the first secretary.

House Rules of Operation

Republican Thomas B. Reed (1839–1902) became Speaker of the House in 1890, and changed the rules of operation to make himself a veritable tsar with absolute control in running the House.

Force Bill (1890)

Senate objections kept Congress from protecting African-American voters in the South through federal supervision of state elections.

Dependent Pensions Act (1890)

Congress granted service pensions to Union veterans and their dependents for the first time.

THE ECONOMY (1887–1892)

Antimonopoly measures, protective tariffs and reciprocal trade, and a billion-dollar budget became the order of the day.

Sherman Antitrust Act (1890)

Corporate monopolies (trusts) which controlled whole industries were subject to federal prosecution if they were found to be combinations or conspiracies in restraint of trade. Although supported by smaller businesses, labor unions, and farm associations, the Sherman Antitrust Act was in time interpreted by the Supreme Court to apply to labor unions and farmers' cooperatives as much as to large corporate combinations. Monopoly was still dominant over laissez-faire, free-enterprise economics during the 1890s.

Sherman Silver Purchase Act (1890)

Prosilver interests passed legislation authorizing Congress to buy 4.5 million ounces of silver each month at market prices and issue treasury notes redeemable in gold and silver. The act created inflation and lowered gold reserves.

McKinley Tariff (1890)

This compromise protective tariff promised by the Republicans in 1888, and introduced by William McKinley of Ohio (1843–1901), was passed and extended to industrial and agricultural goods. Subsequent price increases led to a popular backlash and a Democratic House victory in the 1890 congressional elections.

SOCIAL AND CULTURAL DEVELOPMENTS (1887–1892)

Popular Amusements

In addition to the legitimate stage, vaudeville shows presenting variety acts became immensely popular. The circus expanded when Barnum and Bailey formed a partnership to present "the greatest show on earth." Distinctively American Wild West shows toured North America and Europe. To record these activities, George Eastman's (1854–1932) newly invented roll-film camera became popular with spectators.

Sports

In 1888, professional baseball sent an all-star team to tour the world. Croquet and bicycle racing were new crazes. Basketball was invented in 1891 by James Naismith, a Massachusetts Y.M.C.A. instructor. Organized intercollegiate sports such as football, basketball, and baseball created intense rivalries between colleges which attracted mass spectator interest.

Childrearing Practices

Parents became more supportive and sympathetic to their children and less authoritarian and restrictive. The 1880s were something of a golden age in children's literature. Mary Wells Smith depicted an agrarian ideal; Sidney Lanier (1842–1881) wrote tales of heroic boys and girls; Howard Pyle's *Robin Hood* gained wide readership and Joel Chandler Harris's (1848–1908) characters Brer Rabbit, Brer Fox, and Uncle Remus became very popular.

Religion

Many churches took issue with the growing emphasis on materialism in American society. By 1890, there were about 150 religious denominations in the United States.

FOREIGN RELATIONS (1887–1892)

Pan-Americanism

As secretary of state, James G. Blaine was concerned with international trade, political stability, and excessive militarism in Latin America. His international Bureau of American Republics was designed to promote a Pan-American customs union and peaceful conflict resolution. To achieve his aims, Blaine opposed U.S. military intervention in the hemisphere.

Asia and the Pacific

The medical missionary and diplomat Horace Allen promoted peaceful American investment and trade with Korea.

In 1889, the United States upheld its interests against German expansion in the Samoan Islands by establishing a three-party protectorate over Samoa with Britain and Germany. The United States retained the port of Pago Pago.

In 1891, Queen Liliuokalani (1838–1917) resisted American attempts to promote a protectorate over Hawaii. By 1893, pro-American sugar planters overthrew the native Hawaiian government and established a new government friendly to the United States.

Theoretical Works

In 1890, Naval Captain Alfred Thayer Mahan (1840–1914) published *The Influence of Sea Power on History*, which argued that control of the seas was the means to world power. Josiah Strong's *Our Country* presented the thesis that Americans had a mission to fulfill by exporting the word of God around the world, especially to non-white populations. Frederick Jackson Turner's (1861–1932) "Frontier Thesis" (1893) justified overseas economic expansion as a way to secure political power and prosperity. In *The Law of Civilization and Decay* (1895), Henry Brooks Adams (1838–1918) postulated that a nation must expand or face inevitable decline.

ECONOMIC DEPRESSION AND SOCIAL CRISIS (1892–1897)

The economic depression that began in 1893 brought about a collective response from organized labor, militant agriculture, and the business community. Each group called for economic safeguards and a more humane free-enterprise system which would expand economic opportunities in an equitable manner.

POLITICS OF THE PERIOD (1892–1897)

The most marked development in American politics was the emergence of a viable third-party movement in the form of the essentially agrarian Populist Party.

Election of 1892

Democrat Grover Cleveland (New York) and his vice-presidential running mate Adlai E. Stevenson (1835–1914) (Illinois) regained the White House by defeating Republican president Benjamin Harrison (Indiana) and Vice President Whitelaw Reid (1837–1912) (New York). Voters reacted against the inflationary McKinley Tariff. Cleveland's conservative economic stand in favor of the gold standard brought him the support of various business interests. The Democrats won control of both houses of Congress.

Populist Party

The People's party (Populist) nominated James Weaver (Iowa) for president and James Field (Virginia) for vice president in 1892. The party platform put together by such Populist leaders as Ignatius Donnelly (Minnesota), Thomas Watson (Georgia), Mary Lease (Kansas), and "Sockless" Jerry Simpson (Kansas) called for the enactment of a program espoused by agrarians, but also for a coalition with urban workers and the middle class. Specific goals were the coinage of silver to gold at a ratio of 16 to 1; federal loans to farmers; a graduated income tax; postal savings banks; public ownership of railroads and telephone and telegraph systems; prohibition of alien land ownership; immigration restriction; a ban on private armies used by corporations to break up strikes; an eight-hour working day; a single six-year term for president and direct election of senators; the right of initiative and referendum; and the use of the secret ballot.

Although the Populists were considered radical by some, they actually wanted to reform the system from within and allow for a fairer distribution of wealth. In a society in which 10 percent of the population controlled 90 percent of the nation's wealth, the Populists were able to garner about one million votes (out of 11 million votes cast) and 22 electoral votes. By 1894, Populists had elected 4 senators, 4 congressmen, 21 state executive officials, 150 state senators, and 315 state representatives, primarily in the West and South. After the 1893 depression, the Populists planned a serious bid for national power in the 1896 election.

Repeal of Sherman Silver Purchase Act (1893)

After the economic panic of 1893, Cleveland tried to limit the outflow of gold reserves by asking Congress to repeal the Sherman Silver Purchase Act, which had provided for notes redemptive in either gold or silver. Congress did repeal the act, but the Democratic party split over the issue.

Election of 1896

The Republicans nominated William McKinley (Ohio) for president and Garrett Hobart (1844–1899) (New Jersey) for vice president on a platform which promised to maintain the gold standard and protective tariffs. The Democratic party repudiated Cleveland's conservative economics and nominated William Jennings Bryan (1860–1925) (Nebraska) and Arthur Sewell (Maine) for president and vice president on a platform similar to the Populists. Bryan delivered one of the most famous speeches in American history when he declared that the people must not be "crucified upon a cross of gold."

The Populist party also nominated Bryan, but chose Thomas Watson (Georgia) for vice president. Having been outmaneuvered by the Silver Democrats, the Populists lost the opportunity to become a permanent political force.

McKinley won a hard-fought election by only about one-half million votes, as Republicans succeeded in creating the fear among business groups and middle-class voters that Bryan represented a revolutionary challenge to the American system. A warning to labor unions that they would face unemployment if Bryan won the election also helped McKinley. An often forgotten issue in 1896 was the Republican promise to stabilize the ongoing Cuban revolution. This pledge would eventually lead the United States into war with Spain (1898) for Cuban independence. The Republicans retained control over Congress, which they had gained in 1894.

THE ECONOMY (1892–1897)

The 1890s was a period of economic depression and labor agitation.

Homestead Strike (1892)

Iron and steel workers went on strike in Pennsylvania against the Carnegie Steel Company to protest salary reductions. Carnegie employed strikebreaking Pinkerton security guards. Management-labor warfare led to a number of deaths on both sides.

Depression of 1893

The primary causes for the depression of 1893 were dramatic growth of the federal deficit, withdrawal of British investments from the American market and the outward transfer of gold, and loss of business confidence. The bankruptcy of the National Cordage Company was the first among thousands of U.S. corporations

Twenty percent of the work force was eventually unemployed. The depression would last four years. Recovery would be helped by war preparation.

March of Unemployed (1894)

The Populist businessman Jacob Coxey (1854–1951) led a march of hundreds of unemployed workers on Washington asking for a government work-relief program. The government met the marchers with force and arrested their leaders.

Pullman Strike (1894)

Eugene Debs's (1855–1926) American Railway Union struck the Pullman Palace Car Co. in Chicago over wage cuts and job losses. President Cleveland broke the violent strike with federal troops.

Wilson-Gorman Tariff (1894)

This protective tariff did little to promote overseas trade as a way to ease the depression. A provision amended to create a graduated income tax was stricken by the Supreme Court as unconstitutional (*Pollack v. Farmers' Loan and Trust Co.*, 1895).

Dingley Tariff (1897)

The Dingley Tariff raised protection to new highs for certain commodities.

SOCIAL AND CULTURAL DEVELOPMENTS (1892–1897)

Economic depression and war dominated thought and literature in the 1890s.

Literature

William Dean Howells's *A Hazard of New Fortunes* (1890) was a broad attack on urban living conditions in industrial America and the callous treatment of workers by wealthy tycoons. Stephen Crane (1871–1900) wrote about the abuse and control of women in *Maggie: A Girl of the Streets* (1892) and the pain of war in *The Red Badge of Courage* (1895).

Americans also began to read such European realists as Dostoyevsky, Ibsen, Tolstoy, and Zola.

William James's (1842–1910) *Principles of Psychology* introduced the discipline to American readers as a modern science of the human mind.

Prohibition of Alcohol

The Anti-Saloon League was formed in 1893. Women were especially concerned about the increase of drunkenness during the depression.

Immigration

Immigration declined by almost 400,000 during the depression. Jane Addams's Hull House in Chicago continued to settle poor immigrants into American society. Lillian Wald's (1867–1940) Henry Street Settlement in New York and Robert

Wood's South End House in Boston performed similar functions. Such institutions also lobbied against sweatshop labor conditions, and for bans on child labor.

Chautaugua Movement

Home study courses growing out of the Chautaugua Movement in New York State became popular.

Chicago World's Fair (1893)

Beautifying the cities was the fair's main theme. A lasting development was the expansion of urban public parks.

Radio and Film

Nathan Stubblefield transmitted voice over the air without wires in 1892. Thomas Edison's kinetoscope permitted the viewing of motion pictures in 1893.

FOREIGN RELATIONS (1892–1897)

Cuba and Spain

The Cuban revolt against Spain in 1895 threatened American businessmen's $100 million worth of annual business activity and $50 million in investments in Cuba. During the election of 1896, McKinley promised to stabilize the situation and work for an end to hostilities. Sensational "yellow" journalism, and nationalistic statements from officials such as Assistant Secretary of the Navy Theodore Roosevelt (1858–1919), encouraged popular support for direct American military intervention on behalf of Cuban independence. President McKinley, however, proceeded cautiously through 1897.

Britain and Venezuela (1895)

The dispute over the border of Britain's colony of Guiana threatened war with Venezuela, especially after gold was discovered in the area. Although initially at odds with Britain, the United States eventually came to support British claims against Venezuela when Britain agreed to recognize the Monroe Doctrine in Latin America.

The Sino-Japanese War (1894–1895)

Japan's easy victory over China signaled to the United States and other nations trading in Asia that China's weakness might result in its colonization by industrial powers, and thus in the closing of the China market. The United States resolved to seek a naval base in the Pacific to protect its interests. The decision to annex the Philippines after the war with Spain was partly motivated by the desire to protect America's trade in Asia. This concern would also lead the United States to announce the Open Door policy with China, designed to protect equal opportunity of trade and China's political independence (1899 and 1900).

Latin America

When revolutions broke out in 1894 in both Brazil and Nicaragua, the United

States supported the existing governments in power to maintain political stability and favorable trade treaties. Secretaries of State Walter Q. Gresham, Richard Olney, and John Sherman continued to support James G. Blaine's Pan-American policy.

The Pacific

The United States intervened in the Hawaiian revolution (1893) to overthrow the anti-American government of Queen Liliuokalani. President Cleveland rejected American annexation of Hawaii in 1894, but President McKinley agreed to annex it in 1898.

WAR AND THE AMERICANIZATION OF THE WORLD (1897–1902)

In 1900, an Englishman named William T. Stead wrote a book entitled *The Americanization of the World,* in which he predicted that American productivity and economic strength would propel the United States to the forefront of world leadership in the 20th century. Few, however, would have predicted that as early as 1920 the United States would achieve the pinnacle of world power as a result of the debilitating policies pursued by European political leaders during World War I (1914–1919). A modern professional foreign service developed to advance U.S. interests.

POLITICS OF THE PERIOD (1897–1902)

President McKinley's wartime leadership and tragic assassination closed one door in American history, but opened another door to the leadership of Theodore Roosevelt, the first "progressive" president.

Election of 1900

The unexpected death of Vice President Garrett Hobart led the Republican party to choose the war hero and reform governor of New York, Theodore Roosevelt, as President William McKinley's vice-presidential running mate. Riding the crest of victory against Spain, the G.O.P platform called for upholding the gold standard for full economic recovery, promoting economic expansion and power in the Caribbean and the Pacific, and building a canal in Central America. The Democrats once again nominated William Jennings Bryan and Adlai Stevenson on a platform condemning imperialism and the gold standard. McKinley easily won reelection by about 1 million votes (7.2 million to 6.3 million), and the Republicans retained control of both houses of Congress.

Other Parties

The fading Populists nominated Wharton Barker (Pennsylvania) and Ignatius Donnelly (Minnesota) on a proinflation platform, but only received 50,000 votes. The Socialist Democratic party nominated Eugene V. Debs (Indiana) and Job Harriman (California) on a platform urging the nationalization of major industries.

Debs received 94,000 votes. The Prohibition party nominated John Woolley (Illinois) and Henry Metcalf (Rhode Island), and called for a ban on alcohol production and consumption. They received 209,000 votes.

McKinley Assassination (1901)

While attending the Pan American Exposition in Buffalo, New York, the president was shot on September 6 by Leon Czolgosz, an anarchist sworn to destroy all governments. The president died on September 14, after many officials thought he would recover. Theodore Roosevelt became the nation's 25th president, and at age 42, its youngest to date.

THE ECONOMY (1897–1902)

The war with Spain provided the impetus for economic recovery. The war cost $250,000,000. President Roosevelt promised a "square deal" for all Americans, farmers, workers, consumers, and businessmen. Progressive economic reform was geared to the rejuvenation of free-enterprise capitalism following the 1893 depression and the destruction of illegal monopolies. In this way, radicals would be denied an audience for more revolutionary and violent change.

Federal Bankruptcy Act (1898)

This act reformed and standardized procedures for bankruptcy and the responsibilities of creditors and debtors.

Erdman Act (1898)

This act provided for mediation, by the chair of the Interstate Commerce Commission and the commissioner of the Bureau of Labor, in unresolved railroad labor controversies.

Currency Act (1900)

The United States standardized the amount of gold in the dollar at 25.8 grains, 9/10s fine. A separate gold reserve was set apart from other general funds, and government bonds were sold to maintain the reserve.

Technology

Between 1860 and 1900, railroad trackage grew from 36,800 miles to 193,350 miles. U.S. Steel Corp. was formed in 1901, Standard Oil Company of New Jersey in 1899.

SOCIAL AND CULTURAL DEVELOPMENTS (1897–1902)

Yellow Journalism

Joseph Pulitzer's *New York World* and William Randolph Hearst's (1863–1951) *New York Journal* competed fiercely to increase circulation by exaggerating Spanish atrocities in Cuba. Such stories whipped up popular resentment of Spain and helped to create a climate of opinion receptive to war.

De Lôme Letter and Sinking of the Maine

On February 9, 1898, the newspapers published a letter written by the Spanish minister in Washington, Depuy de Lôme, criticizing President McKinley in insulting terms. On February 15, the battleship U.S.S. *Maine* was blown up in Havana harbor with a loss of 250 Americans. The popular demand for war with Spain grew, even though it was likely that the *Maine* was blown up by accident.

U.S. Military

The U.S. Army was not prepared for a full-scale effort in 1898. Sadly, more deaths resulted from disease and food poisoning than from battlefield casualties. The U.S. Navy (26,000 men) was better prepared for war as a result of years of modernization.

Territories

After the United States had defeated Spain, it was faced with the issue of what to do with such captured territories as the Philippines, Puerto Rico, the Isle of Pines, and Guam. A major public debate ensued, with critics of land acquisition forming the Anti-Imperialist League; it was supported by Mark Twain, William James, William Jennings Bryan, Grover Cleveland, Charles Francis Adams (1807–1886), Carl Schurz, Charles W. Eliot (1834–1926), David Starr Jordan (1851–1917), Andrew Carnegie, and Samuel Gompers among others. Supporters of colonialism included Theodore Roosevelt, Mark Hanna (1837–1904), Alfred Thayer Mahan (1840–1914), Henry Cabot Lodge (1850–1924), Albert Beveridge (1862–1927), and President McKinley.

Literature

Thorstien Veblen's (1857–1929) *Theory of the Leisure Class* (1899) attacked the "predatory wealth" and "conspicuous consumption" of the new rich in the Gilded Age. Veblen added evidence and argument to a critique begun by Jacob Riis (1849–1914) in *How the Other Half Lives* (1890), which documented the gnawing poverty, illness, crime, and despair of New York's slums. Frank Norris's (1870–1902) *McTeague* (1899) chronicled a man's regression to brutish animal behavior in the dog-eat-dog world of unbridled and unregulated capitalist competition. His novel *The Octopus* (1901) condemned monopoly.

FOREIGN POLICY (1897–1902)

McKinley's Ultimatum

On March 27, President McKinley asked Spain to call an armistice, accept American mediation to end the war, and end the use of concentration camps in Cuba. Spain refused to comply. On April 21, Congress declared war on Spain with the objective of establishing Cuban independence (Teller Amendment).

Cuba

After the first U.S. forces landed in Cuba on June 22, 1898, the United States proceeded to victories at El Caney and San Juan Hill. By July 17, Admiral

Sampson's North Atlantic Squadron destroyed the Spanish fleet, Santiago surrendered, and American troops quickly captured Puerto Rico.

The Philippines

As early as December 1897, Commodore George Dewey's (1837–1917) Asiatic Squadron was alerted to possible war with Spain. On May 1, 1898, the Spanish fleet in the Philippines was destroyed, and Manila surrendered on August 13. Spain agreed to a peace conference to be held in Paris in October 1898.

Treaty of Paris

Secretary of State William Day (1849–1923) led the American negotiating team, which secured Cuban independence, the ceding of the Philippines, Puerto Rico, and Guam to the United States, and the payment of $20 million to Spain for the Philippines. The treaty was ratified by the Senate on February 6, 1900.

Philippines Insurrection

Filipino nationalists under Emilio Aguinaldo (1869–1964) rebelled against the United States (February 1899) when they learned the Philippines would not be given independence. The United States used 70,000 men to suppress the revolutionaries by June 1902. A special U.S. commission recommended eventual self-government for the Philippines.

Hawaii and Wake Island

During the war with Spain, the United States annexed Hawaii on July 7, 1898. In 1900, the United States claimed Wake Island, 2,000 miles west of Hawaii.

China

Fearing the breakup of China into separate spheres of influence, Secretary of State John Hay (1838–1905) called for acceptance of the Open Door Notes by all nations trading in the China market. He wanted to guarantee equal opportunity of trade (1899) and the sovereignty of the Manchu government of China (1900).

Boxer Rebellion (1900)

Chinese nationalists ("Boxers") struck at foreign settlements in China, and at the Ch'ing dynasty's Manchu government in Beijing, for allowing foreign industrial nations large concessions within Chinese borders. An international army helped to put down the rebellion and aided the Chinese government to remain in power.

Platt Amendment (1901)

Although Cuba was granted its independence, the Platt Amendment guaranteed that it would become a virtual protectorate of the United States. Cuba could not: 1) make a treaty with a foreign state impairing its independence, or 2) contract an excessive public debt. Cuba was required to: 1) allow the United States to preserve order on the island, and 2) lease a naval base for 99 years to the United States at Guantanamo Bay.

Hay-Pauncefote Treaty (1901)

This treaty between the United States and Britain abrogated an earlier agreement (1850, Clayton-Bulwer Treaty) to jointly build an isthmian canal. The United States was free to unilaterally construct, fortify, and maintain a canal that would be open to all ships.

Supreme Court

The Supreme Court decided that constitutional rights did not extend to territorial possessions; thus the Constitution did not follow the flag.

THEODORE ROOSEVELT AND PROGRESSIVE REFORMS (1902–1907)

Theodore Roosevelt restored the presidency to the high eminence it had held through the Civil War era, and redressed the balance of power with old guard leaders in Congress.

POLITICS OF THE PERIOD (1902–1907)

President Roosevelt did much to create a bipartisan coalition of liberal reformers whose objective was to restrain corporate monopoly and promote economic competition at home and abroad.

Roosevelt's Antitrust Policy (1902)

The president pledged strict enforcement of the Sherman Antitrust Act (1890), which was designed to break up illegal monopolies and regulate large corporations for the public good.

Progressive Reform in the States

Taking their cue from Washington, many states enacted laws creating honest and efficient political and economic regulatory standards. Political reforms included laws establishing primary elections (Mississippi, Wisconsin), initiative and referendum (South Dakota, Oregon), and the rooting out of political bosses on the state and municipal levels (especially in New York, Ohio, Michigan, and California).

Commission Form of Government (1903)

After a hurricane and tidal wave destroyed much of Galveston, Texas, progressive businessmen and Texas state legislators removed the ineffective and corrupt mayor and city council and established a city government of five elected commissioners who were experts in their fields to rebuild Galveston. Numerous other cities adopted the commission form of government to replace the mayor/council format.

State Leaders

Significant state reformers in this period were Robert LaFollette (1855–1925) of Wisconsin, Albert Cummins of Iowa, Charles Evans Hughes (1862–1948) of New

York, James M. Cox of Ohio, Hiram Johnson of California, William S. U'ren of Oregon, Albert Beveridge of Indiana, and Woodrow Wilson of New Jersey.

City Reformers

Urban leaders included John Purroy Mitchell of New York City, Tom L. Johnson and Newton Baker of Cleveland, Hazen Pingree of Detroit, Sam Jones of Toledo, and Joseph Folk of St. Louis.

Election of 1904

Roosevelt was nominated for president, with Charles Fairbanks (Indiana) for vice president. The Democratic party nominated New York judge Alton B. Parker for president and Henry G. Davis (West Virginia) for vice president. Roosevelt easily defeated Parker by about two million votes, and the Republicans retained control of both houses of Congress.

Hepburn Act (1906)

Membership of the Interstate Commerce Commission was increased from five to seven. The I.C.C. could set its own fair freight rates, had its regulatory power extended over pipelines, bridges, and express companies, and was empowered to require a uniform system of accounting by regulated transportation companies. This act and the Elkins Act (1903—reiterated illegality of railroad rebates) gave teeth to the original Interstate Commerce Act of 1887.

Pure Food and Drug Act (1906)

This prohibited the manufacture, sale, and transportation of adulterated or fraudulently labeled foods and drugs in accordance with consumer demands.

Meat Inspection Act (1906)

This provided for federal and sanitary regulations and inspections in meat packing facilities. Wartime scandals in 1898 involving spoiled canned meats were a powerful force for reform.

Immunity of Witness Act (1906)

Corporate officials could no longer make a plea of immunity to avoid testifying in cases dealing with their corporation's illegal activities.

Conservation Laws

From 1902 to 1908, a series of laws and executive actions were enacted to create federal irrigation projects, national parks and forests, develop water power (Internal Waterways Commission), and establish the National Conservation Commission to oversee the nation's resources.

THE ECONOMY (1902–1907)

Antitrust Policy (1902)

Roosevelt ordered the Justice Department to prosecute corporations pursuing monopolistic practices. Attorney General P. C. Knox (1853–1921) first brought suit against the Northern Securities Company, a railroad holding corporation put together by J. P. Morgan (1837–1913), and then moved against Rockefeller's Standard Oil Company. By the time he left office in 1909, Roosevelt had indictments against 25 monopolies.

Department of Commerce and Labor (1903)

A new cabinet position was created to address the concerns of business and labor. Within the department, the Bureau of Corporations was empowered to investigate and report on the illegal activities of corporations.

Coal Strike (1902)

Roosevelt interceded with government mediation to bring about negotiations between the United Mine Workers union and the anthracite mine owners after a bitter strike over wages, safety conditions, and union recognition. This was the first time that the government intervened in a labor dispute without automatically siding with management.

Panic of 1907

A brief economic recession and panic occurred in 1907 as a result, in part, of questionable bank speculations, a lack of flexible monetary and credit policies, and a conservative gold standard. This event called attention to the need for banking reform which would lead to the Federal Reserve System in 1913. Although Roosevelt temporarily eased the pressure on antitrust activity, he made it clear that reform of the economic system to promote free-enterprise capitalism would continue.

St. Louis World's Fair (1904)

The World's Fair of 1904 celebrated the centennial of the Louisiana Purchase.

SOCIAL AND CULTURAL DEVELOPMENTS (1902–1907)

Debate and discussion over the expanding role of the federal government commanded the attention of the nation.

Progressive Reforms

There was not one unified progressive movement, but a series of reform causes designed to address specific social, economic, and political problems. Progressive reforms might best be described as evolutionary change from above rather than revolutionary upheaval from below.

Muckrakers

Muckrakers (a term coined by Roosevelt) were investigative journalists and authors who were often the publicity agents for reforms. Popular magazines included *McClure's, Collier's, Cosmopolitan,* and *Everybody's.* Famous articles that led to reforms included "The Shame of the Cities" by Lincoln Steffens (1866–1936), "History of Standard Oil Company" by Ida Tarbell (1857–1944), "The Treason of the Senate" by David Phillips, and "Frenzied Finance" by Thomas Lawson.

Literature

Works of literature with a social message included *Following the Color Line* by Ray Stannard Baker (1870–1946), *The Bitter Cry of the Children* by John Spargo, *Poverty* by Robert Hunter, *The Story of Life Insurance* by Burton Hendrick, *The Financier* by Theodore Dreiser (1871–1945), *The Jungle* by Upton Sinclair (1878–1968), *The Boss* by Henry Lewis, *The Call of the Wild, The Iron Heel,* and *The War of the Classes* by Jack London (1876–1916), *A Certain Rich Man* by William Allen White (1868–1944), and *The Promise of American Life* by Herbert Croly.

Inventions

The Wright brothers made their first air flight at Kitty Hawk, North Carolina, in 1903.

FOREIGN RELATIONS (1902–1907)

Panama Canal

Roosevelt engineered the separation of Panama from Colombia and the recognition of Panama as an independent country. The Hay-Bunau-Varilla Treaty of 1903 granted the United States control of the canal zone in Panama for $10 million and an annual fee of $250,000, beginning nine years after ratification of the treaty by both parties. Construction of the canal began in 1904 and was completed in 1914.

Roosevelt Corollary to the Monroe Doctrine

The United States reserved the right to intervene in the internal affairs of Latin American nations to keep European powers from using military force to collect debts in the Western Hemisphere. The United States, brandishing the "big stick" against Europeans and Latin Americans, by 1905, had intervened in the affairs of Venezuela, Haiti, the Dominican Republic, Nicaragua, and Cuba.

Rio de Janeiro Conference (1906)

Secretary of State Elihu Root (1845–1937) attempted to de-emphasize U.S. military and political intervention in order to promote economic and political goodwill, economic development, trade, and finances in Latin America. President Roosevelt was actually moving away from "big stick" diplomacy toward "dollar diplomacy" before he left office. The United States also promoted the Pan-American Railway project.

Russo-Japanese War (1904–1905)

With American encouragement and financial loans, Japan pursued and won a war against tsarist Russia. Roosevelt negotiated the Treaty of Portsmouth, New Hampshire, which ended the war, and which ironically won the president the Nobel Peace Prize in 1906. Japan, however, was disappointed at not receiving more territory and financial compensation from Russia and blamed the United States.

Taft-Katsura Memo (1905)

The United States and Japan pledged to maintain the Open Door principles in China. Japan recognized American control over the Philippines, and the United States granted a Japanese protectorate over Korea.

Gentleman's Agreement with Japan (1907)

After numerous incidents of racial discrimination against Japanese in California, Japan agreed to restrict the emigration of unskilled Japanese workers to the United States.

Great White Fleet (1907)

In order to show American strength to Japan and China, Roosevelt sent the great white naval fleet to Asian ports.

Algeciras Conference (1906)

The United States, along with eight European states, guaranteed Morocco equal opportunity for trade and the independence of its sultan.

The Second Hague Conference (1907)

Forty-six nations including the United States met in the Netherlands to discuss disarmament and the creation of an international court of justice. Little was accomplished except for the adoption of a resolution banning the use of military force for the collection of foreign debts.

THE REGULATORY STATE AND THE ORDERED SOCIETY (1907–1912)

The nation increasingly looked to Washington to protect the less powerful segments of the republic from the special interests that had grown up in the late 19th century. A persistent problem for the federal government was how best to preserve order and standards in a complex technological society without interfering with the basic liberties Americans had come to cherish. The strain of World War I after 1914 would further complicate the problem.

Election of 1908

Deciding not to run for reelection, Theodore Roosevelt opened the way for William H. Taft (1857–1930) (Ohio) and James S. Sherman (1855–1912) (New York) to run on a Republican platform calling for a continuation of anti-trust enforcement, environmental conservation, and a lower tariff policy to promote international trade. The Democrats nominated William Jennings Bryan for a third time, with John Kern (Indiana) for vice president, on an antimonopoly and low tariff platform. The Socialists once again nominated Eugene Debs. Taft easily won by over a million votes, and the Republicans retained control of both houses of Congress. For the first time, the American Federation of Labor entered national politics officially with an endorsement of Bryan. This decision began a long alliance between organized labor and the Democratic Party in the 20th century.

Antitrust Policy

In pursuing anti-monopoly law enforcement, Taft chose as his attorney general George Wickersham (1858–1936), who brought 44 indictments in antitrust suits.

Political Rift

Taft was less successful in healing the Republican split between conservatives and progressives over such issues as tariff reform, conservation, and the almost dictatorial power held by the reactionary Republican Speaker of the House, Joseph Cannon (Illinois). Taft's inability to bring both wings of the party together led to the hardened division which would bring about a complete Democratic victory in the 1912 elections.

Ballinger-Pinchot Dispute (1909–1910)

Progressives backed Gifford Pinchot (1865–1946), chief of the U.S. Forest Service, in his charge that the conservative secretary of the interior, Richard Ballinger, was giving away the nation's natural resources to private corporate interests. A congressional investigatory committee found that Ballinger had done nothing illegal, but did act in a manner contrary to the government's environmental policies. Taft supported Ballinger through the controversy, but negative public opinion forced Ballinger to resign in 1911. Taft's political standing with progressive Republicans was hurt going into the election of 1912.

Government Efficiency

Taft promoted the idea of a national budgetary system. Although Congress refused to cooperate, the president used executive action to save over $40 million for the government and set an example for many state and local governments.

The Sixteenth Amendment

Congress passed in 1909 a graduated income tax amendment to the Constitution which was ratified in 1913.

Mann-Elins Act (1910)

This act extended the regulatory function of the Interstate Commerce Commission.

Election of 1912

This election was one of the most dramatic in American history. President Taft's inability to maintain party harmony led Theodore Roosevelt to return to national politics. When denied the Republican nomination, Roosevelt and his supporters formed the Progressive (Bull Moose) party and nominated Roosevelt for president and Hiram Johnson (California) for vice president on a political platform nicknamed "The New Nationalism." It called for stricter regulation on large corporations, creation of a tariff commission, women's suffrage, minimum wages and benefits, direct election of senators, initiative, referendum and recall, presidential primaries, and prohibition of child labor. Roosevelt also called for a Federal Trade Commission to regulate the economy, a stronger executive, and more government planning. Theodore Roosevelt did not see big business as evil, but as a permanent development that was necessary in a modern economy.

The Republicans

President Taft and Vice President Sherman were nominated on a platform of "Quiet Confidence," which called for a continuation of the progressive programs pursued by Taft.

The Democrats

A compromise nominated New Jersey governor Woodrow Wilson for president. Thomas Marshall (1854–1925) of Indiana was selected as vice president. Wilson called his campaign the "New Freedom"; it was similar to programs in the Progressive and Republican parties. Wilson, however, did not agree with Roosevelt on the issue of big business, which Wilson saw as morally evil. Therefore, Wilson called for breaking up large corporations rather than just regulating them. He differed from the other two party candidates by favoring independence for the Philippines, and by advocating the exemption from prosecution of labor unions under the Sherman Antitrust Act. Wilson also supported such measures as lower tariffs, a graduated income tax, banking reform, and direct election of senators. Philosophically, Wilson was skeptical of big business and big government. In some respects, he hoped to return to an earlier and simpler concept of a free-enterprise republic. After his selection, however, he would modify his views to conform more with those of Theodore Roosevelt.

Election Results

The Republican split paved the way for Wilson's victory. Wilson received 6.2 million votes, Roosevelt 4.1 million, Taft 3.5 million, and the Socialist Debs 900,000 votes. In the electoral college, Wilson received 435 votes, Roosevelt 88, and Taft 8. Although a minority president, Wilson garnered the largest electoral majority in American history up to that time. Democrats won control of both houses of Congress.

The Wilson Presidency

The Wilson administration brought together many of the policies and initiatives of the previous Republican administrations with the reform efforts in Congress by both parties. Before the outbreak of World War I in 1914, President Wilson, working with cooperative majorities in both houses of Congress, achieved much of the remaining progressive agenda, including lower tariff reform (Underwood-

Simmons Act, 1913), the 16th Amendment (graduated income tax, 1913), the 17th Amendment (direct election of senators, 1913), the Federal Reserve banking system (which provided regulation and flexibility to monetary policy, 1913), the Federal Trade Commission (to investigate unfair business practices, 1914), and the Clayton Antitrust Act (improving the old Sherman act and protecting labor unions and farm cooperatives from prosecution, 1914).

Other goals such as the protection of children in the work force (Keating-Owen Act, 1916), credit reform for agriculture (Federal Farm Loan Act, 1916), and an independent tariff commission (1916) came later. By the end of Wilson's presidency, the New Freedom and the New Nationalism had merged into one government philosophy of regulation, order, and standardization in the interest of an increasingly diverse nation.

THE ECONOMY (1907–1912)

National Monetary Commission (1908)
Chaired by Senator Nelson Aldrich (Rhode Island), the 18-member commission in 1913 recommended what later became the basis for the Federal Reserve system: a secure treasury reserve and branch banks to add and subtract currency from the monetary supply depending on the needs of the economy.

Payne-Aldrich Tariff (1909)
Despite the intention of lowering the tariff, enough amendments were added in the Senate to turn the bill into a protective measure.

Postal Savings Banks (1910)
Certain U.S. post offices were authorized to receive deposits and pay interest.

New Battleship Contract (1910)
The State Department arranged for Bethlehem Steel Corporation to receive a large contract to build battleships for Argentina. This was an example of Taft's "dollar diplomacy" in action.

Antitrust Proceedings
Although a friend to the business community, President Taft ordered 90 legal proceedings against monopolies, and 44 antitrust suits, including the one that broke up the American Tobacco Trust (1911). Under Taft, the government succeeded with its earlier suit against Standard Oil.

New Cabinet Posts (1913)
The Department of Commerce and Labor was divided into two separate autonomous cabinet level positions.

SOCIAL AND CULTURAL DEVELOPMENTS (1907–1912)

Social Programs

States led the way with programs such as public aid to mothers of dependent children (Illinois, 1911), and the first minimum wage law (Massachusetts, 1912).

Race and Ethnic Attitudes

Despite the creation of the NAACP in 1909, many progressive reformers were Anglo-Saxon elitists critical of the lack of accomplishments of immigrants and minorities. In 1905, the African-American intellectual militant W.E.B. DuBois (1868–1963) founded the Niagara Movement which called for federal legislation to protect racial equality and for full rights of citizenship.

Radical Labor

A radical labor organization called the Industrial Workers of the World (I.W.W., or Wobblies, 1905–1924) was active in promoting violence and revolution. Led by such colorful figures as Carlo Tresca, Elizabeth Gurley Flynn (the Red Flame), Daniel DeLeon, "Mother" Mary Harris Jones, the maverick priest Father Thomas Hagerty, and Big Bill Haywood, among others, the I.W.W. organized effective strikes in the textile industry in 1912, and among a few western miners groups, but had little appeal to the average American worker. After the Red Scare of 1919, the government worked to smash the I.W.W. and deported many of its immigrant leaders and members.

White Slave Trade

In 1910, Congress made interstate prostitution a federal crime with the passage of the Mann Act.

Motion Pictures

By 1912, Hollywood had replaced New York and New Jersey as the center for silent-film production.

Science

The X-ray tube was developed by William Coolidge in 1913. Robert Goddard (1882–1945) patented liquid rocket fuel in 1914. Plastics and synthetic fibers such as rayon were developed in 1909 by Arthur Little and Leo Baekeland, respectively. Adolphus Busch applied the diesel engine to the submarine in 1912. In 1913, Henry Ford (1863–1947) introduced the continuous flow process on the automobile assembly line.

FOREIGN RELATIONS (1907–1915)

"Dollar Diplomacy"

President Taft sought to avoid military intervention, especially in Latin America, by replacing "big stick" policies with "dollar diplomacy" in the expectation that American financial investments would encourage economic, social, and political stability. This idea proved an illusion as investments never really filtered through all levels of Latin American societies, nor did such investments generate democratic reforms.

Mexican Revolution (1910)

Francisco I. Madero overthrew the dictator Porfirio Diaz (1911), declaring himself a progressive revolutionary akin to reformers in the United States. American and European corporate interests (especially oil and mining) feared interference with their investments in Mexico. President Taft recognized Madero's government, but stationed 10,000 troops on the Texas border (1912) to protect Americans from the continuing fighting. In 1913, Madero was assassinated by General Victoriano Huerta. Wilson urged Huerta to hold democratic elections and adopt a constitutional government. When Huerta refused his advice, Wilson invaded Mexico with troops at Veracruz in 1914. A second U.S. invasion came in northern Mexico in 1916. War between the United States and Mexico might have occurred had not World War I intervened.

Latin American Interventions

Although Taft and Secretary of State P.C. Knox created the Latin American division of the State Department in 1909 to promote better relations, the United States kept a military presence in the Dominican Republic and Haiti, and intervened militarily in Nicaragua (1911) to quiet fears of revolution and help manage foreign financial problems.

Lodge Corollary to the Monroe Doctrine (1911)

When a Japanese syndicate moved to purchase a large tract of land in Mexico's Lower California, Senator Lodge introduced a resolution to block the investment. The corollary excluded non-European powers from the Western Hemisphere under the Monroe Doctrine.

Bryan's Arbitration Treaties (1913–1915)

Wilson's secretary of state William Jennings Bryan continued the policies of Roosevelt and Taft to promote arbitration of disputes in Latin America and elsewhere. Bryan negotiated about 30 such treaties.

Root-Takahira Agreement (1908)

This agreement reiterated the status quo in Asia established by the United States and Japan in the Taft-Katsura memo (1905).

Chinese Revolution (1911)

Chinese nationalists overthrew the Manchu dynasty and the last emperor of China, Henry Pu Yi. Although the military war lord Yuan Shih-Kai seized control, decades of factionalism, revolution, and civil war destabilized China and its market potential for American and other foreign investors.

16 WILSON AND WORLD WAR I (1912–1920)

IMPLEMENTING THE NEW FREEDOM: THE EARLY YEARS OF THE WILSON ADMINISTRATION

The New President

Wilson was only the second Democrat (Cleveland was the first) elected president since the Civil War. He was born in Virginia in 1856, the son of a Presbyterian minister, and was reared and educated in the South. After earning a doctorate at Johns Hopkins University, he taught history and political science at Princeton, and in 1902 became president of that university. In 1910, he was elected governor of New Jersey as a reform, or progressive, Democrat.

The Cabinet

Key appointments were William Jennings Bryan as secretary of state and William Gibbs McAdoo (1863–1941) as secretary of the treasury.

The Inaugural Address

Wilson called the Congress, now controlled by Democrats, into a special session beginning April 7, 1913, to consider three topics: reduction of the tariff, reform of the national banking and currency laws, and improvements in the antitrust laws. On April 8, he appeared personally before Congress, the first president since John Adams to do so, to promote his program.

The Underwood-Simmons Tariff Act of 1913

Average rates were reduced to about 29 percent from 37 to 40 percent under the previous Payne-Aldrich Tariff. A graduated income tax was included in the law to compensate for lost tariff revenue. The 16th Amendment to the Constitution, ratified in February 1913, authorized the income tax.

The Federal Reserve Act of 1913

The law divided the nation into 12 regions, with a Federal Reserve bank in each region. Commercial banks in the region owned the Federal Reserve bank by purchasing stock equal to six percent of their capital and surplus. They also elected the directors of the bank. National banks were required to join the system, and state banks were invited to join. The Federal Reserve banks held the gold reserves of their members. Federal Reserve banks loaned money to member banks by rediscounting their commercial and agricultural paper; that is, the money was loaned at interest less than the public paid to the member banks, and the notes of indebtedness of businesses and farmers to the member banks were held as collateral. This allowed the Federal Reserve to control interest rates by raising or lowering the discount rate.

The money loaned to the member banks was in the form of a new currency, Federal Reserve notes, which was backed 60 percent by commercial paper and 40 percent by gold. This currency was designed to expand and contract with the volume of business activity and borrowing. Checks on member banks were cleared through the Federal Reserve system.

The Federal Reserve system serviced the financial needs of the federal government. The system was supervised and policy was set by a national Federal Reserve Board composed of the secretary of the treasury, the comptroller of the currency, and five other members appointed by the president of the United States.

The Clayton Antitrust Act of 1914

This law supplemented and interpreted the Sherman Antitrust Act of 1890. Under its provisions, stock ownership by a corporation in a competing corporation was prohibited, and the same persons were prohibited from managing competing corporations. Price discrimination (charging less in some regions than in others to undercut the competition) and exclusive contracts which reduced competition were prohibited. Officers of corporations could be held personally responsible for violations of antitrust laws. Lastly, labor unions and agricultural organizations were not to be considered "combinations or conspiracies in restraint of trade" as defined by the Sherman Antitrust Act.

The Federal Trade Commission Act of 1914

The law prohibited all unfair trade practices and created a commission empowered to issue cease and desist orders to corporations to stop actions considered to be in restraint of trade, and to bring suit in the courts if the orders were not obeyed. Firms could also contest the orders in court. Under previous antitrust legislation, the government could act against corporations only by bringing suit.

THE TRIUMPH OF NEW NATIONALISM

Political Background

The Progressive party dissolved rapidly after the election of 1912. Early in 1916, Wilson and the Democrats abandoned most of their limited government and states' rights positions in favor of a legislative program of broad economic and social reforms designed to win the support of the former Progressives for the Democratic party in the election of 1916. The urgency of their concern was increased by the fact that Theodore Roosevelt intended to seek the Republican nomination in 1916.

The Brandeis Appointment

Wilson's first action after the adoption of the new program was the appointment on January 28, 1916, of Louis D. Brandeis (1856–1941), considered by many to be the principal advocate of social justice in the nation, as an associate justice of the Supreme Court.

The Federal Farm Loan Act of 1916

The law divided the country into 12 regions and established a Federal Land bank in each region. Funded primarily with federal money, the banks made farm mortgage loans at reasonable interest rates. Wilson had threatened to veto similar legislation in 1914.

The Child Labor Act of 1916

This law, earlier opposed by Wilson, forbade shipment in interstate commerce of some products whose production had involved the labor of children under 14 or 16. The legislation was especially significant because it was the first time that Congress regulated labor within a state using the interstate commerce power. The law was declared unconstitutional by the Supreme Court in 1918 on the grounds that it interfered with the powers of the states.

The Adamson Act of 1916

This law mandated an eight-hour day for workers on interstate railroads with time and a half for overtime and a maximum of 16 hours in a shift. Its passage was a major victory for railroad unions, and averted a railroad strike in September 1916.

The Kerr-McGillicuddy Act of 1916

This law initiated a program of workmen's compensation for federal employees.

THE ELECTION OF 1916

The minority party nationally in terms of voter registration, the Democrats nominated Wilson and adopted his platform calling for continued progressive reforms and neutrality in the European war. "He kept us out of war" became the principal campaign slogan of Democratic politicians.

The convention bypassed Theodore Roosevelt and chose Charles Evans Hughes (1862–1948), an associate justice of the Supreme Court and formerly a progressive Republican governor of New York.

Wilson won the election with 277 electoral votes and 9,129,000 popular votes, almost three million more than he received in 1912.

SOCIAL ISSUES IN THE FIRST WILSON ADMINISTRATION

Blacks

In 1913, Treasury Secretary William G. McAdoo and Postmaster General Albert S. Burleson segregated workers in some parts of their departments with no objection from Wilson. Many northern blacks and whites protested, especially black leader W.E.B. DuBois (1868–1963), who had supported Wilson in 1912. No further segregation in government agencies was initiated, but Wilson had gained a reputation for being inimical to civil rights.

Women

The movement for women's suffrage, led by the National American Woman Suffrage Association, was increasing in momentum at the time Wilson became president, and several states had granted the vote to women. Wilson opposed a federal women's suffrage amendment, maintaining that the franchise should be controlled by the states. Later, he changed his view and supported the 19th Amendment.

Immigration

Wilson opposed immigration restrictions and vetoed a literacy test for immigrants in 1915, but in 1917, Congress overrode a similar veto.

WILSON'S FOREIGN POLICY AND THE ROAD TO WAR

Wilson's Basic Premise: New Freedom Policy

Wilson promised a more moral foreign policy than that of his predecessors, denouncing imperialism and dollar diplomacy, and advocating the advancement of democratic capitalist governments throughout the world.

Wilson signaled his repudiation of Taft's dollar diplomacy by withdrawing American involvement from the six-power loan consortium of China.

The Caribbean

Like his predecessors, Wilson sought to protect the Panama Canal, which opened in 1914, by maintaining stability in the area. He also wanted to encourage diplomacy and economic growth in the underdeveloped nations of the region. In applying his policy, he became as interventionist as Roosevelt and Taft.

In 1912, American marines had landed in Nicaragua to maintain order, and an American financial expert had taken control of the customs station. The Wilson administration kept the marines in Nicaragua and negotiated the Bryan-Chamorro Treaty of 1914, which gave the United States an option to build a canal through the country. In effect, Nicaragua became an American protectorate, although treaty provisions authorizing such action were not ratified by the Senate.

Claiming that political anarchy existed in Haiti, Wilson sent marines in 1915 and imposed a treaty making the country a protectorate, with American control of its finances and constabulary. The marines remained until 1934.

In 1916, Wilson sent marines to the Dominican Republic to stop a civil war and established a military government under an American naval commander.

Wilson feared in 1915 that Germany might annex Denmark and its Caribbean possession, the Danish West Indies or Virgin Islands. After extended negotiations, the United States purchased the islands from Denmark by treaty on August 4, 1916, for $25 million and took possession of them on March 31, 1917.

In 1913, Wilson refused to recognize the government of Mexican military dictator Victoriano Huerta, and offered unsuccessfully to mediate between Huerta and his Constitutionalist opponent, Venustiano Carranza. When the Huerta government arrested several American seamen in Tampico in April 1914, American forces occupied the port of Veracruz, an action condemned by both Mexican political factions. In July 1914, Huerta abdicated his power to Carranza, who was soon opposed by his former general Francisco "Pancho" Villa (1878–1923). Seeking American intervention as a means of undermining Carranza, Villa shot 16 Americans on a train in northern Mexico in January 1916 and burned the border town of Columbus, New Mexico, in March 1916, killing 19 people. Carranza reluctantly consented to Wilson's request that the United States be allowed to pursue and capture Villa in Mexico, but did not expect the force of about 6,000 army troops under the command of General John J. Pershing which crossed the Rio Grande on March 18. The force advanced more than 300 miles into Mexico, failed to capture Villa, and became, in effect, an army of occupation. The Carranza government demanded an American withdrawal, and several clashes with Mexican troops occurred. War threatened, but in January 1917 Wilson removed the American forces.

Pan-American Mediation (1914)

John Barrett, head of the Pan-American Union (formerly Blaine's International Bureau of American Republics), called for multilateral mediation to bring about a solution to Mexico's internal problems and remove the United States from Mexico. Although Wilson initially refused, Argentina, Brazil, and Chile did mediate among the Mexican factions and Wilson withdrew American troops. Barrett hoped to replace the unilateral Monroe Doctrine with a multilateral Pan-American policy to promote collective responses and mediation to difficult hemispheric problems. Wilson, however, refused to share power with Latin America.

THE ROAD TO WAR IN EUROPE

American Neutrality

When World War I broke out in Europe, Wilson issued a proclamation of American neutrality on August 4, 1914. The value of American trade with the Central Powers fell from $169 million in 1914 to almost nothing in 1916, but trade with the Allies rose from $825 million to $3.2 billion during the same period. In addition, the British and French had borrowed about $3.25 billion from American sources by 1917. The United States had become a major supplier of Allied munitions, food, and raw materials.

The Submarine Crisis of 1915

The sinking of the British liner *Lusitania* off the coast of Ireland on May 7, 1915, with the loss of 1,198 lives, including 128 Americans, brought strong protests from Wilson. Secretary of State Bryan, who believed Americans should stay off belligerent ships, resigned rather than insist on questionable neutral rights and was replaced by Robert Lansing. Following the sinking of another liner, the *Arabic*, on August 19, the Germans gave the "*Arabic* pledge" to stop attacks on unarmed passenger vessels.

The House-Grey Memorandum

Early in 1915, Wilson sent his friend and adviser Colonel Edward M. House on an unsuccessful visit to the capitals of the belligerent nations on both sides to offer American mediation in the war. Late in the year, House returned to London to propose that Wilson call a peace conference; if Germany refused to attend or was uncooperative at the conference, the United States could enter the war on the Allied side. An agreement to that effect, called the House-Grey memorandum, was signed by the British foreign secretary, Sir Edward Grey, on February 22, 1916.

Preparedness

In November 1915, Wilson proposed a major increase in the army and the abolition of the National Guard as a preparedness measure. Americans divided on the issue, with organizations like the National Security League proposing stronger military forces, and others like the League to Enforce Peace opposing military growth. After opposition by southern and western antipreparedness Democrats, Congress passed a modified National Defense Act in June 1916 which increased the army from about 90,000 to 220,000 and enlarged the National Guard under federal control. In August, over $500 million was appropriated for naval construction. The additional costs were met by increased taxes on the wealthy.

Wilson's Final Peace Efforts (1916–1917)

On December 12, 1916, the Germans, confident of their strong position, proposed a peace conference, but were evasive and stated that they did not want Wilson at the conference. In an address to Congress on January 22, 1917, Wilson made his last offer to serve as a neutral mediator. He proposed a "peace without victory," based not on a "balance of power" but on a "community of power."

Unlimited Submarine Warfare

Germany announced on January 31, 1917, that it would sink all ships, belligerent or neutral, without warning in a large war zone off the coasts of the Allied nations in the eastern Atlantic and the Mediterranean. The Germans realized that the United States might declare war, but they believed that, after cutting the flow of supplies to the Allies, they could win the war before the Americans could send any sizable force to Europe. Wilson broke diplomatic relations with Germany on February 3. During February and March several American merchant ships were sunk by submarines.

The Zimmerman Telegram

The British intercepted a secret message from the German foreign secretary, Arthur Zimmerman, to the German minister in Mexico, and turned it over to the United States on February 24, 1917. The Germans proposed that, in the event of a war between the United States and Germany, Mexico attack the United States. After the war, the "lost territories" of Texas, New Mexico, and Arizona would be returned to Mexico. In addition, Japan would be invited to join the alliance against the United States. When the telegram was released to the press on March 1, many Americans became convinced that war with Germany was necessary.

The Declaration of War

A declaration of war against Germany was passed by the Senate on April 4 by a vote of 82 to 6, and by the House on April 6 by a vote of 373 to 50. It was signed by Wilson on April 6.

Wilson's Reasons

Wilson believed that the Zimmerman telegram showed that the Germans were not trustworthy and would eventually go to war against the United States. He also felt that armed neutrality could not adequately protect American shipping. The democratic government established in Russia after the revolution in March 1917 also proved more acceptable as an ally than the tsarist government. Finally, he was convinced that the United States could hasten the end of the war and ensure a major role for itself in designing a lasting peace.

WORLD WAR I: THE MILITARY CAMPAIGN

Raising an Army

Despite the enlistment of many volunteers, it was apparent that a draft would be necessary. The Selective Service Act was passed on May 18, 1917, after bitter opposition in the House led by the speaker, "Champ" Clark. Only a compromise outlawing the sale of liquor in or near military camps secured passage. The first drawing of 500,000 names was made on July 20, 1917. By the end of the war, 24,231,021 men had been registered and 2,810,296 had been inducted. In addition, about two million men and women volunteered.

Women and Minorities in the Military

Some women served as clerks in the navy or in the Signal Corps of the army. Originally nurses were part of the Red Cross, but eventually some were taken into the army. About 400,000 black men were drafted or enlisted, despite the objections of southern political leaders. They were kept in segregated units, usually with white officers, which were used as labor battalions or for other support activities. Some black units did see combat, and a few African Americans became officers but did not command white troops.

The American Expeditionary Force

The soldiers and marines sent to France under command of Major General John J. Pershing (1860–1948) were called the American Expeditionary Force, or the AEF. From a small initial force which arrived in France in June 1917, the AEF increased to over two million by November 1918. Pershing resisted efforts by European commanders to amalgamate the Americans with the French and British armies, insisting that he maintain a separate command.

Major Military Engagements

The American force of about 14,500, which had arrived in France by September 1917, was assigned a quiet section of the line near Verdun. As numbers increased, the American role became more significant. When the Germans mounted a major drive toward Paris in the spring of 1918, the Americans experienced their first important engagements. In June, they prevented the Germans from crossing the Marne at Chateau-Thierry, and cleared the area of Belleau Woods. In July, eight American divisions aided French troops in attacking the German line between

Reims and Soissons. The American First Army, with over half a million men under Pershing's immediate command, was assembled in August 1918, and began a major offensive at St. Mihiel on the southern part of the front on September 12. Following the successful operation, Pershing began a drive against the German defenses between Verdun and Sedan, an action called the Meuse-Argonne offensive. He reached Sedan on November 7. During the same period the English in the north and the French along the central front also broke through the German lines. The fighting ended with the armistice on November 11, 1918.

MOBILIZING THE HOME FRONT

Industry

In July 1917, the council created the War Industries Board to control raw materials, production, prices, and labor relations. The military forces refused to cooperate with the civilian agency in purchasing their supplies, and the domestic war effort seemed on the point of collapse in December 1917, when a congressional investigation began. In 1918, Wilson took stronger action under his emergency war powers, which were reinforced by the Overman Act of May 1918. In March 1918, Wilson appointed Wall Street broker Bernard M. Baruch (1870–1965) to head the WIB. He was assisted by an advisory committee of 100 businessmen. The WIB allocated raw materials, standardized manufactured products, instituted strict production and purchasing controls, and paid high prices to businesses for their products. Even so, American industry was just beginning to produce heavy armaments when the war ended. Most heavy equipment and munitions used by the American troops in France were produced in Britain or France.

Food

The United States had to supply not only its own food needs but those of Britain, France, and some of the other Allies as well. The problem was compounded by bad weather in 1916 and 1917. The Lever Act of 1917 gave the president broad control over the production, price, and distribution of food and fuel. Herbert Hoover (1874–1964) was appointed by Wilson to head a newly created Food Administration. Hoover fixed high prices to encourage the production of wheat, pork, and other products, and encouraged the conservation of food through such voluntary programs as "Wheatless Mondays" and "Meatless Tuesdays." Despite the bad harvests in 1916 and 1917, food exports by 1919 were almost triple those of the prewar years, and real farm income was up almost 30 percent.

Fuel

The Fuel Administration under Harry A. Garfield was established in August 1917. "Fuelless Mondays," for nonessential industries to conserve coal, and "Gasless Sundays," for automobile owners to save gasoline, were instituted. Coal production increased about 35 percent from 1914 to 1918.

Railroads

The American railroad system, which provided most of the intercity transportation in the country, seemed near collapse in December 1917 because of the wartime demands and heavy snows that slowed service. Wilson created the United States Railroad Administration under William G. McAdoo, the secretary of the treasury, to take over and operate all the railroads in the nation as one system. The government paid the owners rent for the use of their lines, spent over $500 million on improved tracks and equipment, and achieved its objective of an efficient railroad system.

Maritime Shipping

The U.S. Shipping Board was authorized by Congress in September 1916, and in April 1917 it created a subsidiary, the Emergency Fleet Corporation, to buy, build, lease, and operate merchant ships for the war effort. Edward N. Hurley became the director in July 1917, and the corporation constructed several large shipyards which were just beginning to produce vessels when the war ended. By seizing German and Dutch ships, and by the purchase and requisition of private vessels, the board had accumulated a large fleet by September 1918.

Labor

To prevent strikes and work stoppages in war industries, the War Labor Board was created in April 1918 under the joint chairmanship of former president William Howard Taft and attorney Frank P. Walsh. It had members from both industry and labor. The WLB in effect prohibited strikes, but it also encouraged higher wages, the eight-hour day, and unionization. Union membership doubled during the war from about 2.5 million to about 5 million.

War Finance and Taxation

The war is estimated to have cost about $33.5 billion by 1920, excluding such future costs as veterans' benefits and debt service. Of that amount at least $7 billion was loaned to the Allies, with most of the money actually spent in the United States for supplies. The government raised about $10.5 billion in taxes, and borrowed the remaining $23 billion. Taxes were raised substantially in 1917 and again in 1918. The Revenue Act of 1918, which did not take effect until 1919, imposed a personal income tax of six percent on incomes up to $4,000, and twelve percent on incomes above that amount. In addition, a graduated surtax went to a maximum of 65 percent on large incomes, for a total of 77 percent. Corporations paid an excess profits tax of 65 percent, and excise taxes were levied on luxury items. Much public, peer, and employer pressure was exerted on citizens to buy Liberty Bonds, which covered a major part of the borrowing. An inflation rate of about 100 percent from 1915 to 1920 contributed substantially to the cost of the war.

The Committee on Public Information

The committee, headed by journalist George Creel, was formed by Wilson in April 1917. Creel established a successful system of voluntary censorship of the press and a propaganda campaign to build support for the American cause. The CPI set up volunteer Liberty Leagues in every community, and urged their members, and citizens at large, to spy on their neighbors, especially those with foreign names, and to report any suspicious words or actions to the Justice Department.

War Hysteria

A number of volunteer organizations sprang up around the country to search for draft dodgers, enforce the sale of bonds, and report any opinion or conversation considered suspicious. Perhaps the largest such organization was the American Protective League with about 250,000 members, which claimed the approval of the Justice Department. Such groups publicly humiliated people accused of not buying war bonds, and persecuted, beat, and sometimes killed people of German descent. As a result of the activities of the CPI and the vigilante groups, German language instruction and German music were banned in many areas, German measles became "liberty measles," pretzels were prohibited in some cities, and so on. The anti-German and antisubversive war hysteria in the United States far exceeded similar public moods in Britain and France during the war.

The Espionage and Sedition Acts

The Espionage Act of 1917 provided for fines and imprisonment for persons who made false statements which aided the enemy, incited rebellion in the military, or obstructed recruitment or the draft. Printed matter advocating treason or insurrection could be excluded from the mails. The Sedition Act of May 1918 forbade any criticism of the government, flag, or uniform, even if there were not detrimental consequences, and expanded the mail exclusion. The laws sounded reasonable, but they were applied in ways that trampled on civil liberties. Eugene V. Debs, the perennial Socialist candidate for president, was given a 10-year prison sentence for a speech at his party's convention in which he was critical of American policy in entering the war and warned of the dangers of militarism. Movie producer Robert Goldstein released the movie *The Spirit of '76* about the Revolutionary War. It naturally showed the British fighting the Americans. Goldstein was fined $10,000 and sentenced to 10 years in prison because the film depicted the British, who were now fighting on the same side as the United States, in an unfavorable light. The Espionage Act was upheld by the Supreme Court in the case of *Schenck v. United States* in 1919. The opinion, written by Justice Oliver Wendell Holmes, Jr. (1841–1935), stated that Congress could limit free speech when the words represented a "clear and present danger," and that a person cannot cry "fire" in a crowded theater. The Sedition Act was similarly upheld in *Abrams v. United States* a few months later. Ultimately 2,168 persons were prosecuted under the laws, and 1,055 were convicted, of whom only 10 were charged with actual sabotage.

WARTIME SOCIAL TRENDS

Women

Large numbers of women, mostly white, were hired by factories and other enterprises in jobs never before open to them. They were often resented and ridiculed by male workers. When the war ended, almost all returned to traditional "women's jobs" or to homemaking. Returning veterans replaced them in the labor market. Women continued to campaign for women's suffrage. In 1917, six states, including New York, Ohio, Indiana, and Michigan, gave the vote to women. Wilson changed his position in 1918 to advocate women's suffrage as a war measure. In January 1918, the House of Representatives adopted a suffrage amendment to the constitution which was defeated later in the year by southern forces in the Senate. The way was paved for the victory of the suffragists after the war.

Racial Minorities

The labor shortage opened industrial jobs to Mexican Americans and to African Americans. W.E.B. DuBois, the most prominent African-American leader of the time, supported the war effort in the hope that the war to make the world safe for democracy would bring a better life for African Americans in the United States. About half a million rural southern African Americans migrated to cities, mainly in the North and Midwest, to obtain employment in war and other industries, especially in steel and meatpacking. In 1917, there were race riots in 26 cities in the North and South, with the worst in East St. Louis, Illinois.

Prohibition

In December 1917, a constitutional amendment to prohibit the manufacture and sale of alcoholic beverages in the United States was passed by Congress and submitted to the states for ratification. While alcohol consumption was being attacked, cigarette consumption climbed from 26 billion in 1916 to 48 billion in 1918.

PEACEMAKING AND DOMESTIC PROBLEMS (1918–1920)

The Fourteen Points

From the time of the American entry into the war, Wilson had maintained that the war would make the world safe for democracy. He insisted that there should be peace without victory, meaning that the victors would not be vindictive toward the losers, so that a fair and stable international situation in the postwar world would ensure lasting peace. In an address to Congress on January 8, 1918, he presented his specific peace plan in the form of the Fourteen Points. The first five points called for open rather than secret peace treaties, freedom of the seas, free trade, arms reduction, and a fair adjustment of colonial claims. The next eight points were concerned with the national aspirations of various European peoples and the adjustment of boundaries, as, for example, in the creation of an independent Poland. The fourteenth point, which he considered the most important and had espoused as early as 1916, called for a "general association of nations" to preserve the peace. The plan was disdained by the Allied leadership, but it had great appeal for many people on both sides of the conflict in Europe and America.

The Versailles or Paris Peace Conference

Wilson decided that he would lead the American delegation to the peace conference which opened in Paris on January 12, 1919. In doing so he became the first president to leave the country during his term of office. The other members of the delegation were Secretary of State Robert Lansing, General Tasker Bliss, Colonel Edward M. House, and attorney Henry White. Wilson made a serious mistake in not appointing any leading Republicans to the commission and in not consulting the Republican leadership in the Senate about the negotiations. In the negotiations, which continued until May 1919, Wilson found it necessary to make many compromises in forging the text of the treaty.

The Senate and the Versailles Treaty

Following a protest by 39 senators in February 1919, Wilson obtained some changes in the League of Nations structure to exempt the Monroe Doctrine and domestic matters from League jurisdiction. Then, on July 26, 1919, he presented the treaty with the League within it to the Senate for ratification. Almost all of the 47 Democrats supported Wilson and the treaty, but the 49 Republicans were divided. About a dozen were "irreconcilables" who thought that the United States should not be a member of the League under any circumstances. The remainder included 25 "strong" and 12 "mild" reservationists who would accept the treaty with some changes. The main objection centered on Article X of the League Covenant, where the reservationists wanted it understood that the United States would not go to war to defend a League member without the approval of Congress. The leader of the reservationists was Henry Cabot Lodge of Massachusetts, the chairman of the Foreign Relations Committee. More senators than the two-thirds necessary for ratification favored the treaty either as written or with reservations.

Wilson and the Senate

On September 3, 1919, Wilson set out on a national speaking tour to appeal to the people to support the treaty and the League and to influence their senators. He collapsed after a speech in Pueblo, Colorado, on September 25, and returned to Washington, where he suffered a severe stroke on October 2 which paralyzed his left side. He was seriously ill for several months, and never fully recovered. In a letter to the Senate Democrats on November 18, Wilson urged them to oppose the treaty with the Lodge reservations. In votes the next day, the treaty failed to get a two-thirds majority either with or without the reservations.

The Final Vote

Many people, including British and French leaders, urged Wilson to compromise with Lodge on reservations, including the issue of Article X. Wilson, instead, wrote an open letter to Democrats on January 8, 1920, urging them to make the election of a Democratic president in 1920 a "great and solemn referendum" on the treaty as written. Such partisanship only exacerbated the situation. Many historians think that Wilson's ill health impaired his judgment, and that he would have worked out a compromise had he not had the stroke. The Senate took up the treaty again in February 1920, and on March 19 it was again defeated both with and without the reservations. The United States officially ended the war with Germany by a resolution of Congress signed on July 2, 1921, and a separate peace treaty was ratified on July 25. The United States did not join the League.

DOMESTIC PROBLEMS AND THE END OF THE WILSON ADMINISTRATION

Demobilization

The AEF was brought home as quickly as possible in early 1919, and members of the armed forces were rapidly discharged. Congress provided for wounded veterans through a system of veteran's hospitals under the Veteran's Bureau, and funded relief, especially food supplies, for war-torn Europe. The wartime agencies were soon disbanded. During 1919, Congress considered various plans to nationalize the railroads or continue their public operation, but then passed the Esch-Cummings or Transportation Act of 1920 that returned them to private ownership and operation.

Final Reforms of the Progressive Era

In January 1919, the 18th Amendment to the Constitution prohibiting the manufacture, sale, transportation, or importation of intoxicating liquors was ratified by the states, and it became effective in January 1920. The 19th Amendment providing for women's suffrage, which had been defeated in the Senate in 1918, was approved by Congress in 1919. It was ratified by the states in time for the election of 1920.

The Postwar Economy

Despite fear of unemployment with the return of veterans to the labor force and the end of war purchases, the American economy boomed during 1919 and the first half of 1920. Consumers had money from high wages during the war, and the European demand for American food and manufactured products continued for some months after the war. The demand for goods resulted in a rapid inflation.

Strikes

The great increase in prices prompted 2,655 strikes in 1919, involving about four million workers, or 20 percent of the labor force. Unions were encouraged by the gains they had made during the war and thought they had the support of public opinion. However, the Communist revolution in Russia in 1917 soon inspired a fear of violence and revolution by workers. While most of the strikes in early 1919 were successful, the tide of opinion gradually shifted against the workers.

The Red Scare

Americans feared the spread of the Russian Communist revolution to the United States, and many interpreted the widespread strikes of 1919 as Communist-inspired and the beginning of the revolution. Bombs sent through the mail to prominent government and business leaders in April 1919 seemed to confirm their fears, although the origin of the bombs has never been determined. The membership of the two Communist parties founded in the United States in 1919 was less than 100,000, but many Americans were sure that many workers, all foreign-born persons, radicals, and members of the International Workers of the World, a radical union in the western states, were Communists. The anti-German hysteria of the war years was transformed into the anti-Communist and antiforeign hysteria of 1919 and 1920, and continued in various forms through the 1920s.

The Palmer Raids

Attorney General A. Mitchell Palmer, who aspired to the 1920 presidential nomination, was one of the targets of the anonymous bombers in the spring of 1919. In August 1919, he named J. Edgar Hoover (1895–1972) to head a new Intelligence Division in the Justice Department to collect information about radicals. In November 1919, Palmer's agents arrested almost 700 persons, mostly anarchists, and deported 43 of them as undesirable aliens. On January 2, 1920, Justice Department agents, local police, and vigilantes in 33 cities arrested about 4,000 people accused of being Communists. Many people caught in the sweep were neither Communists nor aliens. Eventually 556 were shown to be Communists and aliens, and were deported. Palmer then announced that huge Communist riots were planned for major cities on May Day (May 1, 1920). Police and troops were alerted, but the day passed with no radical activity. Palmer was discredited and the Red Scare subsided.

The Race Riots of 1919

White hostility based on competition for lower-paid jobs and black encroachment into neighborhoods led to race riots in 25 cities, with hundreds killed or wounded and millions of dollars in property damage. The Chicago riot in July was the worst, lasting 13 days and leaving 38 dead, 520 wounded, and 1,000 families homeless. Fear of returning African-American veterans in the South led to an increase of lynchings from 34 in 1917 to 60 in 1918 and 70 in 1919. Some of the victims were veterans still in uniform.

17 THE ROARING TWENTIES AND ECONOMIC COLLAPSE (1920–1929)

THE ELECTION OF 1920

The Political Climate

It seemed to many political observers in 1920 that the Republicans had an excellent chance of victory. The Wilson administration was blamed by many for the wartime civil liberties abuses, the League of Nations controversy, and the strikes and inflation of the postwar period.

The Republican Convention

Senator Warren G. Harding (1865–1923) of Ohio was nominated as a dark-horse candidate, and Governor Calvin Coolidge (1872–1933) of Massachusetts was chosen as the vice presidential nominee. The platform opposed the League and promised low taxes, high tariffs, immigration restriction, and aid to farmers.

The Democratic Convention

Governor James Cox was nominated on the 44th ballot, and Franklin D. Roosevelt (1882–1945), an assistant secretary of the Navy and distant cousin of Theodore, was selected as his running mate. The platform endorsed the League, but left the door open for reservations.

The Election

Harding struck a responsive chord in many people when he urged that the nation should abandon heroics, nostrums, and experiment, and return to what he called "normalcy."

Harding received 16,152,200 popular votes, 61 percent of the total, for 404 electoral votes. Cox received 9,147,353 popular votes for 127 electoral votes. Socialist candidate Eugene V. Debs, in federal prison in Atlanta for an Espionage Act conviction, received 919,799 votes. It appears that people voted Republican more as a repudiation of Wilson's domestic policies than as a referendum on the League. Wilson had alienated German Americans, Irish Americans, antiwar progressives, civil libertarians, and midwestern farmers, all groups which had given the Democrats considerable support in 1916.

THE TWENTIES: ECONOMIC ADVANCES AND SOCIAL TENSIONS

The Recession of 1920–1921

The United States experienced a severe recession from mid-1920 until the end of 1921. Europe returned to normal and reduced its purchases in America, and domestic demand for goods not available in wartime was filled. Prices fell, and unemployment exceeded 12 percent in 1921.

Prosperity and Industrial Productivity

The economy improved rapidly in 1922, and continued to be strong until 1929. Improved industrial efficiency, which resulted in lower prices for goods, was primarily responsible. Improved machinery increased output. Industry changed from steam to electric power, allowing the design of more intricate machines which replaced the work of human hands. The moving assembly line, first introduced by Henry Ford in the automobile industry in 1913 and 1914, was widely adopted. Scientific management, exemplified by the time and motion studies pioneered by Frederick W. Taylor before the war, led to more efficient use of workers and lower labor costs. Larger firms began, for the first time, to fund major research and development activities to find new and improved products, reduce production costs, and utilize by-products.

The Automobile

The principal driving force of the economy of the 1920s was the automobile. There were 8,131,522 motor vehicles registered in the United States in 1920, and 26,704,825 in 1929. By 1925, the price of a Ford Model T had been reduced to $290, less than three months pay for an average worker. Ford plants produced nine thousand Model Ts per day. Automobile manufacturing stimulated supporting industries such as steel, rubber, and glass, as well as gasoline refining and highway construction. During the 1920s, the United States became a nation of paved roads. The Federal Highway Act of 1916 started the federal highway system and gave matching funds to the states for construction. One estimate stated that the automobile industry directly or indirectly employed 3.7 million people in 1929.

Other Leading Industries

A host of electrical appliances such as stoves, vacuum cleaners, refrigerators, toasters, and radios became available. About two-thirds of American homes had electricity by 1929, leaving only those in rural areas without it. Home and business construction also experienced a boom from 1922 to 1928. The chemical, printing, and movie industries grew rapidly. Industries that began in the period include radio and commercial aviation.

Consumer Credit and Advertising

Unlike earlier boom periods, which had involved large expenditures for capital investments such as railroads and factories, the prosperity of the 1920s depended heavily on the sale of consumer products. Purchases of "big ticket" items such as automobiles, refrigerators, and furniture were made possible by installment or time payment credit. The idea was not new, but the availability of consumer credit expanded tremendously during the 1920s. Consumer interest and demand was spurred by the great increase in professional advertising, which used newspapers, magazines, radio, billboards, and other media.

The Dominance of Big Business

There was a trend toward corporate consolidation during the 1920s. In most fields, an oligopoly of two to four firms dominated. This is exemplified by the automobile industry, where Ford, General Motors, and Chrysler produced 83 percent of the vehicles in 1929. Government regulatory agencies such as the Federal Trade Commission and the Interstate Commerce Commission were passive and generally controlled by persons from the business world. The public generally accepted the situation and viewed businessmen with respect. Illustrating the attitudes of the time, *The Man Nobody Knows,* a book by advertising executive Bruce Barton published in 1925, became a best-seller. It described Jesus as the founder of modern business and his apostles as an exemplary business management team.

Banking and Finance

There was also a trend toward bank consolidation. Because corporations were raising much of their money through the sale of stocks and bonds, the demand for business loans declined. Commercial banks then put more of their funds into real estate loans, loans to brokers against stocks and bonds, and the purchase of stocks and bonds themselves. By doing so they made themselves vulnerable to economic disaster when the depression began in late 1929. Even during the prosperous 1920s, 5,714 banks failed, most of them in rural areas or in Florida. Banks in operation in 1929 numbered 25,568.

Labor

The National Association of Manufacturers and its state affiliates began a drive in 1920 to restore the "open shop," or nonunion workplace. The alternative used was "welfare capitalism," whereby the firm sought to provide job satisfaction so that the workers would not want a union. Company-sponsored pension and insurance plans, stock-purchase plans, efforts to insure worker safety and comfort, social and sporting events, and company magazines were undertaken. Company unions, designed to give workers some voice with management, were organized by 317 firms. Unions, which had prospered during World War I, found themselves on the defensive. Leaders, especially William Green, president of the American Federation of Labor after 1924, were conservative and nonaggressive. Union membership dropped about 20 percent, from five million to about four million, during the decade. The most violent labor confrontations occurred in the mining and southern textile industries. The United Mine Workers of America, headed by John L. Lewis (1880–1969), was involved in bitter strikes in Pennsylvania, West Virginia, Kentucky, and Illinois, but by 1929 had lost most of its power. The United Textile Workers failed to organize southern textile workers in a campaign from 1927 to 1929, but violent strikes occurred in Tennessee, North Carolina, and Virginia.

The Farm Problem

Farmers did not share in the prosperity of the 1920s. Farm prices had been high during World War I because of European demand and government price-fixing. By 1920, the European demand dropped considerably, and farm prices were determined by a free market. During the same period farm expenses rose.

AMERICAN SOCIETY IN THE 1920s

Population

During the 1920s, the population of the United States increased by 16.1 percent, from 105,710,620 in 1920 to 122,775,046 in 1930, a slower percentage of growth than in previous decades. The birthrate was also lower than in former times, dropping from 27.7 per 100,000 in 1920 to 21.3 per 100,000 in 1930. About 88 percent of the people were white.

Urbanization

By 1920, for the first time, a majority of Americans (51 percent) lived in an urban area with a population of 2,500 or more. A new phenomenon of the 1920s was the tremendous growth of suburbs and satellite cities, which grew more rapidly than the central cities. Streetcars, commuter railroads, and automobiles contributed to the process, as well as the easy availability of financing for home construction. The suburbs had once been the domain of the wealthy, but the technology of the 1920s opened them to working-class families.

The Standard of Living

Improved technology and urbanization led to a sharp rise in the standard of living. Urban living improved access to electricity, natural gas, telephones, and piped water. The use of indoor plumbing, hot water, and central heating increased dramatically. Improved machinery produced better-fitting and more comfortable ready-made clothing and shoes. Yet enjoyment of the new standard of living was uneven. For those who had access, the new standard of living required more money than had been necessary in former times. In 1929, about 12 million families, or 43 percent of the total, had annual incomes under $1,500, which was considered by many to be the poverty line. About 20 million families, or 72 percent, had incomes under $2,500, the family income deemed necessary for a decent standard of living.

The Sexual Revolution

Traditional American moral standards regarding premarital sex and marital fidelity were widely questioned for the first time during the 1920s. There was a popular misunderstanding by people who had not read his works that Sigmund Freud had advocated sexual promiscuity. Movies, novels, and magazine stories were more sexually explicit. The "flaming youth" of the Jazz Age emphasized sexual promiscuity and drinking, as well as new forms of dancing considered erotic by the older generation. The automobile, by giving people mobility and privacy, was generally considered to have contributed to sexual license. Journalists wrote about "flappers," young women who were independent, assertive, and promiscuous. Birth control, though illegal, was promoted by Margaret Sanger (1883–1966) and others and was widely accepted. But compared with the period from 1960 to the present, it was a relatively conservative time.

Women

Many feminists believed that the passage of the 19th Amendment in 1920 providing women's suffrage would solve all problems for women. When it became apparent that women did not vote as a block, political leaders gave little additional attention to the special concerns of women. The sexual revolution brought some emancipation. Women adopted less bulky clothing, and could smoke and socialize with men in public more freely than before. Divorce laws were liberalized in many states at the insistence of women. Domestic service was the largest job category. Most other women workers were in traditional female occupations such as secretarial and clerical work, retail sales, teaching, and nursing. Rates of pay were below those for men. Most women still pursued the traditional role of housewife and mother, and society accepted that as the norm.

Blacks

The migration of southern rural African Americans to the cities continued, with about 1.5 million moving during the 1920s. By 1930, about 20 percent of American blacks lived in the North, with the largest concentrations in New York, Chicago, and Philadelphia. While they were generally better off economically in the cities than they had been as tenant farmers, they generally held low-paying jobs and were confined to segregated areas of the cities. The Harlem section of New York City, with an African American population of 73,000 in 1920 and 165,000 in 1930, was the largest African American urban community. It became the center for African American writers, musicians, and intellectuals. African Americans throughout the country developed jazz and blues. W.E.B. DuBois, the editor of *The Crisis*, continued to call for integration, and to attack segregation despite his disappointment with the lack of progress after World War I. The National Association for the Advancement of Colored People was a more conservative but active voice for civil rights, and the National Urban League concentrated on employment and economic advancement.

A native of Jamaica, Marcus Garvey (1887–1940) founded the Universal Negro Improvement Association there in 1914. He moved to New York in 1916. Garvey advocated African American racial pride and separatism rather than integration, and called for a return of African Americans to Africa. Some of his ideas soon alienated the older African American organizations. He developed a large following, especially among southern African Americans. He urged his followers to buy only from African Americans, and founded a chain of businesses, including grocery stores, restaurants, and laundries. In 1921, he proclaimed himself the provisional president of an African empire, and sold stock in the Black Star Steamship Line which would take migrants to Africa. The line went bankrupt in 1923, and Garvey was convicted and imprisoned for mail fraud in the sale of the line's stock and then deported. His legacy was an emphasis on African American pride and self-respect.

Mexicans and Puerto Ricans

Mexicans had long migrated to the southwestern part of the United States as agricultural laborers, but in the 1920s they began to settle in cities such as Los Angeles, San Antonio, and Denver. Like other immigrants, they held low-paying jobs and lived in poor neighborhoods. The 1920s also saw the first large migration of Puerto Ricans to the mainland, mostly to New York City. There they were employed in manufacturing, in service industries such as restaurants, and in domestic work.

Education

Free elementary education was available to most students in 1920, except for many African American children. High school education became more available, and shifted from an emphasis on college preparation to include vocational education, which was funded in part by the Smith-Hughes Act of 1917 which gave federal funds for agricultural and technical studies. There was also a substantial growth in enrollment in higher education.

Religion

Church and synagogue membership increased more rapidly than the population during the 1920s, despite much religious tension and conflict. Most Protestant sects had been divided into Northern and Southern branches since before the Civil War. By the 1920s, there was another major division between the modernists who accommodated their thinking to include biblical criticism and evolution, and fundamentalists who stressed the literal truth of the Bible and creationism. There was also division on social issues such as support of labor. The only issue which united most Protestants (except Lutherans) was prohibition.

Popular Culture

Movie attendance averaged 40 million a week in 1922 and 90 million a week in 1929. Introduction of sound with *The Jazz Singer* in 1927 generated even more interest. Stars like Douglas Fairbanks, Gloria Swanson, Rudolph Valentino, Clara Bow, and Charlie Chaplin were tremendously popular. Americans spent ten times more on movies than on all sports, the next biggest attraction. The 1920s were called the Golden Age of major-league baseball. Millions followed the exploits of George Herman "Babe" Ruth and other stars. Boxing was popular and made Jack Dempsey and others famous. College football began to attract attention, with Knute Rockne coaching at Notre Dame and Harold "Red" Grange playing for the University of Illinois. When Grange signed with the Chicago Bears in 1926, professional football began to grow in popularity. Commercial radio began when station KDKA in Pittsburgh broadcast the election results in November 1920. By 1929, more than one-third of all families had radios. National network broadcasting began when the National Broadcasting Company was organized in 1926, followed by the Columbia Broadcasting System in 1927. Radio was free entertainment, paid for by advertising. Despite the many new diversions, Americans continued to read, and millions of popular magazines were sold each week. Popular books of the period included the Tarzan series and Zane Grey's (1875–1939) Westerns, as well as some literary works.

Literary Trends

Many writers of the 1920s were disgusted with the hypocrisy and materialism of contemporary American society. Often called the "Lost Generation," many of them, such as novelists Ernest Hemingway (1899–1961) and F. Scott Fitzgerald (1896–1940) and poets Ezra Pound (1885–1972) and T. S. Eliot (1888–1965) , moved to Europe. Typical authors and works include Ernest Hemingway's *The Sun Also Rises* (1926) and *A Farewell to Arms* (1929); Sinclair Lewis' (1885–1951) *Babbitt* (1922), *Arrowsmith* (1925), and *Elmer Gantry* (1927); F. Scott Fitzgerald's *The Great Gatsby* (1925) and *Tender Is the Night* (1929); John Dos Passos's (1896–1970) *Three Soldiers* (1921); and Thomas Wolfe's (1900–1938) *Look Homeward, Angel* (1929). H. L. Mencken (1880–1956), a journalist who began publication of the *American Mercury* magazine in 1922, ceaselessly attacked the "booboisie," as he called middle-class America, but his literary talent did not match that of the leaders of the period.

SOCIAL CONFLICTS

A Conflict of Values

Many white Protestant families saw their traditional values gravely threatened. The traditionalists were largely residents of rural areas and small towns, and the clash of farm values with the values of an industrial society of urban workers was evident. The traditionalist backlash against modern urban industrial society expressed itself primarily through intolerance.

The Ku Klux Klan

On Thanksgiving Day in 1915, the Knights of the Ku Klux Klan, modeled on the organization of the same name in the 1860s and 1870s, was founded near Atlanta by William J. Simmons. Its purpose was to intimidate African Americans, who were experiencing an apparent rise in status during World War I. The Klan remained small until 1920, when two advertising experts, Edward Y. Clark and Elizabeth Tyler, were hired by the leadership. Clark and Tyler used modern advertising to recruit members. By 1923, the Klan had about five million members throughout the nation. The largest concentrations of members were in the South, the Southwest, the Midwest, California, and Oregon. The use of white hoods, masks, and robes, and the secret ritual and jargon, seemed to appeal mostly to lower middle-class men in towns and small cities. The Klan stood for "native, white, Protestant supremacy." It opposed African Americans, Catholics, Jews, Asians, and other foreigners. It also attacked bootleggers, drunkards, gamblers, and adulterers for violating moral standards. The Klan's methods of repression included cross burnings, tar and featherings, kidnappings, lynchings, and burnings. The Klan was not a political party, but it endorsed and opposed candidates and exerted considerable control over elections and politicians in at least nine states. The Klan began to decline after 1925 when it was hit by scandals, especially the murder conviction of Indiana Grand Dragon David Stephenson. The main reason for its decline was the staunch opposition of courageous editors, politicians, and other public figures who exposed its lawlessness and terrorism in the face of great personal danger. Many historians see the Klan as the American expression of fascism, which was making headway in Italy, Germany, and other European nations during the 1920s.

Immigration Restriction

There had been calls for immigration restriction since the late 19th century. Labor leaders believed that immigrants depressed wages and impeded unionization. Some progressives believed that they created social problems. In June 1917, Congress, over Wilson's veto, had imposed a literacy test for immigrants and excluded many Asian nationalists. During World War I and the Red Scare, almost all immigrants were considered radicals and Communists. With bad economic conditions in postwar Europe, over 1.3 million came to the United States between 1919 and 1921. As in the period before the war, they were mostly from south and east Europe and mostly Catholics and Jews, the groups most despised by nativist Americans. In 1921, Congress passed the Emergency Quota Act, which limited immigration by nation to three percent of the number of foreign-born persons from that nation in the United States in 1910. In practice, the law admitted about as many as wanted to come from such nations as Britain, Ireland, and Germany, while severely restricting Italians, Greeks, Poles, and east European Jews. It became effective in 1922 and reduced the number of immigrants annually to about 40 percent of the 1921 total. Congress then passed the National Origins Act of 1924, which set the quotas at two percent of the number of foreign-born persons of that nationality in the United States in 1890, excluded all Asians, and imposed an annual maximum of 164,000.

Immigration from Western Hemisphere nations was not limited. The law further reduced the number of south and east Europeans, and cut the annual immigration to 20 percent of the 1921 figure. In 1927, the annual maximum was reduced to 150,000.

Prohibition

The 18th Amendment, which prohibited the manufacture, sale, or transportation of intoxicating liquors, took effect in January 1920. It was implemented by the Volstead Act of October 1919, which defined intoxicating beverages as containing one-half of one percent alcohol by volume, and imposed criminal penalties for violations. Enforcement was reasonably effective in some rural southern and midwestern states which had been dry before the amendment. In urban areas, neither the public nor their elected officials were interested in enforcement. Speakeasies, supposedly secret bars operated by bootleggers, replaced saloons. Smuggled liquor flowed across the nation, and the manufacture of "bathtub gin" and similar beverages was undertaken by thousands. Organized crime, which previously had been involved mainly with prostitution and gambling, grew tremendously to meet the demand. Al Capone of Chicago was perhaps the most famous of the bootlegging gangsters. Women, who had not gone to saloons in the preprohibition period, frequented speakeasies and began to drink in public. By the mid-1920s, the nation was divided on the prohibition issue. Support continued from rural areas and almost all Republican office-holders. The Democrats divided between the urban northerners who advocated repeal, and rural, especially southern, Democrats who supported prohibition.

Creationism and the Scopes Trial

Fundamentalist Protestants, under the leadership of William Jennings Bryan, began a campaign in 1921 to prohibit the teaching of evolution in the schools, and thus protect belief in the literal biblical account of creation. The idea was especially well received in the South. In 1925, the Tennessee legislature passed a law that forbade any teacher in the state's schools or colleges to teach evolution. The American Civil Liberties Union found a young high school biology teacher, John Thomas Scopes, who was willing to bring about a test case by breaking the law. Scopes was tried in Dayton, Tennessee, in July 1925. Bryan came to assist the prosecution, and Chicago trial lawyer Clarence Darrow (1857–1938) defended Scopes. The trial attracted national attention through newspaper and radio coverage. The judge refused to allow expert testimony, so the trial was a duel of words between Darrow and Bryan. As was expected, Scopes was convicted and fined $100. Bryan died of exhaustion a few days after the trial. Both sides claimed a moral victory. The antievolution crusaders secured enactment of a statute in Mississippi in 1926, which was followed by statutes in several other states.

Sacco and Vanzetti

On April 15, 1920, two unidentified gunmen robbed a shoe factory and killed two men in South Braintree, Massachusetts. Nicola Sacco and Bartolomeo Vanzetti, Italian immigrants and admitted anarchists, were tried for the murders. Judge Webster Thayer clearly favored the prosecution, which based its case on the political radicalism of the defendants. After they were convicted and sentenced to death in July 1921, there was much protest in the United States and in Europe that they had not received a fair trial. After six years of delays, there were executed on August 23, 1927. Controversy about the trial continues today.

GOVERNMENT AND POLITICS IN THE 1920s: THE HARDING ADMINISTRATION

Warren G. Harding

Harding was a handsome and amiable man of limited intellectual and organizational abilities. He had spent much of his life as the publisher of a newspaper in the small city of Marion, Ohio. He recognized his limitations, but hoped to be a much-loved president. He showed compassion by pardoning socialist Eugene V. Debs for his conviction under the Espionage Act and by inviting him to dinner at the White House. He also persuaded U.S. Steel to give workers the eight-hour work day. A convivial man, he liked to drink and play poker with his friends, and kept the White House stocked with bootleg liquor despite prohibition. He was accused of keeping a mistress named Nan Britton. His economic philosophy was conservative.

The Cabinet and Government Appointments

Harding appointed some outstanding persons to his cabinet, including Secretary of State Charles Evans Hughes, a former Supreme Court justice and presidential candidate; Secretary of the Treasury Andrew Mellon (1855–1937), a Pittsburgh aluminum and banking magnate and reportedly the richest man in America; and Secretary of Commerce Herbert Hoover, a dynamic multimillionaire mine owner famous for his wartime relief efforts. Less impressive was his appointment of his cronies Albert B. Fall as secretary of the interior and Harry M. Daugherty as attorney general. Other cronies, some dishonest, were appointed to other government posts.

Tax Reduction

Mellon believed in low taxes and government economy to free the rich from "oppressive" taxes and thus encourage investment. The farm bloc of midwestern Republicans and southern Democrats in Congress prevented cuts in the higher tax brackets as great as Mellon recommended. The Revenue Acts of 1921 and 1924 cut the maximum tax rates to 50 percent and then to 48 percent. Taxes in lower brackets were also reduced, but inheritance and corporate income taxes were retained. Mellon was able to reduce the federal debt by an average of $500 million a year.

The Fordney-McCumber Tariff

Mellon sought substantial increases in tariffs, but again there was a compromise with the farm bloc. The Fordney-McCumber Tariff of September 1922 imposed high rates on farm products and protected such infant industries as rayon, china, toys, and chemicals. Most other items received moderate protection, and a few items, including farm equipment, were duty-free. The president could raise or lower rates to a limit of 50 percent on the recommendation of the Tariff Commission. The average rate was about 33 percent, compared with about 26 percent under the previous tariff.

The Budget

As a result of the Budget and Accounting Act of 1921, the federal government had a unified budget for the first time. The law also provided for a director of the budget to assist in its preparation, and a comptroller general to audit government accounts.

The Harding Scandals

Harding apparently was honest, but several of his friends whom he appointed to office became involved in major financial scandals. Most of the information about the scandals did not become public knowledge until after Harding's death.

The Teapot Dome Scandal began when Secretary of the Interior Albert B. Fall in 1921 secured the transfer of several naval oil reserves to his jurisdiction. In 1922, he secretly leased reserves at Teapot Dome in Wyoming to Harry F. Sinclair of Monmouth Oil and at Elk Hills in California to Edward Doheny of Pan-American Petroleum. A Senate investigation later revealed that Sinclair had given Fall $305,000 in cash and bonds and a herd of cattle, while Doheny had given him a $100,000 unsecured loan. Sinclair and Doheny were acquitted in 1927 of charges of defrauding the government, but in 1929, Fall was convicted, fined, and imprisoned for bribery.

Another scandal involved Charles R. Forbes, appointed by Harding to head the new Veterans' Bureau. It was later estimated that he had stolen or squandered about $250 million in bureau funds.

Scandal also tainted Attorney General Daugherty, who through his good friend Jesse Smith took bribes from bootleggers, income tax evaders, and others in return for protection from prosecution. When the scandal began to come to light, Smith committed suicide in Daugherty's Washington apartment in May 1923. There was also evidence that Daugherty received money for using his influence in returning the American Metal Company, seized by the government during the war, to its German owners.

Harding's Death

Depressed by the first news of the scandals, Harding left in June 1923 for an extended trip, including a tour of Alaska. On his return to California, he died suddenly in San Francisco on August 2, 1923, apparently of a heart attack. Rumors of foul play or suicide persisted for years.

Coolidge Becomes President

Vice President Calvin Coolidge became president. He had a reputation for honesty, although he did not remove Daugherty from the cabinet until March 1924.

THE ELECTION OF 1924

The Republicans

Calvin Coolidge was nominated, and Charles G. Dawes (1865–1951) was his running mate. The platform endorsed business development, low taxes, and rigid economy in government. The party stood on its record of economic growth and prosperity since 1922.

The Democrats

After a deadlock between the eastern wing and the southern and western wing of the party, John W. Davis, a conservative Wall Street lawyer, was finally chosen as a dark horse; Charles W. Bryan, brother of William Jennings Bryan, was chosen as the vice-presidential candidate. The platform favored a lower tariff, but otherwise was similar to the Republican document.

The Progressives

Robert M. LaFollette, after failing in a bid for the Republican nomination, formed a new Progressive party, with support from Midwest farm groups, socialists, and the American Federation of Labor. The platform attacked monopolies, and called for the nationalization of railroads, the direct election of the president, and other reforms.

The Election

Coolidge received 15,725,016 votes and 382 electoral votes, more than his two opponents combined. Davis received 8,385,586 votes and 136 electoral votes, while

LaFollette had 4,822,856 votes and 36 electoral votes from his home state of Wisconsin.

THE COOLIDGE ADMINISTRATION

Calvin Coolidge

Coolidge was a dour and taciturn man. Born in Vermont, his adult life and political career were spent in Massachusetts. "The business of the United States is business," he proclaimed, and "the man who builds a factory builds a temple." His philosophy of life was stated in the remark that "four-fifths of all our troubles in this world would disappear if only we would sit down and keep still." Liberal political commentator Walter Lippmann wrote that "Mr. Coolidge's genius for inactivity is developed to a very high point." He intentionally provided no presidential leadership.

The McNary-Haugen Bill

Coolidge vetoed a plan passed by Congress in 1927–1928 to raise prices for basic farm products. The plan was a forerunner of the agricultural programs of the 1930s.

Muscle Shoals

During World War I, the government constructed a dam and two nitrate plants on the Tennessee River at Muscle Shoals, Alabama. A proposal for government operation was vetoed by Coolidge in 1928. The facility was to become the nucleus of the Tennessee Valley Authority in the 1930s.

Veterans' Bonus

Legislation to give veterans of World War I 20-year endowment policies, with values based on their length of service, was passed over Coolidge's veto in 1924.

The Revenue Act of 1926

Mellon's tax policies were finally implemented by this law, which reduced the basic income tax, cut the surtax to a maximum of 20 percent, abolished the gift tax, and cut the estate tax in half.

THE ELECTION OF 1928

The Republicans

Coolidge did not seek another term, and the convention quickly nominated Herbert Hoover, the secretary of commerce, for president, and Charles Curtis (1860–1936) as his running mate. The platform endorsed the policies of the Harding and Coolidge administrations.

The Democrats

Governor Alfred E. Smith (1873–1944) of New York, a Catholic and an antiprohibitionist, controlled most of the nonsouthern delegations. Southerners supported his nomination with the understanding that the platform would not advocate repeal of prohibition. Senator Joseph T. Robinson of Arkansas, a Protestant and a prohibitionist, was the vice-presidential candidate. The platform differed little from the Republican, except in advocating lower tariffs.

The Election

Hoover received 21,392,190 votes and 444 electoral votes. Smith had 15,016,443 votes for 87 electoral votes in eight states.

FOREIGN POLICY IN THE TWENTIES

The Washington Conference

At the invitation of Secretary of State Charles Evans Hughes, representatives of the United States, Great Britain, France, Japan, Italy, China, the Netherlands, Belgium, and Portugal met in Washington in August 1921 to discuss naval limitations and Asian affairs. Three treaties resulted from the conference: the Five Power Pact or Treaty, signed in February 1922, the Nine Power Pact or Treaty, and the Four Power Pact or Treaty.

War Debts, Reparations, and International Finance

The United States had loaned the Allies about $7 billion during World War I and about $3.25 billion in the postwar period, and insisted on full payment of the debts. Meanwhile, Germany was to pay reparations to the Allies, but by 1923 Germany was bankrupt. The Dawes plan, proposed by American banker Charles G. Dawes (1865–1951) and accepted in 1924, structured a new schedule of debt payments for Germany.

Latin America

American investment in Latin America almost doubled during the 1920s, and relations with most nations in the region improved. Coolidge removed the marines from Nicaragua in 1925, but a revolution erupted and the marines were returned. Revolutionary General Augusto Sandino fought against the marines until they were replaced by an American-trained national guard under Anastasio Somoza. The Somoza family ruled Nicaragua until 1979, when they were overthrown by revolutionaries called the Sandinistas.

THE GREAT DEPRESSION: THE CRASH

Hoover Becomes President

Herbert Hoover, an Iowa farm boy and an orphan, graduated from Stanford University with a degree in mining engineering. He became a multimillionaire from mining and other investments around the world. After serving as the director of the Food Administration under Wilson, he became secretary of commerce under Harding and Coolidge. He believed that cooperation between business and government would enable the United States to abolish poverty through continued economic growth.

The Stock-Market Boom

Stock prices increased throughout the decade. The boom in prices and volume of sales was especially active after 1925, and was intensive during 1928–29. The Dow-Jones Industrial Average for the year 1924 was 120; for the month of September 1929 it was 381; and for the year 1932 it dropped to 41. Stocks were selling for more than 16 times their earnings in 1929, well above the rule of thumb of 10 times their earnings.

The Stock-Market Crash

Careful investors, realizing that stocks were overpriced, began to sell to take their profits. During October 1929, prices declined as more stock was sold. On "Black Thursday," October 24, 1929, almost 13 million shares were traded, a large number for that time, and prices fell precipitously. Investment banks tried to boost the market by buying, but on October 29, "Black Tuesday," the market fell about 40 points, with 16.5 million shares traded.

18 THE GREAT DEPRESSION AND THE NEW DEAL (1929–1941)

REASONS FOR THE DEPRESSION

A stock-market crash does not mean that a depression must follow. A similar crash in October 1987 did not lead to depression. In 1929, a complex interaction of many factors caused the decline of the economy.

Many people had bought stock on a margin of 10 percent, meaning that they had borrowed 90 percent of the purchase through a broker's loan and put up the stock as collateral. Broker's loans totaled $8.5 billion in 1929, compared with $3.5 billion in 1926. When the price of a stock fell more than 10 percent, the lender sold the stock for whatever it would bring and thus further depressed prices. The forced sales brought great losses to the banks and businesses that had financed the broker's loans, as well as to the investors.

There were already signs of recession before the market crash in 1929. Because the gathering and processing of statistics was not as advanced then as now, some factors were not so obvious to people at the time. The farm economy, which involved almost 25 percent of the population, had been depressed throughout the decade. Coal, railroads, and New England textiles had not been prosperous. After 1927, new construction declined and auto sales began to sag. Many workers had been laid off before the crash of 1929.

Many scholars believe that there was a problem of underconsumption, meaning that ordinary workers and farmers, after using their consumer credit, did not have enough money to keep buying the products which were being produced. One estimate says that the income of the top 1 percent of the population increased at least 75 percent during the decade, while that of the bottom 93 percent increased only 6 percent. The process continued after the depression began. After the stock market crash, people were conservative and saved their money, thus reducing the demand for goods. As demand decreased, workers were laid off or had wage reductions, further cutting their purchasing power and bringing another decrease in demand.

With the decline in the economy, Americans had less money for foreign loans and bought fewer imported products. That meant that foreign governments and individuals were not able to pay their debts in the United States. The whole reparations and war debts structure collapsed. American exports dropped, further hurting the domestic economy. The depression eventually spread throughout the world.

Economic Effects of the Depression

During the early months of the depression, most people thought it was just an adjustment in the business cycle which would soon be over. As time went on, the worst depression in American history set in, reaching its bottom point in early 1932. The gross national product fell from $104.6 billion in 1929 to $56.1 billion in 1933. Unemployment reached about 13 million in 1933, or about 25 percent of the labor force, excluding farmers. Industrial production dropped about 51 percent. The banking system suffered; 5,761 banks, more than 22 percent of the total, failed by the end of 1932.

HOOVER'S DEPRESSION POLICIES

The Agricultural Marketing Act

Passed in June 1929, before the market crash, this law, proposed by the president, created the Federal Farm Board. It had a revolving fund of $500 million to lend agricultural cooperatives to buy commodities, such as wheat and cotton, and hold them for higher prices. Until 1931, it did keep agricultural prices above the world level. Then world prices plummeted, the board's funds ran out, and there was no period of higher prices in which the cooperatives could sell their stored commodities.

The Hawley-Smoot Tariff

This law, passed in June 1930, raised duties on both agricultural and manufactured imports. It did nothing of significance to improve the economy, and historians argue over whether it contributed to the spread of the international depression.

Voluntarism

Hoover believed that voluntary cooperation would enable the country to weather the depression. He held meetings with business leaders at which he urged them to avoid layoffs of workers and wage cuts, and secured no-strike pledges from labor leaders. He urged all citizens to contribute to charities to help alleviate the suffering. While people were generous, private charity could not begin to meet the needs.

Public Works

In 1930, Congress appropriated $750 million for public buildings, river and harbor improvements, and highway construction in an effort to stimulate employment.

The Reconstruction Finance Corporation

Chartered by Congress in 1932, the RFC had an appropriation of $500 million, and authority to borrow $1.5 billion for loans to railroads, banks, and other financial institutions. It prevented the failure of basic firms, on which many other elements of the economy depended, but was criticized by some as relief for the rich.

The Federal Home Loan Bank Act

This law, passed in July 1932, created home-loan banks, with a capital of $125 million, to make loans to building and loan associations, savings banks, and insurance companies to help them avoid foreclosures on homes.

Relief

Hoover staunchly opposed the use of federal funds for relief for the needy. In

July 1932, he vetoed a bill that would have appropriated funds for relief. He compromised by approving legislation authorizing the RFC to lend $300 million to the states for relief, and to make loans to states and cities for self-liquidating public works.

The Bonus Army

The Bonus Expeditionary Force, which took its name from the American Expeditionary Force of World War I, was a group of about 14,000 unemployed veterans who went to Washington in the summer of 1932 to lobby Congress for immediate payment of the bonus that had been approved in 1926 for payment in 1945. At Hoover's insistence, the Senate did not pass the bonus bill, and about half of the BEF accepted a congressional offer of transportation home. The remaining five or six thousand, many with wives and children, continued to live in shanties along the Anacostia River and to lobby for their cause. After two veterans were killed in a clash with the police, Hoover, calling them insurrectionists and Communists, ordered the army to remove them. On July 28, 1932, General Douglas MacArthur, the army chief of staff, assisted by majors Dwight D. Eisenhower (1890–1969) and George S. Patton (1885–1945), personally commanded the removal operation. With machine guns, tanks, cavalry, infantry with fixed bayonets, and tear gas, MacArthur drove the veterans from Washington and burned their camp.

The Farm Holiday Association

Centered in Iowa, the association, headed by Milo Reno and others, called a farm strike in August 1932. They urged farmers not to take their products to market in an effort to raise farm prices. The picketing of markets led to violence, and the strike collapsed.

THE ELECTION OF 1932

The Republicans

At the convention in Chicago, Hoover was nominated on the first ballot. The platform called for a continuation of his depression policies.

The Democrats

Franklin D. Roosevelt (1882–1945), the popular governor of New York, gained the support of many southern and western delegates. House Speaker John Nance Garner (1868–1967) (Texas) became the vice-presidential candidate. Roosevelt took the unprecedented step of flying to the convention to accept the nomination in person, declaring that he pledged a "new deal" for the American people. The platform called for the repeal of prohibition, government aid for the unemployed, and a 25 percent cut in government spending.

The Election

Roosevelt received 22,809,638 votes, for 57.3 percent of the total, and 472 electoral votes. Hoover had 15,758,901 votes and 59 electoral votes. Despite the hard times, Norman Thomas (1884–1968), the Socialist candidate, received only 881,951 votes. The Democrats also captured the Senate and increased their majority in the House.

THE FIRST NEW DEAL

Franklin D. Roosevelt

The heir of a wealthy family and a fifth cousin of Theodore Roosevelt, Franklin was born in 1882 on the family estate at Hyde Park, New York, graduated from Harvard and Columbia Law School, married his distant cousin Anna Eleanor Roosevelt (1884–1962) in 1905, and practiced law in New York City. He entered state politics, then served as assistant secretary of the navy under Wilson, and was the Democratic vice-presidential candidate in 1920. In 1921, he suffered an attack of polio which left him paralyzed for several years and on crutches or in a wheelchair for the rest of his life. In 1928, he was elected governor of New York to succeed Al Smith. He was reelected in 1930. As governor, his depression programs for the unemployed, public works, aid to farmers, and conservation attracted national attention.

The Cabinet

Important cabinet appointments included Senator Cordell Hull (1871–1955) of Tennessee as secretary of state; Henry A. Wallace (1888–1960) as secretary of agriculture; Harold L. Ickes (1874–1952) as secretary of the interior; Frances Perkins (1882–1965), a New York social worker, as secretary of labor (the first woman appointed to a cabinet post); and James A. Farley (1888–1976), Roosevelt's political manager, as postmaster general.

The Brain Trust

Roosevelt's inner circle of unofficial advisers, first assembled during the campaign, was more influential than the cabinet. Prominent in it were agricultural economist Rexford G. Tugwell, political scientist Raymond Moley, lawyer Adolph A. Berle, Jr., the originators of the McNary-Haugen Bill—Hugh S. Johnson and George Peek—and Roosevelt's personal political advisor, Louis Howe.

The New Deal Program

Roosevelt did not have a developed plan of action when he took office. He intended to experiment and to find what worked. As a result, many programs overlapped or contradicted others and were changed or dropped if they did not work.

Repeal of Prohibition

In February 1933, before Roosevelt took office, Congress passed the 21st Amendment to repeal prohibition, and sent it to the states. In March, the new Congress legalized light beer. The amendment was ratified by the states and took effect in December 1933.

The Banking Crisis

In February 1933, as the inauguration approached, a severe banking crisis developed. Banks could not collect their loans or meet the demands of their depositors for withdrawals and runs occurred on many banks. Eventually banks in 38 states were closed by the state governments, and the remainder were open for only limited operations. An additional 5,190 banks failed in 1933, bringing the depression total to 10,951.

The Inaugural Address

When Roosevelt was inaugurated on March 4, 1933, the American economic system seemed to be on the verge of collapse. Roosevelt assured the nation that "the only thing we have to fear is fear itself," called for a special session of Congress to convene on March 9, and asked for "broad executive powers to wage war against the emergency." Two days later, he closed all banks and forbade the export of gold or the redemption of currency in gold.

LEGISLATION OF THE FIRST NEW DEAL

The Hundred Days and the First New Deal

The special session of Congress, from March 9 to June 16, 1933, passed a great body of legislation which has left a lasting mark on the nation. The period has been referred to ever since as the "Hundred Days." Historians have divided Roosevelt's legislation into the First New Deal (1933–1935), and a new wave of programs beginning in 1935 called the Second New Deal.

Economic Legislation of the Hundred Days

The Emergency Banking Relief Act was passed on March 9, the first day of the special session. The law provided additional funds for banks from the RFC and the Federal Reserve, allowed the Treasury to open sound banks after 10 days and to merge or liquidate unsound ones, and forbade the hoarding or export of gold. Roosevelt on March 12 assured the public of the soundness of the banks in the first of many "fireside chats," or radio addresses. People believed him, and most banks were soon open with more deposits than withdrawals.

The Banking Act of 1933, or the Glass-Steagall Act, established the Federal Deposit Insurance Corporation (FDIC) to insure individual deposits in commercial banks, and separated commercial banking from the more speculative activity of investment banking.

The Truth-in-Securities Act required that full information about stocks and bonds be provided by brokers and others to potential purchasers.

The Home Owners Loan Corporation (HOLC) had authority to borrow money to refinance home mortgages and thus prevent foreclosures. Eventually it lent more than three billion dollars to more than one million home owners.

Gold was taken out of circulation following the president's order of March 6, and the nation went off the gold standard. Eventually, on January 31, 1934, the value of the dollar was set at $35 per ounce of gold, 59 percent of its former value. The object of the devaluation was to raise prices and help American exports.

Later Economic Legislation of the First New Deal

The Securities and Exchange Commission was created in 1934 to supervise stock exchanges and to punish fraud in securities trading.

The Federal Housing Administration (FHA) was created by Congress in 1934 to insure long-term, low-interest mortgages for home construction and repair.

Relief and Employment Programs of the Hundred Days

These programs, intended to provide temporary relief for people in need, were to be disbanded when the economy improved.

The Federal Emergency Relief Act appropriated $500 million for aid to the poor to be distributed by state and local governments. It also established the Federal Emergency Relief Administration under Harry Hopkins (1890–1946).

The Civilian Conservation Corps enrolled 250,000 young men aged 18 to 24 from families on relief to go to camps where they worked on flood control, soil conservation, and forest projects under the direction of the War Department. A small monthly payment was made to the family of each member. By the end of the decade, 2.75 million young men had served in the corps.

The Public Works Administration, under Secretary of the Interior Harold Ickes, had $3.3 billion to distribute to state and local governments for building projects such as schools, highways, and hospitals. The object was to "prime the pump" of the economy by creating construction jobs. Additional money was appropriated later.

Later Relief Efforts

In November 1933, Roosevelt established the Civil Works Administration to hire four million unemployed workers. The temporary and makeshift nature of the jobs, such as sweeping streets, brought much criticism, and the experiment was terminated in April 1934.

Agricultural Programs of the Hundred Days

The Agricultural Adjustment Act of 1933 created the Agricultural Adjustment Administration (AAA), headed by George Peek. It sought to return farm prices to parity with those of the 1909 to 1914 period. Farmers agreed to reduce production of principal farm commodities and were paid a subsidy in return. The money came from a tax on the processing of the commodities. Farm prices increased, but tenants and sharecroppers were hurt when owners took land out of cultivation. The law was repealed in January 1936 on the grounds that the processing tax was not constitutional.

The Federal Farm Loan Act consolidated all farm credit programs into the Farm Credit Administration to make low-interest loans for farm mortgages and other agricultural purposes.

Later Agricultural Programs

The Commodity Credit Corporation was established in October 1933 by the AAA to make loans to corn and cotton farmers against their crops so that they could hold them for higher prices.

The Frazier-Lemke Farm Bankruptcy Act of 1934 allowed farmers to defer foreclosure on their land while they obtained new financing, and helped them to recover property already lost through easy financing.

The National Industrial Recovery Act

This law, passed on June 16, 1933, the last day of the Hundred Days, was viewed as the cornerstone of the recovery program. It sought to stabilize the economy by preventing extreme competition, labor-management conflicts, and overproduction. A board composed of industrial and labor leaders in each industry or business drew up a code for that industry which set minimum prices, minimum wages, maximum work hours, production limits, and quotas. The antitrust laws were temporarily suspended. The approach was based on the idea of many economists at the time that a mature industrial economy produced more goods than could be consumed, and that it would be necessary to create a relative shortage of goods in order to raise prices and restore prosperity. The idea was proved wrong by the expansion of consumer goods after World War II. Section 7a of the law also provided that workers had the right to join unions and to bargain collectively. The National Recovery Administration (NRA) was created under the leadership of Hugh S. Johnson to enforce the law and generate public enthusiasm for it. In May 1935, the law was declared unconstitutional in the case of *Schechter v. United States* on the grounds that Congress had delegated legislative authority to the code-makers, and that Schechter, who slaughtered chickens in New York, was not engaged in interstate commerce. It was argued later that the NRA had unintentionally aided big firms to the detriment of smaller ones because the representatives of the larger firms tended to dominate the code-making process. It was generally unsuccessful in stabilizing small businesses such as retail stores, and was on the point of collapse when it was declared unconstitutional.

The Tennessee Valley Authority

The TVA, a public corporation under a three-member board, was proposed by Roosevelt as the first major experiment in regional public planning. Starting from the nucleus of the government's Muscle Shoals property on the Tennessee River, the TVA built 20 dams in an area of 40,000 square miles to stop flooding and soil erosion, improve navigation, and generate hydroelectric power. It also manufactured nitrates for fertilizer, conducted demonstration projects for farmers, engaged in reforestation, and attempted to rehabilitate the whole area. It was fought unsuccessfully in the courts by private power companies. Roosevelt believed that it would serve as a yardstick to measure the true cost of providing electric power.

Effects of the First New Deal (1933–1935)

The economy improved but did not recover. The GNP, money supply, salaries, wages, and farm income rose. Unemployment dropped from about 25 percent of nonfarm workers in 1933 to about 20.1 percent, or 10.6 million, in 1935. But it was a long way from the 3.2 percent of predepression 1929, and suffering as a result of unemployment was still a major problem.

THE SECOND NEW DEAL: OPPOSITION FROM THE RIGHT AND LEFT

Criticism of the New Deal

Conservatives and businessmen frequently charged that the New Deal was socialist or communist in form, and some conservative writers labeled the wealthy Roosevelt "a traitor to his class." People on the lower end of the economic scale thought that the New Deal, especially the NRA, was too favorable to big business. The elderly thought that nothing had been done to help them. Several million people who were or had been tenant farmers or sharecroppers were badly hurt. Several opposition organizations and persons actively opposed Roosevelt's policies.

The American Liberty League was formed in 1934 by conservatives to defend business interests and promote the open shop. While many of its members were Republicans, and it was financed primarily by the Du Pont family, it also attracted conservative Democrats like Alfred E. Smith and John W. Davis. It supported conservative congressional candidates of both parties in the election of 1934, but with little success.

The Old Age Revolving Pension Plan was advanced by Dr. Francis E. Townsend (1867–1960), a retired California physician. The plan proposed that every retired person over 60 receive a pension of $200 a month, about double the average worker's salary, with the requirement that the money be spent within the month. The plan would be funded by a national gross sales tax. Some three to five million older Americans joined Townsend Clubs.

The Share Our Wealth Society was founded in 1934 by Senator Huey "The Kingfish" Long (1893–1935) of Louisiana. Long was a populist demagogue who was elected governor of Louisiana in 1928, established a practical dictatorship over the state, and moved to the United States Senate in 1930. He supported Roosevelt in 1932, but then broke with him, calling him a tool of Wall Street for not doing more to combat the depression. Long called for the confiscation of all fortunes over five million dollars and a tax of one hundred percent on annual incomes over one million. With the money, the government would provide subsidies so that every family would have a "homestead" of house, car, and furnishings, a minimum annual income of $2,000, and free college education for those who wanted it. His slogan was "Every Man a King." Long talked of running for president in 1936, and published a book entitled *My First Days in the White House.* His society had more than five million members when he was assassinated on the steps of the Louisiana Capitol on September 8, 1935. The Reverend Gerald L. K. Smith appointed himself Long's successor as head of the society, but he lacked Long's ability.

The National Union for Social Justice was headed by Father Charles E. Coughlin, a Catholic priest in Royal Oak, Michigan, who had a weekly radio program. Beginning as a religious broadcaster, in 1926, Coughlin later turned to politics and finance, attracting an audience of millions of many faiths. He supported Roosevelt in 1932, but then turned against him. He advocated an inflationary currency and was anti-Semitic, but beyond that his fascist-like program was not clearly defined.

THE SECOND NEW DEAL BEGINS

Roosevelt's Position

With millions of Democratic voters under the sway of Townsend, Long, and Coughlin, with the destruction of the NRA by the Supreme Court imminent, and with the election of 1936 approaching, Roosevelt began to push through a series of new programs in the spring of 1935. Much of the legislation was passed during the summer of 1935, a period sometimes called the Second Hundred Days.

Legislation and Programs of the Second New Deal

The Works Progress Administration (WPA) was started in May 1935, following the passage of the Emergency Relief Appropriations Act of April 1935. Headed by Harry Hopkins, the WPA employed people from the relief rolls for 30 hours of work a week at pay double the relief payment but less than private employment. There was not enough money to hire all of the unemployed, and the numbers varied from time to time, but an average of 2.1 million people per month were employed. By the end of the program in 1941, 8.5 million people had worked at some time for the WPA, at a total cost of $11.4 billion. Most of the projects undertaken were in construction. The WPA built hundreds of thousands of miles of streets and roads, and thousands of schools, hospitals, parks, airports, playgrounds, and other facilities. Hand work was emphasized so that the money would go for pay rather than equipment, provoking much criticism for inefficiency. Unemployed artists painted murals in public buildings; actors, musicians, and dancers performed in poor neighborhoods; and writers compiled guidebooks and local histories.

The National Youth Administration (NYA) was established as part of the WPA in June 1935, to provide part-time jobs for high school and college students to enable them to stay in school, and to help young adults not in school to find jobs.

The Rural Electrification Administration (REA) was created in May 1935, to provide loans and WPA labor to electric cooperatives so they could build lines into rural areas not served by private companies.

The Resettlement Administration (RA) was created in the Agriculture Department in May 1935 under Rexford Tugwell. It relocated destitute families from seemingly hopeless situations to new rural homestead communities or to suburban greenbelt towns.

The National Labor Relations or Wagner Act was passed in May 1935 to replace the provisions of Section 7a of the NIRA. It reaffirmed labor's right to unionize, prohibited unfair labor practices, and created the National Labor Relations Board (NLRB) to oversee and ensure fairness in labor-management relations.

The Social Security Act was passed in August 1935. It established a retirement plan for persons over age 65, which was to be funded by a tax on wages paid equally by employee and employer. The first benefits, ranging from $10 to $85 per month, were paid in 1942. Another provision of the act had the effect of forcing the states to initiate unemployment insurance programs. It imposed a payroll tax on employers which went to the state if it had an insurance program, and to the federal government if it did not. The act also provided matching funds to the states for aid to the blind, handicapped, and dependent children, and for public health services. The American Social Security system was limited compared to those of other industrialized nations, and millions of workers were not covered by it. Nonetheless, it marked a major change in American policy.

The Banking Act of 1935 created a strong central Board of Governors of the Federal Reserve system with broad powers over the operations of the regional banks.

The Public Utility Holding Company or Wheeler-Rayburn Act of 1935 empowered the Securities and Exchange Commission to restrict public-utility holding companies to one natural region and to eliminate duplicate holding companies. The Federal Power Commission was created to regulate interstate electrical power rates and activities, and the Federal Trade Commission received the same kind of power over the natural gas companies.

The Revenue Act of 1935 increased income taxes on higher incomes, and also inheritance, large gift, and capital gains taxes.

The Motor Carrier Act of 1935 extended the regulatory authority of the Interstate Commerce Commission to cover interstate trucking lines.

THE ELECTION OF 1936

The Democrats

At the convention in Philadelphia in June, Roosevelt and Garner were renominated by acclamation on the first ballot. The convention also ended the requirement of a two-thirds vote for nomination. The platform promised an expanded farm program, labor legislation, more rural electrification and public housing, and enforcement of the antitrust laws. In his acceptance speech, Roosevelt declared that "this generation of Americans has a rendezvous with destiny."

The Republicans

Governor Alfred M. Landon (1887–1987) of Kansas, a former progressive supporter of Theodore Roosevelt, was nominated on the first ballot at the convention in Cleveland in June. Frank Knox, a Chicago newspaper publisher, was chosen as his running mate. The platform criticized the New Deal for operating under unconstitutional laws, and called for a balanced budget, higher tariffs, and lower corporate taxes. It did not call for the repeal of all New Deal legislation, and promised better and less expensive relief, farm, and labor programs. In effect, Landon and the Republicans were saying that they would do the same thing, but do it better.

The Union Party

Dr. Francis Townsend, Father Charles Coughlin, and the Reverend Gerald L. K. Smith, Huey Long's successor in the Share Our Wealth Society, organized the

Union party to oppose Roosevelt. The nominee was Congressman William Lemke of North Dakota, an advocate of radical farm legislation. Vicious attacks by Smith and Coughlin on Roosevelt brought a backlash against them, and American Catholic leaders denounced Coughlin.

The Election

Roosevelt carried all of the states except Maine and Vermont with 27,757,333 votes, or 60.8 percent of the total, and 523 electoral votes. Landon received 16,684,231 votes and 8 electoral votes. Lemke had 891,858 votes for 1.9 percent of the total. Norman Thomas, the Socialist candidate, received 187,000 votes, only 21 percent of the 881,951 votes he received in 1932.

The New Deal Coalition

Roosevelt had put together a coalition of followers who made the Democratic party the majority party in the nation for the first time since the Civil War. While retaining the Democratic base in the South and among white ethnics in the big cities, Roosevelt also received strong support from midwestern farmers. Two groups that made a dramatic shift into the Democratic ranks were union workers and African Americans. Unions took an active political role for the first time since 1924, providing both campaign funds and votes. African Americans had traditionally been Republican since emancipation, but by 1936 about three-fourths of the African American voters, who lived mainly in the northern cities, had shifted into the Democratic party.

THE LAST YEARS OF THE NEW DEAL

Court Packing

Frustrated by a conservative Supreme Court which had overturned much of his New Deal legislation, Roosevelt, after receiving his overwhelming mandate in the election of 1936, decided to curb the power of the court. In doing so, he overestimated his own political power. In February 1937, he proposed to Congress the Judicial Reorganization Bill, which would allow the president to name a new federal judge for each judge who did not retire by the age of $70^1/2$. The appointments would be limited to a maximum of 50, with no more than six added to the Supreme Court. At the time, six justices were over the proposed age limit. The president was astonished by the wave of opposition from Democrats and Republicans alike, but he uncharacteristically refused to compromise. In doing so, he not only lost the bill but control of the Democratic Congress, which he had dominated since 1933. Nonetheless, the Court changed its position, as Chief Justice Charles Evans Hughes and Justice Owen Roberts began to vote with the more liberal members. The National Labor Relations Act was upheld in March 1937, and the Social Security Act in April. In June, a conservative justice retired, and Roosevelt had the opportunity to make an appointment.

The Recession of 1937–1938

Most economic indicators rose sharply between 1935 and 1937. The gross national product had recovered to the 1930 level, and unemployment, if WPA workers were considered employed, had fallen to 9.2 percent. During the same period, there were huge federal deficits. Roosevelt decided that the recovery was sufficient to warrant a reduction in relief programs and a move toward a balanced budget. The budget for fiscal year 1938 was reduced from $8.5 billion to $6.8 billion, with the WPA experiencing the largest cut. During the winter of 1937–1938, the economy slipped rapidly and unemployment rose to 12.5 percent. In April 1938, Roosevelt requested and received from Congress an emergency appropriation of about $3 billion for the WPA, as well as increases for public works and other programs. In July 1938, the economy began to recover, and it regained the 1937 levels in 1939.

Legislation of the Late New Deal

The Bankhead-Jones Farm Tenancy Act, passed in July 1937, created the Farm Security Administration (FSA) to replace the Resettlement Administration. The FSA continued the homestead projects, and loaned money to farmers to purchase farms, lease land, and buy equipment. It also set up camps for migrant workers and established rural health care programs.

The National Housing or Wagner-Steagall Act, passed in September 1937, established the United States Housing Authority (USHA), which could borrow money to lend to local agencies for public housing projects.

The Second Agricultural Adjustment Act of February 1938 appropriated funds for soil conservation payments to farmers who would remove land from production. The law also empowered the Agriculture Department to impose market quotas to prevent surpluses in commodities if two-thirds of the farmers producing that commodity agreed.

The Fair Labor Standards Act, popularly called the minimum-wage law, was passed in June 1938. It provided for a minimum wage and a gradual reduction to a work week of 40 hours, with time and a half for overtime. Workers in small businesses and in public and nonprofit employment were not covered. The law also prohibited the shipment in interstate commerce of manufactured goods on which children under 16 had worked.

SOCIAL DIMENSIONS OF THE NEW DEAL ERA

African Americans and the New Deal

Unemployment for African Americans was much higher than for the general population, and before 1933 they were often excluded from state and local relief efforts. African Americans did benefit from many New Deal relief programs, but about 40 percent of African American workers were sharecroppers or tenants who suffered from the provisions of the first Agricultural Adjustment Act. Roosevelt seems to have given little thought to the special problems of African Americans, and he was afraid to endorse legislation such as an antilynching bill for fear of alienating the southern wing of the Democratic party. Eleanor Roosevelt and Harold Ickes strongly supported civil rights, and a "Black Cabinet" of advisors was assembled in the Interior Department. More African Americans were appointed to government positions by Roosevelt than ever before, but the number was still small. When government military contracts began to flow in 1941, A. Philip Randolph (1889– 1979), the president of the Brotherhood of Sleeping Car Porters, proposed a march on Washington to demand equal access to defense jobs. To forestall such an action, Roosevelt issued an executive order on June 25, 1941, establishing the Fair Employment Practices Committee to ensure consideration for minorities in defense employment.

Native Americans and the New Deal

John Collier, the commissioner of the Bureau of Indian Affairs, persuaded Congress to repeal the Dawes Act of 1887 by passing the Indian Reorganization Act of 1934. The law restored tribal ownership of lands, recognized tribal constitutions and government, and provided loans to tribes for economic development. Collier also secured the creation of the Indian Emergency Conservation Program, a Native American CCC for projects on the reservations. In addition, he helped Native Americans secure entry into the WPA, NYA, and other programs.

Mexican Americans and the New Deal

Mexican Americans benefited least from the New Deal, for few programs covered them. Farm owners turned against them as farm workers after they attempted to form a union between 1933 and 1936. By 1940, most had been replaced by whites. Many returned to Mexico, and the Mexican American population dropped almost 40 percent from 1930 to 1940.

Women During the New Deal

Wives and mothers found themselves responsible for stretching meager budgets by preparing inexpensive meals, patching old clothing, and the like. "Making do" became a slogan of the period. In addition, more women had to supplement or provide the family income by going to work. There was much criticism of working women based on the idea that they deprived men of jobs. Male job losses were greatest in heavy industry, while areas of female employment such as retail sales were not as hard hit. Unemployed men seldom sought jobs in the traditional women's fields.

LABOR UNIONS

Unions During the First New Deal

Labor unions lost members and influence during the 1920s and early 1930s. The National Industrial Recovery Act gave them new hope when it guaranteed the right to unionize, and during 1933 about 1.5 million new members joined unions. But enforcement of the industrial codes by the NRA was ineffective, and labor leaders began to call it the "National Run Around." As a result, in 1934, there were many strikes, sometimes violent ones.

Craft versus Industrial Unions

The passage of the National Labor Relations or Wagner Act in 1935 resulted in a massive growth of union membership, but at the expense of bitter conflict within the labor movement. The American Federation of Labor was made up primarily of craft unions. Some leaders, especially John L. Lewis, the dynamic president of the United Mine Workers, wanted to unionize the mass-production industries, such as automobiles and rubber, with industrial unions. In November 1935, Lewis and others established the Committee for Industrial Organization to unionize basic industries, presumably within the AFL. President William Green of the AFL ordered the CIO to disband in January 1936. When the rebels refused, they were expelled by the AFL executive council in March 1937. The insurgents then reorganized the CIO as the independent Congress of Industrial Organizations.

The Growth of the CIO

During its organizational period, the CIO sought to initiate several industrial unions, particularly in the steel, auto, rubber, and radio industries. In late 1936 and early 1937, it used a tactic called the sit-down strike, with the strikers occupying the workplace to prevent any production. There were 477 sit-down strikes involving about 400,000 workers. The largest was in the General Motors plant in Flint, Michigan, where the union sought recognition by that firm. In February 1937, General Motors recognized the United Auto Workers as the bargaining agent for its 400,000 workers. By the end of 1941, the CIO had about 5 million members, the AFL about 4.6 million, and other unions about one million. Union members comprised about 11.5 percent of the work force in 1933 and 28.2 percent in 1941.

CULTURAL TRENDS OF THE 1930s

Literary Developments

Some writers and intellectuals turned to communism, including the 53 writers who signed an open letter endorsing the Communist presidential candidate in 1932. Some turned to proletarian novels, such as Jack Conroy in *The Disinherited* (1933) and Robert Cantwell in *The Land of Plenty* (1934). Ernest Hemingway seemed to have lost his direction in *Winner Take All* (1933) and *The Green Hills of Africa* (1935), but in *To Have and Have Not* (1937), a strike novel, he turned to social realism, and in *For Whom the Bell Tolls* (1941) he expressed his concern about fascism. Sinclair Lewis also dealt with fascism in *It Can't Happen Here* (1935). John Dos Passos depicted what he saw as the disintegration of American life from 1900 to 1929 in his trilogy *U.S.A.* (1930–1936). William Faulkner (1897–1962) sought values in southern life in *Light in August* (1932), *Absalom! Absalom!* (1936), and *The Unvanquished* (1938). The endurance of the human spirit and personal survival were depicted in James T. Farrell's (1904–1979) trilogy *Studs Lonigan* (1936), about the struggles of lower-middle-class Irish Catholics in Chicago, Erskine Caldwell's

(1903–1987) *Tobacco Road* (1932), about impoverished Georgia sharecroppers, and John Steinbeck's (1902–1968) *The Grapes of Wrath* (1939), about "Okies" migrating from the dust bowl to California in the midst of the depression.

Popular Culture

The depression greatly reduced the amount of money available for recreation and entertainment. The WPA and the CCC constructed thousands of public recreation areas. Roosevelt and Harry Hopkins, the director of the WPA, hoped to develop a mass appreciation of culture through murals in public buildings, traveling plays, concerts, and exhibits, and community arts centers. Beyond some revival of handicrafts, it is doubtful that the program had much effect.

While radio was the form of entertainment most used, the movies were the most popular. The movie industry was one of the few industries that did not suffer financially from the depression. Movies were the great means of escape. Spectacular musicals with dozens of dancers and singers, such as *Broadway Melody of 1936*, were popular. The dance team of Fred Astaire and Ginger Rogers thrilled millions in *Flying Down to Rio* and *Shall We Dance?* Shirley Temple charmed the public as their favorite child star. Judy Garland rose to stardom in *The Wizard of Oz*, while animated films like *Snow White* appealed to children of all ages. People enjoyed the triumph of justice and decency in *Mr. Smith Goes to Washington* and *You Can't Take It With You* with Jimmy Stewart. Dozens of light comedies starred such favorites as Cary Grant, Katharine Hepburn, Clark Gable, and Rosalind Russell, while Errol Flynn played such larger-than-life roles as Robin Hood. A different kind of escape was found in gangster movies, with Edward G. Robinson, James Cagney, or George Raft. *Gone With the Wind*, released in 1939 starring Clark Gable and Vivien Leigh, was destined to become a timeless classic, while *The Grapes of Wrath* in 1940 commented on the depression itself.

The popular music of the decade was swing, and the big bands of Duke Ellington, Benny Goodman, Glenn Miller, Tommy Dorsey, and Harry James vied for public favor. The leading popular singer was Bing Crosby. City blacks refined the country blues to city blues, and interracial audiences enjoyed both city blues and jazz. Black musicians were increasingly accepted by white audiences.

Comic strips became a standard newspaper feature and a source of comic books.

NEW DEAL DIPLOMACY AND THE ROAD TO WAR

The Good Neighbor Policy

Roosevelt and Secretary of State Cordell Hull continued the policies of their predecessors by endeavoring to improve relations with Latin American nations, and formalized their position by calling it the Good Neighbor Policy.

Nonintervention

At the Montevideo Conference of American Nations in December of 1933, the United States renounced the right of intervention in the internal affairs of Latin American countries. In 1936, in the Buenos Aires Convention, the United States agreed to submit all American disputes to arbitration. The marines were removed from Haiti, Nicaragua, and the Dominican Republic by 1934. The Haitian protectorate treaty was allowed to expire in 1936, the right of intervention in Panama was ended by treaty in 1936, and the receivership of the finances of the Dominican Republic ended in 1941.

Cuba

The United States did not intervene in the Cuban revolution in the spring of 1933, but it did back a coup by Fulgencio Batista to overthrow the liberal regime of Ramon Grau San Martin in 1934.

The London Economic Conference

An international conference was held in London in June 1933 to obtain tariff reduction and currency stabilization for the industrialized nations. It failed for lack of American cooperation.

Recognition of the USSR

In an effort to open trade with the Soviets, mutual recognition was negotiated in November 1933. The financial results were disappointing.

Philippine Independence

The Tydings-McDuffie Act of March 1934 forced the Philippines to become independent on July 4, 1946, rather than granting the dominion status which the Filipinos had requested.

The Reciprocal Trade Agreement Act

This law allowed the president to negotiate agreements which could vary from the rates of the Hawley-Smoot Tariff by up to 50 percent. By 1936, lower rates had been negotiated with 13 nations, and by 1941, almost two-thirds of all American foreign trade was covered by agreements.

UNITED STATES NEUTRALITY LEGISLATION

Isolationism

Belief that the United States should stay out of foreign wars and problems began in the 1920s and grew in the 1930s. Examinations of World War I profiteering and revisionist history that asserted Germany had not been responsible for World War I and that the United States had been misled were also influential during the 1930s. A Gallup poll in April 1937 showed that almost two-thirds of those responding thought that American entry into World War I had been a mistake. Leading isolationists included Congressman Hamilton Fish (1888–1946) of New York, Senator William Borah (1865–1940) of Idaho, and Senator George Norris (1861–1944) of Nebraska, all Republicans. Pacifist movements, such as the Fellowship of Christian Reconciliation, were influential among college and high school students and the clergy.

The Johnson Act of 1934

This law prohibited any nation in default on World War I payments from selling securities to any American citizen or corporation.

The Neutrality Acts of 1935

On outbreak of war between foreign nations, all exports of American arms and munitions to them would be embargoed for six months. In addition, American ships were prohibited from carrying arms to any belligerent, and the president was to warn American citizens not to travel on belligerent ships.

The Neutrality Acts of 1936

The laws gave the president authority to determine when a state of war existed, and prohibited any loans or credits to belligerents.

The Neutrality Acts of 1937

The laws gave the president authority to determine if a civil war was a threat to world peace and if it was covered by the Neutrality Acts. It also prohibited all arms sales to belligerents, and allowed the cash-and-carry sale of nonmilitary goods to belligerents.

THREATS TO WORLD ORDER

The United States looked on as Japan invaded Manchuria, Italy invaded Ethiopia, and Germany occupied the Rhineland.

The "Quarantine the Aggressor" Speech

In a speech in Chicago in October 1937, Roosevelt proposed that the democracies unite to quarantine aggressor nations, but when public opinion did not pick up the idea, he did not press the issue.

THE AMERICAN RESPONSE TO THE WAR IN EUROPE

Preparedness

Even before the outbreak of World War II, Roosevelt began a preparedness program to improve American defenses. Congress greatly increased defense appropriations. In August 1939, Roosevelt created the War Resources Board to develop a plan for industrial mobilization in the event of war. The next month, he established the Office of Emergency Management in the White House to centralize mobilization activities.

The Neutrality Act of 1939

Roosevelt officially proclaimed the neutrality of the United States on September 5, 1939. He then called Congress into special session on September 21 and urged it to allow the cash-and-carry sale of arms. Despite opposition from isolationists, the Democratic Congress, in a vote that followed party lines, passed a new Neutrality

Act in November. It allowed the cash-and-carry sale of arms and short-term loans to belligerents, but forbade American ships to trade with belligerents or Americans to travel on belligerent ships. The new law was helpful to the Allies because they controlled the Atlantic.

Changing American Attitudes

Almost all Americans recognized Germany as a threat. They divided on whether to aid Britain, or to concentrate on the defense of America. The Committee to Defend America by Aiding the Allies was formed in May 1940, and the America First Committee, which opposed involvement, was incorporated in September 1940.

In April 1940, Roosevelt declared that Greenland, a possession of conquered Denmark, was covered by the Monroe Doctrine, and he supplied military assistance to set up a coastal patrol there.

Defense Mobilization

In May 1940, Roosevelt appointed a Council of National Defense, chaired by William S. Knudson (1879–1948), the president of General Motors, to direct defense production and to build 50,000 planes. The Office of Production Management was created to allocate scarce materials, and the Office of Price Administration was established to prevent inflation and protect consumers. In June, Roosevelt made Republicans Henry L. Stimson (1867–1950) and Frank Kellogg (1856–1937) secretaries of war and navy, respectively, partly as an attempt to secure bipartisan support.

Selective Service

Congress approved the nation's first peacetime draft, the Selective Service and Training Act, in September 1940. Men 21 to 35 were registered, and many were called for one year of military training.

Destroyers for Bases

Roosevelt determined that to aid Britain in every way possible was the best way to avoid war with Germany. In September 1940, he signed an agreement to give Britain 50 American destroyers in return for a 99-year lease on air and naval bases in British territories in Newfoundland, Bermuda, and the Caribbean.

THE ELECTION OF 1940

The Republicans

Passing over their isolationist front-runners, Senator Robert A. Taft (1889–1953) of Ohio and New York attorney Thomas E. Dewey (1902–1971), the Republicans nominated Wendell L. Willkie (1892–1944) of Indiana, a dark-horse candidate. Willkie, a liberal Republican who had been a Democrat most of his life, was the head of an electric utility holding company which had fought against the TVA. The platform supported a strong defense program, but severely criticized New Deal domestic policies.

The Democrats

Roosevelt was nominated for a third term, breaking a tradition which had existed since George Washington. Only with difficulty did Roosevelt's managers persuade the delegates to accept his choice of vice president, Secretary of Agriculture Henry A. Wallace, to succeed Garner. The platform endorsed the foreign and domestic policies of the administration. Roosevelt told the public, "Your boys are not going to be sent to any foreign wars."

The Election

Roosevelt won by a much narrower margin than in 1936, with 27,243,466 votes, 54.7 percent, and 449 electoral votes. Willkie received 22,304,755 votes and 82 electoral votes. Socialist Norman Thomas had 100,264 votes, and Communist Earl Browder (1891–1973) received 48,579.

AMERICAN INVOLVEMENT WITH THE EUROPEAN WAR

The Lend-Lease Act

This let the United States provide supplies to Britain in exchange for goods and services after the war. It was signed on March 11, 1941. In effect, the law changed the United States from a neutral to a nonbelligerent on the Allied side.

The Patrol of the Western Atlantic

In April 1941, Roosevelt started the American Neutrality Patrol. The American navy would search out but not attack German submarines in the western half of the Atlantic and warn British vessels of their location. Also in April, U.S. forces occupied Greenland, and in May, the president declared a state of unlimited national emergency.

American marines occupied Iceland, a Danish possession, in July 1941 to protect it from seizure by Germany. The American navy began to convoy American and Icelandic ships between the United States and Iceland.

On August 9, 1941 Roosevelt and Winston Churchill issued the Atlantic Charter.

Germany invaded Russia in June 1941, and in November the United States extended lend-lease assistance to the Russians.

The Shoot-on-Sight Order

The American destroyer *Greer* was attacked by a German submarine near Iceland on September 4, 1941. Roosevelt ordered the American military forces to shoot on sight any German or Italian vessel in the patrol zone. An undeclared naval war had begun. The American destroyer *Kearny* was attacked by a submarine on October 16, and the destroyer *Reuben James* was sunk on October 30, with 115 lives lost. In November, Congress authorized the arming of merchant ships.

THE ROAD TO PEARL HARBOR

The Embargo of 1940

To halt Japanese expansion in Asia, the Vichy government granted the Japanese government the right to build military bases and station troops in French Indochina. In late July, the United States placed an embargo on the export of aviation gasoline, lubricants, and scrap iron and steel to Japan, and granted an additional loan to China. In December, the embargo was extended to include iron ore and pig iron, some chemicals, machine tools, and other products.

The Embargo of 1941

In July 1941, Japan obtained military control of southern Indochina. Roosevelt reacted by freezing Japanese funds in the United States, closing the Panama Canal to Japan, activating the Philippine militia, and placing an embargo on the export of oil and other vital products to Japan.

Japanese-American Negotiations

Negotiations to end the impasse between the United States and Japan were conducted in Washington between Secretary Hull and Japanese Ambassador Kichisaburo Nomura. Hull demanded that Japan withdraw from Indochina and China, promise not to attack any other area in the western Pacific, and withdraw from its pact with Italy and Germany in return for the reopening of American trade. The Japanese offered to withdraw from Indochina when the Chinese war was satisfactorily settled, to promise no further expansion, and to agree to ignore any obligation under the Tripartite Pact to go to war if the United States entered a defensive war with Germany. Hull refused to compromise.

A Summit Conference Proposed

The Japanese proposed in August 1941 that Roosevelt meet personally with the Japanese prime minister, Prince Konoye, in an effort to resolve their differences. Such an action might have strengthened the position of Japanese moderates, but Roosevelt replied in September that he would do so only if Japan agreed to leave China. No meeting was held.

Final Negotiations

In October 1941, a new military cabinet headed by General Hideki Tojo took control of Japan. The Japanese secretly decided to make a final effort to negotiate, and to go to war if no solution was found by November 25. A new round of talks followed in Washington, but neither side would make a substantive change in its position, and on November 26, Hull repeated the American demand that the Japanese remove all their forces from China and Indochina immediately. The Japanese gave final approval on December 1 for an attack on the United States.

Japanese Attack Plans

The Japanese planned a major offensive to take the Dutch East Indies, Malaya, and the Philippines in order to obtain the oil, metals, and other raw materials they needed. At the same time, they would attack Pearl Harbor in Hawaii to destroy the American Pacific fleet to keep it from interfering with their plans.

American Awareness of Japanese Plans

The United States had broken the Japanese diplomatic codes and knew that trouble was imminent. Between December 1 and December 6, 1941, it became clear to administration leaders that Japanese task forces were being ordered into battle. American commanders in the Pacific were warned of possible aggressive action there, but not forcefully. Apparently most American leaders thought that Japan would attack the Dutch East Indies and Malaya, but would avoid American territory so as not to provoke action by the United States. Some argue that Roosevelt wanted to let the Japanese attack so that the American people would be squarely behind the war.

The Pearl Harbor Attack

At 7:55 a.m. on Sunday, December 7, 1941, the first wave of Japanese carrier-based planes attacked the American fleet in Pearl Harbor. A second wave followed at 8:50 a.m. American defensive action was almost nil, but by the second wave a few anti-aircraft batteries were operating and a few army planes from another base in Hawaii engaged the enemy. The United States suffered the loss of two battleships sunk, six damaged and out of action, three cruisers and three destroyers sunk or damaged, and a number of lesser vessels destroyed or damaged. All of the 150 aircraft at Pearl Harbor were destroyed on the ground. Worst of all, 2,323 American servicemen were killed and about 1,100 wounded. The Japanese lost 29 planes, five midget submarines, and one fleet submarine.

19 WORLD WAR II AND THE POSTWAR ERA (1941–1960)

DECLARED WAR BEGINS

The Declaration of War

On December 8, 1941, Roosevelt told a joint session of Congress that the day before had been a "date that would live in infamy." Congress declared war on Japan, with one dissenting vote. On December 11, Germany and Italy declared war on the United States. Great Britain and the United States then established the Combined Chiefs of Staff, headquartered in Washington, to direct Anglo-American military operations.

Declaration of the United Nations

On January 1, 1942, representatives of 26 nations met in Washington, D.C., and signed the Declaration of the United Nations, pledging themselves to the principles of the Atlantic Charter and promising not to make a separate peace with their common enemies.

THE HOME FRONT

War Production Board

The WPD was established in 1942 by President Franklin D. Roosevelt for the purpose of regulating the use of raw materials.

Wage and Price Controls

In April 1942, the General Maximum Price Regulation Act froze prices and extended rationing. In April 1943, prices, wages, and salaries were frozen.

Revenue Act of 1942

The Revenue Act of 1942 extended the income tax to the majority of the population. Payroll deduction for the income tax began in 1944.

Social Changes

Rural areas lost population, while population in coastal areas increased rapidly. Women entered the work force in increasing numbers. African Americans moved from the rural South to northern and western cities, with racial tensions often resulting, most notably in the June 1943 racial riot in Detroit.

Smith-Connolly Act

Passed in 1943, the Smith-Connolly Antistrike Act authorized government seizure of a plant or mine idled by a strike if the war effort was impeded. It expired in 1947.

Korematsu v. United States

In 1944, the Supreme Court upheld President Roosevelt's 1942 order that Issei (Japanese Americans who had emigrated from Japan) and Nisei (native born Japanese Americans) be relocated to concentration camps. The camps were closed in March 1946.

Smith v. Allwright

In 1944, the Supreme Court struck down the Texas primary elections, which were restricted to whites, for violating the 15th Amendment.

Presidential Election of 1944

President Franklin D. Roosevelt, together with new vice-presidential candidate Harry S. Truman (1884–1972) of Missouri, defeated his Republican opponent, Governor Thomas E. Dewey of New York.

Death of Roosevelt

Roosevelt died on April 12, 1945, at Warm Springs, Georgia. Harry S. Truman became president.

THE NORTH AFRICAN AND EUROPEAN THEATRES

Nearly 400 ships were lost in American waters of the Atlantic to German submarines between January and June 1942.

The United States joined in the bombing of the European continent in July 1942. Bombing increased during 1943 and 1944 and lasted to the end of the war.

The Allied army under Dwight D. Eisenhower attacked French North Africa in November 1942. The Vichy French forces surrendered.

In the Battle of Kassarine Pass, February 1943, North Africa, the Allied army met General Erwin Rommel's Africa Korps. Although the battle is variously interpreted as a standoff or a defeat for the United States, Rommel's forces were soon trapped by the British moving in from Egypt. In May 1943, Rommel's Africa Korps surrendered.

Allied armies under George C. Patton (1885–1945) invaded Sicily from Africa in July 1943, and gained control by mid-August. Moving from Sicily, the Allied armies invaded the Italian mainland in September. Benito Mussolini had already fallen from power, and his successor, Marshal Pietro Badoglio, surrendered. The Germans, however, put up a stiff resistance, with the result that Rome did not fall until June 1944.

In March 1944, the Soviet Union began pushing into eastern Europe.

On "D-Day," June 6, 1944, Allied armies under Dwight D. Eisenhower, now commander in chief of the Allied Expeditionary Forces, began an invasion of Normandy, France. Allied armies under General Omar Bradley (1893–1981) took the transportation hub of St. Lo, France, in July.

Allied armies liberated Paris in August. By mid-September, they had arrived at the Rhine, on the edge of Germany.

Beginning December 16, 1944, at the Battle of the Bulge, the Germans counterattacked, driving the Allies back about fifty miles into Belgium. By January, the Allies were once more advancing toward Germany. The Allies crossed the Rhine in March 1945. In the last week of April, Eisenhower's forces met the Soviet army at the Elbe. On May 7, 1945, Germany surrendered.

THE PACIFIC THEATRE

By the end of December 1941, Guam, Wake Island, the Gilbert Islands, and Hong Kong had fallen to the Japanese. In January 1942, Raboul, New Britain, fell, followed in February by Singapore and Java, and in March by Rangoon, Burma.

The U.S. air raids on Tokyo in April 1942 were militarily inconsequential, but they raised Allied morale.

U.S. forces surrendered at Corregidor, Philippines, on May 6, 1942.

In the Battle of the Coral Sea, May 7–8, 1942 (northeast of Australia, south of New Guinea and the Solomon Islands), planes from the American carriers *Lexington* and *Yorktown* forced Japanese troop transports to turn back from attacking Port Moresby. The battle stopped the Japanese advance on Australia.

At the Battle of Midway, June 4–7, 1942, American air power destroyed four Japanese carriers and about 300 planes. The United States lost the carrier *Yorktown* and one destroyer. The battle proved to be the turning point in the Pacific.

A series of land, sea, and air battles took place around Guadalcanal in the Solomon Islands from August 1942 to February 1943, stopping the Japanese.

The Allied strategy of island hopping, begun in 1943, sought to neutralize Japanese strongholds with air and sea power and then move on. General Douglas MacArthur commanded the land forces moving from New Guinea toward the Philippines, while Admiral Chester W. Nimitz directed the naval attack on important Japanese islands in the central Pacific.

U.S. forces advanced into the Gilberts (November 1943), the Marshalls (January 1944), and the Marianas (June 1944).

In the Battle of the Philippine Sea, June 19–20, 1944, the Japanese lost three carriers, two submarines, and more than 300 planes, while the Americans lost 17 planes. After the American capture of the Marianas, General Tojo resigned as premier of Japan.

The Battle of Leyte Gulf, October 25, 1944, involved three major engagements which resulted in Japan's loss of most of its remaining naval power. It also brought the first use of the Japanese kamikaze or suicide attacks by Japanese pilots who crashed into American carriers.

Forces under General Douglas MacArthur (1880–1964) liberated Manila in March 1945.

Between April and June 1945, in the battle for Okinawa, nearly 50,000 American casualties resulted from the fierce fighting, but the battle virtually destroyed Japan's remaining defenses.

THE ATOMIC BOMB

The Manhattan Engineering District was established by the army engineers in August 1942 for the purpose of developing an atomic bomb (it eventually became known as the Manhattan Project). J. Robert Oppenheimer directed the design and construction of a transportable atomic bomb at Los Alamos, New Mexico.

On December 2, 1942, Enrico Fermi (1901–1954) and his colleagues at the University of Chicago produced the first atomic chain reaction.

On July 16, 1945, the first atomic bomb was exploded at Alamogordo, New Mexico.

The *Enola Gay* dropped an atomic bomb on Hiroshima, Japan, on August 6, 1945, killing about 78,000 persons and injuring 100,000 more. On August 9, a second bomb was dropped on Nagasaki, Japan.

On August 8, 1945, the Soviet Union entered the war against Japan.

Japan surrendered on August 14, 1945. The formal surrender was signed on September 2.

DIPLOMACY

Casablanca Conference

On January 14–25, 1943, Franklin D. Roosevelt and Winston Churchill, prime minister of Great Britain, declared a policy of unconditional surrender for "all enemies."

Moscow Conference

In October 1943, Secretary of State Cordell Hull obtained Soviet agreement to enter the war against Japan after Germany was defeated, and to participate in a world organization after the war was over.

Declaration of Cairo

Issued on December 1, 1943, after Roosevelt met with General Chiang Kai-shek in Cairo from November 22 to 26, the Declaration of Cairo called for Japan's unconditional surrender and stated that all Chinese territories occupied by Japan would be returned to China and that Korea would be free and independent.

Teheran Conference

The first "Big Three" conference met at Casablanca in January 1943. They later met at Teheran, Yalta, and Potsdam.

THE EMERGENCE OF THE COLD WAR AND CONTAINMENT

Iron Curtain

In a speech in Fulton, Missouri, in 1946, Winston Churchill stated that an "Iron Curtain" had spread across Europe, separating the democratic from the authoritarian Communist states.

Containment

In 1946, career diplomat and Soviet expert George F. Kennan warned that the Soviet Union had no intention of living peacefully with the United States. The next year, in July 1947, he wrote an anonymous article for *Foreign Affairs* in which he called for a counterforce to Soviet pressures, for the purpose of "containing" communism.

Truman Doctrine

In February 1947, Great Britain notified the United States that it could no longer aid the Greek government in its war against Communist insurgents. The next month President Harry S. Truman asked Congress for $400 million in military and economic aid for Greece and Turkey. In what became known as the "Truman Doctrine," he argued that the United States must support free peoples who were resisting Communist domination.

Marshall Plan

Secretary of State George C. Marshall (1880–1959) proposed in June 1947 that the United States provide economic aid to help rebuild Europe. Meeting in July, representatives of the European nations agreed on a recovery program jointly financed by the United States and the European countries. The following March, Congress passed the European Recovery Program, popularly known as the Marshall Plan, which provided more than $12 billion in aid.

Berlin Crisis

After the United States, France, and Great Britain announced plans to create a West German Republic out of their German zones, the Soviet Union in June 1948 blocked surface access to Berlin. The United States then instituted an airlift to transport supplies to the city until the Soviets lifted their blockade in May 1949.

NATO

In April 1949, the North Atlantic Treaty Organization was signed by the United States, Great Britain, France, Italy, Belgium, the Netherlands, Luxembourg, Denmark, Norway, Portugal, Iceland, and Canada. The signatories pledged that an attack against one would be considered an attack against all. Greece and Turkey joined the alliance in 1952, and West Germany in 1954. The Soviets formed the Warsaw Treaty Organization in 1955 to counteract NATO.

NATO was strengthened by the Korean War.

Atomic Bomb

The Soviet Union exploded an atomic device in September 1949.

INTERNATIONAL COOPERATION

Bretton Woods, New Hampshire

Representatives from Europe and the United States, at a conference held July 1–22, 1944, signed agreements for an international bank and a world monetary fund to stabilize international currencies and rebuild the economies of war-torn nations.

At Yalta in February 1945, Roosevelt, Churchill, and Stalin called for a conference on world organization to meet in April 1945 in the United States.

United Nations

From April to June 1945, representatives from 50 countries met in San Francisco to establish the United Nations. The U.N. charter created a General Assembly composed of all member nations which would act as the ultimate policy-making body. A Security Council, made up of 11 members, including the United States, Great Britain, France, the Soviet Union, and China as permanent members and six additional nations elected by the General Assembly for two-year terms, would be responsible for settling disputes among U.N. member nations.

CONTAINMENT IN ASIA

Japan

General Douglas MacArthur headed a four-power Allied Control Council which governed Japan, allowing it to develop economically and politically.

China

Between 1945 and 1948, the United States gave more than $2 billion in aid to the Nationalist Chinese under Chiang Kai-shek, and sent George C. Marshall to settle the conflict between Chiang's Nationalists and Mao Tse-tung's Communists. In 1949, however, Mao defeated Chiang and forced the Nationalists to flee to Formosa (Taiwan). Mao established the People's Republic of China on the mainland.

Korean War

On June 25, 1950, North Korea invaded South Korea. President Truman committed U.S. forces commanded by General MacArthur, but under United Nations auspices. By October, the U.N. forces (mostly American) had driven north of the 38th parallel, which divided North and South Korea. Chinese troops attacked MacArthur's forces on November 26, pushing them south of the 38th parallel, but by spring 1951, the U.N. forces had recovered their offensive. MacArthur called for a naval blockade of China and bombing north of the Yalu River, criticizing the president for fighting a limited war. In April 1951, Truman removed MacArthur from command.

Armistice

Armistice talks began with North Korea in the summer of 1951. In June 1953, an armistice was signed, leaving Korea divided along virtually the same boundary that had existed prior to the war.

EISENHOWER-DULLES FOREIGN POLICY

John Foster Dulles

Dwight D. Eisenhower, elected president in 1952, chose John Foster Dulles (1888–1959) as secretary of state. Dulles talked of a more aggressive foreign policy, calling for "massive retaliation" and "liberation" rather than containment. He wished to emphasize nuclear deterrents rather than conventional armed forces. Dulles served as secretary of state until ill health forced him to resign in April 1959. Christian A. Herter (1895–1961) took his place.

Hydrogen Bomb

The United States exploded its first hydrogen bomb in November 1952. The Soviets followed in August 1953.

Soviet Change of Power

Josef Stalin died in March 1953. After an internal power struggle that lasted until 1955, Nikita Khrushchev emerged as the Soviet leader. He talked of both "burying" capitalism and "peaceful coexistence."

Asia

In 1954, the French asked the United States to commit air forces to rescue French forces at Dien Bien Phu, Vietnam, where they were being besieged by the nationalist forces led by Ho Chi Minh. Eisenhower refused. In May 1954, Dien Bien Phu surrendered.

Geneva Accords

France, Great Britain, the Soviet Union, and China signed the Geneva Accords in July 1954, dividing Vietnam along the 17th parallel. The North would be under Ho Chi Minh and the South under Emperor Bao Dai. Elections were scheduled for 1956 to unify the country, but Ngo Dinh Diem overthrew Bao Dai and prevented the elections from taking place. The United States supplied economic aid to South Vietnam.

Southeast Asia Treaty Organization

Dulles attempted to establish a Southeast Asia Treaty Organization parallel to NATO, but was able to obtain only the Philippine Republic, Thailand, and Pakistan as signatories in September 1954.

Quemoy and Matsu

The small islands of Quemoy and Matsu off the coast of China were occupied by the Nationalist Chinese under Chiang Kai-shek, but claimed by the People's Republic of China. In 1955, after the mainland Chinese began shelling these islands,

Eisenhower obtained authorization from Congress to defend Formosa (Taiwan) and related areas.

Eisenhower Doctrine

President Eisenhower announced in January 1957 that the United States was prepared to use armed force in the Middle East against Communist aggression. Under this doctrine, U.S. marines entered Beirut, Lebanon, in July 1958 to promote political stability during a change of governments. The marines left in October.

Summit Conference with the Soviet Union

In July 1955, President Eisenhower met in Geneva with Anthony Eden, prime minister of Great Britain, Edgar Faure, premier of France, and Nikita Khrushchev and Nikolai Bulganin, at the time coleaders of the Soviet Union. They discussed disarmament and reunification of Germany, but made no agreements.

Atomic Weapons Test Suspension

In October 1958, Eisenhower and Khrushchev voluntarily suspended atmospheric tests of atomic weapons.

Soviet-American Visitations

Vice President Richard M. Nixon visited the Soviet Union and Soviet Vice-Premier Anastas I. Mikoyan came to the United States in the summer of 1959. In September, Premier Khrushchev toured the United States and agreed to another summit meeting.

U-2 Incident

On May 1, 1960, an American U-2 spy plane was shot down over the Soviet Union, and pilot Francis Gary Powers was captured. Eisenhower ultimately took responsibility for the spy plane, but Khrushchev angrily called off the Paris summit conference which was to take place in a few days.

Latin America

The United States supported the overthrow of President Jacobo Arbenz Guzman of Guatemala in 1954 because he began accepting arms from the Soviet Union.

Vice President Nixon had to call off an eight-nation goodwill tour of Latin America after meeting hostile mobs in Venezuela and Peru in 1958.

In January 1959, Fidel Castro overthrew Fulgencio Batista, dictator of Cuba. Castro soon began criticizing the United States and moved closer to the Soviet Union, signing a trade agreement with the Soviets in February 1960. The United States prohibited the importation of Cuban sugar in October 1960, and broke off diplomatic relations in January 1961.

THE POLITICS OF AFFLUENCE: DEMOBILIZATION AND DOMESTIC POLICY

Truman Becomes President

Harry S. Truman, formerly a senator from Missouri and vice president of the United States, became president on April 12, 1945. In September 1945, he proposed a liberal legislative program, including expansion of unemployment insurance, extension of the Employment Service, a higher minimum wage, a permanent Fair Employment Practices Commission, slum clearance, low-rent housing, regional TVA-type programs, and a public-works program, but was unable to put it through Congress.

Employment Act of 1946

This act established a three-member Council of Economic Advisors to advise the president, and set up a Congressional Joint Committee on the Economic Report. The act declared that the government was committed to maintaining maximum employment.

Atomic Energy

Congress created the Atomic Energy Commission in 1946, establishing civilian control over nuclear development and giving the president sole authority over the use of atomic weapons in warfare.

Price Controls

Truman vetoed a weak price-control bill passed by Congress, thereby ending the wartime price control program. When prices quickly increased about 6 percent, Congress passed another bill in July 1946. Although Truman signed this bill, he used its powers inconsistently, especially when—bowing to pressure—he ended price controls on beef. In late 1946, he lifted controls on all items except rents, sugar, and rice.

Labor

In early 1946, the United Auto Workers, under Walter Reuther, struck General Motors, and steelworkers, under Philip Murray, struck U.S. Steel, demanding wage increases. Truman suggested an 18-cents-per-hour wage increase and in February allowed U.S. Steel to raise prices to cover the increase. This formula became the basis for settlements in other industries. After John L. Lewis's United Mine Workers struck in April 1946, Truman ordered the government to take over the mines and then accepted the union's demands, which included safety and health and welfare benefits. The president averted a railway strike by seizing the railroads and threatening to draft strikers into the army.

Demobilization

The army fell to 600,000 from a WW II peak of 8 million. The Serviceman's Readjustment Act (G.I. Bill of Rights) of 1944 provided $13 billion in aid ranging from education to housing.

Taft-Hartley Act (1947)

The Republicans, who had gained control of Congress in 1946, sought to control the power of the unions through the Taft-Hartley Act. This act made the "closed-shop" illegal; labor unions could no longer force employers to hire only union members. The act did allow the "union-shop," in which newly-hired employees were required to join the union. It also established an 80-day cooling-off period for strikers in key industries, ended the practice of employers collecting dues for unions, forbade such actions as secondary boycotts, jurisdictional strikes, featherbedding, and contributing to political campaigns, and required an anti-Communist oath from union officials. The act slowed down efforts to unionize the South, and by 1954, 15 states had passed "right to work" laws, forbidding the "union-shop."

Reorganization of Armed Forces

In 1947, Congress passed the National Security Act, creating a National Military Establishment, National Security Council, Joint Chiefs of Staff, and Central Intelligence Agency (CIA). Together these organizations were intended to coordinate the armed forces and intelligence services.

Government Reorganization

Truman in 1947 appointed former President Herbert Hoover to head a Commission on Organization of the Executive Branch. The commission's 1949 report led to the Organization Act of 1949, which allowed the president to make organizational changes subject to congressional veto.

Civil Rights

In 1946, Truman appointed the President's Committee on Civil Rights, which one year later produced its report *To Secure These Rights*. The report called for the elimination of all segregation. In 1948, the president banned racial discrimination in federal government hiring practices and ordered desegregation of the armed forces.

Presidential Succession

The Presidential Succession Act of 1947 placed the Speaker of the House and the president pro tempore of the Senate ahead of the secretary of state and after the vice president in the line of succession. The 22nd Amendment to the Constitution, ratified in 1951, limited the president to two terms.

Election of 1948

Truman was the Democratic nominee, but the Democrats were split by the States' Rights Democratic party (Dixiecrats) which nominated Governor Strom Thurmond of South Carolina, and the Progressive party, which nominated former Vice President Henry Wallace. The Republicans nominated Governor Thomas E. Dewey of New York. After traveling widely, and attacking the "do-nothing Congress," Truman won a surprise victory.

THE FAIR DEAL

The Fair Deal Program

Truman sought to enlarge and extend the New Deal, including extending Social Security to more people, rural electrification, and farm housing. He also introduced bills dealing with civil rights, national health insurance, federal aid to education, and repeal of the Taft-Hartley Act. A coalition of Republicans and Southern Democrats prevented little more than the maintenance of existing programs.

Farm Policy

Because of improvements in agriculture, overproduction continued to be a problem. Secretary of Agriculture Charles F. Brannan proposed a program of continued price supports for storable crops, and guaranteed minimum incomes to farmers of perishable crops. It was defeated in Congress, and surpluses continued to pile up.

ANTICOMMUNISM

Smith Act

The Smith Act of 1940 made it illegal to advocate the overthrow of the government by force or to belong to an organization advocating such a position. It was used by the Truman administration to jail leaders of the American Communist party.

Loyalty Review Board

In response to criticism, particularly from the House Committee on Un-American Activities, that his administration was "soft on communism," Truman established this board in 1947 to review government employees.

The Hiss Case

In 1948, Whittaker Chambers, formerly a Communist and now an editor of *Time*, charged Alger Hiss, president of the Carnegie Endowment for International Peace and a former State Department official, with having been a Communist who supplied classified American documents to the Soviet Union. In 1950, Hiss was convicted of perjury, the statute of limitations on his alleged spying having run out.

McCarran Internal Security Act (1950)

This act required Communist-front organizations to register with the attorney general, and prevented their members from defense work and travel abroad. It was passed over Truman's veto.

Rosenberg Case

In 1950, Julius and Ethel Rosenberg and Harry Gold were charged with giving atomic secrets to the Soviet Union. The Rosenbergs were convicted and executed in 1953.

Joseph McCarthy

On February 9, 1950, Senator Joseph R. McCarthy (1908–1957) of Wisconsin stated that he had a list of known Communists who were working in the State Department. He later expanded his attacks to diplomats and scholars and contributed to the electoral defeat of two senators. After making charges against the army, he was censured by the Senate in 1954. He died in 1957.

EISENHOWER'S DYNAMIC CONSERVATISM

1952 Election

The Republicans nominated Dwight D. Eisenhower, most recently NATO commander, for the presidency and Richard M. Nixon, senator from California, for the vice presidency. The Democrats nominated Governor Adlai E. Stevenson (1900–1965) of Illinois for president. Eisenhower won by a landslide; for the first time since Reconstruction, the Republicans won some southern states.

Conservatism

Eisenhower sought to balance the budget and lower taxes but did not attempt to roll back existing social and economic legislation. Eisenhower first described his policy as "dynamic conservatism," and then as "progressive moderation." The administration abolished the Reconstruction Finance Corporation, ended wage and price controls, and reduced farm price supports. It cut the budget and in 1954 lowered tax rates for corporations and individuals with high incomes; an economic slump, however, made balancing the budget difficult.

Social Legislation

Social Security was extended in 1954 and 1956 to an additional 10 million people, including professionals, domestic and clerical workers, farm workers, and members of the armed services. In 1959, benefits were increased 7 percent. In 1955, the minimum wage was raised from 75 cents to $1.00 an hour.

Farm Policy

The Rural Electrification Administration announced in 1960 that 97 percent of American farms had electricity. In 1954, the government began financing the export of farm surpluses in exchange for foreign currencies, and later provided surpluses free to needy nations and to the poor in exchange for governmentally issued food stamps.

Public Works

In 1954, Eisenhower obtained congressional approval for joint Canadian-U.S. construction of the St. Lawrence Seaway, which was to give oceangoing vessels access to the Great Lakes. In 1956, Congress authorized construction of the Interstate Highway System, with the federal government supplying 90 percent of the cost and the states 10 percent.

Supreme Court

Eisenhower appointed Earl Warren (1891–1974), formerly governor of California, chief justice of the Supreme Court in 1953. That same year, he appointed William J. Brennan associate justice. Although originally perceived as conservatives, both justices used the Court as an agency of social and political change.

Election of 1956

The 1956 election once again pitted Eisenhower against Stevenson. The president won easily, carrying all but seven states.

Space and Technology

The launching of the Soviet space satellite *Sputnik* on October 4, 1957, created fear that America was falling behind technologically. Although the United States launched *Explorer I* on January 31, 1958, the concern continued. In 1958, Congress established the National Aeronautics and Space Administration (NASA) to coordinate research and development, and passed the National Defense Education Act to provide grants and loans for education.

Sherman Adams Scandal

In 1958, the White House chief of staff resigned after it was revealed that he had received a fur coat and an oriental rug in return for helping a Boston industrialist.

Labor

The Landrum-Griffen Labor-Management Act of 1959 sought to control unfair union practices by establishing such rules as penalties for misuse of funds.

New States

On January 3, 1959, Alaska became the 49th state, and on August 21, 1959, Hawaii became the 50th.

CIVIL RIGHTS

Initial Eisenhower Actions

Eisenhower completed the formal integration of the armed forces, desegregated public services in Washington, D.C., naval yards, and veteran's hospitals, and appointed a Civil Rights Commission.

Legal Background to Brown

In *Ada Lois Sipuel v. Board of Regents* (1948) and *Sweatt v. Painter* (1950), the Supreme Court ruled that African Americans must be allowed to attend integrated law schools in Oklahoma and Texas.

Brown v. Board of Education of Topeka

In this 1954 case, NAACP lawyer Thurgood Marshall challenged the doctrine of "separate but equal" (*Plessy v. Ferguson*, 1896). The Court declared that separate educational facilities were inherently unequal. In 1955, the Court ordered states to integrate "with all deliberate speed."

Although at first the South reacted cautiously, by 1955 there were calls for "massive resistance"; White Citizens Councils emerged to spearhead the resistance. State legislatures used a number of tactics to get around *Brown.* By the end of 1956, desegregation of the schools had advanced very little.

Although he did not personally support the Supreme Court decision, Eisenhower sent 10,000 National Guardsmen and 1,000 paratroopers to Little Rock, Arkansas, to control mobs and enable African Americans to enroll at Central High in September 1957. A small force of soldiers was stationed at the school throughout the year.

Emergence of Nonviolence

On December 11, 1955, in Montgomery, Alabama, Rosa Parks, a black woman, refused to give up her seat to a white and was arrested. Under the leadership of Martin Luther King (1929–1968), an African American pastor, African Americans of Montgomery organized a bus boycott that lasted for a year, until in December 1956, the Supreme Court refused to review a lower court ruling that stated that separate but equal was no longer legal.

Civil Rights Acts

Eisenhower proposed the Civil Rights Act of 1957, which established a permanent Civil Rights Commission and a Civil Rights Division of the Justice Department empowered to prevent interference with the right to vote. The Civil Rights Act of 1960 gave the federal courts power to register African American voters.

Ending "Massive Resistance"

In 1959, state and federal courts nullified Virginia laws that prevented state funds from going to integrated schools. This proved to be the beginning of the end for "massive resistance."

Sit-Ins

In February 1960, four African American students staged a sit-in at a Woolworth lunch counter in Greensboro, North Carolina. This inspired sit-ins elsewhere in the South and led to the formation of the Student Nonviolent Coordinating Committee (SNCC).

THE ELECTION OF 1960

Vice President Richard M. Nixon won the Republican presidential nomination, and the Democrats nominated Senator John F. Kennedy (1917–1963) for the presidency, with Lyndon B. Johnson (1908–1973), majority leader of the Senate, as his running mate.

Kennedy's Catholicism was a major issue until, on September 12, Kennedy told a gathering of Protestant ministers that he accepted separation of church and state and that Catholic leaders would not tell him how to act as president.

A series of televised debates between Kennedy and Nixon helped create a positive image for Kennedy and may have been a turning point in the election.

Kennedy won the election by slightly more than 100,000 popular votes and 94 electoral votes, based on majorities in New England, the Middle Atlantic, and the South.

SOCIETY AND CULTURE

Gross National Product

The GNP almost doubled between 1945 and 1960, growing at an annual rate of 3.2 percent from 1950 to 1960. Inflation meanwhile remained under 2 percent annually throughout the 1950s. Defense spending was the most important stimulant, and military-related research helped create or expand the new industries of chemicals, electronics, and aviation. The United States had a virtual monopoly in international trade because of the devastation of the world war. Technological innovations contributed to productivity, which jumped 35 percent between 1945 and 1955. After depression and war, Americans had a great desire to consume. Between 1945 and 1960, the American population grew by nearly 30 percent, which contributed greatly to consumer demand.

Consumption Patterns

Home ownership grew by 50 percent between 1945 and 1960. These new homes required such appliances as refrigerators and washing machines, but the most popular product was television, which increased from 7,000 sets in 1946 to 50 million sets in 1960. Advertising found the TV medium especially powerful. Teenagers became an increasingly important consumer group, making—among other things—a major industry of rock 'n' roll music by the mid-1950s. Elvis Presley was its first star.

DEMOGRAPHIC TRENDS

Aided by use of air conditioning, Florida, the Southwest, and California grew rapidly, with California becoming the most populous state by 1963. The Northeast, however, remained the most densely populated area.

Suburbs

Suburbs grew six times faster than cities in the 1950s. William Levitt pioneered the mass-produced housing development when he built 10,600 houses (Levittown) on Long Island in 1947, a pattern followed widely elsewhere in the country. The Federal Housing Administration helped builders by insuring up to 95 percent of a loan and buyers by insuring their mortgages. Car production increased from 2 million in 1946 to 8 million in 1955, which further encouraged the development of suburbia. As blacks moved into the northern and midwestern cities, whites moved to the suburbs, a process dubbed "white flight."

Jobs

The number of farm workers dropped from 9 million to 5.2 million between 1940 and 1960. By 1960, more Americans held white-collar than blue-collar jobs.

CONFORMITY AND SECURITY

Corporate Employment

Employees worked for large organizations. By 1960, 38 percent of the work force was employed by organizations with more than 500 employees. Such environments encouraged the managerial personality and corporate cooperation rather than individualism.

Homogeneity

Observers found that the expansion of the middle class encouraged conformity. David Riesman argued in *The Lonely Crowd* (1950) that Americans were moving from an inner-directed to an outer-directed orientation. William Whyte's *The Organization Man* (1956) saw corporate culture as emphasizing the group rather than the individual. Sloan Wilson's *The Man in the Grey Flannel Suit* (1955) expressed similar concerns in fictional form.

Leisure

The standard work week shrank from six to five days. Television became the dominant cultural medium, with more than 530 stations by 1961. Books, especially paperbacks, increased in sales annually.

Women

A cult of feminine domesticity reemerged after World War II. Marynia Farnham and Ferdinand Lundberg published *Modern Woman: The Lost Sex* in 1947, which suggested that science supported the idea that women could only find fulfillment in domesticity. Countless magazine articles also promoted the concept that a woman's place was in the home.

SEEDS OF REBELLION

Intellectuals

Intellectuals became increasingly critical of American life. In *The Affluent Society* (1958), John Kenneth Galbraith argued that the public sector was underfunded. John Keats's *The Crack in the Picture Window* (1956) criticized the homogeneity of suburban life in the new mass-produced communities. James B. Conant questioned the adequacy of American education in *The American High School Today* (1959).

Theatre and Fiction

Arthur Miller's *Death of a Salesman* (1949) explored the theme of the loneliness of the other-directed person. Novels also took up the conflict between the individual and mass society. Notable works included J. D. Salinger's *The Catcher in the Rye*

(1951), James Jones's *From Here to Eternity* (1951), Joseph Heller's *Catch-22* (1955), Saul Bellow's *The Adventures of Augie March* (1953), and John Updike's *Rabbit, Run* (1960).

Art

Painter Edward Hopper portrayed isolated, anonymous individuals. Jackson Pollock, Robert Motherwell, Willem de Kooning, Arshile Gorky, and Mark Rothko were among the leaders in abstract expressionism, in which they attempted spontaneous expression of their subjectivity.

The Beats

The Beats were a group of young men alienated by 20th-century life. Their movement began in Greenwich Village, New York, with the friendship of Allen Ginsburg, Jack Kerouac, William Burroughs, and Neal Cassady. They emphasized alcohol, drugs, sex, jazz, Buddhism, and a restless vagabond life, all of which were vehicles for their subjectivity. Ginsberg's long poem *Howl* (1956) and Kerouac's novel *On the Road* (1957) were among their more important literary works.

20 THE NEW FRONTIER, VIETNAM, AND SOCIAL UPHEAVAL (1960–1972)

KENNEDY'S "NEW FRONTIER" AND THE LIBERAL REVIVAL

Legislative Failures

Kennedy was unable to get much of his program through Congress because of an alliance of Republicans and southern Democrats. He proposed plans for federal aid to education, urban renewal, medical care for the aged, reductions in personal and corporate income taxes, and the creation of a Department of Urban Affairs. None of these proposals passed.

Kennedy did gain congressional approval for raising the minimum wage from $1.00 to $1.25 an hour and extending it to 3 million more workers.

Area Redevelopment Act

The Area Redevelopment Act of 1961 made available nearly $400 million in loans to "distressed areas."

Housing Act

The 1961 Housing Act provided nearly $5 billion over four years for the preservation of open urban spaces, development of mass transit, and the construction of middle-class housing.

Steel Prices

In 1961, Kennedy "jawboned" the steel industry into overturning a price increase after having encouraged labor to lower its wage demands.

CIVIL RIGHTS

Freedom Riders

In May 1961, blacks and whites, sponsored by the Congress on Racial Equality, boarded buses in Washington, D.C., and traveled across the South to New Orleans to test federal enforcement of regulations prohibiting discrimination. They met violence in Alabama but continued to New Orleans. Others came into the South to test the segregation laws.

Justice Department

The Justice Department, under Attorney General Robert F. Kennedy (1925–1968), began to push for civil rights, including desegregation of interstate transportation in the South, integration of schools, and supervision of elections.

Mississippi

In the fall of 1962, President Kennedy called the Mississippi National Guard to federal duty to enable an African American, James Meredith, to enroll at the University of Mississippi.

March on Washington

Kennedy presented a comprehensive civil rights bill to Congress in 1963. It banned racial discrimination in public accommodations, gave the attorney general power to bring suits on behalf of individuals for school integration, and withheld federal funds from state-administered programs that practiced discrimination. With the bill held up in Congress, 200,000 people marched, demonstrating on its behalf on August 28, 1963, in Washington, D.C. Martin Luther King gave his "I Have a Dream" speech.

THE COLD WAR CONTINUES

Bay of Pigs

Under Eisenhower, the Central Intelligence Agency had begun training some 2,000 men for an invasion of Cuba to overthrow Fidel Castro, the left-leaning revolutionary who had taken power in 1959. On April 19, 1961, this force invaded at the Bay of Pigs, but was pinned down and forced to surrender. Some 1,200 men were captured.

Berlin Wall

After a confrontation between Kennedy and Khrushchev in Berlin, Kennedy called up reserve and National Guard units and asked for an increase in defense funds. In August 1961, Khrushchev responded by closing the border between East and West Berlin and ordering the erection of the Berlin Wall.

Nuclear Testing

The Soviet Union began the testing of nuclear weapons in September 1961. Kennedy then authorized resumption of underground testing by the United States.

Cuban Missile Crisis

On October 14, 1962, a U-2 reconnaissance plane brought photographic evidence that missile sites were being built in Cuba. Kennedy, on October 22, announced a blockade of Cuba and called on Khrushchev to dismantle the missile bases and remove all weapons capable of attacking the United States from Cuba. Six days later, Khrushchev backed down, withdrew the missiles, and Kennedy lifted the blockade. The United States promised not to invade Cuba, and removed missiles from bases in Turkey, claiming they had planned to do so anyway.

Afterwards, a "hot line" telephone connection was established between the White House and the Kremlin to effect quick communication in threatening situations.

Nuclear Test Ban

In July 1963, a treaty banning the atmospheric testing of nuclear weapons was signed by all the major powers except France and China.

Alliance for Progress

In 1961, Kennedy announced the Alliance for Progress, which would provide $20 million in aid to Latin America.

Peace Corps

The Peace Corps, established in 1961, sent young volunteers to third-world countries to contribute their skills in locally sponsored projects.

JOHNSON AND THE GREAT SOCIETY

Kennedy Assassination

On November 22, 1963, Kennedy was assassinated by Lee Harvey Oswald in Dallas, Texas. Jack Ruby, a nightclub owner, killed Oswald two days later. Conspiracy theories emerged. Chief Justice Earl Warren led an investigation of the murder and concluded that Oswald had acted alone, but questions continued.

Lyndon Johnson

Succeeding Kennedy, Johnson had extensive experience in both the House and Senate, and as a Texan, was the first southerner to serve as president since Woodrow Wilson. He pushed hard for Kennedy's programs, which were languishing in Congress.

A tax cut of more than $10 billion passed Congress in 1964, and an economic boom resulted.

Civil Rights Act

The 1964 Civil Rights Act outlawed racial discrimination by employers and unions, created the Equal Employment Opportunity Commission to enforce the law, and eliminated the remaining restrictions on black voting.

Economic Opportunity Act

Michael Harrington's *The Other America* (1962) showed that 20 to 25 percent of American families were living below the governmentally defined poverty line. This poverty was created by increased numbers of old and young, job displacement produced by advancing technology, and regions bypassed by economic development. The Economic Opportunity Act of 1964 sought to address these problems by establishing a Job Corps, community action programs, educational programs, work-study programs, job training, loans for small businesses and farmers, and Volunteers in Service to America (VISTA), a "domestic peace corps." The Office of Economic Opportunity administered many of these programs.

Election of 1964

Lyndon Johnson was nominated for president by the Democrats, with Senator Hubert H. Humphrey of Minnesota for vice president. The Republicans nominated Senator Barry Goldwater, a conservative from Arizona. Johnson won more than 61 percent of the popular vote and could now launch his own "Great Society" program.

Health Care

The Medicare Act of 1965 combined hospital insurance for retired people with a voluntary plan to cover physician's bills. Medicaid provided grants to states to help the poor below retirement age.

Education

In 1965, the Elementary and Secondary Education Act provided $1.5 billion to school districts to improve the education of poor people. Head Start prepared educationally disadvantaged children for elementary school.

Immigration

The Immigration Act of 1965 discontinued the national origin system, basing immigration instead on such things as skills and the need for political asylum.

Cities

The 1965 Housing and Urban Development Act provided 240,000 housing units and $2.9 billion for urban renewal. The Department of Housing and Urban Affairs was established in 1966, and rent supplements for low-income families also became available.

Appalachia

The Appalachian Regional Development Act of 1966 provided $1.1 billion for isolated mountain areas.

Space

Fulfilling a goal established by Kennedy, Neil Armstrong and Edwin Aldrin, on July 20, 1969, became the first humans to walk on the moon.

EMERGENCE OF BLACK POWER

Voting Rights

In 1965, Martin Luther King announced a voter registration drive. With help from the federal courts, he dramatized his effort by leading a march from Selma to Montgomery, Alabama, between March 21 and 25. The Voting Rights Act of 1965 authorized the attorney general to appoint officials to register voters.

Racial Riots

Seventy percent of African Americans lived in city ghettos. It did not appear that the tactics used in the South would help them. Frustration built up. In August 1965, Watts, an area of Los Angeles, erupted in riot. More than 15,000 National Guardsmen were brought in; 34 people were killed, 850 wounded, and 3,100 arrested. Property damage reached nearly $200 million. In 1966, New York and Chicago experienced riots, and the following year there were riots in Newark and Detroit. The Kerner Commission, appointed to investigate the riots, concluded that they were directed at a social system that prevented African Americans from getting good jobs and crowded them into ghettos.

Black Power

Stokely Carmichael, chairman of SNCC, was by 1964 unwilling to work with white civil-rights activists. In 1966, he called for the civil rights movements to be "black-staffed, black-controlled, and black-financed." Later, he moved on to the Black Panthers, self-styled urban revolutionaries based in Oakland, California. Other leaders such as H. Rap Brown also called for Black Power.

King Assassination

On April 4, 1968, Martin Luther King was assassinated in Memphis by James Earl Ray. Riots in more than 100 cities followed.

Black Officials

Despite the rising tide of violence, the number of African Americans achieving elected and appointed office increased. Among the more prominent were Associate Justice of the Supreme Court Thurgood Marshall, Secretary of Housing and Urban Affairs Robert Weaver, and Senator Edward W. Brooke.

ETHNIC ACTIVISM

Hispanics

The number of Hispanics grew from 3 million in 1960 to 9 million in 1970 to 20 million in 1980.

United Farm Workers

Cesar Chavez founded the United Farm Workers' Organizing Committee to unionize Mexican American farm laborers. He turned a grape pickers strike in Delano, California, into a national campaign by attacking the structure of the migrant labor system through a boycott of grapes.

Native Americans

The American Indian Movement (AIM) was founded in 1968. At first it staged sit-ins to dramatize Native American demands. By the early 1970s, it was turning to the courts.

THE NEW LEFT

Demographic Origins

By the mid-1960s, the majority of Americans were under age 30. College enrollments increased fourfold between 1945 and 1970.

Students for a Democratic Society

SDS was organized by Tom Hayden and Al Haber of the University of Michigan in 1960. Hayden's Port Huron Statement (1962) called for "participatory democracy." SDS drew much of its ideology from the writings of C. Wright Mills, Paul Goodman, and Herbert Marcuse.

Free-Speech Movement

Students at the University of California, Berkeley, staged sit-ins in 1964 to protest the prohibition of political canvassing on campus. Led by Mario Savio, the movement changed from emphasizing student rights to criticizing the bureaucracy of American society. In December, police broke up a sit-in; protests spread to other campuses.

Vietnam

Student protests began focusing on the Vietnam war. In the spring of 1967, 500,000 gathered in Central Park in New York City to protest the war, many burning their draft cards. SDS became more militant and willing to use violence. It turned to Lenin for its ideology.

1968

More than 200 large campus demonstrations took place in the spring, culminating in the occupation of buildings at Columbia University to protest the university's involvement in military research and relations with minority groups. Police wielding clubs eventually broke up the demonstration. In August, thousands gathered in Chicago to protest the war during the Democratic convention. Although police violence against the demonstrators aroused anger, the antiwar movement began to split between those favoring violence and those opposed to it.

Decline

Beginning in 1968, SDS began breaking up into rival factions. After the more radical factions began using bombs, Tom Hayden left the group. By the early 1970s, the New Left had lost political influence, having abandoned its original commitment to democracy and nonviolence.

THE COUNTERCULTURE

Origins

Like the New Left, the founders of the counterculture were alienated by bureaucracy, materialism, and the Vietnam war, but they turned away from politics in favor of an alternative society. In many respects, they were heirs of the Beats.

Counterculture Expression

Many young people formed communes in such places as San Francisco's Haight-Ashbury district or in rural areas. "Hippies," as they were called, experimented with Eastern religions, drugs, and sex, but most were unable to establish a self-sustaining lifestyle. Leading spokesmen included Timothy Leary, Theodore Roszak, and Charles Reich.

Woodstock

Rock music was a major element of the counterculture. The Woodstock Music Festival, held in August 1969 in upstate New York, featured such musicians as Joan Baez, Jimi Hendrix, and Santana. In contrast to the joy of Woodstock, a California festival a few months later at the Altamount Speedway experienced a murder in full view of the audience. By the early 1970s, the counterculture was shrinking, either the victim of its own excesses or through its members reentering the mainstream.

WOMEN'S LIBERATION

Betty Friedan

In *The Feminine Mystique* (1963), Betty Friedan argued that middle-class society stifled women and did not allow them to use their individual talents. She attacked the cult of domesticity.

National Organization for Women

Friedan and other feminists founded the National Organization for Women (NOW) in 1966, calling for equal employment opportunities and equal pay.

Expanding Demands

In 1967, NOW advocated an Equal Rights Amendment to the Constitution, changes in divorce laws, and legalization of abortion. In 1972, the federal government required colleges receiving federal funds to establish "affirmative action" programs for women to ensure equal opportunity, and the following year the Supreme Court legalized abortion in *Roe v. Wade*.

Problems

The women's movement was largely limited to the middle class. The Equal Rights Amendment failed to pass. Abortion rights stirred up a counter "right-to-life" movement.

THE SEXUAL REVOLUTION

Sexual Practices

In 1948, Alfred C. Kinsey published pioneering research indicating widespread variation in sexual practices. In the 1960s, new methods of birth control, particularly the "pill," and antibiotics encouraged freer sexual practices and challenged traditional taboos against premarital sex.

Homosexual Rights

Gay and lesbian rights activists emerged in the 1960s and 1970s, particularly after a 1969 police raid on the Stonewell Inn, an establishment frequented by homosexuals in Greenwich Village, New York.

CULTURAL EXPRESSIONS

American films achieved a higher level of maturity. *Who's Afraid of Virginia Woolf* (1966) and *The Graduate* (1967) questioned dominant social values. *Dr. Strangelove* (1964) satirized the military establishment, while *Bonnie and Clyde* (1969) glorified two bank robbers. *Easy Rider* (1969) portrayed the counterculture. The dehumanizing aspects of technology appeared in *2001: A Space Odyssey* (1968).

In literature, Truman Capote's *In Cold Blood* (1965), Norman Mailer's *Armies of the Night* (1968), and Tom Wolfe's *Electric Kool-Aid Acid Test* (1968) combined factual and fictional elements.

Pop artists such as Andy Warhol, Roy Lichtenstein, and Claes Oldenburg drew their subjects from such elements of popular culture as advertising, comics, and hamburgers.

Much theatre became experimental, as exemplified by the San Francisco Mime Troupe. Some plays, including Barbara Garson's *MacBird* (1966) and Arthur Kopit's *Indians* (1969), took an explicitly radical political stance.

VIETNAM

Background

After the French defeat in 1954, the United States sent military advisors to South Vietnam to aid the government of Ngo Dinh Diem. The pro-Communist Vietcong forces gradually grew in strength, partly because Diem failed to follow through on promised reforms. They received support from North Vietnam, the Soviet Union, and China. The U.S. government supported a successful military coup against Diem in the fall of 1963.

Escalation

In August 1964—after claiming that North Vietnamese gunboats had fired on American destroyers in the Gulf of Tonkin—Lyndon Johnson pushed the Gulf of Tonkin resolution through Congress, authorizing him to use military force in Vietnam. After a February 1965 attack by the Vietcong on Pleiku, Johnson ordered operation "Rolling Thunder," the first sustained bombing of North Vietnam. Johnson then sent combat troops to South Vietnam; under the leadership of General William C. Westmoreland, they conducted search and destroy operations. The number of troops increased to 184,000 in 1965, 385,000 in 1966, 485,000 in 1967, and 538,000 in 1968.

Defense of American Policy

"Hawks" defended the president's policy and, drawing on containment theory, said that the nation had the responsibility to resist aggression. Secretary of State Dean Rusk became a major spokesman for the domino theory, which justified government policy by analogy with England's and France's failure to stop Hitler prior to 1939. If Vietnam should fall, it was said, all Southeast Asia would eventually go. The administration stressed its willingness to negotiate the withdrawal of all "foreign" forces from the war.

Opposition

Opposition began quickly, with "teach-ins" at the University of Michigan in 1965 and a 1966 congressional investigation led by Senator J. William Fulbright. Antiwar demonstrations were gaining large crowds by 1967. "Doves" argued that the war was a civil war in which the United States should not meddle. They said that the South Vietnamese regimes were not democratic, and opposed large-scale aerial bombings, use of chemical weapons, and the killing of civilians. "Doves" rejected the domino theory, pointing to the growing losses of American life (over 40,000 by 1970) and the economic cost of the war.

Tet Offensive

On January 31, 1968, the first day of the Vietnamese new year (Tet), the Vietcong attacked numerous cities and towns, American bases, and even Saigon. Although they suffered large losses, the Vietcong won a psychological victory, as American opinion began turning against the war.

ELECTION OF 1968

Eugene McCarthy

In November 1967, Senator Eugene McCarthy of Minnesota announced his candidacy for the 1968 Democratic presidential nomination, running on the issue of opposition to the war.

New Hampshire

In February, McCarthy won 42 percent of the Democratic vote in the New Hampshire primary, compared with Johnson's 48 percent. Robert F. Kennedy then announced his candidacy for the Democratic presidential nomination.

Johnson's Withdrawal

Lyndon Johnson withdrew his candidacy on March 31, 1968, and Vice President Hubert H. Humphrey took his place as a candidate for the Democratic nomination.

Kennedy Assassination

After winning the California primary over McCarthy, Robert Kennedy was assassinated by Sirhan Sirhan, a young Palestinian. This event assured Humphrey's nomination.

The Nominees

The Republicans nominated Richard M. Nixon, who chose Spiro T. Agnew, governor of Maryland, as his running mate in order to appeal to southern voters. Governor George C. Wallace of Alabama ran for the presidency under the banner of the American Independent party, appealing to fears generated by protestors and big government.

Nixon's Victory

Johnson suspended air attacks on North Vietnam shortly before the election. Nonetheless Nixon, who emphasized stability and order, defeated Humphrey by a margin of 1 percent. Wallace's 13.5 percent was the best showing by a third-party candidate since 1924.

THE NIXON CONSERVATIVE REACTION

Civil Rights

The Nixon administration sought to block renewal of the Voting Rights Act and delay implementation of court-ordered school desegregation in Mississippi. After the Supreme Court ordered busing of students in 1971 to achieve school desegregation, the administration proposed an antibusing bill, which was blocked in Congress.

Supreme Court

In 1969, Nixon appointed Warren E. Burger, a conservative, as chief justice, but ran into opposition with the nomination of southerners Clement F. Haynesworth, Jr., and G. Harrold Carswell. After these nominations were defeated, he nominated Harry A. Blackmun, who received Senate approval. He later appointed Lewis F. Powell, Jr., and William Rehnquist as associate justices. Although more conservative than the Warren court, the Burger court did declare the death penalty, as used at the time, unconstitutional in 1972, and struck down state antiabortion legislation in 1973.

Revenue Sharing

The heart of Nixon's "New Federalism," passed by Congress in 1972, was a five-year plan to distribute $30 billion of federal revenues to the states.

Congressional Legislation

Congress passed bills giving 18-year-olds the right to vote (1970), increasing Social Security benefits and funding for food stamps (1970), the Occupational Safety and Health Act (1970), the Clean Air Act (1970), acts to control water pollution (1970, 1972), and the Federal Election Campaign Act (1972). None were supported by the Nixon administration.

Economic Problems and Policy

Unemployment climbed to 6 percent in 1970, real gross national product declined in 1970, and in 1971 the United States experienced a trade deficit. Inflation reached 12 percent by 1974. These problems resulted from federal deficits in the 1960s, international competition, and rising energy costs.

In 1969, Nixon cut spending and raised taxes. He encouraged the Federal Reserve Board to raise interest rates. The economy worsened. In 1970, Congress gave the president the power to regulate prices and wages. Nixon used this power in August 1971 by announcing a 90-day price and wage freeze and taking the United

States off the gold standard. At the end of the 90 days, he established mandatory guidelines for wage and price increases. Finally, in 1973, he turned to voluntary wage and price controls, except on health care, food, and construction. When inflation increased rapidly, Nixon cut back on government expenditures, refusing to spend (impound) funds already appropriated by Congress.

VIETNAMIZATION

Nixon proposed that all non-South Vietnamese troops be withdrawn in phases, and that an internationally supervised election be held in South Vietnam. The North Vietnamese rejected this plan.

The president then turned to "Vietnamization," the effort to build up South Vietnamese forces while withdrawing American troops. In 1969, Nixon reduced American troop strength by 60,000, but at the same time ordered the bombing of Cambodia, a neutral country.

Protests

Two Moratorium Days in 1969 brought out several hundred thousand protestors, and reports of an American massacre of Vietnamese at My Lai reignited controversy over the nature of the war, but Nixon continued to defend his policy. Troop withdrawals continued, and a lottery system was instituted in 1970 to make the draft more equitable. In 1973, Nixon abolished the draft and established an all-volunteer army.

Cambodia

In April 1970, Nixon announced that Vietnamization was succeeding and that another 150,000 American troops would be out of Vietnam by the end of the year. A few days later, he sent troops into Cambodia to clear out Vietcong sanctuaries and resumed bombing of North Vietnam.

Kent State

Protests against escalation of the war were especially strong on college campuses. During a May 1970 demonstration at Kent State University in Ohio, the National Guard opened fire on protestors, killing four students. Soon after, two black students were killed by a Mississippi state policeman at Jackson State University. Several hundred colleges were soon closed down by student strikes, as moderates joined the radicals. Congress repealed the Gulf of Tonkin Resolution.

Pentagon Papers

The publication in 1971 of classified Defense Department documents, called "The Pentagon Papers," revealed that the government had misled the Congress and the American people regarding its intentions in Vietnam during the mid-1960s.

Mining

Nixon drew American forces back from Cambodia but increased bombing. In

March 1972, after stepped-up aggression from the North, Nixon ordered the mining of Haiphong and other northern ports.

End of U.S. Involvement

In the summer of 1972, negotiations between the United States and North Vietnam began in Paris. A draft agreement was developed by October which included a cease-fire, return of American prisoners of war, and withdrawal of U.S. forces from Vietnam. A few days before the 1972 presidential election, Henry Kissinger, the president's national security advisor, announced that "peace was at hand."

Resumed Bombing

Nixon resumed bombing of North Vietnam in December 1972, claiming that the North Vietnamese were not bargaining in good faith. In January 1973, the opponents reached a settlement in which the North Vietnamese retained control over large areas of the South and agreed to release American prisoners of war within 60 days. After the prisoners were released, the United States would withdraw its remaining troops. Nearly 60,000 Americans had been killed and 300,000 more wounded and the war had cost Americans $109 billion. On March 29, 1973, the last American combat troops left South Vietnam.

FOREIGN POLICY

China

With his national security advisor, Henry Kissinger, Nixon took some bold diplomatic initiatives. Kissinger traveled to China and the Soviet Union for secret sessions to plan summit meetings with the Communists. In February 1972, Nixon and Kissinger went to China to meet with Mao Tse-tung and his associates. The United States agreed to support China's admission to the United Nations and to pursue economic and cultural exchanges.

Soviet Union

At a May 1972 meeting with the Soviets, a Strategic Arms Limitation Treaty (SALT) was signed. The signatories agreed to stop making nuclear ballistic missiles and to reduce the number of antiballistic missiles to 200 for each power.

Détente

Nixon and Kissinger called their policy *détente*, a French term meaning a relaxation in the tensions between two governments. The agreements were significant in part because they were made before the United States withdrew from Vietnam.

Middle East

Following the Arab-Israeli war of 1973, the Arab states established an oil boycott to push the Western nations into forcing Israel to withdraw from lands controlled since the Six Day War of 1967. Kissinger, now secretary of state, negotiated the withdrawal of Israel from some of the lands and the Arabs lifted their boycott. The Organization of Petroleum Exporting Countries (OPEC)—Venezuela, Saudi Arabia, Kuwait, Iraq, and Iran—then raised the price of oil from about $3.00 to $11.65 a barrel. U.S. gas prices doubled and inflation shot above 10 percent.

ELECTION OF 1972

George McGovern

The Democrats nominated Senator George McGovern of South Dakota for president and Senator Thomas Eagleton for vice president. After the press revealed that Eagleton had previously been treated for psychological problems, McGovern eventually forced him off the ticket, replacing him with Sargent Shriver. McGovern was also hampered by a party divided over the war and social policies, as well as his own relative radicalism.

George Wallace

Wallace ran once again as the American Independent party candidate, but was shot on May 15 and left paralyzed below the waist.

Richard M. Nixon

Richard M. Nixon and Spiro T. Agnew, who had been renominated by the Republicans, won a landslide victory, receiving 521 electoral votes to McGovern's 17.

21 WATERGATE, CARTER, AND THE NEW CONSERVATISM (1972–1991)

THE WATERGATE SCANDAL

The Break-In

What became known as the Watergate crisis began during the 1972 presidential campaign. Early on the morning of June 17, James McCord, a security officer for the Committee to Reelect the President (CREEP), and four other men broke into Democratic headquarters at the Watergate apartment complex in Washington, D.C., and were caught while going through files and installing electronic eavesdropping devices. On June 22, Nixon announced that the administration was in no way involved in the burglary attempt.

James McCord

The trial of the burglars began in early 1973, with all but McCord (who was convicted) pleading guilty. Before sentencing, McCord wrote a letter to Judge John J. Sirica, arguing that high Republican officials had known in advance about the burglary and that perjury had been committed at the trial.

Further Revelations

Soon Jeb Stuart Magruder, head of CREEP, and John W. Dean, Nixon's attorney, stated that they had been involved. Dean testified before a Senate Watergate investigating committee that Nixon had been involved in covering up the incident. Over the next several months, extensive involvement of the administration, including payment of "hush" money to the burglars, destruction of FBI records, forgery of documents, and wiretapping, was revealed. Dean was fired and H.R. Haldeman and John Ehrlichman, who headed the White House staff, and Attorney General Richard Kleindienst, resigned. Nixon claimed that he had not personally been involved in the cover-up but refused, on the grounds of executive privilege, to allow investigation of White House documents.

White House Tapes

Under considerable pressure, Nixon agreed to the appointment of a special prosecutor, Archibald Cox of Harvard Law School. When Cox obtained a subpoena for tape recordings of White House conversations (whose existence had been revealed during the Senate hearings)—and the administration lost an appeal in the appellate court—Nixon ordered Elliot Richardson, the attorney general, to fire Cox. Both Richardson and his subordinate, William Ruckelshaus, resigned, leaving Robert Bork, the solicitor general, to carry out the order. This "Saturday Night Massacre," which took place on October 20, 1973, aroused a storm of controversy. The House Judiciary Committee, headed by Peter Rodino of New Jersey, began looking into the possibilities of impeachment. Nixon agreed to turn the tapes over to Judge Sirica and named Leon Jaworski as the new special prosecutor. But it soon became known that some of the tapes were missing and that a portion of another had been erased.

The Vice Presidency

Vice President Spiro Agnew was accused of income tax fraud and having accepted bribes while a local official in Maryland. He resigned the vice presidency in October 1973 and was replaced by Congressman Gerald R. Ford of Michigan under provisions of the new 25th Amendment.

Nixon's Taxes

Nixon was accused of paying almost no income taxes between 1969 and 1972, and of using public funds for improvements to his private residences in California and Florida. The IRS reviewed the president's tax return and assessed him nearly $500,000 in back taxes and interest.

Indictments

In March 1974, a grand jury indicted Haldeman, Ehrlichman, former Attorney General John Mitchell, and four other White House aides and named Nixon an unindicted coconspirator.

Calls for Resignation

In April, Nixon released edited transcripts of the White House tapes, the contents of which led to further calls for his resignation. Jaworski subpoenaed 64 additional tapes, which Nixon refused to turn over, and the case went to the Supreme Court.

Impeachment Debate

Meanwhile, the House Judiciary Committee televised its debate over impeachment, adopting three articles of impeachment. It charged the president with obstructing justice, misusing presidential power, and failing to obey the committee's subpoenas.

Resignation

Before the House began to debate impeachment, the Supreme Court ordered the president to release the subpoenaed tapes to the special prosecutor. On August 5, Nixon, under pressure from his advisors, released the tape of June 23, 1972, to the public. This tape, recorded less than a week after the break-in, revealed that Nixon had used the CIA to keep the FBI from investigating the case. Nixon announced his resignation on August 8, 1973, to take effect at noon the following day. Gerald Ford then became president.

Legislative Response

Congress responded to the Vietnam War and Watergate by enacting legislation intended to prevent such situations. The War Powers Act (1973) required congressional approval of any commitment of combat troops beyond 90 days. In 1974,

Congress limited the amounts of contributions and expenditures in presidential campaigns. It also strengthened the 1966 Freedom of Information Act by requiring the government to act promptly when asked for information and to prove its case for classification when attempting to withhold information on grounds of national security.

THE FORD PRESIDENCY

Gerald Ford

Gerald Ford was in many respects the opposite of Nixon. Although a partisan Republican, he was well liked and free from any hint of scandal. Ford almost immediately encountered controversy when in September 1974 he offered to pardon Nixon. Nixon accepted the offer, although he admitted no wrongdoing and had not yet been charged with a crime.

The Economy

Ford also faced major economic problems, which he approached somewhat inconsistently. Saying that inflation was the major problem, he called for voluntary restraints and asked citizens to wear WIN (Whip Inflation Now) buttons. The economy went into decline. Ford asked for tax cuts to stimulate business and argued against spending for social programs.

When New York City approached bankruptcy in 1975, Ford at first opposed federal aid, but changed his mind when the Senate and House Banking Committees guaranteed the loans.

Vietnam

As North Vietnamese forces pushed back the South Vietnamese, Ford asked Congress to provide more arms for the South. Congress rejected the request, and in April 1975 Saigon fell to the North Vietnamese.

The Mayaguez

On May 12, 1975, Cambodia, which had been taken over by Communists two weeks earlier, seized the American merchant ship *Mayaguez* in the Gulf of Siam. After demanding that the ship and crew be freed, Ford ordered a marine assault on Tang Island, where the ship had been taken. The ship and crew of 39 were released, but 38 marines were killed.

Election of 1976

Ronald Reagan, formerly a movie actor and governor of California, opposed Ford for the Republican nomination, but Ford won by a slim margin. The Democrats nominated James Earl Carter, formerly governor of Georgia, who ran on the basis of his integrity and lack of Washington connections. Carter, with Senator Walter Mondale of Minnesota as the vice-presidential candidate, defeated Ford narrowly.

CARTER'S MODERATE LIBERALISM

Jimmy Carter

Carter sought to conduct the presidency on democratic and moral principles. His administration gained a reputation for proposing complex programs to Congress and then not continuing to support them through the legislative process.

The Economy

Carter approached economic problems inconsistently. In 1978, he proposed voluntary wage and price guidelines. Although somewhat successful, the guidelines did not apply to oil, housing, and food. Carter then named Paul A. Volcker as chairman of the Federal Reserve Board. Volcker tightened the money supply in order to reduce inflation, but this action caused interest rates to go even higher. High interest rates depressed sales of automobiles and houses, which in turn increased unemployment. By 1980, unemployment stood at 7.5 percent, interest at 20 percent, and inflation at 12 percent.

Energy

Attempting to reduce America's growing dependence on foreign oil, in 1977, Carter proposed raising the tax on gasoline and taxing automobiles that used fuel inefficiently, among other things, but obtained only a gutted version of his bill. Near the end of his term, Carter proposed coupling deregulation of the price of American crude oil with a windfall profits tax, a program that pleased neither liberals nor conservatives. Energy problems were further exacerbated by a second fuel shortage in 1979.

Domestic Achievements

Carter offered amnesty to Americans who had fled the draft and gone to other countries during the Vietnam War. He established the Departments of Energy and Education and placed the civil service on a merit basis. He created a "superfund" for cleanup of chemical waste dumps, established controls over strip mining, and protected 100 million acres of Alaskan wilderness from development.

CARTER'S FOREIGN POLICY

Human Rights

Carter sought to base foreign policy on human rights, but was criticized for inconsistency and lack of attention to American interests.

Panama Canal

Carter negotiated a controversial treaty with Panama, affirmed by the Senate in 1978, that provided for the transfer of ownership of the canal to Panama in 1999 and guaranteed its neutrality.

China

Carter ended official recognition of Taiwan and in 1979 recognized the People's Republic of China. Conservatives called the decision a "sell-out."

Salt II

In 1979, the administration signed the Strategic Arms Limitation Treaty (SALT II) with the Soviet Union. The treaty set a ceiling of 2,250 bombers and missiles for each side, and established limits on warheads and new weapons systems. It never passed the Senate.

Camp David Accords

In 1978, Carter negotiated the Camp David Agreement between Israel and Egypt. Bringing Anwar Sadat, president of Egypt, and Menachem Begin, prime minister of Israel, to Camp David for two weeks in September 1978, Carter sought to end the state of war that existed between the two countries. Israel promised to return occupied land in the Sinai to Egypt in exchange for Egyptian recognition, a process completed in 1982. An agreement to negotiate the Palestinian refugee problem proved ineffective.

Afghanistan

The policy of détente went into decline. Carter criticized Soviet restrictions on political freedom and reluctance to allow dissidents and Jews to emigrate. In December 1979, the Soviet Union invaded Afghanistan. Carter stopped shipments of grain and technology to the Soviet Union, withdrew SALT II from the Senate, and barred Americans from competing in the 1980 summer Olympics held in Moscow.

THE IRANIAN CRISIS

The Iranian Revolution

In 1978, a revolution forced the shah of Iran to flee the country, replacing him with a religious leader, Ayatollah Ruhollah Khomeini. Because the United States had supported the shah with arms and money, the revolutionaries were strongly anti-American, calling the United States the "Great Satan."

Hostages

After Carter allowed the exiled shah to come to the United States for medical treatment in October 1979, some 400 Iranians broke into the American embassy in Teheran on November 4, taking the occupants captive. They demanded that the shah be returned to Iran for trial and that his wealth be confiscated and given to Iran. Carter rejected these demands; instead, he froze Iranian assets in the United States and established a trade embargo against Iran. He also appealed to the United Nations and the World Court. The Iranians eventually freed the African American and women hostages, but retained 52 others.

In April 1980, Carter ordered a marine rescue attempt, but it collapsed after several helicopters broke down and another crashed, killing 8 men. Secretary of State

Cyrus Vance resigned in protest before the raid began, and Carter was widely criticized for the attempted raid.

THE ELECTION OF 1980

The Democrats

Carter, whose standing in polls had dropped to about 25 percent in 1979, successfully withstood a challenge from Senator Edward M. Kennedy for the Democratic presidential nomination.

The Republicans

The Republicans nominated Ronald Reagan of California, who had narrowly lost the 1976 nomination and was the leading spokesman for American conservatism. Reagan chose George Bush, a New Englander transplanted to Texas and former CIA director, as his vice-presidential candidate. One of Reagan's opponents, Congressman John Anderson of Illinois, continued his presidential campaign on a third-party ticket.

The Campaign

While Carter defended his record, Reagan called for reductions in government spending and taxes and said he would transfer more power from the federal government to the states. He advocated what were coming to be called traditional values—family, religion, hard work, and patriotism.

Reagan's Victory

Reagan won by a large electoral majority, and the Republicans gained control of the Senate and increased their representation in the House.

American Hostages

After extensive negotiations with Iran, in which Algeria acted as an intermediary, Carter released Iranian assets and the hostages were freed on January 20, 1980, 444 days after being taken captive and on the day of Reagan's inauguration.

SOCIAL TRENDS

Minorities and Women

A two-tier black social structure was emerging, composed of a middle class and an "underclass" living in the ghettos. Single-parent families, usually headed by females, grew disproportionately among the African American underclass.

Hispanics grew 61 percent during the 1970s. Many were "undocumented" immigrants who worked in low-paying service jobs.

The number of Asians—Chinese, Japanese, Filipinos, Koreans, and Vietnamese—increased rapidly during the 1970s. Disciplined and hardworking, many of them moved into the middle class in a single generation.

The Equal Rights Amendment, approved by Congress in 1972, aroused opposition among traditionalists, led by Phillis Schlafly, and was never ratified by the required 38 states.

Abortion

After the Supreme Court in *Roe v. Wade* (1973) legalized abortion during the first three months of pregnancy, conflict arose between "pro-choice" (those who wished to keep abortion legal) and "pro-life" (those who were anti-abortion) groups. The issue affected many local and state political campaigns.

Population Shift

Population was shifting from the Northeast to the "Sunbelt." The Sunbelt tended to be politically conservative.

Narcissism

In contrast to the social consciousness of the 1960s, the 1970s were often described as the "Me Generation." Writers such as Tom Wolfe and Christopher Lasch described a "culture of narcissism" in which preoccupation with the self appeared in the popularity of personal-fulfillment programs, health and exercise fads, and even religious cults.

Religion

During the 1970s, the United States experienced a major revival of conservative Christianity, spread among both the fundamentalists and the more moderate evangelicals. A 1977 survey suggested that some 70 million Americans considered themselves "born-again" Christians, the most prominent of whom was President Jimmy Carter, a devout Baptist. Many of these Christians, led by Reverend Jerry Falwell's "Moral Majority," became politically active, favoring prayer and the teaching of creationism in the public schools, opposing abortion, pornography, and the ERA, and supporting a strong national defense.

THE REAGAN PRESIDENCY: ATTACKING BIG GOVERNMENT

Tax Policy

An ideological though pragmatic conservative, Ronald Reagan acted quickly and forcefully to change the direction of government policy. He placed priority on cutting taxes. His approach was based on "supply-side" economics, the idea that if government left more money in the hands of the people, they would invest rather then spend the excess on consumer goods. The results would be greater production, more jobs, and greater prosperity, and thus more income for the government despite lower tax rates.

Economic Recovery Tax Act

Reagan asked for a 30 percent tax cut, and despite fears of inflation on the part of Congress, in August 1983 obtained a 25 percent cut, spread over three years. The percentage was the same for everyone; hence high-income people received greater savings than middle- and low-income individuals. To encourage investment, capital gains, gift, and inheritance taxes were reduced and business taxes liberalized. Anyone with earned income was also allowed to invest up to $2,000 a year in an individual retirement account (IRA), deferring all taxes on both the principle and its earnings until retirement.

Government Spending

Congress passed the Budget Reconciliation Act in 1981, cutting $39 billion from domestic programs, including education, food stamps, public housing, and the National Endowments for the Arts and Humanities. While cutting domestic programs, Reagan increased the defense budget by $12 billion.

Economic Response

By December 1982, the economy was experiencing recession because of the Federal Reserve's "tight money" policy, with over 10 percent unemployment. From a deficit of $59 billion in 1980, the federal budget was running $195 billion in the red by 1983. The rate of inflation, however, helped by lower demand for goods and services and an oversupply of oil as non-OPEC countries increased production, fell from a high of 12 percent in 1979 to 4 percent in 1984. The Federal Reserve Board then began to lower interest rates, which, together with lower inflation and more spendable income because of lower taxes, resulted in more business activity. Unemployment fell to less than 8 percent.

Increasing Revenue

Because of rising deficits, Reagan and Congress increased taxes in various ways. The 1982 Tax Equity and Fiscal Responsibility Act reversed some concessions made to business in 1981. Social Security benefits became taxable income in 1983. In 1984, the Deficit Reduction Act increased taxes by another $50 billion. But the deficit continued to increase.

Air Traffic Controllers

The federally employed air traffic controllers entered an illegal strike in August 1981. After Reagan ordered them to return to work and most refused to do so, the president fired them, 11,400 in all, effectively destroying their union, and began training replacements.

Assassination Attempt

John W. Hinckley shot Reagan in the chest on March 30, 1981. The president was wounded but made a swift recovery. His popularity increased, possibly helping his legislative program.

Antitrust

Reagan ended ongoing antitrust suits against International Business Machines and American Telephone and Telegraph, thereby fulfilling his promise to reduce government interference with business.

Women and Minorities

Although Reagan appointed Sandra Day O'Connor to the Supreme Court, his administration gave fewer of its appointments to women and minorities than had the Carter administration. The Reagan administration also opposed "equal pay for equal work" and renewal of the Voting Rights Act of 1965.

Problems with Appointed Officials

A number of Reagan appointees were accused of conflict of interest, including Anne Gorsuch Burford and Rita Lavelle of the Environmental Protection Agency, Edwin Meese, presidential advisor and later attorney general, and Michael Deaver, the deputy chief of staff. Ray Donovan, secretary of labor, was indicted but acquitted of charges that he had made payoffs to government officials while he was in private business. By the end of Reagan's term, more than 100 of his officials had been accused of questionable activities.

ASSERTING AMERICAN POWER

Soviet Union

Reagan took a hard line against the Soviet Union, calling it an "evil empire." He placed new cruise missiles in Europe, despite considerable opposition from Europeans.

Latin America

Reagan encouraged the opposition (*contras*) to the leftist Sandinista government of Nicaragua with arms, tactical support, and intelligence, and supplied aid to the government of El Salvador in its struggles against left-wing rebels. In October 1983, the president also sent American troops into the Caribbean island of Grenada to overthrow a newly established Cuban-backed regime.

Middle East

As the Lebanese government collapsed and fighting broke out between Christian and Islamic Lebanese in the wake of the 1982 Israeli invasion, Reagan sent American troops into Lebanon as part of an international peacekeeping force. Soon, however, Israel pulled out and the Americans came under continual shelling from the various Lebanese factions. In October 1983, a Muslim drove a truck filled with explosives into a building housing marines, killing 239. A few months later, Reagan removed all American troops from Lebanon.

ELECTION OF 1984

The Democrats

Walter Mondale, a former senator from Minnesota and vice president under Carter, won the Democratic nomination over Senator Gary Hart and Jesse Jackson, an African American civil-rights leader. Mondale chose Geraldine Ferraro, a congresswoman from New York, as his running mate. Mondale criticized Reagan for his budget deficits, high unemployment and interest rates, and reduction of spending on social services.

The Reagan Victory

The Republicans renominated Ronald Reagan and George Bush. Reagan drew support from groups such as the Moral Majority. Reagan appealed to other voters because of his strong stand against the Soviet Union and the lowering of inflation, interest rates, and unemployment. He defeated Mondale by gaining nearly 60 percent of the vote, breaking apart the Democratic coalition of industrial workers, farmers, and the poor that had existed since the days of Franklin Roosevelt. Reagan's success did not help Republicans in Congress, however, where they lost two seats in the Senate and gained little in the House.

SECOND-TERM FOREIGN CONCERNS

Achille Lauro

In October 1985, Arab terrorists seized the Italian cruise ship *Achille Lauro* in the Mediterranean, threatening to blow up the ship if 50 jailed Palestinians in Israel were not freed. They killed an elderly Jewish American tourist and surrendered to Egyptian authorities on the condition that they be sent to Libya on an Egyptian airliner. Reagan ordered navy F-14 jets to intercept the airliner and force it to land in Italy, where the terrorists were jailed.

Libya

Reagan challenged Muammar al-Qadhafi, the anti-American leader of Libya, by sending Sixth Fleet ships within the Gulf of Sidra, which Qadhafi claimed. When Libyan gunboats challenged the American ships, American planes destroyed the gunboats and bombed installations on the Libyan shoreline. Soon after, a West German night club popular among American servicemen was bombed, killing a soldier and a civilian. Reagan, believing the bombing was ordered directly by Qadhafi, launched an air strike from Great Britain against Libyan bases in April 1986.

Soviet Union

After Mikhail S. Gorbachev became the premier of the Soviet Union in March 1985 and took a more flexible approach toward both domestic and foreign affairs, Reagan softened his anti-Soviet stance. Nonetheless, although the Soviets said that they would honor the unratified SALT II agreement, Reagan argued that they had not adhered to the pact and sought to expand and modernize the American defense system.

SDI

Reagan concentrated on obtaining funding for the development of a computer-controlled strategic defense initiative system (SDI), popularly called "Star Wars" after the widely seen movie, that would destroy enemy missiles from outerspace. Congress balked, skeptical about the technological possibilities and fearing enormous costs.

Arms Control

SDI also appeared to prevent Reagan and Gorbachev from reaching an agreement on arms limitations at summit talks in 1985 and 1986. Finally, in December 1987, they signed an agreement eliminating medium-range missiles from Europe.

Iran-Contra

Near the end of 1986, a scandal arose involving William Casey, head of the CIA, Lieutenant Colonel Oliver North of the National Security Council, Admiral John Poindexter, national security advisor, and Robert McFarlane, former national security advisor. In 1985 and 1986, they had sold arms to the Iranians in hopes of encouraging them to use their influence in getting American hostages in Lebanon released. The profits from these sales were then diverted to the Nicaraguan *contras* in an attempt to get around congressional restrictions on funding the *contras*. The president was forced to appoint a special prosecutor, and Congress held hearings on the affair in May 1987.

Nicaragua

The Reagan administration did not support a peace plan signed by five Central American nations in 1987, but the following year the Sandinistas and the *contras* agreed on a cease-fire.

SECOND-TERM DOMESTIC AFFAIRS

Tax Reform

The Tax Reform Act of 1986 lowered tax rates, changing the highest rate on personal income from 50 percent to 28 percent and on corporate taxes from 46 percent to 34 percent. At the same time, it removed many tax shelters and tax credits. The law did away with the concept of progressive taxation, the requirement that the percentage of income taxed increased as income increased. Instead, over a two-year period it established two rates, 15 percent on incomes below $17,850 for individuals and $29,750 for families and 28 percent on incomes above these amounts. The tax system would no longer be used as an instrument of social policy.

Economic Patterns

Unemployment declined, reaching 6.6 percent in 1986, while inflation fell as low as 2.2% during the first quarter of that year. The stock market was bullish through mid-1987.

Oil Prices

Falling oil prices hit the Texas economy particularly hard, as well as other oil-producing states of the Southwest. Oil-producing countries had to cut back on their purchases of imports, which in turn hurt all manufacturing nations. American banks suffered when oil-related international loans went unpaid.

Agriculture

With the general slowing of inflation, and the decline of world agricultural prices, many American farmers began to descend into bankruptcy in the mid-1980s, often dragging the rural banks that had made them the loans into bankruptcy as well. Although it lifted the ban on wheat exports to the Soviet Union, the Reagan administration reduced price supports and opposed debt relief passed by Congress.

Deficits

The federal deficit reached $179 billion in 1985. At about the same time, the United States experienced trade deficits of more than $100 billion annually, partly because management and engineering skills had fallen behind Japan and Germany, and partly because the United States provided an open market to foreign businesses. In the mid-1980s, the United States became a debtor nation for the first time since World War I. Consumer debt also rose from $300 billion in 1980 to $500 billion in 1986.

Mergers

The merging of companies, encouraged by the deregulation movement of Carter and Reagan as well as the emerging international economy, was fueled by funds released by new tax breaks and became a widespread phenomenon. Twenty-seven major companies merged between 1981 and 1986. Multinational corporations, which produced goods in many different countries, also began to characterize the economy.

Black Monday

On October 19, 1987, the Dow-Jones stock-market average dropped more than 500 points. Between August 25 and October 20, the market lost over a trillion dollars in paper value. Fearing a recession, Congress in November 1987 reduced 1988 taxes by $30 billion.

NASA

The explosion of the shuttle *Challenger* soon after take-off in February 1986 damaged NASA's credibility and reinforced doubts about the complex technology required for the SDI program.

Supreme Court

Reagan reshaped the Court, in 1986 replacing Chief Justice Warren C. Burger with Associate Justice William H. Rehnquist, probably the most conservative member of the Court. Although failing in his nomination of Robert Bork for associate justice, Reagan did appoint other conservatives to the Court: Sandra Day O'Connor, Antonin Scalia, and Anthony Kennedy.

ELECTION OF 1988

The Candidates

After a sex scandal eliminated Senator Gary Hart from the race for the Democratic presidential nomination, Governor Michael Dukakis of Massachusetts emerged as the victor over his major challenger, Jesse Jackson. He chose Senator Lloyd Bentsen of Texas as his vice-presidential running mate. Vice President George Bush, after a slow start in the primaries, won the Republican nomination. He chose Senator Dan Quayle of Indiana as his running mate. Bush easily defeated Dukakis, but the Republicans were unable to make any inroads in Congress.

BUSH ABANDONS REAGANOMICS

Budget Deficit

Soon after George Bush took office as president on January 20, 1989, the budget deficit for 1990 was estimated at $143 billion. With deficit estimates continuing to grow, Bush held a "budget summit" with congressional leaders in May 1990, and his administration continued talks throughout the summer. In September, the administration and Congress agreed to increase taxes on gasoline, tobacco, and alcohol, establish an excise tax on luxury items, and raise medicare taxes. Cuts were also to be made in medicare and other domestic programs. The 1991 deficit was now estimated to be over $290 billion. The following month, Congress approved the plan, hoping to cut a cumulative amount of $500 billion from the deficit over the next five years. In a straight party vote, Republicans voting against and Democrats voting in favor, Congress in December transferred the power to decide whether new tax and spending proposals violated the deficit cutting agreement from the White House Office of Management and Budget to the Congressional Budget Office.

Defense Budget

The Commission on Base Realignment and Closure proposed in December 1989 that 54 military bases be closed. In June 1990, Secretary of Defense Richard Chaney sent to Congress a plan to cut military spending by 10 percent and the armed forces by 25 percent over the next five years. The following April, Chaney recommended the closing of 43 domestic military bases, plus many more abroad.

Minimum Wage

After Bush vetoed in May 1989 an increase in the minimum wage from $3.35 to $4.55 an hour, the following November Congress approved and Bush signed an increase to $4.25 an hour, to be effective in 1991.

Savings and Loan Debacle

With the savings and loan industry in financial trouble in February 1989, largely because of bad real-estate loans, Bush proposed to close or sell 350 institutions, to be paid for by the sale of government bonds. In July, he signed a bill which created the Resolution Trust Corporation to oversee the closure and merging of S & Ls, and which provided $166 billion over 10 years to cover the bad debts. Estimates of the total costs of the debacle were over $300 billion.

Scandals in the Financial Markets

Charges of insider trading, stock manipulation, and falsification of records resulted in Drexel Burnham Lambert, a major securities firm, pleading guilty in December 1988 to six violations of federal law. The company filed for bankruptcy and Michael Milken, its "junk bond king" (junk bonds are bonds below an investment grade of BB or Bb, which because of their risk carry a two to three point interest advantage) pleaded guilty to conspiracy, among other charges, in 1990. Meanwhile, in July 1989, 46 futures traders at the Chicago Mercantile Exchange were charged with racketeering.

Economic Slowdown

The gross national product slowed from 4.4 percent in 1988 to 2.9 percent in 1989. Unemployment gradually began to increase, reaching 6.8 percent in March 1991, a three-year high. Every sector of the economy except for medical services and all geographical areas experienced the slowdown. The "Big Three" automakers posted record losses and Pan American and Eastern Airlines entered bankruptcy proceedings. In September 1991, the Federal Reserve lowered the interest rate.

OTHER DOMESTIC ISSUES UNDER BUSH

Exxon Valdez

After the *Exxon Valdez* spilled more than 240,000 barrels of oil into Alaska's Prince William Sound in March 1989, the federal government ordered Exxon Corporation to develop a clean-up plan, which it carried out until the weather prevented them from continuing in September. *Valdez* captain, Joseph Hazelwood, was found guilty of negligence the following year. Exxon Corporation, the state of Alaska, and the Justice Department of the federal government reached a settlement in October 1991 requiring Exxon to pay $1.025 billion in fines and restitution through the year 2001.

Congressional Ethics Violations

After the House Ethics Committee released a report charging that Speaker of the House Jim Wright had violated rules regulating acceptance of gifts and outside income, Wright resigned in May 1989. A short time later, the Democratic whip Tony Coelho resigned because of alleged improper use of campaign funds.

Flag Burning

In May 1989, the Supreme Court ruled that the Constitution protected protesters who burned the United States flag. Bush denounced the decision and supported an amendment barring desecration of the flag. The amendment failed to pass Congress.

HUD Scandal

In July 1989, Secretary of Housing and Urban Development Jack Kemp revealed that the department had lost more than $2 billion under his predecessor, Samuel Pierce. A special prosecutor was named in February 1990 to investigate the case, and the House held hearings on HUD during the next two months.

Medicare

In July 1988, the Medicare Catastrophic Coverage Act had placed a cap on fees medicare patients paid to physicians and hospitals. After many senior citizens, particularly those represented by the American Association of Retired Persons (AARP), objected to the surtax that funded the program, Congress repealed the act in November 1989.

Pollution

The Clean Air Act, passed in October 1990 and updating the 1970 law, mandated that the level of emissions was to be reduced 50 percent by the year 2000. Cleaner gasolines were to be developed, cities were to reduce ozone, and nitrogen oxide emissions were to be cut by one-third.

Civil Rights

The Americans with Disabilities Act, passed in July 1990, barred discrimination against people with physical or mental disabilities. In October 1990, Bush vetoed the Civil Rights Act on the grounds that it established quotas, but a year later he accepted a slightly revised version that, among other things, required that employers in discrimination suits prove that their hiring practices are not discriminatory.

Supreme Court Appointments

Bush continued to reshape the Supreme Court in a conservative direction when, upon the retirement of Justice William J. Brennan, he successfully nominated Judge David Souter of the U.S. Court of Appeals in 1989. Two years later, Bush nominated a conservative African American, Judge Clarence Thomas, also of the U.S. Court of Appeals, upon the retirement of Justice Thurgood Marshall. Thomas's nomination stirred up opposition from the NAACP and other liberal groups which supported affirmative action and abortion rights. Dramatic charges of sexual harassment against Thomas from Anita Hill, a University of Oklahoma law professor, were revealed only days before the nomination was to go to the Senate. The charges provoked a reopening of Judiciary Committee hearings, which were nationally televised. Nonetheless, Thomas narrowly won confirmation in October 1991.

BUSH'S ACTIVIST FOREIGN POLICY

Panama

Since coming to office, the Bush administration had been concerned with Panamanian dictator Manuel Noriega because he allegedly provided an important link in the drug traffic between South America and the United States. After economic sanctions, diplomatic efforts, and an October 1989 coup failed to oust Noriega, Bush ordered 12,000 troops into Panama on December 20. The Americans installed a new government headed by Guillermo Endara, who had earlier apparently won a presidential election which was then nullified by Noriega. On January 3, 1990, Noriega surrendered to the Americans and was taken to the United States to stand trial on drug-trafficking charges, a trial that began in September 1991. Twenty-three United States soldiers and three American civilians were killed in the operation. The Panamanians lost nearly 300 soldiers and more than 500 civilians.

Nicaragua

After years of civil war, Nicaragua held a presidential election in February 1990. Because of an economy largely destroyed by civil war and large financial debt to the United States, Violetta Barrios de Chamorro of the National Opposition Union defeated Daniel Ortega of the Sandinistas, thereby fulfilling a longstanding American objective. The United States lifted its economic sanctions in March and put together an economic aid package for Nicaragua. In September 1991, the Bush administration forgave Nicaragua most of its debt to the United States.

China

After the death in April 1989 of reformer Hu Yaobang, formerly general secretary and chairman of the Chinese Communist party, students began pro-democracy marches in Beijing. By the middle of May, more than one million people were gathering in Beijing's Tiananmen Square, and others elsewhere in China, calling for political reform. Martial law was imposed and in early June the army fired on the demonstrators. Estimates of the death toll in the wake of the nationwide crackdown on demonstrators ranged between 500 and 7,000. In July 1989, U.S. National Security Advisor Brent Scowcroft and Deputy Secretary of State Lawrence Eagleburger secretly met with Chinese leaders. When they again met the Chinese in December and revealed their earlier meeting, the Bush administration faced a storm of criticism for its policy of "constructive engagement" from opponents arguing that sanctions were needed. Although establishing sanctions on China in 1991 on high-technology satellite-part exports, Bush continued to support renewal of China's Most Favored Nation trading status.

Africa

To rescue American citizens threatened by civil war, Bush sent 230 marines into Liberia in August 1990, evacuating 125 people. South Africa in 1990 freed Nelson Mandela, the most famous leader of the African National Congress, after 28 years of imprisonment. South Africa then began moving away from apartheid, and in 1991, Bush lifted economic sanctions imposed five years earlier. Mandela and his wife Winnie toured the United States in June 1990 to a tumultuous welcome, particularly from African Americans. During their visit, they also addressed Congress.

COLLAPSE OF EAST EUROPEAN COMMUNISM

Bush-Gorbachev Summits

Amid the collapse of communism in Eastern Europe, Bush met with Mikhail Gorbachev in Malta from December 1 through 3, 1989; the two leaders appeared to agree that the Cold War was over. On May 30 and 31, 1990, Bush and Gorbachev met in Washington to discuss the possible reunification of Germany, and signed a trade treaty between the United States and the Soviet Union. The meeting of the two leaders in Helsinki on September 9 addressed strategies for the developing Persian Gulf crisis. At the meeting of the "Group of 7" nations (Canada, France, Germany, Italy, Japan, United Kingdom, and the United States) in July 1991, Gorbachev requested economic aid from the West. A short time later, on July 30 and 31, Bush met Gorbachev in Moscow where they signed the START treaty, which cut United States and Soviet nuclear arsenals by 30 percent, and pushed for Middle Eastern talks.

PERSIAN GULF CRISIS

July 1990

Saddam Hussein of Iraq charged that Kuwait had conspired with the United States to keep oil prices low and began massing troops at the Iraq-Kuwait border.

August 1990

On August 2, Iraq invaded Kuwait, an act that Bush denounced as "naked aggression." One day later, 100,000 Iraqi soldiers were poised south of Kuwait City, near the Saudi Arabian border. The United States quickly banned most trade with Iraq, froze Iraq's and Kuwait's assets in the United States, and sent aircraft carriers to the Persian Gulf. After the U.N. Security Council condemned the invasion, on August 6, Bush ordered the deployment of air, sea, and land forces to Saudi Arabia, dubbing the operation "Desert Shield." At the end of August, there were 100,000 American soldiers in Saudi Arabia.

September 1990

Bush encouraged Egypt to support American policy by forgiving Egypt its debt to the United States. He also obtained pledges of financial support from Saudi Arabia, Kuwait, and Japan, among other nations, to help pay for the operation.

October 1990

On October 29, the Security Council warned Hussein that further actions might be taken if he did not withdraw from Kuwait.

November 1990

In November, Bush ordered that U.S. forces be increased to more than 400,000. On November 29, the United Nations set January 15, 1991, as the deadline for Iraqi withdrawal from Kuwait.

January 1991

On January 9, Iraq's foreign minister, Tariq Aziz, rejected a letter written by Bush to Hussein. Three days later, after an extensive debate, Congress authorized the use of force in the gulf. On January 17, an international force including the United States, Great Britain, France, Italy, Saudi Arabia, and Kuwait launched an air and missile attack on Iraq and occupied Kuwait. The United States called the effort "Operation Desert Storm." Under the overall command of army general H. Norman Schwarzkopf, the military effort emphasized high-technology weapons, including F-15 E fighter bombers, F-117 A stealth fighters, Tomahawk cruise missiles, and Patriot antimissile missiles. Beginning on January 17, Iraq sent SCUD missiles into Israel in an effort to draw that country into the war and hopefully break up the U.S.-Arabian coalition. On January 22 and 23, Hussein's forces set Kuwaiti oil fields on fire and spilled oil into the gulf.

February 1991

On February 23, the allied ground assault began. Four days later, Bush announced that Kuwait was liberated and ordered offensive operations to cease. The United Nations established the terms for the cease-fire: Iraqi annexation of Kuwait to be rescinded, Iraq to accept liability for damages and return Kuwaiti property, Iraq to end all military actions and identify mines and booby traps, and Iraq to release captives.

April 1991

On April 3, the Security Council approved a resolution to establish a permanent cease-fire; Iraq accepted U.N. terms on April 6. The next day the United States began airlifting food to Kurdish refugees on the Iraq-Turkey border who were fleeing the Kurdish rebellion against Hussein, a rebellion that was seemingly encouraged by Bush, who nonetheless refused to become militarily involved. The United States estimated that 100,000 Iraqis had been killed during the war, while the Americans had lost about 115 lives.

Toward a Middle East Conference

On February 6, 1991, the United States had set out its postwar goals for the Middle East. These included regional arms control and security arrangements, international aid for reconstruction of Iraq and Kuwait, and resolution of the Israeli-Palestinian conflict. Immediately after cessation of the conflict, Secretary of State James Baker toured the Middle East attempting to promote a conference to address the problems of the region. After several more negotiating sessions, Saudi Arabia, Syria, Jordan, and Lebanon had accepted the United States proposal for an Arab-Israeli peace conference by the middle of July; Israel conditionally accepted in early August. Despite continuing conflict with Iraq, including U.N. inspections of its nuclear capabilities, and new Israeli settlements in disputed territory which kept the conference agreement tenuous, the nations met in Madrid, Spain, at the end of October. Bilateral talks in early November between Israel and the Arabs concentrated on procedural issues.

BREAK UP OF THE SOVIET UNION

Collapse of Soviet Communism

In the aftermath of the Soviet coup attempt on August 19, 1991, much of the Communist structure came crashing down, including the prohibition of the Communist party in Russia. The remaining Baltic republics of Latvia and Estonia declared their independence, which was recognized by the United States several days after other nations had done so. Most of the other Soviet republics then followed suit in declaring their independence. The Bush administration wanted some form of central authority to remain in the Soviet Union; hence, it did not seriously consider recognizing the independence of any republics except the Baltics. Bush also resisted offering economic aid to the Soviet Union until it presented a radical economic reform plan to move toward a free market. However, humanitarian aid such as food would be given in order to preserve stability during the winter.

Arms Reduction

In September 1991, George Bush announced unilateral removal and destruction of ground-based tactical nuclear weapons in Europe and Asia, removal of nuclear-armed Tomahawk cruise missiles from surface ships and submarines, immediate destruction of intercontinental ballistic missiles covered by START, and an end to the 24-hour alert for strategic bombers that the United States had maintained for decades. Gorbachev responded the next month by announcing the immediate deactivation of intercontinental ballistic missiles covered by START, removal of all short-range missiles from Soviet ships, submarines, and aircraft, and destruction of all ground-based tactical nuclear weapons. He also said that the Soviet Union would reduce its forces by 700,000 troops, and he placed all long-range nuclear missiles under a single command.

SOCIAL AND CULTURAL DEVELOPMENTS

AIDS

In 1981, scientists announced the discovery of Acquired Immune Deficiency Syndrome (AIDS), which was especially widespread among homosexual males and intravenous drug users. Widespread fear resulted, including an upsurge in homophobia. The Centers for Disease Control and National Cancer Institute, among others, pursued research on the disease. By 1990, 600,000 Americans had the virus, 83,000 had died, and another 136,000 were sick. The FDA responded to calls for faster evaluation of drugs by approving the drug AZT in February 1991. With the revelation that a Florida dentist had infected five patients, there were calls for mandatory testing of health-care workers. Supporters of testing argued before a House hearing in September 1991 that testing should be regarded as a public-health issue, rather than a civil-rights issue.

Religious Right

In 1987, it was revealed that popular TV preacher Jim Bakker had been involved in a sex and money scandal. A short time later, one of his major critics, evangelist Jimmy Swaggart, was also discovered to be involved in a sex scandal. With the influence of TV evangelists on the wane, Jerry Falwell announced that he was abandoning political activism to concentrate on preaching. In October 1991, Jim Bakker was convicted of fraud and conspiracy.

Labor

Labor-union membership dropped to about 19 percent of the labor force, largely because the economy was shifting from heavy industry to electronics and service industries.

Abortion

In a July 1989 decision, *Webster v. Reproductive Health Services,* the Supreme Court upheld a Missouri law prohibiting public employees from performing abortions, unless the mother's life was threatened. With this decision shifting the abortion focus from the courts to the state legislatures, pro-life (antiabortion) forces moved in several states to restrict the availability of abortions, but their results were mixed. Florida rejected abortion restrictions in October 1989, the governor of Louisiana vetoed similar legislation nine months later, and in early 1991 Maryland adopted a liberal abortion law. In contrast, Utah and Pennsylvania enacted strict curbs on abortion during the same period. At the national level, Bush, in October 1989, vetoed funding for medicaid abortions. The conflict between pro-choice and pro-life forces gained national attention through such events as a pro-life demonstration held in Washington in April 1990, and the blockage of access to abortion clinics by Operation Rescue, a militant antiabortion group, in the summer of 1991.

Rich and Poor

Kevin Phillips's *The Politics of Rich and Poor* (1990) argued that the 40 million Americans in the bottom fifth of the population experienced a 1 percent decline in income between 1973 and 1979 and a 10 percent decline between 1979 and 1987. Meanwhile, the top fifth rose by 7 percent and 16 percent during the same periods. The number of single-parent families living below the poverty level of $11,611 for a family of four rose by 46 percent between 1979 and 1987. Nearly one-quarter of the children under age six were poor.

Censorship

The conservative leaning of the electorate for the past decade revealed its cultural dimension in a controversy that erupted over the National Endowment for the Arts in September 1989. Criticism of photographer Robert Mapplethorpe's homoerotic and masochistic pictures, among other artworks which had been funded by the endowment, led Senator Jesse Helms of North Carolina to propose that grants for "obscene or indecent" projects, or those derogatory of religion, be cut off. Although the proposal ultimately failed, it raised questions about the government's role as a sponsor of art in an increasingly pluralistic society. The Mapplethorpe photographs also became an issue the following summer when Cincinnati's Contemporary Art Center was indicted on charges of obscenity when it exhibited the artist's work. A jury later struck down the charges. Meanwhile, in March 1990, the Recording Industry Association of America agreed to place new uniform warning labels on recordings that contained potentially offensive language. The issue of language was dramatized when a federal judge in Florida ruled in June 1990 that the 2 Live Crew album, *As Nasty as They Wanna Be*, was obscene. A few days later two of the band members and a record store owner were arrested for violating state obscenity laws. Civil liberties groups protested. The band members were later acquitted, while the businessman was convicted.

Crisis in Education

The National Commission on Excellence in Education, appointed in 1981, argued in "A Nation at Risk" that a "rising tide of mediocrity" characterized the nation's schools. In the wake of the report, many states instituted reforms, including higher teacher salaries, competency tests for teachers, and an increase in required subjects for high school graduation. In September 1989, Bush met with the nation's governors in Charlottesville, Virginia, to work on a plan to improve the schools. The meeting called for the establishment of national performance goals to be measured by achievement tests. In February 1990, the National Governors Association adopted specific performance goals, stating that achievement tests should be administered in grades four, eight, and twelve.

GRE History – Test 1

TIME: 170 Minutes
190 Questions

DIRECTIONS: The following incomplete statements and questions have five answer choices. Select the best choice.

(*Answer sheets appear in the back of this book.*)

1. All of the following were New Deal reforms EXCEPT

    (A) the National Industrial Recover Act.

    (B) the Tennessee Valley Authority.

    (C) the Reconstruction Finance Corporation.

    (D) the Agricultural Adjustment Act.

    (E) the Works Progress Administration.

2. The Heptarchy consisted of the following Anglo-Saxon states

    (A) Essex, Wessex, Sussex, Kent, East Anglia, Mercia, and Northumbria

    (B) West Cornwall, Essex, Wessex, Sussex, East Anglia, Mercia, and Northumbria

    (C) Wales, West Anglia, Kent, Essex, Wessex, Sussex, and Mercia

    (D) The Danelaw, Cumbria, Essex, Wessex, Sussex, Kent, and East Anglia

    (E) Strathclyde, Wessex, Sussex, Kent, East Anglia, Mercia, and Northumbria

3. All of the following were contributors in the Realist-Nominalist Controversy EXCEPT

    (A) Peter Abelard.   (D) Thomas Aquinas.

    (B) Peter Lombard.   (E) Hildebrand.

    (C) Albertus Magnus.

4. Lenin's "retreat" from communism was embodied in the

   (A) Kornilov Affair.
   (D) Second Five-Year Plan.
   (B) New Economic Policy.
   (E) April Theses.
   (C) First Five-Year Plan.

QUESTIONS 5–6 refer to the following passage.

An Act of Congress which deprives a person of the United States of his liberty or property merely because he came himself or brought his property into a particular Territory of the United States, and who had committed no offense against the laws, could hardly be dignified with the name of due process of law . . . .

5. The preceding passage is most likely to have been written by

   (A) Roger B. Taney.
   (D) Zachary Taylor.
   (B) Abraham Lincoln.
   (E) Thomas Jefferson.
   (C) Stephen A. Douglas.

6. The author wants primarily to convince readers that

   (A) each territory has the right to allow or prohibit slavery within its boundaries.

   (B) the Constitution protects slavery in all U.S. territories.

   (C) slavery is a moral evil that should not be allowed to spread into any new territories.

   (D) slavery is a necessary evil, the spread of which should be limited as much as possible.

   (E) the constitutional requirement of due process of law mandates that slaves brought into free territories be immediately liberated.

7. The Cluniac Movement was an effort to

   (A) reform the Church from within.

   (B) humiliate William I of England.

   (C) establish a network of universities throughout Europe.

   (D) denounce the ideas advanced by John Hus and his followers.

   (E) validate the writings of the Fathers of the Church.

8. During the early 1930s the Spanish Republican government initiated a program to

    I. expel the Jesuits.

    II. nationalize the railroads.

    III. confiscate large estates.

    IV. introduce the eight-hour work day and social insurance.

    V. reform and enlarge the army.

    (A) I and IV only

    (B) I, II, and III only

    (C) I, II, III, and IV only

    (D) Only IV

    (E) I, II, III, IV, and V

9. All of the following leaders attended the Congress of Vienna EXCEPT

    (A) Talleyrand.

    (B) Metternich.

    (C) Castlereagh.

    (D) Louis Napoleon.

    (E) Wellington.

10. The primary cause of the Price Revolution of the 16th century was

    (A) the collapse of agriculture through crop failures.

    (B) the influx of specie (gold and silver) into the European economies.

    (C) the decline in population.

    (D) the impact of the early stages of industrialism.

    (E) the rise of national economies.

11. Which of the following were characteristics of the U.S. economy during the 1980s?

    I. Declining foreign investment

    II. Declining unemployment rates

    III. Declining stock prices

    IV. Declining inflation

    V. Declining imbalance between imports and exports

(A) I and V only

(D) I, III, IV, and V only

(B) II and IV only

(E) I, II, III, IV, and V

(C) II, III, and V only

12. Which of the following was most crucial in bringing about U.S. participation in the First World War?

(A) British propaganda

(B) German violation of Belgian neutrality

(C) German use of submarines against merchant and passenger ships

(D) German atrocities against French and Belgian civilians in the occupied areas of those countries

(E) Revelation of a German proposal to Mexico for a joint war against the United States

13. Essential documents in the growth of representative government in England include the

   I. Magna Carta.

   II. Edict of Nantes.

   III. Confirmation of the Charters.

   IV. Peace of Wedmore.

   V. Assize of Arms.

(A) I, II, and III

(D) Only I

(B) I, III, and V

(E) I, II, III, IV, and V

(C) I and III only

14. At the Congress of Berlin, the British prime minister Benjamin Disraeli gained all of the following objectives EXCEPT

(A) British possession of Cyprus.

(B) a small Bulgaria.

(C) the independence of the Ottoman Empire.

(D) Russian exclusion from the Mediterranean.

(E) the introduction of democratic reforms within the Ottoman Empire.

15. The Turkish advances into Central Europe during the 17th century were thwarted primarily by

(A) Louis XIV.

(B) Oliver Cromwell.

(C) Leopold I.

(D) Charles V.

(E) Elector Frederick William.

16. *The Decline of the West*, which expressed the depth of intellectual despair after the First World War, was written by

(A) Arnold Toynbee.

(B) Oswald Spengler.

(C) William McNeil.

(D) Tristan Tzara.

(E) Jose Ortega y Gasset.

17. Theodore Roosevelt could have read all of the following EXCEPT

(A) Lincoln Steffens' *The Shame of the Cities.*

(B) John Steinbeck's *The Grapes of Wrath.*

(C) Edward Bellamy's *Looking Backward.*

(D) Henry George's *Progress and Poverty.*

(E) Upton Sinclair's *The Jungle.*

18. The Compromise of 1850 included all of the following provisions EXCEPT

(A) a tougher fugitive slave law.

(B) the admission of California as a free state.

(C) the prohibition of slavery in areas of the Mexican Cession not yet admitted as states.

(D) the prohibition of the slave trade in the District of Columbia.

(E) federal assumption of Texas's pre-annexation debt.

19. How should the following phases of the French Revolution be listed in chronological order, from earliest to latest?

    I. Directory

    II. Legislative Assembly

    III. National Assembly

    IV. Consulate

    V. Convention

(A) I, III, II, IV, V

(B) III, II, V, I, IV

(C) III, V, II, I, IV

(D) III, V, II, IV, I

(E) III, V, I, II, IV

20. Based on the maps below, what does the growth of the Midlands and Liverpool most probably suggest?

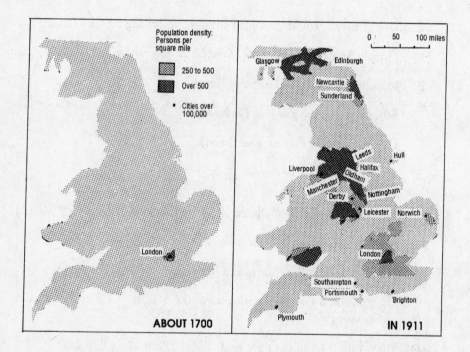

(A) The Commercial Revolution

(B) The growth of the consumption of luxury items

(C) The Industrial Revolution

(D) The strength of medieval agricultural rights and practices such as usufruct

(E) The impact of 18th century imperialism

21. Renaissance neoplatonism was significantly advanced by

    I.   Marsiglio Ficino.

    II.   Pico della Morandola.

    III. Machiavelli.

    IV. Boccaccio.

    V.   Erasmus of Rotterdam.

(A) I, II, and III only   (D) I and II only

(B) I, II, III, and IV only   (E) I, II, III, IV, and V

(C) II, III, and IV only

22. The mutual assistance defensive arrangement, NATO, was formed in direct response to the

(A) failure of the United Nations to adequately address the mounting crisis in Korea.

(B) fall of China to Mao and the Communists.

(C) Russian threat to Greece.

(D) Russian policies in Germany and Czechoslovakia.

(E) emergence of Titoism in Yugoslavia.

23. All of the following are true of 18th century British mercantilism EXCEPT

(A) encouragement of manufacturing in America.

(B) requirement that trade between Britain and the colonies be carried in British or American ships.

(C) prohibition on the importation of certain items from non-British sources into the colonies.

(D) requirement that items imported into the colonies be shipped through Britain first.

(E) encouragement of staple-crop production in America.

24. All of the following helped shape the development of colonial American agriculture EXCEPT

(A) availability of land.

(B) abundance of capital.

(C) limitations of climate and land.

(D) shortage of labor.

(E) European demand for agricultural products.

25. Which of the following would an 1850s Southern plantation owner have been most likely to approve of?

(A) George Fitzhugh's *Cannibals All!*

(B) Hinton Rowan Helper's *The Impending Crisis of the South.*

(C) Frederick Law Olmstead's *The Cotton Kingdom.*

(D) William Lloyd Garrison's *Liberator.*

(E) Harriet Beecher Stowe's *Uncle Tom's Cabin.*

QUESTIONS 26–27 refer to the following passage.

But as the earth bringeth not forth fruit except first it be watered and made fruitful from above . . . even so by the righteousness of the law, in doing many things we do nothing, and in fulfilling of the law we fulfill it not, except first, without any merit or work of ours, we be made righteous by the Christian righteousness, which nothing appertaineth to the righteousness of the law, or to the earthly and active righteousness. But this righteousness is heavenly and passive; which we have not of ourselves, but receive it from heaven; which we work not, but apprehend it by faith; whereby we mount up above all laws and works.

26. The passage above most nearly represents the view of

(A) Erasmus.   (D) Wolsey.

(B) Luther.   (E) Calvin.

(C) Henry of Navarre.

27. The author of this passage is describing the theological argument known as

    (A) predestination.

    (B) transubstantiation.

    (C) justification by faith.

    (D) supremacy.

    (E) conciliarism.

    _____

28. During the ministry of Clement Atlee, the British government introduced a wide range of social and economic legislation which included

    I. National Health Service.

    II. National Insurance.

    III. nationalization of all industry.

    IV. the Cable and Wireless Act.

    V. the end of rationing.

    (A) I, II, III, and V only

    (B) I, II, III, and IV only

    (C) I, II, and IV only

    (D) I, II, IV, and V only

    (E) I, II, III, IV, and V

29. The primary cause of Khruschev's fall from power was

    (A) the Bay of Pigs affair.

    (B) the cost of the Soviet missile program.

    (C) the failure of his agricultural plan.

    (D) his frequent absences from the Soviet Union.

    (E) lack of support for the Soviet military.

30. Which of the following statements does NOT express the attitudes or beliefs of the founders of the Massachusetts Bay Colony?

    (A) They had a special covenant relationship with God.

    (B) Their colony should be a moral example to the entire world, especially to England.

    (C) Migrating to America was the best way to reform England.

(D) The Church of England had become so corrupt that all true Christians were obligated to separate from it.

(E) God would reward their obedience with temporal blessings.

31. Which of the following statements is LEAST true about immigration to the U.S. between 1880 and 1900?

(A) Most immigrants were unskilled day laborers.

(B) Immigration increased steadily during these years.

(C) Immigrants tended to be Catholic, Eastern Orthodox, or Jewish.

(D) Most immigrants came from northern and western Europe.

(E) Chinese immigrants were excluded by law during most of these years.

32. Which of the following peace settlements concluded wars during the reign of Louis XIV?

    I. Peace of Augsburg

   II. Treaty of Nimwegen

  III. Treaty of Ryswick

   IV. Peace of Utrecht

    V. Treaty of Paris

(A) I, II, III, and IV only   (D) III and IV only

(B) I, III, IV, and V only   (E) I, II, III, IV, and V

(C) II, III, and IV only

33. The primary cause of the Hungarian revolution of 1848 was

(A) the demand for a liberal constitution.

(B) the desire to establish control over the Slavs in the East and South.

(C) nationalism.

(D) economic and social change.

(E) hatred of the Hohenzollern dynasty.

34. All of the following contributed to the development of the heliocentric theory EXCEPT

    (A) Nicholas of Cusa.   (D) Da Vinci.

    (B) Nicholaus Copernicus.   (E) William Harvey.

    (C) Galileo.

35. Which of the following gave the greatest impetus to national civil service reform?

    (A) President Hayes's halt to Southern Reconstruction

    (B) The renomination of President Arthur in 1884

    (C) The continued Stalwart-Half Breed battles of the Republican party

    (D) The assassination of President Garfield

    (E) The prosecution and eventual conviction of Boss Tweed

36. During the early 1930s, French fascism manifested itself in radical groups such as the

    I.   Francistes.

    II. Solidarité Française.

    III. "Cagoulards."

    IV. Parti Populaire Française.

    V.   Annales.

    (A) I and II only   (D) I, II, III, and IV only

    (B) I and V only   (E) I, II, III, IV, and V

    (C) I, II, and III only

37. The Kronstadt Rebellion was caused by

    (A) the economic disaster and social upheaval of the Russian Civil War.

    (B) the desire of Ukrainian naval officers to secede from the new Soviet Union.

    (C) the collapse of Germany in October/November 1918.

(D)   the influence of the Spartacist movement.

(E)   troops sympathetic to Poland.

38.   The Credit Mobilier Scandal involved

(A)   a dummy construction company used by railroad magnates to defraud the government.

(B)   a tax-collection contract sold in exchange for a kickback to Republican campaign coffers.

(C)   a conspiracy to defraud the government of large amounts of money from the excise tax on whiskey.

(D)   an attempt by Congress to raise its own pay retroactively.

(E)   the use of a dummy corporation to raise funds on the French stock exchange for the Confederacy.

39.   "Political power is that power, which every man having in the state of nature, has given up into the hands of the society, and therein to the governors, whom the society hath set over itself, with this express or tacit trust, that it shall be employed for their good, and the preservation of their property: now this power, which every man has in the state of nature, and which he parts with to the society in all cases where the society can secure him, is to use such means, for the preserving of his own property, as he thinks good, and nature allows him; and to punish the breach of the law of nature in others, so as (according to the best of his reason) may most conduce to the preservation of himself, and the rest of mankind."

The passage above most nearly represents the views of

(A)   Thomas Hobbes.   (D)   George III.

(B)   Francis Bacon.   (E)   Voltaire.

(C)   John Locke.

40.   The Pact of Locarno included all of the following provisions EXCEPT

(A)   mutual guarantees between Germany, Belgium, France, Great Britain, and Italy.

(B)   arbitration agreements between Germany and Belgium.

(C)   disarmament agreements based on pre–World War I armament levels.

(D) a guarantee of mutual support between France and Czechoslovakia.

(E) a guarantee of the German-Belgian border as fixed in 1918.

41. The Dawes Plan was

(A) a British plan to stabilize the gold standard.

(B) an American plan which confronted the crisis associated with the Ruhr invasion.

(C) a British plan to limit the level of naval weapons.

(D) a British plan to nationalize the coal industry.

(E) a British plan to manage postwar demobilization.

QUESTIONS 42–44 refer to the map below.

EXPANSION OF THE UNITED STATES

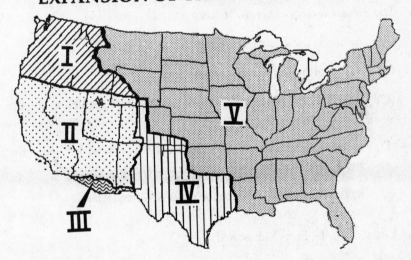

42. In which areas of the map was slavery in existence prior to its annexation by the United States?

(A) II, III, and IV

(B) II and III

(C) IV only

(D) II only

(E) III only

43. Which areas of the map became part of the United States as a direct result of the Mexican War?

    (A) IV only

    (B) III and IV

    (C) III only

    (D) II, III, and IV

    (E) II only

44. Which of the following is true of Area III?

    (A) Its acquisition was a direct result of the Mexican-American war.

    (B) It contained a possible route for a southern transatlantic railroad.

    (C) Its purchase was authorized by President Polk.

    (D) It automatically entered the Union as slave territory.

    (E) The area gained statehood during the Cleveland and Harrison administrations.

45. The Fabian Society in Great Britain

    (A) advanced the Chartist program.

    (B) was an orthodox Marxist organization.

    (C) embodied the Marxist revisionist sentiment of the Left at the close of the 19th century.

    (D) advocated the idea of Tory Democracy advanced by Benjamin Disraeli and Randolph Churchill.

    (E) was established to advance the cause of a free Ireland.

46. Lenin's "April Theses" advocated

    I.   seizure of the land by the peasants.

    II. control of industry by committees of workers.

    III. withdrawal from the war.

    IV. the elimination of Nicholas II and his family.

    V.   the continuance of the provisional government.

    (A) I, II, and V only

    (B) II and V only

(C)   II, III, and V only   (D)   I, II, and III only

(E)   I, II, III, IV, and V

47.   Zwingli radicalized Protestantism beyond Luther's positions by

(A)   his emphasis on predestination and his view of the Eucharist.

(B)   denouncing the corruption of the Roman Catholic church.

(C)   his alliance with the Unitarians.

(D)   defeating the Catholic Swiss Cantons in the Kappel War.

(E) · infiltrating the Hapsburg court of Charles V.

48.   How should the following pre–First World War diplomatic arrangements be listed in chronological order, from earliest to latest?

   I.   Dual Entente

  II.   Dual Alliance

 III.   Triple Alliance

 IV.   Anglo-Russian Entente

  V.   Entente Cordiale

(A)   I, II, III, V, IV   (D)   II, III, V, IV, I

(B)   I, IV, II, III, V   (E)   II, III, V, I, IV

(C)   II, III, I, V, IV

49.   The Marshall Plan could best be understood as part of an American desire to

(A)   make communism less appealing to Europeans by creating economic prosperity.

(B)   assemble a military alliance against the Soviet Union.

(C)   maintain Western Europe in a state of permanent economic dependence on the United States.

(D)   permanently eliminate the possibility of a threat from an industrialized Germany.

(E)   end the nation's postwar depression by creating viable economic competitors in Europe.

50. Which of the following inventors had the most direct effect on agriculture?

    I. Elias Howe

    II. Cyrus McCormick

    III. Chrisopher Sholes

    IV. Eli Whitney

    V. Henry Bessemer

(A) I, II, and III

(B) II, III, and IV

(C) II, III, and V

(D) II, IV, and V

(E) II and IV

QUESTIONS 51–55 refer to the following passage.

29 March 1789, Bailliage, France: [The people of Bailliage] wish:

1. That his subjects of the third estate equal by such status to all other citizens, present themselves before the common father without other distinction which might degrade them.

2. That all the orders [the three estates], already united by duty and common desire to contribute equally to the needs of the State, also deliberate in common concerning its needs.

3. That no citizen lose his liberty except according to law; that consequently, no one be arrested by virtue of special orders, or, if imperative circumstances necessitate such orders, that the prisoner be handed over to the regular courts of justice within forty-eight hours at the latest . . .

5. That the property of all citizens be inviolable, and that no one be required to make sacrifice thereof for the public welfare, except upon assurance of indemnification based upon the statement of freely selected appraisers . . .

16. That such tax be borne equally, without distinction, by all classes of citizens and by all kinds of property, even feudal and contingent rights.

51. The above statement was

(A) an element in a petition which would be placed before Louis XVI.

(B) the advice of the people of Bailliage on the new constitution.

(C) part of the *cahiers de doléances* or lists of grievances which were advanced in the spring of 1789.

(D)   representative of radical Jacobin sentiment.

(E)   written by Abbé Sieyès.

52.   The above statement suggests that the authors

(A)   supported the current practices of the regime.

(B)   intended to overthrow the government.

(C)   wanted to minimize their tax burden.

(D)   wanted to reform the existing system through a universal recognition of basic rights and the principle of equal responsibility.

(E)   did not understand the development of nationalism in France.

53.   The ideas advanced in the passage were considered and, in many instances, implemented under the jurisdiction of

(A)   the Estates-General.

(B)   Louis XVI.

(C)   Robespierre.

(D)   the National Assembly.

(E)   the Legislative Assembly.

54.   The underlying political concepts upon which these statements are based most closely represent the views of

(A)   Voltaire.   (D)   Montesquieu.

(B)   Robespierre.   (E)   Louis XIV.

(C)   Quesnay.

55.   The above statement was drafted while representatives were being selected for the

(A)   Directory.   (D)   Convention.

(B)   Legislative Assembly. (E)   Estates-General.

(C)   National Assembly.

56. Grover Cleveland's 1887 State of the Union address dealt entirely with

    (A) the agricultural crisis and the gold standard.

    (B) the abuse of Union army pension rolls.

    (C) the tariff question.

    (D) civil service reform.

    (E) government regulation of big business.

QUESTIONS 57–59 refer to the following passage.

"Our constitution is called a democracy for the administration is in the hands of the many and not of the few. But while the law secures equal justice to all alike in their private disputes, the claim of excellence is also recognized; and when a citizen is in any way distinguished, he is preferred to the public service, not as a matter of privilege, but as the reward of merit. Neither is poverty a bar, but a man may benefit his country whatever be the obscurity of his condition. There is no exclusiveness in our public life, and in our private intercourse we are not suspicious of one another, nor angry with our neighbor if he does what he likes. . . ."

57. In this statement Pericles advanced the view of democracy which was held in

    (A) Sparta.   (D) Athens.

    (B) Syracuse.   (E) Mycenae.

    (C) Alexandria.

58. The Athenians eulogized by Pericles had perished in the war with

    (A) Persia.

    (B) Sparta and its allies.

    (C) Philip of Macedon.

    (D) Carthage.

    (E) Darius.

59. Pericles' statement was reported in an early historical work written by

    (A) Herodotus.   (D) Xenophon.

    (B) Thucydides.   (E) Livy.

    (C) Tacitus.

60. All of the following were fully or partially realized points of Woodrow Wilson's Allied peace plan EXCEPT

    (A) the creation of an independent Poland.

    (B) the extensive readjustment of national boundaries in the Middle East to create independent nations.

    (C) the restoration of Alsace-Lorraine to France.

    (D) the creation of a League of Nations to settle international disputes.

    (E) the creation of nations in the Balkans according to the principle of self-determination of peoples.

61. In 1662, Puritan ministers in New England "created a new class of membership for those who had not had the intense 'converting experience' but who were descended from those who had had the experience. In this way they kept the church-benches filled without abandoning their ideal of a purified church where only 'Visible Saints' could be full members."

    The above passage refers to the

    (A) "Old Deluder Satan" Act.

    (B) "Half-Way Covenant."

    (C) Fundamental Orders of Connecticut.

    (D) Mayflower Compact.

    (E) New England Confederation.

QUESTION 62 refers to the following map.

62. The map indicates the status of Germany in

    (A) 1871.   (D) 1815.

    (B) 1919.   (E) 1989.

    (C) 1945.
    _____

63. All of the following political leaders opposed the Stuart monarchs EXCEPT

    (A) Sir Edward Coke.   (D) John Hampton.

    (B) John Pym.   (E) Edward Hyde.

    (C) Oliver Cromwell.

64. Reformation documents which contributed to the growth of vernacular literatures included

    I. Luther's German *Bible*.

    II. Calvin's *Institutes of the Christian Religion*.

    III. Henry VIII's *Defense of the Seven Sacraments*.

    IV. Ignatius Loyola's *Spiritual Exercises*.

    V. *The Index of Prohibited Books*.

    (A) Only I   (D) I, II, III, and IV only

    (B) I and II only   (E) I, II, III, IV, and V

    (C) I, II, and III only

65. Which of the following gave the president the most power in directing American foreign policy during the post–World War II era?

    (A) The Tonkin Gulf Resolution

    (B) The Civil Rights Act of 1964

    (C) The Boland Amendments of 1982 and 1984

    (D) The War Powers Act

    (E) The Good Neighbor Policy

66. Prior to 1848, the leaders of the Italian nationalist movement were

    I. Cavour.

    II. Garibaldi.

    III. Pius IX.

    IV. Mazzini.

    V. de Maistre.

    (A) I, II, and IV only

    (B) III and IV only

    (C) III, IV, and V only

    (D) I, II, III, and IV only

    (E) I, II, III, IV, and V

67. Baroque philosophical thought and values were embodied most profoundly in the work of

    (A) Bernini.

    (B) Vasari.

    (C) Montaigne.

    (D) Montesquieu.

    (E) Jean Bodin.

68. The War of the Three Henrys concluded with the

    I. ascendence of Henry of Navarre to the throne.

    II. end of the Valois dynasty.

    III. triumph of the Catholics.

    IV. rise of the Bourbon dynasty.

    V. Fronde.

    (A) I, II, and III only

    (B) I, III, and IV only

    (C) I, II, III, and IV only

    (D) I, II, IV, and V only

    (E) I, II, III, IV, and V

QUESTIONS 69–70 refer to the following passage.

'Tis repugnant to reason, to the universal order of things, to all examples from former ages, to suppose that this Continent can long remain subject to any external power. The most sanguine in Britain doth not think so. The utmost stretch of human wisdom cannot, at this time, compass a plan, short of separation, which can promise the Continent even a year's security. Reconciliation is *now* a fallacious dream. Nature hath deserted the connection, and art cannot supply her place.

69. This passage can be found in which of the following?

    (A) Thomas Jefferson's *Declaration of Independence*

    (B) George Washington's *Farewell Address*

    (C) Thomas Paine's *Crisis Papers*

    (D) Thomas Paine's *Common Sense*

    (E) John Dickinson's *Letters from a Farmer in Pennsylvania*

70. The author wants primarily to convince readers that

    (A) it is a necessity of nature that America should be independent of Great Britain.

    (B) America should keep itself free from entangling alliances with European powers.

    (C) Great Britain will soon give up the struggle to retain her North American colonies.

    (D) parliamentary attempts to tax Americans without the consent of colonial legislatures are violations of the English constitution.

    (E) Britain has given ample provocation for the colonies to declare their independence.

QUESTION 71 refers to the following three maps.

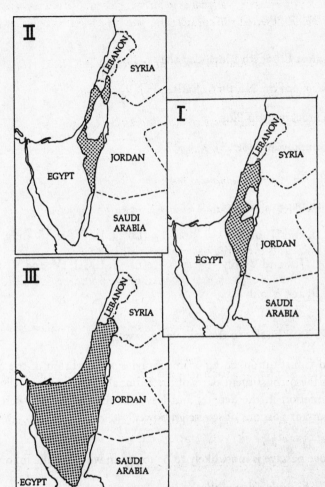

71. The correct chronological sequence of the development of modern Israel, as indicated by the maps, is

    (A) II, I, III

    (B) III, I, II

    (C) II, III, I

    (D) I, II, III

    (E) III, II, I

    _____

72. The Act of Abjuration is the declaration of independence of

    (A) the Kingdom of the Two Sicilies.

    (B) Belgium.

    (C) the Netherlands.

(D) Portugal.

(E) Luxembourg.

73. Plots against Elizabeth I included the

   I. Rising of the Northern Earls.

   II. Throckmorton Plot.

   III. Gunpowder Plot.

   IV. Popish Plot.

   V. Babington Plot.

   (A) I, II, and III only   (D) I, II, IV, and V only

   (B) I, II, III, and V only   (E) I, II, III, IV, and V

   (C) I, II, and V only

QUESTIONS 74–75 refer to the following passage.

The proposed Constitution, so far from implying an abolition of the State governments, makes them constituent parts of the national sovereignty, by allowing them a direct representation in the Senate, and leaves in their possession certain exclusive and very important portions of sovereign power.

74. The above passage is most likely to be found in which of the following?

   (A) Washington's *Farewell Address*

   (B) Jefferson's *Kentucky Resolutions*

   (C) Montesquieu's *Spirit of the Laws*

   (D) Tocqueville's *Democracy in America*

   (E) Hamilton, Madison, and Jay's *The Federalist* papers

75. The author wants primarily to convince readers that

   (A) a balanced government is the best form of government.

   (B) the U.S. Constitution would preserve the rights and powers of the states.

   (C) the U.S. Constitution is a form of government uniquely suited to the American character.

    (D)   the U.S. Constitution would effectively eliminate state governments.

    (E)   the United States should keep itself free from entangling alliances with European countries.

76.   Which of the following political philosophers are correctly paired based upon the similarity of their views?

    (A)   Hobbes and Voltaire   (D)   Locke and Voltaire

    (B)   Rousseau and Montesquieu   (E)   Rousseau and Quesnay

    (C)   Quesnay and Montesquieu

77.   In England, the free trade movement achieved a victory with

    (A)   the repeal of the Corn Laws (1846) and the Navigation Acts (1849).

    (B)   the implementation of the Corn Laws.

    (C)   the Factory Act of 1833.

    (D)   the adoption of Joseph Chamberlain's preferential trade scheme.

    (E)   the rise of the Chartist movement.

78.   The major issues confronting the European powers at the time of the Treaty of Paris were

    (A)   the dominant power of France and the rigid class system.

    (B)   German dualism and the imperial rivalry between France and Britain.

    (C)   the rise of Russia as a great power and the overwhelming power of Britain.

    (D)   the collapse of Central and Eastern European dynasties and the rapid development of democracy in Western Europe.

    (E)   the economic struggle between the Western and Central European states and the collapse of the feudal order.

79.   The Ruhr Crisis was caused by

    (A)   abuse of French and Belgian citizens in this German district.

    (B)   German border conflicts with the French and Belgians.

    (C)   an economic conflict associated with reparations and war debts.

(D) German militarization of the Ruhr Valley.

(E) Hitler's march into the Rhineland.

QUESTION 80 refers to the following picture.

80. The picture above is representative of

(A) artistic realism.

(B) the Ashcan School.

(C) regional painting.

(D) the Hudson River School.

(E) the New York School.

81. All of the following contributed to the development of Deism EXCEPT

  I. John Toland.

  II. Lord Shaftesbury.

  III. Matthew Tindal.

  IV. Anthony Collins.

  V. Bernard de Mandeville.

(A) I only

(B) I and II only

(C) II, III, and V only

(D) II and V only

(E) IV only

82. The right of the Union of South Africa to establish apartheid was based primarily on the British statute known as the

(A) Reform Bill of 1867.

(B) Parliament Act of 1911.

(C) British Nationality Act of 1948.

(D) Reform Bills of 1884–5.

(E) Education Act of 1902.

QUESTION 83 refers to the following map.

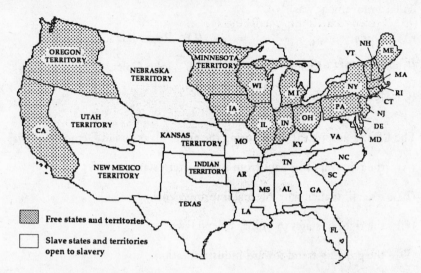

83. The map above depicts the status of slavery in America after the

(A) Dred Scott decision.

(D) Kansas-Nebraska Act.

(B) Missouri Compromise.

(E) Civil War.

(C) Compromise of 1850.

84. The disestablishment of the Church of Ireland and the passage of laws to protect the Irish tenant farmer occurred during the first ministry of

(A) Benjamin Disraeli.

(D) Herbert Asquith.

(B) William Gladstone.

(E) Lord Palmerston.

(C) Lord Salisbury.

85. "Life is more than reasoning, more than "simply extracting square roots," declares the Underground Man. The will, which is "a manifestation of all life," is more precious than reason. Simply to have their own way, human beings will do something stupid, self-destructing, irrational. Reason constitutes only a small part of the human personality."

The above passage most nearly represents the views of

(A) Herbert Spencer.

(D) Leo Tolstoy.

(B) Auguste Comte.

(E) Peter Kropotkin.

(C) Fyodor Dostoyevsky.

86. The English reformer of the 14th century whose views were embodied in the Lollard movement was

    (A) Duns Scotus.

    (B) William Ockham.

    (C) John Wycliffe.

    (D) Roger Bacon.

    (E) John Colet.

87. The LEAST important issue during the era of "Jacksonian Democracy" was

    (A) the removal of Indians from southeastern states.

    (B) federal financing of internal improvements.

    (C) the right of states to nullify federal laws.

    (D) the growing trend toward industrialization.

    (E) the reopening of trade with the British West Indies.

88. Which of the following are decisions of the Warren Court?

    I.   *Edwards v. Aguillard*

    II. *Reynolds v. Sims*

    III. *Miranda v. State of Arizona*

    IV. *Roe v. Wade*

    V.   *Watkins v. United States*

    (A) I and II

    (B) II, III, and IV

    (C) I, IV, and V

    (D) II, III, and V

    (E) II, III, IV, and V

89. The Physiocrats based their program on the

    (A) development of the new industrial order.

    (B) reform of the agrarian order.

    (C) new urban contract designed by Quesnay.

    (D) return to the values of the *Ancien Régime.*

    (E) cooperation of Louis XVI.

90. Bismarck's *Kulturkampf* constituted

    (A) an assault on the remnants of Hapsburg support within the German Empire.

    (B) an attack upon the Social Democratic party.

    (C) a provocation intended to lead to war with France.

    (D) an attack on the Catholic church and the Center party.

    (E) an effort to assure Russian neutrality in any future struggle with Austria.

91. The Yalta conference determined

    I. the Soviet Union's role as the liberator of Berlin.

    II. the postwar political arrangements in Central and Eastern Europe.

    III. the structure of the United Nations.

    IV. American/British control of Western Europe.

    V. the United States as the only nuclear power.

    (A) I, II, and IV only   (D) I and II only

    (B) I, II, IV, and V only   (E) I, II, III, IV, and V

    (C) I, II, and III only

92. In which of the following colonies was the economy in the 18th century dependent on the cultivation of rice and indigo?

    (A) Pennsylvania   (D) North Carolina

    (B) Maryland   (E) South Carolina

    (C) Virginia

93. "The rule that a British subject shall not be bound by laws, or liable to taxes, but what he has consented to by his representatives, must be confined to the inhabitants of Great Britain only; and is not strictly true even there."

    The above statement is most likely to have been made by

    (A) Samuel Adams in denouncing the Stamp Act.

    (B) Francis Bernard as royal governor of Massachusetts.

(C)   John Adams in defending British soldiers accused of murder in the Boston Massacre.

(D)   John Dickinson in counseling against haste in declaring independence.

(E)   Thomas Paine in *Common Sense.*

QUESTION 94 refers to the following cartoon.

94.   The cartoon comments on

(A)   Mussolini's prostration before King Victor Emmanuel III.

(B)   the subjugation of the post–World War II Italian Republic to the Catholic church.

(C)   Garibaldi's presentation of the Kingdom of the Two Sicilies to King Victor Emmanuel II.

(D)   Pope Pius IX's approval of the "Roman Republic" of 1848.

(E)   D'Annunzio's presentation of territory accumulated after World War I, which completed Italian unification.

95. New approaches to the understanding of human behavior were advanced by all of the following EXCEPT

    (A) Carl Jung.

    (B) John Dewey.

    (C) Sigmund Freud.

    (D) Thomas Huxley.

    (E) Arnold Toynbee.

96. During the late 19th and early 20th centuries, revolutionary developments in science were realized through

    I.   Charles Darwin's *The Origin of Species*.

    II. Max Planck's *Quantum Physics*.

    III. Albert Einstein's *Theory of Relativity*.

    IV. Henri Bergson's *Positivism*.

    V.   the Michelson-Morley Experiment.

    (A) I, II, III, and V only

    (B) II, III, IV, and V only

    (C) II, III, and V only

    (D) II and III only

    (E) I, II, III, IV, and V

QUESTIONS 97–98 refer to the following passage.

All combinations and associations, under whatever plausible character, with the real design to direct . . . the constituted authorities, are destructive of this fundamental principle and of fatal tendency. They serve to organize faction; to give it an artificial and extraordinary force; to put in the place of the delegated will of the nation the will of a party, often a small but artful and enterprising minority of the community, and, according to the alternate triumphs of different parties, to make the public administration the mirror of the ill-considered and incongruous projects of faction rather than the organ of consistent and wholesome plans, digested by common counsels and modified by mutual interests.

97. The above passage is most likely to be found in which of the following?

    (A) Hamilton, Madison, and Jay's *The Federalist* papers

    (B) Washington's farewell address

    (C) Jefferson's first inaugural address

    (D) Lincoln's first inaugural address

    (E) Jefferson's Declaration of Independence

98. The author wants primarily to convince his audience that

    (A) political parties are harmful.

    (B) the British have undermined free government in America.

    (C) party strife need not lead to civil conflict.

    (D) party strife should be forgotten once the will of the people has been expressed in an election.

    (E) the Constitution contains adequate safeguards against the dangers of faction.

99. Among the revisionists of the late 19th century were

    I. Sidney Webb.

    II. Keir Hardie.

    III. Beatrice Webb.

    IV. Herbert Spencer.

    V. Peter Kropotkin.

    (A) I and III only   (D) I, II, III, and V only

    (B) I, II, and III only   (E) I, II, III, and IV only

    (C) II and III only

100. All of the following advanced the development of a European Economic Community after 1945 EXCEPT

    (A) Harold Macmillan.   (D) Jean Monnet.

    (B) Paul-Henri Spaak.   (E) Charles de Gaulle.

    (C) Robert Schuman.

QUESTION 101 refers to the following painting.

101. In this painting, *Guernica,* Pablo Picasso condemned

   (A) the German use of gas during World War I.

   (B) the German bombardment of a defenseless town during the Spanish Civil War.

   (C) the loss of noncombatants at the hands of Spanish republicans.

   (D) the German attack on Poland.

   (E) the characteristics of German art during the inter-war era.

102. Historians generally consider which of the following to have been an advocate of a strong national government?

   (A) Thomas Jefferson   (D) Roger B. Taney

   (B) John C. Calhoun   (E) John Marshall

   (C) Jefferson Davis

103. The Kennedy/Johnson policy of "flexible response" directly relied on

   (A) the application of Keynesian economic concepts to Cold War spending.

   (B) the necessity of discriminating between the importance of conflicts.

   (C) the use of the Peace Corps to discourage Third World nations from embracing communism.

   (D) the necessity of immediate escalation in fighting foreign wars.

   (E) the mutual exclusivity of domestic and foreign spending.

104. The most dynamic advocate of republicanism during the first decade of the Third Republic was

    (A)   Adolphe Thiers.

    (B)   Marshall MacMahon.

    (C)   Leon Gambetta.

    (D)   Victor Hugo.

    (E)   Louis Blanc.

105. The English Bill of Rights

    I.   required the monarchs to be members of the Church of England.

    II.   established the Protectorate.

    III.   established parliamentary control over revenues.

    IV.   maintained the monarch as the commander of armed forces.

    V.   was acceptable to William and Mary.

    (A)   I, II, and III only

    (B)   I, III, and IV only

    (C)   I, II, and IV only

    (D)   I, III, IV, and V only

    (E)   I, II, III, IV, and V

106. Which of the following would NOT have supported the late 19th century drive for bimetallism in the United States?

    (A)   Those who thought inflation would benefit the economy

    (B)   Those who owned stock in silver mines

    (C)   Those who held large amounts of government securities

    (D)   Those who were deeply in debt

    (E)   Those who came from predominantly agricultural states

107. Which of the following pairs combine opposing economic philosophies?

    (A)   Alexander Hamilton and Mark Hanna

    (B)   The "American System" and the "Great Society"

    (C)   Woodrow Wilson and Andrew Mellon

    (D)   The Interstate Commerce Act and the Hepburn Act

    (E)   The Square Deal and the New Deal

108. Which of the following opposed the Compromise of 1850?

    (A) Henry Clay   (D) Millard Fillmore

    (B) John C. Calhoun   (E) Stephen A. Douglas

    (C) Daniel Webster

109. In 1956, the American government differed sharply with Britain and France in addressing the

    (A) Hungarian Revolution.

    (B) Polish riots.

    (C) Suez Crisis.

    (D) change in the Soviet Union following Khruschev's Secret Speech.

    (E) Algerian Crisis.

110. Simonides of Ceos, Bacchylides of Ceos, and Pindar were great lyric poets and contemporaries of

    (A) Aristotle.   (D) Theocritus.

    (B) Aeschylus.   (E) Ptolemy.

    (C) Horace.

111. The Eleusinian Mysteries consisted chiefly of

    I.   ceremonies devised by the Athenian worshipers of Dionysus, Demeter, and Persephone.

    II. a passion play which represented the sorrows of Demeter.

    III. ceremonies which contributed to the progress of democratization in Athens.

    IV. the belief that the soul is suffering the punishment of sin.

    V.   the belief that through pure living one can cleanse themselves from sin.

    (A) I, II, and III only   (D) I and II only

    (B) I, II, III, and IV only   (E) I, II, III, IV, and V

    (C) I, II, and IV only

112. A pillar of President Taft's Latin American "dollar diplomacy" policy was

    (A) the use of diplomacy to improve the business climate.

    (B) the threat of military intervention to protect American investments in the region.

    (C) the use of American investment as a diplomatic tool.

    (D) the offer of foreign aid as an inducement for cooperation.

    (E) the development of the Latin American economies to promote regional stability.

113. British violations of American shipping rights played the greatest role in which of the following?

    (A) The outbreak of World War I

    (B) The Monroe Doctrine

    (C) The Venezuela/British Guiana controversy in 1895

    (D) The outbreak of the War of 1812

    (E) The Roosevelt Corollary

114. Popular anticlericalism, a major theme of Renaissance literature, was evident in

    (A) Baccaccio's *Decameron.*

    (B) Henry VIII's *Defense of the Seven Sacraments.*

    (C) *Summa Theologica* by Thomas Aquinas.

    (D) Copernicus's *The Revolutions of the Heavenly Bodies.*

    (E) Pope Leo X's *Exsurge Domine.*

115. English Puritanism developed during the reign of Elizabeth I

    (A) in reaction to the failure of the Elizabethan Religious Settlement to implement the reforms of the Council of Trent.

    (B) because of Elizabeth I's intention to extend Protestant sentiment throughout the realm.

    (C) because of the dissatisfaction with the scope and breadth of the Elizabethan Religious Settlement among the Marian Exiles and others who were influenced by Calvinist views.

(D)   as a direct reaction to the Jesuit Mission led by Edmund Campion.

(E)   to maintain the hierarchical and ceremonial aspects of the previous era.

116. The Bloc National in post-World War I France was a coalition of

(A)   moderates and conservatives.

(B)   socialists and republicans.

(C)   Syndicalists and Nationalists.

(D)   moderates and socialists.

(E)   agrarian liberals and socialists.

QUESTION 117 refers to the following map.

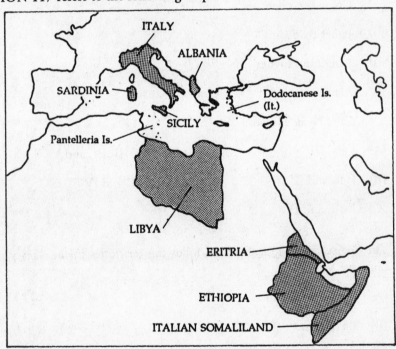

117. The map indicates the extent of the Italian territories in Europe and Africa in

(A)   1870.   (D)   1940.

(B)   1914.   (E)   1919.

(C)   1945.

118. Which of the following BEST describes the election of 1860?

    (A) Democrat Douglas ran far behind Republican Lincoln in the popular vote, but much closer in the electoral vote.

    (B) Lincoln polled a clear majority of all votes cast.

    (C) Southern Democrat Breckenridge was a secessionist who carried most of the slave states.

    (D) The Southern states were prepared to secede if Lincoln won.

    (E) Union candidate Bell received no support in the South.

119. Which of the following were prominent members of the Harlem Renaissance literary movement?

     I. Countee Cullen

    II. James Baldwin

   III. Langston Hughes

    IV. Alain Locke

     V. Zora Neale Hurston

    (A) I and III

    (B) I, II, and III

    (C) I, III, and IV

    (D) I, III, IV, and V

    (E) III and IV

120. The Soviet Union lost all of the following territories in the Treaty of Brest-Litovsk EXCEPT

    (A) the Baltic provinces.

    (B) the Ukraine.

    (C) Finland.

    (D) Byelorussia.

    (E) the land adjacent to the White Sea.

121. The Allied treaty with Austria at the end of the First World War was the

    (A) Treaty of St. Germain.

    (B) Treaty of Neuilly.

(C)   Treaty of Trianon.

(D)   Treaty of Sevres.

(E)   Treaty of Rapallo.

122. The most forceful advocate of German nationalism was

(A)   Johann Schiller.   (D)   Johann G. Herder.

(B)   Immanuel Kant.   (E)   Karl Marx.

(C)   Ludwig von Beethoven.

123. The French Revolution of 1830 was primarily caused by

(A)   the desire for a dynastic change.

(B)   fierce French nationalism.

(C)   the need for a liberal government.

(D)   the collapse of the French economy.

(E)   the failure of French foreign policy.

124. The 1968 Tet Offensive

(A)   was depicted in the American news media as a major victory for U.S. forces.

(B)   was a military victory for the communist North Vietnamese forces.

(C)   brought an immediate end to the Vietnam War.

(D)   led to the belief in the United States that the Vietnam War was unwinnable.

(E)   had little appreciable effect on the course of the Vietnam War.

125. Which of the following statements is NOT true of the 1947 Taft-Hartley Act?

(A)   It made the "closed shop" illegal.

(B)   It established an 80-day cooling-off period for delaying strikes in key industries.

(C)   It banned the practice of forcing newly hired employees to join a union.

(D)   It prohibited secondary boycotts.

(E)   It required the administration of an anti-communist oath to union officials.

126. The 1832–3 Nullification Crisis involved all of the following EXCEPT

    (A) federal tariff policy.

    (B) Southern fear of federal tampering with slavery.

    (C) federal land policy.

    (D) personal animosity between Andrew Jackson and John C. Calhoun.

    (E) the rights of individual states versus those of the federal government.

127. Which of the following novels deals LEAST with World War II and its issues?

    (A) Norman Mailer's *The Naked and the Dead*

    (B) Saul Bellow's *Herzog*

    (C) James Jones's *From Here to Eternity*

    (D) Thomas Pynchon's *Gravity's Rainbow*

    (E) Joseph Heller's *Catch-22*

128. Mussolini's syndicalist-corporate system included

    I. organizations of workers and employers.

    II. worker-employer syndicates.

    III. outlawing strikes and walkouts.

    IV. programs to promote private initiatives.

    V. an arrangement with the Vatican.

    (A) Only I   (D) I, II, and V only

    (B) I and II only   (E) I, II, III, IV, and V

    (C) I, II, and III only

QUESTION 129 refers to the following cartoon.

129. This cartoon ridicules the

    (A)   German occupation of Austria.

    (B)   German occupation of Czechoslovakia.

    (C)   Nazi-Soviet Non-Aggression Pact.

    (D)   Nazi-Soviet Alliance.

    (E)   Soviet attack on the Baltic states.

130. The statement "*Esse est percipi:* to exist is to be perceived" reflects the thought of

    (A)   David Hume.   (D)   George Berkeley.

    (B)   Leibnitz.   (E)   Quesnay.

    (C)   Pascal.

QUESTION 131 refers to the following chart.

THE GREAT DEPRESSION

Indices of Industrial Production, 1929–1938, in Major European Countries (1937 = 100)

	1929	1930	1931	1932	1933	1934	1935	1936	1937	1938
France	123	123	105	91	94	92	88	95	100	92
Germany	79	69	56	48	54	67	79	90	100	92
Italy	90	85	77	77	82	80	86	86	100	100
Great Britain	77	74	69	69	73	80	82	94	100	101

Unemployment (in thousands)

	1929	1930	1931	1932	1933	1934	1935	1936	1937	1938
France	neglig.	13	64	301	305	368	464	470	380	402
Germany	1,899	3,070	4,520	5,575	4,804	2,718	2,151	1,593	912	429
Italy	301	425	734	1,006	1,019	964	–	–	874	810
Great Britain	1,216	1,917	2,630	2,745	2,521	2,159	2,036	1,755	1,484	1,791

131. The data given by the chart supports all of the following assertions EXCEPT

(A) The Great Depression hit France later than its European neighbors.

(B) Every country except France returned to 1929 production levels by 1938.

(C) In 1938, unemployment was still a major problem in every country except Germany.

(D) By 1936, the Allied countries in Western Europe were closer to prewar industrial production rates.

(E) Germany doubled its industrial production between 1932 and 1938.

---

132. Which of the following did NOT characterize the early 19th century religious movement known as the Second Great Awakening?

(A) Extreme displays of emotion

(B) An emphasis on individual conversion

(C) Increased interest in social reforms such as the temperance movement

(D) Acceptance of slavery as ordained by God

(E) Extensive involvement by women and African Americans

133. Which of the following circumstances was most significant in bringing an end to Reconstruction in 1877?

(A) The installation of a Republican administration

(B) The deaths of many leading Radical politicians in the North

(C) The increasing interest in economic issues rather than racial or sectional ones

(D) The violent resistance of Southerners in such organizations as the Ku Klux Klan

(E) The Northern electorate's fatigue with the effort to remake Southern society

134. The political party that ran on a strong antiforeign platform was

(A) the American party of 1856.

(B) the Liberty party of 1844.

(C) the Free Soil party of 1848 and 1852.

(D) the States' Rights Democratic party of 1948.

(E) the People's party of 1892.

135. Which of these military thinkers were proponents of defensive warfare between the two world wars?

I. B. H. Liddell Hart

II. Henri Pétain

III. J. F. C. Fuller

IV. Charles de Gaulle

(A) I and II

(B) I, II, and III

(C) II only

(D) II and IV

(E) II and III

136. By the 13th century, the wealthiest of the Italian city-states was

    (A) Pisa.   (D) Venice.

    (B) Florence.   (E) Genoa.

    (C) Milan.

137. All of the following are considered national epics EXCEPT

    (A) *The Song of Roland.*   (D) *Divine Comedy.*

    (B) *Beowulf.*   (E) *Volsgungasga.*

    (C) *El Cid.*

138. Shortly after Columbus's discovery of the New World, the Treaty of Tordesillas

    (A) allowed Spain to take over Scandinavian claims to the New World.

    (B) regularized relations between the Spaniards and the Indian tribes of the Caribbean.

    (C) divided newly discovered lands between Spain and Portugal.

    (D) adjusted the New World claims of France, Spain, England, and Portugal.

    (E) ended the war between England and Spain.

139. President Tyler broke with the Whig party on all of the following issues EXCEPT

    (A) the creation of the Second Bank of the United States.

    (B) the ending of the Independent Treasury system.

    (C) the sale of public lands in the West.

    (D) a high protective tariff.

    (E) federal financing of internal improvements.

140. Barbarian tribes which penetrated the Roman Empire included the

    I.   Vandals.

    II. Huns.

    III. Magyars

IV. Ostrogoths.

V. Visigoths.

(A) I, IV, and V only   (D) I, II, III, and IV only

(B) I, II, and III only   (E) I, II, III, IV, and V

(C) I, II, IV, and V only

141. In 1951, West Germany, France, Italy, Belgium, the Netherlands, and Luxembourg entered into an agreement known as the

(A) European Economic Community (EEC).

(B) Euratom.

(C) Steel and Coal Agreement.

(D) Brussels Pact.

(E) Treaty of Rome.

142. English Utilitarianism was supported by

I. David Ricardo.

II. James Mill.

III. Horatio Hunt.

IV. Jeremy Bentham.

V. John Stuart Mill.

(A) I, II, IV, and V only   (D) IV and V only

(B) II, III, and IV only   (E) III and IV only

(C) II, IV, and V only

143. All of the following spurred serious states' rights conflicts EXCEPT

(A) the Alien and Sedition Laws.

(B) the Supreme Court's ruling in *Brown v. Board of Education.*

(C) the New Deal reforms.

(D) the Hawley-Smoot Tariff Act.

(E) the Tariff of 1932.

144. As president, Theodore Roosevelt believed in all of the following EXCEPT

    (A) unbridled freedom for big business.

    (B) a strong and aggressive foreign policy.

    (C) an active presidency.

    (D) a large, strong, and active federal government.

    (E) acquisition of overseas possessions.

145. *The Journal of Modern History* publishes articles on

    (A) history in all fields.

    (B) American and European history.

    (C) European history.

    (D) American history.

    (E) public history.

146. The most noted practitioner (writing in English) of the New Historicism is

    (A) Simon Schama.   (D) Jonathan Spence.

    (B) Stephen Greenblatt.   (E) G. D. H. Cole.

    (C) G. R. Elton.

147. Fear of a Bolshevik upheaval contributed to the emergence of fascism in

    I. Italy.

    II. Spain.

    III. Germany.

    IV. Hungary.

    V. Austria.

    (A) I and III only   (D) I, II, and IV only

    (B) I, II, III, and IV only   (E) I, II, III, IV, and V

    (C) I, II, and III only

148. The most significant development in British constitutional history during the first half of the 18th century was the

    (A)   installation of the Hanoverian dynasty.

    (B)   emergency of the Cabinet system of government.

    (C)   development of a reformed judiciary.

    (D)   appearance of journalism as a monitor of the regime.

    (E)   redistribution of seats in the House of Commons.

149. Spanish explorers Hernan de Soto and Francisco Vasquez de Coronado sought

    (A)   an all-water route to the Orient.

    (B)   rich Indian civilizations to plunder.

    (C)   a route to East Asia.

    (D)   sources of raw materials for Spain.

    (E)   scientific and geographic knowledge about the interior of North America.

150. Which of the following is true of the last Whig presidential candidate in 1852?

    (A)   He was assailed for his illegitimate birth.

    (B)   He came out strongly against the Fugitive Slave Law.

    (C)   As in 1840 and 1848, he was a war hero.

    (D)   He lost to a much more well-known Democratic candidate.

    (E)   He enjoyed the full support of all elements of his party.

151. Solon's constitutional reforms included

    I.   the establishment of a property class known as the "500-bushel men."

    II.   substituting the drachma for the *medimnus.*

    III.   the creation of the *heliaea.*

    IV.   use of circuit judges.

    V.   economic and commercial measures to support the wine and oil trade.

(A)   I and II only   (D)   I, II, and IV only

(B)   I, II, and III only   (E)   I, II, III, IV, and V

(C)   I, II, III, and IV only

152. In 1989, the Velvet Revolution occurred in

(A)   Poland.   (D)   Hungary.

(B)   Bulgaria.   (E)   Czechoslovakia.

(C)   Romania.

153. Which of the following was NOT one of the purposes of the Lewis and Clark expedition?

(A)   Establishing friendly relations with the western Indians

(B)   Gaining geographic knowledge about the western part of North America

(C)   Discovering sources of gold

(D)   Gaining scientific knowledge about the flora and fauna of western North America

(E)   Finding a water route to the Pacific Ocean across North America

154. All of the following improved the situation of the American farmer during the late 19th century EXCEPT

(A)   an expanding money supply based on the gold standard.

(B)   the escalating food demands of a growing urban population.

(C)   the declining rate at which new acreage became available for cultivation.

(D)   early government programs subsidizing farmers and stabilizing commodities markets.

(E)   a constant supply of farm laborers.

155. A respected journal dedicated to the study of general medieval history is

(A)   *The Journal of Ecclesiastical History.*

(B)   *Annales.*

(C)   *Speculum.*

(D) *Historical Journal.*

(E) *ISIS.*

156. Under the feudal arrangement, *aids* were due to the lord when

   I.   the lord's father died.

   II. the lord's eldest son was knighted.

   III. the lord's eldest daughter was married.

   IV. the lord needed to raise an army.

   V.   the lord was being held for ransom.

   (A) I, IV, and V only   (D) II, III, and V only

   (B) I, II, and IV only   (E) I, II, III, IV, and V

   (C) II, III, and IV only

157. The purpose of Franklin D. Roosevelt's "Four Freedoms" speech was to

   (A) obtain a congressional declaration of war against Germany.

   (B) gain support for his Lend-Lease program.

   (C) obtain a congressional declaration of war against Japan.

   (D) assert complete American neutrality in the war in Europe.

   (E) set forth the terms under which Germany's surrender would be accepted.

158. Explorers who established French claims to the eastern United States included

   I.   Giovanni da Verrazano.

   II. Martin Frobisher.

   III. Jacques Cartier.

   IV. John Cabot.

   V.   Henry Hudson.

   (A) I only   (D) I, III, IV, and V

   (B) I and III   (E) II only

   (C) I, II, and V

159. The Whig interpretation of history was advanced by

    I. G. M. Trevelyan.

    II. Thomas Babington Macauley.

    III. Winston Churchill.

    IV. R. H. Tawney.

    V. Arnold Toynbee.

(A) I and II only

(B) I, II, and III only

(C) I, II, III, and IV only

(D) I, II, IV, and V only

(E) I, II, III, IV, and V

160. The Black Death of the 14th century resulted in the

(A) decline of the movement toward nation-states in Western Europe.

(B) rise of modern medicine.

(C) enhancement of the value of labor.

(D) flight of millions of Europeans overseas.

(E) collapse of the feudal economies in Central and Eastern Europe.

161. Which of the following were profoundly influenced by Calvinism?

    I. Edgar Allan Poe's *The Poetic Principle*

    II. Nathaniel Hawthorne's *The Scarlet Letter*

    III. Anne Bradstreet's *The Tenth Muse Lately Sprung Up in America*

    IV. Benjamin Franklin's *Poor Richard's Almanac*

    V. William Bradford's *Of Plymouth Plantation*

(A) I and IV

(B) I, II, and V

(C) II, III, IV, and V

(D) II, III, and V

(E) I, III, and V

162. The international incident known as the XYZ Affair involved

    (A) a French foreign minister's demand for a bribe before he would meet with American envoys.

    (B) the British refusal to evacuate their forts on American territory.

    (C) General Andrew Jackson's incursion into Spanish-held Florida.

    (D) the British seizure of American crewmen from a U.S. Navy warship in Chesapeake Bay.

    (E) Aaron Burr's secret plot to detach the western United States in order to create a new nation of which he would be ruler.

163. The battle that influenced France to become involved in the American War of Independence was

    (A) Yorktown.   (D) Lexington.

    (B) Saratoga.   (E) Bunker Hill.

    (C) Guilford Court House.

164. The Lay Investiture Controversy was primarily a

    (A) struggle between German nobles and their emperor.

    (B) liturgical debate within the Church.

    (C) conflict concerning the appointment of German bishops.

    (D) conflict over the selection of new popes.

    (E) struggle concerning the selection of a new emperor.

165. The purpose of the "Olive Branch Petition" was to

    (A) end the undeclared naval war with France during the late 1790s.

    (B) demand that the federal government end the War of 1812.

    (C) persuade Americans to return to colonial status under Great Britain after the defeats at Brandywine and Germantown.

    (D) persuade Parliament to repeal the Stamp Act.

    (E) persuade the king to intercede with Parliament to restore peace in 1775.

166. Late 19th century works by American naturalists included

    I. Henry James's *The Portrait of a Lady.*

    II. Frank Norris' *The Octopus.*

    III. Herman Melville's *Billy Budd.*

    IV. Theodore Dreiser's *Sister Carrie.*

    V. Thomas Nelson Page's "Marse Chan."

    (A) I, II, and IV   (D) II and IV

    (B) I, II, and III   (E) II and V

    (C) II, III, and IV

167. "He sulkily admitted now that there was no more escape, but he lay and detested the grind of the real-estate business, and disliked his family, and disliked himself for disliking them. The evening before, he had played poker at Vergil Gunch's till midnight, and after such holidays he was irritable before breakfast. It may have been the tremendous home-brewed beer of the prohibition-era and the cigars to which that beer enticed him; it may have been resentment of return from this fine, bold man-world to a restricted region of wives and stenographers, and of suggestions not to smoke so much."

    This passage was most likely written by

    (A) William Dean Howells.   (D) F. Scott Fitzgerald.

    (B) David Phillips.   (E) Washington Irving.

    (C) Sinclair Lewis.

168. Thomas Jefferson's philosophy of government, as expressed in the Declaration of Independence, most closely reflects the views of

    (A) Thomas Hobbes.   (D) Jean Paul Marat.

    (B) Jean Jacques Rousseau.   (E) Karl Marx.

    (C) John Locke.

169. At the Peace of Augsburg in 1555, the Catholic and Lutheran leaders agreed to

    I. the principle of *cuius regio, cuius religio.*

    II. recognize the existence of Lutheranism.

III. recognize the existence of Calvinism.

IV. recognize the independence of the Netherlands.

V. attend the next session of the Council of Trent.

(A) II, III, and IV only

(D) III only

(B) II, III, and V only

(E) I, II, III, IV, and V

(C) I and II only

170. The high-tariff policy of the United States between the two world wars

(A) triggered economic growth in the United States but stagnation in Europe.

(B) created an abnormal speculative spiral on the U.S. stockmarket.

(C) hindered European nations from repaying their war debts to the U.S.

(D) retarded the growth of manufacturing in the U.S.

(E) enabled the U.S. to recover from the Depression more rapidly than other countries.

171. The battle that marked the shift of power in the naval struggle between the United States and Japan in World War II was

(A) Leyte Gulf.

(D) Coral Sea.

(B) Guadalcanal.

(E) Midway.

(C) Pearl Harbor.

172. Which of the following battles of the American Civil War was NOT a Confederate victory?

(A) Antietam

(D) Fredericksburg

(B) Chickamauga

(E) First Bull Run

(C) Chancellorsville

173. De Gaulle's leadership of the Fifth French Republic was weakened by the

(A) rise of the European Common Market.

(B) Paris Spring uprising.

    (C)   Soviet invasion of Czechoslovakia.

    (D)   devaluation of the French currency.

    (E)   collapse of the French auto industry.

174. "For abolishing the free System of English Laws in a neighbouring Province, establishing therein an Arbitrary government, and enlarging its Boundaries so as to render it at once an example and fit instrument for introducing the same absolute rule into these Colonies."

In the above passage, Thomas Jefferson indicts King George III and Parliament for the

    (A)   Quartering Act.   (D)   Stamp Act.

    (B)   Prohibitory Act.   (E)   Townshend Acts.

    (C)   Quebec Act.

175. The "Anaconda Plan" was

    (A)   a scheme for building an American canal across the Isthmus of Panama.

    (B)   an attempted compromise to avoid fighting between North and South in 1861.

    (C)   President James K. Polk's strategy for defeating Mexico.

    (D)   Winfield Scott's proposed strategy for the North in the Civil War.

    (E)   a scheme for the construction of a transcontinental railroad.

176. The concept of "Tory Democracy" was advanced initially by

    (A)   Palmerston.   (D)   Salisbury.

    (B)   Randolph Churchill   (E)   Roseberry.

    (C)   Disraeli.

177. The best illustration of the change in the spirit of European intellectuals at the beginning of the 20th century is

    (A)   Thomas Mann's *Buddenbrooks.*

    (B)   Leo Tolstoy's *War and Peace.*

    (C)   Dostoyevsky's *Notes from the Underground.*

(D)   Thomas Mann's *Death in Venice*.

(E)   Winston Churchill's *Savonrola*.

178. Which of the following would be LEAST likely to approve of William Lloyd Garrison's career?

(A)   David Walker

(B)   Ralph Waldo Emerson

(C)   Theodore Dwight Weld

(D)   Harriet Tubman

(E)   Nat Turner

179. The "Spirit of Locarno" was reflected in the

(A)   Dawes Plan.

(B)   Hoover Moratorium.

(C)   London Naval Conference.

(D)   Washington Naval Conference.

(E)   Kellogg-Briand Pact.

180. In writing "He has abdicated Government here, by declaring us out of his Protection and waging War against us," about which act or acts by King George III and Parliament is Thomas Jefferson complaining?

(A)   The Declaratory Act

(B)   The Coercive Acts

(C)   The Intolerable Acts

(D)   The Townshend Acts

(E)   The Prohibitory Act

181. The Thirty Years' War became primarily a political conflict during the

(A)   Danish phase.

(B)   Swedish phase.

(C)   Bohemian phase.

(D)   Swedish-French phase.

(E)   Italian phase.

182. The principle that imperial claims had to be supported by occupation emerged at the

(A)   Congress of Berlin.

(B)   Berlin Conference.

(C)   London Naval Conference.

(D)   Versailles Conference.

(E)   Plombieres Conference.

183. Purposes of Alexander Hamilton's tax, tariff, and debt manipulation schemes during the presidency of George Washington included

(A) ridding the federal government of debt as soon as possible.

(B) ending undue government interference in the economy.

(C) binding the interests of the moneyed class to the new federal government.

(D) maintaining the United States as an agrarian society.

(E) promoting the importation of British manufactured goods.

QUESTIONS 184–185 refer to the following passage.

During the contest of opinion through which we have passed the animation of discussions and of exertions has sometimes worn an aspect which might impose on strangers unused to think freely and to speak and to write what they think; but this being now decided by the voice of the nation, announced according to the rules of the Constitution, all will, of course, arrange themselves under the will of the law, and unite in common efforts for the common good. . . . Let us, then, fellow-citizens, unite with one heart and one mind. . . . We have called by different names brethren of the same principle.

184. The above passage is most likely to be found in which of the following?

(A) Washington's farewell address

(B) Lincoln's first inaugural address

(C) Jackson's first inaugural address

(D) Jefferson's first inaugural address

(E) the Declaration of Independence

185. The author wants primarily to convince his audience that

(A) political parties are harmful.

(B) political strife is foreign to the American character.

(C) party strife is indicative of fundamental philosophical differences.

(D) party strife should be forgotten once the will of the people has been expressed in an election.

(E) only the members of his party are acting in accordance with the rules of the Constitution.

186. All of the following sets of thinkers are matched by period and discipline EXCEPT

    (A) Descartes and Bacon.

    (B) Wilde and Mann.

    (C) Planck and Einstein.

    (D) Kant and Ricardo.

    (E) Erasmus and Colet.

187. After 1945, West Germany was confronted with a multitude of problems including the

    I. immigration of thousands of East Germans.

    II. postwar War Trials.

    III. destroyed industrial and transportation systems.

    IV. occupation by foreign troops.

    V. continuing problems associated with managing German foreign investments and colonies.

    (A) II, III, and IV only

    (B) II, III, IV, and V only

    (C) I, II, III, and IV only

    (D) II, IV, and V only

    (E) I, II, III, IV, and V

188. Intellectual currents existing in pre–Reformation Europe included

    I. humanism.

    II. Scholasticism.

    III. popular anticlericalism.

    IV. growing nationalism.

    V. mysticism.

    (A) I, II, and III only

    (B) II, III, and IV only

    (C) I, III, IV, and V only

    (D) I, II, III, and V only

    (E) I, II, III, IV, and V

189. The Nixon-Kissinger policy of détente took into account all of the following "ambiguous tendencies" in international affairs EXCEPT

    (A) rivalries within international communism.

    (B) the achievement of Soviet military parity.

    (C) Soviet frustration with negotiated settlements.

    (D) the emergence of a Soviet industrial economy.

    (E) Soviet expansion into the Third World.

190. The event that was most important in transforming the U.S. from international debtor status to international creditor status was

    (A) the Civil War.

    (B) the formation of J. P. Morgan and Company.

    (C) the First World War.

    (D) the passage of the Fordney-McCumber Tariff.

    (E) the Depression of the 1930s.

GRE History – Test 1

ANSWER KEY

1.	(C)	26.	(B)	51.	(C)	76.	(A)
2.	(A)	27.	(C)	52.	(D)	77.	(A)
3.	(E)	28.	(C)	53.	(D)	78.	(B)
4.	(B)	29.	(C)	54.	(D)	79.	(C)
5.	(A)	30.	(D)	55.	(E)	80.	(A)
6.	(B)	31.	(D)	56.	(C)	81.	(D)
7.	(A)	32.	(C)	57.	(D)	82.	(C)
8.	(C)	33.	(C)	58.	(B)	83.	(D)
9.	(D)	34.	(E)	59.	(B)	84.	(B)
10.	(B)	35.	(D)	60.	(B)	85.	(C)
11.	(B)	36.	(D)	61.	(B)	86.	(C)
12.	(C)	37.	(A)	62.	(B)	87.	(D)
13.	(C)	38.	(A)	63.	(E)	88.	(D)
14.	(E)	39.	(C)	64.	(B)	89.	(B)
15.	(C)	40.	(C)	65.	(A)	90.	(D)
16.	(B)	41.	(B)	66.	(C)	91.	(C)
17.	(B)	42.	(C)	67.	(C)	92.	(E)
18.	(C)	43.	(E)	68.	(C)	93.	(B)
19.	(B)	44.	(B)	69.	(D)	94.	(C)
20.	(C)	45.	(C)	70.	(A)	95.	(E)
21.	(D)	46.	(D)	71.	(A)	96.	(C)
22.	(D)	47.	(A)	72.	(C)	97.	(B)
23.	(A)	48.	(C)	73.	(C)	98.	(A)
24.	(B)	49.	(A)	74.	(E)	99.	(B)
25.	(A)	50.	(E)	75.	(B)	100.	(A)

101.	(B)	126.	(C)	151.	(B)	176.	(C)
102.	(E)	127.	(B)	152.	(E)	177.	(D)
103.	(A)	128.	(C)	153.	(C)	178.	(C)
104.	(C)	129.	(C)	154.	(D)	179.	(E)
105.	(D)	130.	(D)	155.	(C)	180.	(E)
106.	(C)	131.	(C)	156.	(D)	181.	(D)
107.	(C)	132.	(D)	157.	(B)	182.	(B)
108.	(B)	133.	(E)	158.	(A)	183.	(C)
109.	(C)	134.	(A)	159.	(B)	184.	(D)
110.	(B)	135.	(C)	160.	(C)	185.	(D)
111.	(A)	136.	(D)	161.	(D)	186.	(D)
112.	(C)	137.	(D)	162.	(A)	187.	(C)
113.	(D)	138.	(C)	163.	(B)	188.	(C)
114.	(A)	139.	(B)	164.	(C)	189.	(C)
115.	(C)	140.	(C)	165.	(E)	190.	(C)
116.	(A)	141.	(C)	166.	(D)		
117.	(D)	142.	(C)	167.	(C)		
118.	(D)	143.	(D)	168.	(C)		
119.	(D)	144.	(A)	169.	(C)		
120.	(E)	145.	(C)	170.	(C)		
121.	(A)	146.	(B)	171.	(E)		
122.	(D)	147.	(C)	172.	(A)		
123.	(C)	148.	(B)	173.	(B)		
124.	(D)	149.	(B)	174.	(C)		
125.	(C)	150.	(C)	175.	(D)		

DETAILED EXPLANATIONS OF ANSWERS

Test 1

1. **(C)**   The Reconstruction Finance Corporation was not part of the New Deal but was created in 1932, during the presidency of Herbert Hoover, as an attempt to reexpand credit by extending loans to distressed businesses. This was part of Hoover's response to the Depression. The National Industrial Recovery Act (A) (1933), the Tennessee Valley Authority (B) (1933), the Agricultural Adjustment Act (D) (1933), and the Works Progress Administration (E) (1935), were all part of Roosevelt's New Deal program.

2. **(A)**   During the 6th century, the Heptarchy of Anglo-Saxon England included Essex, Wessex, Sussex, Kent, East Anglia, Mercia, and Northumbria. By the end of the 6th century Kent emerged as the primary power in Britain. West Cornwall (B), Wales (C), the Danelaw, Cumbria (D), and Strathclyde (E) were not organized political entities during the 6th century and so were not part of the Heptarchy.

3. **(E)**   Hildebrand (E) was a medieval church reformer who became pope. Peter Abelard (A) (*Sic et Non*), Peter Lombard (B) (*Four Books of Sentences*), Albertus Magnus (C), and Thomas Aquinas (D) (*Summa Theologica*) were all significant contributors to the Realist-Nominalist Controversy. While this controversy was initiated over Plato's Doctrine of Ideas, it was transformed into a discussion of whether truth obtained through reason was reconcilable with truth obtained through revelation.

4. **(B)**   Confronting the devastation resulting from the Civil War, the diplomatic isolation of most powers, and the recent withdrawal of foreign armies, Lenin "retreated" from some of the espoused purposes of communism in his New Economic Policy of 1921 (B). This policy was in effect through 1927, and was replaced in 1928 with the initiation of Stalin's program of collectivization in the First Five-Year Plan (C). The Kornilov Affair of September 1917 (A) demonstrated the absence of effective leadership in the Kerensky government. The Second Five-Year Plan (D) was announced by Stalin during the 1930s. Lenin's April Theses (E) was a prerevolutionary statement advanced in April 1917.

5. **(A)**   The passage was written by U.S. Chief Justice Roger B. Taney as part of the Supreme Court's majority opinion in the 1857 case of *Dred Scott v. Sanford*. Taney held 1) that slaveholders could take up residence with their slaves in free

states without thereby losing title to their human chattels; and 2) that neither Congress nor any territorial legislature could prohibit slavery in any territory of the United States. He justified this opinion on the basis that 1) the U.S. Constitution recognized slaves as property; and 2) forbidding the ownership of slaves in territories amounted to depriving the slaveholders of their property without due process of law.

6. **(B)** As in number 5 above, Taney's argument was that slavery, as a form of property recognized by the Constitution, could not be prohibited by Congress or any other authority, in any of the territories of the United States.

7. **(A)** The Cluniac Movement, which emerged during the 10th century, was directed at eliminating corruption within the Church and at emphasizing the spiritual, rather than secular, mission of the Church. The Cluniac Movement started in eastern France. William I of England (B) was not directly affected by this movement, nor was it involved with the establishment of universities (C) or with validating the Fathers of the Church (E). John Hus (D) was a radical reformer within the Church in the 15th century.

8. **(C)** The Spanish Republican government of President Alcala Zamora and Prime Minister Manuel Azaña was committed to a program of liberal reforms which included expelling the Jesuits (I), the nationalization of railroads (II), the confiscation of large estates (III), and the introduction of the eight-hour work day and a system of social insurance (IV). They labored to reduce the size and authority of the Spanish army which supported the old order.

9. **(D)** Louis Napoleon (D), a nephew of Napoleon Bonaparte, did not attend the Congress of Vienna in 1815. He would later serve as the president of the Second French Republic (1849–51) and emperor of the Second French Empire (1851–70). Baron Talleyrand (A) represented France at the Vienna meeting, which was hosted by the Austrian foreign minister, Prince Metternich (B). Foreign Secretary Lord Castlereagh (C) and the Duke of Wellington (E) represented England at the meeting.

10. **(B)** The influx of great quantities of gold and silver (specie) into the European economies (B) was the primary cause of the Price Revolution of the 16th century. Most of the gold and silver came from Latin America and entered Europe through Spain. The 16th century did not witness the collapse of European agriculture (A), nor a decline in population (C). While the early national economies (E) were emerging in 16th century Western Europe, they did not affect inflation. Industrialism (D) did not have any substantive impact on Europe until the end of the 18th century.

11. **(B)** The economy of the 1980s was generally characterized by declining inflation (IV) and falling unemployment rates (II). On the other hand, stock prices (III) generally increased, despite a sharp drop in October 1987, while the imbalance

between imports and exports (V), the so-called "trade deficit," and the level of foreign investment in the U.S. economy (I) remained high.

12. (C) The German use of submarines against merchant and passenger ships was the most crucial factor in bringing the United States into the First World War. German violation of Belgian neutrality (B) helped bring Britain into the war, and British propaganda (A), which did play a role in securing U.S. involvement, made much of German atrocities in Belgium (D). The Zimmerman note, in which Germany suggested to Mexico a joint war against the United States, with promises of generous annexations by Mexico (E), was also a factor. However, torpedoing unarmed ships without giving warning and making provision for the safety of passengers and crew—which a submarine was incapable of doing in 1917—was seen as akin to piracy.

13. (C) The Magna Carta of 1215 (I) and the Confirmation of the Charters (III) of 1297 were major events in the development of representative government in England; they curtailed the authority of the monarch through law. The Edict of Nantes (II) was approved by Henry IV in 1598, and extended freedoms to the French Huguenots. The Peace of Wedmore (IV) marked the victory of Alfred the Great over Guthrun the Dane. Through the Assize of Arms (V) of 1181, Henry II created a national militia which was independent of the feudal nobility.

14. (E) In June 1878, the Congress of Berlin was convened to resolve the crisis which had developed as a consequence of the Russo-Turkish War. Benjamin Disraeli was determined to reverse the Russian gains conceded by the Turks at San Stephano. His success in Berlin resulted in the establishment of a small Bulgaria rather than the large Bulgaria desired by the Russians (B), in maintaining the integrity and independence of the Ottoman Empire (C) as a buffer to Russian expansionism, in continuing the exclusion of Russian ships from entering the Mediterranean through the Straits (D), and in gaining Cyprus (A) from the Turks in return for British support. The acquisition of Cyprus solidified British control of the eastern Mediterranean. However, Disraeli made no attempt to impose democratic reforms on the Ottoman Empire (E).

15. (C) Leopold I (C), Holy Roman Emperor (1658–1705), the leader of Hapsburg Austria and son of Ferdinand III, succeeded in repelling the Turkish offensives of the 1660s and 1680s. Louis XIV (A) was the king of France from 1643 to 1715 and focused his attention on Western Europe. Oliver Cromwell (B), who died in 1658, led England during the Protectorate. Charles V (D) was the Holy Roman Emperor during the first half of the 16th century. Elector Frederick William (E) of Brandenburg-Prussia was developing his disparate state during the 17th century.

16. (B) *The Decline of the West* was written by the German intellectual Oswald Spengler (B). The British historian Arnold J. Toynbee (A) produced a massive work,

A Study of History, and William McNeil (C) of the University of Chicago wrote the scholarly *The Rise of the West.* Tristan Tarza (D), a Hungarian Swiss, was one of the founders of Dadaism and a contributor to the early development of literary surrealism. Jose Ortega y Gasset's (E) *The Revolt of the Masses* was a denunciation of European decadence.

17. **(B)** Theodore Roosevelt, who died in 1919, could not have read John Steinbeck's *The Grapes of Wrath,* a 1939 book depicting the plight of poor Oklahomans during the Depression. He could have read a number of other books in this genre of social commentary, including Lincoln Steffens' 1904 work, *The Shame of the Cities* (A), which depicted political corruption in major cities; Edward Bellamy's utopian and socialistic 1888 novel *Looking Backward* (C); Henry George's 1879 condemnation of economic progress, *Progress and Poverty* (D); and *The Jungle,* Upton Sinclair's 1906 fictional depiction of conditions in the Chicago stockyards and meat-packing plants (E).

18. **(C)** The Compromise of 1850 did not include the prohibition of slavery in all areas of the Mexican Cession not yet admitted as states. It provided that the status of slavery in these areas, the Utah and New Mexico Territories, be decided according to the doctrine of "Popular Sovereignty," that is, by those who actually settled there. The Compromise did include admission of California as a free state (B), allocation to New Mexico of lands claimed by Texas, abolition of the slave trade in the District of Columbia (D), a guarantee that slavery itself would not be abolished in the District of Columbia without the consent of both Maryland and Virginia, federal assumption of Texas's preannexation debt, (E) and a tougher fugitive slave law (A).

19. **(B)** During the French revolutionary era the National Assembly (III) existed from 1789 to 1791, the Legislative Assembly (II) from 1791 to 1792, the Convention (V) from 1792 to 1795, the Directory (I) from 1795 to 1799, and the Consulate (IV) from 1799 to 1804.

20. **(C)** These maps indicate the impact of the Industrial Revolution (C) on English society; note the growth in the Midlands and the Liverpool areas which provided ready access to raw materials and transport. The Commercial Revolution (A) occurred during the 16th century; 18th-century imperialism (E) had no major impact upon the development of the Midlands. Medieval rights and practices such as usufruct and open lands (D) gave way to the growth of technology and the Enclosure Movement. While the increase in luxury items (B) was a result of the Industrial Revolution, it did not cause the population increase.

21. **(D)** While most Italian Renaissance thinkers associated themselves with the emerging neoplatonism of the era, Marsiglio Ficino (I) and Pico della Mirandola (II) provided major arguments in the confrontation with the neoAristotelianism of the Scholastics. Machiavelli's *The Prince* (III) constituted a major work in political

theory, and Boccaccio's *Decameron,* (IV) advanced a criticism of 14th-century political values. Erasmus of Rotterdam (V) is remembered for his satire *The Praise of Folly,* and his outstanding translations of the Old and New Testaments.

22.   **(D)**   In 1949, the Western European states joined the United States and Canada in forming the North Atlantic Treaty Organization (NATO). NATO has served as the central defensive instrument for the West and opposed Russian policies in Germany and Czechoslovakia. Crises in Korea (A) and China (B) were not directly related to the establishment of NATO. The Communist threat in Greece (C) had been eliminated by 1949. Marshall Tito's variance of communism and independence from Moscow (E) was an internal Communist issue and did not pose a threat to the West.

23.   **(A)**   As adherents of mercantilism, British colonial authorities during the 18th century had no desire to encourage manufacturing in America, preferring America to be a ready market for British manufactured goods. The British did encourage the production in America of staple crops (E)—particularly those which otherwise would have to be imported from foreign suppliers. They also required that goods be carried in British shipping (B), that items bound for the colonies be shipped through Britain first (D), and that certain items be bought only from British sources (C), in an attempt to boost the British economy by cutting out foreign competition. These provisions were imposed by a series of Navigation Acts.

24.   **(B)**   Though land was abundant (A), capital (B) and labor (D) were scarce in early America. Limitations of climate and land (C) prevented New England from developing the staple-crop agriculture in demand in Europe (E).

25.   **(A)**   George Fitzhugh's *Cannibals All!,* in which he argued that slavery was more humane than wage-labor, would have been far more likely to be approved by an 1850s Southern planter than any of the other books listed. *Uncle Tom's Cabin* (E) and *The Impending Crisis of the South* (B) were both 1850s books attacking slavery. *The Cotton Kingdom* (C) was not flattering in its depiction of Southern culture, and the *Liberator* (D) was an abolitionist newspaper so hated in the South that a man found in the South with a copy in his possession risked being killed.

26.   **(B)**   The statement most nearly represents the view of Martin Luther (B), who formulated this concept during the period 1510–14. Erasmus of Rotterdam (A), a contemporary of Luther, is remembered for his scholarly *Praise of Folly* and his translations of the Old and New Testaments. Henry of Navarre (C) led the French Huguenots in the War of the Three Henrys and became Henry IV of France in 1589. Cardinal Thomas Wolsey (D) served as chancellor of England under Henry VIII and was loyal to the Roman Catholic church. John Calvin (E) moved further to the left than Luther theologically; he emphasized and developed the Zwinglian view of the Eucharist and predestination.

27.   (C)   Luther's sense of sin and inner conflict were diminished through the development of the concept of justification by faith (C). He came to this position through his reading of St. Paul's "Epistles to the Romans." Transubstantiation (B) was the Catholic concept that the actual body and blood of Christ are embodied in the Eucharist. Predestination (A) was emphasized by Ulrich Zwingli and John Calvin. The Act of Supremacy of 1534 (D) is associated with Henry VIII's break with Rome, and conciliarism (E) was a movement within the Roman Catholic church which emphasized the power of assembled bishops *vis à vis* the papacy.

28.   (C)   The Labour Ministry of Clement Atlee (1945–51) introduced a wide range of social and economic legislation which radically transformed British society. Among the measures enacted were the National Health Service (I), National Insurance (II), and the Cable and Wireless Act (IV). While the coal and utility industries were nationalized, there was no effort to nationalize all of British industry (III). Rationing, which had been imposed during the Second World War, did not end until 1954 (V).

29.   (C)   The primary cause of Khrushchev's fall from power in 1964 was the continuing failure of his agricultural plan (C). The Russian leader gained some internal support as a result of the American failure in the Bay of Pigs invasion of Cuba in 1961 (A). There was general support of the expansion of the Soviet missile program because of its military uses and Khruschchev had the general support of the Soviet military (B), (E). Foreign trips were not related to the coup, which led to the ascendancy of Leonid Brezhnev (D).

30.   (D)   The founders of the Massachusetts Bay Colony were Puritans; they wanted to purify the Church of England. But they did not believe that the Church of England was so corrupt that all true Christians were obligated to separate themselves from it. They did believe that they had a special covenant relationship with God (A), that God would reward them with temporal blessings in recognition of their obedience (E), that the colony was a moral example to England and the world (B) of what a true biblical commonwealth could and should be, and that the power of this example represented the best way to reform England (C).

31.   (D)   The "New Immigration" of 1880–1900 predominantly consisted of immigrants from eastern and southern Europe, rather than northern and western Europe. The "New Immigrants" were largely unskilled day laborers (A) and came from non-Protestant religions (C); as a result, quotas were established to keep these "inferior" immigrants out. Immigration did increase steadily over these years (B), although the Chinese remained excluded (E) from the immigration boom by the Chinese Exclusion Act of 1882, which was renewed upon its expiration in 1892 and remained in effect for the rest of the century.

32.   (C)   The Treaty of Nimwegen (II) (1678–9) concluded the Dutch War of Louis XIV and resulted in losses from both Spain and Austria to France. The Treaty

of Ryswick (III) (1697) ended the War of the League of Augsburg; France was forced to make concessions to the allies. The Peace of Utrecht (IV) (1713) constituted a major setback for France and a victory for Britain and the Netherlands. The Peace of Augsburg (I) (1555) concluded the German wars of religion which were associated with the emergence of Lutheranism; Lutheranism was recognized and the power of the Northern German princes was enhanced. The Treaty of Paris (V) (1763) concluded the Seven Years' War; this occurred after the death of Louis XIV in 1715.

33. **(C)** Louis Kossuth was the leader of the Hungarian nationalists during the Revolution of 1848. While certain elements in Hungarian society were motivated by their desire for a liberal constitution (A), their intent to control the region and the Slavs (B), or by calls for drastic economic and social changes (D), the majority revolted because of nationalist aspirations (C). Many Hungarians were displeased with the Hapsburg dynasty which ruled them; the Hohenzollern dynasty (E) was the royal family of Prussia.

34. **(E)** William Harvey (E) first postulated the theory of the circulatory system and published a treatise on it in 1628. In 1610, Galileo (C) wrote a report on his telescopic observation of the moons of Jupiter; his statement supported the heliocentric theory which had emerged through the laborious efforts of Nicholas of Cusa (A), Leonardo Da Vinci (D), and most importantly Nicholaus Copernicus (B), whose *On the Revolutions of the Heavenly Spheres* was published upon his death in 1547.

35. **(D)** The assassination of Garfield by a disgruntled office seeker shocked the nation and provoked the Pendleton Act of 1883, which, among other reforms, required a competitive test for entry into jobs "classified" by the president, and prohibited financial assessments of jobholders. While the Stalwart-Half Breed battles in the Republican party exemplified the problems of the spoils system (C), they had been going on for years before Garfield was shot, without reforms. Tweed's conviction (E), while long in coming, spurred no national movement for reform; Hayes's ending of Reconstruction (A) was not a civil service issue. Chester Arthur did not win renomination in 1884 (B).

36. **(D)** The Francistes (I), Solidarité Française (II), the Cagoulards (Comite Secret d'Action Revolutionnaire) (III), and the Parti Populaire Française (IV) were radical groups which emerged during the 1930s. Annales (V) is a school of historians and the title of a prominent French historical journal.

37. **(A)** On March 1, 1921, a rebellion of naval personnel broke out at the Soviet Kronstadt Naval Base. The rebellion, which was brutally suppressed by March 18th, was caused by the impact of the economic disaster and social upheaval of the Russian Civil War (A). Neither Ukrainian nationalist aspirations (B) nor sympathy for Poles (E) were factors in this Soviet rebellion. The collapse of Ger-

many in October/November 1918 (C), and the influence of the Spartacist movement (D), which was also a German development, were not related to the Kronstadt Rebellion.

38.   (A)   Credit Mobilier was the name of a dummy construction company set up by officials of Union Pacific in order to embezzle millions of dollars the government was paying to subsidize the construction of a transcontinental railroad. The contract for the collection of $427,000 in unpaid taxes, for a 50% commission that later found its way into Republican campaign coffers (B), was the centerpiece of a scandal known as the Sanborn Contract Fraud. The Whiskey Ring Fraud was the name given to the conspiracy of distillers and treasury officials to defraud the government of large amounts of money from the excise tax on whiskey (C), and Congress's attempt to raise its own pay retroactively (D) was christened the Salary Grab Act. The exposure of all of these sordid affairs during the presidency of U. S. Grant helped give his administration a reputation for corruption.

39.   (C)   The passage represents the views of John Locke as expressed in his *Second Treatise on Civil Government*. An opposing philosophy was advanced by Thomas Hobbes (A) in *Leviathan*. Francis Bacon's (B) primary work was in the development of empiricism. George III (D) was the reactionary king of England during the American Revolution. Voltaire (E) developed a political philosophy which called for enlightened despotism.

40.   (C)   The Pact of Locarno did not produce any disarmament goals (C). The Locarno Treaties of 1925 consisted of treaties of mutual guarantee of the Franco-German and Belgian-German frontiers (E), which were signed by Germany, France, and Belgium with Great Britain and Italy as guarantors (A). Locarno also provided for arbitration treaties between Germany and Poland, Germany and Czechoslovakia, Germany and Belgium (B), and Germany and France. Further, the Locarno Treaties included mutual assistance pacts between France and Poland, and France and Czechoslovakia (D) in the event of attack by Germany.

41.   (B)   The Dawes Plan was organized by Charles Dawes, a Chicago banker and later vice president of the United States, in 1924 in response to the crisis caused by the French and Belgian occupation of the Ruhr Valley. The focal point of the conflict was the reparations controversy; the Dawes Plan developed a new reparations schedule and resulted in the withdrawal of the French and Belgian troops. The Dawes Plan was not concerned with any English plan to stabilize the gold standard (A), limit the level of naval weapons (C), nationalize the coal industry (D), or manage the postwar demobilization (E).

42.   (C)   Area IV of the map represents the Republic of Texas, which had legalized slavery during the nine years of its existence as an independent nation, prior to its 1845 annexation by the United States. Slavery never existed in the Oregon

country (I), nor did it exist in the Mexican Cession (II) or the Gadsden Purchase (III) before U.S. annexation.

43.   (E)   The only area that became part of the United States as a direct result of the Mexican War was the Mexican Cession (II), purchased by the United States for the sum of $18,250,000 under the terms of the treaty that ended the war. Texas (IV) was annexed in 1845, shortly before the Mexican War. Oregon (I) was acquired in a deal with Great Britain in 1846, the same year that war broke out with Mexico. The Gadsden Purchase (III) was bought from Mexico several years after the end of the war.

44.   (B)   The United States bought Area III, the Gadsden Purchase, from Mexico in 1853, mainly to accomplish the goal of a Southern transcontinental railroad to link the bulk of the United States with the newly acquired territories on the Pacific Coast. The Southern Pacific Railroad, which ran from Houston through El Paso and Tucson to Los Angeles, was completed in 1882. The government made the purchase five years after President Polk left office (C), and six years after the end of the Mexican-American War, through which Polk added much of northern Mexico to the United States (A). The region was not purchased as slave or free territory (D); according to the Compromise of 1850, the decision would be left to the territory. The region became part of the states of Arizona and New Mexico in 1912 (E), almost a quarter of a century after Cleveland and Harrison added seven states to the Union.

45.   (C)   The Fabian Society was established in 1881 as a revisionist Marxist body which maintained that Marxist objectives could be achieved in Britain through evolutionary, i.e., electoral, means rather than through revolutionary means (C). While there was general sympathy with the old Chartist Movement (A) of the 1830s and 1840s, the Fabians were intent on a further radicalization of British society. The concept of Tory Democracy which was advanced by Benjamin Disraeli and Randolph Churchill (D) attempted to align the Conservative party with the irreversible movement of democratization in England. While the Fabians were interested in the Irish Question (E), the Society was not established for that purpose.

46.   (D)   Lenin's "April Theses" of 1917 called for the seizure of the land by the peasants (I), the control of industry by committees of workers (II), and withdrawal from the war (even if as a unilateral act) (III). It called for the elimination, not the continuance, of the provisional government (V). Lenin's decision on the fate of the Romanov family (IV) was deferred until the spring of 1918.

47.   (A)   Ulrich Zwingli extended Protestant thinking through his emphasis on predestination and his interpretation of the Eucharist as a symbolic reenactment of the Last Supper. Zwingli's views on the Eucharist contrasted sharply with the Catholic doctrine of transubstantiation and the Lutheran doctrine of consubstantiation. Zwingli, as well as other reformers, denounced the Roman Catholic church

(B). He denounced the early advocates of Unitarianism (C). He made no attempt to infiltrate the Hapsburg court of Charles V (E). Rather than defeating the Catholic Swiss Cantons (D), Zwingli's force was defeated in the Kappel War and Zwingli was killed.

48. **(C)** Germany agreed to the Dual Alliance (II) in 1879. The Triple Alliance (III) was signed in 1881 by representatives of Italy, Germany, and Austria-Hungary. France and Russia entered the Dual Entente (I) in 1894. The Entente Cordiale (V) between Britain and France was signed in 1904 and settled colonial disputes in North Africa. The Anglo-Russian Entente of 1907 (IV) resolved British-Russian differences over Persia, Tibet, and Afghanistan.

49. **(A)** The Marshall Plan can best be understood as part of an American desire to make communism less appealing to Europeans by creating economic prosperity. A military alliance against the Soviet Union (B) was not part of the plan; although recognition of the new Soviet government had not yet been granted, it was not seen as a threat to the United States. While some Americans might have wanted to make Western Europe permanently dependent on the U.S. economically (C), and believed this would end the nation's postwar Depression (E), these were not goals of the Marshall Plan itself. Rather than perceiving an industrialized Germany as a threat (D), U.S. diplomats recognized that a nonindustrialized Germany would pose a much larger threat to political stability in Western Europe.

50. **(E)** Eli Whitney (IV), inventor of the cotton gin, which separated cotton fiber from seed, and Cyrus McCormick (II), inventor of the mechanical reaper, had the most direct effect on agriculture of those listed. The others invented unrelated items during the latter half of the 19th century—Elias Howe (I), the sewing machine; Christopher Sholes (III), the typewriter; and Henry Bessemer (V), the Bessemer-Kelly method of making cheap steel.

51. **(C)** This statement was part of the *cahiers de doléances,* or lists of grievances, which were advanced by most of the towns in France in the spring of 1789, as part of the process of selecting representatives to the Estates-General, which convened in May 1789 (C). It would be the task of the Third Estate of the Estates-General to raise these issues and then to lead in the formulation of a statement which would be directed to Louis XVI (A), (B). This moderate statement of goals did not reflect the radical tenants of Jacobinism (D) nor was it drafted by Abbé Sieyès, author of *What is the Third Estate?* (E).

52. **(D)** In this statement the people of Bailliage indicated that they were politically sophisticated and that they possessed an understanding of the problems which confronted them and the French nation (D). They did not support the current regime (A), entertain a rather narrow and limited sense of the French nation (E), indicate that they were interested solely in tax issues (C), or express any intent to overthrow the existing government (B).

53. **(D)** Most of the concerns raised in this statement were addressed by the National Assembly (1789–91) (D). The Estates-General (A) ceased to exist after June 1789; Louis XVI (B) became increasingly reactionary and was eliminated in January 1792. The Legislative Assembly of 1791–2 (E) proved to be inefficient, and Robespierre (C) was interested in a more radical agenda.

54. **(D)** The sentiments advanced in this statement most closely represent the views of Baron Montesquieu (D), the author of *The Spirit of the Laws*, who generally argued in favor of a British form of government for France. Voltaire (A) favored enlightened despotism; François Quesnay (C) and the Physiocrats endorsed an agrarian society governed through leaders advised by intellectuals. Robespierre (B), one of the principal Jacobins, advanced a political, social, and economic primitivism based on agriculture. Louis XIV (E) advocated monarchical absolutism.

55. **(E)** The *cahiers de doléances* were directed to the representatives who would serve in the Third Estate of the Estates-General (E). The National Assembly (C) emerged in the summer of 1789; the Legislative Assembly (B) existed from 1791 to 1792, and was followed by the radical Convention (D) from 1792 to 1795. The middle-class oriented Directory (A) was the form of government from 1795 to 1799.

56. **(C)** Although farming (A), Union pensions (B), civil service reform (D), and government regulation of big business (E) were all important issues during President Cleveland's first administration (1884–1888), the all-consuming issue was the tariff, and he devoted his entire 1887 State of the Union address to an argument for lower tariffs to liquidate the Treasury surplus. Cleveland argued for lower tariffs even in the face of severe opposition from big business, Congress, and war veterans, who all benefited from the astronomically high tariffs resulting, in part, from revenue needs during the Civil War. The tariff issue dominated the subsequent presidential campaign, in which Cleveland may have lost votes because of his obstinacy on the issue.

57. **(D)** In this excerpt from his Funeral Oration of 430 BC, Pericles articulated the Athenian (D) view of democracy. Sparta (A), Athens's enemy in the Peloponnesian War, did not have a democratic form of government; neither did Syracuse (B) or Mycenae (E). Alexandria (C) was not organized until the next century.

58. **(B)** Sparta and its allies (B) from the Peloponnesian League went to war against Athens during the 430s BC. This Greek Civil War resulted in the defeat of Athens. The wars against Persia (A), including a war against Darius (E), were fought at the beginning of the 5th century BC. Philip of Macedon (C) stabilized the Greek peninsula during the mid-4th century BC. Carthage (D) was a power in central North Africa and was defeated in a series of wars with Rome known as the Punic Wars.

59. **(B)** Information about this speech and other details concerning this conflict were written by the greatest historian of ancient Greece, Thucydides (B). Herodotus (A), author of *The Persian Wars,* is known as the "Father of History." Xenophon (D) was the leader of a military expedition into the Near East; he wrote an account known as *The Persian Expedition.* Tacitus (C) and Livy (E) were Roman historians.

60. **(B)** While the Treaty of Versailles did forge an independent, though short-lived, Polish nation (A), restore Alsace-Lorraine to France (C), create many nations in the Balkans according to the principle of self-determination (E), and create the League of Nations (D) (albeit without the participation of the United States), Wilson's Fourteen Points did not achieve independence for any Middle Eastern nations, let alone adjust national boundaries. Borders were readjusted and territories changed hands, but future Middle Eastern nations would remain part of European colonial empires until after World War II.

61. **(B)** The passage refers to the Half-Way Covenant, by which Puritan ministers of colonial Massachusetts sought to minimize the decline in spiritual fervor between first and second generation settlers. The "Old Deluder Satan" Act (A) was an attempt to ensure the education of children. The Fundamental Orders of Connecticut (C) formed the first written constitution in America. The Mayflower Compact (D) established the basis for government in the Plymouth colony. The New England Confederation (E) of 1643 united the Massachusetts, Plymouth, Connecticut, and New Haven colonies in an organization to settle boundary disputes and resist attacks from the French, Dutch, and Indians.

62. **(B)** This map illustrates the changes which affected Germany after the First World War. The altered areas would have been included on a post–Franco-Prussian War map in 1871 (A). In 1945 (C), after the Second World War, Germany was dismembered. In 1815 (D), Germany did not exist as a state. In 1989 (E), Germany was reunited (officially in 1990); the designated changes were not applicable in 1989.

63. **(E)** Edward Hyde (E) defended Charles I and Charles II during the 17th century and was named the Earl of Clarendon. In the 1660s his career was ruined when Charles II failed to defend him in the battle over the Clarendon Code. Sir Edward Coke (A), who served as Chief Justice of the Court of Common Pleas, was removed by James I because of his criticisms of the monarchy. John Pym (B), John Hampton (D), and Oliver Cromwell (C) were members of the Long Parliament who opposed the policies of Charles I; Cromwell became Lord Protector in 1653.

64. **(B)** Both Luther's German *Bible* (I) and Calvin's *Institutes of the Christian Religion* (II), in French, contributed to the growth of these respective vernacular literatures. Henry VIII's *Defense of the Seven Sacraments* (III), Ignatius Loyola's *Spiritual Exercises* (IV), and *The Index of Prohibited Books* (V) appeared in Latin in most editions and enjoyed limited circulation.

65. **(A)** The Tonkin Gulf Resolution of 1964, which granted President Johnson vast powers in pursuing the Vietnam War, best exemplifies the post–World War II trend toward executive-directed foreign policy in which Congress plays only a small role. The Civil Rights Act (B), while it enhanced the reputation of President Johnson, was an act of domestic, not foreign, policy. Both the Boland Amendments (C), which forbade the president from providing monetary aid to overthrow the Nicaraguan government and the War Powers Act of 1973 (D), which limited the president's war-making powers to 60 days without congressional approval, represent congressional attempts to curtail executive foreign policy-making power. The Good Neighbor Policy (E) was a complex set of initiatives toward Latin American nations that was part of Franklin D. Roosevelt's foreign policy.

66. **(C)** Prior to the revolutions of 1848, Pope Pius IX (III), Joseph Mazzini (IV), and Joseph de Maistre (V) were the leaders of the Italian nationalist movement. While Camillio Cavour (I) was active in the movement, he did not emerge as a major power until after 1848, when he became prime minister of Piedmont/Sardinia. Garibaldi's (II) contribution to Italian nationalism came in the 1860s with the acquisition of the Kingdom of the Two Sicilies.

67. **(C)** The French essayist Montaigne (C) was the most significant philosopher of the Baroque period. Bernini (A) was a major Baroque architect and sculptor who was known for the fountains and interiors of St. Peter's Basilica. Vasari (B) was the late Italian Renaissance historian and biographer who wrote *Lives of the Most Eminent Architects, Sculptors, and Painters.* Baron Montesquieu (D) wrote *The Spirit of the Laws* during the 18th-century Enlightenment. Jean Bodin (E) was a prominent French political theorist and philosopher.

68. **(C)** The War of the Three Henrys concluded in 1589 with the ascendance of Henry of Navarre to the throne (I). Henry, the leader of the French Huguenots and a member of the Bourbon dynasty (IV), became a Catholic (III) to gain the French crown; he became Henry IV and replaced the Valois line (II). The Fronde (V) was a mid-17th century noble uprising against the young Louis XIV; it was suppressed through the efforts of the regent, Cardinal Mazarin.

69. **(D)** Thomas Paine argued that it was only common sense (the title of his 1776 pamphlet) for the American colonies to become independent from Great Britain. His argument is much more radical than that of John Dickinson in his *Letters from a Farmer in Pennsylvania* (E), written a decade earlier as a protest against the unconstitutional practices of the British government. Paine's *Crisis Papers* (D) were written about a year after *Common Sense* and were aimed not at convincing people to declare independence, which had already been done, but rather at persuading them to make sacrifices in order to win that independence.

70. **(A)** Paine's argument in this passage is that it is a necessity of nature that

"this Continent"—America—should be independent of Great Britain. See also the explanation for number 69 above.

71.   (A)   Map II illustrates the 1947 boundaries of Israel as prescribed under the United Nations Partition Plan. Map I reflects the territories which were conquered by 1949. Map III presents the Israeli boundaries after the Six Days' War in 1967.

72.   (C)   The Act of Abjuration, which rejected Spanish authority, was the declaration of independence of the Netherlands (C). The Kingdom of the Two Sicilies (A) emerged during the 18th century. Portuguese independence from Spain (D) was recognized in 1713 at the Peace of Utrecht. Guarantees of Belgian independence (B) were ratified in 1833–37. Spanish control of Luxembourg (E) was eliminated during the late 17th century.

73.   (C)   The Rising of the Northern Earls (I) and the Throckmorton (II) and Babington (V) Plots were representative of Catholic-led plots to overthrow Elizabeth I. The Popish Plot (IV) of 1678 occurred during the reign of Charles II. The Gunpowder Plot (III) of 1605 was a plan to eliminate most of the leaders of the English government by a small group of Catholic fanatics; it occurred during the early years of the reign of James I.

74.   (E)   The *Federalist* papers were a series of 85 letters written to newspapers by Hamilton, Madison, and Jay. The passage comes from *Federalist* number 10, written by Alexander Hamilton. Its purpose was to explain, and ease people's minds about, the proposed U.S. Constitution.

75.   (B)   In order to set people's minds at ease about the proposed U.S. Constitution and thus secure its ratification, Hamilton sought to demonstrate that the Constitution would preserve the rights and powers of the states (the opposite of (D)). Hamilton, along with the other Federalists, did believe that a balanced government was the best form of government (A) and that the U.S. Constitution offered a form of government especially suited to the American character (C), but these facts are not the point of the argument presented here. That the United States should keep itself free from entangling alliances with European countries (E) was the advice of George Washington in his *Farewell Address.*

76.   (A)   Both Hobbes and Voltaire (A) maintained that an absolute ruler, hopefully enlightened, would provide the best government. Locke and Montesquieu argued that the power of the monarch had to be contained through constitutional restrictions; sovereign power rested in the nation and was not transferable. Rousseau expounded on these notions in his *Social Contract.* Quesnay was the leader of the Physiocrats and believed that an enlightened leader, advised by intellectuals, would provide the optimum government.

77.   (A)   The repeal of the Corn Laws in 1846 and the Navigation Acts in 1849

(A) were major steps in England's movement toward free trade. These economic restraints were lifted in accordance with the principles set out by Adam Smith in his *Wealth of Nations*, which appeared in the preceding century. The Factory Act of 1833 (C) imposed restrictions on the use of child labor in the textile industry. Joseph Chamberlain's concept of preferential trade (D) for British colonies and dominions ran counter to the free trade philosophy; he advocated this policy during the first decade of the 20th century. The Chartist Movement (E) advanced economic positions which ran counter to free trade. The implementation of the Corn Laws (B) during the early 19th century was not an example of free trade economics because they prohibited the importation of foreign grain and imposed no price restraints on domestic grain.

78. **(B)** At the Treaty of Paris in 1763, two major issues became apparent (B). One was the contest between Prussia in the north (Hohenzollern) and Austria in the south (Hapsburg). This struggle would continue until 1866, when Prussia defeated Austria in the German Civil War. The other was the rivalry between Britain and France over colonies in North America and India. Anglo-French colonial conflicts continued until the Entente Cordiale in 1904. By 1763, the dominant power of France (A) was no longer the threat that it had been during the age of Louis XIV. Russia was not a formidable power (C), and democracy was not yet developing in Western Europe (D). While some nations and classes were concerned with the collapse of the feudal order (E), it was not recognized as a problem in the treaty; nor was there an appreciation of the impact of the economic distinctions between Western and Central Europe.

79. **(C)** The Ruhr Crisis (1923–4) was caused by an economic conflict associated with reparations and war debts (C). French and Belgian troops occupied the mineral-rich Ruhr Valley; this action resulted in a crisis which was resolved through an American initiative known as the Dawes Plan (1924), which established a new reparations schedule. There was no abuse of French or Belgian citizens (A), no German border conflicts (B), and no German militarization of the Ruhr Valley (D). Hitler's march into the Rhineland did not occur until 1935 (E).

80. **(A)** The painting is Winslow Homer's "The Fox Hunt," an ironic reversal of nature, depicting the fox as the prey of the birds he had previously hunted, by one of the leading American realists. This irony is not seen in the portrayals of the beauty of nature common to the Hudson River School (D) and regional painting (C). The realists reacted against the emotionalism of the romantics and the rationality of the neoclassicists by painting their subjects as realistically as possible. The bleak cynicism of the Ashcan School (B) was a later development in realism; the New York School (E) an abstract school that developed much later.

81. **(D)** John Toland (I), Matthew Tindal (III), and Anthony Collins (IV) were major contributors to Deism. Lord Shaftesbury (II) advanced arguments supporting ethical theories and Bernard de Mandeville (V) wrote the controversial *Fable of the Bees*, which contended that "private vices are public virtues."

82. (C) The British Nationality Act of 1948 permitted each dominion to determine who could hold citizenship. One of the consequences of this act was that soon after it was passed, the Union of South Africa passed apartheid legislation. The Reform Bills of 1867 (A) and 1884–5 (D) extended the vote to English males over 21. The Parliament Act of 1911 (B) restricted the power of the House of Lords. The Education Act of 1902 (E) constituted a major step in the development of public education in Britain. These acts were all domestic, not imperial, legislation.

83. (D) The map depicts the United States as it was after the passage of the Kansas-Nebraska Act, with the entire expanse of the Kansas and Nebraska territories—virtually the entire Great Plains area north of what is now Oklahoma—opened to slavery under the doctrine of popular sovereignty. The Missouri Compromise (B) admitted Missouri as a slave state and divided the remainder of the Louisiana Purchase territory along the line of 36°30′ latitude, reserving the area south of that line for slavery and north of it (the later Kansas and Nebraska territories) for freedom. The Compromise of 1850 (C) admitted California as a free state, placed the Utah and New Mexico territories (the rest of the Mexican Cession) under the doctrine of popular sovereignty, and left the central and northern Great Plains untouched. The Dred Scott decision (A) of 1857 opened all of the nation's territories to slavery by denying that any government, federal or territorial, had the right to ban it. The Civil War (E), of course, ended slavery in the United States.

84. (B) During his first of four terms as British prime minister (1870–75), the Liberal William Gladstone (B) demonstrated his concern for the problems confronting the Irish through the disestablishment of the Church of Ireland and the passage of laws to protect the rights of Irish tenant farmers. Later, Gladstone would support the Irish Home Rule movement. Lord Palmerston (E) died in 1865, prior to the re-emergence of the Irish Question. Disraeli (A) and Salisbury (C) were Conservative prime ministers who followed policies unsympathetic to native Irish interests. Herbert Asquith (D) was British prime minister and the leader of the Liberal party from 1907 to 1916. His interest in Ireland was deflected by domestic politics and the war effort. The Easter Rebellion in 1916 helped cause Asquith's fall from power.

85. (C) This passage comes from Fyodor Dostoyevsky's *Notes from the Underground*, which presented a rather despondent, though not hopeless, view of Russian life. Herbert Spencer (A) advanced his adaptation of Darwinian principles to society during the end of the 19th century. August Comte (B) has been considered the founder of positivism. Leo Tolstoy (D) was a 19th-century Russian novelist most frequently remembered for his *War and Peace*. Prince Peter Kropotkin (E) was a Russian nobleman who became an anarchist theoretician.

86. (C) During the late 14th century, John Wycliffe (C) (*On Civil Dominion*) raised questions concerning the fundamental purposes of Christianity and the relationship between spiritual and temporal authorities. As a result of his efforts, he was

persecuted. Later, during the proceedings of the Council of Constance (1414), the Roman Catholic church ordered that his body be exhumed and that its remnants be dispersed. Wycliffe's ideas survived in the Lollard movement, which continued to exist as a minor religious underground movement in England throughout the 15th century. Duns Scotus (A), William Ockham (B), and Roger Bacon (D) were prominent medieval intellectuals; John Colet (E) was a major contributor to the English Renaissance during the late 15th century.

87. **(D)** While farms were disappearing and industry was growing during the era of Jacksonian Democracy, industrialization would not become an issue until after the Civil War. Federal financing of internal improvements (B), states' rights (C), trade with the British West Indies (E), and the removal of southeastern Indians to reservations (A) all were, with other issues such as the Second Bank of the United States, important issues during this era.

88. **(D)** *Miranda v. State of Arizona* (III) is probably the most well known of the Warren Court's decisions; it ruled that police must inform suspects of their rights to silence and counsel before questioning them. *Reynolds v. Sims* (II), also known as the "one man, one vote" decision, dictated that representation in state legislatures must be based on population, not area. *Watkins v. United States* (V) upheld the Fifth-Amendment right of a witness to refuse to testify before a congressional committee, even if the committee was investigating subversive activities. *Roe v. Wade* (IV), which declared abortion legal on the basis of a "zone of privacy" implied by several amendments in the Bill of Rights, was a Burger Court decision of 1973. *Edwards v. Aguillard* (I) was a Rehnquist court decision of 1988, prohibiting the state of Louisiana from requiring its schools to give a "balanced treatment" of "creation science" and evolution on the grounds that such a requirement advanced religious teachings in violation of the First Amendment.

89. **(B)** The French Physiocrats, under the leadership of François Quesnay, advanced a program based on the reform of the agrarian order (B). Further, they believed that the monarch should take the advice of enlightened intellectuals. They did not identify with industrialism (A), extended urbanization, or the maintenance of the status quo. They opposed the values of the *Ancien Régime* (D), did not place much hope in Louis XVI (E), nor were they interested in extending urbanization (C) through industrialism (A).

90. **(D)** Bismarck's *Kulturkampf* or "Struggle for the Modern," was directed at curtailing the influence of the Catholic church and the Catholic-dominated Center party (D). Bismarck was confronted with the need to unify the new German Empire and he viewed the Center party and the Catholic church in the South as an obstacle to realizing this goal. At the same time (1875), Bismarck was interested in establishing a positive relationship with Austria-Hungary (A) and Russia (E), and as he feared a war of revenge by the French (C), he did not antagonize them.

91. (C)   The Yalta Conference in February 1945 determined the arrangements for Central and Eastern Europe after the war (II), the Soviet Union's role as the liberator of Berlin (I), and finalized plans for the United Nations (III). Churchill, Stalin, and Roosevelt did not agree to recognize the United States as the only nuclear power (V) nor American/British control of Western Europe (IV).

92. (E)   The colonial economy of South Carolina, unlike those of any of the more northerly colonies, was dependent on the cultivation of rice and indigo, the latter a plant used to make blue dye. Maryland (B), Virginia (C), and North Carolina (D) were primarily tobacco-growing colonies, while Pennsylvania (A) produced grain.

93. (B)   The statement was made by Governor Francis Bernard of Massachusetts in his attempt to convince the Americans that they ought to accept taxation without representation, in the form of the Stamp Act. While Dickinson (D) might have favored caution in approaching the subject of independence and John Adams (C) might have believed that the British soldiers involved in the Boston Massacre were not personally guilty, they would have held to the British political ideal, by then well over a century old, of no taxation without representation.

94. (C)   The cartoon comments on the crucial event in the "creation" of Italy, Garibaldi's surrender of the Kingdom of the Two Sicilies to King Victor Emmanuel II's Sardinian forces. The king marks the act of creation by putting on a boot labeled "Italy." D'Annunzio's acquisition of *Italia Irrendenta* land after the Treaty of Versailles (E) was welcome, but not a "completion" of a process that had really ended in 1870, with the acquisition of Venice and Rome. Benito Mussolini's relationship to King Victor Emmanuel III (A) was hardly one of subservience, and Pope Pius IX's relationship to the Republic of 1848 (D) was antipathetic.

95. (E)   Arnold Toynbee (E) was a British historian and author of *A Study of History*. In his *Origins of Psychoanalysis* and *Civilization and Its Discontents*, Sigmund Freud (C) presented an understanding of human behavior based on psychoanalysis. Carl Jung (A) broke with Freud and developed an alternative approach to psychology which included the idea of the collective unconscious. John Dewey (B) was an American philosopher and educator who is renowned for his *School and Society*. Thomas Huxley (D) was an advocate of Darwinian principles.

96. (C)   Max Planck's *Quantum Physics* (II), Albert Einstein's *Theory of Relativity* (III), and the Michelson-Morley Experiment (V) were significant contributions to the development of the New Science at the end of the 19th and the beginning of the 20th centuries. Charles Darwin's *The Origin of Species* (I) was published in 1859 and advanced an evolutionary hypothesis. Henri Bergson's *Positivism* (IV) represented a philosophy which explained scientific advancement in terms of Comtean logical positivism.

97. **(B)** The passage is from Washington's 1796 farewell address, in which he announced his decision not to accept a third term as president and offered advice for the future shaping of national policy.

98. **(A)** In this passage, Washington wanted to convey that political parties—or "factions" as he called them—were harmful. Along with the rest of the Founding Fathers, Washington did not envision the present system of political parties, so he could not have been discussing party strife (C), (D); by the same token, the Constitution does not address the dangers of faction (E). Washington might have felt that Britain wanted to undermine the American system of government (B), but this passage does not discuss that topic.

99. **(B)** Sidney (I) and Beatrice (III) Webb and Keir Hardie (II) were founding members of the British revisionist group known as the Fabian Society. Hardie would establish the Independent Labour Party. Herbert Spencer (IV) was a Social Darwinist and Peter Kropotkin (V) was the renowned theoretician of the anarchists during the late 19th and early 20th centuries.

100. **(A)** British Prime Minister Harold Macmillan (A) maintained Britain's primary relationships were with the Empire-Commonwealth and the United States. Jean Monnet (D) was the first to advance the concept of a European Economic Community after the Second World War. His efforts were supported by the Frenchman Robert Schuman (C) and the Belgian Paul-Henri Spaak (B). Charles de Gaulle (E) supported the development of the EEC from a French nationalist perspective.

101. **(B)** In *Guernica*, Pablo Picasso condemned the German bombardment of a defenseless town during the Spanish Civil War (B). While Picasso denounced the German invasion of Poland (D), and lamented the loss of hundreds of thousands of noncombatants at the hands of the Fascists (not the republicans) (C), he did not condemn all of German art (E), nor was this work a commentary of the German use of gas (A) during World War I.

102. **(E)** John Marshall, who served as chief justice of the United States for a third of a century, was a steadfast champion of the cause of national sovereignty and an enemy of the doctrine of states' rights. His successor, the almost equally long-tenured Roger B. Taney (D), held the opposite viewpoint. So did Thomas Jefferson (A) and Confederate president Jefferson Davis (C). But by far the most renowned advocate of states rights in 19th-century America was South Carolina politician John C. Calhoun (B).

103. **(A)** "Flexible response," which demanded the widest range of options and means to respond to all possible conflicts, stressed the Keynesian economic concept of infinite growth, which would ostensibly give the Kennedy/Johnson administrations the resources to respond to all threats, anywhere, anytime. As such, flexible response did not rate conflicts in importance (B); the "domino theory" of Secretary

of State Rusk stated that the loss of one country to communism made the loss of neighboring countries more likely. Nor did the Kennedy/Johnson administrations believe, given infinite growth, that increased military spending necessarily meant decreased domestic spending (E), although as the Vietnam War escalated, Johnson's Great Society programs suffered. Flexible response also valued a gradual escalation of military response, not the immediate response of "massive retaliation" (D). The Peace Corps (C), created by the Kennedy administration, was not specifically used as an instrument of foreign policy by either Kennedy or Johnson.

104. **(C)** While Adolphe Thiers (A) and Marshall MacMahon (B) were involved in the early years of the Third French Republic, Leon Gambetta (C), who died in 1882, emerged as the most zealous advocate of republicanism during this period. Victor Hugo (D), who died in 1885, was an author and nationalist. Louis Blanc (E) was a radical who succeeded in implementing a National Workshop Program in Paris during the spring of 1848.

105. **(D)** The English Bill of Rights of 1689 required that all monarchs be members of the Church of England (I) to avoid any more Catholic monarchs; established by law parliamentary control over revenues (III); and maintained the monarch's control of the military (IV). William and Mary (V) accepted the Bill of Rights in April 1689.

106. **(C)** Those who held large amounts of government securities, payable in gold, would not have favored bimetallism since, by monetizing silver at an artificially high, fixed rate relative to gold, it would tend to drain the government's gold reserves and endanger its ability to meet its obligations to pay those securities. Those who thought inflation would benefit the economy (A), those who owned stock in silver mines (B), those who were deeply in debt (D), and those who came from predominantly agricultural states (E), particularly in the South and Great Plains areas, would have seen bimetallism as likely to benefit them financially, and favored it.

107. **(C)** The economic philosophy of President Woodrow Wilson, which attacked the "triple wall of privilege" (i.e., the trusts, the tariff, and the banks), contrasted sharply with the outlook of Treasury Secretary Andrew Mellon (1921–29), who favored noninterference with business. The other pairs are appropriately matched. The Interstate Commerce Act of 1887, intended to help regulate railroads, was given more teeth by the Hepburn Act of 1908 (D). Alexander Hamilton and Mark Hanna (A) were kindred spirits although they lived almost a hundred years apart; both favored big business and laissez-faire economics. Henry Clay's "American System" of tariffs and internal improvements and Lyndon Johnson's "Great Society" (B) both proposed to use vast amounts of federal money on domestic improvements, on manufacturing (Clay) and social reform (Johnson). Theodore Roosevelt's Square Deal (E) was, like Franklin D. Roosevelt's New Deal, a loose

arrangement of executive actions and executive-influenced congressional acts designed to advance a progressive idea.

108. **(B)** John C. Calhoun, representing the Southern extremist position, opposed the Compromise of 1850 as not sufficiently favorable to the South. Henry Clay (A) was sponsor of the Compromise, Daniel Webster (C) all but destroyed his political future by supporting it, and Stephen A. Douglas (E) finally shepherded it through Congress with the aid of President Millard Fillmore (D).

109. **(C)** During the Suez Crisis of 1956 (C), the American president, Dwight Eisenhower, pressured the British and the French to withdraw from the conflict with Egypt. The British and French were allied with Israel. The Hungarian Revolution (A), the Polish riots (B), and Khrushchev's Secret Speech (D), in which he denounced Stalin, occurred in 1956 but did not have any negative impact on the Atlantic alliance. The Algerian crisis (E) was a French affair and intensified until de Gaulle came to power in 1958.

110. **(B)** The great lyric poets Simonides of Ceos, Bacchylides of Ceos, and Pindar were all contemporaries of the poet and playwright Aeschylus (B). They were early contributors to the Golden Age of Athenian literature (5th century BC). Aristotle (A) was a later Greek who lived during a rather dormant literary era. Theocritis (D) was an early 3rd century poet who was the first of the Greek pastoral poets. Ptolemy (E) was a general in Alexander's army; he emerged as the leader of Egypt. Horace (C) was a contributor to the Golden Age of Latin letters.

111. **(A)** The Eleusinian Mysteries consisted chiefly of the ceremonies devised by the Athenian worshipers of Dionysus, Demeter, and Persephone (I); a passion play which represented the sorrows of Demeter (II); and ceremonies which contributed to the progress of democratization in Athens (III). Orphism, in the 6th century BC, advanced the beliefs that the soul is suffering the punishment of sin (IV) and that through pure living one can cleanse oneself from sin (V).

112. **(C)** The basis of President William H. Taft's "dollar diplomacy" was the use of American investment in Latin America as a tool for successful diplomacy, unlike the policies of various European countries or Japan, that often used diplomacy (A) or military force (B) to further their business interests during the same era. It was not an offer of foreign aid (D) or of American development of the Latin American economies (E).

113. **(D)** British violations of American shipping rights, which included the impressment of American seamen, was one of the cause of the War of 1812. While British sea power was occasionally a nuisance thereafter, it never again had such drastic influence on American policy. During the early years of World War I (A), the British blockade of Germany and their confiscation practices (which extended to nonmunition items and materials going to Germany's neutral neighbors) caused

outrage; but this outrage was quickly allayed with monetary compensation and by the activities of the German U-boats. The Venezuelan controversy (C), which increased U.S.-British tensions temporarily, was not a dispute over American shipping rights. The Roosevelt Corollary to the Monroe Doctrine (E) did not result from violation of American shipping rights, but rather from the British blockade of Venezuela and the Dominican Republic. The Monroe Doctrine itself (B) was proclaimed partly at Britain's urging (although it was also aimed to some extent at British sea power in Latin America), and was partially enforced in the short run by British ships.

114. (A)   Boccaccio's *Decameron* was a classic anticlerical work which emphasized the misdeeds of the clergy. Henry VIII's *Defense of the Seven Sacraments* (B), was a response to the Lutheran reformation which supported traditional Catholic sacramental theology. *Summa Theologica* by Thomas Aquinas (C) was the medieval intellectual synthesis which produced Scholasticism. Copernicus' *The Revolutions of the Heavenly Bodies* (D) advanced the heliocentric theory of the universe and Pope Leo X's papal Bull, *Exsurge Domine,* condemned Luther as a heretic (E).

115. (C)   English Puritanism developed during the reign of Elizabeth I because of the dissatisfaction with the scope and breadth of the Elizabethan Religious Settlement among the Marian Exiles and others who were influenced by Calvinist views. Obviously, (A) is incorrect because the Council of Trent advanced Catholic doctrines; Elizabeth I was interested in consolidating, not extending (B), Protestantism in England. The Jesuit Mission (D) occurred in 1580 and was not related to Puritanism; Puritanism (E) opposed the earlier Catholic forms of worship.

116. (A)   After the First World War ended, a coalition of moderates and conservatives, the Bloc National (A), came to power and led French politics from 1919 to 1924. It was led by Premier Alexandre Millerand. Socialists and republicans (B), Syndicalists and Nationalists (C), moderates and socialists (D), and agrarian liberals and socialists (E) did not combine except in the most extreme circumstances.

117. (D)   This map of Italian holdings in Europe and Africa incorporates the Italian seizures of Ethiopia and Albania which took place in the 1930s. The Kingdom of Italy was established in 1870 (A); at that time Italy did not have any extensive imperial holdings. In 1914 (B) and 1919 (E), Albania and Ethiopia were not part of the Italian Empire. By 1945 (C), Italy lost its control over these states.

118. (D)   The Southern states did begin to secede as soon as the election was over; South Carolina seceded four days after Lincoln won, and six more states seceded before Lincoln took office. The other statements are not true. Lincoln, considered one of the greatest presidents, did not even poll 40% of the vote (B). Senator Stephen A. Douglas, the other candidate popularly associated with the campaign, ran second in the popular vote (A), but received only 12 electoral votes. Vice-President John Breckinridge, despite running on the Southern Democratic ticket,

was a well-known moderate Unionist (C). Union candidate John Bell, far from showing badly in the South, took the more moderate states of Virginia, Tennessee, and Kentucky (E), and polled well in North Carolina and Georgia, finishing with more electoral votes than Douglas.

119. **(D)** Major figures in the Harlem Renaissance movement, which flowered during the 1920s, were poet and essayist Langston Hughes (III), poet Countee Cullen (I), and poet Alain Locke (IV). Novelist and anthropologist Zora Neale Hurston (II) was a contemporary of most Harlem Renaissance writers and spent time in Harlem during the Renaissance, even collaborating with Hughes on a play. Novelist and essayist Baldwin (II), born in 1924 in Harlem, was too young to have played a part in the Renaissance, which was cut short by the Great Depression, although he embodied many of its values in his work.

120. **(E)** In the Treaty of Brest-Litovsk between the Soviet Union and Germany, the Soviets lost the Baltic provinces (A), the Ukraine (B), Finland (C), and Byleorussia (D). However, they retained the land adjacent to the White Sea (E) near the Arctic Circle.

121. **(A)** The Treaty of St. Germain of September 10, 1919, concluded the war between the Allies and Austria; it recognized the breakup of the Austro-Hungarian state. The Treaty of Neuilly (B) of November 27, 1919, resulted in the Bulgarians losing territory to Yugoslavia and Greece. The Treaty of Trianon (C) of June 4, 1920, established peace between Hungary and the Allies. The Treaty of Sevres (D) of August 10, 1920, was the Allied peace with Turkey. The Treaty of Rapallo (E) of December 12, 1920, resolved disputes between Yugoslavia and Italy.

122. **(D)** Johann G. Herder (1744–1803) (D), a philosopher, historian, and critic, was the most forceful advocate of German nationalism among those listed. The philosopher Immanuel Kant (B), the poet Johann Schiller (A), and the composer Ludwig von Beethoven (C) supported the concept of German nationalism. Political philosopher Karl Marx (E) denounced nationalism and statism entirely.

123. **(C)** The French Revolution of July 1830 was precipitated by the reactionary policies of Charles X. The French middle class revolted to gain liberal concessions, which resulted in a constitution and in limited guarantees of individual rights. There was no real interest in dynastic change (A), or in a political revolution based on economic (D) or foreign policy (E) issues. While French nationalism (B) was quite visible, it did not constitute the primary cause for this rebellion.

124. **(D)** The Tet Offensive, which was a military victory for U.S. forces but was depicted in the American news media as a success for the Communist North Vietnamese, helped create the impression in the United States that the war was unwinnable. While it did not lead to an immediate end to the war (C), it did have a

profound impact on the course of the conflict (E) by increasing pressure on U.S. authorities to pull out and leave South Vietnam to determine its own fate.

125. **(C)** The Taft-Hartley Act did not ban the practice known as the "union shop," by which newly hired employees are forced to join a union. It did make the "closed shop," in which only union members are hired, illegal (A), establish an 80-day cooling-off period for delaying strikes in key industries (B), prohibit secondary boycotts (D), and require that union officials take an anti-communist oath (E). It also forbade such practices as employers collecting dues for the union, as well as jurisdictional strikes, featherbedding, and forced contributions to political campaigns.

126. **(C)** The Nullification Crisis did not involve federal land policy. It was primarily a question of the constitutionality of tariffs (A) and the right of states to set aside federal laws (E), driven by Southern fear of possible future federal tampering with slavery (B). Animosity between South Carolina politician John C. Calhoun and President Andrew Jackson (D) also played a role in the crisis.

127. **(B)** Saul Bellow's *Herzog* is a largely autobiographical novel about a college professor who suffers from bouts of paranoia. Mailer's *The Naked and the Dead* (A), about the members of an American infantry platoon invading a Japanese island; Jones's *From Here to Eternity* (C), about life in the army before the Japanese attack on Pearl Harbor; and Heller's *Catch-22* (E), about an enlisted man whose attempts to get himself declared insane backfire on him, are perhaps the most famous American postwar novels about the Second World War. Pynchon's *Gravity's Rainbow* (D) is a pessimistic, ambitious novel that begins at the end of World War II; the plot uses the V-2 rocket.

128. **(C)** Mussolini created a syndicalist-corporate system through the Rocco Labor Law of 1926, which established organizations of workers and employers (I) and outlawed strikes and walkouts (III). Other legislation created corporations which coordinated activities between the worker-employer syndicates (II). Mussolini's regime opposed private (uncoordinated) initiatives (IV). Relations with the Vatican were formalized in 1929 through a Concordat which was not related to the syndicalist-corporate system (V).

129. **(C)** In this cartoon, which appeared shortly after the Nazi-Soviet Non-Aggression Pact of August 1939 (C), David Low ridiculed Hitler's and Stalin's lust for power and territory at the expense of ideology. Hitler and Stalin led states which espoused opposing ideological views. It is important to note that this pact was not a formal alliance (D). The German occupation of Austria (A) and Czechoslovakia (B), and the Soviet attack on the Baltic states (E) were not the theme of this cartoon.

130. **(D)** This statement reflects the idealism of George Berkeley (D), who was the 18th century author of *De Motu*, *The Querist*, *Alciphron*, and other works.

Berkeley's views contrasted sharply with the skepticism of David Hume (A), and were not directly related to the thoughts of Leibnitz (B), Pascal (C), or Quesnay (E).

131. (C) The continued problem of unemployment affected all of these countries in 1938. Germany's leap in industrial production (E) and the productive capabilities of France as compared to other nations (B) are evident from the chart. Somewhat less evident, but nonetheless supported by the chart's data, is the relative economic immunity France enjoyed for a time (A) before finally succumbing to the Depression, and the slightly more rapid industrial recovery of France and Great Britain (D).

132. (D) One of the most significant social impacts of the Second Great Awakening was the impetus it gave to the antislavery movement in the North. While the South as a region came to assert that slavery was ordained by God, this view collided with the trend of religious feeling at the time. The Second Great Awakening did include extreme displays of emotion (A), an emphasis on individual conversion (B), an increased interest in social reforms such as the temperance and abolition movements (C), and the involvement of women and African Americans (E).

133. (E) Reconstruction came to an end in 1877, primarily because the Northern electorate had grown tired of the effort to remake Southern society. Many leading Radical politicians in the North had died (B), but it was the electorate's fatigue with Reconstruction (E) that prevented others from rising to take their place. The violence of organizations such as the Ku Klux Klan (D) actually increased after the withdrawal of Federal troops from the South, and it was the end of Reconstruction that allowed the nation to shift its interest from racial and sectional issues to economic ones (C).

134. (A) The American, or Know-Nothing party, which ran ex-President Fillmore as its candidate in 1856, grew out of the Order of the Star-Spangled Banner; it called for rigid naturalization and immigration laws. The Liberty party of 1844 (B) was an antislavery party; the Free Soil party (C) was also antislavery, and stood for federally financed internal improvements and free government homesteads as well. The People's party (E) was a populist party that ran with some success in the election of 1892; its platform demanded the free and unlimited coinage of silver at a ratio of 16 to 1, a graduated income tax, and government ownership of the telephone, telegraph, and railroad industries. The States' Rights Democratic party (E) was a Southern-dominated splinter of the Democratic party that formed largely in reaction to the civil rights policies of President Truman.

135. (C) Marshal Pétain (II), the "Hero of Verdun," was the major proponent of the defensive, trench-based warfare that finally won World War I for the Allied powers. Defensive warfare was French political policy between the wars; the construction of the Maginot line reflected the defensive mentality of generals like Pétain. The other theorists saw more clearly that the next war would be won by

overwhelming offensive firepower. Charles de Gaulle (IV), future president of France, wrote a book heralding tanks as the wave of the future which drew heavily on ideas propounded by British military thinkers Fuller (III) and Hart (I), who visualized the nature of future warfare as "the expanding torrent."

136. **(D)** While the volume of trade had already shifted to the north by the 13th century, Italian city-states were centers of wealth. Pisa (A), Florence (B), Milan (C), and Genoa (E) were significant cities and commanded respect because of their imposing wealth. However, even these cities were humbled by the dynamism and riches of Venice (D).

137. **(D)** Dante's *Divine Comedy* is considered to be one of the most significant literary accomplishments in Italian. However, it is not a national epic. *The Song of Roland* (A) is the national epic of France, *Beowulf* (B) is the English epic, *El Cid* (C) the Spanish epic, and the *Volsgungasga* (E) is the Icelandic epic.

138. **(C)** In 1494, Spain and Portugal signed the Treaty of Tordesillas, stipulating that Spain would respect Portugal's claims in Africa, Asia, and extreme eastern South America and that Portugal would respect those of Spain to the rest of the Americas, thus establishing the preeminent role of Spain in the very early exploration of North America. The Scandinavian countries, though they had reached North America some five centuries before, advanced no claims (A) on the New World. The Spaniards dealt with Indian relations (B) by enslaving and ultimately exterminating the Indians of the Caribbean region. France and England (D) never accepted that the Treaty of Tordesillas excluded them from the New World, and they ignored the treaty. This was especially true of England after the Protestant Reformation, and during the late 1500s England and Spain fought a lengthy war (E); however, as of the 1490s, the two countries had never yet been to war with each other.

139. **(B)** Although he stood at odds with his fellow Whigs on the Bank issue (A); the Whigs' complicated tariff scheme which combined, among other things, the sale of public land (C) and a high tariff rate (D); and federal expenditure on internal improvements (E), President Tyler, realizing the need for financial reform, signed into law the destruction of the Independent Treasury system in early 1841. This measure, however, was only the calm before the storm for Tyler and the Whigs; before the middle of his term not only had his entire cabinet resigned (except Secretary of State Webster), but Tyler had been disowned by his party.

140. **(C)** The Vandals (I), Huns (II), Ostrogoths (IV), and Visigoths (V) penetrated the Roman Empire during the 4th and 5th centuries. The Magyars (III) were active during the 9th century and threatened the frontiers of the Frankish Empire.

141. **(C)** In 1951, West Germany, France, Italy, Belgium, the Netherlands, and Luxembourg entered into an agreement known as the Steel and Coal Agreement (C). It is also known as the Schuman Plan. The European Economic Community

(EEC) (A) and Euratom (B) were established by the Treaty of Rome (E) in 1957. The Brussels Pact (D) was a defensive arrangement between members of the Atlantic community.

142. **(C)** Jeremy Bentham (IV), James Mill (II), and John Stuart Mill (V) were advocates of English Utilitarianism, which maintained the dictum "the greatest good for the greatest number." David Ricardo (I) advanced the Iron Law of Wages; Horatio Hunt (III) was a popular English reformer associated with the Peterloo Massacre.

143. **(D)** The Hawley-Smoot Tariff of 1930, despite having the highest protective tariff rate in history (almost 60%), did not touch off a storm of states' rights protest as previous tariffs had, such as the Tariff of 1832 (E). The 1832 tariff led to the Nullification Crisis of that year, supported by Vice-President Calhoun, in which South Carolina nullified the tariff and President Jackson sent federal troops to intimidate South Carolina into accepting it. The Alien and Sedition Laws of President John Adams (A) caused the earliest states' rights controversy, led by Vice-President Thomas Jefferson and James Madison. Jefferson and Madison, authors of the Virginia and Kentucky Resolutions, believed that states must "nullify" federal laws they saw as unconstitutional (which the Sedition Law, at least, certainly was). Assertions of states' rights have persisted in this century: the states' rights doctrine was unsuccessfully invoked against New Deal reforms (C), and five Southern states nullified the Warren Court's ruling in *Brown v. Board of Education* (B), which desegregated public schools.

144. **(A)** Although Roosevelt's reputation as a "trust-buster" was exaggerated, he was far from believing in a principle of unbridled freedom for big business. In keeping with the Progressive movement, he favored controls, restraints, and regulations on business. He also believed in the "big stick," a strong and aggressive foreign policy (B), the acquisition of overseas possessions (E), and a large, strong, and active federal government (D) led by an active president (C).

145. **(C)** *The Journal of Modern History* directs its attention to European history. It is published by the University of Chicago Press.

146. **(B)** While Simon Schama (A), author of *Citizens*, produces works in the New Historicism, the most noted practitioner in English is Stephen Greenblatt (B), who edited *Representing the English Renaissance*. Jonathan Spence (D) wrote *The Memory Palace of Matteo Ricci*. G. R. Elton (C) is the Cambridge don most noted for his archival studies which resulted in many books such as *The Tudor Revolution in Government*. G. D. H. Cole (E) was a British historian of the early 20th century and author of *Chartist Portraits*.

147. **(C)** Fear of a Bolshevik upheaval was a contributing factor in the emergence of fascism in Italy (I) in 1922, Germany (III) in 1933, and Spain (II) in 1939.

Fascism threatened representative government in Austria (V) and Hungary (IV) during the 1930s.

148. **(B)**   The most significant development in the constitutional history of Britain during the first half of the 18th century was the development of the Cabinet system of government (B). Due to the inadequate leadership of George I and George II, Sir Robert Walpole emerged as the leader of a cabinet and the first prime minister. The installation of the Hanoverian dynasty (A) was not a substantive constitutional development nor was the appearance of journalism as a monitor of the regime (D). The reformed judiciary (C) and the redistribution of seats in the House of Commons (E) did not occur at this time.

149. **(B)**   De Soto and Coronado hoped to repeat the success of Hernando Cortes, who had sacked the rich Aztec Empire of Mexico. For Coronado, the hope first focused on the mythical "Seven Cities of Cibola" and then on the equally fictional "Gran Quivira." Both Spaniards were disappointed but did play important roles in exploring the hitherto unknown interior of North America and in establishing Spain's claims to the southern portions of the continent.

150. **(C)**   The Whig party, by its last presidential campaign in 1852, was clearly in decline. Perhaps out of desperation, the party bypassed President Millard Fillmore and Senator Daniel Webster, who had done much more for the United States, and nominated War of 1812 hero Winfield Scott for president. Scott lost not to a well-known Democrat but to dark-horse candidate Franklin Pierce (D). Scott, like most Whig candidates, did not enjoy unanimous support within his own party (E); for example, Scott favored the Fugitive Slave Law (B), which alienated the Whig Party's anti-slavery wing. The question of illegitimacy was not a topic in the election of 1852 (A), as it would be for Republican candidate John C. Frémont in 1856.

151. **(B)**   During the early 6th century BC, the Athenian reformer Solon introduced a series of measures which included the establishment of a property class known as the "500-bushel men" (I), the creation of the *heliaea* (III), which contributed to the development of a democratic tradition; and the substitution of the drachma for the *medimnus* (II). Pisistratus, an Athenian leader of the mid-6th century BC, initiated economic and commercial measures which supported the wine and oil trade (V) and the use of circuit judges (IV).

152. **(E)**   In 1989, the Velvet Revolution occurred in Czechoslovakia under the leadership of Vaclav Havel. Poland (A), Bulgaria (B), Romania (C), and Hungary (D) also underwent revolutionary changes during this turbulent year.

153. **(C)**   In sending out the Lewis and Clark expedition, President Thomas Jefferson was not concerned with the possibility that they might discover gold (they did not). He did desire that they establish friendly relations with the western Indians

(A), gain both geographic (B) and scientific (D) knowledge about western North America, and find a water route to the Pacific Ocean across the continent (E).

154. **(D)**   Despite the efforts of the Populists, government programs to aid farmers did not become reality during the late 19th century. However, the lot of the farmer was bettered by a combination of circumstances including an expanding money supply based on the gold standard (A), the escalating food demands of a growing urban population (B), a declining rate at which new acreage became available for cultivation (C), and a constant (rather than rapidly growing) supply of farm laborers (E).

155. **(C)**   *Speculum* (C) is a respected journal dedicated to the study of general medieval history. *Annales* (B) is an innovative French historical journal which publishes articles in a wide range of fields. *The Journal of Ecclesiastical History* (A) is a British publication focused on British church history. *The Historical Journal* (D) is another British periodical centered on varying aspects of British history. *ISIS* is a journal of the history of science.

156. **(D)**   *Aids* were due to the lord on three occasions: upon the knighting of the lord's eldest son (II); the marriage of the lord's eldest daughter (III); and when the lord was being held for ransom (V). The feudal inheritance tax (I) was the *relief.* The military obligations due to the lord were specified in the general feudal agreement (IV).

157. **(B)**   The purpose of Roosevelt's 1941 "Four Freedoms" speech was to gain public support for his recently announced Lend-Lease program, giving the Allies fighting against Hitler's Germany "all aid short of war." The speech did say much about the kind of world Roosevelt wanted to create after the war, but it did not herald American entry into the conflict.

158. **(A)**   Giovanni da Verrazano (I), though an Italian by nationality, explored the coasts of what are today the northeastern states under the sponsorship of France, establishing important French claims in the New World. Jacques Cartier (III) explored the Gulf of St. Lawrence as far inland as present-day Montreal but did not touch present-day America. Martin Frobisher (II) explored the east coast of Canada for England. John Cabot (IV) also sailed for England, and Henry Hudson (V) sailed alternately for England and Holland; he discovered the Hudson River while sailing for Holland.

159. **(B)**   The Whig interpretation of history, which argued that the history of England was a progression toward representative government, was advanced by Thomas Babington Macauley (II), G. M. Trevelyan (I), and Winston Churchill (III). R. H. Tawney (IV) (*Religion and the Rise of Capitalism*) wrote history from the perspective of economic determinism. Arnold Toynbee (V) (*A Study of History*) studied the rise and fall of civilizations.

160. **(C)** The devastation of the Black Death enhanced the value of labor during the 14th century because of the enormous depletion of the labor pool. The plague did not have any meaningful impact on the development of nation-states (A), nor was a flight of millions of Europeans overseas (D) associated with this event. Modern medicine (B) did not develop for centuries, and feudal economies in Central and Eastern Europe (E) survived until the modern era.

161. **(D)** Hawthorne's novel (II), about a woman shamed in a Puritan New England community for committing adultery with a minister; Bradstreet's collection of poetry (III), and Bradford's journal (V) all demonstrate, albeit in different ways, the preoccupation with Calvinism that marked so much of early American thought and literature. Franklin's work (IV) was not preoccupied with Calvinist precepts, but with propounding his own ideas. Poe's essay (I), one of the first important works of literary criticism from America, was strongly influenced by romanticism.

162. **(A)** The XYZ Affair involved the demand of French foreign minister Talleyrand that he receive a bribe before he would meet with American envoys. Immediately following the War of Independence the British did refuse to evacuate their forts on American territory, particularly on the northwestern frontier (B). In 1818 Andrew Jackson did lead an incursion into Spanish-held Florida (C) in pursuit of raiding Indians. The 1807 British seizure of American crewmen from a U.S. Navy warship in Chesapeake Bay (D) was the *Cheaspeake-Leopard* Incident. Finally, Aaron Burr did indeed seem to have some sort of bizarre plot in mind during the first decade of the 1800s though nothing came of it (E).

163. **(B)** The battle that influenced France to become involved in the American War of Independence was Saratoga. The surrender there of a British army under General John Burgoyne convinced the cynical leadership of France that the Americans could maintain themselves against British power and thus that assisting them could be a valuable way to harm France's traditional enemy, Great Britain. Lexington (D) was the first battle of the war, Bunker Hill (E) the bloodiest, and Yorktown (A) the last. Guilford Court House (C) was a hard-fought battle in North Carolina during the latter part of the war.

164. **(C)** The Lay Investiture Controversy was primarily a conflict between the papacy and the German emperor concerning the appointment of German bishops (C). While some German nobles (A), (E) exploited the controversy to enhance their local powers, it was an issue between higher authorities. It was not a debate within the Church (B) or over the selection of new popes (D).

165. **(E)** The "Olive Branch Petition" was a last desperate attempt of the American colonists to persuade the king to intercede with Parliament to restore peace with the mother country late in 1775. The king ignored the petition and instead declared the Americans to be in rebellion and prepared for all-out war against them.

166. **(D)** American naturalism in the late 19th and early 20th centuries was an outgrowth of realism, which de-emphasized didactic and moral ends in favor of an "objective" depiction of life. To this end naturalists wrote meditations on evolution, historical determinism, and mechanistic philosophy, along with a concern for social justice. Frank Norris (II), author of *The Octopus* and *McTeague,* and Theodore Dreiser (IV), author of *Sister Carrie* and *An American Tragedy,* are perhaps the most famous American naturalists. Herman Melville (III) addressed metaphysical concerns and often had pessimistic leanings, but did not write in the naturalist tradition. Thomas Nelson Page (V) wrote mainly about the South; he belonged to the realist tradition, although his stories and novels were heavily sentimental. Henry James (I) was perhaps the most famous American writer of the late 19th century, but, as opposed to realists and naturalists who focused strictly on the reproduction of reality in fiction, James was preoccupied with formal problems and aimed for psychological realism in his work.

167. **(C)** The passage, which refers to events of small-town midwestern life in the 1920s, is from Sinclair Lewis's novel *Babbitt* (1922), which describes the life of George Babbitt, a businessman and in many ways the personification of the narrowness of small-town America. David Phillips (B) was a muckraking journalist and author of "The Treason of the Senate" (1906), which exposed special-interest-related corruption in that body. F. Scott Fitzgerald's (D) subjects belonged to the Jazz Age rather than to small-town America. The works of William Dean Howells (A) are concerned with the growth of industrialization that was an issue of Gilded Age politics. Washington Irving (E), author of *The Sketch Book*, wrote during the earliest part of the 19th century.

168. **(C)** The Declaration of Independence reflects a view of government essentially that of the 17th century English philosopher John Locke, whose ideas, by the time of the Revolution, were commonplace among educated Americans. The ideas of Locke's fellow Englishman Thomas Hobbes (A) were quite opposite and were far from popular in America. The ideas of the 18th century Frenchman Jean Jacques Rousseau (B) contributed nothing to the American Revolution but a great deal to the French one, with its reign of terror and subsequent dictatorship. Jean Paul Marat (D), also influenced the French Revolution, and Karl Marx (E) was born half a century after America won the Revolution.

169. **(C)** At the Peace of Augsburg (1555), the Catholic and Lutheran leaders agreed to the principle of *cuius regio, cuius religio* (I) and to recognize the existence of Lutheranism (II). The Lutheran leaders were not invited to nor would they have agreed to attend the next session of the Council of Trent (V), which opened in 1561. The Peace of Westphalia (1648) recognized the existence of Calvinism (III) as a form of Christianity and the independence of the Netherlands (IV).

170. **(C)** High U.S. tariffs during the period between the two world wars had a substantial role in preventing the European debtor nations from marketing their

surpluses in the U.S., thus thwarting their ability to raise the capital needed to repay their enormous First World War debts to American bankers. High tariffs did not create a stockmarket spiral (B), retard the growth of manufacturing (C), or enable the U.S. to recover from the Depression (D) more rapidly. The stagnation of the European economies and the growth of the U.S. economy (A) was not a direct result of the tariff policy.

171. (E) The Battle of Midway marked the end of Japan's early spectacular success in the Pacific war. Pearl Harbor (C) marked the beginning of hostilities. Coral Sea (D), just a few weeks prior to Midway, was a drawn battle. Guadalcanal (B) represented the beginning of American's counteroffensive, and Leyte Gulf (A) finally broke the back of the Japanese navy.

172. (A) Antietam, the bloodiest single day of the Civil War, was at best a draw for the Confederates, and since the Confederate Army of Northern Virginia retreated after the battle it might even be viewed as a defeat. Certainly Lincoln chose to view it so and thus took the occasion to issue his Emancipation Proclamation. First Bull Run (E), the first battle of the war, was a spectacular Confederate victory, as were Fredericksburg (D), Chancellorsville (C), and Chickamauga (B).

173. (B) De Gaulle's leadership of the Fifth French Republic was weakened by the student uprising known as the Paris Spring (B). Students protested the Vietnam War, Gaullist economic and social policies, and the government's program for the universities. In 1968, the year of the Paris Spring, de Gaulle objected to Britain's entrance into the European Economic Community but this did not have any negative impact on his control (A). De Gaulle was not affected by the Soviet invasion of Czechoslovakia (C). There was no devaluation of the French currency (D), nor did the French auto industry collapse (E) at this time.

174. (C) The act Jefferson was attacking in this passage of the Declaration of Independence was the 1774 Quebec Act, establishing Roman Catholicism and authoritarian government in that province and extending it to embrace all of what is now the United States west of the Appalachians, north of the Ohio River, and east of the Mississippi. The Quartering Act (A), also of 1774, provided for the quartering of British troops in America at the expense of the colonists. The Prohibitory Act (B), issued late in 1775, declared the Americans to be no longer under the protection of King George III and amounted to a virtual declaration of war. The Stamp Act (D) of 1765, and the Townshend Acts (E) issued three years later, were attempts by Parliament to tax the American colonies.

175. (D) Winfield Scott's proposed "Anaconda Plan" was to restore the Union by seizing the Mississippi River, blockading southern ports, and waiting for Southern Unionists to reverse their states' secessions. Some aspects of the plan were implemented by the Lincoln administration, though its assumption of widespread latent Unionism in the South proved to be false.

176. **(C)** The concept of "Tory Democracy" was initially advanced by British prime minister Benjamin Disraeli (C). Randolph Churchill (B) championed the concept after Disraeli's death in 1881. Salisbury (D) and Roseberry (E) served as prime ministers during the 1880s and 1890s. Palmerston (A) died in 1865.

177. **(D)** Thomas Mann's novella, *Death in Venice*, is a clear illustration of the changes in the *zeitgeist* at the beginning of the 20th century. His *Buddenbrooks* (A) was an extensive novel about the development of a German family during the 19th century. Leo Tolstoy's *War and Peace* (B) and Fyodor Dostoyevski's *Notes from the Underground* (C) are significant works in Russian literature from the end of the 19th century, but they did not reflect the turmoil which had gripped avant-garde literature in the West. Winston Churchill's *Savonrola* (E) was a minor work by the young British statesman and politician.

178. **(C)** Whereas William Lloyd Garrison, editor of the antislavery weekly *The Liberator*, was an extreme abolitionist who refused to wear cotton, eat cane sugar, or even vote in a political system that allowed slavery, Theodore Weld, author of *American Slavery As It Is* (1839), was a "gradualist" who favored gradual enactments against slavery by Southern legislatures and perhaps even monetary compensation to slaveowners. The philosopher Emerson (B), who demanded that all right-thinking gentlemen break the Fugitive Slave Law "on the earliest occasion," was a nonconformist and would be more likely to have approved of Garrison's methods and sentiments. Nat Turner (E) was the leader of Turner's Rebellion, in which the black preacher killed about 60 white Virginians. David Walker (A) wrote an *Appeal to the Colored Citizens of the World* (1829), advocating a violent end to white domination. Harriet Tubman (D), called "General Tubman" by John Brown, spirited numerous slaves to Canada and Northern states via the "Underground Railroad" and was a Union spy during the Civil War.

179. **(E)** The "Spirit of Locarno"—a spirit of cooperation in maintaining the peace—was reflected in the Kellogg-Briand Pact (E) of 1928. This arrangement was also known as the Pact of Paris; it was an American-French initiative supported by 15 other countries. The Dawes Plan (A) of 1924 was a scheme to resolve the Ruhr Crisis; the Hoover Moratorium (B) of 1931 suspended the payment of war debts. The Washington (D) and London (C) Conferences were efforts to curtail the expansion of naval weaponry in 1921 and 1930 respectively.

180. **(E)** In this passage of the Declaration of Independence, Jefferson was complaining of the Prohibitory Act, by which King George III declared the Americans to be no longer under his protection and virtually declared war on them. Many Americans felt the withdrawal of the king's protection relieved them of their debt of allegiance to the king and saw the Act as his abdication of the government of the colonies.

181. **(D)** The Thirty Years' War (1618–48), which started over religious differences, was transformed into a political conflict during the Swedish-French phase (D), which lasted from 1635 to 1648. During this phase, Catholic France and Protestant Sweden combined with other states to defeat the Hapsburg Empire. The Danish (1625–30) (A), Bohemian (1618–25) (C), and Swedish (B) phases aligned Protestant states against the Catholic Hapsburgs. There was no Italian (E) phase in this war.

182. **(B)** The principle that imperial claims had to be supported by occupation emerged at the Berlin Conference (B), which Bismarck convened in 1885. This policy was a direct attack on British interests; Britain was not represented at the conference. The London Naval Conference of 1930 (C) and the Versailles Conference of 1919 (D) occurred after the promulgation of this principle. The Congress of Berlin (A) in 1878, constituted a major victory for Disraeli in containing Russian expansion into the Balkans and the Mediterranean. The Plombieres Conference (E) was a secret meeting between Cavour and Napoleon III prior to the war with Austria in 1859.

183. **(C)** Perhaps the most important purpose of Hamilton's economic program was binding the interests of the moneyed class to the new federal government. By making the government a banker and, more important, a debtor, the opposite of (A), he would ensure that the federal government's survival would be a condition of the repayment of the deposits of wealthy and powerful men. He also desired to promote manufacturing in America, the opposite of (D), by protecting it from the competition of imports, the opposite of (E). Hamilton did not believe that the government should refrain from "interfering" in the economy (B).

184. **(D)** The passage is from Jefferson's first inaugural address, March 1801. Coming after the extremely heated electoral campaign of 1800, it was followed immediately by Jefferson's famous statement, "We are all Republicans, we are all Federalists."

185. **(D)** Jefferson was trying to convince his audience that party strife should be forgotten once the will of the people has been expressed in an election (D). Jefferson recognized the inevitability of party politics in a democratic system, so he would not have argued against them (A), or that the strife caused by parties is foreign to the American character (B). Fundamental philosophical differences (C) are what give rise to different parties, and are not the topic of this passage, nor is Jefferson arguing that only his party acts in accordance with the Constitution (E).

186. **(D)** Immanuel Kant was a prominent philosopher of the late Enlightenment and the author of *The Critique of Pure Reason*, and David Ricardo was an early political economist. René Descartes and Francis Bacon (A) contributed to the scientific and intellectual revolution of the 17th century. Oscar Wilde and Thomas Mann (B) wrote symbolist literature. Max Planck and Albert Einstein (C) made contributions

to the New Science. Erasmus and John Colet (E) were Christian humanists of the Northern Renaissance.

187. (C) After 1945, West Germany was confronted with many problems, including the immigration of thousands of East Germans into a devastated society (I), the War Trials (II), the reconstruction of a destroyed industrial and transportation system (III), and the impact of the occupation by foreign troops (IV). However, German foreign investments and colonies (V) had been seized and their management was no longer a German problem.

188. (C) Humanism (I), popular anticlericalism (III), growing nationalism (IV), and mysticism (V) were intellectual currents which existed in pre–Reformation Europe. All of them constituted a threat to the Roman Catholic church. Scholasticism (II) was supported only by the Roman Catholic church and had little support among European thinkers of the era.

189. (C) The Soviets were not frustrated with "negotiated settlements"; as Kissinger himself might point out, American Cold War policy before détente focused far more on deterrence and retaliation than negotiation. The policy of détente did count on rivalries within international communism (A), particularly between Russia and China; the achievement of Soviet military parity with America (B), which might, in Kissinger's view, allow the Soviets to negotiate from a position of perceived strength; the emergence of Soviet industry (D), which might be influenced by capitalist/consumerist trends; and continued expansion of Soviet influence into the Third World (E), which would add responsibilities and tensions to the Soviet leadership.

190. (C) The First World War was the single most important event in bringing the transition of the United States from a net international debtor nation to an international creditor, as European nations involved in the war liquidated their investments in the U.S. and then borrowed large sums that they were subsequently unable and/or unwilling to repay.

GRE History – Test 2

TIME: 170 Minutes
190 Questions

> **DIRECTIONS:** The following incomplete statements and questions have five answer choices. Select the best choice.

(Answer sheets appear in the back of this book.)

1. During the American Civil War, which of the following came closest to bringing European intervention on the side of the Confederacy?

    (A) The seizure of Confederate commissioners Mason and Slidell from the British steamer *Trent*

    (B) British connivance at Southern attempts to have warships built in British shipyards

    (C) The North's blockade of Southern ports

    (D) The South's embargo on cotton shipments early in the war

    (E) The Southern victory at the first battle of Bull Run

2. The Fashoda Crisis was an imperial conflict between

    (A) Belgium and Britain.   (D) Italy and France.

    (B) Germany and Britain.   (E) France and Britain.

    (C) Germany and France.

3. Support for imperialism during the 17th and 18th centuries was based on the economic philosophy known as

    (A) free trade.   (D) materialism.

    (B) mercantilism.   (E) neofeudalism.

    (C) commercialism.

4. Which of the following would NOT have been viewed with favor by a member of the Populist movement?

    (A) Free coinage of silver

    (B) Direct election of U.S. senators

    (C) Federal policies that favored farmers

    (D) Federal intervention to break up the sharecropping and crop-lien systems

    (E) Maintenance of the gold standard

5. Lincoln Steffens' *The Shame of the Cities* specifically denounces

    (A) corruption in big-city politics.

    (B) poverty in large cities.

    (C) the growth of large cities.

    (D) dominance of state governments by urban voters at the expense of farmers.

    (E) the increasing reliance of urban economies on manufacturing rather than trade.

6. "Those who have handled science have been either men of experiment or men of dogmas. The men of experiment are like the ant; they only collect and use; they resemble spiders, who make cobwebs out of their own substance. But the bee takes a middle course; it gathers its material from the flowers of the garden and of the field, and transforms and digests it by a power of its own. . . . Therefore, from a close and purer league of these two faculties, the experimental and the rational (such as has never yet been made), much may be hoped."

    This passage is most likely to be found in which of the following?

    (A) John Locke's *A Letter Concerning Toleration*

    (B) Auguste Comte's *Course of Positive Philosophy*

    (C) Adam Smith's *Wealth of Nations*

    (D) Voltaire's *English Letters*

    (E) Francis Bacon's *Novum Organum*

7. Which of the following would a historian be LEAST likely to accept as a cause of World War I?

    (A) The public and open nature of Great Power diplomacy in Europe

    (B) Loss of civilian control over the military establishments of European nations

    (C) A continuing arms race among the Great Powers of Europe

    (D) Rivalry over expanding colonial empires

    (E) Rivalry between the governments of Austria-Hungary and Russia over control of the Balkans

8. "I esteem it above all things necessary to distinguish exactly the business of civil government from that of religion, and to settle the just bounds that lie between the one and the other. If this is not done, there can be no end put to the controversies that will always be arising between those that have, or at least pretend to have, on the one side, a concernment for the interest of men's soul, and on the other side, a care of the commonwealth. . . . The care of souls cannot belong to the civil magistrate, because his power consists only in out-ward force; but true saving religion consists in the inward persuasion of the mind, without which nothing can be acceptable to God."

    The author of the passage would most likely support

    (A) the viewpoint of the *politiques*.

    (B) the Revocation of the Edict of Nantes.

    (C) the Atlantic Charter.

    (D) the Fronde.

    (E) the Toleration Decrees of James I of England.

9. All of the following are works of social protest and/or social Utopianism EXCEPT

    (A) Edward Bellamy's *Looking Backward.*

    (B) William Dean Howell's *Traveler from Altruria.*

    (C) William Vaughn Moody's "Ode in the Time of Hesitation."

    (D) Sherwood Anderson's *Winesburg, Ohio.*

    (E) Ida M. Tarbell's *History of the Standard Oil Company.*

10. Which of the following leaders MOST appealed to the ideal of individual accomplishment in promoting laissez-faire economics?

    (A) Grover Cleveland

    (B) Herbert Hoover

    (C) Alexander Hamilton

    (D) Dwight Eisenhower

    (E) Theodore Roosevelt

11. All of the following were historians of the Age of Reason EXCEPT

    (A) David Hume.

    (B) Edward Gibbon.

    (C) Giambattista Vico.

    (D) Montesquieu.

    (E) Georg Wilhelm Hegel.

12. Kerensky was recognized as the Supreme Commander of the Provisional Government only after the collapse of the

    (A) July Offensive.

    (B) Second Coalition.

    (C) Third Coalition.

    (D) Kornilov Affair.

    (E) new economic policy.

13. The religious thought of all of the following contributed to the growth of Presbyterianism EXCEPT

    (A) John Knox.

    (B) John Calvin.

    (C) William Laud.

    (D) Martin Bucer.

    (E) Ulrich Zwingli.

14. In issuing the Emancipation Proclamation, one of Lincoln's goals was to

    (A) gain the active aid of Britain and France in restoring the Union.

    (B) stir up enthusiasm for the war in such border states as Maryland and Kentucky.

    (C) please the Radicals in the North by abolishing slavery in areas of the South already under the control of Union armies.

    (D) please Russia, one of the Union's few overseas friends, where the serfs had been emancipated the previous year.

    (E) keep Britain and France from intervening on the side of the Confederacy.

15. Which of the following statements is correct about the case of Whitaker Chambers and Alger Hiss?

   (A) Hiss accused Chambers, an important midranking government official, of being a Communist spy.

   (B) The case gained national attention through the involvement of Senator Joseph R. McCarthy.

   (C) Hiss was convicted of perjury for denying under oath that he had been a Communist agent.

   (D) The case marked the beginning of American concern about Communist subversion.

   (E) Chambers denied ever having had any involvement with the Communist party.

16. Thomas Jefferson could have read all of the following EXCEPT

   (A) Thomas Paine's *The Age of Reason*.

   (B) William Byrd's *A Journey to the Land of Eden*.

   (C) Ralph Waldo Emerson's "The American Scholar."

   (D) Washington Irving's *The Sketch Book*.

   (E) Phyllis Wheatley's poems.

17. The Enabling Act of March 1933 resulted in

   (A) the restoration of the Weimar Constitution.

   (B) a challenge to the Nazi leadership.

   (C) the dissolution of the Reichstag.

   (D) the authorization of the rearmament of Germany.

   (E) the repudiation of the Versailles Treaty.

18. All of the following contributed to the commercial development of Europe in the 16th and 17th centuries EXCEPT

   (A) primogeniture in England.

   (B) Dutch innovations in sailing ships.

   (C) the growth of absolutism in England.

(D)   the wealth Spain gained from its colonial empire.

(E)   the guild system in France.

19.   The political and diplomatic goals of the German chancellor Bismarck included all of the following EXCEPT

(A)   limiting the influence of liberalism in Germany.

(B)   establishing an alliance system centered around Germany.

(C)   creating and preserving a united Germany.

(D)   founding a German Empire.

(E)   gaining economic influence over the Ottoman Empire.

20.   Before the Industrial Revolution, most cottage industries produced

(A)   furniture.   (D)   cloth.

(B)   dishes.   (E)   decorative items.

(C)   glassware.

21.   Which of the following could NOT have been read by Franklin D. Roosevelt?

(A)   Arthur Schlesinger, Jr.'s *The Imperial Presidency*

(B)   John F. Kennedy's *Why England Slept*

(C)   John Steinbeck's *The Grapes of Wrath*

(D)   Stuart Chases's *A New Deal*

(E)   Herbert Hoover's *The Challenge to Liberty*

22.   The country, aside from Japan, which President Harry S. Truman desired to impress by dropping atomic bombs on Hiroshima and Nagasaki in August 1945 was

(A)   China.   (D)   France.

(B)   Great Britain.   (E)   the Soviet Union.

(C)   Germany.

23. The 20th century historians Lucien Febvré and Marc Bloch were founding members of the

    (A) Annales school.

    (B) logical positivist school.

    (C) empiricist school.

    (D) New History school.

    (E) neo-Marxist school.

24. Which of the following countries experienced a decline in population during the 19th century?

    (A) Italy

    (B) Ireland

    (C) Austria

    (D) Russia

    (E) France

25. Which of the following factors contributed LEAST to U.S.-Soviet animosity during the 1980s?

    (A) Ronald Reagan's pronouncements during the 1980 campaign

    (B) The continued agitation of the John Birch Society

    (C) The Soviet invasion of Afghanistan in 1979

    (D) The destruction of KAL Flight 007

    (E) The U.S. invasion of Grenada in 1983

26. What is the correct chronological order for the following events in the Industrial Revolution in Great Britain?

    I.   Invention of the steam engine

    II. Production of wrought iron

    III. Invention of the spinning jenny

    IV. Application of steam power to transportation

    V.   Discovery of petroleum as a source of power

    (A) I, II, III, IV, V

    (B) I, III, II, IV, V

    (C) V, IV, I, II, III

    (D) III, II, I, IV, V

    (E) V, I, II, III, IV

27. The Peace of Westphalia (1648) severely limited the expansion of

    (A) Lutheranism.

    (B) Calvinism.

    (C) the Counter-Reformation.

    (D) Sweden.

    (E) the Church of England.

28. The urban riots of the mid-1960s were primarily triggered by

    (A) opposition to the Vietnam War.

    (B) the needs of the rioters for food and clothing.

    (C) opposition to runaway government spending.

    (D) racial tensions.

    (E) the conflicting concerns of the counterculture and traditional society.

29. The "Crime of '73" refers to the

    (A) demonetization of silver.

    (B) incursion of whites into treaty-guaranteed Sioux lands in the Black Hills.

    (C) assassination of President James A. Garfield.

    (D) failure of Congress to pass civil service legislation in that year.

    (E) attempt by Jay Gould and others to corner the gold market.

30. The Renaissance did not occur in Russia for all of the following reasons EXCEPT

    (A) Russia was a mixture of Oriental and European characteristics.

    (B) there was no literature in the Russian language.

    (C) onlike Western Europe, Russia had no tradition of feudalism.

    (D) customs and manners differed widely from those of Western Europe.

    (E) the Russian religion had derived from the Byzantine Empire.

31. All of these advanced Italian commercial interests during the Renaissance EXCEPT

    (A) Italian banking offices throughout Europe.

    (B) joint-stock companies.

    (C) Italy's geographical position.

    (D) the strength of the Italian monarchy.

    (E) the manufacture of silk.

32. Which of the following was accomplished during the presidency of Andrew Johnson?

    (A) Acquisition of Hawaii

    (B) Acquisition of Alaska

    (C) Completion of the first transcontinental railroad

    (D) Completion of the Panama Canal

    (E) Acquisition of Puerto Rico

33. When the English poet John Milton wrote

    "With Centric and Concentric
          scribbled o'er
    Cycle and Epicycle,
             Orb and Orb"

    he was describing a view in

    (A) medicine.   (D) economics.

    (B) political theory.   (E) painting.

    (C) astronomy.

34. What is the correct chronological order for the following discoveries and developments in the history of medicine?

    I. The introduction of antiseptic surgery

    II. The discovery of endocrine glands

    III. The development of antibiotics

IV. The germ theory of disease

V. The discovery of X-rays

(A) I, II, III, IV, V

(B) I, IV, V, II, III

(C) II, I, IV, V, III

(D) III, I, IV, V, II

(E) IV, II, I, V, III

35. All of the following profoundly influenced Transcendentalism EXCEPT

(A) William Wordsworth.

(B) Ralph Waldo Emerson.

(C) George Ripley.

(D) Thomas Aquinas.

(E) Margaret Fuller.

36. Which of the following is true of the Napoleonic Code?

(A) It abolished slavery in the French colonies.

(B) It promoted religious intolerance.

(C) It caused major changes in the French educational system.

(D) It gave inheritance rights to French women.

(E) It had little effect on French law.

37. Which of the following countries was LEAST active in acquiring a colonial empire during the period from 1870 to 1914?

(A) Britain

(B) France

(C) Belgium

(D) Germany

(E) Spain

38. All of the following are true about presidential elections between 1876 and 1900 EXCEPT

(A) twice, the candidate who polled the most popular votes failed to gain a majority of the electoral vote.

(B) the Democrats had the most success with "waving the bloody shirt."

(C) factional infighting within the Republican party produced several "compromise" candidates.

(D) the Republican party won most of these elections.

(E) the major third-party force was eventually absorbed by the Democrats.

39. The economic theory of mercantilism would be consistent with which of the following statements?

(A) Economies will prosper most when trade is restricted as little as possible.

(B) A government should seek to direct the economy so as to maximize exports.

(C) Colonies are of little economic importance to the mother country.

(D) It is vital that a country import more than it exports.

(E) Tariff barriers should be avoided as much as possible.

40. It "outshines everything" since the birth of Jesus and reduces the Renaissance and Reformation to "the rank of mere episodes, mere internal displacements, within the system of medieval Christendom."

This quotation from historian Herbert Butterfield describes an historical period known as the

(A) Enlightenment.   (D) Great Schism.

(B) Scientific Revolution.   (E) Thirty Years' War.

(C) Time of Troubles.

41. The congressional "gag rule" stipulated that

(A) no law could be passed prohibiting slavery in the territories.

(B) no member of Congress could make statements or speeches outside of Congress pertaining to slavery.

(C) no antislavery materials could be sent through the mail to addresses in Southern states.

(D) no antislavery petitions would be formally received by Congress.

(E) no bills pertaining to slavery would be considered.

42. Franklin D. Roosevelt's New Deal programs attempted to do all of the following EXCEPT

(A)   raise farm prices by paying farmers not to plant.

(B)   encourage cooperation within industries so as to raise prices generally.

(C)   invigorate the economy by lowering tariff barriers.

(D)   eliminate the gold standard as it had previously existed.

(E)   restore confidence in the banking system.

43.   The term "Long Hot Summers" refers to

(A)   outdoor rock concerts during the late 1960s and early 1970s.

(B)   major Communist offensives against U.S. troops in Vietnam.

(C)   protests held in large American cities against the Vietnam War.

(D)   a series of warmer-than-usual summers during the 1950s, leading to speculation about climatic change.

(E)   race riots in large American cities during the 1960s.

44.   Which of the following contributed to the political decline of Poland in the 18th century?

I.   *Liberum veto*

II.   The subservience of the nobility to the monarchy

III.   The elected nature of the monarchy

(A)   I only   (D)   I and III

(B)   II only   (E)   III only

(C)   II and III

45.   The primary dispute that delayed ratification of the Articles of Confederation by the newly independent states of the United States was

(A)   disagreement about the nature and composition of the national legislature.

(B)   disagreement about the powers and method of selecting a national president.

(C)   the refusal of some states to give up separate treaties made independently between themselves and foreign countries.

(D) the refusal of some states to give up extensive claims to the land west of the Appalachians.

(E) the reluctance of slaveholding states to join in a union with states that considered slavery to be evil.

46. Which of the following allowed a small number of the British nobility to control Parliament before 1832?

(A) "Pocket boroughs"

(B) Secret voting

(C) The Pragmatic Sanction

(D) Periodic redistricting to reapportion seats in Parliament

(E) The effects of the Industrial Revolution

47. In 18th century England, the greatest threat to the economic security of small farmers was

(A) laissez-faire economic policies.

(B) the Enclosure Movement.

(C) the political influence of the Church of England.

(D) economic competition from French farmers.

(E) the increasing use of agricultural land by industrial interests.

48. Paracelsus and Vesalius were important figures in medieval

(A) theology.

(B) law.

(C) medicine.

(D) debates over the authority of the Holy Roman Emperor.

(E) monasticism.

QUESTIONS 49–50 refer to the following passage.

It [his first theft] marked his adaptability, his capacity to adjust himself to changing conditions, the lack of which would have meant swift and terrible death. It marked, further, the decay or going to pieces of his moral nature, a vain thing and a handicap in the ruthless struggle for existence. It was all well enough in the Southland, under the law of love and fellowship, to respect private property and personal feelings; but in the Northland, under the law of club and fang, whoso took such things into account was a fool, and in so far as he observed them he would fail to prosper.

49. The above passage most likely comes from

(A) Theodore Dreiser's *Sister Carrie.*

(B) Ernest Hemingway's *Winner Take Nothing.*

(C) Jack London's *The Call of the Wild.*

(D) George Fitzhugh's *Cannibals All!*

(E) Frank Norris's *The Octopus.*

50. The author's argument most clearly shows the influence of

(A) Socialism.

(B) Naturalism.

(C) Social Darwinism.

(D) Expressionism.

(E) Progressivism.

51. Russia's social and political development was advanced by all of the following EXCEPT

(A) the Table of Ranks.

(B) the Charter of Nobility.

(C) Ivan IV's policy toward the boyars.

(D) the establishment of the Romanov dynasty.

(E) Tsar Alexander II's emancipation of the serfs.

52. "There is no right to strike against the public safety, anywhere, any time," was said by

(A) Rutherford B. Hayes about the Great Railroad Strike of 1877.

(B) Grover Cleveland on sending federal troops to help put down the Pullman strike.

(C) Calvin Coolidge on calling out the Massachusetts National Guard during the Boston police strike.

(D) Senator Robert A. Taft speaking in favor of the Taft-Hartley Act.

(E) Ronald Reagan about the air traffic controllers' strike.

53. All of the following countries fell victim to military intervention or invasion by Fascist armies during the 1930s EXCEPT

(A) Poland.

(D) Austria.

(B) Spain.

(E) Yugoslavia.

(C) Albania.

54. All of the following economists believed that the value of most products should be determined by market forces EXCEPT

(A) Adam Smith.

(D) Thomas Malthus.

(B) David Ricardo.

(E) Jeremy Bentham.

(C) François Quesnay.

QUESTION 55 refers to the following photograph.

55. The above picture reflects the architectural style favored by which of the following?

    (A) Thomas Jefferson   (D) Dr. William Thornton

    (B) Benjamin Latrobe   (E) William Jenney

    (C) Charles Bullfinch

    _____

56. Which of the following best describes Immanuel Kant's "categorical imperative," as explained in his *Critique of Pure Reason*?

    (A) A self-evident and rational ethical rule

    (B) A call for political revolt

    (C) A diplomatic movement to promote internationalism

    (D) A government-mandated economic measure

    (E) A scientific theory

57. Isaac Newton's theory of gravity would not have been possible without

    (A) the concept of inertia.

    (B) Aristotle's theories of motion.

    (C) the ideas of the Scholastics.

    (D) the Ptolemaic model of the solar system.

    (E) Avogadro's Law.

58. Which of the following was among the objectives of Booker T. Washington?

    (A) Constant agitation about questions of racial equality

    (B) To encourage blacks to be more militant in demanding their rights

    (C) To encourage blacks to work hard, acquire property, and prove they were worthy of their rights

    (D) To urge blacks not to accept separate but equal facilities

    (E) Formation of an organization to advance the rights of blacks

59. Daniel Webster's nationalism and John Calhoun's sectionalism conflicted in all of the following events EXCEPT

    (A) the Compromise of 1850.

    (B) the Hayne-Webster debates.

    (C) Webster's argument in *Dartmouth College v. Woodward*.

    (D) the Tariff of 1828.

    (E) the War of 1812.

60. All of the following help to explain Germany's emergence as an industrial power by the end of the 19th century EXCEPT

    (A) a system of technical and scientific education.

    (B) the founding of the cartel system.

    (C) the rise of a chemical industry in Germany.

    (D) the political influence of the German Junker class.

    (E) the economic importance of the Ruhr area.

61. The motion picture *The Cabinet of Dr. Caligari* and the music of Arnold Schoenberg were examples of the artistic movement known as

    (A) naturalism.   (D) neo-Romanticism.

    (B) cubism.   (E) surrealism.

    (C) expressionism.

62. Pope Leo X's encyclopedic *Rerum Novarum* (Concerning New Things) supported

    (A) the *Syllabus of Errors*.

    (B) labor unions as a way of aiding the working class.

    (C) Marxism.

    (D) laissez-faire economic policies.

    (E) the nationalism of Mazzini.

63. During the Second World War, Soviet leader Joseph Stalin constantly urged that U.S. and British forces should

    (A) open a "Second Front" by landing troops in the Balkans and advancing toward Vienna.

    (B) open a "Second Front" by driving the Germans out of North Africa and subsequently moving into Italy.

    (C) transfer large numbers of troops to join the Soviets in facing the Germans from the east.

    (D) join the Soviet Union in its war against Japan.

    (E) open a "Second Front" by landing troops in France and driving toward Germany from the west.

64. All of the following believed that unconscious motivations were major contributors to human behavior EXCEPT

    (A) Sigmund Freud.   (D) Vilfredo Pareto.

    (B) Arthur Adler.   (E) Charles Maurras.

    (C) Carl Jung.

65. The partitioning of Czechoslovakia at Munich in 1938 violated the French government's commitment to

    (A) the Little Entente.

    (B) the Treaty of Rapallo.

    (C) the Lateran Treaty of 1929.

    (D) the European Recovery Program.

    (E) the Molotov-Ribbentrop Pact.

66. The Bolsheviks succeeded in gaining control of Russia during the years 1917–1922 because of

    (A) support from the Russian Orthodox church.

    (B) support from the monarchists.

    (C) help from foreign armies.

    (D) political differences among their opponents.

    (E) the ineptitude of the Red armies.

67. The British Poor Law of 1834 reflected the ideas of

    (A) John Stuart Mill.

    (B) Karl Marx.

    (C) Aldous Huxley.

    (D) Robert Owen.

    (E) Jeremy Bentham.

68. In founding the colony of Georgia, James Oglethorpe's primary purpose was to

    (A) provide a refuge for persecuted English Quakers.

    (B) provide a refuge for persecuted Christians of all sects from all parts of Europe.

    (C) gain a base for launching English expeditions against Spanish-held Florida.

    (D) make a financial profit.

    (E) provide a refuge for English debtors.

69. The unification of Germany in 1870 represented

    (A) the triumph of liberalism in Germany.

    (B) a gain in prestige for Austria-Hungary.

    (C) a triumph for Russian foreign policy.

    (D) the triumph of the *kleindeutsch* vision.

    (E) a victory for the southern German state of Bavaria over the northern German state of Prussia.

70. In terms of Third Republic politics, the Dreyfus Affair represented a triumph for the

    (A) French army.

    (B) French monarchists.

    (C) radical Republicans.

    (D) Orléans family.

    (E) Roman Catholic church.

71. All of the following factors promoted American industrialization during the early 19th century EXCEPT

    (A) high protective tariffs.

(B) improvements in transportation.

(C) large-scale immigration.

(D) the absence of craft organizations that tied artisans to a single trade.

(E) close and friendly relations with already industrialized Great Britain.

72. What was the significance of the Immigration Acts of 1921 and 1924?

(A) They limited immigration from Mexico for the first time.

(B) They created a category of "special immigrants," which included relatives of U.S. citizens living abroad.

(C) They made immigration requirements qualitative, rather than quantitative.

(D) They set quotas on immigration from certain areas of Europe, Asia, and Africa.

(E) They based annual quotas on a flat one-sixth of one percent of the national population in 1920.

73. The German *Bauhaus* school of the 1920s was a major influence on 20th century

(A) music.   (D) philosophy.

(B) architecture.   (E) drama.

(C) literature.

74. Which sequence is the correct chronological order of events in the French Revolution of 1789?

    I. Storming of the Bastille

    II. Tennis Court Oath

    III. The Directory

    IV. Reign of Terror

    V. Execution of Louis XVI

(A) I, II, III, IV, V   (D) II, I, V, IV, III

(B) V, IV, III, II, I   (E) I, II, V, IV, III

(C) I, II, IV, V, III

75. "...the nation of The Rich and the nation of The Poor...between which there is no social intercourse and no sympathy; they are as ignorant of each other's habits, thoughts, and feelings as if they are dwellers in different time zones, as inhabitants of different planets."

    This quotation expressed the opinion of

    (A) Lord Palmerston.

    (B) William Gladstone.

    (C) Benjamin Disraeli.

    (D) Gabriele d'Annunzio.

    (E) John Stuart Mill.

76. All of the following statements are true of Henry George EXCEPT

    (A) he argued that increasing prosperity was causing increasing poverty.

    (B) he believed government should take a laissez-faire philosophy.

    (C) he asserted that economic inequality was the result of private ownership of land.

    (D) he favored a single tax on the "unearned increment" of land.

    (E) he desired large-scale public works.

77. Jonathan Edwards was

    (A) a preacher of the Great Awakening in New England.

    (B) a mid-18th century pennsylvania Enlightenment philosopher.

    (C) an early opponent of Parliamentary taxation of the American colonies.

    (D) a Transcendentalist thinker and writer.

    (E) the founder of the communitarian experiment at New Harmony.

78. The primary issue in dispute in Shays' Rebellion was

    (A) the jailing of individuals or seizure of their property for failure to pay taxes during a time of economic hardship.

    (B) the underrepresentation of western Massachusetts in the state legislature, leading to accusations of "taxation without representation."

    (C) the failure of Massachusetts to pay a promised postwar bonus to soldiers who had served in its forces during the Revolution.

Test 2

(D) the failure of Massachusetts authorities to take adequate steps to protect the western part of the state from the depredations of raiding Indians.

(E) economic oppression practiced by the banking interests of eastern Massachusetts.

79. Congress's most successful and effective method of financing the War of Independence was

(A) printing large amounts of paper money.

(B) obtaining grants and loans from France and the Netherlands.

(C) levying heavy direct taxes.

(D) issuing paper securities backed by the promise of western land grants.

(E) appealing to the states for voluntary contributions.

QUESTIONS 80–82 refer to the following map.

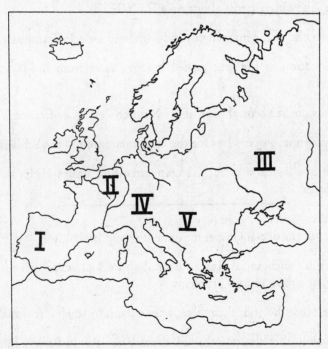

80. Which of the following areas contained multinational states after 1945?

(A) IV only

(B) V only

(C) II, IV, and V

(D) III and V

(E) III, IV, and V

591

81. Which of the following statements are correct for BOTH Area IV and Area V?

   I. Individual nationalities won struggles for independence or unification during the 19th century.

   II. At least part of these areas was occupied by German troops during World Wars I and II.

   III. Prior to World War I, these areas caused tension between Austria-Hungary and Russia.

   IV. World War II began here.

   V. They included most of the "Iron Curtain" countries in 1946.

   (A) I only

   (B) V only

   (C) I and II

   (D) III, IV, and V

   (E) I, II, and V

82. All of the following are true about Area II EXCEPT

   (A) it was one of the most highly industrialized areas in Europe by 1914.

   (B) one nation in the area gained independence from the Netherlands in 1830.

   (C) it was not the central issue of the Munich Peace Conference.

   (D) it was an important area for the implementation of the Schlieffen Plan.

   (E) it was a logical area for German expansion under Hitler's *Lebensraum* theories.

83. A member of the Social Gospel movement would probably

   (A) consider such social sins as alcohol abuse and sexual permissiveness as society's most serious problems.

   (B) assert that the poor themselves were at fault for their circumstances.

   (C) maintain that abuses and social degradation resulted solely from a lack of willpower on the part of those who committed them.

   (D) hold that religion is an entirely individualistic matter.

   (E) argue that Christians should work to reorganize the industrial system and bring about international peace.

84. All of the following were characteristics of Benedictine monasticism in the Middle Ages EXCEPT

    (A) a vow of poverty.

    (B) an ascetic life.

    (C) study and prayer.

    (D) manual labor.

    (E) a rural life.

85. The Latin church and Greek Orthodox church differed during the Middle Ages over

    (A) the use of the Greek language in the mass.

    (B) the participation of women in the mass.

    (C) the relationship between church and state.

    (D) the nature of the Trinity.

    (E) the selection of popes.

86. Sinclair Lewis generally depicted small-town America as

    (A) an island of sincerity amid the cynicism of American life.

    (B) the home of such traditional virtues as honesty, hard work, and wholesomeness.

    (C) merely a smaller-scale version of big-city life.

    (D) dreary, prejudiced, and vulgar.

    (E) open and accepting but naive and easily taken in.

87. All of the following were cardinal features of U.S. foreign policy during the Harding and Coolidge administrations EXCEPT

    (A) a strong interventionist policy in Latin America.

    (B) an aversion to involvement in European political conflicts.

    (C) a concrete naval disarmament treaty.

    (D) rigidity in demanding repayment of Allied war debts.

    (E) the negotiation of independence for the oil-rich Middle Eastern nations.

88. All of the following are true of the "agricultural revolution" in 17th and 18th century Europe EXCEPT

    (A) the amount of land under cultivation increased.

    (B) the horse-drawn hoe helped destroy weeds.

    (C) some seed planting was done with mechanical drills.

    (D) steam-powered plows greatly increased yields.

    (E) the planting of clover and peas increased soil fertility.

89. Which of the following best describes the major issue in debates between nominalists and Scholastic realists during the Middle Ages?

    (A) The validity of indulgences

    (B) The significance of the Crusades

    (C) The celibacy of the clergy

    (D) The existence of universals

    (E) The validity of the Trinity

90. Georgia O'Keeffe, Thomas Hart Benton, and Edward Hopper were all

    (A) American painters of the 1920s.

    (B) pioneers in the field of a distinctly American music.

    (C) known for their abstract paintings of flowers and other objects.

    (D) pioneers in the building of skyscrapers.

    (E) American literary figures of the first decade of the 20th century.

91. All of the following were Christian heresies from the early years of Christianity through the end of the Middle Ages EXCEPT the

    (A) Arians.   (D) Albigensians.

    (B) Waldensians.   (E) Dominicans.

    (C) Cathars.

92. Which one of the following best describes the Augsburg Confession?

    (A) A compromise statement of faith

(B)   A plan to reform the monasteries

(C)   A manifesto asserting papal infallibility

(D)   An anti-Nazi statement by German clergy

(E)   A document justifying separation of church and state

93. Which of these statements is true of religious toleration during the colonial era?

(A)   Maryland's Act of Religious Toleration of 1649 decreed the death penalty for Jews and atheists.

(B)   The Massachusetts Bay colonists extended the right to freedom of worship that was denied them in England.

(C)   French Huguenots were refused entry into South Carolina because of their nationality.

(D)   The Act of Religious Toleration successfully withstood Protestant attempts to overthrow it.

(E)   African-American slaves could be freed by conversion to Christianity.

94. Which of the following is true of the Tonkin Gulf incident?

(A)   It involved a clash of U.S. and Soviet warships.

(B)   In it, two North Vietnamese fighter-bombers were shot down as they neared U.S. Navy ships.

(C)   It involved the seizure, by North Vietnam, of a U.S. Navy intelligence ship in international waters.

(D)   It led to major U.S. involvement in the Vietnam War.

(E)   In it, a U.S. Navy destroyer was damaged by a guided missile fired by a North Vietnamese plane.

95. Which of the following occurred during the Time of Troubles in Russia?

I.   There was no clear rule of succession for the tsars.

II.   The Russian Orthodox church broke away from the Latin church.

III.   The Bolsheviks struggled to maintain control during a civil war.

IV.   The serfs were freed.

V. Attempts were made to revoke the westernization policies of Peter the Great.

(A) I, II, and III

(D) I only

(B) II, III, and IV

(E) II only

(C) III, IV, and V

96. During the Lay Investiture Controversy of the Middle Ages, the pope was pitted against the

(A) Holy Roman Emperor.

(B) leaders of various Protestant sects.

(C) abbots of German monasteries.

(D) political leaders of Byzantium.

(E) Muslimm leaders in Spain.

97. Which of the following best characterizes medieval European trade?

(A) It was predominantly with the Muslim world.

(B) It surpassed agriculture as a source of European wealth.

(C) It involved only overland routes.

(D) It was largely based on the textile industry in France.

(E) It greatly increased in the 11th century.

98. The "White Man's Burden" referred to

(A) the financial cost of running the huge European colonial empires.

(B) the cost in human lives of diseases, such as small pox, to which only white people were susceptible.

(C) the duty of white laborers to rise up and overthrow the wealthy industrialists who were abusing their power and their workers.

(D) the cost of the wars that resulted from 19th-century militarism.

(E) the belief that it was the duty of whites to "civilize" nonwhite people through colonization or economic dominance of nonwhite lands.

99. Which of the following statements are true about economic technology in 19th century America?

    I. Technological advances helped shift thousands of farm workers to service jobs between 1820 and 1850.

    II. Turnpike-building was more difficult, for political and economic reasons, in the Western regions than in the East.

    III. Before the Civil War, railroad track was laid almost exclusively in Northern states.

    IV. Timber-cutting machines were labor-intensive rather than resource-intensive.

    V. Most American canals ran north-south rather than east-west.

    (A) I and II

    (B) I, II, and III

    (C) I, II, and IV

    (D) I, II, III, and V

    (E) I, II, IV, and V

100. "Laws, in their most general signification, are the necessary relations arising from the nature of things. In this sense, all beings have their laws; the Deity, his laws, the material world its laws, the intelligences superior to man their laws; the beasts, their laws, man his laws . . . Law in general is human reason, inasmuch as it governs all the inhabitants of the earth; the political and civil laws of each nation ought to be only the particular cases in which human reason is applied."

    This quotation best represents the views found in

    (A) François de Chateaubriand's *The Genius of Christianity*.

    (B) Cesare di Beccaria's *An Essay on Crime*.

    (C) Benedict de Spinoza's *Ethics Demonstrated in a Geometrical Manner*.

    (D) Baron Charles de Montesquieu's *Spirit of Laws*.

    (E) Voltaire's *Treatise on Toleration*.

QUESTION 101 refers to the following painting.

101. This painting is an example of which school of art?

    (A) Impressionism   (D) Classicism

    (B) Cubism   (E) Pre-Raphaelite

    (C) Post-Impressionism

102. "Here you will ask: If all who are in the Church are priests, by what character are those, whom we now call priests, to be distinguished from the laity? I reply: By the use of these words, 'priest,' 'clergy,' 'spiritual person,' 'ecclesiastic,' an injustice has been done, since they have been transferred from the remaining body of Christ to those few, who are now, by a hurtful custom, called ecclesiastics."

This passage expresses the opinions of

    (A) Ignatius Loyola.   (D) Martin Luther.

    (B) Pope Pius IX.   (E) Erasmus of Rotterdam.

    (C) Martin Buber.

103. What was the reaction of most Filipinos when they were liberated from Spanish control and occupied by American forces following the Spanish-American war?

    (A) They applied for statehood, but their application was rejected by Congress, which feared that the Philippines were too far away to effectively govern.

(B) They welcomed the Americans as heroes and were thrilled when the U.S. government announced that the Philippines would eventually be granted its independence when the people had been educated and trained in running their own government.

(C) Their reaction was relatively neutral. They had known nothing but colonial status for hundreds of years and had become resigned to their fate.

(D) While there was some resentment at the American refusal to grant them immediate independence, there was little violence. Most Philippine hostility was expressed in a few scattered, peaceful protests.

(E) Filipinos, angered at American actions, declared themselves independent and launched a violent rebellion that killed thousands and took two years to quell.

104. The English South Sea Bubble Crisis of the early 18th century involved

(A) a political struggle between Puritans and monarchists.

(B) the economic collapse of a government monopoly.

(C) a rise in the price of agricultural land.

(D) controversy resulting from gold stolen from Spanish ships.

(E) a period of religious fervor.

105. Which of the following best explains why artisans, rather than the working class, were at the forefront of the revolutions of 1848 in Europe?

(A) Nationalism

(B) Political trends

(C) Economic conditions

(D) The popularity of Marxism

(E) Larger wages paid to factory workers

106. The Transcendentalist philosophy espoused by Henry David Thoreau, Nathaniel Hawthorne, and Herman Melville was developed at the

(A) Shaker community in New Lebanon, New York.

(B) Mormon community in Palmyra, New York.

(C) New Harmony community in Indiana.

    (D) Oneida community in upstate New York.

    (E) Brook Farm community in Roxbury, Massachusetts.

107. The Battle of Tours (733 A.D.) was significant for halting the European expansion of

    (A) France.

    (B) Islam.

    (C) monasticism.

    (D) Christian heresies.

    (E) the armies of Emperor Charles V.

108. The medieval rabbi who wrote that the teachings of Judaism were in accord with the results of philosophy and offered insights which reason alone could not furnish was

    (A) Avincenna.   (D) Origen.

    (B) Plotinus.   (E) Maimonides.

    (C) Aurelius Augustus.

109. In the 1830s and 1840s, the primary difference between the Whigs and the Democrats was that

    (A) the Whigs favored economic expansion while the Democrats favored a stable but retracted economy.

    (B) the Democrats favored the abolition of slavery while the Whigs favored retention of the current system of slavery allowed in the Southern states, but no further expansion of slavery north of the Mason-Dixon line.

    (C) the Whigs favored an expanded, activist federal government while the Democrats favored a limited noninterventionist federal government.

    (D) the Democrats were strongly supported by evangelical Christians and supported a wide range of moral reforms while the Whigs were supported by Westerners who favored individual choice over morally based restrictions on behavior.

    (E) the Whigs favored limitations on westward expansion while the Democrats favored the concept of "manifest destiny" and expansion to the Pacific Ocean.

110. All of the following characterized the writing of the "Lost Generation" EXCEPT

   (A) disillusionment with materialism and consumerism.

   (B) heroes as flawed as the villains they struggle against.

   (C) an acceptance of decadence as the best way to survive in post–World War I society.

   (D) a sense of lost values and purpose.

   (E) repugnance at the loss of spirituality in society.

111. The New England colonies were more successful and stable than the Chesapeake Bay colonies for all of the following reasons EXCEPT

   (A) New England colonists tended to arrive in family units while the vast majority of Chesapeake Bay colonists were young single males who arrived as indentured servants.

   (B) the Chesapeake Bay region had a much higher death rate among its colonists than did the New England region.

   (C) women were treated more as equals in the New England colonies than they were in the Chesapeake Bay region, making it more difficult to attract women to Chesapeake Bay.

   (D) the ratio of males to females in Chesapeake Bay was much more imbalanced than in New England, making it more difficult for males in Chesapeake Bay to find wives and start families.

   (E) the population increased faster in New England, allowing for the development of stable communities, than it did in the Chesapeake Bay region.

112. The American system of manufacturing which emerged in the early 1800s was successful because of its use of

   (A) slave labor.

   (B) handmade, individually crafted, high quality items.

   (C) the "putting out" system—distributing raw materials and collecting finished products for distribution.

   (D) early electric power to provide cheap energy for new factories.

   (E) interchangeable parts to allow for mass production of high quality items.

113. "For Machiavelli accepted the political challenge in its entirety; he swept aside every criterion of action not suggested by the concept of *raison d'etat*, i.e., by the exact evaluation of the historical movement and the constructive forces which the Prince must employ in order to achieve his aim . . . hence, he paved the way for absolute governments, which theoretically were completely untrammeled, both in their home and in their foreign policies."

According to the passage, Machiavelli would have approved of which of the following?

(A) A constitutional monarchy

(B) A parliamentary government

(C) Louis XIV

(D) Louis Philippe

(E) A corporative state

114. Which of the following is true about the development of Russian absolutism in the late 18th century?

(A) The Russian aristocracy was able to check the growth of royal authority.

(B) Absolute monarchy was reinforced by a feudal aristocracy.

(C) Serfdom was a major obstacle to the achievement of parliamentary democracy.

(D) Feudalism and absolute monarchism developed along completely separate lines.

(E) Russian absolutism followed the example of Louis XIV in controlling the nobility.

115. The Michelson-Morley experiment of 1887 was a significant test of

(A) the speed of light.

(B) the fission of the atom.

(C) the workings of genetics.

(D) the popular effects of technology.

(E) the atomic weight of hydrogen.

116. Lyndon Johnson's "Great Society" programs did NOT include

    (A) securing civil rights for all Americans.

    (B) eliminating poverty, especially in the inner cities.

    (C) retraining adults who had dropped out of school.

    (D) ensuring voting rights for all minorities.

    (E) providing quality health care for the elderly.

117. The religious hymn

    My thoughts on awful subjects roll,
    Damnation and the dead;
    What horrors seize a guilty soul
    Upon a dying bed!

    alludes to all of the following trends in 19th century American religion
    EXCEPT

    (A) the proliferation of frontier "camp meetings."

    (B) the increasing influence of the Unitarians.

    (C) the increase of missionary work in "primitive" lands.

    (D) the appearance of the Millerites in western New York.

    (E) the rise of the Baptist and Methodist denominations.

118. "In its most literal sense, *Libertaet* referred simply to the rights of the German
    princes within the Holy Roman Empire, but it connoted much more than
    this. It held different overtones which for the princes extended it to cover their
    growing political authority and which for the people extended it to represent
    the political rights of the society as a whole. Involved in the concept was the
    process by which the special chartered liberties of medieval corporations were
    grafted, during the early modern period, onto the sovereign powers of those
    corporations which became territorial states. The internal connection, reflected
    in the notion of *Libertaet*, between the governing rights of the princes and the
    representative rights of the people was the first link in the development which
    was to associate freedom with the very authority of the state in Germany."

    According to this passage, the BEST definition for the word *Libertaet* would
    be

    (A) life, liberty, and property rights.

    (B) the autocratic power of the state.

(C) freedom within a parliamentary democracy.

(D) political rights within a society.

(E) freedom of expression and religion.

119. Which of the following areas did NOT experience a revolution during 1830?

(A) Poland

(D) Western Germany

(B) Belgium

(E) Britain

(C) France

120. Followers of Martin Luther and John Calvin frequently disagreed about

(A) the meaning of the Eucharist.

(B) the extent of papal authority.

(C) the extent of priestly authority.

(D) the importance of clerical celibacy.

(E) interpretations of the Trinity.

121. The European nation MOST committed to maintaining the Treaty of Versailles was

(A) Britain.

(D) France.

(B) Germany.

(E) Italy.

(C) Spain.

122. What was "fragging"?

(A) It was the name given to the practice of soldiers shooting their own officers rather than following them into battle.

(B) It was the name given to the process of killing an enemy by making sure his body was fragmented into several pieces.

(C) It was the name given to the special sarcastic salute U.S. soldiers gave to the politicians when they came to "visit the troops."

(D) It was the name for the effects on a human body of a unique booby trap used by the Viet Cong against U.S. soldiers.

(E) It was the name given to homosexual activity by some soldiers during the Vietnam War.

123. The poems of William Cullen Bryant

    (A) rejected formal European conventions.

    (B) memorialized pastoral Southern settings.

    (C) almost always utilized free verse instead of metered verse.

    (D) were highly esteemed by European literati.

    (E) tended to overshadow the works of fellow Knickerbocker Washington Irving.

124. All of the following were true about the Star Chamber courts of England EXCEPT

    (A) there were no juries.

    (B) the accused could not confront witnesses.

    (C) trials were public.

    (D) Henry VIII used them to control the nobility and others.

    (E) torture was used to obtain confessions.

125. The ideologies of Nazism and Italian Fascism agreed on all of the following points EXCEPT

    (A) the emphasis on anti-Semitism.

    (B) the emphasis on national unity.

    (C) the desire for territorial expansion.

    (D) the emphasis on obedience to the state.

    (E) the need for a government centered around a single leader.

126. The Peasant Revolt of 1525 sought an end to

    (A) mercantilism.   (D) the Inquisition.

    (B) forced religious conversions.   (E) Austrian rule.

    (C) feudal obligations.

127. Colonies such as the Carolinas were known as "restoration colonies" because

(A) their creation was mainly due to the restoration of the Stuarts to the English throne.

(B) they were created as places to send criminals to restore them to civilized behavior and give them a chance to lead decent, honest lives.

(C) their creation was mainly due to an effort by the English government to restore a balance of power in the New World between the thriving English colonies in New England and the less successful English colonies in the South.

(D) their creation was mainly due to the restoration of the power of the English Parliament over the king.

(E) their creation was an attempt to restore the supremacy of the Anglican church in the colonies.

128. Andrew Johnson was nearly impeached primarily because

(A) he was an alcoholic and made several major speeches while very drunk.

(B) angry Northern congressmen resented the fact that Johnson, a Southerner from Tennessee, had become president following Lincoln's death and was administering Southern Reconstruction.

(C) members of Congress felt that Johnson's Reconstruction policies were too harsh and unfairly penalized former Confederate leaders trying to rebuild their homeland.

(D) he demanded suffrage for blacks in addition to the abolition of slavery.

(E) he obstructed the enforcement of congressional Reconstruction policies that he felt were too harsh.

129. The first textile workers in America were primarily

(A) farmers' daughters from New England.

(B) freed slaves who moved North from the repressive labor markets in the South.

(C) Irish immigrants.

(D) ex-soldiers and war veterans who often could find work nowhere else.

(E) uneducated males form the working class who comprised America's first generation of "blue collar" workers.

130. All of the following contributed to the Industrial Revolution on the continent of Europe EXCEPT

    (A) railways and waterways.

    (B) a plentiful labor supply.

    (C) the availability of financial resources.

    (D) support for industrialization from European governments.

    (E) plentiful natural resources.

131. All of the following were characteristics of the German *Gleichschaltung* EXCEPT

    (A) the coordination of all institutions to Nazi principles.

    (B) the purging of Jewish faculty from German universities.

    (C) the burning of books.

    (D) the dissolution of all non-Nazi political parties.

    (E) an alliance of Germany and Italy.

132. Which of the following was the last to be given the right to vote in Britain?

    (A) Women age 30 and older

    (B) Working-class men

    (C) Middle-class men

    (D) Women between the ages of 21 and 30

    (E) Men between the ages of 21 and 30

133. The "Gospel of Wealth" referred to the idea that

    (A) excess wealth would prevent those who possessed it from going to heaven, therefore the only way they could get to heaven was to give away their wealth to charities and philanthropic causes.

    (B) real wealth comes from the love of those around you, not from money.

    (C) money talks.

(D) being wealthy wasn't sinful so long as you didn't hurt other people in the process of gathering that wealth.

(E) rich people obtained their wealth because God gave it to them.

134. In 1830, approximately how many white Southern families owned slaves?

(A) one-fourth

(B) one-third

(C) one-half

(D) two-thirds

(E) three-fourths

135. Which of the following is NOT true of the early years of the reign of Napoleon III in France?

(A) Central Paris was rebuilt.

(B) Legislative aid was given to workers.

(C) French citizens enjoyed free speech and freedom of assembly.

(D) Government subsidies were given to business and industry.

(E) A system of secret police was established.

136. Which of the following consistently opposed Italian unification?

(A) The state of Piedmont

(B) The pope

(C) The Prussian government

(D) The Hapsburg family

(E) Guiseppe Garibaldi

137. Which of the following was a violation of the Kellogg-Briand Pact of 1928?

(A) U.S. sponsorship of the Dawes Plan

(B) League of Nations sanctions against Mussolini's Italy

(C) The Locarno Treaties

(D) German and Italian aid to Falangist forces in Spain

(E) The Washington Naval Conference

138. The Mexican War of 1846 was fought primarily to

    (A) avenge the slaughter of 186 Texans at the Alamo by Santa Anna's Mexican forces.

    (B) drive the Spanish from Mexico and establish Mexican freedom once and for all.

    (C) stop raids by Mexican "bandits" into U.S. territory in Texas and Arkansas.

    (D) acquire California, New Mexico, and disputed territory along Texas' southern and western borders from Mexico.

    (E) depose the Mexican dictator Santa Anna and replace his regime with a democratically elected government friendly to the United States.

139. John Brown's raid on the federal arsenal at Harper's Ferry and his subsequent trial and execution had the effect of

    (A) making a martyr of John Brown and convincing many Southerners that secession from the Union was the only way they could prevent the increasingly abolitionist North from interfering with slavery in the South.

    (B) discrediting the abolitionist movement in the eyes of most people and convincing most Southerners that the North would not support forceful efforts to end slavery, despite verbal attacks on slavery by Northern abolitionists.

    (C) inciting a series of slave revolts that resulted in the deaths of thousands of Southern slaves, further enraging both Northern abolitionists and Southern slaveholders.

    (D) sparking a virtual civil war in the state of Nebraska over the issue of slavery.

    (E) exposing a proslavery plot to assassinate the leaders of several abolitionist groups and discrediting the prosecution despite Brown being found guilty.

140. Which of the following is the most true about European feminists during World War I?

    (A) They were united in opposition to the war.

    (B) They tended to favor the cause of Britain, France, Russia, and Italy.

(C) They condemned both sides of the war.

(D) They were split, even within their own countries, regarding the war.

(E) They tended to agree that imperialism was a major cause of the war.

141. Panslavism in the 19th century sought to unite all of the following into a single entity EXCEPT

(A) Poland.

(B) Bulgaria.

(C) Russia.

(D) Germany.

(E) the Czechs.

142. "The law is the boundary, the measure, betwixt the King's prerogative and the people's liberty; whilst these move in their own orbs, they are a support and a security to one another; the prerogative a cover and defence to the liberty of the people, and the people by their liberty are enabled to be a foundation to the prerogative, but if these grounds be so removed . . . one of these mischiefs must ensue: if the prerogative of the King overwhelm the liberty of the people, it will be turned to tyranny; if liberty undermine the prerogative, it will grow into anarchy."

The author wants to convince readers that

(A) it is important to maintain a balance between government power and individual rights.

(B) the most significant political principle is individual liberty.

(C) individual liberty always takes precedence over royal authority.

(D) government should imitate the rules of geometry.

(E) obedience to the state is the most important duty.

143. "Peace, Land, and Bread" was the slogan of

(A) National Socialism in Germany.

(B) pacifism in Great Britain.

(C) Bolshevism in Russia.

(D) Falangism in Spain.

(E) Royalism in France.

144. At the time of Columbus's voyages, the native societies of the Americas

    (A) probably numbered less than 10 million people.

    (B) shared a common language and cultural heritage.

    (C) reflected the same emerging patterns of feudal organization that characterized European societies in the early Middle Ages.

    (D) believed strongly in the concept of private, individual land ownership.

    (E) generally made a sharp division of labor between men's work and women's work.

145. Which principle best describes Prince Metternich's "Concert of Europe" idea?

    (A) European security was dependent on Great Power cooperation.

    (B) The culture of European nations was more important than their political differences.

    (C) Revolutionary movements would fail without international cooperation.

    (D) Limited constitutional monarchies were the wave of the future.

    (E) Austria should give independence to all nationalities within its borders.

146. All of the following Soviet leaders in the post–World War II years attempted to preserve the "Stalinist system" EXCEPT

    (A) Nikita Khrushchev.   (D) Yuri Andropov.

    (B) Georgi Malenkov.   (E) Konstantin Chernenko.

    (C) Leonid Brezhnev.

147. Italian diplomatic goals after World War I focused on

    (A) building a large military establishment.

    (B) annexing land to Italy.

    (C) naval domination of the Mediterranean Sea.

    (D) creating an alliance against France.

    (E) cooperating with the League of Nations.

148. In *An Economic Interpretation of the Constitution,* what historian argued that the men who wrote the Constitution primarily held their wealth in property, government securities, and other kinds of paper wealth?

    (A)   Charles A. Beard

    (B)   Forrest McDonald

    (C)   Will Durant, in collaboration with Ariel Durant

    (D)   Arthur Schlesinger, Jr.

    (E)   Bruce Catton

149. The Enlightenment philosopher who believed that civilization has been a corrupting influence in history was

    (A)   Jean Jacques Rousseau.

    (B)   Denis Diderot.

    (C)   Baron Charles de Montesquieu.

    (D)   Voltaire.

    (E)   Marquis Marie Jean de Condorcet.

150. Which of the following best describes the Weber Thesis?

    (A)   The British and French governments were as responsible for World War II as Adolf Hitler.

    (B)   The Cold War resulted from misunderstandings on both sides.

    (C)   Social and religious factors tied Calvinism to early capitalism.

    (D)   Early scientists in the Scientific Revolution were predominantly of one religious faith.

    (E)   Medieval society was more dynamic and less static than is commonly assumed.

151. Which of the following was NOT a characteristic belief of many Social Darwinists?

    (A)   Assertion of racial superiority

    (B)   Defense of imperialism or colonialism

    (C)   Defense of wealthy industrialists

(D) Glorification of war

(E) The essential equality of human beings

152. "All men are created equal . . . [and] they are endowed by their Creator with certain unalienable rights . . . among these are life, liberty, and the pursuit of happiness; that to secure these, governments are instituted among men, deriving their just powers from the consent of the governed; that whenever any form of government become destructive of these ends, it is the right of the people to alter or abolish it . . ."

The above passage from the Declaration of Independence most nearly represents the views of

(A) Jean-Jacques Rousseau.

(D) Thomas Paine.

(B) James Harrington.

(E) Thomas Jefferson.

(C) John Locke.

153. A major point of disagreement between Europe and the United States after World War I concerned

(A) the nationalization of U.S. businesses in Europe.

(B) claims of copyright violations.

(C) payment of European debts to the United States.

(D) the recognition of the new Communist government of Russia.

(E) the rearmament of Germany.

154. Of all the European revolutions of 1848, the one MOST oriented toward nationalism was in

(A) Austria.

(D) France.

(B) Spain.

(E) Denmark.

(C) Poland.

155. Which of the following best describes the Hanseatic League?

(A) A religious alliance

(B) A commercial monopoly

(C) A scientific society

(D) An educational association

(E) An alliance against Spain

156. W. C. Handy, Joe "King" Oliver, and "Jelly Roll" Morton were known for their accomplishments in

(A) jazz.

(D) rock and roll.

(B) blues.

(E) swing.

(C) gospel.

157. "My motive and object in all my political works...have been to rescue man from tyranny and false systems of government, and enable him to be free.... The folly of hereditary right in Kings, is that nature disapproves it... by giving mankind an ass for a lion.... Ye that dare oppose not only the tyranny but the tyrant, stand forth! O! Receive the fugitive and prepare... an asylum for mankind."

Which of the following would be MOST likely to agree with the political view expressed in this passage?

(A) Thomas Jefferson

(D) John Adams

(B) Benjamin Franklin

(E) James Madison

(C) Samuel Adams

158. "In 1870 Britain accounted for nearly one-third of the world's manufacturing output while her nearest rival, the United States, produced less than a quarter. By 1913, however, Britain had fallen to third place with only 14.1 per cent, while America and Germany respectively produced 35.3 and 15.9 per cent. A similar decline is apparent in her share of overseas trade...We must take care when making international comparisons, or we may do British industry and industrialists an injustice. For example, Sir John Clapham wrote of the United States that, "Half a continent is more likely in the course of time to raise more coal and make more steel than a small island..." There is (als)o the danger of concentrating our attention solely on areas of British "failure," while ignoring more successful sectors of industry. In shipbuilding, for example, British technical leadership and industrial power remained unchallenged."

The author of this passage believes that

(A) the trade of the United States in 1913 exceeded that of all other countries combined.

(B) by 1900, Germany and the United States had overtaken Britain in manufacturing output.

(C) despite losing preeminence in trade, Britain still produced many technologically advanced products.

(D) british industrial power was the basis for British naval supremacy.

(E) the German chemical industry had given Germany a major advantage in European trade.

159. All of the following became independent nations during the 19th century EXCEPT

(A) Bulgaria.

(B) Poland.

(C) Italy.

(D) Greece.

(E) Belgium.

160. Which of the following posed a political threat to Russian absolutism?

   I. The Old Believers movement

  II. Emelyan Pugachev

 III. The Union of Welfare

 IV. The Strelski

(A) I and III only

(B) I, III, and IV

(C) III and IV only

(D) II, III, and IV

(E) I, II, III, and IV

161. Which of the following describes the Edict of Nantes of 1598?

(A) A mercantilist policy

(B) A censorship policy

(C) A declaration favoring abolition of serfdom

(D) A declaration of religious toleration

(E) A declaration of the rights of the nobility

162. The Magna Carta of 1215 primarily guaranteed liberties to which group?

    (A) The nobility

    (D) Merchants

    (B) All English citizens

    (E) Parliament

    (C) Women

163. The trial of John Peter Zenger in 1735 for seditious libel

    (A) established the government's right to censor the press.

    (B) encouraged editors to be more critical of public officials.

    (C) resulted in a "hung jury" and a dismissal of the charges.

    (D) determined that government censorship of the press was unconstitutional.

    (E) found Zenger guilty.

164. What is the correct chronological order for the development of the following forms of economic organization during the Renaissance?

    I. Regulated companies

    II. Joint-stock companies

    III. Partnerships

    IV. Individual enterpreneurs

    (A) I, II, III, IV

    (D) IV, II, I, III

    (B) IV, III, I, II

    (E) II, III, IV, I

    (C) I, II, IV, III

165. The 20th century movement emphasizing that the universe is absurd, structureless, and without inherent meaning is

    (A) structuralism.

    (D) positivism.

    (B) symbolism.

    (E) existentialism.

    (C) Chartism.

166. The Physiocrats were critics of which economic system?

    (A) Keynesianism

    (B) Mercantilism

    (C) Laissez-faire

    (D) Cartels

    (E) Marxism

167. According to the Pirenne Thesis,

    (A) by the 9th century, the center of Europe had shifted from the Mediterranean to northern Europe.

    (B) the Muslim world had little impact on Europe during the late Middle Ages.

    (C) monasticism was essentially unimportant in northern Europe until the 12th century.

    (D) trade declined throughout the Middle Ages.

    (E) the disappearance of Roman coinage caused economic disruption during the 7th and 8th centuries.

168. The establishment of penitentiaries in the United States during the 1840s reflected an attitude

    (A) that criminals should be separated from society so that decent citizens would not have to interact with them.

    (B) that criminals were dangerous and should be confined to protect society from their depradations.

    (C) that emphasized corporal punishment for criminals rather than the previous efforts at rehabilitation.

    (D) that criminals should be put to work via "hard labor" so that something productive could emerge from their incarceration.

    (E) that looked upon criminals as misguided souls in need of reform.

169. "Throughout the world of astronomy, geology, physics, and chemistry, there is no question today of a 'moral order,' or a personal God whose hand 'hath disposed of all things in wisdom and understanding.' And the same must be said of the field of biology, the whole constitution and history of organic nature, if we set aside the question of man for the moment. Darwin had not only proved by his theory of selection that the orderly processes in the life and

structure of animals and plants have arisen by mechanical laws without any preconceived design, but he has shown us in the 'struggle for life' the powerful natural force which has exerted supreme control over the entire course of organic evolution for millions of years."

Historians refer to the viewpoint expressed above as

(A) positivism.

(D) scientism.

(B) uniformitarianism.

(E) anarchism.

(C) syndicalism.

170. "To each according to his needs; from each according to his abilities."

This paraphrase from the Bible was made famous by

(A) Karl Marx.

(D) Auguste Comte.

(B) Georges Sorel.

(E) Fyodor Dostoyevsky.

(C) Louis Blanc.

171. Other than Charles Darwin himself, the most widely read author on evolution in Darwin's lifetime was

(A) Herbert Spencer.

(D) Ludwig Feuerbach.

(B) Charles Lyell.

(E) Leslie Stephen.

(C) Marcel Proust.

172. Which of the following books could NOT have been read by Voltaire?

(A) John Milton's *Paradise Lost*

(B) Victor Hugo's *Les Miserables*

(C) Thomas Hobbes' *Leviathan*

(D) Edmund Spenser's *The Faerie Queen*

(E) Giovanni Boccacio's *The Decameron*

173. Which of the following did the 18th century historian Edward Gibbon consider to be a cause of the fall of the Roman Empire?

(A) The spread of immorality

(B) Luxurious living

(C) The influence and spread of Christianity

(D) Military weakness

(E) Economic problems

174. Henry Kissinger is most closely associated with the

 (A) "Vietnamization" of the war effort in Indochina.

 (B) flexible response policy.

 (C) policy of detente.

 (D) U.S. rapprochement with China.

 (E) Watergate break-in.

175. Which of the following alliance systems included non-European countries as members?

 (A) The Triple Alliance

 (B) The Axis Pact

 (C) The North Atlantic Treaty Organization

 (D) The League of Augsburg

 (E) The European Economic Community

176. All of the following statements about Europe at the end of World War II are true EXCEPT

 (A) the border between Germany and Poland was moved westward.

 (B) Communist governments assumed control of Eastern European nations.

 (C) a treaty was negotiated with Germany.

 (D) Berlin was made a four-power city in the middle of the Communist sector of Germany.

 (E) the border between the Soviet Union and Poland was moved westward.

177. During the 1920s and 1930s, most Eastern European nations had

    (A) democratic governments.   (D) Christian Socialist governments.

    (B) authoritarian governments.   (E) Fascist governments.

    (C) Communist governments.

178. Which of the following best describes the movement called Pietism?

    (A) A scientific movement

    (B) An antipapal movement in Italy

    (C) A Protestant movement in Germany

    (D) An anti-Communist movement in Romania

    (E) A nationalist movement in Spain

179. The Enlightenment philosopher Voltaire sought to accomplish all of the following EXCEPT

    (A) religious toleration.

    (B) ridicule the English political system.

    (C) win sympathy for the Calas family.

    (D) win acceptance of Enlightened Despotism.

    (E) decrease the power of the French nobility.

180. The Church of Jesus Christ of Latter-day Saints (Mormons) originated

    (A) in Germany during the Protestant Reformation.

    (B) in the manufacturing districts of England during the Industrial Revolution.

    (C) in the colleges of New England.

    (D) in the "Burned-Over District" of upstate New York in the 1830s.

    (E) during the American Revolution as a protest to Anglican dogma.

181. All of the following are characteristics of European economies in the 18th century EXCEPT

    (A) an increased demand for land due to a population increase.

(B) the enrichment of French nobility through renting land rather than raising crops.

(C) peasant ownership in eastern Germany of many of the larger farms.

(D) the English nobility's acquisition of land from the peasants and enclosure of common land.

(E) the predominance of the small farm in western Germany.

182. All of the following caused a return to a stronger executive power in France EXCEPT

(A) the Algerian Crisis.

(B) the Great Depression.

(C) the French surrender to Germany in 1940.

(D) the Franco-Prussian War.

(E) the fall of the Second Republic.

183. During the 14th century, Europeans were fascinated by the vivid descriptions of Asia in *The Travels* of

(A) Amerigo Vespucci.   (D) Hernando Cortes.

(B) Ferdinand Magellan.   (E) Marco Polo.

(C) Prince Henry the Navigator.

184. Which of the following was MOST supportive of the republican form of government in ancient Rome?

(A) Publius Crassus   (D) Cicero

(B) Pompey   (E) Sulla

(C) Julius Caesar

185. Which of the following would have been LEAST likely to support Lincoln's war policies after 1862?

(A) Abolitionists   (D) Mainstream Republicans

(B) Copperheads   (E) Free Soilers

(C) Scalawags

QUESTIONS 186–187 refer to the following passage.

"Hence it was necessary for the salvation of man that certain truths which need human reason should be known to him by Divine Revelation. Even as regards these truths about God which human reason could have discovered, it was necessary that man should be taught by a Divine Revelation; because the Truth about God such as reason could discover, would only be known by a few, and that after a long time, and with the admixture of many errors…It was therefore necessary that, besides philosophical science built up by reason, there should be a sacred science learnt through Revelation."

186. The author wants to convince the reader that

    (A) no one person can know all of the truth.

    (B) Christianity should be tolerant of theological disagreements.

    (C) the Puritan role in the English Civil War was wrong.

    (D) truth is more important than Divine Right of Kings.

    (E) Revelation is a more reliable source of truth than Reason.

187. One European who would probably have disagreed with the views expressed in the passage was

    (A) John Henry Newman.   (D) Pope Pius XII.

    (B) Jacques Maritain.   (E) Galileo Galilei.

    (C) Pope John XXIII.

188. Which of the following thinkers identified most closely with the following statement "renounce notions, and begin to form an acquaintance with things"?

    (A) Galileo   (D) Spinoza

    (B) Bacon   (E) Boyle

    (C) Descartes

189. The Revisionist Marxist movement

    (A) failed to gain a following during the late 19th century.

    (B) supported the Marxist concept of revolution but differed with numerous other Marxist prescriptions.

(C) encompassed the Fabian Society, the Social Democratic Party in Germany, and the French Socialist movement led by Jean Jaurès.

(D) was the base upon which Lenin developed his support for the deployment of Communism in Russia.

(E) never attracted much support in such Asian societies as China and Vietnam.

190. In *Hard Times,* Charles Dickens depicted an English community which

(A) was enjoying the fruits of progress based on industrialization.

(B) was preoccupied with religious constraints.

(C) was characterized by difficult personal, class, and environmental adjustments caused by the industrial order.

(D) prevailed through its repudiation of the Industrial Revolution.

(E) emphasized British nationalism.

GRE History – Test 2

ANSWER KEY

1.	(A)	26.	(B)	51.	(B)	76.	(B)
2.	(E)	27.	(C)	52.	(C)	77.	(A)
3.	(B)	28.	(D)	53.	(E)	78.	(A)
4.	(E)	29.	(A)	54.	(C)	79.	(B)
5.	(A)	30.	(C)	55.	(A)	80.	(D)
6.	(E)	31.	(D)	56.	(A)	81.	(C)
7.	(A)	32.	(B)	57.	(A)	82.	(E)
8.	(A)	33.	(C)	58.	(C)	83.	(E)
9.	(D)	34.	(B)	59.	(E)	84.	(A)
10.	(B)	35.	(D)	60.	(D)	85.	(C)
11.	(E)	36.	(D)	61.	(C)	86.	(D)
12.	(D)	37.	(E)	62.	(B)	87.	(E)
13.	(C)	38.	(B)	63.	(E)	88.	(D)
14.	(E)	39.	(B)	64.	(E)	89.	(D)
15.	(C)	40.	(B)	65.	(A)	90.	(A)
16.	(C)	41.	(D)	66.	(D)	91.	(E)
17.	(C)	42.	(C)	67.	(E)	92.	(A)
18.	(C)	43.	(E)	68.	(E)	93.	(A)
19.	(E)	44.	(D)	69.	(D)	94.	(D)
20.	(D)	45.	(D)	70.	(C)	95.	(D)
21.	(A)	46.	(A)	71.	(E)	96.	(A)
22.	(E)	47.	(B)	72.	(D)	97.	(E)
23.	(A)	48.	(C)	73.	(B)	98.	(E)
24.	(B)	49.	(C)	74.	(D)	99.	(C)
25.	(B)	50.	(C)	75.	(C)	100.	(D)

101.	(B)	126.	(C)	151.	(E)	176.	(C)
102.	(D)	127.	(A)	152.	(C)	177.	(B)
103.	(E)	128.	(E)	153.	(C)	178.	(C)
104.	(B)	129.	(A)	154.	(A)	179.	(B)
105.	(C)	130.	(B)	155.	(B)	180.	(D)
106.	(E)	131.	(E)	156.	(A)	181.	(C)
107.	(B)	132.	(D)	157.	(C)	182.	(D)
108.	(E)	133.	(E)	158.	(C)	183.	(E)
109.	(C)	134.	(B)	159.	(B)	184.	(D)
110.	(C)	135.	(D)	160.	(E)	185.	(B)
111.	(C)	136.	(D)	161.	(D)	186.	(E)
112.	(E)	137.	(D)	162.	(A)	187.	(E)
113.	(C)	138.	(D)	163.	(A)	188.	(B)
114.	(B)	139.	(A)	164.	(B)	189.	(C)
115.	(A)	140.	(D)	165.	(E)	190.	(C)
116.	(C)	141.	(D)	166.	(B)		
117.	(B)	142.	(A)	167.	(A)		
118.	(D)	143.	(C)	168.	(E)		
119.	(E)	144.	(E)	169.	(D)		
120.	(A)	145.	(A)	170.	(A)		
121.	(D)	146.	(A)	171.	(A)		
122.	(A)	147.	(B)	172.	(B)		
123.	(D)	148.	(A)	173.	(C)		
124.	(C)	149.	(A)	174.	(C)		
125.	(A)	150.	(C)	175.	(C)		

DETAILED EXPLANATIONS OF ANSWERS

Test 2

1.   **(A)**   The seizure of Confederate commissioners Mason and Slidell from the British steamer *Trent* late in 1861 came the closest of any event to bringing European intervention on the side of the Confederacy. It brought the United States and Great Britain to the brink of war, though actual conflict was averted through the statesmanship of Lincoln and Britain's Prince Albert. British connivance at Southern attempts to have warships built in British shipyards (B) brought the threat of war from U.S. Ambassador Charles Francis Adams, but the British government was quick to seize the most powerful of the ships in question (though others had already reached Confederate hands). The South's embargo on cotton shipments early in the war (D) was intended to gain British support, but its failure was so complete and its effect on the South so negative that it ranks as one of the most spectacular policy blunders in history.

2.   **(E)**   The Fashoda Crisis of 1898–1889 was a conflict between France and Britain on the White Nile in the Sudan. In the end, the French backed down and the crisis was resolved in such a way that within five years the two nations agreed to the Entente Cordiale. Belgium (A), Germany (B), (C), and Italy (D) did not participate in this conflict.

3.   **(B)**   Mercantilism (B), which maintained a static concept of wealth and measured national wealth by a favorable balance of trade and self-sufficiency, provided a conceptual basis for imperial expansion during the 17th and 18th centuries. Earlier commercialism (C), and later free trade (A), affected imperial activity. Neofeudalism (E) was limited to isolated European communities. Materialism (D) was an Epicurean philosophy adopted by some 17th century Catholic thinkers to explain the existence of God in scientific terms.

4.   **(E)**   The Populists, who wanted inflation as a boost to the economy and aid to badly indebted farmers, opposed the maintenance of the gold standard. They did favor free coinage of silver (A), direct election of U.S. senators (B), federal policies that favored farmers (C), and federal intervention to break up the sharecropping and crop-lien systems (D).

5.   **(A)**   The book *The Shame of the Cities*, originally published by Steffens as a series of articles for periodicals, denounced corruption in big-city politics and the reign of the big-city political machines.

6.   (E)   Bacon's *Novum Organum* (1620) portrayed science as primarily an inductive system, drawing general conclusions from particular or specific facts, as opposed to the highly deductive methods of the medieval Scholastic philosophers, whom Bacon ridiculed. Bacon also placed great emphasis on experimentation as the core of natural science, even asserting that all the secrets of nature might be discovered through a few hundred experiments. Locke's *A Letter Concerning Toleration* (A) dealt primarily with religious and political dissent; Adam Smith's *Wealth of Nations* (C) was concerned with the importance of individual freedom in the conduct of business transactions; and Voltaire's *English Letters* (D) extolled English political traditions. Comte's *Course of Positive Philosophy* (B) predicted the emergence of a new scientifically oriented society in the 19th century.

7.   (A)   Prewar diplomatic agreements were largely secret (something criticized by the American President Woodrow Wilson when he proposed "open covenants openly arrived at." The other answers are generally accepted as causes of the war. By 1914, Europe had become divided into two systems of alliances, the Triple Entente and the Triple Alliance. While Germany's role in starting the war remains a matter of controversy, there is general agreement that the overall causes of the war included the lack of civilian control over military establishments (B), an arms escalation during the twenty to thirty years preceding the war (C), rivalries and border disputes over European colonies in Africa and Asia (D), and the rivalry between Austria-Hungary and Russia over control of the Balkans, which were slowly being relinquished by the declining Ottoman Empire (E).

8.   (A)   The *politiques* emerged during France's 16th century dynastic and religious war, the War of the Three Henrys, as advocates of religious toleration and the separation of church and state. The major achievement of Henry of Navarre, who was the victor of this war, was the Edict of Nantes, a declaration of toleration for French Huguenots. It was later revoked by Louis XIV (B). The Atlantic Charter (C) was issued during World War II by the U.S. President Franklin D. Roosevelt and the British prime minister Winston Churchill. The Fronde (D) was the name given to periodic revolts of the French nobility in the 18th century. The Toleration Decrees of King James I (E) were political documents meant to assert the king's independence from Parliament; they upheld the king's right to appoint Catholic political advisers.

9.   (D)   Anderson's collection of short fiction, written in 1919, derides the narrowness of small-town life, but it is not a work of protest per se, nor does it present a more ideal world. Bellamy's 1888 novel (A) and Howells's 1894 novel (B) both posited a Utopian state. Moody's song (C) denounced growing U.S. imperialism. Tarbell's work (E) about the Rockefeller empire was of the genre Theodore Roosevelt would have called "muckraking."

10.   (B)   Herbert Hoover, an orphan who worked his way up from poverty to become the thirty-first president of the United States, made the idea of "rugged

individualism" a large part of his appeal for laissez-faire economic policies. Other leaders who emphasized hands-off economic policies tended to de-emphasize the "pull yourself up by your bootstraps" appeal in favor of the "what's best for business is best for America" appeal, which dominated the Gilded Age and the presidency of Grover Cleveland (A). Theodore Roosevelt (E), although arguably the strongest individualist of the choices given, also encouraged more government regulation of business than any of the other choices. Eisenhower (D) was a fiscal conservative whose philosophy emphasized the need for free markets and the fight against "creeping socialism." President Washington's treasury secretary Alexander Hamilton (C) combined laissez-faire philosophy with a hearty disbelief in the idea that anyone could "climb the ladder" as Hoover would.

11.   (E)   David Hume's (A) *History of England*, Edward Gibbon's (B) *Decline and Fall of the Roman Empire*, Giambattista Vico's (C) writings on the philosophy of history, and Baron Montesquieu's (D) *L'Esprit des lois* and *Persian Letters* constituted important contributions to the historiography of the Enlightenment. Georg Wilhelm Hegel's *Reason in History* was a 19th century work.

12.   (D)   Only after the collapse of General Kornilov's abortive coup (D) was Alexander Kerensky recognized as the Russian Supreme Commander; he held that position for less than sixty days. Kerensky's plan for the July Offensive (A) failed with the advance of Austro-German forces. As a result of this failure, the Second Coalition (B) was formed in August 1917 to stabilize the political situation. A Third Coalition (C) was established after the Kornilov Affair in September 1917. Lenin advanced the new economic policy (E) in 1921.

13.   (C)   William Laud (C) served as the Anglican Archbishop of Canterbury during the tenure of Charles I; he was intent upon destroying Presbyterianism in Scotland. John Knox (A) established the Presbyterian Church in Scotland. He was influenced by Calvin (B) and Zwingli (E) during the period of his Marian exile and incorporated many Calvinist doctrines into his new sect. Martin Bucer (D), the Protestant leader of Strasbourg and a friend of Calvin and Knox, contributed indirectly to the spread of Protestantism in Scotland.

14.   (E)   One of Lincoln's reasons for issuing the Emancipation Proclamation was keeping Britain and France from intervening on the side of the Confederacy. Lincoln neither needed nor could have obtained the active aid of these countries in restoring the Union (A), and Russia, which had indeed freed its serfs the previous year, would have been a U.S. ally regardless (D). The Radicals in the North would indeed have been pleased had Lincoln freed the slaves in areas of the South under the control of Union armies (C), but it was precisely that which the Emancipation Proclamation did not do, largely out of concern for the more-or-less loyal slaveholding border states such as Maryland and Kentucky (B).

15.   (C)   Hiss, a midranking government official, was convicted of perjury for denying under oath that he had been a Communist agent, after being accused as

such by admitted former Communist Whitaker Chambers (E), not the other way around (A). The case gained national attention through the involvement of young Congressman Richard Nixon, not Senator Joseph R. McCarthy (B), and while it did increase American concern about Communist subversion, it was by no means the beginning of such concern (D).

16.　(C)　The Age of Jefferson, if measured by his own life span, stretched over the publication of Paine's revolutionary-era polemic (A), Byrd's colonial history of Virginia (B), and even Irving's work of 1821 (D), which has often been called the first uniquely American work of great literature. Phyllis Wheatley (E) was a self-educated African-American slave who, upon being taken to England in the mid-1770s, published a volume of poetry; her work is usually counted among the best of the colonial American canon. Emerson delivered his address (C), often called a "Declaration of Independence" for American letters, in 1837, eleven years after Jefferson's death.

17.　(C)　The Enabling Act of March 1933 resulted in the dissolution of the Reichstag, which resulted in Hitler's dictatorship (C). It did not restore the Weimar Constitution (A), authorize the rearmament of Germany (D), challenge the Nazi leadership (B), or denounce the Versailles Treaty (E).

18.　(C)　English absolute monarchs, like those on the continent of Europe, tended to favor the agricultural interests of the nobility over commercial interests. The movement toward constitutionalism in the 17th century would reverse this trend. All of the other choices advanced commercial development. Primogeniture (A), which mandated passage of the landed estates of the aristocracy to the oldest son, forced younger sons to seek their fortunes elsewhere; often their commercial ventures would be funded by capital from the oldest son's estates. By the late 1500s, the Dutch had strengthened their economy by the use of flyboats (B), which moved grain at low cost and contributed to Dutch domination of Baltic trade. Although wealth from the New World might have been used extensively for commercial development, commercial ventures were held in low regard in Spain (D). The guild system of France (E) served to restrict competition and production.

19.　(E)　Bismarck demonstrated little interest in German economic involvement in the Ottoman Empire, and after the Russo-Turkish War of 1877, he attempted to act as an "honest broker" between the two sides. Answers (A) through (D) are true. The chief minister of the Prussian monarchy in the 1860s, Bismarck united Germany through three wars (C), the last of which, the Franco-Prussian war of 1870, allowed Bismarck to unite Germany under an imperial government. Bismarck wrote the constitution of the new German empire (D), giving the Prussian monarch the office of emperor of Germany and reserving for himself the pivotal position of German chancellor. Worried that a future European war would splinter his newly united nation, and convinced that France sought such a war as a means of revenge, Bismarck attempted, after 1870, to tie all of the other Great Powers to Germany through a series of alliances (B). Domestically, he worked to curb the influence of German liberalism, which he saw as a threat to the monarchical principle (A).

20. **(D)** Cottage industries, so named because they were generally domestic industries centered around a single household, were organized on a "putting-out" system involving entrepreneurs who furnished the raw materials and purchased the finished products. Working for the entrepreneurs, individual families processed the raw materials into finished goods—most often into cloth, with a family dividing the labor of cleaning fibers, spinning thread, and weaving cloth. The system often supplemented the meager income of small farm families. The economic security of domestic industries was lost during the early Industrial Revolution.

21. **(A)** Franklin D. Roosevelt, who died in 1945, could not have read *The Imperial Presidency*, written in 1973 by Arthur Schlesinger, Jr., which criticized the powerful executive branch FDR had done much to create. Roosevelt could have read each of the other works. *Why England Slept* (B) was John F. Kennedy's 1940 senior thesis at Harvard, heavily edited by members of his father's staff and published the same year. *The Grapes of Wrath* (C) was a 1939 novel by John Steinbeck, lamenting the plight of the poor in the Depression. *A New Deal* (D) by Stuart Chase was published shortly before FDR came into the presidency in 1933, and advocated many of the programs he later embraced. *The Challenge to Liberty* (E) was former president Herbert Hoover's 1934 assessment and critique of the New Deal.

22. **(E)** Truman's reason for dropping the atomic bombs on Hiroshima and Nagasaki, aside from the desire to save the 1,000,000 American lives that would probably have been lost in an invasion of the Japanese mainland, was to impress the Soviet Union with American power and thus curb Stalin's appetite for military aggression.

23. **(A)** The Annales school, named after the French journal *Annales d'histoire economique et sociale*, rejects purely narrative and political forms of history and attempts to study social structures for a given time and place. The school prefers to ignore traditional historical periods and national boundaries, utilizing instead theoretical models for society and statistical studies. Logical positivism (B) is a 20th century movement in philosophy which attempts to bring scientific precision to language and communication. Empiricism (C) is the view that all knowledge arises from the senses; the brain merely processes sensory information. The New History (D) is a 20th century school of economic historians in the United States.

24. **(B)** In all European nations except Ireland, the Industrial Revolution not only helped increase food production through the mechanization of agriculture, but also increased the number of available jobs. Although the British Isles as a whole (of which Ireland was a part in the 19th century) gained population during the 19th century, the population in Ireland declined during that time. Troubled by overpopulation, the lack of factory jobs, and the harsh realities of British rule and British landlords, many Irish chose to emigrate, especially to the United States.

25. **(B)** While the John Birch Society, led by Robert Welch, agitated against suspected Communist subversion (and, indirectly, against the civil rights movement) during the 1960s, its influence had almost entirely disappeared by the 1980s. Republican candidate Reagan's pronouncements against the Soviet "evil empire" during the 1980 campaign (A) set the tone for U.S.-Soviet antagonism during the decade, while the Soviet destruction of KAL Flight 007 (D) in 1982, and the U.S. invasion of Grenada in 1983 (E), where Cuban influence was allegedly growing, also fed the flame of antagonism. The Soviet invasion of Afghanistan (C), although it happened under President Carter, continued to be an irritant in U.S.-Soviet relations until the Soviet Union pulled out in 1987.

26. **(B)** The steam engine (I) was first put in practical use pumping water from English mines, by Thomas Newcomen in 1712. Invented by James Hargreaves in 1767, the spinning jenny (III), essentially a more complicated version of the spinning wheel, produced 16 threads at a time. Wrought iron (II) was first produced in the late 1700s through a new method of processing metal. George Stephenson used a railroad system to transport coal in England in 1822 (IV). After Edwin Drake sank the first oil well in Pennsylvania in 1859, petroleum was used largely as kerosene, until the development of the first successful internal combustion engine in the 1870s (V).

27. **(C)** The Peace of Westphalia allowed local monarchs in Germany to determine the religion of their realms for all their subjects. The treaty strengthened Lutheran and Calvinist holds on parts of Germany (the opposites of answers (A) and (B)), blunting the attempts of the Counter-Reformation—the Catholic church's movement of renewal in response to the Protestant Reformation—to return those lands to the Catholic faith. France emerged from the war as the dominant power in Europe; Sweden (D), which had been given aid by France to enter the war on the Protestant side, also gained in stature as a European power.

28. **(D)** The urban riots of the mid-1960s, such as the famous 1965 Watts riot in Los Angeles, were primarily triggered by racial tensions (D). The Vietnam War (A) became a cause for rioting in the late 1960s and early 1970s. The need for food and clothing (B), opposition to runaway government spending (C), and the conflicting concerns of the counterculture and traditional society (E), while often subsidiary reasons, were not primary causes of the urban riots of the mid-1960s.

29. **(A)** The "Crime of '73," so-called by factions desiring an inflationary monetary policy, was the Grant administration's demonetization of silver (A) and return to a straight gold standard. The assassination of President Garfield (C) took place in 1881, not 1873. Neither the incursion of whites into Sioux territory in the Black Hills (B), nor the failure of Congress to pass civil service legislation (D), nor the attempts by Gould and others to corner the gold market (E) were ever known as the "Crime of '73."

30.   (C)   The Russia of the Renaissance period, with its boyars and serfs, was not dissimilar to feudal Europe in social structure. All of the other answers are differences between Russia and Western Europe. For example, answer (D) is correct because Russian women of the upper classes were veiled and kept in seclusion, while men wore elaborate beards and robes. The Russian Orthodox church was a branch of Byzantine Christianity (E).

31.   (D)   Divided among strife-ridden city states, Italy had no central government during the Renaissance; unification did not come until 1870. The other answers all advanced Italian commercial interests during the Renaissance. Italian bankers, particularly in Florence, established bank branches throughout Europe to aid Italian merchants (A). Italy's geographical position (C), midway between the Middle East and Europe, and its location on the Mediterranean Sea with access to the Atlantic ports of France and Britain, also contributed to Italy's emergence as a commercial power. The Italians were the first to create joint-stock companies (B) in which investment money from several individuals was pooled into one large company; profits were distributed according the the number of "shares" investors owned. The Italians exported silk (E) to compensate for the decline in wool exports.

32.   (B)   The acquisition of Alaska, called "Seward's Folly" after William Seward, Johnson's secretary of state, was accomplished during the term of the United States' seventeenth president. The first transcontinental railroad (C) was completed a few months after Johnson left office. Hawaii (A) and Puerto Rico (E) were acquired during the presidency of Willam McKinley. The Panama Canal (D) was opened for shipping during the presidency of Woodrow Wilson.

33.   (C)   Milton's words refer to the Ptolemaic view of the solar system. This view was prevalent until the Scientific Revolution of the 1600s and 1700s, when it was replaced by the Copernican system, named after the 16th century Polish astronomer who proposed it. Claudius Ptolemy, a 2nd century astronomer, had accepted Aristotle's theory that the Earth was the center of the universe and the sun, moon, and planets revolved around it. The words "orb and orb" refer to the planetary orbits, while the word "epicycles" refers to extra orbits added to the Ptolemaic system in the Middle Ages to account for discrepancies in planetary motion across the sky. Although the Copernican system would prove to be almost as complicated, the increasing complexity of the Ptolemaic system (as shown by the ever-increasing number of epicycles being added) was a major argument cited in favor of the Copernican system.

34.   (B)   The British physician Joseph Lister first used antisepsis in operations in the 1860s (I). Robert Koch and Louis Pasteur promoted the germ theory of disease in the second half of the 19th century (IV). Wilhelm Roentgen discovered x-rays in 1895 (V). The first discovery of the functioning of the endocrine glands came in the early 20th century (II). Alexander Fleming discovered the first antibiotic in the late 1920s (III).

35.   (D)   St. Thomas Aquinas, a rationalist thinker who valued the intellect over emotion and imagination, was precisely the kind of figure Transcendentalists rebelled against. The Romantic poet Wordsworth (A) had a profound effect on Transcendentalism, which valued intuition and spiritual truth. Three of Transcendentalism's major figures were poet and philosopher Emerson (B); Fuller (E), editor of *The Dial* for two years; and the Reverend Ripley (D), founder of the Transcendental Club and president of the community of Brook Farm.

36.   (D)   The Napoleonic Code, a major modernization and rewriting of French law, was authorized by Napoleon Bonaparte during his reign as emperor of France. The Code gave full rights of inheritance to French women for the first time (D). It would be the basis of French law for the remainder of the 19th century. It continued slavery in French colonies (the opposite of (A)), but, reflecting Napoleon's acceptance of Enlightenment views on religion, it also committed the French government to religious tolerance (the opposite of (B)). Although Napoleon reformed French education at the high school level, the Code itself did not address these changes (C).

37.   (E)   During the years 1870–1914, Spain was losing, rather than acquiring, a colonial empire. The Spanish colonial empire was a remnant of the exploration following the discovery of the New World by Columbus, who was financed by the Spanish monarchy. Most of the empire had been lost as South American countries asserted their independence; the Philippine Islands were lost in a war with the United States in the late 19th century. All of the other nations listed were active participants in the Age of Imperialism. Britain (A) had the largest empire, with France (B) a close second. Although a small country, Belgium (C) held sizable parts of Africa. Germany (D) had become involved in parts of East Africa and small parts of Asia.

38.   (B)   "Waving the bloody shirt," or invoking the memory of the Civil War, was something the Democrats, the "party of disunion," rarely succeeded with. Northern—and Republican—success in the Civil War accounts at least in part for Republican domination of presidential elections in this era (D), which occurred despite infighting between the Stalwart and Half-Breed factions that occasionally produced "compromise" candidates such as Presidents Hayes and Garfield (C). Only twice did the Democrats manage victory, both times with Grover Cleveland. The Populist party was a third-party option in 1892, but the Democratic party ultimately absorbed the Populist agenda and most of its supporters (E) with the candidacy of William Jennings Bryan. On two occasions, in 1876 (Hayes over Tilden) and 1888 (Harrison over Cleveland), the winner of the popular vote lost the electoral vote (A).

39.   (B)   The economic theory of mercantilism advocated government direction of the economy to maximize exports. Mercantilism also advocated government restrictions on trade, the possession of colonies as both a source of raw material and as a market for products, high tariff barriers, and a high export-to-import ratio (the opposites of (A), (C), (D), and (E)).

40. **(B)** The quotation is from *The Origin of Modern Science* (1949) by British historian Herbert Butterfield, which asserted that the significance of the Scientific Revolution had been overlooked. Butterfield outlined the ways in which the new science of the 16th and 17th centuries modified or rejected medieval Scholasticism and Aristotelian theories of motion. The Enlightenment (A), a period of intense intellectual activity and reform efforts in late 16th and 17th century England, France, and Germany, might also fit Butterfield's description, but it is not the historical period he was describing. The Time of Troubles (C) was a period of civil strife and foreign intervention in 16th century Russia. The Great Schism (D) of the 1400s came at the end of the Babylonian Captivity, a period when the popes were dominated by the French monarchy. During the Great Schism, two men claimed to be pope and traveled throughout Europe trying to claim the allegiance of Christians everywhere. The Thirty Years' War (E), from 1618 to 1648, was the last European war in which religion played a major role.

41. **(D)** The congressional "gag rule" held that no antislavery petitions would be formally received by Congress. It did not directly govern the laws that could be considered (A) and (E), nor did it limit what a member could say outside of Congress (B). Antislavery materials sent through the mail would not be delivered to Southern addresses (C), but this was a separate matter.

42. **(C)** Franklin D. Roosevelt's New Deal programs were designed to help the United States break out of the Great Depression. Many economic strategies were tried, including raising prices by reducing farm production (A), encouraging cooperation within industries (B), altering the gold standard (D), and endeavoring to restore confidence in the banking system (E). However, tariff reductions (C) were not part of the New Deal.

43. **(E)** The "Long Hot Summers" were filled with race rioting in America's large cities during the 1960s. Major outdoor rock concerts (A), such as the 1969 Woodstock concert, did not occur during these years. The large Communist offensive against U.S. troops in Vietnam (B) was known as the Tet offensive. The protests (C), which were many, were antiwar protests. Concern about warm summer weather and the possibility of climatic change (D) was a phenomenon of the late 1980s.

44. **(D)** For more than a century before it was partitioned among three powerful neighbors in three separate steps during the late 1700s, Poland was dominated by a noble class which sought to weaken the monarchy while providing increasing independence for themselves. In electing the monarchs, the nobility often compromised among themselves, seeking to satisfy dissident factions rather than to create a centralized government. The representative body of the Polish nobility, the *Diet*, was rendered ineffectual by the tradition of the *Liberum Veto*: any objection to topics under discussion brought an immediate adjournment. The need for unanimity, along with the election of many monarchs from outside the borders of Poland (one of

whom did not speak Polish), prepared the way for the division of the country by its powerful neighbors, Prussia, Russia, and Austria.

45. **(D)** The ratification of the Articles of Confederation was delayed while some states, such as Maryland, refused approval until others, such as Virginia, agreed to give up their extensive Western land claims. Disagreement about the nature and composition of the national legislature (A) was present but was less significant in delaying ratification. There could be no disagreement on the powers of the president under the Articles (B), since they provided for none. State treaties with other countries (C) did not exist, and the slavery issue (E) was not yet heated enough to prevent union.

46. **(A)** Pocket boroughs were election districts in which a dominant family exerted sufficient influence to select the area's parliamentary representative. This was made possible by the fact that instead of being secret, voting was open and oral (the opposite of (B)); wealthy families might bribe, blackmail, or otherwise influence the small number of citizens who were eligible to vote for Parliament. The Pragmatic Sanction of 1723 (C), issued by the Austrian emperor Charles VI in hopes of guaranteeing the succession of his daughter Maria Theresa, made a single legal entity of lands acquired by the Hapsburg family through wars, inheritance, or marriage. As the political influence of the nobility waned and the number of eligible voters was expanded, pocket boroughs were greatly reduced in number. Periodic redistricting (D) did not take place until after 1832, and the Industrial Revolution (E) had little effect on upper-class political control until much later.

47. **(B)** In the middle of the 18th century, the price of wool increased so much that it was more profitable to convert farmland to grazing land rather than continue to raise crops on the land. By passing a series of laws known as the Enclosure Acts, the British Parliament, which was largely under the control of the British nobility, provided for the fencing in, or enclosing, of large areas of common land. The enclosed areas became grazing areas for sheep, mostly owned by the nobility. The laws worked to the detriment of small farmers, who lost the use of these common areas and frequently lost their livelihood.

48. **(C)** Paracelsus (the pseudonym of Philippus von Hohenheim, 1493–1541) broke with the theories of the ancient Greek physician Galen by arguing that disease was the result of chemical influences in the body and that chemicals might therefore alter the course of a disease. Andreas Vesalius (1514–1564), an anatomist, differed from Galen less than Paracelsus, although he rejected Galen's idea that all blood vessels lead to the liver, proposing instead that the heart was central to the circulatory system.

49. **(C)** The passage comes from Jack London's *The Call of the Wild* (1903), concerning the travails of a dog, Buck, transplanted from serene, southern California to the rugged Alaska/Yukon environment during the Alaskan gold rush. Buck can

only survive the subfreezing temperatures, backbreaking sledding, harsh treatment from sledders and trainers, and fighting between dogs by abandoning the morals that served him in California and observing "the law of club and fang." Dreiser's novel (A), while perhaps as bleak, concentrated on characters' lack of control in an urban environment; Norris's work (E) used railroad corruption as a backdrop.

50. (C) Social Darwinism, a sociological counterpart of Charles Darwin's theories of natural selection in biology, claims that in society and culture, as in nature, only the strongest and most adaptable creatures survive. London's Buck survives in his harsh environment only because he is strong and able to adapt. Advocates of big business often used Social Darwinism to justify the fortunes of industry's barons ("they fought for it, they earned it, they deserved it"). Although Naturalism (B) influenced London somewhat, formal concerns were secondary to social concerns in London's art. While the collectivist ideals of Socialism (A) appealed to London for a time, *The Call of the Wild* extols the power of the individual. London was not a Progressive (E), although he was a contemporary of the Progressives. Expressionism (D) is an early 20th century movement in visual art that gives primacy to the expression of the artist's subjective world, rather than external stimuli, in the creation of the work of art.

51. (B) Married to Peter III, the tsar of Russia, the German Catherine the Great had no legal claim to the Russian throne. After gaining the throne through the murder of her husband, Catherine, who was aware of the tenuity of her claim to the throne, became increasingly concerned with winning the support of the Russian nobility. She attempted to win this support through the Charter of Nobility of 1785, which guaranteed rights and privileges to the Russian noble class and expanded the institution of serfdom in Russia. Although technically freed by an emancipation proclamation issued by Tsar Alexander II in 1861 (E), the serfs won total freedom only with the Russian Revolution of 1917, making Russia the last of the great European powers to take that step. The Table of Ranks (A) was Peter the Great's method of basing his civil service on merit. Ivan IV, the first Russian ruler to hold the title of tsar, brutally suppressed the boyars, the older Russian nobility, as a means of asserting his own sovereignty and advancing the cause of absolutism (C). The Romanov dynasty (D), founded by Michael Romanov at the end of the Time of Troubles, brought a clear line of succession to the throne, lending stability to the monarchy in a country where soldiers or noblemen often selected the next tsar.

52. (C) Calvin Coolidge made this statement. Reagan took a similar attitude in his handling of the 1981 air traffic controllers' strike (E). Hayes and Cleveland also took uncompromising attitudes toward such labor disturbances as the Great Railroad Strike of 1877 (A) and the Pullman Strike (B). Senator Robert A. Taft was co-sponsor of the Taft-Hartley Act (D), aimed at restraining the excesses of labor unions.

53. (E) Yugoslavia fell victim to Fascist invasion only after World War II had

begun. The Fascist forces of Italy and Germany cooperated together in the Spanish Civil War of the mid-1930s (B); the war provided an opportunity for new weapons and military tactics to be tested, and the German leader Adolf Hitler and the Italian leader Benito Mussolini favored the Royalist, or Falangist, cause in that war. German troops forcibly annexed Austria to Germany in 1938 (D) and began World War II with an invasion of Poland in 1939 (A). Albania (C) was a victim of Mussolini's aggression in 1939.

54.   (C)   François Quesnay, the leader of the 18th century school of economics known as the Physiocrats, believed that all wealth should be based on land and that only agriculture could increase a nation's wealth. All of the others are associated with the laissez-faire free-market beliefs originated by Adam Smith (A) in his *An Inquiry into the Nature and Causes of the Wealth of Nations* (1776). David Ricardo (B) was the author of the *Principles of Political Economy* (1817); Thomas Malthus (D) was the author of *An Essay on the Principle of Population* (1798); and Jeremy Bentham (E) was the founder of Utilitarianism.

55.   (A)   The architectural style depicted is known as the Romanesque style, and it was favored by America's most renowned architect of the early 19th century, Thomas Jefferson. The building shown is the old state capital building in Richmond, Virginia, which was designed by Jefferson and is still standing. Its soaring front columns and undecorated facade, its narrow but deep floor plan, and its solid, simple, classical lines are typical of the Romanesque style. This style was quite popular during Jefferson's time, largely because Jefferson favored it. It was supplanted by the similar, but more elegant Greek Revival style which was favored by Benjamin Latrobe (B) and Dr. William Thornton (D). Charles Bullfinch (C) of Boston, another prominent early American architect, was known for his Georgian designs. William Jenney (E) was an American architect who lived in the second half of the 19th century and was responsible for using cast iron and steel to design and construct America's first skyscrapers.

56.   (A)   In his *Critique of Pure Reason* (1781), Kant tackled a major problem for Enlightenment philosophers: if the influence of Christianity was reduced, how might a new, nonreligious morality be constructed which would gain popular acceptance? Kant's solution was the "categorical imperative," which was based on rational qualities held by everyone; its logic would be so self-evident that all would assent to it. Individuals would feel compelled to follow rules which were universal precedents. Unfortunately, Kant was not specific when it came to listing categorical imperatives. His most famous formulation of a categorical imperative—"So act as you would will others to act"—is essentially a reformulation of the Golden Rule.

57.   (A)   Although Isaac Newton arrived at his theories of gravity through mathematical equations, his work would not have been possible without the concept of inertia, the tendency of all bodies to continue to move at the same speed and direction unless an outside force alters them. Applying this principle to the solar

system, Newton perceived that the Earth would normally continue into space in a straight line unless the sun exerted a force to pull the Earth back toward the center. Newton's theories rejected Aristotle's theories of motion (B), such as his idea that a ball moved through the air because the air in front moved around it and pushed it. The Scholastic philosophers of the Middle Ages (C) used methods quite different from those of natural science, preferring to use a deductive system based on syllogistic reasoning. Answer (D) is incorrect because Newton's theories of gravity helped confirm the Copernican (sun-centered) theory of the solar system, rather than the opposing Ptolemaic (earth-sun) view. Avogadro's Law (E), named after the 19th century physicist Amadeo Avogadro, held that equal volumes of gases hold equal numbers of molecules if they are under the same conditions of pressure and temperature.

58.   (C)   Booker T. Washington encouraged his fellow blacks to work hard, acquire property, and prove they were worthy of their rights. Washington's contemporary and critic W. E. B. du Bois urged his fellow blacks to agitate on questions of racial equality (A), be more militant in demanding their rights (B), not to accept separate but equal facilities (D), and to form an organization to advance the rights of blacks (E).

59.   (E)   The conflict between the pro-Union stance of the Whig statesman Daniel Webster and the states' rights stance of Democrat John Calhoun erupted often. Webster argued against the Calhounian doctrine of states' rights in *Dartmouth College v. Woodward* (C); in his famous debates with the southern Senator Robert Hayne (B), and in supporting the Tariff of 1828 (or, to Calhoun, the "Tariff of Abominations"), the passage of which eventually forced Calhoun to resort to the doctrine of Nullification (D). Even though Webster supported the legislation under the Compromise of 1850 (A) that was so dear to Calhoun—a tougher Fugitive Slave Law and popular sovereignty for the territories in New Mexico and Utah—he did so in the name of preserving the Union, whereas Calhoun acted wholly on behalf of the South. Their positions on the War of 1812, (E), were exact opposites. Calhoun, who made his name as one of Congress's "War Hawks," supported the "nationalist" position of war with Britain, while Webster took the "sectional" New England position and sided with the rest of New England against the war.

60.   (D)   The Junker class, a noble class which originated in Prussia, held a strong influence in German politics after 1870. The owners of large landed estates in eastern Prussia, they insisted that all foreign commercial agreements, including tariff arrangements, provide protection for German agricultural interests over and above the industrial interests of Germany. The iron ore and coal deposits in the area of the Ruhr (E), combined with the proximity of the Rhine River, gave Germany a natural industrial center. The strong scientific and technological education (A) provided by many German universities aided in the rise of specific industries, such as the electrical and chemical industries (C). The cartel system (B), although under attack in the

United States at the turn of the century, flourished in Germany during its industrialization.

61.   (C)   Expressionism, an early 20th century rebellion against prevalent aesthetic standards, led to atonality and dissonance in music, such as the music of the Austrian composer Schoenberg. Expressionism is suggested by the stylized and exaggerated sets in the German motion picture *The Cabinet of Dr. Caligari*, where the inner world of a mental patient is projected onto the outside world, and buildings and objects are distorted to reflect the patient's inner mind. Naturalism (A) was a 19th century literary movement in which writers rebelling against romanticized views presented darkly realistic portraits of society. Cubism (B), a 20th century school in art, portrayed the human form as a series of geometric figures. Surrealism (E), also a 20th century artistic school, resulted in dreamlike, distorted portraits of reality.

62.   (B)   *Rerum Novarum* was an encyclopedic of social concern, placing the Catholic church on record as favoring labor unions as a means to aid the working class. In effect, it rejected the laissez-faire principle that government should not interfere in the business world, since in many countries legislation to authorize unions would be necessary. The tone of *Rerum Novarum* was completely different from the *Syllabus of Errors* issued by Pope Pius IX in 1846 (A), which condemned many trends of the time, including parliamentary democracy. Although he was originally a strong Italian nationalist, Pius IX came to regard Italian nationalists such as Guiseppe Mazzini (E) with suspicion, and *Rerum Novarum* did not comment on the nationalist question in Italy.

63.   (E)   Stalin wanted the Allies to open a "Second Front" in France to drive Germany from the west (E). He did not want to open a second front in the Balkans (A) or North Africa (B), nor did he want large numbers of Allied troops to join the Soviets fighting from the east (C). The Soviets were not at war with Japan (D), despite Allied pressure.

64.   (E)   Charles Maurras (E), the founder of the pre-Fascist French political movement *Action Française*, admired the classicism and rationalism of the Enlightenment, with its emphasis on the rational bases of human behavior. The other individuals emphasized nonrational or unconscious motivations of behavior. Freud's (A) emphasis on the unconscious as a major motivating factor in human behavior is well known. The psychologist Arthur Adler (B) wrote about the individual's inner needs for power and self-preservation. Carl Jung (C), a psychologist, was interested in myths that were important to human behavior, an influence he termed the "unobserved self." The sociologist Vilfredo Pareto (D) studied the basic emotional causes of action, which he termed "residues."

65.   (A)   In 1920, Czechoslovakia, Romania, and Yugoslavia had banded together in the Little Entente; France allied itself with some of these nations, as well as Poland. When Hitler demanded part of Czechoslovakia in 1938, and was given half

of the country in agreements signed by French and British diplomats at the subsequent Munich Peace Conference, the action directly violated French agreements with the Little Entente. The Treaty of Rapallo (B) was a 1922 agreement between Weimar Germany and the Soviet Union, providing Soviet territory to secretly train German troops in the use of tanks and airplanes (an activity forbidden by the Treaty of Versailles). The Lateran Treaty of 1929 (C) was signed by the Vatican and Mussolini's government; it promised, among other things, government noninterference in Church affairs. The European Recovery Program (D) was the official name of the "Marshall Plan" for U.S. aid to European nations after World War II. The Molotov-Ribbentrop Pact (E), a nonaggression agreement between Stalin's Soviet government and Hitler's German government, was signed days before the German invasion of Poland in 1939.

66. **(D)** The Bolsheviks benefited from the divided nature of their opposition, which was separated into socialists and revolutionaries, liberal reformers, and conservative monarchists. The Red armies (E) were those of the Bolsheviks. French, British, Japanese, and American armies were deployed in Russia after the 1917 revolution, but their purpose was to hinder, not to aid, the new Bolshevik government. The leaders of the Russian Orthodox church (A) tended to side with the Russian monarchy.

67. **(E)** Bentham, the founder of Utilitarianism, believed that his pain-pleasure "calculus" might solve problems in the British welfare system, which relied on periodic monetary payments to the poor. Although Bentham's laissez-faire beliefs often prescribed a hands-off approach to economic and social issues, he came to favor a more active governmental role regarding the problem of poverty. Those unable to pay their creditors were to be placed in workhouses established by the Poor Law of 1834. The standard of living for inmates of the workhouse would be very low, and would discourage poverty and motivate the poor to escape their circumstances. John Stuart Mill (A) was a 19th century British political writer and liberal. Marx (B) had no impact on British law in the 19th century. Aldous Huxley (C) was the author of the 20th century dystopian novel *Brave New World*. Robert Owen (D), a factory owner, was a prominent 19th century Utopian Socialist who sought to help the working class in the early stages of the Industrial Revolution.

68. **(E)** Oglethorpe's primary purpose was providing a refuge for English debtors. A secondary purpose was carrying on war against Spain (C). Making a financial profit (D) came relatively far down the list for Oglethorpe and his fellow trustees. Some persecuted Christians from various parts of Europe did come to Georgia (B), but Oglethorpe had distinctly mixed feelings about the presence of such "religious enthusiasts." Fifty years prior to the founding of Georgia, Pennsylvania had been founded as a refuge for Quakers (A).

69. **(D)** Before the unification of Germany, statesmen had been divided on whether to include the Austrian Empire, which contained 11 nationalities. Under

Bismarck's leadership, the Prussian government chose to exclude these non-Germans and did not include even the German parts of Austria in the new German nation. The *kleindeutsch* ("small German") solution of a united Germany without Austria prevailed; the *grossdeutsch* ("big German," including Austria) solution was preferred by many Germans, including the Austrian Adolf Hitler, who annexed Austria to Germany in 1938. The unification of Germany proved to be a dilemma for German liberals (A), who felt forced to choose between patriotic nationalism and their liberal political instincts. Unification was also a setback for Austria (B), which had hoped to unite Germany itself. Unification caused apprehension in Russia (C), where diplomats had kept their country officially neutral on the issue but worried about the impact of a powerful new state in the center of Europe. The predominantly Catholic southern states of Germany were wary of domination by the Protestant north and were the last area to be incorporated into a united Germany (the opposite of (E)).

70. (C) The arrest in 1894 of Colonel Alfred Dreyfus, a French military intelligence officer accused of selling military secrets to a German agent, proved to be the most tumultuous political affair of the early Third Republic. Dreyfus was convicted of treason by a military tribunal and imprisoned. As it became increasingly apparent that Dreyfus was innocent, the radical Republicans protested his imprisonment. Unlike the more moderate Republicans, the radical Republicans were strongly anticlerical and saw both the Catholic church and the army as obstacles to the achievement of parliamentary democracy in France. Led by the politician Georges Clemenceau and the journalist Emile Zola, the radical Republicans used the "Dreyfus Affair" to destroy the credibility of the monarchists in France, whose power was centered in the high officer corps of the army (A). Because of the affair, antirepublican sentiment was crushed and the radical Republicans moved toward control of the Republic. The Orléans family (D) held the French throne from 1830 to 1848.

71. (E) The *absence* of anything like close or friendly relations with Great Britain did, in fact, help promote industrialization in America by spurring desire for protective tariffs (A) to make America economically independent of Great Britain. Industrialization was also boosted by improvements in transportation (B), which allowed goods to reach a larger market; large-scale immigration (C), which brought both workers and consumers; and the absence of craft organizations that would have tied artisans to a single trade and smothered economic creativity (D).

72. (D) The Immigration Acts of 1921 and 1924 were a watershed in immigration law because they were the first to set limits on the immigration of certain groups, including natives of Eastern Europe, Africa, Asia, and Oceania. Qualitative determinants (C), such as fitness of health and character, had previously been the determinants of immigration levels. Under the laws of 1921 and 1924, however, the overall quota of immigrants was to be 150,000 by 1927, and quotas for individual groups were to be set at the percentage of the 150,000 figure that each group constituted in the total population. Western Hemisphere immigrants, including

Mexicans and Canadians (A), were, however, exempt from these quotas; thus the actual immigration figures of these years regularly exceeds 150,000. The McCarran-Walter Act of 1952 (E) simplified the quota formula so that the limit was one-sixth of one percent of the population, which usually amounted to about 160,000. In 1965, the United States began to admit nuclear relatives of citizens, returning resident aliens, certain former citizens, and families of Western Hemisphere countries as "special immigrants" (B), who were exempt from numerical ceilings.

73. **(B)** With the motto "form follows function," the *Bauhaus* school of 1920s Germany rebelled against the opulent decorative style of the Victorian age, insisting on clean and simple lines in both buildings and furniture. It flourished in the climate of Weimar Germany, but many of its leading members, such as Mies van der Rohe, fled when National Socialism came to power in Germany; some eventually emigrated to the United States.

74. **(D)** The Tennis Court Oath (II) was taken by representatives of the Third Estate in 1789, when they thought they had been locked out of their scheduled meeting place by King Louis XVI. They pledged to continue meeting until the monarchy had been converted into a limited constitutional monarchy. Violent mob riots in the streets followed, such as the storming of the Bastille prison (I). After the king was executed in 1793 (V), a power struggle emerged in the parliament of the revolutionary government, the National Assembly. This struggle, known as the Reign of Terror (IV) because of the large numbers of people executed during the period, was followed by a period in which the Assembly tried to restore order and credibility to the Revolution. In this stage of the Revolution, decisions were often made by a small steering committee known as the Directory (III).

75. **(C)** The quotation is from *Sybil* (1845), written by the British politician and prime minister Benjamin Disraeli. The leader of the Conservative party in the later years of the 19th century, Disraeli reformed the party to give it a broader appeal than its traditional electoral base, the nobility. Domestically, he favored legislation to help the working class, including laws to authorize and encourage the formation of labor unions. Both William Gladstone (B), a political rival of Disraeli's, and John Stuart Mill (E) were 19th century liberals, who traditionally showed little concern for the working-class poor. Lord Palmerston (A) was a prominent British politician and diplomat. Gabriele D'Annunzio (D) was an early 20th century Italian nationalist and poet.

76. **(B)** Henry George definitely did not believe in laissez-faire government. He did, however, assert that increasing prosperity was causing increasing poverty (A), that economic inequality was the result of private land ownership (C), and that the government should wipe out this unfair advantage by a single tax on the "unearned" profits of land ownership (D), wuth the money to be used to various public works (E).

77. **(A)** Jonathan Edwards was a preacher of the Great Awakening in New England. A well-known 18th century Pennsylvania Enlightenment philosopher (B) of sorts was Benjamin Franklin. There were a number of early opponents of parliamentary taxation of the American colonies, among whom John Dickinson and Patrick Henry were prominent. Prominent as a thinker and writer of the Transcendentalist movement of the early 1800s was Ralph Waldo Emerson. The founder of the communitarian experiment at New Harmony, Indiana (E), was Scottish industrialist and socialist Robert Owen.

78. **(A)** The primary issue in Shays' Rebellion was the jailing of individuals or seizure of their property for failure to pay taxes during a time of economic hardship. Economic oppression by eastern Massachusetts bankers (E) and underrepresentation of the western part of the state (B) may have been contributing factors. Indians were by this time not a serious problem in Massachusetts (D) and there was no unpaid bonus (C).

79. **(B)** The most successful method of financing the War of Independence was obtaining grants from foreign countries. Printing large amounts of paper money (A), issuing paper securities backed by the promise of Western land grants (D), and appealing to the states for voluntary contributions (E) were tried with very little success. Congress did not have the power to levy direct taxes (C).

80. **(D)** Area III comprises the European section of the Soviet Union, or the Union of Soviet Socialist Republics, a multinational federal state composed of more than 100 ethnic groups, represented through 15 "socialist republics" from the 1920s through the early 1990s. Area V includes the multinational state of Yugoslavia, created after World War I as a panslavic state. It encompasses Serbians, Montenegrins, and Croatians, among others. Another multinational state in Area V is Czechoslovakia, whose name was originally hyphenated ("Czecho-slovakia") to indicate the dual union of Czech and Slovak nationalities. Area IV includes the multilingual state of Switzerland, which, although various segments of the population speak French, German, or Italian, has a single national identity.

81. **(C)** Area IV includes Germany and Switzerland; Area V includes Austria (prior to 1918, an empire which included 11 different nationalities) and the Balkan nations. Germany was unified in 1871. The Balkans were the scene of a number of successful struggles for national independence (I) from the Ottoman Empire, beginning with the Greek revolt of the 1820s. German troops were present in both areas during both world wars; they entered the Balkans during World War I to aid Austria-Hungary and occupied much of the Balkan peninsula (II) during World War II. Points III, IV, and V apply only to Area V.

82. **(E)** Hitler's demands for additional living space for Germany (*Lebensraum*) envisioned German expansion into Eastern Europe rather than into lands west of Germany. Area II includes France and the Low Countries of Belgium and the

Netherlands, and was the scene of some of the earliest industrialization activities in Europe (A). Before 1870, Britain and Belgium were the two most highly industrialized areas in the world. During the revolutions of 1830, the Belgian people successfully gained their independence from the Netherlands (B). The Schlieffen Plan, the military contingency plan followed by the German army in its invasion of France in 1914, called for the army to march through Belgium to reach the northern border of France (D). The Munich Peace Conference of 1938 (C) debated the fate of Czechoslovakia, not the Low Countries.

83. (E) A member of the Social Gospel movement would probably argue that Christians should work to reorganize the industrial system and bring about international peace. He would probably not be very concerned about such "ordinary" sins as alcohol abuse and sexual permissiveness (A), nor would he hold the poor at fault for their plight (B) or suggest that those who committed abuses simply lacked will-power (C)—all this was society's fault. He did not see religion as individualistic (D) but rather as a social matter.

84. (A) Benedictine monasticism, based on the Rule of St. Benedict and formalized in the 6th century, offered an ascetic life of manual labor (B), (D), generally in a rural community (E), with much contemplation and prayer (C). However, a vow of poverty was not a requirement. St. Francis of Assisi would make that part of the Franciscan order he founded in the late Middle Ages.

85. (C) The major difference between the two branches of Christianity in the Middle Ages was over the role of the state in church life. In Byzantium, the patriarch, the predominant church figure, was nominated by the Byzantine emperor. The emperor thought of himself as a protector of the Church, and the Eastern church often looked to the emperor for guidance. In the Latin church, the pope, as "Vicar of Christ on Earth," often disputed with political authorities; the frequent arguments between medieval popes and Holy Roman Emperors is one example.

86. (D) Sinclair Lewis depicted small-town America as dreary, prejudiced, and vulgar, rather than in any of the more traditional and positive ways reflected in the other answer choices.

87. (E) Despite friction with Britain over oil rights, the Harding and Coolidge administrations apparently preferred Middle Eastern lands to remain in the hands of European powers, and secured such rights via the negotiations of Secretary of State Charles Evans Hughes. The United States generally took an "isolationist" line toward European political conflicts, such as the Ruhr Crisis, during this time (B). But they also had to contend with Allied war debts (D), which they did not forgive, and were slow to restructure. In the Five-Power Naval Treaty of 1921–1922, the United States negotiated naval parity with Britain and superiority to Japan (C) based on a 5-5-3 ratio. The Coolidge years are also notorious for armed intervention and occupation of the Dominican Republic, Haiti, Mexico, and Nicaragua (A) at various times.

88. **(D)** A plow powered by a steam engine would not be used until the 1830s; its development belonged to an age of machine-driven agricultural advancement which began as the 18th century drew to a close. During the "agricultural revolution," the amount of cultivated land did increase (A), and new crops such as clover and peas (D) improved the soil by storing nitrogen from the air in their roots. Also by the 18th century, some seeds were planted with mechanical drills (C), and the horse-drawn hoe helped weed and maintain the soil (B).

89. **(D)** By the late Middle Ages, the predominant school in theology was Scholastic realism, a theory of knowledge and education which mixed elements of the philosophies of Plato and Aristotle. From Plato, the Scholastics derived the idea that the ultimate things of the world, such as the soul, are invisible and immaterial. These ultimate ideas they called "universals." From Aristotle, they derived syllogistic or deductive methods of reasoning, based on premises which were, essentially, the citing of "authorities." Scholastic realism predominated until the 13th century, when the nominalist William of Ockham complained that realism was an unnecessarily complicated view of the world. To Ockham, only the specific or particular existed; he was skeptical of the existence of universals. Indulgences (A), a papal transfer of "merits" from dead saints to living persons, lessened the amount of time a person might spend in purgatory; the sale of indulgences in Martin Luther's area of Germany was one of the causes of the Reformation.

90. **(A)** Georgia O'Keeffe, Thomas Hart Benton, and Edward Hopper were all American painters of the 1920s (A). This was the age of jazz (B) and of skyscrapers (D). Georgia O'Keeffe was known for her abstract paintings of flowers and animal skulls against the background of the New Mexico desert (C).

91. **(E)** The Dominicans (E) were a Catholic order with the specific purpose of combating heresy. Various heresies, often centering around the existence of the Trinity or a rejection of the authority of the Church, flourished at various times in the Middle Ages. In southern France, the Waldensians (B) and the Cathars (C) (also called Albigensians (D)) were prominent. Arianism (A), a heresy which questioned the divinity of Jesus, had emerged at the Council of Nicaea in 325 A.D.

92. **(A)** Written by Martin Luther's friend Philip Melanchthon, the Augsburg Confession was an attempt to find a compromise statement of religious faith that both the Lutheran and Catholic princes of the Holy Roman Empire might unite behind. Rejected by the Catholic princes, who condemned the Lutherans as negativists whose only activity was to protest (hence the term "Protestant"), the Augsburg Confessions became the traditional statement of belief for Lutheran churches around the world.

93. **(A)** Although the Act of Toleration was a landmark of religious freedom for Catholics in Lord Baltimore's colony, it proscribed the death penalty for groups that did not accept Jesus Christ as their savior. Catholics in Maryland secured the passage

of this act because Protestants still outnumbered them (D). Puritans in Massachusetts were noted for the rigidity of their beliefs and their intolerance toward the faiths of others (B), while colonists in South Carolina held relatively tolerant beliefs, which allowed the emigration of the persecuted French Protestant Huguenots (C), although not very many others. Conversion to Christianity (E), though intermittently a goal of slaveowners for its own value, could not free slaves.

94. (D) The Tonkin Gulf incident led to major U.S. involvement in the Vietnam War. In the Gulf of Sidra during the 1980s, two clashes occurred involving the shooting down of Libyan, not Vietnamese, jets approaching U.S. ships (B). Off the coast of North Korea in 1968, Korean, not Vietnamese, forces seized the U.S. intelligence ship *Pueblo* (C). In an incident in the Persian Gulf in 1987 the U.S. Navy frigate, not destroyer, *Stark*, was struck by a guided missile fired by an Iraqi, not North Vietnamese, plane (E).

95. (D) The first ruler of Russia to use the title of tsar, the 16th century ruler Ivan IV ("Ivan the Terrible") had suppressed the old Russian nobility, they boyars, and broken the power of the Mongols, Asian invaders who had dominated Russia during the Middle Ages. Left undecided, however, was the question of the rule of succession, or how future tsars were to be chosen. During the Time of Troubles (1604–1613), a pretender to the throne appeared, civil wars racked the country, and foreign invaders meddled in Russian political affairs. Answer (V) must be incorrect because the westernization policies of Peter the Great come later, during the late 17th and early 18th centuries. The Bolshevik triumph in 1917, and a subsequent civil war (III), also occur much later in history, as does the emancipation of the serfs (IV). The Russian Orthodox church was a branch of the Byzantine church, not the Latin church (II).

96. (A) The Lay Investiture Controversy of the Middle Ages pitted the pope against the Holy Roman Emperor, who was, technically, a creation of the papacy. In 1075, Pope Gregory VII decreed that bishops or abbots must be invested by ecclesiastical authorities; he insisted that appointment or installation by lay authorities was not valid. When the Holy Roman Emperor, Henry IV, refused to accept the rule, the pope responded with excommunication, which meant that all Christians were required to withhold food, shelter, and obedience from Henry. When Henry stood barefoot for three days in the snow in front of the pope's palace in Canossa, Italy, Gregory felt compelled, as a priest, to grant him absolution and restore recognition of his status as emperor. Both sides counted the outcome as a victory.

97. (E) The growth of European trade in the 11th century was a prelude to the Commercial Revolution (the period when Italian merchants established joint-stock companies). Medieval trade was largely confined to Europe (A) and the Mediterranean area. Although agriculture remained the major occupation (B) and land was the main source of wealth, trade was significant, both via overland routes and at sea

(C), where Muslim ships were a threat on the Mediterranean Sea and Viking ships were feared on the Atlantic Ocean.

98. (E) Nineteenth century Europeans and Americans fully believed in the superiority of their cultures, of the white race, and of Christianity. In their minds, it was perfectly acceptable to go into undeveloped nonwhite lands and do what they pleased with the lands and the natives. Since the natives of these lands were overwhelmingly nonwhite, non-Christian and technologically undeveloped, Americans and Europeans rationalized their domination of these lands and the subjugation of the natives. They viewed their actions as a noble mission to "civilize" the "savages" and give them the benefits of Western culture. This "mission" was called the "white man's burden" because it was characterized as a burden that only the shoulders of the Western white male were big enough to handle.

99. (C) In 1820, over three-quarters of all Americans worked on farms; in forty years, that number had decreased to just over half (I); the decrease was caused by the movement of these workers to new service-oriented positions developed technological advances. Timber machinery, which helped to clear dense forests but did not conserve timber, was one of these labor-reducing advances (IV). Turnpike building in the West faced states' righters' opposition to federal aid for such projects, as well as Eastern fears that road-building would bleed their populations (II). It is not true that railroad track was entirely a Northern phenomenon (III); almost a quarter of all American railroad track lay in Southern states. Canals, however, ran mostly east-west rather than north-south (V).

100. (D) Montesquieu's *Spirit of Laws* sought to identify patterns, or "laws," of human political behavior. The title of his book contains the one word most often used in the quotation, "laws." Chateaubriand's *The Genius of Christianity* (A) was a Romantic view of the Catholic church. Beccaria's *An Essay on Crime* (B) advocated more enlightened prison policies in the 18th century. Spinoza's *Ethics Demonstrated in a Geometrical Manner* (C) reflected the philosopher's belief that God was the essence of mathematical law in the universe. Voltaire's *Treatise on Toleration* (E) continued, in the tradition of the English writer John Locke, the argument that religious intolerance harms society as a whole.

101. (B) Cubism, a 20th century movement, sought to reduce the structure of objects to their most fundamental geometric forms, a characteristic clearly shown in this painting by Picasso entitled *Three Musicians*. Impressionism (A) and Post-Impressionism (C) were both 19th century movements. Impressionists such as Claude Monet sought to represent the immediate impressions made on the senses; the treatment of light was emphasized, but solid forms were de-emphasized in favor of patches of color. Post-Impressionists such as Paul Cezanne painted more solidly defined forms. Classicism (D), predominant in Europe before the 19th century, was modeled after ancient Roman and Greek styles and emphasized restraint and bal-

ance. The Pre-Raphaelites (E) were a mid-19th century association of painters and poets protesting what they saw as low standards in British art.

102. (D) The quotation summarizes Luther's doctrine of the "priesthood of the believer," which held that individuals must justify themselves before God, without intervention or intermediaries. Luther objected to the priesthood not only as an obstacle to salvation, but also as a group inaccurately thought to have a special relationship with God. Erasmus (E), a Renaissance Christian Humanist, agreed with Luther that reforms were necessary in the Catholic church, but he refused to leave the Church, believing that reform would be more effectively accomplished from within. Ignatius Loyola (A) was a founder of the Society of Jesus, or Jesuits, a group founded to combat the spread of Protestantism during the Reformation. Pope Pius IX (B) issued the famous *Syllabus of Errors* in the mid-19th century. It condemned many modern movements, including parliamentary democracy. Martin Buber (C), a 20th century philosopher, was the author of the "I-thou" philosophy often summarized as "Personalism."

103. (E) Philippine nationalists believed that when the United States drove out the Spanish, the Philippines would be given independence. Comments by the commander of the U.S. naval forces in the region, Commodore Dewey, were interpreted as promises of independence. When the United States began formal occupation of the islands and it became clear that independence was not forthcoming, the nationalists began agitating against U.S. rule. In addition, Americans treated the Filipinos with contempt. Much of this was due to latent racism against the nonwhite Filipinos. Racial slurs were commonly used and they were treated in much the same manner as Southerners treated ex-slaves after the Civil War. Frustration soon reached a boiling point and in 1899 the leader of the nationalists, Emilo Aguinaldo, declared Philippine independence and launched an insurrection against American control. The rebellion took over two years to control and it resulted in countless atrocities by both Filipinos and Americans. In the ensuing bloodbath over 500,000 Filipinos were killed and approximately 5,000 Americans died. While the Filipinos lost the revolution, it did lead to reforms in U.S. policy. In 1916, the Filipinos were promised that they would be granted their independence, when the United States felt they were capable of successfully governing themselves.

104. (B) In 18th century England, the South Sea Company agreed to take over part of the national debt if the government would grant the company exclusive trading rights in South America and the islands of the Pacific Ocean. The potential profits for the company were immense, and excited investors raised the stock of the company to a level 10 times its original price. As the realization set in that the stock was overpriced, its value fell rapidly. The "bubble" ended in economic collapse and greatly embarrassed the English government.

105. (C) Although liberalism and nationalism (A) were factors in most revolutions of 1848, the participation of European craftsmen, or artisans, resulted from the

increasing unemployment rates of the group (C) as the European public came to prefer the standardized look of machine-made goods over handcrafted merchandise. Answer (E) is incorrect because many of the skilled artisans drew higher earnings than factory workers in the middle of the 19th century.

106. **(E)**   All of the choices are utopian communities which evolved as part of the religious revivals, or the Second Great Awakening, of the 1820s, 1830s, and 1840s. But only one of those communities, Brook Farm, was the source of the Transcendentalist philosophy espoused by Thoreau, Melville, and others who lived and worked there. Brook Farm focused on the importance of spiritualism over materialism. Members of the community lived a communal lifestyle and all shared in the upkeep of the community. The writers who lived there explored the workings of nature and the individual and became some of the most prominent American writers of the 19th century. During their prime they were a part of what is now called the American Renaissance.

107. **(B)**   When the armies of Islam swept rapidly across northern Africa in the 8th and 9th centuries, some crossed the Straits of Gibraltar into Spain. During the Middle Ages, half of Spain was under Muslim control, leaving a strong Muslim or "Moorish" influence and extensive Moorish architecture in the country. This forced the first Christian rulers of Spain to regain their country in a process that is known as the *Reconquista*. When the armies of Islam threatened to sweep into France in the 8th century, Charles Martel defeated them with a Christian army near the southern French city of Tours in 733. Charlemagne completed the process of expelling Muslim armies from France. Charles V (E), as king of Spain, emperor of Austria, and Holy Roman Emperor, was the most powerful European political figure during the Reformation, eight centuries after the battle of Tours.

108. **(E)**   Moses Ben Maimon, also known as "Maimonides" (1135–1204), influenced Christian writers such as Thomas Aquinas and the jurist Hugo Grotius, but found it necessary to flee religious persecution in Spain and move to Muslim areas. He frequently wrote in Arabic. Avincenna (A) was a 9th and 10th century Arab philosopher. Plotinus (B), a 3rd century pagan philosopher and neoplatonist, influenced early Christian theologians. Aurelius Augustus (C) was the given name for St. Augustine, a seminal Christian theologian of the 4th and 5th centuries. Origen (D), also a Christian theologian, lived in the 3rd century.

109. **(C)**   In the 1830s and 1840s, the Democrats supported the Jeffersonian principles of limited power to the federal government. They felt that what power the government wielded should be exercised at the state and local level. Democrats distrusted a strong, centralized government and opposed policies which would give the federal government too much control, such as a national bank, protective tariffs, or government support for private industry. Their opponents, the Whigs, favored all of these policies. The Whigs believed in using the power of the federal government

to help build the country and expand the nation's economy. The Whigs supported policies favored by business owners, the middle class, and the wealthy.

110. **(C)** Most Americans welcomed the economic growth and prosperity of the mid-1920s. However, some found the collapse of Progressivism, the subsequent dominance of materialistic consumerism, laissez-faire capitalism with its greed, corruption, and conspicuous consumption, as well as the emphasis on social conformity and dearth of spirituality to be morally repugnant. This repugnance and cynicism regarding America's social framework were captured most poignantly in the works of several young American authors. F. Scott Fitzgerald, H. L. Mencken, Ernest Hemingway, and Sinclair Lewis wrote stories of heroes as flawed as the villains they sought to conquer (B). Their works raised questions about traditional assumptions of right and wrong and often left those questions unanswered. They painted unsettling pictures of American society, frequently with a sharply critical, sometimes satirical, portrayal of American hypocrisy and decadence (the opposite of (C)). Their unsettling works, with the inherent crying out at the loss of ideals, values, and purpose (D), as well as the interwoven criticism of the current dominance of materialism (A), led critics and historians to label them the "Lost Generation." A whole generation of young writers faced what they believed to be a spiritually lost America (E) desperately needing to find new and meaningful goals and values. These writers' works attempted to point out the folly of 1920s America and rekindle the idealism and sense of deeper purpose they felt necessary for America to live up to its potential for all its citizens.

111. **(C)** All of the other choices were true. Most New England immigrants arrived as family units. This provided the New England colonies with a relatively stable social structure from their inception. In Chesapeake Bay, most colonists were single young males, many of whom were indentured servants. The ratio of men to women was 6 to 1 before 1640. This made it exceedingly difficult to find eligible mates and start families. In addition, the climate in the Chesapeake Bay region was an unhealthy climate. Men and women died between 10 to 20 years earlier on average than they did in New England, leaving them little time to start families when they did find mates. This severely limited population growth in Chesapeake Bay, where the population increases were entirely due to continued immigration rather than indigenous colonists. A population whose growth depends on a continuous flood of newcomers is not nearly as stable as a population whose growth is based on established couples having children and raising them in stable family environments, as occurred in New England. The only choice that was untrue was choice (C). There were basically no differences in the way women were viewed (in terms of their social role or their rights) in New England or Chesapeake Bay. In fact, some historians argue that because women were so rare and in such demand in the Chesapeake region, they were more likely to be treated as equals than women in New England, who were plentiful and more likely to be locked into the traditional wifely role. A woman in Chesapeake Bay might succeed in rebelling against social norms simply because she was so badly needed that males couldn't afford to reject

her. A woman in New England who rebelled against social expectations had no chance of being accepted by males who could find plenty of other women who were willing to "accept their place" in society.

112. (E)   Innovations by Eli Whitney and Simeon North in the use of interchangeable parts to produce small arms for the military pioneered the beginnings of the machine tool industry. The use of precision engineered high quality interchangeable parts led to the mass production of a wide variety of high quality products not previously available to consumers. This brought the United States slowly but steadily into the Industrial Revolution and laid the groundwork for the American manufacturing colossus that emerged by the end of the 19th century.

113. (C)   Machiavelli's writings have been subject to varying interpretations. This passage gives the most common view: that Machiavelli was one of the first advocates of the principle of *raison d'etat,* which held that since the state was an entity unto itself, statesmen might properly act in ways which would promote the interests and needs of the state. The most famous proponent of *raison d'etat* was Cardinal Richelieu who, as chief minister to Louis XIV of France, supported Protestant forces in the Thirty Years' War (1618–1648) because he believed that it was in France's best interest to weaken the forces of the rival Hapsburg rulers of Austria, Spain, and, at times, the Holy Roman Empire. A constitutional monarchy (A) and parliamentary government (B) would be opposites to the kind of absolute government that the author argues Machiavelli favored. Louis Philippe (D), who ruled France from 1830–1848, was the "bourgeois monarch," the middle class's concept of an ideal limited monarch who was more a symbol of stability than an actual ruler. In the Fascist Italy of Mussolini, capital and labor were represented in the government through corporations or political unions, leading to the term "the corporative state" (E).

114. (B)   What sets Russia off from the rest of Europe during this time is not only the persistence of feudalism, but the ways in which the Russian monarchy used the feudal system to further its own ends. In Russia, the monarchs generally bought the loyalty of the nobility through expanding the rights of the nobility to hold serfs, specifically through Catherine the Great's Charter of Nobility of 1785. It is not true, then, that feudalism and absolutism were completely separate developments in Russia (D), nor that the Russian nobility, co-opted as it was by the Charter of Nobility, was able to successfully challenge the power of the monarch (A). It also follows that the Russian way of controlling the nobility was not the way of Louis XIV (E), who merely embroiled the French nobility in the endless ceremony of life at Versailles. The problem of serfdom in parliamentary democracy (C) would not become apparent until the 19th century.

115. (A)   Conducted by the American scientists Albert Michelson and Edward Morley, this famous experiment attempted to determine if the speed of light is different for light rays traveling in the same direction as the earth than it is for rays

traveling away from the earth. Their discovery that the speed of light was the same in both situations seemed illogical; if a light ray left the earth traveling in the same direction as the earth, it received no "boost" in speed from the motion of the earth. The results of the experiment carried implications for much subsequent work in physics, including Albert Einstein's theory of relativity.

116. **(C)** Lyndon Johnson's "Great Society" was the collective name for several separate programs aimed at ending civil rights abuses (A) and combating poverty (B). In the area of civil rights, the Civil Rights Act of 1964 was a piece of landmark legislation. It forbade discrimination based on racial, ethnic, or sexual origin or religious beliefs in job hiring, promotion, and firing. It also forbade such discrimination in access to public accommodations and gave the federal government powers to cut funding to federally aided industries or agencies found guilty of discrimination. It also actively involved the U.S. government in attacking segregated school systems and forcing them to desegregate. Related to this, the Voting Rights Act of 1965 gave the government the power to intervene and supervise voter registration in areas where minorities had been illegally restricted or discouraged from registering to vote in significant numbers (D). Economically, Johnson declared a war on poverty, backing several bills to combat poverty and its causes in the United States. Medicare, followed by Medicaid, was aimed at providing quality medical care to the elderly (E). Several programs were initiated to increase the quality of teachers and education in poverty-stricken areas. Most notably, Project Headstart, which attempted to provide quality preschool training for impoverished preschoolers, involved the government in attacking the failure to succeed in school which marked the lives of so many of the nation's poor. Johnson also initiated the Neighborhood Youth Corps and the Job Corps to provide job training and experience for inner-city youths. There were also tax cuts and economic aid programs to provide increased welfare benefits, especially to mothers with young children. However, none of the Great Society programs sought to retrain adults who had dropped out of school (C).

117. **(B)** The cool, rational Unitarians, who rejected the concept of the Trinity, embraced the liberal beliefs flowing from the American Revolution, and rebelled against Calvinism, clearly were not cut out for the Second Great Awakening, to which the hymn refers. The Baptists and Methodists (E) were the main progenitors of the revivalist spirit embodied by "camp meetings" (A), as were the Millerites in western New York (D), whose emotion could not be dampened even by the failure of the world to end on October 22, 1844, as they predicted. Missionary work in the Indian backwoods, Hawaii, and Asia (C) were also a part of the new religious fervor.

118. **(D)** The word *Libertaet* as the Germans used it in medieval times is a difficult word because it does not translate directly into "freedom" and does not have all the connotations that "freedom" has for an English-speaking culture. The passage indicates that the closest translation would be the political rights within a society (D), which included the rights of princes within the Holy Roman Empire and those of medieval corporations. As such *Libertaet* does not carry the connotation of autoc-

racy (B), nor does it conceive of "freedom" in terms of expression (E), property (A), or parliamentary democracy (C).

119. **(E)**   Britain, which had a reformist tradition so strong that citizens boasted it had successfully achieved "progress and order," had no revolution in the 19th century. Beginning with the July Revolution in France (C) against King Charles X (who had tried to ignore France's constitution, the Charter of 1814), the revolutions of 1848 swept northward to Belgium (B), where the Catholic and Flemish-speaking Belgians successfully revolted to win their independence from the predominantly Protestant Dutch Republic. Revolutionary fervor also spread eastward to small monarchies in western Germany (D) where the first constitutional monarchies in that country were established and to the Russian-controlled section of Poland (A), where a revolt of Polish army officers led Tsar Nicholas I, in 1833, to revoke Poland's liberal constitution, which had been granted by a previous tsar.

120. **(A)**   The Eucharist, or Communion, was the major part of the Catholic mass retained in the new Protestant services of the Reformation. The Catholic doctrine of transubstantiation, or the teaching that the wine and bread of the service were physically converted to the body of Christ, was replaced by Luther with the doctrine of consubstantiation, the belief that Christ was physically present during the service but was not part of the bread and wine. Calvin rejected both views, portraying Communion as a pious and commemorative memorial service. Luther and Calvin both rejected the authority of popes (B) and priests (C) and allowed the clergy to marry (D), and there were no substantial differences in their views on the Trinity (E).

121. **(D)**   The Treaty of Versailles provided advantages and protections for France, the country whose industrial capacity had been largely decimated by fighting on the western front in World War I. The treaty limited the size of the German army and banned training in airplanes or tanks within Germany; returned control of the area of Alsace-Lorraine to France (territories taken by Germany after the Franco-Prussian War of 1870); and required the German government to pay substantial war reparations, particularly to France. France was the country most resistant to German demands for revision of the Treaty during the 1920s. Britain (A) was a close second to France in its commitment to the Treaty of Versailles, even though it shared no common border with Germany and the English Channel protected the British Isles from a land attack. Germany (B) was the nation most diligently seeking revisions of the treaty during the 1920s. Italy (E), which had failed to gain land along the Adriatic Sea during the peace settlements of World War I, came under the Fascist dictatorship of Benito Mussolini, an eventual German ally, during the 1920s. Spain (C) had not been involved in the peace settlement.

122. **(A)**   "Fragging" was the practice of killing an officer who was seen as too "gung ho" and who gave risky orders. Instead of following the order, someone under his command would shoot him and his death would be blamed on enemy fire.

While it is difficult to estimate how much of this actually occurred, as the stories about it undoubtedly exaggerate the actual frequency of occurrence, it happened enough to be a serious concern for many American officers as the American involvement in the war wound down in the late 1960s and early 1970s.

123. **(D)** Bryant's poems, including the epic "Thanatopsis," were among the first American works to be received favorably by cultured European society. They did not overshadow nor outsell Irving's more celebrated works, however (E), as evidenced by the fact that Bryant had to edit the *New York Evening Post* to earn his keep. Bryant's work also did not reject European classicism (A) but rather showed the influence first of the 18th century poets and then of Wordsworth and the Romantics. Nor did Bryant utilize the free verse experimentation (C) that began in America with Walt Whitman. Bryant, born in Massachusetts, memorialized New England scenes, not Southern ones (B); the memorialization of the "pastoral South" through art is largely a post–Civil War phenomenon.

124. **(C)** The Star Chamber courts of England, so named because of stars painted on the ceiling of the meeting room, met in secret, using no juries (A); did not allow accused persons to see the evidence against them (B), and used torture to exact confessions (E). Originally used by English monarchs against their political opponents, the Star Chamber courts of England were utilized by Henry VIII (D) to suppress opposition to his marriage to Anne Boleyn and to force acceptance of his position as the new titular head of the Church of England.

125. **(A)** The Italian fascism of Benito Mussolini (whose party actually assumed the name "Fascist") and the German fascism of Adolf Hitler (termed National Socialism or Nazism) were similar in many respects. Both cited their nation's past history as omens that their countries would achieve true national unity and greatness (B). Both sought territorial expansion (C), shown by Hitler's annexation of Austria and part of Czechoslovakia in the 1930s and Mussolini's invasions of Ethiopia and Albania in the 1930s and early 1940s. For both, obedience to the state was a prime duty (D), especially personal obedience to the leader or *Duce* (Mussolini) and *Fuehrer* (Hitler) (E). On the subject of anti-Semitism, there was less agreement, at least until the early years of World War II. While anti-Semitism was central to Hitler's racial theories, it did not become official government policy in Italy until after the Axis Pact between Germany and Italy was signed in 1936.

126. **(C)** In the turbulent early years of the Reformation, the Peasant Revolt of 1525 was centered in southwestern Germany, where many peasants had almost achieved landowner status and were better off than peasants in eastern Germany. The revolt was directed primarily against the feudal manorial system. The peasants' demands, drafted by sympathetic Christian Humanists, called for the right to hunt in forests formally reserved for the sport of the lords, an end to annual dues paid to the overlord, and an end to other abuses by the overlords, such as exorbitant rents.

127. **(A)** The Carolinas were granted to supporters of the Stuarts as a reward for their loyalty during the Stuarts' exile during the English civil war. With the Stuarts' restoration to the throne, eight courtiers loyal to the Stuarts were granted proprietorship of the land extending from Virginia to Florida.

128. **(E)** Under 'Johnson's Reconstruction policies, many Southern states attempted to reenter the Union led by former Confederates pardoned by Johnson. Once in office, these ex-Confederates helped legislate a new wave of "black codes" that limited the rights of blacks. They also did little or nothing to ensure that the rights of freed slaves were protected. Johnson was willing to let the old Southern ruling elites take power again as long as they understood that they could not reinstitute slavery, nor could they secede. Since Johnson himself did not see blacks as equals, he was not willing to demand any further guarantees that black rights be protected. Northern congressmen saw the new black codes as a new type of economic and political slavery. They felt that the old ruling elites of the South should be punished for their actions and should be forbidden from holding public office. Efforts by Southern leaders to restrict black rights convinced many congressional leaders that Southern leaders had failed to learn from their military defeat. When Congress implemented its own tougher reconstruction policy, Johnson fought it by replacing appointed officials who attempted to enforce congressional Reconstruction policy. When Johnson attempted to replace a member of his cabinet, Edward Stanton, in disregard of congressional legislation requiring Senate approval of the removal of any cabinet member by the president, the House of Representatives voted for impeachment. The impeachment trial was close but Johnson survived it by one vote. After his close victory in the trial, Johnson enforced congressional Reconstruction policies for the remainder of his tern.

129. **(A)** The textile industry was one of the few 19th century industries to employ females on a large scale. This was because when the first textile mills opened there was a shortage of labor in their locations. Since there were not enough males to fill the positions, companies recruited young, single females. While most Americans still believed females should ultimately strive for marriage and children, widows and young unmarried women were accepted as workers because of their circumstances. Since most textile mills were located in southern New England, most of the workers were recruited from the farms and cities in that region. Females had traditionally hand spun most fabrics and clothing in America, so it was natural to recruit them into the new textile mills as workers, since they already understood fabrics and principles of weaving cloth. Factory work was not a socially acceptable choice for married women, so choosing widows and young single women was the best available option. People still worried about protecting their daughters as they went to work in the mills, so a paternalistic system called the Lowell System, was set up to guide and protect them. Women lived in company-sponsored boardinghouses. They were chaperoned and provided with a good salary and education. Working at the mills was not seen as a permanent option for women. It was, rather, a temporary stop on the way to their true goal of marriage and family. Eventually the use of young

women cloistered in these company dormitories was phased out as an influx of cheaper labor from repeated waves of immigration provided companies with an adequate supply of cheaply paid male workers.

130. **(B)** Unlike Britain, where economic changes during the 1700s threw many small farmers off their lands and created a labor supply for the early factories, no similar trends on the Continent created a supply of available factory workers. The availability of rail and water transportation (A) facilitated industrialization, and there was also significant government support (D), as shown by such developments as the *Zollverein*, a tariff union of many German states which was created even before political unification came to that country. Natural resources (E) in Western and Central Europe were abundant; capital (C) was not a problem, either.

131. **(E)** The *Gleichschaltung*, or "coordination" of German society, took place during the first two years of Nazi rule in Germany, from 1933 through 1935. As part of this systematic reorganization of Germany, all institutions and associations were to become branches of the Nazi party (A) and all government employees were to become personal employees of the *Fuehrer*, Adolf Hitler. Political opponents and Jews were systematically weeded from government and university positions (B), particularly after the anti-Semitic Nuremberg Laws of 1935. Books deemed politically or morally objectionable, and books by Jewish writers, were publicly burned by Hitler's storm troopers (C). National Socialism was declared the sole national party (D). The Axis Pact, a military alliance between Mussolini's Italy and Hitler's Germany, was not signed until 1936.

132. **(D)** All adult British males were granted the right to vote in a slow process that began in 1832, when an Electoral Reform Bill granted suffrage to some midde-class males. By 1919, reform legislation had extended the suffrage to all males 21 and older (B), (C), and (E). In the aftermath of World War I, during which women had worked in munitions factories and other war-related industries, pressure to grant suffrage to women resulted in a provision extending the electorate to all women age 30 and over (A). Women between the ages of 21 and 30 were finally granted the vote in 1929 (D).

133. **(E)** In the late 19th and early 20th centuries, many Americans such as Carnegie, Morgan, and Rockefeller amassed fortunes unlike anything previously seen in American history. They often built their fortunes on the backs of poor and middle-income workers. Many Americans looked at money as the "root of all evil," forcing these rich magnates to defend their accumulated wealth. One way some of these wealthy leaders of industry defended themselves was through the "Gospel of Wealth." This gospel stated that the rich got rich because it was "God's will" that they be rich. In other words, they were rich because they had received God's blessing in the form of fabulous wealth. From their point of view, God approved of their riches and must have approved of how they obtained it. So, to be this wealthy, they must be good people or God wouldn't have let them accumulate their wealth.

Andrew Carnegie, who espoused this theory quite vocally, also added that this meant the rich had a social responsibility to use the wealth wisely to help society. Unfortunately, most others who preached the Gospel of Wealth did not feel the social obligations Carnegie felt. So, while giving some of your money to charity, etc., was a social obligation to some, it was not a central part of the Gospel of Wealth.

134. **(B)** Contrary to most stereotypes, only about one-third of white Southerners owned slaves. Most white Southerners were frontier farmers who owned small plots of land which they worked themselves. They were relatively poor and uneducated, and placed a high priority on their self-reliance. This attitude limited their desire for slaves; in fact, many of them opposed slavery and the size of their farms made slaveowning economically unprofitable. Most slaveowners were middle class farmers moving up in Southern society. They too were relatively uneducated, but they typically farmed larger plots of land and controlled more wealth than non-slaveholding farmers. Only about 7% of Southerners were the stereotypic large plantation owners with dozens of slaves. In fact, during the Civil War, one of the biggest complaints from Confederate soldiers and civilians was that they were being asked to fight and sacrifice in a rich man's war for a rich man's institution (slavery).

135. **(D)** During the first eight years of his rule, Napoleon II (1852–1870), the last monarch of France and nephew of Napoleon Bonaparte, attempted to rule as an absolute monarch, creating a system of secret police to spy on political enemies (E), restricting political meetings and imposing press censorship, and using the rebuilding of downtown Paris (A), to eliminate the narrow medieval streets which had facilitated the successful Revolution of 1830. This period of his reign is generally termed the Authoritarian Empire. As opposition slowly gained ground in national elections, Napoleon III in 1860 converted to a style of rule dubbed the Liberal Empire, in which he relaxed restrictions on public meetings and the press and actively courted the middle class with subsidies to businesses (C), and the working class with promises of legislation authorizing the formation of labor unions (B).

136. **(D)** As rulers of an empire which combined 11 nationalities, the Austrian Hapsburg family dreaded the possibility of widespread movements for national independence. They were particularly alarmed by the independence movement in Italy, since Austria held land in the northern section of the Italian peninsula and was dislodged only when Prussia (C), the victor over Austria in the Seven Weeks' War of 1866, made an Austrian withdrawal part of the peace settlement. All of the other choices were supporters of unification, at least at some time. Pope Pius IX (B) was an Italian nationalist when he assumed the papacy, although the behavior of revolutionaries in Rome during the Revolution of 1848 made him more cautious. Piedmont (A), a northern Italian state, guided the process of unification with help from the southern Italian farmer Garibaldi (E), whose peasant armies overwhelmed one of the largest Italian states, the Kingdom of the Two Sicilies.

137. **(D)** When Hitler's Germany and Mussolini's Italy provided armament and military advisers to the antirepublican forces of Francisco Franco in the Spanish Civil War of the 1930s, their intervention was a violation of the Kellogg-Briand Pact of 1928, which attempted to outlaw war. The Pact was compatible with the Dawes Plan (A), which liberalized Germany's reparations payment schedule under the Treaty of Versailles. There was also no conflict with the sanctions which the League of Nations imposed on Mussolini's Italy after the Italian invasion of Ethiopia in 1936 (B); with the Locarno Treaties, by which Germany, France, and Belgium guaranteed their mutual borders (C); and with the Washington Naval Conference of 1921–1922 (E), which preceded the Kellogg-Briand Pact and committed the United States, Britain, France, Italy, and Japan to forego the construction of battleships for a decade.

138. **(D)** When the independent Republic of Texas asked to be admitted to the United States, the government of Mexico threatened war if Texas were admitted. When the United States admitted Texas a confrontation between the U.S. and Mexico rapidly developed over the southwestern border of Texas. President Polk sent American forces to guard the disputed lands claimed by Texas. Mexican forces attacked a small contingent of those forces. America retaliated by declaring war.

139. **(A)** John Brown's raid climaxed the growing hostility between proslavery Southerners and antislavery Northerners. His execution made him a martyr in many people's eyes. Despite the condemnations of Brown's tactics issued by several Northern leaders, such as Abraham Lincoln, most Southerners were convinced that Northerners agreed with Brown's goals and were upset only because he had failed. After John Brown's raid, both sides' views polarized further and many Southerners became convinced that the North would not rest until slavery had been abolished. Therefore, the only way they could preserve their "peculiar institution" was to secede from the Union and establish their own confederacy where slavery could continue unimpeded.

140. **(D)** Women's organizations and politically active women in Europe had been markedly pacifist before World War I. Two prominent examples are the popular anti-war novel *Lay Down Your Arms* (*Nie Wieder Krieg!*, 1889), which won a Nobel Peace Prize for the Austrian writer Bertha Suttner, and the Women's International League for Peace and Freedom, which met in early 1915 and sent delegations to European capitals in an attempt to stop the war. As the war progressed, however, major splits developed within the women's movement of some countries. In Britain, Emmeline Pankhurst, the most famous suffragette leader, declared that a German victory would destroy all that the women's movement sought. She condemned pacifists as "shirkers" and quarreled with one of her daughters, Christabel, who supported the peace movement. The idea that imperialism was a cause of the war was a postwar development (E).

141. **(D)** Panslavism, a movement to unite all the Slavic peoples of Eastern Eu-

rope and Russia under one leadership, was articulated in the 19th century by the novelist Fyodor Dostoyevsky (1821–1881) and the political writer N. I. Danilevsky (1822–1885), whose book *Russia and Europe* predicted an eventual warbetween Russian and Europe, culminating in a great Slavic federation. Portraying industrialized Western Europe as a morally corrupt and declining area of the Continent, the Panslavists envisioned the Slavs as a youthful and vigorous people who would lead Europe to a new greatness. Some 19th century Polish writers also advocated Panslavism, although under Polish leadership. Germany (D), the only non-Slavic nation mentioned, was often portrayed by Panslavists as the traditional enemy of all of the Slavic peoples.

142. **(A)**   This quotation by Chief Prosecutor John Pym at the trial of the Earl of Stratford, a supporter of Charles I, argues for a constitutional monarchy. Citing the opportunities for the abuse of royal power, it asserts that limits on absolutism are necessary; insisting that liberty cannot be absolute, lest anarchy follow, it argues for a balance between royal authority and individual rights. Since answers (B), (C), and (E) assert the precedence of either individual liberty or state authority, they cannot be correct. The passage says nothing about the need for politics to imitate the rules of geometry (D).

143. **(C)**   "Peace, Land, and Bread" was the slogan used by the Bolshevik leader Vladimir Lenin during the summer of 1917, when, in the aftermath of the February Revolution of that year, Tsar Nicholas II abdicated. In preparing for a second revolution against the Provisional Government, Lenin fashioned a slogan which carried a broad appeal. "Peace" was an appeal to Russians hostile to participation in World War I, which went badly for Russian forces and was an enormous drain on the limited industrial capacity of the country. "Land" was an appeal to the peasants, the overwhelming majority of the population. "Bread" referred to the inept and socially discriminatory food policies of the government, which required farmers to turn harvests over to government agents who favored urban areas when they redistributed the food.

144. **(E)**   Indian men generally did the heavy work of clearing the land and building shelters; the Indian women did the cultivating, planting, and harvesting. When Indians observed the European men planting seeds and weeding their fields, they scoffed at them for doing woman's work.

145. **(A)**   Prince Clement Metternich, Austrian foreign minister from 1809 through 1848, was a dominant figure at the Congress of Vienna, where he worried that new revolutions might topple monarchies, particularly absolute monarchies. He was even more concerned, however, with Russian expansionism. He was suspicious that Tsar Alexander I aspired to dominate the diplomatic scene and advance Russian interests in Europe. His "Concert of Europe" slogan underlined his desire that the Great Powers which had combined to defeat Napoleon Bonaparte continue that cooperation after the Congress was disbanded, in order to guarantee continued

peace in Europe. He was a principal author of the Quadruple Alliance of the countries which had defeated Napoleon, which met regularly after the Congress adjourned.

146. **(A)** Following Stalin's death in 1953, Soviet leaders vacillated between the view that Stalinism was too brutal and the view that only the bureaucratic rigidity and brutality of the Stalinist era would hold the many nationalities of the Soviet Union together. The Stalinist style of rule was represented by his successor, Georgi Malenkov (1953–1955) (B); Leonid Brezhnev (1964–1982) (C); Yuri Andropov (1982–1984) (D); and Konstantin Chernenko (1984–1985) (E). Before the accession of Mikhail Gorbachev to power in 1985, the ruler who proclaimed himself an anti-Stalinist was Nikita Khrushchev (1955–1964), who condemned the excesses of Stalin in a secret speech to the Soviet party congress in 1956.

147. **(B)** Under the motto of *Italia Irrendenta,* Italian nationalists during this period lamented that some of their countrymen had been excluded from the borders of Italy during the unification process completed in 1870, particularly those Italians left under the control of the Austro-Hungarian Empire. The Italian representative to the Versailles Peace Conference following World War I attempted to secure land in the area of Fiume, which had been Italy's price for joining the Allies during the war, but American President Woodrow Wilson blocked the move, arguing that it violated the principle of self-determination as enunciated in the Fourteen Points of January 1918.

148. **(A)** In 1913, Charles A. Beard advanced the thesis that the delegates to the Constitutional Convention were not true patriots but selfish men out to protect their own interests. According to Beard, the delegates held large amounts of depreciated government securities and stood to gain financially from a strong national government. Forrest McDonald announced in his book *We the People: The Economic Origins of the Constitution,* published in 1958, that Beard's economic interpretation of the Constitution does not work.

149. **(A)** Rousseau came to prominence in the French Enlightenment, when he entered an essay contest sponsored by the Dijon Academy on the topic "What have the arts and sciences done to advance mankind?" Rousseau's winning essay, published as *Discourse on the Moral Effects of the Arts and Sciences* (1750), argued that both had corrupted human nature. This attitude, plus his skepticism of both reason and natural science, distinguished him from other philosophers such as Denis Diderot, publisher of the famous *Encyclopedia* (B); Baron Charles de Montesquieu, whose *Persian Letters* ridiculed official corruption and whose *Spirit of Laws* argued that laws are naturally variable according to time and place (C); Voltaire, whose designation of Christianity as a cause of social ills was accompanied by a hatred of the French nobility (D); and Condorcet (E), whose *Essay on the Progress of the Human Mind* predicted eventual human perfectability.

150. **(C)**   The 20th century German sociologist Max Weber argued that Calvinism and early capitalism shared a common ethic, the so-called "Protestant Ethic," which saw industriousness, seriousness, sobriety, thrift, and respectability as important virtues. Weber believed that the Protestant Ethic reinforced the emerging capitalist economy. Since many businessmen believed that this ethic was the key to success in business, it was not surprising that middle-class merchants were attracted to Calvinism. Weber's thesis attempted to explain: (1) the close association of early capitalism and Calvinism, culminating in Puritan influences in modern capitalist societies; and (2) why Calvinism drew many of its early adherents from the business-oriented elements of the European middle class.

151. **(E)**   Social Darwinism was originally a derisive term coined by opponents who accused Social Darwinists of slavish imitation of Darwin. Few of the Social Darwinists were scientists; most were political or social writers who attempted to appropriate Darwin's reputation in order to give credence to their own preconceived ideas. A few Social Darwinists of the Left, such as the Russian writer Michael Kropotkin, argued that evolution was a process in which whole species struggled against hostile environments. His book *Mutual Aid* (1902) argued that cooperation was more important than competition. Most Social Darwinists, however, were of the Right, and argued that in a competitive society, the winners—whether races (A), colonizers (B), captains of industry (C), or armies (D)—were clearly the "fittest."

152. **(C)**   The contract theory of government was developed by political philosophers during the Middle Ages. It challenged the existing absolutism based on the theory of the divine right of kings. The new doctrine gradually gained adherents, and the absolute power of some monarchs was mildly curtailed. The advocacy of the contract theory by John Locke (C), Jean Jacques Rousseau (A), and James Harrington (B) helped to gain the support of the intellectual classes and laid the foundations for the English, American, and French Revolutions. The Declaration of Independence, described by Thomas Jefferson as "pure Locke," based its justification of revolution on the violation of the contract by the English government. John Locke's *Two Treatises on Government* (1690) deeply influenced the thinking of the revolutionary generation. Locke maintained that life, liberty, and property were the inalienable rights of every individual, and that man's happiness and security were the ends for which government came into existence. In his *Letters on Toleration*, Locke declared that in some circumstances that revolution is not only right but is also necessary.

153. **(C)**   When the United States withdrew diplomatically from Europe at the end of World War I, American demands that European nations repay money borrowed from American sources during the war was a major issue. European nations saw this demand as an example of "Uncle Scrooge," who collected from his allies for his own war contributions. There were no discussions of the nationalization of industries (A); copyright violations (B); or the rearmament of Germany (E). In general, most of America's allies in the war did not consider recognition of the

Communist government of Russia (D) immediately, although recognition came from Britain and France in the 1920s and the United states in 1933. In fact, during this period from 1918 to 1922, when civil war broke out between monarchists and Bolsheviks, the United States, Britain, France, and Japan sent troops into Russia, ostensibly to aid in restoring order but with the secondary goal of toppling the Bolshevik government.

154. (A)   Beginning in France, where unemployed artisans were major participants, the revolutions of 1848 spread eastward to Austria, Italy, and Germany. Many of these revolutions were liberal revolutions, in which the middle class sought to strengthen its claim to political power, often at the expense of monarchy and nobility. Many revolutions in Germany became nationalist as a German parliament met in the city of Frankfurt with the goal of uniting the country under a single monarch. But the majority of nationalist revolts occurred in Austrian territory (A), where Louis Kossuth led a Hungarian independence movement, the Czech people revolted in Prague, and there were protests against Austrian rule in northern Italy.

155. (B)   The Hanseatic League, a mercantile association of northern German cities founded in the 13th century, bound its member cities together for mutual protection and the exchange of trade privileges. It held a virtual monopoly on Baltic trade in the 15th century. Diplomatically, it became a great power in Europe, even going to war against Denmark in 1362. It was largely destroyed in the Thirty Years' War, the remnant being three German cities which retained the rank of independent Imperial cities until German unification in 1870.

156. (A)   Jazz is the result of a three-hundred-year blending of European and West African musical traditions, and it is an art form indigenous to the United States. It originated during the last part of the 19th century in New Orleans, where predominantly European music patterns drew upon rhythms brought in from the West Indies. W. C. Handy, Joe "King" Oliver, and "Jelly Roll" Morton, black Americans, were known for their accomplishments in jazz.

157. (C)   The passage is from Thomas Paine's pamphlet *Common Sense*, which attacked the entire system by which England and King George III ruled the American colonies. It called for Americans to stand against the tyranny outlined within its pages and pulled Americans closer to a full-scale revolt against England. The passage is quite similar to the writings and speeches of Samuel Adams, who was noted for his outspoken criticism of the crown and its misuse of power. Samuel Adams was one of the most radical of the delegates to the First Continental Congress, and one of the first to call for military preparations to oppose British attempts to collect taxes and enforce regulations. In the aftermath of Lexington and Concord, he was one of the first colonial leaders to openly call for American independence from Britain. Thomas Jefferson (A), most notably in *The Declaration of Independence*, also called for Americans to break free from British rule. He did so in a more formal argument, outlining a case against the way in which King George III ruled, not England's right

to rule nor George's hereditary right to rule England. While it referred to the king's actions as those of a tyrant, it did not resort to the name-calling (i.e., "an ass for a lion") freely used by Paine. While Benjamin Franklin (B) may have agreed with parts of Paine's message, he never engaged in the type of fiery oratory against King George III presented in the above passage. He was much more low-key and diplomatic in his approach and, like Jefferson, disagreed with the manner in which George III ruled, not his right to rule. John Adams (D) supported some attempt at compromise with England until there was no longer any hope of compromise left. His famous work *The Olive Branch* was one of the last efforts to reconcile the differences between revolutionary colonists and the British crown, and the language in it had a more conciliatory tone than the language in *Common Sense*. It spoke in terms of resolving problems and preserving common interests. James Madison (E), would almost certainly have taken the same approach as Jefferson and Franklin; a more diplomatic and sophisticated attack on the methods of King George's rule rather than a personal attack on George himself. Madison's keen intellect and writing style would have certainly offered a more refined and smoothly written argument than the one presented in *Common Sense*. Madison did not become well known until after the American Revolution was over, with his publication of the *Federalist Papers* in 1787, which attempted to win support for the newly written U.S. Constitution.

158. (C)   The author argues that while statistics show that other nations had surpassed Britain's share of world trade by 1913, the statistics are misleading, since, among other things, British products were sought for their high technology. The passage gives no facts or statistics in support of United States trade exceeding all other nations (A), or of Germany and the U.S. overtaking Great Britain before 1913 (B). British naval supremacy (D) and the German chemical industry (E) are not discussed in this passage.

159. (B)   As European nationalities gained independence in the 19th century, some from the Ottoman Empire in the Balkan peninsula, such as Bulgaria (A) and Greece (D), and some in northern Europe such as Belgium (E), Poland remained partitioned. The division of Poland among its neighbors Germany, Austria, and Russia, which occurred in the late 17th century, continued until after World War I, when the American President Woodrow Wilson, who had called for "self-determination of peoples" in his Fourteen Points, helped engineer the reemergence of Poland as an independent nation. Italian unification (C), achieved in 1870, involved pulling together disparate states and the acquisition of papal land.

160. (E)   The Old Believers movement (I) consisted of Russians who rejected changes in the Russian Orthodox church made by Tsar Peter the Great. Emelyan Pugachev (II), insisting that he was the dead tsar Peter III, gathered a peasant army which nearly succeeded in toppling Catherine the Great. The Union of Welfare (III), one of several liberal groups which sprang up among army officers who had occupied Paris after the defeats of Napoleon Bonaparte in 1814 and 1815, carried

out the only attempted revolution in 19th century Russia, the Decembrist Revolt of 1825. The Strelski (IV), a Russian military corps that served as personal bodyguards to some early tsars, exerted considerable political influence in 17th century Russia.

161. **(D)** Elevated to the throne as a compromise candidate after France's religious and dynastic war of the Reformation era, the War of the Three Henrys, Henry Navarre took the throne as Henry IV (1589–1610). A Huguenot, he agreed to convert to Roman Catholicism, the predominant religion in France. His Edict of Nantes was a model of religious toleration. The Edict granted the Huguenots not only freedom of worship but also the right to maintain fortresses in the countryside. When Louis XIV revoked the Edict in 1698, he argued that such independent Huguenot fortresses were a violation of his royal sovereignty.

162. **(A)** The Magna Carta of 1215, which had been forced upon the English King John by a nobility driven to rebellion by what it saw as his abuses of royal prerogatives, primarily guaranteed that the monarch would not encroach on the powers and privileges of the nobility. Beginning with the period of Puritan opposition to the Stuart monarchs of the 1600s, its guaranteed liberties were reinterpreted as applying to all citizens.

163. **(A)** John Peter Zenger was accused of seditious libel for publishing criticisms of New York's governor. Zenger was imprisoned for ten months and brought to trial in 1735. Ignoring the established rule in English common law that one might be punished for criticism which fostered "an ill opinion of the government," the jury considered the attack on the governor to be true and found Zenger innocent. Although the libel law remained the same, the jury's verdict emboldened editors to criticize officials more freely.

164. **(B)** The successful expansion of European trade during the Commercial Revolution of the Renaissance was made possible by increasingly sophisticated forms of organized business activity. The disadvantages of conducting trade by single entrepreneurs (IV)—the limited amount of money available for capital and the personal risks of undergoing trade voyages personally—led first to pooling money and sharing risks through partnerships (III). Partnerships were replaced by regulated companies (I), groups of investors who received some monopolistic protection from governments and who shared their capital to hire or build ships. Merchandise carried by the ships was still owned and sold by individuals or partners, however. Joint-stock companies (II) evolved from the regulated companies. Although joint-stock companies, in which investors created a separate large corporation by pooling their capital, were first created for only a single voyage, they soon became permanent organizations.

165. **(E)** A loosely organized 20th century movement with variable beliefs, existentialism, flourished among many European literary and philosophic writers during the two decades preceding and the two decades following World War II. Most

existentialists saw their philosophy as a sign of hope in a meaningless and bleak post-war world. Most also emphasized the difficulty of moral choice in a universe characterized by endless absurdities. Structuralism (A) is a 20th century movement in anthropology which insists that there are universal patterns in human culture which reflect the common structures of all human minds. Symbolism (B) was a late 19th century literary and artistic movement which attempted to express emotions through the subtle use of symbols. Chartism (C) was a mid-19th century British movement which sought to expand the right to vote in Britain. Positivism (D), advocated by the 19th century French writer Auguste Comte, held that only scientifically verifiable information was "knowledge" and that scientists and philosophers would provide the political leadership of the future.

166. **(B)** The French Physiocrats of the 18th century carried the spirit of the French Enlightenment to the field of economic policy. Arguing that the laws of nature should not be restrained in economics, they attacked mercantilism (B) and guild rules as hindrances to the free operation of agriculture and trade; in this sense, they were forerunners of 19th century laissez-faire ideology (C). Physiocrats such as François Quesnay (1694–1744) differed from laissez-faire principles, however, by emphasizing that a healthy agriculture was the basis for the entire economic order. Keynesianism (A) describes the economics of the 20th century British economist John Maynard Keynes, who argued for government involvement in the economy. Cartels (D) were late 19th and early 20th century alliances of corporations, often for the purpose of controlling raw materials and fixing prices. Marxism (E) rejected both the Physiocrats and the tenets of laissez-faire.

167. **(A)** The Belgian scholar Pirenne theorized that the real turning point of Western civilization had occurred in the 8th century. The Roman Empire had stretched across the Mediterranean world, from the Straits of Gibraltar to the Middle East. Muslim conquests during the 7th and 8th centuries had forced Europeans to shift the center of their civilization northward. Charlemagne's empire became the center of European culture; Europe became centered around the primarily agrarian, isolated economy of the north. Some scholars have challenged Pirenne's thesis, arguing that considerable trade existed during the Middle Ages between the Christian and Muslim worlds.

168. **(E)** The establishment of penitentiaries in the 1840s reflected a dramatic shift in public opinion toward criminals. Until this time, criminals were viewed as sinners. Punishments were usually public and corporal. Jails were used as temporary holding facilities to house criminals until they could be tried and properly punished. People believed that public punishment, or fear of it, would prevent most people from engaging in criminal behavior and would deter criminals from repeating their offenses. No thought was given to any rehabilitation beyond punishment. By the 1840s, many people had concluded that crime was a social disease that should be "cured" with education and rehabilitation. Criminals were now perceived as misguided souls in need of reform. Penitentiaries were to be places where criminals

could spend time in isolation, reflecting on their crimes and exploring how they could improve themselves for a better future life. While penitentiaries were not a perfect solution, most people felt that they represented a true shift toward rehabilitation of criminals and a marked improvement over the public punishments used previously.

169. **(D)** "Scientism" is the label applied to the work of 19th century writers (in this case, the German zoologist Ernst Haeckel) who argued that scientific progress had become so impressive that science should be made a model for government and society to copy, and an oracle to solve political or social problems. Positivism (A) is a specific philosophy which fits under the general label of "scientism," founded in the early 19th century by the writer Auguste Comte; it argued for a government composed of great scientists and philosophers. Uniformitarianism (B) was the 19th century geologist Charles Lyell's theory that the same forces which shape the earth's geology today had been at work in the past. Syndicalism (C), a theory of the early 20th century French writer Georges Sorel, argued for general strikes to secure government aid for the working class. Anarchism (E) was a 19th century movement which sought to help the working class by rejecting all government measures based on force.

170. **(A)** Portraying the working class as downtrodden and "in chains," Marx argued that capitalist societies ignored their responsibilities to the needy ("to each according to his needs"). "From each according to his abilities" reflects Marx's call for a fairer division of labor in future Communist societies; it is also a criticism of the long working hours (up to 10 or 12 hours a day) required of women and children who worked in the factory system of Marx's time. Sorel (B), an early 20th century French political writer, advocated systematic popular violence as a means of promoting continual reforms in government. Blanc (C), a 19th century French Utopian Socialist, sought to improve the condition of the working class through the establishment of a series of national workshops. Comte (D), the founder of Positivism, projected that future governments would consist of councils of scientists and learned philosophers; his motto was "Progress and Order." Dostoyevsky (E), Russian novelist and occasional political writer, was famous for *Crime and Punishment* (1866) and *The Brothers Karamazov* (1880).

171. **(A)** Herbert Spencer, a philosopher, was the best-selling author on evolution in Europe until Darwin's *Origin* was published. Spencer argued that evolution was a process in which living matter progressed from the simple to the complex or, in his words, from the "homogeneous" to the "heterogeneous." Lyell (B) a 19th century British geologist, was the founder of Uniformitarianism, the theory that past geological forces on the earth are the same ones we see at work today. Proust (C), a 20th century French novelist, was the author of the influential *Remembrance of Things Past* (1913–1927). Feuerbach (D), a 19th century German philosopher, influenced Marx with his idea that God is an imaginary projection of human aspirations and personal qualities. Stephen (E) was a noted 19th century British writer and agnostic.

172. **(B)** Hugo's *Les Miserables* was a tale of social injustice in France; it was published in 1862, after Voltaire's death. Milton's *Paradise Lost* (1667) (A) was a poem using the fall of Adam from God's grace to raise issues about human nature. Thomas Hobbes' *Leviathan* (1651) (C), written after the English Civil War between Charles I and partisans of Parliament and Puritanism, argued for the restoration of the monarchy as the best way to avoid anarchy. Edmund Spenser's *The Faerie Queen* (1590) (D) was an historical allegory with chivalric elements dedicated to Queen Elizabeth I. Giovanni Boccaccio's *The Decameron* (1353–1384) (E) comprised one hundred witty, and sometimes ribald, tales.

173. **(C)** Gibbon, whose *History of the Decline and Fall of the Roman Empire* (1776–1788) was very much in the Enlightenment spirit, saw Christianity as a "vile superstition." He blamed the Christian religion for the fall of Rome, arguing that Christian virtues such as piety and humility were inappropriate for the maintenance of a far-flung, diverse, vigorous empire.

174. **(C)** Henry Kissinger was secretary of state under Presidents Nixon and Ford from 1973 to 1977. One of his most notable accomplishments, in addition to negotiating an end to the war in Vietnam, was drafting Nixon's policy of détente with the Soviet Union. This policy combined a series of scientific and economic incentives for the Soviets with political moves designed to move China out of the Soviet "sphere of influence" and into a closer relationship with the United States, with the purpose of making the Soviets more dependent on the West economically and isolating them politically. Kissinger's hope was that he could establish a rapprochement between the superpowers that could end the Cold War. While détente failed to end the Cold War, it did ease tensions between the superpowers for a few years until a combination of Soviet moves in Africa and Afghanistan and a harder American attitude under the Reagan administration effectively ended it by 1982. While Kissinger was noted for negotiating a peace agreement that allowed the United States to withdraw from the war in Vietnam, he was not publicly associated with Nixon's "Vietnamization" of the war (A). He was not publicly associated with the development of the flexible response policy (B). Although he was involved in setting up Nixon's official visit to China in 1974 that opened the door to rapprochement with China (D), the actual rapprochement is associated much more with Nixon himself than with Kissinger, since much of Kissinger's work was done secretly. Finally, Henry Kissinger was one of the few high-level members of Nixon's administration who was not tarnished by the Watergate scandal (E), and therefore he is not usually associated with it.

175. **(C)** The North Atlantic Treaty Organization (NATO), based on the North Atlantic Treaty signed in 1949, committed the United States to full participation in the diplomacy of the continent of Europe. The United States was committed to military action if any one alliance member was attacked. The other organizations mentioned included only European nations. The Triple Alliance (A) was a pre–World War I alliance of Germany, Austria-Hungary, and Italy. The Axis Pact (B)

united Hitler's Germany and Mussolini's Italy into a military alliance in 1936. The League of Augsburg (D) was an alliance of European nations determined to halt the expansion of Louis IV's France into Germany. The European Economic Community (E), based upon economic agreements of the early 1950s, is the official name for the "Common Market," which does not include the United States.

176. **(C)** Because of the desire to eliminate fascism in Europe, and because of the troublesome way in which World War I ended, when a promised "negotiated treaty" never materialized, only unconditional surrender was allowed Germany. At the close of World War II, the Soviet Union annexed part of eastern Poland (E); the Polish border was moved westward to encompass some former German territory (A). The postwar Soviet military occupation of Eastern Europe provided support and protection for new Communist governments in Eastern Europe (B). The victorious countries—the United States, Britain, France, and Russia—decided on joint occupation of Berlin, which was located in the section of Germany occupied by Soviet troops (D).

177. **(B)** Although most of the new nations of Eastern Europe established parliamentary governments immediately after World War I, internal problems resulted in a variety of *coup d'états* during the 1920s and, in most cases, rule by military dictatorships or by oligarchies. Poland was placed under the dictatorship of General Josef Pilsudski in 1926. Similar authoritarian governments arose in Romania, Bulgaria, and in Hungary, where Admiral Nicholas Horthy replaced a short-lived Communist government.

178. **(C)** A 17th century movement in the German Protestant community, Pietism stressed religious emotions or inner feeling over religious doctrines and ceremonies. It had no connection with German nationalism (E). Pietism had nothing to do with antipapism (B) or Communism (D), and did not stress science (A).

179. **(B)** During a stay in England, Voltaire came to admire the British system, although he doubted that the French could copy it easily. Voltaire was heavily involved in the Calas affair (C), an incident in which a Huguenot father was accused of murdering his son because the boy was allegedly planning to convert to the Catholic faith. The conviction and execution of the father reinforced Voltaire's belief that France was religiously intolerant (A). His hatred of the nobility (E) led him to conclude that the monarchy was the only institution that might implement the reform plans of the philosophes; his theory that monarchs educated in philosophic ideas might transform their countries in "revolutions from above" was called Enlightened Despotism (D).

180. **(D)** The Church of Jesus Christ of Latter-day Saints (Mormons) was founded in 1830 by Joseph Smith in upstate New York. The dedication and economic efficiency of the Mormons attracted a large number of converts, but his close-knit body of poor farmers and artisans was regarded with suspicion by nonbelievers. Smith was eventually murdered by a mob.

181. **(C)** The large landed estates of eastern Prussia, owned by the Junkers, or Prussian nobility, were largely worked by the peasants. Peasants were more likely to own land in western Germany, where the farms were small (E). All of the other answers are characteristic of 18th century European economies. Population increases during the century drove up both demand for land and land prices (A). The French nobility, which derived most of its income from fees paid by peasants who used the land (B), raised rents throughout the century, thus helping precipitate the French Revolution of 1789. Through the Enclosure Movement of the 1700s, the English nobility gained peasant and common land and fenced it in, or enclosed it, for grazing (D).

182. **(D)** The Franco-Prussian War of 1870 was a deathblow to an imperial system of government and the structure of the Third Republic indicated a revolt against the idea of a "strongman" at the top. The other historical events led either directly or indirectly, with varying results, to the ascension of such a strongman. The short-lived Second Republic (E) that followed the 1848 Revolution eventually fell to a *coup d'état* led by Louis Napoleon. French humiliation at the hands of Germany in 1940 (C) also led to a strong (i.e., autocratic) leader in the Vichy premier Henri Pétain, whose attempts to create a dictatorial French government were hampered by Vichy's second-rate status as a pawn of Nazi Germany. The Algerian struggle for independence in the late 1950s (A), and the inability of Fourth Republic politicians to contain it, led directly to the return of General Charles de Gaulle as the strong leader of a Fifth Republic. The Great Depression (B) provoked the rise of the nominally strong, and largely unsuccessful, Gaston Doumergue in 1934.

183. **(E)** Marco Polo (1254?–1324?) was a member of a Venetian merchant family who crossed the Middle East, Persia, and India on the way to China. His *Travels* (1296–1298) described the grandeur and wealth of the Far East, which eventually influenced Columbus, whose exploration attempted to find a shortcut to the East. Vespucci (1451–1512) (A) and Magellan (1480–1521) (B) attempted to prove that Columbus had not, in fact, reached India. Prince Henry (1394–1460) (C) sponsored explorations of Africa for Portugal. Cortes (1485–1547) (D) was the Spanish conqueror of Mexico.

184. **(D)** The only person named who consistently supported the Roman Republic was Cicero, a first century B.C. politician who worked to unite diverse groups in the Senate in support of the Republic. Working toward an oligarchy or monarchy were the triumvirate of Publius Crassus (A), a member of a wealthy family who plotted attacks on the Senate; Pompey (B), a general who held similar views of the Senate and the Republic; and Julius Caesar (C), whose autocratic style in government led to fears that he wished to end the Republic and declare himself emperor. Sulla (E), a first century B.C. general, massacred opponents in an attempt to make himself dictator of Rome.

185. **(B)** Copperheads were Northern Democrats who opposed Lincoln's war

policies. Many of them were even more opposed to those policies after the announcement of the Emancipation Proclamation in 1862. Most of these antiwar Democrats were not pro-slavery, but they felt that if the South wanted slavery, it should be allowed to go its own way and not be forced to remain a part of the Union. They believed that the war to recapture the South was foolish, wasteful, and unconstitutional. The Emancipation Proclamation convinced many of them that the South would now fight even more determinedly to remain independent of the Union and that the war could not be won. All of the other choices basically supported Lincoln's policies, even if they did not completely agree with them. Abolitionists (A) resented the fact that Lincoln had not made freeing the slaves an issue in the war. But after 1862, with the Emancipation Proclamation, they gave more support to Lincoln's policies than they had previously. Free Soilers (C) had opposed the expansion of slavery into Western lands, and while they did not actively push to eliminate slavery entirely, they supported Lincoln's call to free slaves in territories controlled by Union forces. Scalawags (E) were poor and middle-class farmers, mostly from the mountainous interior regions of the South, such as eastern Tennessee, Kentucky, and western Virginia, who opposed secession and supported the Union. Few of them owned slaves and they resented the arrogance of the rich slave-holding plantation owners, who called for war and then drafted poor workers and farmers to do their fighting for them. While their opinions on slavery varied greatly, most of them supported Lincoln's policies to preserve the Union through war. Mainstream Republicans (D) were antisecessionists and were often abolitionists too. Lincoln's strongest political support came from mainstream Republicans and he owed his election to them. While they may have had serious reservations about his handling of the war, most of the time they gave his policies public support.

186. **(E)** Taken from the writings of Thomas Aquinas (1225–1274), this passage illustrates Aquinas' famous argument that both reason and revelation come from God. Both will ultimately agree, but if they do not, revelation is the more reliable path to truth. The passage illustrates Aquinas' work to integrate the newly rediscovered writings of Aristotle into established Christian theology.

187. **(E)** Galileo, an astronomer during the Scientific Revolution, angered Roman Catholic church authorities in his native Italy by his spirited defense of the Copernican model of the solar system. His church trial, in which he was required to recant his pro-Copernican teachings, illustrated the clash between the Aquinan view of the reliability of revelation, generally accepted by the Church, and the outlook of the emerging field of natural science, represented by Galileo. The other figures are prominent within Catholic theology and history. Newman (A), a member of the Oxford movement within the Church of England in the 19th century, became a convert to the Roman Catholic church and, eventually, a Cardinal. Jacques Maritain (B) was a 20th century Catholic Existentialist writer. Pope John XXIII (C) called into session the reformist Vatican Council II of the 1960s. Pope Pius XII (D), another 20th century pope, declared the Assumption of the Virgin Mary into heaven, the only new Roman Catholic dogma to be proclaimed in this century.

188. **(B)** The correct response is Francis Bacon (B), who advanced his empiricism during early 17th century. While Galileo (A) accomplished much in the development of science, he did not provide substantive contributions to the philosophy of science. Descartes' (C) *Discourse on Method* (1637) approaches science from a more deductive mathematically oriented approach; Baruch Spinoza's (D) contributions occurred later and were in mathematics and ethics. In addition to formulating Boyle's Law (concerning gas and temperature), Robert Boyle (E) was a chemist who did much to discredit alchemy during the second half of the 17th century.

189. **(C)** The Revisionist Marxist movement encompassed the Fabian Society (Sidney and Beatrice Webb, George Bernard Shaw, Keir Hardie, et al.), the Social Democratic Party (Eduard Berstein), and the French socialist movement led by Jean Jaurès. Revisionist Marxism gained a significant following (A) during the late 19th century; it opposed the Marxist imperative of revolution; Lenin was an orthodox Marxist and opposed (D) the revisionists; most Asian Marxists did not identify with the revisionist movement.

190. **(C)** In *Hard Times*, Charles Dickens depicted an English community which (C) was characterized by difficult personal, class, and environmental adjustments caused by the industrial order. Certainly, Dickens' portrait of English industrial life during the 1850s did not indicate that the people were enjoying the fruits of an industrialized-based progress (A), that the people of Coketown were preoccupied with religious constraints (B), that this society repudiated the industrial order (D), nor that it was a society which emphasized British nationalism (E),

GRE History – Test 3

TIME: 170 Minutes
190 Questions

> **DIRECTIONS:** The following incomplete statements and questions have five answer choices. Select the best choice.

(Answer sheets appear in the back of this book.)

1. The reasons for the formation of the Delian League included

    I. the Greek victory over Xerxes.

    II. the Athenian intent to develop a defensive and offensive alliance against Persia.

    III. Athenian strategy to control all of the eastern Mediterranean.

    IV. an imminent Spartan threat to Athens.

    V. more than twenty years of crisis caused by Persian aggression.

    (A) I and II only

    (B) I, II, and III only

    (C) II and III only

    (D) I, II, and V only

    (E) I, II, III, IV, V

2. "Peasant" or "public" uprisings broke out in all of the following places on the dates listed EXCEPT

    (A) France in 1358.

    (B) Sicily in 1282.

    (C) Flanders in 1302.

    (D) England in 1381.

    (E) Holy Roman Empire in 1190.

3. In *A Study of History*, a religious-based philosophy of history is advanced by

    (A) Oswald Spengler.

    (B) William McNeill.

    (C) Arnold Toynbee.

    (D) T. S. Eliot.

    (E) Christopher Dawson.

4. Poor and middle-income Southern farmers who supported Reconstruction governments in the postwar South were called

   (A) carpetbaggers.

   (B) scalawags.

   (C) copperheads.

   (D) freedmen.

   (E) redeemers.

5. All of the following statements about Cardinal Richelieu are correct EXCEPT

   (A) he opposed the Huguenots at La Rochelle.

   (B) he supported the Swedes during the Thirty Years' War.

   (C) he was the principal adviser to Louis XIII.

   (D) he opposed the Hapsburgs during the Thirty Years' War.

   (E) he dictated the terms of the Peace of Westphalia.

6. Under Lenin's New Economic Policy (NEP) of 1921, there was

   I. a partial restoration of capitalism.

   II. state control and ownership of large industries.

   III. state control of transportation and foreign trade.

   IV. private retail trade.

   V. private operation of small industries.

   (A) I, IV, and V only

   (B) I and IV only

   (C) I, II, and IV only

   (D) I, II, IV, and V only

   (E) I, II, III, IV, V

7. The Peloponnesian War was caused by all of the following EXCEPT

   (A) fear of Athenian power.

   (B) the Greek love of liberty.

   (C) rivalry in trade.

   (D) Athenian advocacy of revolutionary policies.

   (E) Corinthian interest in dominating the Greek world.

8. As a result of the Italian-Turkish War of 1911–12, Italy obtained

    (A) islands in the eastern Mediterranean.

    (B) the East African colony of Yemen.

    (C) Tripoli (Libya).

    (D) trading rights throughout the Ottoman Empire.

    (E) None of the above.

9. Historians would be MOST likely to compare Ronald Reagan's presidency with the presidency of

    (A) Teddy Roosevelt.   (D) John Kennedy.

    (B) Herbert Hoover.   (E) Richard Nixon.

    (C) Warren Harding.

10. Based on their political ideals, which of the following comparisons is analogous to comparing Cicero to Octavian?

    (A) Aristotle to Plato   (D) Marcus Aurelius to Octavian

    (B) Pericles to Plato   (E) Virgil to Octavian

    (C) Plato to Aristotle

QUESTIONS 11–12 refer to the following passage.

If they see that our national government is efficient and well administered, our trade prudently regulated, our militia properly organized and disciplined, our finances discreetly managed, our credit re-established, our people free, contented, and united, they will be much more disposed to cultivate our friendship than provoke our resentment. If, on the other hand, they find us either destitute of an effectual government (each state doing right or wrong, as to its rulers may seem convenient), or split into three or four independent and probably discordant republics or confederacies, . . . what a poor, pitiful figure will America make in their eyes.

11. The passage presents a view most similar to that of

    (A) John Adams.   (D) Patrick Henry.

    (B) Thomas Jefferson.   (E) James Monroe.

    (C) George Clinton.

12. The views expressed in the passage are most likely to be found in which of the following?

    (A) The Declaration of Independence

    (B) The Articles of Confederation

    (C) The Monroe Doctrine

    (D) *The American Crisis*

    (E) *The Federalist* Papers

13. All of the following are considered "Fathers of the Church" EXCEPT

    (A) St. Jerome.

    (B) St. Augustine.

    (C) St. Gregory the Great.

    (D) St. Ambrose.

    (E) St. Paul.

14. The "Silver Age of Latin Letters" is most frequently identified with the reign of

    (A) Trajan.

    (B) Diocletian.

    (C) Marcus Aurelius.

    (D) Tiberius.

    (E) Octavian.

15. The Doctrine of Nullification was most similar to the personal philosophy of

    (A) Andrew Jackson.

    (B) Robert Hayne.

    (C) Daniel Webster.

    (D) Martin Van Buren.

    (E) John H. Eaton.

16. Which of the following is true of colonial families in mid-18th century America?

    I. Physical punishment was the normal method of enforcing unquestioned obedience from children.

    II. Most families bore children who lived long enough to bear children of their own.

III. Women, while subservient to their husbands, set the moral standards by which children were raised and decided how the children would be educated and trained.

(A) I only

(B) III only

(C) I and II only

(D) I and III only

(E) I, II, and III

17. The economic theories of Adam Smith are most similar to

(A) supply-side theory.

(B) mercantilism.

(C) Keynesian theory.

(D) Progressivism.

(E) Socialism.

18. In 1848, revolutions broke out in all of the European states EXCEPT

(A) France.

(B) England and Russia.

(C) France and Spain.

(D) Russia.

(E) Italy and Poland.

19. During the Hellenistic period, all of the following trade routes from east to west were used EXCEPT

(A) a northern route from Bactria across the Caspian Sea to the Black Sea.

(B) a central route by sea from India to the Persian Gulf and up the Tigris River to Seleucia.

(C) a southern route from India by sea around Arabia and up through the Red Sea.

(D) a northern route from the Aral Sea along the northern shore of the Caspian Sea to the west through the Sea of Azov.

(E) a northern route from the Caspian and Black Seas through the Danubian valley.

20. Britain's relationship with its dominions was addressed in the

(A) Balfour Report of 1926.

(B) Balfour Declaration of 1917.

(C) Government of India Act.

(D) Beveridge Report.

(E) British Nationality Act.

21. During the late 2nd century BC, Roman political life was dominated by the

(A) First Triumvirate.

(B) prevailing political parties; *Populares, Optimates,* and *Equites.*

(C) Gracchi.

(D) end of the Punic Wars.

(E) dictatorship of Sulla.

22. The Mexican-American War of 1846 was primarily provoked by

(A) Mexico's refusal to recognize Texas as an independent republic.

(B) Mexico's refusal to accept American annexation of disputed territory in west Texas when Texas joined the United States.

(C) Mexico's refusal to accept American settlements in southern Arizona, New Mexico, and California.

(D) American desires to annex all of Mexico and make it part of the United States.

(E) Mexico's refusal to recognize Texas as a part of the United States.

QUESTION 23 refers to the following cartoon.

23. The above cartoon illustrates the nature of the controversy over

    (A) German dualism and the Civil War.

    (B) the War in Sight Crisis between Germany and France.

    (C) the *Kulturkampf* crisis between Bismarck and the Catholic church.

    (D) Petrine Supremacy and the concept of papal infallibility.

    (E) the triumph of secularism.

---

24. Commercial centers of the Portuguese Empire included all of the following EXCEPT

    (A) Goa.   (D) Macao.

    (B) Malacca.   (E) Trinidad.

    (C) Canton.

25. James I's most serious affront to the English political system was his

    (A) lack of support for the Hampton Court Conference.

    (B) publication of *The True Law of Free Monarchy*.

    (C) dismissal of Edward Coke.

    (D) behavior towards the Addled Parliament.

    (E) relationship with the Duke of Buckingham.

26. Benjamin Franklin epitomized which movement in colonial America?

    (A) The Enlightenment   (D) The abolitionist movement

    (B) The Great Awakening   (E) The prohibition movement

    (C) The loyalist movement

27. In general, state governments in the South during Reconstruction

    (A) were ineffective compared to pre–Civil War governments because they were dominated by freed slaves and others who were not competent to hold office.

    (B) were ineffective compared to pre–Civil War governments because of the restrictive rule of the Union military bureaucracy, which kept a tight reign on state governments.

(C)   accomplished some notable achievements, but basically squandered their opportunity to effectively rebuild the South because of the greed and corruption of scalawags and Yankee carpetbaggers.

(D)   were much more successful than the pre–Civil War governments that preceded them.

(E)   accomplished some notable achievements, and were comparable in their effectiveness to the pre–Civil War governments that preceded them.

28.   After the death of Alexander, which of the following Hellenistic kingdoms emerged?

I.   Antigonid Macedonia

II.   Seleucid Asia

III.   Ptolemaic Egypt

IV.   Bactria

V.   India

(A)   I and II only

(B)   I, II, and III only

(C)   I, II, III, and IV only

(D)   I, III, and IV only

(E)   I, II, III, IV, V

29.   The establishment of transcontinental rail lines and the construction of America's massive rail network had all of the following effects EXCEPT

(A)   rapid industrialization of the Old South following the Civil War.

(B)   rapid distribution of goods throughout the country.

(C)   spurring a series of important technical advances.

(D)   making the country smaller by dramatically reducing the time needed to traverse the continent.

(E)   the establishment of standardized time zones throughout the country.

30.   World War II brought about all of the following changes EXCEPT

(A)   dramatic changes in the roles and expectations of women.

(B)   accelerating long-developing social changes for black Americans.

(C)   accelerating the legal migration of Mexicans to southern California.

(D) increasing the number of Americans who moved from rural areas to cities.

(E) increasing the gap between the wealthiest and the poorest Americans.

31. Which of the following is true about the European middle class in the 19th century?

(A) Its political influence decreased throughout the century

(B) It was most sizable in Russia

(C) It called for government aid to business

(D) It held great wealth in the form of land

(E) It espoused liberalism

32. Which of the following statements best characterizes the differences between John Locke's "state of nature" and Rousseau's "state of nature"?

(A) Locke called for reform; Rousseau was satisfied with the status quo.

(B) Rousseau's "state of nature" did not have political connotations.

(C) Rousseau's "state of nature" was one of economic equality.

(D) Locke's "state of nature" included a "social contract," while Rousseau's did not.

(E) Locke's "state of nature" was a violent and dangerous society.

33. An important source of labor for the new factories of an industrialized England was the

(A) workers freed by the abolition of serfdom.

(B) importation of slaves.

(C) influx of new immigrants.

(D) workers left unemployed as a result of the Second Enclosure Movement.

(E) indentured laborers.

34. The correct chronological order of these events of the English Civil War is

(A) Short Parliament, Long Parliament, Petition of Rights, Death of Charles I, Instrument of Government.

(B) Petition of Rights, Short Parliament, Long Parliament, Death of Charles I, Instrument of Government.

(C) Instrument of Government, Petition of Rights, Short Parliament, Long Parliament, Death of Charles I.

(D) Short Parliament, Petition of Rights, Long Parliament, Death of Charles I, Instrument of Government.

(E) Instrument of Government, Short Parliament, Petition of Rights, Long Parliament, Death of Charles I.

QUESTION 35 refers to the following map.

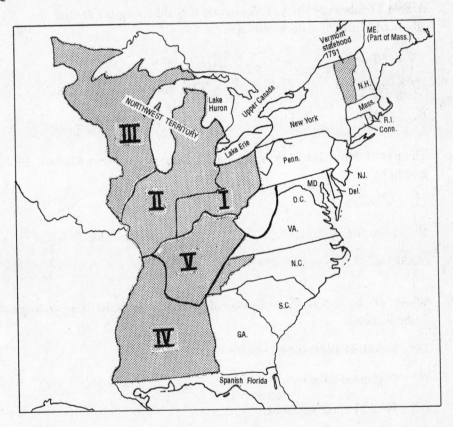

35. As depicted on the map, which of the following was ceded to the United States by the Treaty of Greenville in 1795?

(A) Territory I

(B) Territory II

(C) Territory III

(D) Territory IV

(E) Territory V

36. All of the following were terms or consequences of the Peace of Augsburg EXCEPT the

    (A) recognition of Lutheranism as a second form of Christianity.

    (B) northern German nobles were granted greater independence from the Holy Roman Emperor.

    (C) recognition of the principles of *cuius regio, cuius religio.*

    (D) recognition of Calvinism as a form of Christianity.

    (E) abdication of Charles V.

37. Arnold Toynbee's *A Study of History* and Oswald Spengler's *Decline of the West* advanced a form of history known as

    (A) narrative.   (D) static.

    (B) scientific.   (E) economic determinism.

    (C) cyclical.

38. Thomas Malthus, David Ricardo, Nassau Senior, and James Mill are considered to be

    (A) positivists.   (D) Utilitarians.

    (B) romantic idealists.   (E) Utopian socialists.

    (C) classical economists.

39. Which of the following groups would have been most likely to support Tammany Hall?

    (A) Industrial and business leaders

    (B) Organized religion

    (C) Wealthy rural landowners

    (D) Middle-class shopowners

    (E) Poor urban immigrants

40. Charles Fourier, Robert Owen, and Claude Saint-Simon can best be described as

    (A) anarchists.

    (B) Marxists.

    (C) advocates of capitalism.

    (D) pre-Marxist socialists.

    (E) revisionists.

41. Keynesian theory most similarly reflects the policies and beliefs of

    (A) Thomas Jefferson.

    (B) John Kennedy.

    (C) Ronald Reagan.

    (D) Herbert Hoover.

    (E) Andrew Jackson.

42. The deliberate rejection of activist government is most closely associated with which age?

    (A) The Jacksonian era

    (B) The Gilded Age

    (C) Post–Civil War Reconstruction

    (D) The New Deal Era

    (E) The 1960s

43. The primary reason for the vast differences between the societies that developed in the New England colonies and the Virginia-area colonies was that

    (A) the mortality rate was lower in the New England colonies than in Virginia and the Carolinas.

    (B) Native Americans had a more significant impact on the colonists in Virginia and the Carolinas than they did on the colonists in New England.

    (C) settlers in Virginia were usually wealthier than settlers in New England.

    (D) the colonies in Virginia were founded earlier than the colonies in New England.

    (E) families were more likely to settle in Virginia than in New England.

QUESTIONS 44–45 refer to the following passage.

With the October Revolution the working class had hoped to achieve its emancipation. But there resulted an even greater enslavement of human personality. . . . The power of the police and gendarme monarchy fell into the hands of usurpers—the Communists—who, instead of giving the people liberty, have instilled in them only the constant fear of the Tcheka [secret police], which by its horrors surpasses even the gendarme regime of Tsarism. . . . Worst and most criminal of all is the spiritual cabal of the Communists: they have laid their hand also on the internal world of the laboring masses, compelling everyone to think according to Communist prescription.

44. The above statement represented

    (A) the disillusionment of the Kronstadt sailors and their working class allies in 1921.

    (B) a condemnation of Lenin's policies by his former colleague, Leon Trotsky.

    (C) the position of the Kronstadt-based Russian Orthodox church.

    (D) the views of the Whites near the end of the Russian Civil War.

    (E) the position of the occupying European powers.

45. Leaders of the Catholic Counter-Reformation included all of the following EXCEPT

    (A) Robert Bellarmine.   (D) Reginald Pole.

    (B) Ignatius Loyola.   (E) Pius IX.

    (C) William Allen.

46. "By pursuing his own interest (every individual) frequently promotes that of society more effectively than when he really intends to promote it. I have never known much good done by those who affected to trade for the public good."

The views presented in this passage are most likely to be those expressed by

    (A) Thomas Malthus in *Essay on Population*.

    (B) Adam Smith in *Wealth of Nations*.

    (C) Karl Marx in *Das Kapital*.

(D)   Charles Darwin in *The Origin of Species.*

(E)   Jane Austen in *Pride and Prejudice.*

47.   Elector Frederick William's development of Brandenburg-Prussia during the 17th century was based on

I.   the development of a strong military.

II.   an expanding economy.

III.   the defeat of Sweden in the struggle for dominance in Northern Europe.

IV.   the defeat of Catholic Austria.

V.   the defeat of Poland.

(A)   I, II, and III only

(B)   I, II, and IV only

(C)   I, II, and V only

(D)   I and II only

(E)   I, II, III, IV, V

48.   The "black codes" of many Southern states in the 1830s were intended to

(A)   force Northern states to return runaway slaves to their Southern masters.

(B)   prevent slave rebellions by allowing the execution of any slave found guilty of attempting to gain his or her freedom.

(C)   limit the rights of freed blacks and force them to migrate to Northern states where they couldn't serve as models for slaves to emulate.

(D)   keep all blacks in servitude by refusing to recognize any black as free and allowing so-called "free blacks" to be rounded up and enslaved whenever a shortage of slave labor occurred.

(E)   deal with the increased number of people of mixed race by setting up strict standards defining who was genetically white and who was genetically black.

49.   The St. Bartholemew's Day Massacre

(A)   was successful and led to the collapse of French Protestantism.

(B)   demonstrated that the Counter-Reformation in France was essentially a dynastic and class struggle.

(C) decimated the ranks of the Protestant leadership but failed to suppress the anti-Catholic movement.

(D) was followed by an English effort to assist the Huguenots.

(E) resulted directly in Henry of Navarre's ascension to the French throne.

50. The correct chronological listing for the emergence of the following Reformation leaders is

(A) Luther, Calvin, Zwingli, Bucer, Hus.

(B) Hus, Luther, Zwingli, Bucer, Calvin.

(C) Zwingli, Hus, Bucer, Luther, Calvin.

(D) Luther, Bucer, Hus, Calvin, Zwingli.

(E) Hus, Bucer, Luther, Zwingli, Calvin.

51. Which of the following were terms of the Navigation Acts?

 I. Prohibiting the colonies from issuing their own paper currencies, greatly limiting their trading capabilities

 II. All foreign goods bound for the colonies had to be shipped through England, to be taxed with British import duties

 III. The colonists could not build or import products that directly competed with British export products

(A) I only

(B) II only

(C) I and II only

(D) II and III only

(E) I, II, and III

52. All of the following were colonial wars fought during the 18th century EXCEPT

(A) the French and Indian War.

(B) the Anglo-Franco India War.

(C) King George's War.

(D) King William's War.

(E) the Great Northern War.

53. The primary reason for the emergence of Puritanism in England during the second half of the 16th century was

    (A) the continuing influence of John Wycliffe and the Lollard movement.

    (B) the impact of Lutheranism.

    (C) the influence of the Marian Exiles who returned to England with a Calvinist approach to reform.

    (D) the impact of John Knox.

    (E) the Vestments Controversy.

QUESTIONS 54–55 refer to the following passage.

I am directly opposed to any purpose of secession. The Constitution was made, not merely for the generation which then existed, but for posterity, undefined, unlimited, permanent, and perpetual . . . and for every subsequent state which might come into the Union, binding themselves by that indissoluble bond.

54. The passage most nearly represents the views of

    I.   Henry Clay.

    II. John C. Calhoun.

    III. Daniel Webster.

    (A) I only   (D) I and III only

    (B) II only   (E) I, II, and III

    (C) I and II only

55. The passage is from the only debate in which William Seward, Henry Clay, John C. Calhoun, Daniel Webster, Stephen A. Douglas, Salmon Chase, and Jefferson Davis all took part. This debate resulted in

    (A) the secession of South Carolina from the Union in 1861.

    (B) the Kansas-Nebraska Acts of 1854.

    (C) the Missouri Compromise of 1820.

    (D) the Compromise of 1850.

    (E) the location of the Mason-Dixon line.

56. A comprehensive explanation of the causes for the French Revolution of 1789 was advanced by the historian

    (A) Jules Michelet.

    (B) Georges Lefebvre.

    (C) Victor Hugo.

    (D) Karl Marx.

    (E) H. A. Taine.

57. All of the following factors in 15th and 16th century Europe contributed to the exploration and colonization of the New World EXCEPT

    (A) an increase in Europe's population.

    (B) an increase in the wealth of the major European powers.

    (C) major technical advances in navigational equipment.

    (D) the overthrow of the traditional hierarchical social structure.

    (E) an increase in the power of Europe's absolute monarchs.

58. The 'cold war' resulted from mutual misunderstandings between the United States and the Soviet Union following World War II. Americans believed that Russian attempts to surround themselves with friendly 'buffer states' were the first steps in an insidious plan for Soviet domination of the world and eventual conquest of the United States. Russian leaders viewed American responses such as the Truman Doctrine and the formation of NATO as part of an American plan to strangle the Soviet Union. Both sides became trapped in their misunderstandings of the other side's intentions.

    This passage most closely represents the views of

    (A) orthodox Western historians.

    (B) orthodox Soviet historians.

    (C) early revisionist Western historians.

    (D) later revisionist Western historians.

    (E) post-revisionist Western historians.

59. The Luddite rebellion against the abuses of industrialism manifested itself through

    I. formation of a trade-union movement.

    II. blaming machine industry for low wages and unemployment.

III. attacks on machinery to render it useless.

IV. advocacy of free trade.

V. support for the Corn Laws.

(A) I, II, III, IV, V

(B) I and II only

(C) II and III only

(D) II, III, and V only

(E) Only III

60. Palmerston's foreign policy was characterized by

I. an aggressive defense of Britain's interests.

II. a policy which was designed not to offend Britain's allies.

III. the occasional use of force.

IV. a policy of support for revolutionaries on the Continent.

V. active involvement in European affairs.

(A) I, III, and V only

(B) I and III only

(C) II and IV only

(D) II, IV, and V only

(E) V only

61. *The English Historical Review*, which was the first scholarly journal to address the national and cultural history of Britain, was established through the efforts of

(A) William Stubbs.

(B) Thomas Babington Macaulay.

(C) Lord Acton.

(D) G. M. Trevelyan.

(E) James Anthony Froude.

62. A major impact of the French and Indian War on the attitudes of Americans was that it

(A) led many Americans to question the superiority of English colonial rule and to support French colonial rule.

(B) convinced most Americans to avoid further exploration and settlement of the Ohio and Mississippi valleys until after the American Revolution.

(C) bound the American colonists more tightly to England and made most of them realize they needed English protection from foreign powers such as France.

(D) led many colonists who had previously supported independence from England to call for moderation, because they feared that the huge British military presence in the colonies could now be turned on rebellious colonists.

(E) removed France as a political force in North America, and also allowed the colonists to gain confidence and to see that British troops were not invincible.

63. Which of the following did turn-of-the-century American artists tend to make the subject of most of their paintings?

(A) Realistic urban scenes

(B) Romanticized images of the American frontier

(C) Realistic portrayals of rural family life

(D) Rapidly disappearing pristine natural landscapes

(E) Abstract images

QUESTION 64 refers to the following illustration.

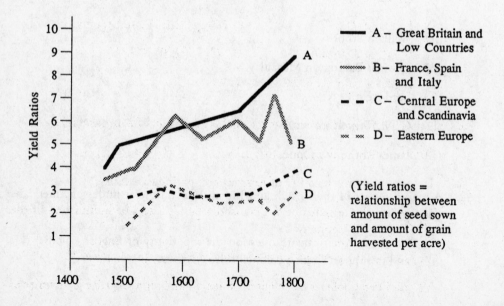

64. The data given in the above chart supports all of the following conclusions EXCEPT

    (A) Great Britain and the Low Countries had the highest yield ratio by 1800.

    (B) yield ratios for France, Spain, Italy, and Eastern Europe declined in the 16th century.

    (C) the greatest rate of increased yield ratio during the second half of the 18th century was achieved by France, Spain, and Italy.

    (D) Western and southern Europe enjoyed higher yields than other sections of Europe.

    (E) Eastern Europe generally had the lowest yields, despite having more available acreage.

---

65. The Holy Alliance was

    I. established to maintain Catholic leaders in power.

    II. designed to secure the arrangements of the Congress of Vienna.

    III. a Russian-based device to suppress revolutionary forces such as nationalism and liberalism.

    IV. used effectively by Metternich during the first decade after the Congress of Vienna.

    V. supported by the victorious powers of Russia, Austria, Prussia, and England.

    (A) I, II, and III only   (D) II, III, IV, and V only

    (B) II, III, and IV only   (E) I, II, III, IV, V

    (C) I, III, IV, and V only

66. Leopold I's major achievements during his leadership of Austria were

    I. the defeat of the Ottoman Turks.

    II. the economic recovery of Austria through industrialism.

    III. restoring the status of the Hapsburg family after the humiliation of the Peace of Westphalia.

    IV. serving as a principal power in the coalition against Louis XIV.

    V. his liberal policies on religion, ethnicity, and representative government.

(A) I, II, III, IV, V   (D) I, III, and IV only

(B) I and II only   (E) I, II, III, and IV only

(C) I, II, and V only

67. Which of the following people would have been most likely to support the Galloway Plan?

(A) Samuel Adams   (D) Patrick Henry

(B) John Adams   (E) Richard Henry Lee

(C) John Jay

68. According to most authorities, the founder of "modern history" was

(A) Georg Wilhelm Hegel.   (D) Arnold Toynbee.

(B) Giovanni Battista Vico.   (E) Oswald Spengler.

(C) Karl Marx.

69. The preeminent advocate of Italian nationalism during the first half of the 19th century was

(A) Garibaldi.   (D) Mazzini.

(B) Cavour.   (E) Pius IX.

(C) Charles Albert.

70. All of the following writers were associated with the "Lost Generation" EXCEPT

(A) H. L. Mencken.   (D) Ernest Hemingway.

(B) John Steinbeck.   (E) Sinclair Lewis.

(C) F. Scott Fitzgerald.

71. All of the following are true of the early Confederate war effort during the Civil War EXCEPT

(A) Confederate industry was unable to supply its soldiers with the armaments needed to adequately fight the war.

(B) Confederate agriculture was never able to adequately supply the people of the South with the food they needed.

(C)   inflation became a major problem in the South as the Confederate government was forced to print more paper currency than it could support with tangible assets.

(D)   the inadequate railroad system of the South hindered the movement of soldiers, supplies, and food from the places they were stationed (or produced) to the places where they were most needed.

(E)   tremendous resentment at the military draft developed among poor and middle class Southerners because wealthy Southern males could pay to have a substitute take their place in the army.

72.   The transformation of the British textile industry and its subsequent dominance of the world market was realized through technological advances developed by all of the following EXCEPT

(A)   John Kay.   (D)   Henry Cort.

(B)   James Hargreaves.   (E)   Samuel Crompton.

(C)   Richard Arkwright.

73.   During the early 1800s, American fashions, ideals, and cultural norms in the coastal cities were most heavily affected by

(A)   British aristocratic standards.

(B)   French republicanism.

(C)   classical Greek influences.

(D)   French aristocratic standards.

(E)   Native American influences.

74.   John Foster Dulles is most closely associated with the

(A)   policy of mutually assured destruction.

(B)   flexible response policy.

(C)   zero option policy.

(D)   Strategic Defense Initiative.

(E)   policy of massive retaliation.

QUESTION 75 refers to the following map.

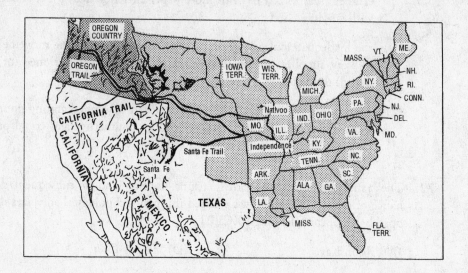

75. The map depicts the United States as it existed in

(A) 1820.   (D) 1850.

(B) 1830.   (E) 1860.

(C) 1840.

76. From the European perspective, the principal outcome of the Seven Years' War was the

(A) continuing Anglo-French colonial rivalry.

(B) containment of British involvement on the Continent.

(C) end of Sweden as a great power.

(D) recognition of Dutch independence.

(E) subsequent struggle between Prussia and Austria for hegemony in Central Europe.

77. The primary English opponent of slavery during the late 18th and early 19th centuries and the leader of the successful effort to prohibit the slave trade was

(A) Jeremy Bentham.   (D) William Wilberforce.

(B) James Mill.   (E) David Ricardo.

(C) Robert Owen.

78. In the Humiliation of Olmutz

    I. Prussia accepted Austria's demand for the reestablishment of the German Confederation.

    II. Austria accepted Prussia's demand for the reestablishment of the German Confederation.

    III. the advocates of the *Kleindeutsch* plan prevailed.

    IV. the advocates of the *Grossdeutsch* plan prevailed.

    V. the Frankfurt Assembly was defeated.

    (A) I and IV only

    (B) I, IV, and V only

    (C) II and III only

    (D) II, III, and V only

    (E) None of the above.

79. The Roman Catholic church responded to the rise of Protestantism through

    I. efforts to mediate the crisis with Luther and Calvin.

    II. the establishment of new religious orders such as the Jesuits.

    III. the Council of Trent.

    IV. repudiation of its relationships with European princes.

    V. an effort of spiritual renewal and internal reform.

    (A) I, II, and III only

    (B) II, III, and IV only

    (C) I and V only

    (D) II, III, and V only

    (E) I, II, III, IV, V

80. Perhaps George Washington's biggest military blunder during the American Revolution was

    (A) the order to transfer cannon from Fort Ticonderoga to Boston.

    (B) his defense of New York City.

    (C) his attack on Hessian forces at Trenton, New Jersey.

    (D) his attack on British forces at Princeton, New Jersey.

    (E) his attack on the British at Germantown.

81. Venetia was annexed by Italy

    (A) through the Peace of Villafranca.

    (B) immediately after Garibaldi's expedition.

    (C) after the German Civil War.

    (D) after the Franco-Prussian War.

    (E) when Pius IX recognized the new Italian kingdom.

82. Bismarck was involved in negotiating all of the following diplomatic arrangements EXCEPT the

    (A) Dual Alliance.   (D) Dual Entente.

    (B) Triple Alliance.   (E) Congress of Berlin.

    (C) Reinsurance Treaty.

83. Luther supported all of the following EXCEPT

    (A) the doctrine of consubstantiation.

    (B) publication of the scripture in the vernacular.

    (C) elimination of the indulgence system.

    (D) the significance of predestination.

    (E) revision of sacramental theology.

QUESTION 84 refers to the following illustration.

84. The painting is an example of the school of

(A) romanticism.

(D) symbolism.

(B) impressionism.

(E) realism.

(C) expressionism.

85. Henry David Thoreau, Nathaniel Hawthorne, Ralph Waldo Emerson, James Fenimore Cooper, Herman Melville, Margaret Fuller, and Theodore Parker were all involved in developing the transcendentalist philosophy of the

(A) Shaker community in New Lebanon, New York.

(B) Mormon community in Palmyra, New York.

(C) New Harmony community in Indiana.

(D) Oneida community in upstate New York.

(E) Brook Farm community in Roxbury, Massachusetts.

86. Woodrow Wilson's "New Freedom" and Teddy Roosevelt's "New Nationalism" were similar in that both

I. removed restrictions on the rights of unions to organize the workplace.

II. expanded the rights of states to regulate business operations within state borders.

III. expanded the government's role in regulating businesses and business monopolies.

(A) I only

(B) III only

(C) I and III only

(D) II and III only

(E) I, II, and III

87. In response to the Kronstadt Rebellion, Lenin

I. crushed the rebellion with the use of Red troops.

II. instituted a reign of terror across the country.

III. responded by initiating the New Economic Policy.

IV. removed Trotsky supporters from the government.

V. negotiated a settlement with the dissenters.

(A) I, II, and IV only

(B) I and III only

(C) III, IV, and V only

(D) IV and V only

(E) IV only

88. Which of the following characteristics best describe the values of the Baroque period?

(A) Symmetry, harmony, order

(B) Gigantism, spectacular, lack of symmetry

(C) Flatness, otherworldliness, spirituality

(D) Introspective, psychoanalytical, independence

(E) Materialistic, order, harmony

89. During the Second French Empire, the authority of the Church over the state for the control of education was realized through the

(A) Cobden-Chevalier Treaty.

(B) Falloux Law.

(C) *Credit Focier.*

(D) efforts of Baron Haussmann.

(E) Article 45 of the Constitution.

90. Prior to the opening of the Congress of Berlin, British prime minister Disraeli and his Foreign Secretary Salisbury had concluded

    I.   an Anglo-Russian understanding.

    II. an Anglo-Turkish accord.

    III. an Anglo-Austrian agreement.

    IV. an Anglo-German accord.

    V.   an Anglo-Dutch accord.

    (A) I only

    (B) I and II only

    (C) I, II, and III only

    (D) I, II, III, and V only

    (E) I, II, III, IV, V

91. A major reason for prejudice against Irish immigrants to America in the 1840s and 1850s was

    (A) their historic animosity to the British.

    (B) difficulty in understanding them because of their accent.

    (C) their Roman Catholic faith.

    (D) their education and skills allowed them to take jobs away from less-skilled American workers.

    (E) their tendency to gravitate toward rural areas and take over the most desired farmland, often dominating the communities in which they settled.

92. Through the October Manifesto, Nicholas II

    (A) established a democratic regime with the creation of the *Duma*.

    (B) reformed the economic system to make it more competitive with the West.

    (C) denounced the revolutionary forces and reaffirmed the status quo.

    (D) established a universal education system in Russia.

    (E) extended civil liberties to include freedom of speech, assembly, and the press.

QUESTIONS 93–94 refer to the following passage.

The major problems of this country today are the result of too many immigrants and the corrupt influence of Papists (Roman Catholics). The immigrants are stealing jobs that belong to the native-born American citizens. Their low moral values threaten the very fabric of our society. The Papists serve Rome, not the United States. They would turn governmental power over to the Pope in a second, if given the chance. Therefore we believe that Papists should not be allowed to hold political office in the United States. Immigrants should be required to live in the United States for at least 21 years before being eligible to vote.

93. The passage most closely represents the views of which political party?

   (A) The Free Soil party   (D) The Republican party

   (B) The Know-Nothing party   (E) The Whig party

   (C) The Populist party

94. The political philosophy represented in this passage achieved its peak in popularity around

   (A) 1825.   (D) 1855.

   (B) 1835.   (E) 1865.

   (C) 1845.

---

95. The Third French Republic was endangered by which of the following internal crises?

   I. Panama Scandal

   II. Boulanger Crisis

   III. War in Sight Crisis

   IV. Paris Commune

   V. the Dreyfus Affair

   (A) I and II only   (D) I, II, and V only

   (B) I, II, and III only   (E) I, II, III, IV, V

   (C) I, II, IV, and V only

96. In the development of the Reparations plan after the First World War, the correct chronological order of events was

    (A) Dawes Plan, Young Plan, Hoover Moratorium, Ruhr Crisis.

    (B) Young Plan, Dawes Plan, Hoover Moratorium, Ruhr Crisis.

    (C) Ruhr Crisis, Dawes Plan, Young Plan, Hoover Moratorium.

    (D) Dawes Plan, Ruhr Crisis, Young Plan, Hoover Moratorium.

    (E) Hoover Moratorium, Dawes Plan, Ruhr Crisis, Young Plan.

97. Thomas Hobbes' political philosophy most clearly resembles that of

    (A) Rousseau.   (D) Montesquieu.

    (B) Voltaire.   (E) Robespierre.

    (C) Quesnay.

98. The Anglo-Russian agreement of 1907

    I. resolved colonial disputes in Persia, Tibet, and Afghanistan.

    II. resulted in an alliance between the two powers.

    III. was inspired by the success of the Entente Cordiale.

    IV. normalized Anglo-Russian relations in the wake of the Russo-Japanese war.

    V. resulted in British support for Russian expansion in the Balkans.

    (A) I and II only   (D) I, II, III, and IV only

    (B) I, II, and III only   (E) I, II, III, IV, V

    (C) I, III, and IV only

99. The American manufacturing system which emerged in the early 1800s was successful because of its

    (A) use of slave labor.

    (B) individually crafted, high quality items.

    (C) use of the "putting out" system for distributing raw materials to and collecting finished products from individual craftsmen.

(D)   use of early electric power to provide cheap energy for new factories.

(E)   use of interchangeable parts to allow for mass production of high quality items.

100.   During the 17th century, the European population declined because

(A)   plagues killed more than one-third of the population.

(B)   the food supply could not sustain the population.

(C)   general wars devastated the population.

(D)   birth control practices were introduced.

(E)   infant mortality increased tenfold.

101.   Syndicalism was a manifestation of anarchism founded by

(A)   Kroptkin.

(B)   Sorel.

(C)   Bakunin.

(D)   Sidney Webb.

(E)   Mazzini.

102.   All of the following were included in the reforms of Alexander II EXCEPT

(A)   the elimination of serfdom.

(B)   peasant independence from the lords.

(C)   the convocation of a representative assembly.

(D)   the right of peasants to enter into contracts and to own property.

(E)   freedom of movement for all people and freedom to change their means of livelihood.

QUESTION 103 refers to the following map.

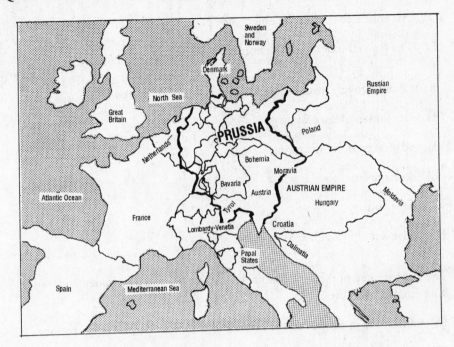

103. The map depicts European political borders after the

    (A) Congress of Berlin.   (D) Treaty of Paris.

    (B) Congress of Vienna.   (E) Munich Crisis.

    (C) Versailles Treaty.

104. The goals of the Niagara movement of 1905 were most similar to those of

    (A) prohibitionists.

    (B) gradualists.

    (C) white supremacists.

    (D) civil rights activists.

    (E) women's suffrage advocates.

105. Which of the following was NOT a factor in the collapse of the Asquith ministry in 1916?

    (A) The Easter Rebellion

    (B) The human devastation on the western front

(C) Opposition to Asquith's intervention in Russia

(D) His failure to exploit the emergency powers which were at his disposal

(E) The general lack of confidence in his leadership

106. The Wilmot Proviso would most likely have been supported by

(A) Jacksonian Democrats.

(B) advocates of nullification.

(C) secessionists.

(D) Free Soilers.

(E) advocates of popular sovereignty.

107. The primary reason slavery flourished in the Southern colonies and not in New England was the

(A) difference in the size of the farms and the staple crops of each region.

(B) tolerance of black slaves to the local diseases and climates in the Southern colonies.

(C) greater initial wealth of Southern farmers, allowing them to better afford the costs associated with the importation and upkeep of slaves.

(D) greater availability of white indentured servants in New England.

(E) Stono uprising of 1739 convinced New Englanders that the cost of controlling slaves was not worth the marginal economic benefits.

108. The American hostage crisis in Iran was precipitated by

(A) the American government allowing the deposed Shah of Iran to come to the United States for cancer treatment.

(B) the American government arranging for the deposed Shah of Iran to receive political asylum in Egypt.

(C) American support for Iraq after it invaded Iran and attempted to bring down the newly established government of Ayatollah Khomeini.

(D) the movement of American warships into the Persian Gulf in an attempt to intimidate the newly established government of Ayatollah Khomeini.

(E) American attempts to overthrow the newly established government of Ayatollah Khomeini.

109. The definitive "Whig" interpretation of British history was advanced in the 19th century by

    (A) David Hume.

    (B) Edward Gibbon.

    (C) Thomas Babington Macaulay.

    (D) John Stuart Mill.

    (E) Jeremy Bentham.

110. The Washington Conference of 1921–22 resulted in agreements between European powers, the United States, China, and Japan which

    I.   established a ratio for capital ships among the five great naval powers.

    II. stabilized the postwar title to islands previously held by Germany.

    III. conformed to the standards of the Reparations Commission established at the Versailles Peace Conference.

    IV. reaffirmed the integrity and independence of China.

    V.   recognized Manchuria as a Japanese sphere of influence.

    (A) I and III only

    (B) III and IV only

    (C) I, II, and IV only

    (D) I, II, and V only

    (E) I, II, III, IV, V

111. During the second half of the 19th century, traditional religion was attacked by science through all of the following EXCEPT

    (A) the application of historical criticism to the Bible.

    (B) the rise of materialistic philosophies which appealed to physical science for evidence.

    (C) the availability of new geological data on the age of the earth and life.

    (D) the theory of evolution.

    (E) the philosophy of positivism.

112. The tenets of Utilitarianism, the social doctrine espoused by such men as Jeremy Bentham, James Mill, and John Stuart Mill, are best characterized as

    (A) the belief that the government should supervise all aspects of the individual's life, as a paternalistic arbiter of social and moral standards.

(B) the belief that the only necessary government institutions are those that promote the greatest good for the greatest number.

(C) the belief that only those government institutions that are absolutely necessary for the maintenance of civil order should be allowed; all other aspects of government are seen as extraneous.

(D) the belief that only those who can be useful to society have a place in it, and those who are too poor or too weak to be useful have no claim to governmental support or protection.

(E) the belief that the only necessary government institutions are those that utilize the natural resources of the country, and that the government should exercise sole control of those resources.

113. Samuel Slater

(A) developed a technique for the mass production of steel at a reasonable cost.

(B) founded the Hudson River school in American art.

(C) opened the first successful factory in the United States.

(D) founded the first successful American settlement west of the Mississippi.

(E) painted many Native American tribes in their traditional settings before they were exterminated by disease, warfare, and white settlement.

QUESTIONS 114–115 refer to the following passage.

The late troubles in the eastern states . . . do not appear to threaten serious consequences. Even this evil is productive of good. It prevents the degeneracy of government, and nourishes a general attention to the public affairs. I hold it, that a little rebellion, now and then, is a good thing, and as necessary in the political world as storms in the physical. Unsuccessful rebellions, indeed, generally establish encroachments on the rights of the people, which have produced them . . . It is a medicine necessary for the sound health of government.

114. The above passage most closely represents the views of

(A) George Washington.

(D) John Jay.

(B) Abraham Lincoln.

(E) Thomas Jefferson.

(C) Alexander Hamilton.

115. The views expressed in the passage represent a reaction to

    (A)   the American Revolution.
    (B)   the Civil War.
    (C)   the Whiskey Rebellion.
    (D)   Shay's Rebellion.
    (E)   the War of 1812.

116. Contributors to German romantic idealism included

    I.   Immanuel Kant.
    II.   Johann G. Fichte.
    III. Georg Wilhelm Hegel.
    IV.   Auguste Comte.
    V.   Thomas Mann.

    (A)   I and III only
    (B)   I, II, and III only
    (C)   I, III, and V only
    (D)   II, III, and IV only
    (E)   I, II, III, IV, V

117. Points of contention with the Republican government that led to the Spanish Civil War included all of the following EXCEPT

    (A)   state control of education.
    (B)   the restriction of military influence.
    (C)   Catalonian autonomy.
    (D)   the seizure of Gibraltar.
    (E)   the extension of democracy throughout Spanish society.

118. The first American offensive operation in World War II took place at

    (A)   Wake Island.
    (B)   Guadalcanal.
    (C)   Midway Island.
    (D)   Tarawa.
    (E)   Saipan.

119. The major cities in Jeffersonian America functioned chiefly as

    (A) depots for international trade.

    (B) marketplaces for farmers to sell their goods.

    (C) transportation centers for the nation's growing railroad system.

    (D) centers of heavy industry and production of manufactured goods.

    (E) freight terminals for the nation's burgeoning canal systems.

120. European radicals and organizations identified with Syndicalism include

     I. Georges Sorel.

    II. *Confederacion Nacional del Trabajo.*

   III. Filippo Corridoni.

    IV. Pierre Laval.

     V. Michael Bakunin.

    (A) I and III only   (D) I, III, and IV only

    (B) I, II, and III only   (E) I, II, III, IV, V

    (C) II, III, and IV only

121. A 19th century novel which asserted the superiority of science to traditional ways of thinking was

    (A) *Les Misérables* by Hugo.

    (B) *Crime and Punishment* by Dostoyevsky.

    (C) *Degeneration* by Nordau.

    (D) *Frankenstein* by Shelley.

    (E) *Fathers and Sons* by Turgenev.

122. The Ballot Act, Civil Services Reform, the Education Act, and the Irish Land Act were accomplishments of

    (A) Benjamin Disraeli.   (D) Lord Roseberry.

    (B) Lord Salisbury.   (E) Arthur James Balfour.

    (C) William Gladstone.

123. The Battle of Antietam was important because

    I. it allowed Lincoln to announce the Emancipation Proclamation.

    II. it let Lincoln to fire General McClellan as commander of the Army of the Potomac.

    III. it successfully ended General Lee's first offensive into Union territory.

    (A) I only   (D) II and III only

    (B) III only   (E) I, II, and III

    (C) I and II only

124. Which one of the following individuals was an example of 19th century liberalism?

    (A) Pierre Joseph Proudhon   (D) Napoleon II

    (B) Benjamin Disraeli   (E) John Stuart Mill

    (C) François Fourier

125. World War I had all of the following effects on the United States EXCEPT

    (A) the creation of conditions which allowed prohibitionists to get the Eighteenth Amendment passed.

    (B) the creation of conditions which allowed women to get the right to vote.

    (C) the creation of conditions which made the United States the dominant international political power during the postwar years.

    (D) the creation of conditions which led thousands of blacks to migrate from southern plantations to northern factories.

    (E) the suppression of free speech, which was supported by the courts.

QUESTION 126 refers to the following illustration.

126. The above cartoon presents

   I. an argument in support of Britain's free trade policy.

   II. a criticism of Britain's free trade policy.

   III. a representation of the abuse of Britain's free trade policy by nations with restrictive tariffs.

   IV. a rationale for Britain to abandon its free trade policy.

   V. an image of the collapse of the British economy.

   (A) I Only

   (B) I, II, and III only

   (C) II, III, and IV only

   (D) II, III, IV, and V only

   (E) I, IV, and V only

127. All of the following are characteristic of the Stuart kings' attitudes toward England's North American colonies EXCEPT

   (A) they felt the colonies provided a method for rewarding court favorites for their loyalty with large grants of land.

   (B) they encouraged the development of the colonies as a valuable source of tax revenue for the crown.

   (C) they saw colonial demands for basic political rights as a treason that had to be halted before it spread.

   (D) they used the colonies as a dumping ground for troublesome political dissidents.

   (E) they encouraged the development of new colonies as a means of enhancing England's stature in Europe.

128. Grover Cleveland's 1884 election to the presidency was largely due to pivotal support from

   (A) the Mugwumps.

   (B) the Ku Klux Klan.

   (C) the Know-Nothings.

   (D) Tammany Hall.

   (E) organized labor.

129. All of the following contributed to the Great Depression EXCEPT

   (A) excessive stock and securities speculation.

    (B)   protectionist trade measures.

    (C)   huge farm debts resulting from collapsed crop prices.

    (D)   lack of credit to help consumers sustain economic growth.

    (E)   an imbalanced distribution of wealth in which the rich controlled far too much of the available income.

130. The Weber Thesis attempted to explain the connections between the rise of Calvinism and the rise of

    (A)   absolute monarchies.   (D)   Anglicanism.

    (B)   capitalism.   (E)   Catholicism.

    (C)   the nation-state.

131. The correct chronological order of German chancellors between 1890 and 1914 is

    (A)   Prince Hohenlohe, Count von Caprivi, Prince Bernhard von Bulow, and Bethmann-Hollweg.

    (B)   Count von Caprivi, Prince Hohenlohe, Prince Bernhard von Bulow, and Bethmann-Hollweg.

    (C)   Prince Bernhard von Bulow, Count von Caprivi, Prince Hohenlohe, and Bethmann-Hollweg.

    (D)   Prince Bernhard von Bulow, Prince Hohenlohe, Count von Caprivi, and Bethmann-Hollweg.

    (E)   Prince Hohenlohe, Prince Bernhard von Bulow, Bethmann-Hollweg, and Count von Caprivi.

132. The War of 1812 had all of the following effects EXCEPT

    (A)   strengthening American industrial and manufacturing production.

    (B)   virtually destroying the Federalist party as a credible opposition to the Republican party.

    (C)   restoring a sense of pride in most Americans that led to a wave of nationalism throughout the country.

    (D)   destroying the power of the Native-American tribes in the Northwest Territory.

    (E)   an increased and more active American role in world politics.

133. The most consistent supporter of Darwin's views on evolution was

    (A) Herbert Spencer.

    (B) George Bernard Shaw.

    (C) Samuel Butler.

    (D) Thomas Huxley.

    (E) Aldous Huxley.

134. "He seduced Heloise, the niece of an influential clergyman of Paris, which was bad enough for an influential theologian, and then made matters worse (by medieval standards) by marrying her, thus barring himself from promotion in the Church. As a result, when he was accused of heresy by St. Bernard, he had few friends."

    The person described in this passage is

    (A) William of Ockham.

    (B) Boniface VIII.

    (C) Philip Augustus.

    (D) Peter Abelard.

    (E) Frederick II.

135. The Tet Offensive is considered the decisive military operation by the North Vietnamese during the war for all of the following reasons EXCEPT

    (A) it was the first significant military victory by the North Vietnamese over U.S. military forces.

    (B) it significantly widened the credibility gap between the U.S. military's public statements and the public's beliefs about the war.

    (C) it resulted in American media coverage of the war taking a decidedly negative turn.

    (D) it prompted most Americans to stop thinking about winning the war and to start thinking about how to get out of the war.

    (E) it led Lyndon Johnson to offer to enter into peace negotiations with the North Vietnamese at any time or place.

136. The leadership of the Conservative and Labour parties in Britain was changed during the early 1960s as a result of the

    (A) deaths of Hugh Gaitskell and Sir Alec Douglas-Home.

    (B) death of Hugh Gaitskell and the Profumo affair.

    (C) collapse of the British economy and the Profumo affair.

(D) Profumo affair and the ascendancy of a new generation of leaders such as Edward Heath.

(E) death of Sir Alec Douglas-Home and the Profumo affair.

QUESTION 137 refers to the following illustration.

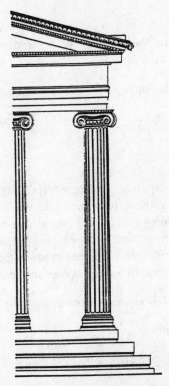

137. The illustration is representative of the Mycenaean and Egyptian influences and the delicate grace which are characteristic of the

(A) Doric column.

(B) Corinthian column.

(C) Ionic column.

(D) Attic column.

(E) None of the above.

138. The Persian threat to the independence of the Greek city-states concluded with

(A) the Peace of Callias.

(B) the Peace of Nicias.

(C) the victory at Zama.

(D) Xenophon's expedition.

(E) the triumph of Alexander.

139. The combination of European and African musical influences came together in 1890s New Orleans to form a new, distinctly American musical style called

    (A) gospel.

    (B) jazz.

    (C) folk.

    (D) country.

    (E) blues.

140. All of the following leaders may be viewed as "Enlightened" monarchs EXCEPT

    (A) Charles III of Spain.

    (B) Frederick the Great.

    (C) Joseph II.

    (D) Louis XV.

    (E) Catherine the Great.

141. "God has not been preparing the English-speaking and Teutonic peoples for a thousand years for nothing but vain, idle self-admiration. No! He has not made us the master organizers of the world to establish a system where chaos reigns. He has given us the spirit of progress to overwhelm the forces of reaction throughout the earth. He has made us adept in government that we may administer government among savage and senile peoples."

    The passage most nearly represents the philosophy of

    I. Manifest Destiny.

    II. American exceptionalism.

    III. Social Darwinism.

    (A) I only

    (B) III only

    (C) I and III only

    (D) II and III only

    (E) I, II, and III

142. The United States Supreme Court case of *Brown v. Board of Education of Topeka*

    (A) underscored the willingness of the federal government to strictly enforce civil rights legislation.

    (B) demonstrated the power of the Supreme Court to change public attitudes and behaviors in regard to civil rights.

    (C) led to street demonstrations by black Americans convinced that the courts would not support their efforts to achieve racial equality.

(D) demonstrated the inability of the Supreme Court to enforce anti-discrimination rulings without decisive government action to support those rulings.

(E) forced an immediate end to the practice of maintaining segregated public schools.

143. The German decision to implement the 'Final Solution"—the destruction of European Jewry—was made

(A) by Hitler soon after he came to power in 1933.

(B) at the Wanasee Conference.

(C) after the Normandy invasion.

(D) at a Nazi Party Congress held after the 1936 Berlin Olympics.

(E) by Hitler without consultation or support from others.

144. All of the following were 18th century French philosophers whose writings had a distinct impact on the political thinking of leaders of America's independence movement EXCEPT

(A) Montesquieu.

(B) Rousseau.

(C) Diderot.

(D) Descartes.

(E) Voltaire.

145. Jane Addams was a turn-of-the-century activist best known for her work in

(A) settlement houses.

(B) the temperance movement.

(C) nursing home care for war veterans.

(D) the suffrage movement.

(E) children's literature.

146. The Locarno Conference (1925)

I. was led by Briand and Stresemann.

II. resulted in treaties which affirmed existing boundaries.

III. resulted in agreements by the participants never to go to war against each other.

IV. outlawed war.

V. limited armaments.

(A) I and II only

(D) II, III, IV, and V only

(B) I, II, and III only

(E) I, II, III, IV, V

(C) I, III, and IV only

147. America's most polished and successful writer during the early 1800s was

(A) Sir Walter Scott.

(D) Washington Irving.

(B) Mark Twain.

(E) Edgar Allan Poe.

(C) James Fenimore Cooper.

148. Wladyslaw Gomulka, Alexander Dubcek, and Marshal Tito (Josip Broz) had in common the fact that they

(A) stood in opposition to de-Stalinization.

(B) abandoned socialism.

(C) saw their countries occupied by Soviet troops under the Brezhnev Doctrine.

(D) came into conflict with the Soviet Union.

(E) supported Mao Tse-tung in his conflict with Stalin.

QUESTION 149 refers to the following illustration.

149. The above painting, *The Starry Night* by Vincent van Gogh, is representative of the school of art known as

    (A) impressionism.

    (B) post-impressionism.

    (C) expressionism.

    (D) pointilism.

    (E) symbolism.

150. Historical research indicates that the long-term consequence of the Industrial Revolution for the working class was to

    (A) reduce their standard of living by removing them from their agricultural roots.

    (B) increase the length of their work day.

    (C) reduce the financial contribution of women to the family income.

    (D) increase their standard of living.

    (E) leave their standard of living at about the same level, but deprive them of the advantages provided by rural life.

151. Which of the following characterizes an important trend in family life in Europe in the 19th century?

    (A) Many middle-class mothers had their own business careers.

    (B) Two or three children per family became the norm.

    (C) Child mortality increased.

    (D) Large families became increasingly common.

    (E) The quality of medical care declined.

152. Churchill's removal from the position of First Lord of the Admiralty during the First World War was precipitated by the defeat at

    (A) Jutland.

    (B) Antwerp.

    (C) Gallipoli.

    (D) the Second Battle of the Marne.

    (E) Verdun.

153. The only senior member of Lyndon Johnson's administration to openly speak out against expansion of the American effort in Vietnam BEFORE the expansion was carried out was

    (A) Robert McNamara.   (D) Nicholas Katzenbach.

    (B) Dean Rusk.   (E) McGeorge Bundy.

    (C) George Ball.

154. "If slavery is not wrong, nothing is wrong! Slavery is a moral evil that cannot be allowed to expand into the western territories although we should not forcefully attempt to eliminate it in states that already allow it. Black Americans are the equal of every living man in their right to life, liberty and the fruit of their own labor. But they are not yet educated enough nor qualified for the full legal rights of citizenship."

    This passage most nearly represents the views of

    (A) Stephen A. Douglas.   (D) Abraham Lincoln.

    (B) John Brown.   (E) Dred Scott.

    (C) John C. Breckenridge.

155. The "Red Scare" of 1919 was primarily caused by

    (A) the release of the Zimmerman papers.

    (B) bombings of government facilities and industrial plants by agents of the Comintern.

    (C) Lenin's promise to bury capitalism, starting with the United States.

    (D) a rash of massive labor strikes and disputes affecting millions of American workers.

    (E) the invasion of Poland by Soviet military forces.

156. The principal advocate for adopting a British-style government for 18th century France was

    (A) Voltaire.   (D) Montesquieu.

    (B) Rousseau.   (E) Diderot.

    (C) Quesnay.

157. Which colonial group would have been most likely to agree with the statement "All men are created equal"?

(A) The Pilgrims

(B) The Puritans

(C) Dutch Patroons

(D) The Quakers

(E) Colonial Anglicans

158. "The only way to erect such a common power as may be able to defend them from the invasion of foreigners and the injuries of one another, and thereby secure them in such sort as that by their own industry and by the fruits of the earth they may nourish themselves and live contentedly, is to confer all their power and strength upon one man, or upon one assembly of men, that they may reduce their wills by plurality of voices unto one will . . . ."

This theory of government most nearly represents the views of

(A) John Locke.

(B) Jean Bodin.

(C) John Napier.

(D) Baron de Montesquieu.

(E) Thomas Hobbes.

159. The first state in Europe to initiate social legislation such as old age, accident, and workmen's compensation was

(A) Switzerland.

(B) Britain.

(C) France.

(D) Germany.

(E) Belgium.

160. Which of the following would a Fabian Socialist be most likely to approve of?

(A) Adam Smith's *Wealth of Nations*

(B) Government-owned utilities

(C) Laissez-faire policies.

(D) An increase in the budget for the British navy

(E) Government subsidies to private corporations

161. Which of the following would historians find LEAST acceptable as an explanation of why the Union had such a difficult time defeating the Confederacy?

(A) Many of the nation's most skilled military leaders joined the Confederacy when the Southern states seceded.

(B) Southerners were more motivated to fight and make sacrifices because they were fighting to defend their own rights and territories.

(C) To win the war, the South had only to defend itself and survive, while the Union had to mount an invasion force to militarily defeat Southern armies and occupy Southern territory.

(D) The South's emphasis on states' rights allowed more decision making at the local level, which allowed it to adjust more flexibly to the changing war situation.

(E) Political interference from Washington often hindered the development and implementation of effective military action against the South.

162. The primary cause of the large increase in the population of Europe from 1700 to 1900 was

(A) better medical care.

(B) increases in the food supply.

(C) immigration from the New World.

(D) government policies encouraging a high birth rate.

(E) increasing urbanization.

163. The turn-of-the-century black leader who refused to accept second-class citizenship for blacks and founded the National Association for the Advancement of Colored People (NAACP) for the purpose of fighting racial disrimination through the courts was

(A) Marcus Garvey.   (D) W. E. B. DuBois.

(B) Booker T. Washington.   (E) Hiram Revels.

(C) George Washington Carver.

164. The early support for Mussolini's Fascist regime was NOT based upon

(A) fear of communism.   (D) industrialists and landowners.

(B) labor unrest.   (E) the Church.

(C) the anxiety of the middle class.

165. The concept of Irish Home Rule was supported by

    I. Daniel O'Connell.

    II. Charles Stewart Parnell.

    III. Lord Salisbury.

    IV. William Gladstone.

    V. Joseph Chamberlain.

    (A) I, II, III, IV, V

    (B) I and II only

    (C) I, II, and III only

    (D) I, II, and IV only

    (E) I, IV, and V only

166. Beginning in the 1830s, paintings ranging from George Caleb Bingham's "The Verdict of the People" to William Sydney Mount's "Rustic Dance After a Sleigh Ride" to the thousands of sentimental prints produced by Currier and Ives most clearly reflected the spirit of

    (A) Alexander Hamilton's political philosophy.

    (B) John Adams' political philosophy.

    (C) Andrew Jackson's political philosophy.

    (D) George Washington's political philosophy.

    (E) Abraham Lincoln's political philosophy.

167. One of the chief reasons for the failure of the Articles of Confederation was

    (A) their focus on the separation of powers within the federal branch of government.

    (B) their failure to adequately curb the powers of the executive branch of government.

    (C) their failure to provide women and free blacks with the right to vote.

    (D) their lack of an adequate mechanism for Congress to force states to comply with its decisions.

    (E) their strict tax collection provisions, which raised resentments among the smaller states who believed that they were being overtaxed while the larger states were being undertaxed.

QUESTION 168 refers to the following illustration.

168. The painting by Salvador Dali illustrates the 20th century style of painting known as

    (A) Dadaism.

    (B) Fauvism.

    (C) cubism.

    (D) surrealism.

    (E) impressionism.

169. As president, Woodrow Wilson could have been influenced in his Progressivist ideals by all of the following EXCEPT

    (A) Thorstein Veblen's *The Theory of the Leisure Class.*

    (B) Sinclair Lewis's *Babbitt.*

    (C) Thorstein Veblen's *The Instinct of Workmanship.*

    (D) Upton Sinclair's *The Jungle.*

    (E) Frederick Taylor's *Dynamic Sociology.*

170. The success of the Liberal party in 1906 cannot be attributed to the party's

    (A) advocacy of a land reform policy which would aid the lower classes.

    (B) commitment to expanding the defense budget.

(C) condemnation of the Boer War.

(D) identification with a free trade policy.

(E) recognition that some restrictions had to be introduced to regulate working conditions.

171. While Puritanism encompassed a number of religious groups, its core was based upon the doctrines of

(A) Martin Luther.

(B) Jacob Hutter.

(C) Zwingli and Calvin.

(D) John Hus.

(E) Michael Servetus.

172. The permanency of the Franco-German boundary was guaranteed by the

(A) Munich Accord.

(B) Kellogg-Briand Pact.

(C) Paris-Berlin Peace Pact.

(D) Dawes Plan.

(E) Geneva Conference.

173. Benedict Arnold was involved in which of the following?

I. The American victory over the British at Saratoga

II. The American victory over the British at Cowpens

III. An abortive attempt to help the British capture West Point

(A) II only

(B) III only

(C) I and III only

(D) II and III only

(E) I, II, and III

174. From 1815 through 1830, American industrial development was LEAST impeded by which of the following barriers to growth?

(A) British tariffs on American goods

(B) Resistance to technological advancement by most American citizens

(C) An inadequate system of higher education

(D) A poor communications network

(E) Lack of a cheap and reliable transportation system

175. All of the following were considered liberal developments during the first half of the 19th century EXCEPT

    (A) the *Statuto*.

    (B) Chartism.

    (C) the Factory Act of 1833.

    (D) the July Ordinances.

    (E) the July Monarchy.

176. The wave of French anticlerical legislation, which included the Association Act and the repudiation of the Concordat of 1801, was identified with the

    (A) Boulanger Crisis.

    (B) Dreyfus Affair.

    (C) Panama Scandal.

    (D) War in Sight Crisis.

    (E) Paris Commune.

QUESTIONS 177–178 refer to the following graph.

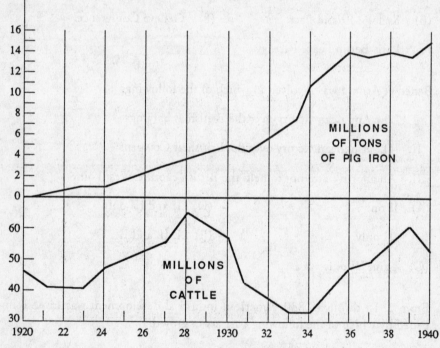

177. The nation most likely depicted by the graph is

    (A) France.

    (B) Germany.

    (C) the Soviet Union.

    (D) Portugal.

    (E) Spain.

178. Which of these can be reasonably concluded from the above graph?

    (A) The Great Depression was the major cause of production declines from 1928 to 1934.

    (B) The precipitous rise in pig iron production was a response to German rearmament.

    (C) Low pig iron production at the beginning of the 1920s reflects the destruction wrought by World War I.

    (D) High pig iron production and high cattle production are mutually exclusive.

    (E) Between 1923 and 1933, cattle production increases and then decreases in five-year intervals.

___

179. All of the following were characteristic of the 1920s EXCEPT

    (A) liberal trends in fashion and morality.

    (B) prohibition and bootlegging.

    (C) consumerism and easy credit.

    (D) massive union power and growth.

    (E) Klu Klux Klan power and popularity.

180. During the late 1940s, the United Nations urged its members to remove their diplomats from

    (A) Argentina.   (D) North Korea.

    (B) Spain.   (E) South Africa.

    (C) Portugal.

181. Anti-clericalism was a theme in all of the following works EXCEPT

    (A) Boccaccio's *Decameron.*

    (B) Chaucer's *Canterbury Tales.*

    (C) Thomas More's *Utopia.*

    (D) Erasmus's *Praise of Folly.*

    (E) Thomas à Kempis's *The Imitation of Christ.*

182. The English Chartist's "People's Charter" demanded

    I.   secret ballots.

    II. universal male suffrage.

    III. equal electoral districts.

    IV. annual Parliaments.

    V.   salary payments for members of Parliament.

    (A) I, II, and III only   (D) I, IV, and V only

    (B) I, II, III, and IV only   (E) I, II, III, IV, V

    (C) II, III, and IV only

183. The policies of Harry Truman were most likely to have been supported by

    (A) urban ethnic groups.   (D) southern democrats.

    (B) organized labor.   (E) industry leaders.

    (C) northern liberals.

184. During the "Liberal Regime" of Louis Philippe, radical economic and social plans were advanced by all of the following EXCEPT

    (A) Saint-Simon.   (D) Auguste Blanqui.

    (B) Charles Fourier.   (E) Pierre Joseph Proudhon.

    (C) Louis Blanc.

185. The "Fifty Million Bill" represented a diplomatic philosophy most similar to that of

    (A) Grover Cleveland.   (D) William Howard Taft.

    (B) Teddy Roosevelt.   (E) Woodrow Wilson.

    (C) William McKinley.

186. Italian Renaissance art can be most appropriately described as

    (A) neoclassicism in which the traditional characteristics of harmony and symmetry were valued.

(B) a revolt against the classical style and the advancement of a new artistic standard based on humanism.

(C) characterized by the spectacular and the deliberately nonsymmetrical.

(D) romantic idealism predicated upon notions of secular fantasy.

(E) the triumph of symbolism.

187. Which of the following explanations would historians find LEAST acceptable for Colonel G. A. Custer's defeat at the Little Bighorn?

(A) Custer split his force into three separate forces who were unable to support each other in the face of a numerically superior enemy, virtually guaranteeing defeat.

(B) Custer attacked the Sioux encampment on the Little Bighorn without effectively scouting the disposition of the entire encampment.

(C) Custer's men panicked when they found themselves being surrounded by overwhelming numbers of Sioux warriors and their panic prevented them from mounting an effective defense.

(D) Custer disobeyed orders from his superiors by attacking the Sioux encampment with his regiment before infantry support under the command of General Terry arrived.

(E) The Sioux were much better armed and led than Custer and the rest of the U.S. army realized.

188. Construed as an intellectual threat to the Church, early 16th century Humanism

(A) argued that the episcopal order of the Roman church should be altered.

(B) maintained that the true source of authority within the Church was scripture.

(C) condemned the Church for not addressing the needs of the poor.

(D) identified with the "New Science," which the Church opposed.

(E) challenged papal supremacy.

189. All of these were important experimental dramatists between the two world wars EXCEPT

    (A) Maxwell Anderson.   (D) Clifford Odets.

    (B) Elmer Rice.   (E) Eugene O'Neill.

    (C) Edward Albee.

190. Which of these statements accurately describes American voting rights during the colonial era?

    I. Since the land requirement could be easily met, about three-quarters of adult freedmen could vote.

    II. Many colonies proscribed non-Protestants from voting, and some proscribed radical Protestant sects as well.

    III. American voting rights were based on British voting rights.

    IV. A group of five American slaves counted for three votes.

    V. Women were barred from voting in only a few colonies.

    (A) I, II, and III   (D) I, II, III, and V

    (B) I, III, and IV   (E) I, II, and V

    (C) II, III, and IV

GRE History – Test 3

ANSWER KEY

1.	(D)	26.	(A)	51.	(D)	76.	(E)
2.	(E)	27.	(E)	52.	(E)	77.	(D)
3.	(C)	28.	(B)	53.	(C)	78.	(B)
4.	(B)	29.	(A)	54.	(D)	79.	(D)
5.	(E)	30.	(E)	55.	(D)	80.	(B)
6.	(E)	31.	(E)	56.	(B)	81.	(C)
7.	(E)	32.	(C)	57.	(D)	82.	(D)
8.	(C)	33.	(D)	58.	(E)	83.	(D)
9.	(C)	34.	(B)	59.	(C)	84.	(A)
10.	(B)	35.	(A)	60.	(B)	85.	(E)
11.	(A)	36.	(E)	61.	(C)	86.	(B)
12.	(E)	37.	(C)	62.	(E)	87.	(B)
13.	(E)	38.	(C)	63.	(A)	88.	(B)
14.	(C)	39.	(E)	64.	(E)	89.	(B)
15.	(B)	40.	(D)	65.	(B)	90.	(C)
16.	(C)	41.	(B)	66.	(D)	91.	(C)
17.	(A)	42.	(B)	67.	(C)	92.	(E)
18.	(B)	43.	(A)	68.	(B)	93.	(B)
19.	(E)	44.	(A)	69.	(D)	94.	(D)
20.	(A)	45.	(E)	70.	(B)	95.	(D)
21.	(B)	46.	(B)	71.	(A)	96.	(C)
22.	(B)	47.	(C)	72.	(D)	97.	(B)
23.	(C)	48.	(C)	73.	(B)	98.	(C)
24.	(E)	49.	(C)	74.	(E)	99.	(E)
25.	(D)	50.	(B)	75.	(C)	100.	(B)

101.	(B)	126.	(C)	151.	(B)	176.	(B)
102.	(C)	127.	(C)	152.	(C)	177.	(C)
103.	(B)	128.	(A)	153.	(C)	178.	(E)
104.	(D)	129.	(D)	154.	(D)	179.	(D)
105.	(C)	130.	(B)	155.	(D)	180.	(B)
106.	(D)	131.	(B)	156.	(D)	181.	(E)
107.	(A)	132.	(E)	157.	(D)	182.	(E)
108.	(A)	133.	(D)	158.	(E)	183.	(A)
109.	(C)	134.	(D)	159.	(D)	184.	(D)
110.	(C)	135.	(A)	160.	(B)	185.	(B)
111.	(E)	136.	(B)	161.	(D)	186.	(A)
112.	(B)	137.	(C)	162.	(B)	187.	(C)
113.	(C)	138.	(A)	163.	(D)	188.	(B)
114.	(E)	139.	(B)	164.	(E)	189.	(C)
115.	(D)	140.	(D)	165.	(D)	190.	(D)
116.	(B)	141.	(E)	166.	(C)		
117.	(D)	142.	(D)	167.	(D)		
118.	(B)	143.	(B)	168.	(D)		
119.	(A)	144.	(D)	169.	(B)		
120.	(B)	145.	(A)	170.	(B)		
121.	(E)	146.	(B)	171.	(C)		
122.	(C)	147.	(D)	172.	(C)		
123.	(E)	148.	(D)	173.	(C)		
124.	(E)	149.	(B)	174.	(A)		
125.	(C)	150.	(D)	175.	(D)		

DETAILED EXPLANATIONS OF ANSWERS

Test 3

1.   (D)   The Delian League was established in 477 BC after more than two decades of war (V) with Persian armies led by Darius and Xerxes (I). Under Athenian leadership, the Delian League was intended to provide a defensive and offensive alliance directed against Persia. Not until later was the Delian League interpreted as an Athenian attempt to dominate the Greek, not Mediterranean, world (III) for its own gain. The Spartan threat to Athens (IV) did not materialize until the early years of the Peloponnesian War in the late 430s.

2.   (E)   In 1190, the Holy Roman Empire (E) was preoccupied with the Third Crusade and did not experience any peasant uprisings. A popular uprising known as the Jacquerie broke out in France in 1358 (A), and in England in 1381 (D) the Great or Peasant Revolt occurred, as the lower classes protested the immense tax burdens imposed by the fiscal demands of the Hundred Years' War. The "Sicilian Vespers" took place in Sicily in 1282 (B) when the people rebelled against French rule, and the peasants and laborers in Flanders in 1302 (C) followed the Sicilian example and expelled French rulers from Flanders.

3.   (C)   In *A Study of History,* a religious-based philosophy of history was advanced by Arnold Toynbee (C). William McNeill (B) wrote *The Rise of the West;* Oswald Spengler (A) wrote *The Decline of the West;* T. S. Eliot (D) and Christopher Dawson (E) were influenced by religion and religious values.

4.   (B)   Scalawags were poor and middle-income Southerners, mostly farmers from the mountainous interior of the Southern states, who supported the Republican-led Reconstruction governments. These people had generally opposed secession, as they rarely owned slaves, and did not usually agree with the states' rights positions taken by the wealthy aristocrats who dominated Southern state governments. They also resisted Confederate efforts to force them to fight in what they saw as a "rich man's war." As a result, they often suffered greatly under the rule of Confederate leaders during the Civil War, and it was only natural that they would support Republicans, Northern or Southern, when the war ended and the Democratic-led Confederate administrations were removed. Carpetbaggers (A) were Northerners who moved to the South after the Civil War and ran Southern businesses and Southern governments. The term reflects Southern hostility toward the North and toward Yankees in general. Copperheads (C) were Northern Democrats who, during

the Civil War, favored some sort of peace agreement with the Southern states rather than fighting to force the South to return to the Union. Freedmen (D) were former slaves who were freed by the Union victory in the Civil War. The term is most closely associated with the Freedman's Bureau, which worked throughout the South during the first years of Reconstruction to help former slaves resettle themselves and protect their rights. During the waning years of Reconstruction, when Southern voters voted Reconstructionist Republicans out of office and replaced them with Democrats, Southerners said that the state had been redeemed from the clutches of Yankee Reconstructionism. The leaders of these new post-Reconstruction Democratic administrations were called "redeemers" (E).

5.   (E)   Cardinal Richilieu opposed the Huguenots at La Rochelle (A), supported the Swedes during the third phase of the Thirty Years' War (B), and opposed the Catholic Hapsburgs (D) during the same struggle. He was the adviser to Louis XIII (C), and was the most powerful man in France for many years. Richilieu died six years before the Peace of Westphalia (E).

6.   (E)   Lenin's New Economic Policy of 1921 reflected the practical realization that capitalism, at least on a small scale, was necessary for the survival of the new Soviet state. Under this policy, Lenin encouraged a partial restoration of capitalism (I), allowing a limited amount of private retail trade (IV) and some private operation of small industries. Lenin realized that the state needed to concentrate on larger issues, such as state control of large industries (II) and transportation and foreign trade (III).

7.   (E)   Based on the accounts of Thucydides and subsequent historians, the Peloponnesian War was caused by several factors, including fear of Athenian power as exercised through the Delian League (A), the general Greek love of liberty (B) for the independent city-states, trade rivalry (C) between Athens and some of the other city-states, particularly Corinth, and Athenian advocacy of revolutionary policies (D), such as democracy and Ionian cultural values. While the leaders of Corinth were ambitious, they were more interested in containing Athens than dominating the Greek world (E).

8.   (C)   As a result of the Italian-Turkish War of 1911–12, Italy obtained Tripoli (Libya) (C). Italy did not acquire islands in the eastern Mediterranean (A), the East African colony of Yemen (B), or trading rights throughout the Ottoman Empire (D). During the early 20th century, Italian political leaders expressed the national ambition for empire which, with the failure of Versailles to expand Italian dominions, contributed to the ascendency of Italian fascism and Mussolini.

9.   (C)   Many historians have already compared Ronald Reagan's presidency to that of Warren Harding. Both men were charismatic Republicans who were elected after discredited Democratic administrations. Both men supported laissez-faire economic and business policies. Both men were well liked and seen as honest, yet were

surrounded by corruption and political scandal. Both men survived these political scandals with their reputations and popularity intact. Both men set economic trends in motion that would lead to problems after they left office—Harding's policies eventually led to the Great Depression, while Reagan's policies eventually led to the Savings and Loan scandal and the huge budget deficits which plagued the United States in the early 1990s.

10. **(B)** In Roman political thought and history, Cicero has been identified as a defender of the Republic and Octavian as the founder of the Empire. An appropriate analogy within Greek history would be Pericles, who supported the basic tenets of Athenian democracy, and Plato, who opposed democracy as unworkable and unworthy (B). Aristotle (A) and (C), while differing from Plato in process and form, concurred with the basic political philosophy of his teacher. Marcus Aurelius (D) was a Roman emperor and philosopher during the 2nd century AD. In his *Meditations*, he explored alternatives and advanced prescriptions for leading a sound life; nonetheless, he supported the imperial system. Virgil (E), author of *The Aeneid* and the leading figure of the "Golden Age of Latin Letters," supported the establishment of the Empire.

11. **(A)** The passage was written by John Jay, a leader of the Federalist political faction that favored a strong central government. John Adams (A) was another leading spokesman for this group, and the above passage also represents his views. Each of the remaining choices, Thomas Jefferson (B), George Clinton (C), Patrick Henry (D), and James Monroe (E) were supporters of the opposing viewpoint, and were known as the Anti-Federalists. These people believed in a very weak central government with few powers. They believed in states' rights, and that government power should be maintained at the local level as much as possible, to protect the rights of the people from potential abuse.

12. **(E)** The passage is a quotation from the writings of John Jay, in *The Federalist* Papers (*The Federalist*, Number 4), in which he argued for the need for a strong central government to prevent European contempt and protect against European intervention in the United States. The Declaration of Independence (A) dealt with reasons for the American colonies to break free from British control. It did not specifically deal with the role of a new American government. The Monroe Doctrine (C) dealt with American foreign policy toward European intervention in the Americas outside of the United States, not the type of government the United States needed to avoid European meddling in U.S. domestic policy. *The American Crisis* (D), a pamphlet by Thomas Paine, dealt with the then current difficulties posed by the American Revolution. It did not deal specifically with the role of an American government because events had not yet progressed far enough for that type of discussion. It was the lack of powers allowed the federal government by the Articles of Confederation (B) that led to the demands for a new Constitution. The Articles do not discuss a federal government with the powers implied in the above passage.

13. **(E)** St. Jerome (A) (*The Vulgate*), St. Augustine (B) (*City of God* and *Confessions*), St. Gregory the Great (C), and St. Ambrose (D), the courageous Bishop of Milan during the 4th century, were Fathers of the Church. St. Paul (E) was an early disciple of Christ who lived in the first century. As Fathers of the Church, the writings and thoughts of these early Christians have endured the turbulence of the Reformation and the impact of secularism.

14. **(C)** The "Silver Age of Latin Letters" is most frequently identified with the reign of Marcus Aurelius (161–180 AD). During this period, the value of cultural accomplishments and activities was appreciated. Marcus Aurelius was a philosopher and the author of *Meditations*. Other contributors to the Silver Age include the historians Tacitus, Suetonius, Pliny the Younger, the biographer Plutarch, and the satirist Lucian.

15. **(B)** The Doctrine of Nullification was developed by John C. Calhoun in 1828, as a means of protection from what many Southerners saw as the "tyranny of the (Northern) majority." This doctrine claimed that individual states could choose to ignore federal mandates or laws if they found those laws offensive or unfair. A leading spokesman for this philosophy was South Carolina Senator Robert Hayne. He led an impassioned argument for nullification in the United States Senate in 1830, in which he debated the issue head-to-head with Senator Daniel Webster (C), who led the forces opposing nullification. In 1832, Hayne led South Carolina to vote for nullification in response to an unpopular federal tariff. Andrew Jackson (A), despite his sympathy for Southern concerns, was a nationalist and vehemently opposed the entire concept of nullification. He ordered the tariff to be collected and threatened military action if Southerners resisted collection efforts. Some South Carolinians began discussing secession. The crisis was resolved through the passage of a compromise tariff, leading to repeal of the nullification law by South Carolina. Martin Van Buren (D) was Andrew Jackson's vice-president and never took a decisive stand on the nullification issue. As president, Van Buren was never forced to confront the issue and, again, never took a strong position either way. John H. Eaton (E) was Jackson's secretary of war. He did not take a strong public position on the nullification issue; however, as the person who would have to enforce any military action taken against states invoking nullification, he expressed no reservations about carrying out such enforcement.

16. **(C)** Physical punishment (I) was the norm for disciplining children, as most religions preached the "spare the rod, spoil the child" philosophy. Children were treated as miniature adults and were expected to conform to adult standards of behavior. Behavioral standards were strict and punishments were severe for both adults and children when those standards were broken. Most families bore children who did survive until adulthood to bear their own children (II). Life expectancies, particularly in the South, increased during this period, as did the population in the colonies. Women, however, did not set the moral standards for their children, nor did they decide how the children were to be educated or trained (III). Those duties

were considered to be the husband's responsibilities, although it was the wife's duty to enforce her husband's decisions where children were concerned.

17.   **(A)**   The theory of supply-side economics most closely resembles the ideas of Adam Smith. This theory was embraced by Ronald Reagan as a key part of his solution to the economic problems facing the United States in 1981. Reagan's approach came to be called "Reaganomics" and was largely based on Adam Smith's ideas of laissez-faire economics, which emphasized the need for a free market unhindered by cumbersome government regulations. Smith believed that the laws of supply and demand would force the market to regulate itself and if government would leave the market unregulated then business leaders would be free to make the best investments for the good of all, resulting in economic prosperity over the long run. Reagan's supply-side economics focused on reducing the size of government and deregulating the marketplace as much as possible, in addition to lowering the tax burdens on both individuals and industries; just the prescription Adam Smith had written about in his laissez-faire philosophy. Mercantilism (B) dealt mainly with the idea of a mother country controlling the economy of its colonies as a way to increase the wealth of the mother country and increase economic control over the colony. This philosophy required strict regulation of economic activity, at least in colonial territories, and in many ways was the antithesis of Adam Smith's arguments. Keynesian theory (C), Progressivism (D), and Socialist theory (E) are all dissimilar to the ideas of Adam Smith in that they argue for massive government spending and government regulation of economic activity.

18.   **(B)**   Liberal and/or nationalist revolutions broke out in all of the major countries of Europe in 1848 except England and Russia. The English had developed representative institutions and had a clear understanding of national identity; the Russian regime had suppressed liberal and nationalist dissenters.

19.   **(E)**   During the Hellenistic period, the principal trade routes from east to west were the northern route from Bactria across the Caspian Sea to the Black Sea (A), a central route by sea from India to the Persian Gulf and up the river Tigris to Seleuceia (B), and a southern route from India by sea around Arabia and up the Red Sea (C). The northern route from the Aral Sea along the northern shore of the Caspian Sea to the west through the Sea of Azov (D) was used less frequently. The northern route (E) from the Caspian and Black Seas through the Danube Valley did not exist during this period.

20.   **(A)**   Britain's relationship with its dominions was addressed in the Balfour Report of 1926 (A). The Balfour Declaration of 1917 (B) supported the concept of an Israeli state. The Government of India Act of 1933 (C) stated that the independence of India would be recognized. The Beveridge Report (D) of 1943 was a plan for the socialization of Britain. The British Nationality Act of 1948 (E) stipulated that citizens of the empire were citizens of Great Britain and that each dominion could determine the terms for citizenship.

21. **(B)** During the late 2nd century BC, Roman political life was dominated by the prevailing political parties: *Populares*, the so-called "people's party"; *Optimates*, the "best men"; and the *Equites*, rich knights (B). The First Triumvirate (A) did not appear until the next century. The Gracchi (C), Tiberius and Gaius Gracchus, were significant public figures but did not hold substantive power. The Punic Wars (D) concluded in 146 BC; they did not dominate Roman political life. Finally, the dictatorship of Sulla (E) did not occur until 82–79 BC.

22. **(B)** While Mexico had recognized Texas as an independent republic in 1845 (A), the Mexican government refused to recognize Texas claims that it controlled the land between the Nueces River and the Rio Grande. The dispute simmered until Texas joined the United States in December 1845, and the United States also claimed the disputed land. Mexico did not like, but was reluctantly willing to accept, American annexation of Texas (E). However, Mexican leaders refused to accept American annexation of the disputed lands south and west of the Nueces River. When the United States laid claim to the land, Mexico broke diplomatic relations (B) and both sides geared for war. While Mexican authorities did not like the increasing flow of Americans into California, New Mexico, and Arizona, this influx of Anglos did not yet constitute a large enough threat to cause a war (C). However, once war started, many Americans in the region joined efforts to overthrow Mexican rule. While some Americans welcomed war with Mexico as an opportunity to annex all of Mexico (D), most did not. Many feared, due to racial bias, that the large native population could not be assimilated into the American mainstream. Others refused to support American annexation of land already densely populated with nonwhite peoples, believing it would have to be ruled as a colony rather than join the Union as an equal state.

23. **(C)** The cartoon illustrates the struggle between Bismarck and the Catholic church, known as the *Kulturkampf* (C). Bismarck wanted to break the power of the Catholic Center party; he initiated a series of anti-Catholic policies in an attempt to do so. German dualism and the German Civil War (A) of 1866 refer to the Austrian-Prussian alliance known as the German Confederation and the war that first annexed the territories of Schleswig and Holstein and then became the so-called Seven Weeks' War, in which Bismarck permanently destroyed Austrian power in Germany. The War in Sight Crisis (B) with France was a result of Bismarck's attempts to implicate France in an international Catholic conspiracy against Germany. Britain and Russia insisted that Bismarck put an end to his warmongering, and war was averted. Petrine Supremacy and the concept of papal infallibility (D) were long-standing points of contention between the Roman Catholic church and the Protestants and the Eastern branches of the Church. Secularism (E) was not a theme of this cartoon.

24. **(E)** During the 15th and 16th centuries, Portugal established a series of commercial centers in its colonial empire. Goa (A) in India, Malacca (B) in Southeast Asia, and Canton (C) and Macao (D) in China served as such centers. Trinidad

(E), off the northern coast of South America, was a Spanish settlement which supported trade in the region.

25. **(D)** English political leaders were aware of James I's support of Divine Right prior to his ascendency to the throne in 1603; his *The True Law of Free Monarchy* (B) was published in 1601. He offended Puritan leaders with his lack of support at the Hampton Court Conference (A); alienated the general public with his relationship with the Duke of Buckingham (E); and outraged the legal community with his dismissal of Sir Edward Coke (C) as the chief justice of the Court of Common Pleas. However, his failure to recognize the historic right of Parliament was most evident in his treatment of the Addled Parliament (D) of 1614.

26. **(A)** The Enlightenment was an intellectual revolution which judged the ability of human reasoning to be supreme. This period is often called the Age of Reason. The great thinkers of the Enlightenment described a world of physical, natural, and social laws; one could achieve a perfect and complete understanding of these laws through the consistent application of reason. Benjamin Franklin, probably more than any other American of his time, was the embodiment of this philosophy. Franklin was a brilliant writer and inventor. He often refused large sums of money, giving away his inventions so that they could be used to better the lives of his fellow Americans. He was a philosopher who spent time in Paris with many of the European leaders of the Enlightenment. He actively promoted Enlightenment positions in his speeches and conversations in the United States. Franklin had little to do with the Great Awakening (B), which was a widespread conversion to more traditional religious beliefs during the mid-1700s in America. Franklin's belief that human reason was supreme was in direct contradiction to the dependence on God promoted by the Great Awakening. As a leader of the American Revolution, Franklin could not have been a representative of the loyalist movement (C), which called for the colonies to remain a part of the British Empire. Neither the abolitionist (D) or prohibition (E) movements would gain significant momentum in the United States until well after Franklin's death.

27. **(E)** The state governments during Reconstruction were not ineffective and actually did a surprisingly effective job, beginning the Herculean task of rebuilding the South's infrastructure. Housing, roads, railroads, and industry all needed to be rebuilt, almost from scratch. The plantation system was in ruins, as was the entire Southern economy. Reconstruction governments founded the South's first adequate public education systems and helped establish a whole range of public services, such as facilities to care for the poor and the mentally ill. Voting rights were expanded for the first time, resulting in poor and middle class voters electing representatives from their own economic class. While these governments were not demonstrably superior to those which preceded them (D), they were certainly no less efficient, and managed to accomplish much that pre–Civil War governments did not (E). Many of the problems that kept Reconstruction governments from doing a better job stemmed from active resistance to needed reforms by Southern whites, who resented being represented by Yankees or blacks. Many of the notable reforms enacted by these

governments were eliminated by the conservative white Democrats who regained power after Reconstruction ended. Reconstruction office holders were just as qualified, albeit less experienced, as those who preceded them, and while white Democrats portrayed all of their problems as resulting from illiterate blacks running the government, the evidence does not support this racist argument (A). While greed and corruption certainly existed in Reconstruction governments (C), there is no evidence that it was worse than the corruption that existed in Southern state governments before or during the Civil War, or that it made Reconstruction governments less efficient. Finally, there is no evidence that tight restrictions associated with Union military control prevented Reconstruction governments from operating effectively (B).

28. **(B)** After Alexander the Great's death in 323 BC, his empire was divided into three major units: Antigonid Macedonia (I), with a monarchy limited by an armed population; Seleucid Asia (II), with a monarchy restricted by autonomous cities; and Ptolemaic Egypt (III), with an unrestricted monarchy. As the Seleucid Empire later disintegrated, Bactria (IV) emerged as a buffer against the barbarians of the East. Most of India (V) was not included in Alexander's empire, although he did penetrate northwest India during his campaigns.

29. **(A)** The industrialization of the Old South is the only effect listed that was not a direct result of the railroad building in the last half of the 19th century. Most railroad construction linked factories and consumers in the Northeast with Midwest farmers and Far West miners and farmers. Railroad construction lagged in the South by comparison. The South remained primarily a rural agricultural region well into the 20th century; industrialization would not flourish there until the rail industry had passed its peak and was beginning its mid-20th century decline. The completion of America's rail network was a feat of monumental proportions, leading to dramatic changes in the lives of most Americans. Goods could now be shipped from the most distant corner of the land to virtually anywhere else in the country within a few days (B). This allowed farmers access to markets which would otherwise have been denied them. It allowed for more efficient distribution of goods throughout the country. It also made the country smaller in that one could now travel from coast to coast in just six to ten days (D), whereas the trip could take weeks or months by horse and wagon. Before the railroads, time was kept by individual communities according to the position of the sun overhead. This led to confusion as a traveler went from one community to the next, and made it nearly impossible for the railroads to draw up workable timetables for their trains. In response, the railroads drew up plans for a national system of time zones, in which every community within a specific zone would share the same local time (E). Eventually this system was universally adopted and evolved into the four time zones which exist today. Finally, railroad construction and development led to some important technical improvements in areas like boiler construction, air brakes, automatic coupling devices, steel construction techniques, and bridge building (C).

30. (E) World War II brought about dramatic social and economic changes that affected virtually every group of Americans in one way or another. During the war, more than 7 million women entered the military and industrial labor force. Despite severe criticism from sociologists and others who blamed everything from divorce to juvenile delinquency on working women, most women hoped to keep working after the war ended. World War II sparked changes in women's expectations and roles (A) that eventually led to the women's liberation movement of the 1960s. World War II also accelerated social changes for black Americans. More than 1 million blacks migrated to cities to find employment during the war and more than 2.5 million blacks either served in the military or worked in industrial jobs (both record numbers). While the government paid only lip service to civil rights, blacks joined civil rights organizations in droves, and the raised expectations of this era laid much of the groundwork for the civil rights crusades of the late 1950s and early 1960s. World War II also led to the legal migration of hundreds of thousands of Mexicans to the United States to meet the need for farm workers in the American Southwest. During the war, the United States established the "work hands" program in 1942 to encourage Mexicans to migrate northward to fill the need for farm laborers. Finally, World War II reignited the mass movement of Americans from rural areas to the cities. This trend had stalled in the 1930s during the Depression, but the war effort led to the creation of millions of jobs in urban areas, and people flocked from rural areas to seek employment opportunities in the cities. During the war, the percentage of Americans who lived in cities swelled from 46% to 63%. The one trend the war did not start was an increasing gap between rich and poor. While this trend had dominated the 1920s and 1930s, World War II reversed it. The enormous number of high-paying factory jobs created by the war led to substantial economic gains for the poor. In 1939, the top 5% of individuals in the United States controlled 23% of the disposable income; by 1945, they controlled only 17% of the disposable income. The 6% loss suffered by the wealthy went into the pockets of the poor and middle classes. This, combined with changes in tax laws that made tax rates more progressive, helped decrease the gap between rich and poor.

31. (E) The European middle class in the 19th century espoused liberalism (E), largely as a means to gain a stronger political voice in systems that were dominated by the aristocratic upper class. As a result, its political influence increased (the opposite of (A)) throughout the century. Contrary to (B), the Russian middle class was proportionally smaller than those in other European countries. The middle classes generally rejected the idea of government aid to business (C), in accordance with the theory of laissez-faire economics. The bulk of the land throughout Europe was still owned by the upper class, not the middle class (D).

32. (C) Locke envisioned the "state of nature" as a time of relative peace and harmony. The "social contract," by which the first government was established, was necessary only because certain tasks, such as road building, might best be done collectively. Rousseau also used the term "social contract," but his "state of nature" was a time of economic equality; insisting that "property is theft," Rousseau argued that economic inequality began when human beings began to place value on objects

that might be hoarded, such as gold or precious stones (unlike food, which was perishable).

33. (D) The Second Enclosure Movement, which consolidated small farms into extensive holdings for the upper class, forced many peasants from the land into the cities and the urban labor pool (D). Serfdom was never "abolished"—that term implies legislation outlawing serfdom was passed, and no such legislation was ever passed in England. Serfdom gradually disappeared as England developed from a feudal economy to a more capitalistic one. Former serfs (A) generally became small farmers or craftsmen, not urban laborers. Slavery was never very widespread in England after the early Middle Ages, and therefore slaves did not make up a signifi- cant industrial labor force (B). There was no real influx of immigrants (C) during the industrial period in England; if anything, the trend was the opposite: many people emigrated from England during this period. It was fairly common for emi- grants to America to become indentured servants, but indenture was not very wide- spread in England itself (E).

34. (B) The correct chronological order of the events listed is the Petition of Rights (1628–29), the Short Parliament (April/May 1640), the Long Parliament (November 1640), the death of Charles I (1649), and the Instrument of Govern- ment (1653).

35. (A) The Treaty of Greenville was between the United States and the Miami Confederacy, which consisted of the Native American tribes living in the Northwest Territory. The treaty ceded lands in the eastern part of the Northwest Territory (I), most in what is today the state of Ohio. The Miami Confederation ceded the lands to the United States in return for cash, supplies, and promises of fair negotiations in future land dealings. The treaty was important because it helped open up the North- west Territory for American settlement and reduced the influence of the British in the area by neutralizing the Native American threat in the eastern one-third of the territory.

36. (E) The Peace of Augsburg of 1555 recognized Lutheranism as a second form of Christianity (A), granted the northern German nobles greater independence from the Holy Roman Empire (B), recognized the principle of *cuius regio, cuius religio* (C), and was followed by the abdication of Charles V (E). Calvinism was not fully recognized until the Peace of Westphalia in 1648.

37. (C) Arnold Toynbee's *A Study of History* and Oswald Spengler's *Decline of the West* promoted a view of history known as cyclical (C). This historical view perceives human institutions as organisms that experience the cycle of birth, devel- opment, maturity, decline, and death, just as living organisms do.

38. (C) Thomas Malthus, David Ricardo, Nassau Senior, and James Mill are known as classical economists (C). Mill was also associated with the Utilitarians (D),

but the others were not. None of these men could be described as positivists (A), romantic idealists (B), or Utopian socialists (E).

39. **(E)** Political machines such as Tammany Hall dominated many city governments at the turn of the century. These organizations stayed in power through bribery, graft, and other corrupt practices. In return, the machines took care of the interests of their most influential constituents. Frequently, they provided services which helped the poor survive, in return for support at the polls. Many middle and upper class reformers demanding changes to end political corruption found themselves stymied at the polls by large blocks of poor and immigrant voters who supported the political machines. The machines often successfully portrayed themselves as protectors of the poor fighting against upper class reformers who were really only interested in themselves. While the political machines were able to enlist the support of some industrial leaders (A), and sometimes got indirect support from organized religion (B), such support was weak and inconsistent. They got little support from middle class shopowners (D), who often found themselves paying the increased costs associated with the corruption promulgated by the political machines. They had virtually no support from wealthy rural landowners (C), who lived outside the urban operating base of most machines and derived no benefits from machine activities.

40. **(D)** Charles Fourier, Robert Dawn, and Claude Saint-Simon can best be described as pre-Marxist socialists (D); some authorities identify them as Utopian socialists. Anarchism (A) was introduced by Pierre Joseph Proudhon in *What is Property?*; Marx and Engels developed scientific socialism or Marxism (B); and the term revisionist (E) is applied to Marxists who differ with one or more of the basic Marxist notions. All of these individuals and groups were opposed to capitalism (C).

41. **(B)** Keynesian economics, based on the work of the British Lord Keynes, calls for massive government spending combined with the lowest tax rates possible to spur consumer demand and help boost a sagging economy. This approach demands a large, active government to administer the various necessary government spending programs. John F. Kennedy (B) actively adopted this approach. In an effort to deal with the recession of the early 1960s, Kennedy's administration enacted a tax reform plan that returned over $11 billion to taxpayers over a three-year period, while increasing federal government spending by 35% over a four-year period. This combination of tax cuts and spending increases represents classic Keynesian ideas for stimulating an economy. Thomas Jefferson (A) was philosophically opposed to industrialization itself, as well as a large powerful government. His writings make it clear that he would never have supported the policies necessitated by Keynesian theory. Andrew Jackson (E) also supported a limited role for the federal government and would never have supported economic policies that guaranteed the increased dependence of average citizens on the federal government. Herbert Hoover (D) was faced, in the Great Depression, with a situation in which Keynesian economics demanded massive increases in federal spending along with substantial tax cuts. While Hoover did not oppose tax cuts, he vehemently opposed

the massive federal spending needed to "jump start" the nation's economy. When Ronald Reagan (C) took office in 1981, he argued for "supply-side" economics, which demands substantial cuts in both tax revenues and in federal spending. Reagan argued for a smaller federal budget and a smaller federal bureaucracy. These policies are almost the theoretical opposite of Keynesian theories.

42. **(B)** The Gilded Age was characterized by an overwhelming rejection of activist government, especially at the national level. The presidents of this age, Hayes, Arthur, Garfield, Cleveland, and Harrison, all resembled corporate managers more than active political leaders. The dominant philosophies of the age were Social Darwinism and laissez-faire economics, both of which emphasized an ethos of people making or losing their own fortunes. Politicians translated these into a political philosophy of limited, hands-off government which did little to intervene in local affairs. Grover Cleveland summed up this philosophy with his statement "people support the government, the government should not support the people." While Andrew Jackson (A) talked of popular sovereignty and limits to the power of the federal government, he used his presidential powers more actively than had any previous president, and federal power actually increased during Jackson's presidency. The federal government, particularly Congress, during the Reconstruction era (C) was quite activist, especially toward governing the postwar South and the developing West. Some people in the Gilded Age supported nonactivist leaders precisely because of the abuses of activist leaders during the Reconstruction era. Franklin Roosevelt was arguably the most activist president in U.S. history, with his massive expansion of the federal government in the 1930s and 1940s to manage New Deal (D) economic programs and to manage the war effort during World War II. The New Deal fundamentally altered the relationship between the government and American citizens in ways that radically increased the role of government in people's daily lives. The 1960s (E) were characterized by increased expansion of the federal government in response to issues such as civil rights and Lyndon Johnson's "War on Poverty" programs. During this period, people increasingly turned toward the federal government and courts to seek clarification and protection of their rights and liberties. The result of these efforts was a larger federal government and more regulation at the federal level than ever before.

43. **(A)** The mortality rate was much lower among colonists in New England than in Virginia. While New England's winters could be brutal, they were rarely fatal, and English colonists were accustomed to dealing with the cold weather. The steamy climate of the Virginia coast, however, was host to various diseases such as malaria, for which the colonists were not prepared, and they died in droves. Women died sooner than men, accentuating an already acute shortage of women in Virginia. This made it difficult to establish and maintain stable family units. Since intact families were more likely to settle in New England than in Virginia (contrary to (E)), New England society developed along the lines of the traditional family unit, with very conservative values the norm and women subordinate to men. In Virginia, however, where men outnumbered women by as much as 6 to 1, society developed

along more diverse lines. The shortage of women gave them more voice in choosing their marital partners and roles. The fact that there were fewer women, and that the ones who were there did not live as long, meant that population growth was more rapid in New England and land ownership patterns developed accordingly, with relatively larger land grants in Virginia than in New England. Native Americans had a significant impact on colonists in both New England and the Virginia area and it would be difficult to conclude, as suggested by (B), that Native Americans had a more significant impact on either of the two regions. Also, while some of the patrons who founded colonial settlements in Virginia and the Carolinas were wealthier than the founders of most colonial settlements in New England, the colonists themselves were not. In fact, contrary to (C), they were often poorer and more of them came to Virginia and the Carolinas as indentured servants than to New England. Finally, although colonial settlement of Virginia began earlier than in New England (E), the 11 years between the establishment of the Jamestown colony and the Plymouth colony in Massachusetts was insignificant in the overall development of these two regions.

44. **(A)** This passage from the "Proclamation of the Kronstadt Rebels" illustrates the disillusionment of the Kronstadt sailors and their working class allies in 1921 (A) with the hardships and the restrictions of the Lenin regime. Trotsky (B) supported the suppression of the Kronstadt revolt, which was not associated with the past occupation of the European powers (E), the Russian Orthodox church (C), or the all-but-over war with the Whites (D).

45. **(E)** Robert Bellarmine (A) was a major figure of the Catholic Counter-Reformation on the Continent during the late 16th and early 17th centuries. Ignatius Loyola (B) established the Society of Jesus in 1530. William Allen (C) and Reginald Pole (D) were leaders of the Catholic cause in England during the 16th century. Pius IX (E) was a conservative pontiff during the 19th century who was associated with the issue of papal infallibility and who wrote the *Syllabus of Errors*.

46. **(B)** Adam Smith's *Wealth of Nations* (B), published in 1776, opposed mercantilism and claimed that to achieve economic prosperity, governments should interfere and regulate business as little as possible, a doctrine that became known as laissez-faire economics. Thomas Malthus's *Essay on Population* (A) predicted that the human population would someday outrun the food supply, and claimed that social welfare programs would only accelerate the population increase. Karl Marx's *Das Kapital* (C) was an indictment of the capitalist economic system as exploitive, and advocated socialism as a means of effecting a more equitable society. In *The Origin of Species*, Charles Darwin (D) presented his theory of evolution and natural selection. *Pride and Prejudice*, by Jane Austen (E), is considered one of the first literary classics written by a woman; it is a novel depicting the lives of the English upper-middle class in the early 19th century.

47. **(C)** Between 1640 and 1688, Elector Frederick William of Brandenburg-Prussia presided over the transformation of his country. Through the development

of a strong military (I) and an expanding economy (II), he was able to institute a series of policies which enhanced Prussian power. The defeat of Poland (V) in the 1650s contributed to Prussian authority. It would be left to Bismarck to defeat Austria (IV) in 1866, and to the Russian Peter the Great to eliminate Swedish power (III) in the Great Northern War.

48.   (C)   "Black codes" were designed to so limit the rights of free blacks in the South that they would move North where they couldn't threaten the Southern slave system. These codes ranged from bans on assembly to laws forbidding blacks from learning to read or write. By driving out freed blacks, Southern whites hoped to remove role models whom enslaved blacks could emulate. There was also the fear that freed blacks would use their freedom to help foment slave uprisings. The codes were quite effective in driving large numbers of blacks northward, but the number of slaves freed for one reason or another continually outnumbered the number of blacks who emigrated to the North, so the codes were never completely successful. The black codes did not deal with the return of runaway slaves (A); that issue was addressed at the federal level. They also were not aimed at stopping slave rebellions through executions (B), as slaveholders already had the right to execute slaves at will. Neither did they deny blacks the right to be free (D); they just limited the rights of those who were free. Finally, they did not deal with the mixed race issue (E). In the pre–Civil War South, anyone with any black ancestry, even if it was two or three generations back, was considered black and treated as such.

49.   (C)   The St. Bartholomew's Day Massacre of 1572 decimated the ranks of the Protestant leadership but failed to suppress the anti-Catholic movement (C). During the 1580s, the War of the Three Henrys resulted in a civil war which ended with the ascension of Henry of Navarre (Henry IV) to the French throne in 1589. While Henry IV became a Catholic, he extended liberties and guarantees to the Huguenots through the Edict of Nantes of 1598.

50.   (B)   The correct chronological order of the leaders of the Reformation is John Hus (early 15th century), who was executed by order of the Council of Constance in 1414, Martin Luther (*Ninety-Five Theses*, 1517), Ulrich Zwingli (leader of Zurich, 1521), Martin Bucer (Strasbourg, 1532), and John Calvin (Geneva, 1536–64).

51.   (D)   The Navigation Acts forced the colonies to trade exclusively with England and gave the British government extensive regulatory control over all colonial trade. The Navigation Acts required all goods shipped to England's American colonies to be shipped through British ports where they could be taxed with British import duties (II). They also prohibited colonists from building or importing goods that competed directly with British exports (III). However, they did not prohibit the colonies from issuing paper currencies (III). That prohibition was the focal point of the Currency Act of 1764, approximately 100 years after the Navigation Acts.

52. **(E)** The French and Indian War (A), the Anglo-Franco Indian War (B), and King George's War (C) paralleled the Seven Years' War in the mid-18th century. The predominant reasons for this worldwide struggle were: 1) limiting the influence of France in Europe, 2) the struggle between Austria and Prussia for control over central Europe, and 3) the colonial conflict between Britain and France. King William's War (D) was a conflict in the colonies during the War of the Spanish Succession. The Great Northern War (E) was a prolonged struggle between Sweden and Russia which ran from 1699 to 1721 and was not a colonial war.

53. **(C)** While recent research indicates that the Lollards (A) sustained the ideas of the 14th century reformer John Wycliffe, and that Lutheran theological positions had some influence on the evolution of English religious thought (B), the primary reason for the rise of Puritanism in 16th century England was the influence of the Marian Exiles (C) who returned after the Elizabethan Settlement (1558–59); while in their exile in Geneva, Strasbourg, and other communities in the Rhineland and Switzerland, these Protestant leaders were introduced to the "extended" Protestant positions of John Calvin and his colleagues. The Vestments Controversy (E) of the early 1580s was an early manifestation of Puritan interest in eliminating the vestiges of Roman Catholicism. John Knox (D) was influenced by Calvinist thought and succeeded in radicalizing the Reformation in Scotland with the establishment of Presbyterianism.

54. **(D)** Both Henry Clay (I) and Daniel Webster (III) were ardent supporters of the Union and believed that once a state had joined the Union that state could never secede. They felt that all grievances must be resolved within the framework of the Constitution, which in their view did not allow states to secede when grievances were not resolved to their liking, or for any other reason. John C. Calhoun (II), however, was a leader in the states' rights movement and believed states could secede whenever they wanted to. His views were diametrically opposed to those expressed in the passage.

55. **(D)** The passage is from a speech made by Henry Clay during the debate over the Compromise of 1850. The Compromise sought to resolve differences between Northern and Southern states over the issues of slavery and prohibition against its expansion into western territories such as New Mexico and California. This debate was the only one in which all of the people named were present. While Henry Clay was present for the debate of the Missouri Compromise in 1820 (C), younger statesmen such as Stephen A. Douglas, Jefferson Davis, Salmon Chase, and Wiliam Seward were not. The Missouri Compromise debate, as well as the decision over the location of the Mason-Dixon line (E), never raised the issue of secession as openly as the debate over the Compromise of 1850, and while impassioned speeches such as the one quoted were given on the issue of slavery, they were not given on the issue of secession. While both the Kansas-Nebraska Acts (B) and the secession of South Carolina (A) sparked impassioned speeches, they both occurred after the

deaths of Calhoun and Webster, so they could not have participated in these debates.

56. **(B)** While the French Revolution attracted the attention of 19th century French nationalist historians such as Jules Michelet (A) and H. A. Taine (E), the literary giant Victor Hugo (C), and the political philosopher Karl Marx (D), it was Georges Lefebvre (B) in *The Coming of the French Revolution* who presented a comprehensive explanation for the causes of the French Revolution of 1789.

57. **(D)** By the late 15th and early 16th centuries, Europe's population was bursting at the seams as the result of rapid increases in population (A). There was not enough land for everyone and many people scratched out marginal existences in the cities. While population growth was not a major reason for the initial explorations of the New World, once the vastness of the American landscape was realized in Europe, the impetus to relieve population pressure by shipping people off to colonize these new lands was enormous. During this time, the leaders of Europe were consolidating their power through the creation of modern nation-states. Most of the explorations of the early 16th century would not have been possible 100 years previously because the political stability and the funding necessary to pay for these expensive explorations would not have been available (B), (E). In addition, several new navigational instruments were developed during this period that allowed sailors to estimate their latitude and longitude (C). These instruments allowed sailors to sail long distances out of sight of land, whereas until then the majority of exploratory voyages were carried out by hugging the African coastline or sailing near known islands off the main coasts. However, during this time the traditional social structure grew more rigid with the rise of absolute monarchs and their intolerance of dissent of any sort. Thus, social upheaval did not contribute to the exploration and colonization of the Western Hemisphere (D).

58. **(E)** The passage represents the current thinking of the latest group of Western historians to study the Cold War, the post-revisionists. Orthodox Western historians (A) portrayed the Cold War as a result of American reactions to Soviet attempts at world domination. In this view, the Soviets were solely to blame for postwar tensions between the superpowers, and American actions were justified by Soviet aggression. This view persisted through the 1960s. By the late 1960s, a new group of historians examining declassified U.S. government documents concluded that the Cold War was primarily Harry Truman's fault. This group, the early revisionists (C), blamed Truman's lack of experience in dealing with the Russians for his over-reacting to and misreading of Russian motives and for pushing the United States into an aggressive, confrontational policy toward the Soviets. Orthodox Russian historians (B) portrayed the Cold War as the result of American desire to surround and destroy the Soviet Union because the existence of a powerful Soviet Union was too large a threat to capitalist greed and American desire for world control. This view is not all that different from the view of late revisionist Western historians (D), who also blamed the Cold War on the United States. These writers

claimed that America began the Cold War out of a need to dominate world markets to protect itself from its own economic weaknesses, and that Russian actions stemmed from legitimate security concerns and realistic reactions to American aggression.

59.   (C)   During the early years of the 19th century, the English Luddites blamed machine industry for low wages and unemployment (II); as part of their protest, they attacked machinery to render it useless (III). While organized, the Luddites did not form a trade union (I). They did not support the Corn Laws (V), which raised the price of grain; nor did they identify with free trade (IV). Labor and class unrest in England were manifested by other, non-Luddite, developments such as the Anti-Corn League and the Peterloo Massacre.

60.   (B)   As foreign secretary and then as prime minister, Lord Palmerston pursued an aggressive defense of his understanding of British interests (I); occasionally, Palmerston threatened and used force (III) as an instrument of foreign policy. During Palmerston's mid-19th century tenure, Britain was not allied to any other power (II) except during the Crimean War. While Palmerston was not aloof from European diplomacy, Britain was not actively involved in European affairs (V) nor did Palmerston actively support European revolutionary movements or leaders (IV).

61.   (C)   *The English Historical Review* was founded by the 19th century English historian Lord Acton (C). Bishop William Stubbs (A) was a renowned constitutional historian; Thomas Babington Macaulay (B) was a 19th century historian and politician; G. M. Trevelyan (D) was a 20th century British historian who promoted the views of the Whigs; and James Anthony Froude was a 19th century historian of Tudor England.

62.   (E)   The French and Indian War was an overwhelming victory for the English and the American colonies. It resulted in the French being eliminated as a major political force in North America. It ended the Native American tactic of playing one European power against another. The result was that the American colonists no longer had to fear direct threats by a major foreign power. Colonists gained confidence in themselves and gained a corps of well-trained officers. Rather than binding America more closely to England (C), this led to a more independent, knowledgeable, and assertive attitude by Americans who now felt more free to challenge and resist British efforts to restrict their activities. While many colonists questioned English policies, especially economic policies toward the colonies, very few Americans saw French rule as equal or superior to British rule (A). The French and Indian War did nothing to change this attitude. While Native American activities temporarily curtailed further westward exploration in some areas after the war (B), the war actually opened up the American West for further explorations, because the French were no longer blocking exploration and the Native Americans, although dangerous, were not strong or united enough to block exploration for long. Finally, the number of British soldiers brought to the colonies (D) to fight the French was

not overwhelming. Large numbers of Americans were enlisted in the fight and fought side by side with British regulars.

63.   **(A)**   Throughout the 19th century, most American artists celebrated American frontier life (B), rural family life (C), and the natural landscapes of the unconquered American frontier (D). Very few works commemorated city life, but as American cities revolutionized both their size and nature by the end of the 19th century, American artists began to take notice. The emerging realism school of art dramatically portrayed the hustle-bustle, the dynamism, and often the urban squalor, of American cities. The construction of skyscrapers, elevated railways, trolley cars, and the advent of electric lighting provided artists with a vast array of new subjects. Often the contrast between the glamorous new technological advances of the modern city with the adjacent city ghettos made for poignant artistic themes. Abstract images (E) were not yet a major artistic theme in the United States and it would be decades before they would have a major impact on American art.

64.   **(E)**   The chart indicates that Great Britain and the Low Countries had the highest yield ratio by 1800 (A), that the yield ratios for France, Spain, Italy, and Eastern Europe declined in the 16th century (B), and Western and Southern Europe enjoyed higher yields than other sections of Europe (D). During the second half of the 18th century, France, Spain, and Italy enjoyed the greatest rate of increase in the yield ratio (C). There is no data to suggest that there is more available acreage in Eastern Europe (E).

65.   **(B)**   The Holy Alliance was a Russian-based device to suppress revolutionary forces such as nationalism and liberalism (III). It was also designed to secure the arrangements of the Congress of Vienna (II), and as such was used effectively by Metternich during the first decade after the Congress (IV). Since England was rather reluctant to join the Holy Alliance, it did not enjoy the support of all of the victorious powers (V). It was not intended to support Catholic powers (I). The Holy Alliance was motivated by the rebellions in Latin America against Spain and the Revolutions of 1820; it led to the development of the "Concert" system in European diplomacy.

66.   **(D)**   The Austrian Leopold I's major achievements were the defeat of the Ottoman Turks after his two successful defenses of Vienna (I), restoring the status of the Hapsburg family after the humiliation of the Peace of Westphalia (III), and serving as a principal power in the coalition against Louis XIV in the Wars of the League of Augsburg and the War of the Spanish Succession (IV) during the late 17th and early 18th centuries. The Austrian economy (II) was not industrialized until the 19th century; however, Austrian urban life was quite sophisticated and diverse during the 18th century. Leopold I cannot be viewed as a "liberal" on matters of religion, ethnicity, and representative government (V).

67.   **(C)**   The Galloway Plan was proposed during the First Continental Congress in 1774, as a means of coping with British abuses of colonial rights while still

maintaining relations with Britain. It involved setting up a central colonial government that would include a unified colonial assembly, which would have to approve royal and parliamentary rules before they could take effect in the colonies. Such a "grand council" would allow the colonies to more effectively deal with British abuses by providing a unified voice and coordinated action. This plan provided an alternative to the more radical ideas of Samuel Adams (A), John Adams (B), Patrick Henry (D), and Richard Henry Lee (E), all of whom preferred a course of open confrontation with the crown, even if it led to warfare and a total break with Britain. John Jay (C) was one of the more moderate members attending the Congress and preferred a more cautious approach. As such, he was much more in agreement with Joseph Galloway's ideas than the other four men. While the Galloway Plan offered perhaps the last chance at a moderate course of action and a peaceful resolution of colonial differences with England, it was voted down and the radicals' more confrontational revolutionary plan was adopted.

68. **(B)** While Georg Wilhelm Hegel (A) (*Reason in History*), Karl Marx (C) (*Das Kapital*), Arnold Toynbee (D) (*A Study of History*), and Oswald Spengler (E) (*The Decline of the West*) made substantial contributions to historiography, the 18th century Neopolitan Giovanni Battista Vico (B) is considered to be the founder of "modern history" because of his contribution to the philosophy of history.

69. **(D)** During the first half of the 19th century, Joseph Mazzini (D) was the preeminent advocate of Italian nationalism. Through his Young Italy movement and other similar organizations throughout Europe, Mazzini championed the concept of national self-determination. Garibaldi (A) influenced Italian unification through his 1860 campaign in the Kingdom of the Two Sicilies. Cavour (B) served as prime minister of Piedmont/Sardinia and planned the 1859 war against Austria. King Charles Albert (C) of Sardinia attempted to move toward a united Italy in 1848, but abdicated in 1849 in favor of his son Victor Emmanuel when the Austrians prevailed. Pius IX (E) supported Italian nationalism prior to the revolutions of 1848, but became a reactionary because of his experiences in the revolution.

70. **(B)** The "Lost Generation" refers to a group of writers who emerged following World War I, whose writings questioned society's traditional prewar values and morality. In the United States, these writers focused particularly on emerging material consumerism, mass advertising, the hypocrisy of American life, and the isolation and meaninglessness of life in modern society. Each of the writers named were an integral part of the Lost Generation except John Steinbeck (B). Steinbeck emerged somewhat later than the Lost Generation writers, with his first successful book in 1935. While many of Steinbeck's themes mirror the concerns raised by the Lost Generation writers, Steinbeck's writing encompassed a much wider range of human conditions, often focusing on life among the poor during the Depression. Steinbeck portrayed humans as having positive, hopeful qualities as well as evil and selfish attributes. Steinbeck achieved his greatest fame with his Nobel Prize–winning *The Grapes of Wrath* in 1940.

71. **(A)** Contrary to popular opinion, Confederate industry did a masterful job in producing weapons and ammunition for the Confederate military during the war. Although it is true that the Confederates never had the abundance of weapons possessed by Union forces, particularly artillery, it was only near the end of the war, when Union forces had overrun many production centers and totally destroyed the South's transportation network, that severe shortages of ammunition and weapons developed. It is also true that at the beginning of the war, Confederate industry could not arm everyone who volunteered for military service, but the Union had the same problem. Confederate agriculture **(B)** never adequately met the food requirements of Southern soldiers and civilians. Many planters refused to plant foodstuffs when they could continue to plant cotton for possible export to Europe for a profit. Those farmers who did plant food crops found that the South's hopelessly outmoded rail system could not transport the food to the cities and armies where it was most needed. By 1863, food riots were occurring in several Southern cities. By 1865, the biggest problem faced by Confederate soldiers was hunger, not Yankees. The South went into the war with a tremendous economic disadvantage; most American banks were in the North. Southern states had very little gold or silver to back up their currency. They also had few industrial assets that could be converted into cash. Most Southern assets were agricultural, the land and the crops produced by the land. The Union naval blockade cut off most cotton export and the cash it could have provided for the South's struggling economy. The South was forced to print huge amounts of paper currency that had no tangible assets to support it **(C)**. The result was massive inflation, which disabled the Southern economy even more. The South's railroad system was inadequate **(D)**; there was only one major Southern rail line connecting the Atlantic Ocean with the Mississippi, and it was easily cut in several places. The North was able to disrupt the South's transportation system throughout the war. This resulted in food shortages, equipment shortages, an inability to transfer soldiers to where they were needed, and an inability to react effectively to unexpected Northern military moves. There was tremendous anger and resentment among poor and middle-class Southerners at the military draft **(E)**. Most of the resentment focused on a provision allowing wealthy Southerners to hire someone as a substitute to serve in the military in their place. Another provision exempted anyone who could prove that he supervised at least 20 slaves.

72. **(D)** From John Kay's **(A)** flying shuttle to the subsequent inventions by James Hargreaves **(B)**, Richard Arkwright **(C)**, and Samuel Crompton **(E)**, the production of British cotton was transformed radically during the second half of the 18th century. Henry Cort **(D)** assisted in improving the production of the iron and steel industry, not the textile industry.

73. **(B)** The United States was strongly affected, particularly in the coastal cities, by the French republic that had replaced the monarchy during the French Revolution. Many Americans saw the French Revolution as an extension of America's revolution against Britain, and they idealized the goals of the new French republic. Wealthy Americans stopped wearing wigs, cut their hair to much shorter lengths,

began wearing full-length trousers with high waists instead of the previous standard knee-length britches, and in general imitated the fashions and cultural ideals of the French republic. While not all Americans admired or trusted the French republic, its influence on American culture and fashion during this period were undeniable and far more profound than any other foreign influence. While British aristocratic standards had a strong influence on Americans in the 1700s (A), they had rapidly lost influence following the American Revolution and had little influence by the early 1800s. Classical Greek influences (C) were noticeable in the architectural style of government buildings and in many American ideals regarding democracy itself, but they were not influential in reshaping American fashions, political ideals, or culture. Since the French aristocracy had been overthrown by the revolution, anything associated with it during the early 1800s was usually portrayed as evil or corrupt, therefore very little of the French aristocracy was admired or copied by Americans at this time (D). Finally, while Native American culture had a profound influence on Americans living on the frontier because of the close proximity of the tribes to frontier settlers, in the coastal cities, most people had no desire to emulate the "Godless" Native American cultures (E). The desire in these cities was to imitate the high culture of European civilization, not the "backward" and "uncivilized" culture of the frontier.

74. (E) John Foster Dulles was secretary of state under President Eisenhower; during his tenure in office, the United States found itself inferior to the Soviet Union and the People's Republic of China in conventional land forces. The United States enjoyed overwhelming superiority, however, in nuclear weapons and their delivery systems. Since the Chinese had no nuclear weapons yet, and the Soviets had far fewer nuclear weapons than the United States, they felt they had no choice but to maintain large conventional forces. The United States did not want to shoulder the massive expense of a huge buildup of conventional military forces; nuclear weapons, by comparison, were much cheaper to build and maintain. Based on this thinking, American defense policy focused on American technological advantages, emphasizing long-range airpower and nuclear weapons. The policy of massive retaliation was enacted to utilize these American advantages and to keep both the Soviets and Chinese off balance. The policy threatened retaliation for any Soviet or Chinese aggression with America's nuclear arsenal. It was hoped that this threat would deter Soviet and Chinese aggression. This policy was replaced in the 1960s when it became clear that the Soviet Union had enough warheads to destroy the United States in a nuclear exchange. The policy replacing it was known as mutually assured destruction (A), which emphasized, but did not promise, that American nuclear weapons would be used only to respond to a nuclear first strike by the Soviets. It focused on the need to maintain enough nuclear weapons to survive a Soviet first strike and still deliver enough retaliatory fire to annihilate Soviet Russia. The zero option policy (C) was the goal of antinuclear groups in the 1970s and 1980s, which had the elimination of all nuclear weapons as its goal. The flexible response policy (B) and the Strategic Defense Initiative (D) were both Reagan administration attempts in the 1980s to break the stalemate and eliminate the unacceptable risks of nuclear annihilation posed by the policy of mutually assured destruction.

75. (C) The map represents the United States as it looked in 1840. In 1820 (A), neither Michigan, Missouri, nor Arkansas had yet been admitted as states. While Missouri had become a state by 1830 (B), Michigan and Arkansas had not. By 1850 (D), Florida, Texas, Iowa, Wisconsin, and California had all achieved statehood, and the map does not show them as states. In 1860 (E), Oregon had become a state with its northern border along the 49th parallel, not the 54th parallel as shown on the map. Also Minnesota had become a state by this time and is not depicted as a state on the map.

76. (E) From the European perspective, the principal outcome of the Seven Years' War was the subsequent struggle between Prussia and Austria for hegemony in Central Europe (E). While the Anglo-French colonial rivalry (A) was historically significant, it did not dominate European diplomacy. The decline of Sweden (C) occurred earlier with the Peace of Nystadt in 1721. Dutch independence (D) was recognized at the Peace of Westphalia in 1648. Britain was not pursuing an aggressive encroachment of Europe during this period (B).

77. (D) William Wilberforce (D) was the primary English opponent of slavery during the late 18th and early 19th centuries and led the movement which resulted in the prohibition of the slave trade. Jeremy Bentham (A) and James Mill (B) were advocates of English Utilitarianism. Robert Owen (C) was a Utopian socialist who established communities in England and the United States. David Ricardo (E) was a British political economist.

78. (B) In the Humiliation of Olmutz in 1850, Prussia accepted Austria's demand for the reestablishment of the German Confederation (I). As a result, the advocates of the *Grossdeutsch* plan prevailed (IV) and the effort of the Frankfurt Assembly was defeated (V). The Prussian plan to move toward a unified Germany without Austria (the *Kleindeutsch* plan) (III) suffered a temporary setback.

79. (D) The Roman Catholic church responded to the rise of Protestantism in a variety of ways, including the establishment of new religious orders such as the Jesuits (II) (others included the Oratorians and the Theatines); a general church meeting, the Council of Trent (III), which met in three sessions from 1545 to 1564; and an effort to bring spiritual renewal and internal reforms (V) through the efforts of such diverse leaders as Teresa of Avila, John of the Cross, Charles Borromeo, and Robert Bellarmine. Initial contacts with Protestant leaders at Leipzig (1519) and Worms (1521) were attempts to suppress the movement, not to mediate with its leaders (I). The Roman Catholic church sought to further secure its position as an "official" religion through enhancing, not repudiating (IV), its relationships with European princes.

80. (B) The order to transfer cannon from the recently captured Fort Ticonderoga to Boston Heights (A) led to the British evacuation of Boston, one of the first major successes for the Americans against the British. The attacks against

the British and Hessians at Princeton and Trenton (D), and (C) were notable successes and helped the Continental army to survive the winter of 1776–77 intact and regain the initiative from the British. While the attack against British forces in Germantown in 1777 (E) was not successful, it was not a major failure either. The Americans had the British on the run, and only a combination of fog, poor communications, and ammunition shortages prevented an American victory. Despite the loss, the Americans gained confidence and the army retreated from the battlefield as cohesive and relatively well-disciplined force. It was the defense of New York City in August 1776 that was Washington's biggest military blunder and very nearly led to the destruction of the Continental army. Washington's defensive set-up divided his forces in the face of a superior enemy and left the entire American army in an exposed position; the British fleet could have cut it off and forced its surrender. Fortunately, the British failed to move quickly and Washington was able to extricate his battered force across the Hudson River to New Jersey, where it could regroup. While both Washington and the Continental army survived the battle, it was the closest Washington and his men came to total military defeat in the entire war.

81.   (C)   Venetia was annexed by Italy after the German Civil War (C). The Italians had fulfilled their obligations under a secret treaty with Bismarck by declaring war against Austria; as a result, they were rewarded with Venetia. Earlier, in 1859, the Italians obtained Lombardy via the Peace of Villafranca (A). Garibaldi's 1860 expedition (B) added the Kingdom of the Two Sicilies to Italy. During the Franco-Prussian War (D), the Italians seized Rome. Pius IX (E) never recognized the new Italian kingdom.

82.   (D)   Bismarck was involved in negotiating the Dual Alliance (A) with Austria-Hungary (1879), the Triple Alliance (B) with Austria-Hungary and Italy (1881), the Reinsurance Treaty (C) with Russia (1887), and the Congress of Berlin (E) in 1878. He was not involved in the Dual Entente (D) of 1894 between France and Russia; it eliminated the basic premise of Bismarck's foreign policy, the diplomatic isolation of France.

83.   (D)   Martin Luther supported the doctrine of consubstantiation (A), the publication of the scripture in the vernacular (B), the elimination of the indulgence system (C), and a revision of sacramental theology (E). While Luther considered predestination significant (D), it was Zwingli and Calvin who made it a focus of their approach to Christianity.

84.   (A)   "Liberty Leading the People" by Eugene Delacroix is an example of romanticism (A); it depicts a French romantic concept of revolution. Impressionism (B), expressionism (C), and symbolism (D) were approaches to art which emerged during the late 19th and early 20th centuries. Realism (E) evolved during the late 17th and the 18th centuries.

85.   (E)   All of the choices were utopian communities which evolved as part of the Second Great Awakening, a series of religious revivals in the 1820s, 1830s, and

1840s, but only one of these communities, Brook Farm, espoused the transcendentalist philosophy of Thoreau, Melville, and the others. Brook Farm focused on the importance of spiritualism over materialism. Members lived a communal lifestyle and all shared in the upkeep of the community. The writers who lived there included many of the most prominent American writers of the 19th century. During their prime they were part of the American Renaissance.

86. **(B)** While Wilson's rhetoric was more idealistic than Roosevelt's, their actual policies were quite similar. Both men pushed for expanded federal regulatory power for controlling the activities of business trusts. Neither man wanted total government control of business, but both wanted to curb business abuses and felt that strong, decisive leadership from Washington was the only way this could be accomplished (III). Both men felt that business monopolies had so much power that true competition was nonexistent. They believed that government regulation was the only way to restore any hope of free competition. Both Roosevelt's "New Nationalism" policy and Wilson's less sweeping "New Freedom" policy emphasized this need for more effective government regulation of business abuses. Neither policy removed restrictions on unions' rights to organize (I) nor gave the states greater powers to regulate businesses within their own borders (II).

87. **(B)** In response to the Kronstadt Rebellion, Lenin crushed the revolt with the use of Red troops (I) and initiated the New Economic Policy (NEP) (III), which tempered the more radical aspects of the Communist system. There was no reign of terror (II), removal of Trotsky supporters (IV), or negotiated settlement with the rebels (V).

88. **(B)** The Baroque period (c. 1570–1630) was a response to the intellectual turmoil which was caused by the Reformation and the subsequent Counter-Reformation. Intellectuals and artists were searching for a new intellectual synthesis, which emerged in the 17th century with the scientific and intellectual revolution. The art of the Baroque era was characterized by gigantism and the spectacular, which was evident in the work of Bernini, and by the lack of symmetry, which was characteristic of El Greco's later works ("The Assumption," c. 1610). Symmetry, harmony, and order (A) were the characteristics of classicism. Flatness, other-worldliness, and spirituality were characteristics of the art of the High Middle Ages. Introspection, psychoanalysis, and independence (D) have been identified with 20th century movements such as symbolism, Dadaism, and others. Materialism, order, and harmony (E) are characteristics of pedestrian art in the 19th and 20th centuries.

89. **(B)** During the Second French Empire, control over education was returned to the Church through the Falloux Law (B). The Cobden-Chevalier Treaty (A) was a commercial treaty. The *Credit Focier* (C), established in 1852, improved the efficiency of the French economy. Baron Haussmann (D) was the prefect of the Seine who was responsible for a major public works program. Article 45 of the Constitu-

tion (E) of the Second French Republic stipulated that the president was limited to one four-year term.

90.   **(C)**   Prior to the Congress of Berlin in June 1878, British prime minister Benjamin Disraeli and his foreign secretary, Lord Salisbury, concluded three arrangements: an Anglo-Russian understanding concerning Bulgaria (I), an Anglo-Turkish accord which addressed the boundaries and the transfer of Cyprus (II), and an Anglo-Austrian agreement concerning Austrian support of Britain at the conference and the recognition of Austrian influence in Bosnia (III). There were no formal Anglo-German (IV) or Anglo-Dutch (V) accords.

91.   **(C)**   Anti-Catholicism had been a factor in American life since the days of the Puritans. Catholicism was identified with religious tyranny and intolerance by most Americans, and there were real fears of the power of the pope and the Catholic church. When Irish immigrants came to America in vast numbers in the 1840s, the overwhelming majority of them were Catholic. This raised Protestant fears that Catholics would launch an insurrection in which the government would be made subservient to papal authority. Fears of Catholicism led many Americans to blame the Irish for virtually every poverty-related problem that existed in the coastal cities. Since the Irish were newcomers and Catholics, they made easy scapegoats and suffered accordingly. The Irish had struggled for centuries against British domination of their island, and the animosity of many Irish people toward the British (A) was well known, but this was not a factor in the prejudice against Irish immigrants; many Americans held fairly strong anti-British attitudes, too. While some people had a difficult time understanding English as spoken by Irish immigrants (B), the difficulties were not insurmountable and language was not a source for discrimination against the Irish. Most Irish immigrants were from rural provinces and were basically unskilled, and many of them were female, eliminating any chance that they would take a skilled American's job away from him (D). Finally, most Irish immigrants settled in cities and towns, not in rural farming communities (E) like German and Scandinavian immigrants.

92.   **(E)**   Through the October Manifesto, Nicholas II extended civil liberties to include freedom of speech, assembly, and the press (E). The October Manifesto was a concession which did not result in genuine reform. The liberalization process did not continue; while a *Duma* was established, it had no real power—it was preoccupied with factionalism. Nicholas II did not denounce the revolutionary forces (C) nor did he establish a democratic regime (A), reform the economic system (B), or establish a universal education system (D).

93.   **(B)**   The passage represents the philosophy and major tenets of the "Know-Nothing" party, which developed in the late 1840s as the culmination of the anti-Catholic and anti-immigrant sentiments which were widespread in the United States at that time. People feared that immigrants were destroying social values, adding to unemployment problems, and disrupting the political process. Many of these immi-

grants were Catholic, and they were particularly targeted because of their supposed subservience to a foreign leader, the pope. The Know-Nothings promised to end this perceived threat by limiting the rights of Catholics and immigrants to vote and to hold elective office. Free Soilers (A) focused on stopping the expansion of slavery into the western territories. The fledgling Republican party (D) focused on the abolition of slavery. The Whig party (E) was a mainstream party that refused to take radical positions on the issues of Catholicism and immigrants, and was destroyed by the development of the more radical parties. The Populist party (C) was formed in the 1890s by farmers seeking to redress economic concerns ignored by the major political parties. The Populists never blamed their problems on immigrants and Catholics and never included restrictive policies against them in their platform.

94. **(D)** The Know-Nothing party evolved out of a secret society known as the "Order of the Star Spangled Banner." It rapidly gained support, especially in coastal cities where the number of immigrants and Catholics were high. The party became the second largest political party in the country by 1855. However, its narrow focus and its lack of nationally recognized, competent, and experienced leaders left it unable to accomplish its stated goals. People quickly grew disillusioned and flocked to other parties focusing on other issues ignored by the Know-Nothings, such as slavery and states' rights, which were rapidly becoming the major issues. By 1860, the Know-Nothings were no longer a major political force.

95. **(D)** The stability of the Third French Republic was endangered by the Panama Scandal (I), the Boulanger Crisis (II), and the Dreyfus Affair (V). The War in Sight Crisis (1875) with Germany (III) was an external threat; the Paris Commune (IV) occurred in 1870–71, prior to the establishment of the Third French Republic.

96. **(C)** The correct chronological order in the development of the Reparations dispute after the First World War was: the Ruhr Crisis of 1923 (caused by the French and Belgian occupation of the Ruhr Valley); the Dawes Plan of 1924, which supported intervention by the United States to establish a reparation schedule and to stabilize German currency; the Young Plan of 1929 (another American-led schedule scheme); and the Hoover Moratorium of 1931, which called for a suspension of payments for one year.

97. **(B)** The political philosophy of Thomas Hobbes most clearly resembles that of Voltaire (B). Voltaire advocated Enlightened Despotism as the best form of government for France; this philosophy concurs with the Hobbesian view that the people need to be governed and that government should be by a qualified few, not by the people. Quesnay's (C) philosophy was similar, but not as directly related to Hobbes. Rousseau (A), Montesquieu (D), and Robespierre (E) advocated more radical philosophies that rejected sovereign authority and the exercise of that authority.

98. (C) The Anglo-Russian agreement of 1907 resolved colonial disputes in Persia, Tibet, and Afghanistan (I); was inspired by the success of the Entente Cordiale between Britain and France in 1904 (III); and normalized Anglo-Russian relations in the wake of the Russo-Japanese war (1904–5) (IV), during which Britain expressed sympathy for Japan. The Anglo-Russian agreement did not result in an alliance between the two powers (II) nor did it result in British support for Russian expansion in the Balkans (V).

99. (E) Innovations by Eli Whitney and Simeon North in the use of interchangeable parts to produce small arms for the military pioneered the beginnings of the machine tool industry. The use of precision-engineered, high-quality interchangeable parts led to the mass production of a wide variety of products not previously available to consumers. This brought the United States slowly but steadily into the industrial age and laid the groundwork for the American manufacturing colossus that emerged by 1900. While slave labor (A) was heavily used on the cotton plantations of the South, it was never a factor in the development of American manufacturing, which thrived primarily in the antislavery Northeast. The technical innovations allowing for the development of the machine tool industry largely replaced individually crafted merchandise (B). With precision engineering, those same goods could now be manufactured in massive numbers with similar or better quality. While skilled artisans continued to play a role in the manufacture of American goods throughout the 19th century, as most people still lived on farms and made many of their own goods, it was mass production tied to machinery with interchangeable parts that led to the success of American manufacturing. The "putting out" system (C) was a system by which manufacturers in the textile industry would send raw materials to workers in their homes, then return to collect the finished goods when the work had been completed. This system declined throughout the 19th century and was replaced by the large factories typical of mass production because they were more cost effective and allowed better quality control of the product. Finally, the factories of New England and the industrial Northeast were run by manual power, steam power, or water power. Electric power (D) would not be available in measurable quantities for another half-century.

100. (B) During the 17th century the European population declined because the food supply could not sustain the population (B). While plagues (A) and wars (C) took a toll of lives, they were not decisive factors in the overall decline of the population. There is no evidence that birth control practices (D) or a nonfood based increase in infant mortality (E) contributed to this demographic development.

101. (B) Syndicalism was a manifestation of anarchism founded by Georges Sorel (B), a French radical. Syndicalism, which was based on control of trade unions and dissident political groups, gained some success in France, Spain, and Italy. Prince Peter Kropotkin (A) and Michael Bakunin (C) were Russian anarchists who espoused a comprehensive anarchist philosophy and strategy. Sidney Webb (D) was a founder of the Fabian Society, a revisionist, and a member of the London municipal

government during the 20th century. Mazzini (E) advanced a liberal nationalism which influenced pre–1848 groups—Young Italy, Young Germany, and the Pan-Slavic movements.

102. (C) Under the reign of Tsar Alexander II (1858–61), Russia began to emerge from the feudal era. Known as the *tsar liberator*, Alexander's reforms included the elimination of serfdom (A), granting the peasants independence from their lords (B), giving peasants the right to enter into legal contracts and to own property (D), and granting all people freedom of movement and the freedom to change (and to choose) their method of livelihood (E). Because of these reforms, Russia was able to begin the transition from a feudal economy to an industrial one, a process that was hastened by the aristocracy's appetite for Westernization, and interrupted by the turmoil of the early decades of the 20th century. Alexander's reforms did not permit convocation of a representative assembly (C).

103. (B) The map describes the European political borders after the Congress of Vienna in 1815 (B). That assembly resolved the prolonged conflicts associated with the French Revolution and the Napoleonic era; there was an attempt made to re-create Europe along the lines of pre-1789. The Congress of Berlin (A) was held in 1878 to settle differences over the Balkans and the eastern Mediterranean. The Versailles Treaty (C) was signed in 1919 after the First World War. The Treaty of Paris of 1763 (D) concluded the Seven Years' War; and the Munich Crisis (E) occurred in 1938 and involved Czechoslovakia.

104. (D) The Niagara movement of 1905 was the result of a meeting of African American political leaders which focused on the problems blacks faced in attaining civil rights, equal access, and equal opportunity in the United States. Frustrated by the failure of the gradualist approach (B) sought by Booker T. Washington, which favored attaining civil rights incrementally over a prolonged period, the Niagara movement favored a more activist, confrontational, but legal and nonviolent approach to demanding civil rights immediately. The movement often ran into violent opposition from white supremacists (C) and many African Americans were killed in the race riots that ensued in cities from Illinois to Alabama. The outrage that followed the deaths of blacks at the hands of white mobs led to calls for a formal organization to work for equality and help protect black Americans. This organization, founded in 1910, was called the National Association for the Advancement of Colored People (NAACP). Both prohibition (A) and women's suffrage (E) were movements dominated primarily by white women. While many members of these movements may have sympathized with the plight of African Americans, their primary concerns were their own causes, which had little to do with civil rights for American blacks.

105. (C) The collapse of the Asquith ministry in 1916 was caused by several factors, including the Easter Rebellion in Ireland (A), the human devastation on the western front (B), Asquith's failure to exploit the emergency powers which were

placed at his disposal (D), and the increasing lack of confidence in his leadership (E). His government was replaced by a coalition led by David Lloyd George. Asquith did not intervene in Russia (C).

106. **(D)** The Wilmot Proviso, an unsuccessful attempt to forbid slavery in any territories acquired as a result of the Mexican-American War, became the slogan for many abolitionist groups who wanted a total end to slavery. It also became a rallying cry for a group known as "Free Soilers." Free Soilers did not necessarily want to abolish slavery, however, they wanted to stop its spread into the western territories. They feared that the expansion of slavery into the West would prevent free whites from obtaining land and the jobs which would be open to them without slavery. While their motives were selfish rather than altruistic, the Wilmot Proviso would have achieved their purpose. They added another voice to the growing chorus of people calling for the restriction or abolition of slavery. All of the other choices listed supported restricted federal power and some form of states' rights; as such, all of them would have opposed the Wilmot Proviso.

107. **(A)** Slavery was never effectively established in New England, largely because the economic system and the large population of New England rendered the need for large numbers of slaves unnecessary. Most New England farms were relatively small and self-sufficient, and the members of farming communities depended on each other to keep their communities economically viable. New England farmers had little need for slaves or indentured servants (D) to run their farms and used neither in significant numbers. In the Southern colonies, there was less cohesion among the colonists, there were fewer people, and there was a constant demand for laborers to cultivate the cash crops necessary to keep the colonies economically afloat. At first, this demand was met by the use of indentured servants, but after the 1660s the supply of potential servants dwindled, and the only immediate replacement was imported slave labor. While few slaves were imported to New England, there is no evidence that they were less able to tolerate New England's climate and the local diseases (B). If anything, the colder climate in New England was healthier and harbored fewer diseases than the steamy climate of the Virginia and Carolina coasts. While some Southern plantation owners of the mid-19th century were certainly wealthier than most New England farmers, this difference came about after the importation of large numbers of slaves into the South, not before. There is no evidence to support the conclusion that greater initial wealth led to the greater importation of slaves into the Southern colonies (C). Finally, while the Stono uprising (E) was the largest slave rebellion of the colonial period, it occurred in South Carolina, not in New England. The incident raised fears of blacks among all white colonists, though it did little to change the attitudes of either Carolinians or New Englanders about the viability of slavery as an economic institution.

108. **(A)** While the United States had helped the Shah get political asylum in Egypt (B), his fleeing to Egypt did not precipitate the hostage crisis. President Carter was warned that admitting the Shah into the United States, for any reason, would

look to the Iranians like America still supported the Shah's regime and would lead to trouble. However, other advisors told Carter that the United States owed the Shah a large debt of gratitude for the favors he had done for America and also because of the lack of support from the U.S. when his government was overthrown. Carter had previously refused to grant the Shah exile in the United States, but when he was told of the Shah's need for cancer treatments (A), he decided to allow the Shah to enter the United States on humanitarian grounds. The Iranians were infuriated and on November 4, 1979, young Iranian males backed by their government and claiming to be students seized the American embassy compound and took 76 hostages, 62 of whom were held for more than a year. The Iran-Iraq War did not begin until after the hostage crisis began, and U.S. support for the Iraqis came largely as a result of the hostage crisis; it was in no way a cause of the crisis (C). Although U.S. naval forces were placed on alert numerous times during the collapse of the Shah's regime, there is no proven link between the actions of U.S. warships in the Persian Gulf and the hostage crisis (D). America did not make any overt attempts to overthrow the new Khomeini government (E).

109. (C)   The definitive "Whig" interpretation of British history was advanced in the 19th century by (C) Thomas Babington Macaulay. Macaulay argued that the rise of Parliament and the corresponding decrease of monarchical power was the central, continuing, and positive theme of British political history. David Hume (A) (*Constitutional History of England*) and Edward Gibbon (B) (*Decline and Fall of the Roman Empire*) were English historians of the 18th century. Jeremy Bentham (E) established English Utilitarianism and John Stuart Mill (D) (*On Civil Government* and *On Liberty*), while identified as a Utilitarian, was a multifaceted political philosopher and reformer of the 19th century.

110. (C)   The Washington Conference of 1921–22 resulted in agreements between European powers, the United States, China, and Japan which established a ratio for capital ships among the five great naval powers (I) (United States, Great Britain, Japan, France, Italy), stabilized the postwar title to islands previously held by Germany (II), and reaffirmed the integrity and independence of China (IV). There was no agreement to recognize Manchuria as a Japanese sphere of influence (V) and the conference was not identified with the standards of the Reparations Commission established at the Versailles Peace Conference (III).

111. (E)   During the second half of the 19th century, traditional religion was attacked by science through the application of historical criticism of the Bible (A), the rise of materialistic philosophies which relied on physical science for all evidence (B), the availability of new geological data on the age of the earth and life, which disputed traditional views advanced by religion (C), and the theory of evolution, which countered the biblical Creation story (D). The philosophy of positivism (E), which was advanced by Auguste Comte, Henri Bergson, and others, was not based on science.

112. **(B)**   The Utilitarians were led by Jeremy Bentham, and he and James Mill raised Mill's son John Stuart Mill, by Utilitarian principles. The most basic of these was the belief that the only justifiable test for a government institution was "How useful is it?" To Bentham and his followers, the definition of "useful" was that it provide the greatest good for the greatest number (B). The idea of a paternalistic government (A) was not accepted by the Utilitarians per se, but if the institutions that provided the greatest good were paternalistic ones, then so be it. However, the Utilitarians did not believe that the government had the right to dictate moral standards. The belief that government's only role was to maintain civil order (C), or that only those who contributed to society had a claim on it (D), or that the only necessary government institutions were those that could manage the nation's natural resources (E) would all be rejected by the Utilitarians.

113. **(C)**   Samuel Slater opened a successful textile mill in Pawtucket, Rhode Island, in 1790, the first successful "modern" factory in the United States. His success was important because it opened up the development of a thriving textile industry in New England, in which new methods of centralized manufacturing and mass production were developed, and it initiated a movement toward centralized factory production in many other areas of manufacturing throughout the northern United States. Slater's mill was a major factor in the development of the United States as a modern industrial power. The technique for mass-producing steel at low cost (A) was developed by Charles Besemer. The Hudson River school of art (B) was founded by Thomas Cole. No single person can be credited with founding the first successful American settlement west of the Mississippi (D), as many of these settlements can be traced back to the Spanish explorers and the missions they established, as well as to trappers and hunters and the trading posts that served them. George Catlin was the American painter known for his portrayals of Native American life before it was destroyed by disease and white settlement (E).

114. **(E)**   The passage represents the reaction of Thomas Jefferson to Shay's Rebellion, as expressed in a letter to James Madison in January 1787. Jefferson, never a fan of large centralized government, truly believed that such uprisings helped keep the government honest and in touch with the needs of those being governed. This view is in opposition to those of George Washington (A), who felt that people's disputes with the government should be resolved through legal, political means. It is also in opposition to the views of Alexander Hamilton (C) and John Jay (D) who were staunch Federalists and firmly believed in a large centralized government with the power to prevent and quash uprisings such as Shay's Rebellion. Abraham Lincoln (C) never publicly expressed the view that an occasional rebellion can be a good thing. As a lawyer, Lincoln believed that disputes and complaints should be handled within the legal framework established by the government.

115. **(D)**   Massachusetts farmers challenged the authority of the government to collect taxes and enforce property laws in Shay's Rebellion. While the rebellion quickly fell apart, it raised questions about the role of a federal government that

highlighted all of the flaws in the Articles of Confederation, under which the United States was being governed. While many Americans were alarmed by Shay's Rebellion and it ignited a drive for a new Constitution, Thomas Jefferson and many others saw it as a sign of an involved populace doing what was necessary to keep the government responsible and in touch with the needs of the people. While Jefferson saw the American Revolution (A) as healthy, there were no "eastern states" to be concerned about at that time, just colonies. Also, the American Revolution was more than just a "little rebellion" in Jefferson's mind. The Whiskey Rebellion (C) occurred in Kentucky, a western state, therefore it could not be the rebellion to which Jefferson referred in the passage. The Civil War (B) occurred long after Jefferson's death. The War of 1812 (E) was a war involving a dispute between two independent nations, and Jefferson would not have referred to it as a rebellion.

116. **(B)** Immanuel Kant (I), author of *The Critique of Pure Reason*, Johann G. Fichte (II), who is identified with German collectivistic nationalism, and Georg Wilhelm Hegel (III), author of *Reason in History*, were significant contributors to German romantic idealism during the late 18th and early 19th centuries. Auguste Comte (IV) was a positivist philosopher who formalized sociology. Thomas Mann (V) was a German writer (*Buddenbrooks* and *Death in Venice*) during the first half of the 20th century.

117. **(D)** The Republican agenda for Spain during the 1930s was outlined in the Constitution of 1931, which called for state control of education (A), as opposed to church control; restricting the influence of the military (B); pursuing the Catalonian request for autonomy (C); and extending democracy throughout Spanish society (E). These positions were opposed by the military, old nobility, and the Church. The issue of the seizure of Gibraltar (D) was not prominent during the 1930s.

118. **(B)** The first American offensive operation in World War II took place at Guadalcanal, in the Solomon Islands, on August 7, 1942. It was a shoestring effort to knock out a Japanese airfield on the island and few people thought it would succeed. However, after four months of bitter fighting, the Japanese were driven from the island and Guadalcanal became the starting point for the famous "island hopping" campaign against the Japanese in the Pacific. Both the Wake Island (A) and Midway Island (C) battles occurred before Guadalcanal but were defensive operations. The Tarawa (D) and Saipan (E) battles were offensive operations that occurred after the battle of Guadalcanal.

119. **(A)** During Jefferson's term as president (1800–1808), American merchant ships comprised a vital part of the nation's economy and transported a large percentage of the world's goods. American coastal cities grew in both size and prosperity from the rich trade brought in from around the world. Artisans associated with the merchant marine grew wealthy from constructing and maintaining the huge fleet of ships based in coastal cities and from constructing the intricate furniture and other

luxury items demanded by the wealthy ship owners and captains living in coastal ports.

120. **(B)** Georges Sorel (I) was the founder of syndicalism; *Confederacion Nacional del Trabajo* (II) was a coalition of Spanish syndicalist groups; and Filippo Corridoni (III) was an Italian syndicalist. Pierre Laval (IV) was a leader of the Third French Republic and the Vichy regime who was executed for assisting the Nazis. Michael Bakunin (V) was the Russian anarchist who established the Social Democratic Action.

121. **(E)** Ivan Turgenev's *Fathers and Sons* (E) asserted the superiority of science over tradition. *Les Misérables* by Victor Hugo (A) was a novel about social injustrice. Fyodor Dostoyevsky's *Crime and Punishment* (B) was a psychological novel. Mary Shelley's *Frankenstein* (D) is often interpreted as a condemnation of science, not an avocation of the superiority of science over tradition. Max Nordau's *Degeneration* (E) was an alarmist portrayal of reverse evolution.

122. **(C)** The Ballot Act, Civil Service Reform, the Education Act, and the Irish Land Act were all accomplishments of Liberal William Gladstone (C) during his first term as prime minister (1868–74). Benjamin Disraeli (A), Lord Salisbury (B), and Arthur James Balfour (E) were Conservative prime ministers. Lord Roseberry (D) led a short-lived Liberal ministry.

123. **(E)** The Battle of Antietam was a crucial event in the American Civil War for many reasons. First, it forced General Robert E. Lee to retreat from Maryland back into northern Virginia, thus ending his first foray into Yankee territory without a major success (III). In many ways, it was the first real victory by the Army of the Potomac over Lee's Army of Northern Virginia, and did much to bolster the sagging morale of Northerners. It also allowed Lincoln to announce the Emancipation Proclamation (I). Lincoln had decided some time previously to free the slaves in Union-controlled territories, but he felt he needed to make the announcement after a substantial Union victory. Lincoln feared that making the announcement while Union armies continued to lose to Confederate forces would seem like a desperate political tactic rather than a forceful moral statement, and would blunt the impact of the Proclamation. But while Antietam was a major victory for the Union, it was not a complete victory. General McClellan, commander of the Army of the Potomac, had had Lee's army in a geographic trap, with its back against the Potomac River. An aggressive, all-out assault on Lee's position could have, and should have, destroyed Lee's army entirely. However, McClellan hesitated to press his advantage and his army launched a series of costly piecemeal attacks that allowed Lee to escape to Virginia with the bulk of his army. Lincoln had criticized McClellan on previous occasions for the same lack of aggressive leadership and was infuriated when McClellan refused to follow Lee's army into northern Virginia. There is no doubt that the Army of the Potomac suffered greatly at Antietam, but McClellan's forces had an entire corps (about 15,000 men) that had been held in reserve throughout

the battle and remained untouched. Two other corps were also in reasonably good fighting condition, and McClellan's forces still maintained an almost two-to-one advantage over Lee's army. Whatever the condition of McClellan's army, Lee's army was in worse condition and was, for awhile, vulnerable as it limped southward with its supplies and wounded. Lee had no reserve to draw upon and of the three corps in his army, only Stonewall Jackson's corps was in any condition to continue the fight. Whether an immediate pursuit of Lee's army would have resulted in the complete victory Lincoln desired can be debated, but Lincoln saw another ruined opportunity. McClellan's refusal to even attempt to pursue Lee was the last straw for Lincoln and he subsequently relieved McClellan of command (III).

124. (E)   Although he was not typical of 19th century liberalism in every respect—he favored trade unions as a means of helping the working class, for example—John Stuart Mill wrote extensively on politics and is generally considered the most notable 19th century liberal writer. His *On Liberty* (1859) is one of the most famous defenses of individual rights. The other answers may be quickly eliminated if the identity of the individuals is known. As the leader of the British Conservative party in the second half of the 19th century, Disraeli opposed many liberal programs. Napoleon III, emperor of France during the 1850s and 1860s, worked to limit one of the major liberal goals, the achievement of true parliamentary government in France. The other answers list lesser-known individuals but are also incorrect. Proudhon was the most famous anarchist of the first half of the 19th century, while Fourier was one of the best-known Utopian socialists of the same period.

125. (C)   World War I had many profound effects on the social and political fabric of the United States. Due to the need for grain to feed the soldiers and allies in Europe, Woodrow Wilson was able to ban the use of grain to produce alcohol. This was the first step in outlawing the production and sale of alcohol altogether (prohibition) (A). Women's rights leaders vowed to refuse to support the American war effort until the government gave women the right to vote (B). Wilson knew that the war effort would be crippled without the full support of American women, so he relented in his opposition to women's suffrage and came out in favor of it in 1917. The need for factory workers to help boost war production led many blacks to leave southern plantations as part of the "great migration" northward in search of factory jobs (D). While many blacks did get jobs in factories and meat-packing plants, prejudice and discrimination prevented them from obtaining anything but the worst jobs available, typically jobs that no one else would take. The effort to promote patriotic support for the war led to a vicious backlash against those who spoke out against the war. Formal and informal sanctions were imposed on those who spoke out against the war and the courts, for the most part, supported these sanctions (E). What the war did not do was to make the United States the dominant international power during the postwar years (C). After the war, American frustration with Wilson's idealistic and internationalist policies was reflected in the rejection of the Versailles Treaty and the American refusal to join the League of Nations. In 1920, Americans elected Warren Harding with his promise of a "return to normalcy,"

which carried with it the promise to return to the isolationist policies of the past. American isolationism during the 1920s and 1930s prevented the United States from becoming the dominant international power during that time. While the United States emerged from World War I as a dominant economic power, it remained a political "sleeping giant" during the postwar years.

126. **(C)** The cartoon, which was published by the Tariff Reform League, was a criticism of Britain's free trade policy (II). Further, it was a call to abandon free trade (IV) because of the abuses which were perpetrated against Britain by nations with restrictive tariffs (III). It was in no way a defense of free trade (I), nor did it advance an image of the collapse of the British economy (V).

127. **(C)** The Stuart kings believed in the Divine Right of Kings and in their power to rule absolutely. When James I dissolved the Virginia company in 1624, he also canceled the Virginia assembly and refused to grant Virginians any basic political rights. They were to be under the absolute rule of the crown. Charles I, James' successor to the throne, followed a similar philosophy. However, as this became an issue in Virginia, Charles changed his policies to fit the situation. Rather than charging the Virginians with treason, as British law entitled him to but which could have led to an economically and politically costly campaign, Charles reasoned that granting the Virginians some measure of self-government could attract more settlers to the crown's colonies. This, in turn, would result in greater economic growth in the colonies, greater tax revenues, and greater North American influence for England. It would also relieve political pressure at home. So rather than moving to crush the efforts of the Virginians, Charles granted them the right to form a representative assembly in 1639. The remaining choices are all true. The Stuarts did view the colonies as a valuable source of potential tax revenue as well as raw materials (B). They frequently used the colonies to reward, or to buy, the loyalty of court favorites (A). They did use the colonies as a dumping ground for troublesome dissident groups, both political and religious, such as the Puritans (D). They saw the development of the British colonial empire in North America as an essential means of enhancing British stature among the major powers in Europe (E).

128. **(A)** The Mugwumps were disenchanted Republicans who bolted from the party when it nominated James G. Blaine as its presidential nominee in 1884. While Blaine was a striking and charismatic candidate, he was seen as someone who could be, and had been, bought by special interests. The Mugwumps wanted an honest candidate, as honesty in office was the only real issue in the 1884 election. The Democrats, sensing mass Mugwump support if they could find the right candidate, selected Grover Cleveland as their presidential nominee. While Cleveland was neither charismatic nor striking, he was honest. The Mugwumps, as hoped, gave Cleveland their support, and it was crucial to his election as president. The Ku Klux Klan (B) and organized labor (E) were not large or organized enough to be major factors in the election. The Know-Nothings (C) no longer existed, and Tammany Hall (D)

hated Cleveland because of his actions against it while he was governor of New York and worked to prevent his election.

129. (D)   Of the choices given, a lack of available credit is the only one that did not contribute to the Great Depression. In fact, just the opposite was true. During the 1920s, to help spread the new ethic of consumerism, banks and industries made new forms of credit and installment loans available to the public. This credit was essential because while industry pushed people to consume, it refused to pay workers the wages they needed to buy the new consumer goods. Credit was also essential to farmers who could not earn enough from their crops to break even because of depressed crop prices. Without the new forms of credit being offered, consumers and farmers could not have sustained the economy as long as they did. Even with the new credit forms, without wage and crop price increases, workers and farmers could not continue to purchase new goods and equipment indefinitely. Eventually they reached their credit limits and often found they couldn't pay off their loans. The resulting foreclosures and bankruptcies weakened the entire banking system, making banks particularly vulnerable when the Stock Market Crash began the collapse of the economic boom of the 1920s.

130. (B)   The thesis proposed by the German sociologist Max Weber theorized a connection between the rise of Calvinism (and Protestantism in general) and the development of capitalism (B). Weber proposed that the two were related because both emphasized thrift, industriousness, self-sufficiency, and the other virtues embodied in what is now known as the "Protestant work ethic." Absolute monarchies (A) and nation-states (C) were in existence long before Calvinism. The rise of Anglicanism (D) is linked to Henry VIII and his rebellion against the restrictions of the Catholic church. Catholicism (E), of course, was also in existence for many centuries before Calvinism rejected many of its basic tenets.

131. (B)   The correct chronological order of these German chancellors is Count von Caprivi (1890–94), Prince Hohenlohe (1894–1900), Prince Bernhard von Bulow (1900–09), and Chancellor Bethmann-Hollweg (1909–17).

132. (E)   The psychological reaction of most Americans to the War of 1812 was one of withdrawal. Most people remembered Washington's advice to be wary of European entanglements and the war confirmed in their minds that Washington had been correct. Rather than seeking a more active and dominant role in European intrigues, most Americans sought isolationism and avoidance of European commitments. Others wished to further reduce U.S. involvement with Europe by keeping Europe out of the Americas. This wish was expressed in the Monroe Doctrine nine years after the conclusion of the 1812 war. While the various trade embargoes during the war hurt American commerce, particularly in maritime New England (A), these same embargoes forced Americans to produce their own goods. In an unintended way, the embargoes served as a form of protectionism for fledgling American manufacturers. Without European imports to compete against, the

Americans developed their own industries and established enough of a foothold to continue to thrive even after trade with Europe resumed. The Federalist party had consistently opposed the war (B), culminating with their disastrous Hartford Convention in 1814. With the conclusion of the war and the resulting wave of nationalism that swept the country, the Federalists were discredited as traitors. They were never again able to effectively challenge the Republican party for political control at the national level. Despite the military and economic blunders throughout the war, the victory at New Orleans and the perception that by holding Britain to a stalemate the U.S. had effectively "won" the war, led to a wave of nationalistic fervor (C). Many people characterized the War of 1812 as a second war of independence and believed that the U.S. "victory" in the war unified the country and pointed the country toward a long-term destiny of greatness. In spite of military failures elsewhere in the war, American actions against the unified Native American tribes in the west were surprisingly successful (D). With the loss of leaders like Tecumseh, and the loss of British support at the end of the war, the tribes had little chance of blunting further westward expansion by the Americans.

133. (D) The most consistent supporter of Darwin's views on evolution was Thomas Huxley (D). Herbert Spencer (A) promoted a philosophy known as Social Darwinism. George Bernard Shaw (B) and Samuel Butler (C) were influenced by Darwinian principles but later modified them. Aldous Huxley (E) (*Brave New World*) was a prominent British writer during the period from the 1920s to 1963.

134. (D) Abelard (1079–1142) was as famous for his scandalous personal life as for his theory of Conceptualism, which was an attempt to find a middle ground between the viewpoints of medieval Realists and Nominalists. William of Ockham (A) was a 13th century Nominalist philosopher who challenged much of the basis of medieval theology. Pope Boniface VIII (B) was kidnapped by agents of the French king Phillip the Fair in the early 1300s; his kidnapping began the Babylonian Captivity, when the popes were under the control of the French monarchy. Philip Augustus, who lived in the late 12th and early 13th centuries, was one of the notable Capetian monarchs of France. Frederick II (E), who lived in the 13th century, was one of the most famous and powerful Holy Roman Emperors.

135. (A) The Tet offensive was a turning point in the Vietnam War in many ways; however, it did not mark the first significant military victory by North Vietnamese forces over American forces. While Tet was certainly a political victory for the North Vietnamese, it was a costly military defeat on the battlefield. The timing of the attack, at the beginning of the 1968 Presidential campaign and immediately following several statements by military leaders that the North Vietnamese were finished, caused military leaders to lose much of their credibility with the public (B). It also resulted in much more negative news coverage of the war by the media (C). Up until Tet the media had not publicly questioned much of what was occurring in Vietnam. After Tet, the media began asking questions and raising the issue of whether or not victory was possible at all. As the media began to question the

chances of victory, so did the general public. Young people in particular openly challenged administration policies and the question now became "How do we get out?" (D). With his popularity plummeting and his advisors telling him there was no victorious way out, short of nuclear war—which would probably bring the Chinese or even the Russians into the conflict, in which case no one would win— Lyndon Johnson withdrew from the presidential race and offered to begin peace negotiations with the North Vietnamese (E) "any time, any place."

136. **(B)** The death of Labour leader Hugh Gaitskell in 1963 brought Harold Wilson to the head of the Labour party, while the Profumo affair of the same year, which triggered fears of Russian espionage when it was discovered that Conservative Minister of War John Profumo had used the same call girl as a Russian naval attaché, hastened the retirement of Conservative Prime Minister Harold Macmillan (B). Sir Alec Douglas-Home (A), (E) was the Conservative leader who became prime minister after Macmillan's resignation, and Edward Heath (D) did not emerge as the Conservative leader until after Douglas-Home's resignation in 1965. The British economy (C) did not collapse during the 1960s, although the rate of growth diminished.

137. **(C)** The diagram is of an Ionic column and entablature; the delicacy of the Ionic column indicates Mycenaen and Egyptian influences. It is named after the location of its development, Ionia. The Doric column (A) was much wider and unadorned at the top. The Corinthian column (C), which was somewhat similar to the Ionic, was characterized by the ornate Corinthian capital at the top. The term Attic (D) refers to Greek art that reflected a combination of Doric and Ionian influences.

138. **(A)** The Peace of Callias in 449 BC terminated the Persian threat to the Greek city-states. This Athenian victory resulted in a challenge to the continuance of the Delian League and the disintegration of the unity of the Greek city-states which had existed, in varying degrees, for five decades. The Peace of Nicias (B) was a truce during the Peloponnesian War. Zama (C) was the site of the Roman victory over Hannibal in the Second Punic War. Xenophon's expedition, which he recounted in several literary works, occurred after the Peloponnesian War. Alexander the Great (E) built his empire during the second half of the 4th century BC.

139. **(B)** New Orleans, in the 1890s, provided the perfect opportunity for the European musical influences followed by wealthy Creoles (people of French, Spanish, and Negro heritage) to intermingle with African musical influences dominating the culture of poor blacks. The result was a distinctly American musical form called jazz. Jazz players of turn-of-the-century New Orleans were among the highest paid "workers" in the South. These almost exclusively black performers were wealthier than virtually any other blacks in the country at the time. They also enjoyed a certain amount of respect and recognition denied to most other blacks. Eventually, New Orleans jazz musicians took their music with them to other parts of the

country. But it was in New Orleans that black musicians gave America its first truly original music form. Blues (E) was a somewhat similar music form that also developed in New Orleans. Its development somewhat preceded jazz and was dominated by African musical influences, but it never integrated the influences of European music in the way jazz did. The development of the other types of music listed in the question were not associated with New Orleans, although gospel (A) also resulted from African American musical influences.

140. **(D)** While Charles III of Spain (A), Frederick the Great of Prussia (B), Joseph II of Austria (C), and Catherine the Great (E) can be identified in some ways as "Enlightened" monarchs, Louis XV of France exhibited no interest in the reform movement. Charles III permitted political innovations in his South American colonies, which contributed to the emergence of revolutions; Frederick the Great of Prussia instituted a series of political, economic, and cultural reforms in Prussia; Joseph II of Austria is identified with "Josephism," a plan for state control of the Church; and Catherine the Great initiated some reforms on the "Enlightened" model.

141. **(E)** The passage is taken from a speech by U.S. Senator Albert Beveridge, an ardent imperialist, and represents a philosophy based on Manifest Destiny (I), American exceptionalism (II), and Social Darwinism (III). The doctrine of Manifest Destiny stated that it was the destiny of the United States to dominate and rule all of the American continent. It was based on the belief that the American people and American democracy were superior to other peoples and governments in the Americas. This is related to the concept of American exceptionalism (II), which stated that America was God's chosen nation and Americans were God's chosen people. The two concepts went hand-in-hand, because if Americans were God's chosen people, then it was God's will that they should someday dominate North America, if not the rest of the world. When Darwin's ideas were published, hypothesizing survival of the fittest, many Americans quickly embraced them because they were easily translated into Social Darwinism, the belief that "superior" cultures will naturally come to dominate "inferior" cultures. This line of reasoning was used to establish "scientific" support for the concepts of Manifest Destiny and American exceptionalism. Together they provided a compelling, even if distorted, rationale for American imperialism.

142. **(D)** The case of *Brown v. Board of Education of Topeka*, in 1954, was a landmark case that some have called the "second Emancipation Proclamation." By ordering an immediate end to segregated schools the Supreme Court, in theory, dismantled the entire separate but equal doctrine that had dominated education in the South since the days of Reconstruction. Unfortunately, in the months and years following the ruling, it became clear that ruling something illegal in the court is much easier than eliminating it outside the court. The ruling did not force an immediate end to segregation (E). The Court's order left it up to local officials to enforce its ruling and they overwhelmingly refused to do so. Southern states filed

suits designed to stall implementation of the ruling, and three years later the majority of schools were still segregated. The case also showed the importance of federal leadership in enforcing civil rights rulings. There is evidence that if Eisenhower's administration acted quickly and decisively in enforcing the decision, Southern states would have grudgingly desegregated. However, Eisenhower disagreed with the decision and did nothing to enforce it, which encouraged Southerners to openly violate the ruling. This behavior made it clear that the federal government was not going to enforce the ruling (A) and led many blacks to lose faith in the ability of the courts to change their situation. While blacks understood that they might count on the courts to support their efforts (C), support wouldn't matter if the government did not follow up with strict enforcement of court rulings. Blacks took to the streets in 1955 in places like Montgomery, Alabama, not because they lost faith in the courts' willingness to support them, but because they lost faith in the willingness of the government to support court decisions. It took a crisis in Little Rock, Arkansas, in 1957 to finally force the federal government to send in the military to enforce the desegregation rulings, and by then resistance to the Court's decision had solidified. The impact of the ruling supported Eisenhower's contention that one can't "change the hearts of men with laws." The Court could rule against desegregation but what was really needed was to change the attitudes of those who believed in segregation. The behavior of whites in the aftermath of *Brown* demonstrated the inability of the court to quickly change the attitudes and personal behaviors of those who were prejudiced (B).

143. **(B)** The German decision to implement the "Final Solution"—the destruction of European Jewry—was made at the Wanasee Conference (B), which was held in 1941. It was a group decision made after the defeat of France and when the defeat of Russia seemed imminent.

144. **(D)** René Descartes was arguably the greatest French philosopher of all time. However, he lived and wrote during the 17th, not the 18th century. His writings dealt with the relationship of the mind and body (dualism) more than with political liberties and the rights of individuals. American political leaders during the period of the American Revolution were much more directly influenced by the French writers of the 18th century Enlightenment. The writings of these individuals offered eager Americans the intellectual ammunition they needed to challenge British authority and to give credence to their own ideas about liberty, human dignity, and American independence. Montesquieu's (A) *The Spirit of Laws*, Rousseau's (B) *Social Contract*, Diderot's (C) *Encyclopedia*, and Voltaire's (E) *Universal Man* all dealt with issues which were the very essence of the American Revolution.

145. **(A)** Jane Addams was a leading Progressivist who was best known for her work in settlement houses. She was a college-educated, pragmatic young woman with an eye for observing the problems of the society around her and a powerful determination to understand and solve those problems. She is most well known for establishing Chicago's Hull House, a settlement house that offered basic amenities

such as showers and food, as well as more sophisticated services such as a medical clinic, child care, a reading room, and educational services. Hull House served as a model for other settlement houses, which were places where middle-class social workers tried to provide the poverty stricken around them with tools to improve their lives. In addition to providing services for the disadvantaged, Addams spent years investigating the people who lived in and around Hull House so that she could better understand their situation and help them more effectively. She found that many were immigrants who suffered not only from poverty but from assorted language and cultural barriers. She worked to help them not only become integrated into the American mainstream, but also to appreciate their own cultural and ethnic roots and to be proud of their traditions. Although temperance (B) was something that was often promoted in settlement houses, it was not the primary focus of Addams' work. The same is true for children's literature (E). Jane Addams was not known for her work in the women's suffrage movement (D), even though she supported it, nor was she involved in nursing care for war veterans (C), aside from those veterans who found their way to Hull House.

146. **(B)** The Locarno Conference of 1925 was dominated by the French foreign minister Briand and the German foreign secretary Stresemann (I), and resulted in treaties which affirmed existing boundaries (II) and agreements never to go to war against each other (III). The Kellogg-Briand Pact of 1928 (IV) outlawed war. Efforts to limit armaments, such as the Geneva Conference (V), failed.

147. **(D)** Washington Irving was internationally recognized as America's most polished and successful writer during the early 1800s. His works were celebrated in Europe as well as in America, in an era when Europeans delighted in criticizing the intellectual ignorance of Americans. *Rip Van Winkle* and *The Legend of Sleepy Hollow* became America's first literary classics and his work *The Sketch Book* became a standard reading text in primary schools throughout the English-speaking world. Irving's contemporary James Fenimore Cooper (C) was second only to Irving in his success as an author during this period. *The Last of the Mohicans* and other works describing the colonial American frontier captured people's imagination as no other work had. While he was internationally renowned, literary critics often attacked his often brittle character development and somewhat clumsy style. The result was that while Cooper and Irving were the most successful American authors of their day, Irving was seen as the more polished. Sir Walter Scott (A) was British, not American; his works inspired both Irving and Cooper. Mark Twain (B) and Edgar Allan Poe (E) wrote later in the 1800s than Washington Irving. Poe did his most famous works in the 1840s, while Twain's work would not be widely publicized until after the Civil War.

148. **(D)** Poland's Gomulka, Czechoslovakia's Dubcek, and Yugoslavia's Tito all came into conflict with the Soviet Union. None of them opposed de-Stalinization (A), and they did not reject socialism (B) or support Mao Tse-tung (E). Yugoslavia never experienced Soviet occupation (C).

149. **(B)** Van Gogh (1853–90) had abandoned Impressionism (A) because he felt that its style limited his freedom of expression. *The Starry Night* is a post-impressionist (B) study which was completed in 1889. Expressionism (C) and pointilism (D) were later variations of Impressionism. Symbolism (E) was a dramatic departure from more traditional schools of art which was characteristic of many early 20th century artists.

150. **(D)** It is important to note that this question refers to the *long-term* consequences of the Industrial Revolution. While it was a very gradual one, studies have shown that the standard of living of the working class in industrialized European countries did increase (D). The standard of living in an agrarian society, though often romanticized, was not necessarily superior to that of an urban one (A), and while in rural areas the length of the workday varied with the amount of sunlight, legislation soon limited the workday for industrial workers (B). The size of the financial contribution made by women actually increased as many women, no longer tied to the home by the plethora of domestic farm chores, went to work in the factories (C). While it can be argued that there were advantages of a rural lifestyle that were lost, the standard of living did not remain at the same level, so (E) is incorrect.

151. **(B)** One of the most important trends in family life in Europe was the shrinking size of the family. Instead of bearing eight or more children, as was common before the 19th century, and often losing two-thirds of the children before adulthood, women began to limit their families to two or three children (B). Many reasons have been suggested to explain this trend, which is the opposite of choice (D). An increase in the number of middle-class women who had careers (A) is not a likely explanation, however. It was not until almost the middle of the 20th century that it became acceptable for middle-class women to work outside the home. The 19th century did not see an increase in child mortality (C) or a decline in the quality of medical care (E). The opposite is true; infant mortality rates decreased dramatically, as new medical techniques and a clearer understanding of disease transmission became widespread.

152. **(C)** Winston Churchill's removal from the position of First Lord of the Admiralty during the First World War was precipitated by the English defeat at Gallipoli (C). Churchill had argued that the opening of a southern front against Turkey was needed to relieve the Russians and to open a pathway to Central Europe. The Gallipoli campaign resulted in defeat for the British and the discrediting of Churchill. The Battle of Jutland of 1916 (A) was the only major naval battle of the war. The Second Battle of the Marne (D), Verdun (E), and Antwerp (B) did not result in Churchill's fall.

153. **(C)** George Ball, Lyndon Johnson's under secretary of state, was the only one of Johnson's senior advisors who openly spoke out against expanding the American effort in Vietnam before the expansion took place. Ball bluntly stated that the

United States would be going into Vietnam for all the wrong reasons and would no more be able to beat the North Vietnamese than the French had in the 1950s. Ball feared a national humiliation and predicted that American forces could not "successfully fight Orientals in an Asian jungle." Ball's prophetic conclusions raised serious concerns for Johnson and caused him to request a reevaluation of the effects of an American expansion in Vietnam. But ultimately, Johnson felt he had no choice but to expand the war in the hopes of putting enough pressure on Hanoi to force the North Vietnamese to strike a deal. Ball understood what Lyndon Johnson never fully comprehended—that to Ho Chi Minh and the North Vietnamese, their efforts in South Vietnam were for national unification and independence. They were not interested in any deal Johnson could offer them and never would have made one that left the South Vietnamese government intact as a separate national government. While some of Johnson's other advisers, most notably Secretary of Defense Robert McNamara (A), eventually changed their minds and urged an American pull-out from Vietnam, none of the other officials listed openly opposed American expansion of its war efforts in Vietnam before the expansion took place.

154. (D)   The paragraph summarizes the position taken by Abraham Lincoln during the Lincoln-Douglas debates in 1856. Lincoln was in a very difficult position throughout these debates and walked a political tightrope, opposing slavery on moral grounds while at the same time trying not to offend a sometimes violent racist electorate. Lincoln truly believed slavery to be a moral wrong that could not be allowed to expand. Politically, he believed that slavery would destroy the Union unless its expansion was halted. At the same time he knew that advocating the elimination of slavery in states that already allowed slavery would amount to political suicide. He knew that any effort to forcefully eliminate slavery would result in a war that could destroy the Union. Also, he knew that advocating full citizenship for blacks, thus supporting the notion that blacks were not inferior to whites but were their equals, would be political suicide given the racism of the electorate. Hence, he adopted the inherently contradictory position of opposing slavery on moral grounds, but refusing to support efforts to eliminate it completely; claiming that blacks were equal to anybody, but refusing to support full citizenship for blacks. Stephen Douglas (A) never denounced slavery as immoral. At best he argued that it would naturally wither away because it could not remain profitable. He took the position that individual states and territories should decide whether or not to allow slavery. Douglas never viewed blacks as the equal of whites and never argued for any rights for blacks. He openly stated during the Lincoln-Douglas debates that he wanted citizenship only for whites. John Brown (B) went to the other extreme. He was an ardent abolitionist who wanted not only an end to slavery and full rights for blacks, he wanted a military invasion of the South to force Southern slaveowners to release their slaves. His ill-conceived occupation of the Federal arsenal in Harpers Ferry, Virginia, was an attempt to begin a national insurrection that would lead to emancipation of the slaves. John Breckinridge (C) was the Kentucky lawmaker who ran as a Southern Democrat against Abraham Lincoln in the 1860 presidential election. As such he led the movement to protect states' rights and to preserve slavery as an

institution. Dred Scott (E) was the center of the controversial Supreme Court decision of March 1857, in which the Court ruled that Scott, a freed slave, had no right to sue in the federal courts and could be returned to slavery.

155. **(D)** When Russia signed a separate peace with Germany in January 1918, the Allies felt betrayed. The Bolshevik government, responsible for the pull out, was ostracized by Western Europe and the United States. In 1919, the Bolsheviks announced the formation of the Communist International Movement (Comintern) to spread the revolution worldwide. This spread fear throughout non-Communist industrial nations and led to suspicions of Communist subversion whenever domestic problems arose, especially when those problems involved labor, where Communist organizers were believed to be most active. In the United States in 1919, many management-labor disputes held in check during the war now boiled to the surface. Workers who didn't feel free to challenge the government or industry while the nation was at war now felt justified in pushing for resolution of their grievances. As a result, more that 4,000,000 workers walked off the job in over 3,000 strikes. Bombs were mailed to several business and political leaders and threats were sent to hundreds more. While the vast majority of these walkouts were due to labor complaints about wages and working conditions, there was just enough involvement by known leftists and Communists to confirm suspicions that all the strikes were part of a massive plot by Communists and anarchists to bring down the U.S. government and economic system. The Federal Bureau of Investigation was created to crush the "insurrection." Working together with state and local police agencies, the FBI arrested thousands of suspected Communists and charged them with sedition. Hundreds of foreign nationals living in the United States were deported, often on very flimsy evidence. However, when alleged plots and predictions of terrorism proved unfounded, the leaders of the anti-Communist crackdown slowly but steadily lost their credibility, and the crackdowns ceased.

156. **(D)** In *The Spirit of the Laws*, Baron Montesquieu (D) indicated that he was influenced by the historical development of the British government. He maintained that France should embark upon a process to emulate the British system. Voltaire (A) was an advocate of Enlightened Despotism; Quesnay (C) was a Physiocrat who admired Chinese government; Rousseau (B) was the author of *The Social Contract*, in which he redefined the relationship between the governor and the governed; and Diderot (E) was the editor of *The Encyclopedia*.

157. **(D)** The Quakers held the philosophy that all humans were equal in the sight of God; this included both men and women. As a result, the Quakers allowed women to serve in all leadership positions, including the clergy. They refused to possess slaves, and eventually condemned the entire practice of slavery, preaching that blacks were not inferior to whites in God's eyes. They were pacifists who saw war as a problem, not a solution to problems. Their beliefs were considered radical and made them very unpopular among most other colonial religious groups, particularly the Puritans. As for the remaining groups, the Pilgrims (A) and the Puritans (B)

denied equal rights to women and were more than willing to limit the rights of anyone who did not share their religious and moral beliefs. To the extent that colonial Anglicans (E) believed in the Divine Right of Kings, as was required by the church, they could not believe in human equality, as the notion of Divine Right was inherently unequal. They were also willing to oppress those who failed to share their beliefs and they too refused to see women as equals. Dutch Patroons (C) were the managers of an inherently unfair Dutch colonial system, in which they ruled over the tenants of their land grants like feudal lords. They were elitists who fully believed in the inferiority of those whom they ruled and certainly disagreed with such radical notions as the equality of women or blacks.

158. **(E)**   The concept of absolutism was supported by Hobbes in his work *Leviathan*. John Locke (A), in his *Two Treatises on Civil Government*, clearly rejected such a concept. Bodin (B) and Montesquieu (D), French political theorists of the 16th and 18th centuries respectively, would also have rejected such a concept of absolutism. Napier (C) was a scientist, the deviser of logarithms.

159. **(D)**   As part of his efforts to weaken the Socialists in the newly unified Germany (D), Chancellor Otto von Bismarck introduced a number of social welfare programs, including old age, accident, and workman's compensation. Britain (B) was the first to follow Bismarck's example. These types of social programs were only gradually introduced in Switzerland (A), France (C), and Belgium (E).

160. **(B)**   The Fabian Society was begun by Beatrice and Sidney Webb, two notable British social reformers. Other Fabian Socialists included the authors George Bernard Shaw and H.G. Wells. The Fabians advocated peaceful social change, particularly the public ownership of private industries. Privately owned utilities, which could charge high rates to the struggling lower classes, were prime targets for the Fabians, who pushed for government ownership and regulation of utilities. Adam Smith's *Wealth of Nations* (A), which proposed laissez-faire economic policies (C), represented everything the Fabians rejected, as did government subsidies to private corporations (E). An increased naval budget (D) would epitomize the imperialistic government that the Fabians were committed to reforming.

161. **(D)**   The South's emphasis on states' rights made running the war against the North an impossible task. Efforts by the Confederate government to draft soldiers, to collect taxes, and to coordinate "national" policies were made almost impossible by fierce resistance from state governments determined to enact their own policies, even if those policies hurt the overall Confederate cause. Many state leaders felt that by "caving in" to the Confederate government they were giving it the same federal powers which had led them to secede from the Union in the first place. This was something many state leaders found hypocritical and ethically unacceptable. Unfortunately, this type of resistance often paralyzed Jefferson Davis's government and virtually guaranteed a Union victory in a prolonged war. All of the remaining

choices were valid reasons why the Union had a difficult time defeating the Confederacy in the Civil War.

162. **(B)** The primary factor in the increase in the European population from 1700 to 1900 was in increase in the food supply (B), brought about by improved agricultural methods. Better medical care (A) was a factor, but not as important as the food supply. During this period, the immigration trend was from Europe to the New World, not the other way around (C). In fact, the pressure from the increasing population contributed to the rise of immigration to the New World. European governments did not adopt policies advocating a high birth rate (D); for the most part, the governments did not concern themselves with the birth rate at all. While increasing urbanization (E) did accompany the increase in population, most historians agree that it was an effect of the population increase, not a cause of it.

163. **(D)** W. E. B. DuBois was a black progressive leader, a well-educated (Ph.D. from Harvard), articulate spokesman for African Americans who refused to accept continued subjugation by whites. He believed that to achieve equality, an elite group of talented, trained, and well-educated African Americans would have to lead the way, setting an example whites could not dismiss and other African Americans could proudly follow. His goals led him to found the NAACP as a vehicle to promote black rights through the courts and to focus concern on black needs and black issues. An idealistic intellectual, his style often alienated him from the majority of impoverished, uneducated African Americans of his day. He found more support among progressive, liberal white intellectuals than among blacks. However, he did set the example his ideals lauded, a strong African American leader whom whites could not easily dismiss and whom blacks could follow proudly. Marcus Garvey (A) was another leading African American. But Garvey felt that blacks would never be accepted as equals by whites nor would they be allowed to fully integrate into white society. As a result, he led a black nationalist group whose goal was the formation of a separate black society. He also headed a "back to Africa" movement in the 1920s, recognizing that his dream of separation would never come true in the United States. He ran the Black Star shipping line and used it to help black Americans emigrate to Liberia as part of his back to Africa campaign. Booker T. Washington (B) founded the Tuskegee Institute in Alabama in 1881. He believed that blacks had to pull themselves out of poverty because they would never get help from white society. He also believed that blacks needed to accept white superiority until they could make themselves economically successful enough to prove to whites that blacks were truly equals. This argument offended many African American leaders, and was flawed in that as long as whites treated blacks as inferiors, it was almost impossible for blacks to get the jobs or acquire the property they needed to fulfill Washington's ideals. George Washington Carver (C) was a chemist employed at the Tuskegee Institute. He was most well known for his scientific advancements in the use of food crops such as peanuts and potatoes, as well as his work on soil enrichment and conservation. Hiram Revels (E) was an African American senator from Mississippi during the Southern Reconstruction. He was involved during the entire

Reconstruction movement to help protect newly won rights for blacks and to establish a solid education system in which all Southern children could receive a decent education.

164. **(E)** During its early years in the 1920s, Mussolini's Fascist regime was based upon fear of communism (A), labor unrest (B), the anxieties of the middle class (C), and industrialists and landowners who desired stability (D). The Church (E) did not reconcile itself with Mussolini's regime until the Concordat of 1929.

165. **(D)** The concept of Irish Home Rule was supported by the Irish leader of the 1830s Daniel O'Connell (I), the brilliant Liberal MP, Charles Stewart Parnell (II), once called "the uncrowned king of Ireland," and Prime Minister William Gladstone (IV), whose support wavered at times. The Conservative Lord Salisbury (III) opposed Irish Home Rule; the Liberal-Unionist turned Conservative Joseph Chamberlain, who served as colonial secretary, also opposed it. Gladstone realized he needed the support of the Irish Parliamentarians to sustain his ministries; Salisbury and Chamberlain were identified with the "imperial" leadership of the Conservative party, who wanted Ireland to accept "colonial" treatment.

166. **(C)** The paintings and prints described were part of an American artistic movement called democratic genre painting, which began in the 1830s in celebration of the "common person" and, more particularly, Andrew Jackson's political concept of "popular sovereignty," which emphasized the importance of the average citizen in the American political process. While all of these paintings and prints may in some way reflect the political philosophies of Lincoln (E), Washington (D), Adams (B), or Hamilton (A), the overall thrust of this artistic genre is clearly associated with Andrew Jackson's glorification of the common people and with the rise of mass democracy associated with Jackson's election as U.S. president in 1828.

167. **(D)** The greatest obstacle faced by the United States Congress operating under the Articles of Confederation was that for any law to be enacted, all of the states had to agree to its enactment. Unanimous consent was difficult to obtain. For example, when American representatives signed treaties, individual states would refuse to obey the treaty provisions if they disagreed with them. The Articles gave Congress no powers to force compliance. This limitation affected taxation, defense, commerce, and foreign relations. Without increased power to the national government, the country could not grow and prosper as a single, unified entity. Concerns about the sovereignty of individual states had led to the Articles being weighted toward states' rights, crippling the national government. (A) is incorrect because there was no separation of powers concept inherent within the Articles of Confederation. The only branch of federal government fully established under the Articles was the Continental Congress. There were no distinctly separate executive (B) or judicial branches at the federal level. The Congress acted as both a legislative and an executive branch. Congress's powers were so limited that there were virtually no powers to curb. While the Articles of Confederation did not deal directly with

voting rights (C), the individual states each set their own voting requirements and restrictions, this omission did not result in the failure of the Articles as a whole. Most states restricted voting to white males, often requiring that they own property. This practice continued well into the 19th and 20th centuries. Finally, under the Articles of Confederation, the Congress had virtually no inherent taxation powers, so there was no conflict between large and small states about fairness in taxation rates (E).

168. **(D)** This painting is an example of surrealism (D), a style popular in the 1920s and 1930s which often produced bizarre, dreamlike images. Dadaism (A) is the style of art that protested the meaninglessness of World War I. The Fauves (B), or "wild beasts," emerged during the 1890s, producing paintings of strong color and intensity that were often based on African or Central American art. Cubism (C) is a form of abstract art that often tries to present objects as if seen from several different angles simultaneously. Impressionism (E) was a 19th century movement that rejected the tradition of presenting the subject as realistically as possible, in favor of softer, more subjective portrayals.

169. **(B)** Each of the books listed dealt with themes related to Progressivist ideas of a more fair and orderly society, and confronted some of the problems posed by laissez-faire, Social Darwinist philosophies as practiced in America. However, *Babbitt* by Sinclair Lewis was not published until 1922, two years after Wilson's presidency had ended. It focused on the corruption of American values at the level of the small-town businessman by the emphasis on making money. Thorstein Veblen's *Theory of the Leisure Class* (A), 1899, and *The Instinct of Workmanship* (C), 1914, attacked laissez-faire and Social Darwinist principles, and demonstrated how imbalanced and destructive these principles were as practiced in the American economy. Frederick Taylor's *Dynamic Sociology* (E), 1883, argued for a focus on the good of society as a whole rather than on the needs of the individual. Finally, Upton Sinclair's *The Jungle* (D), 1906, described the repugnant working conditions in the meat-packing industry in graphic detail. It was a merciless condemnation of management's abuse of labor under turn-of-the-century laissez-faire economics. Each of these works was undoubtedly read by Wilson and could have influenced his Progressivist ideals.

170. **(B)** The success of the Liberals in 1906 has been attributed to their advocacy of a land reform policy which would aid the lower classes (A); condemnation of the Boer War (C); their identification with a free trade policy (D); and recognition that some restrictions had to be introduced to regulate working conditions (E). The Liberals did not desire to expand the defense budget (B); however, circumstances later resulted in such a development.

171. **(C)** Calvin's religious beliefs, which gave rise to such sects as the Calvinists, Puritans, and Presbyterians, drew upon the foundation laid by Zwingli in Geneva. Luther (A) rejected a number of the doctrines of Puritanism, particularly that of

predestination. Hutter (B) was an Anabaptist, while Hus (D) and Servetus (E) were pre-Reformation religious reformers.

172. **(C)** The permanency of the Franco-German boundary was guaranteed by the Paris-Berlin Peace Pact of December 1938 (C). The Munich accord (A) (September 1938) determined the boundaries of Czechoslovakia. The Kellogg-Briand Pact (B) of 1928 outlawed war. The Dawes Plan (D) of 1924 was a reparations scheme; and the Geneva Conference (E) of 1932 was an unsuccessful disarmament meeting.

173. **(C)** Benedict Arnold was one of the American generals who fought bravely in the defeat of the British at Saratoga (I). However, he felt that he did not get the credit he deserved for his efforts in this and other American victories. This, in combination with other frustrations about the way the war was being run, led him to betray the American cause by aiding the British attempt to capture the American base at West Point (III). He did not take part in the battle of the Cowpens (II), which was fought after the incident at West Point.

174. **(A)** Although the British often imposed tariffs on American goods imported to Britain, the United States had developed other markets in Europe, the Caribbean, and the Americas to blunt the impact of British tariffs. While the tariffs did not help the United States grow industrially, they were not a major barrier to growth during this period. America's growth was hindered much more profoundly by its size. There were few adequate roads traversing even the most well-developed parts of the nation, and the vast frontier regions were crossed only by narrow dirt paths that were impassable in bad weather. Railroads and canals had not yet been developed to any large degree, so it was often impossible or extremely expensive and time consuming to travel or ship goods from one part of the country to another. This lack of a cheap and reliable transportation system (E) made it nearly impossible for fledgling industries to get enough market access to expand. The inadequate transportation system also made communications across the nation slow or nonexistent (D). Since an effective communications system is essential for rapid industrial development, the lack of such a system greatly impeded industrial growth. The rural nature of the American population also hindered growth. The United States had few colleges or libraries and no public education system. Most Americans lived on farms and saw no need for formal education beyond the most rudimentary level. Thus, the education system did not produce enough trained graduates to provide the pool of skilled managers and industrial leaders necessary for sustained industrial growth (C). The uneducated population intensely resisted most changes. Most Americans did things the way their grandparents had done them and distrusted new methods that they did not understand (B). Their lack of education meant that they were often unable to see how new devices or methods could improve their lives or their work productivity, thus increasing their resistance to change.

175. **(D)** The July Ordinances (D) of King Charles X of France consisted of restrictions on assembly, speech, and censorship of publications—they were reactionary, not liberal. The *Statuto* (A) of King Charles Albert of Sardinia was a liberal constitution based on the French July Monarchy (E), which deposed Charles X. In Britain, the Factory Act of 1833 (C), which limited the use of child labor in the textile industry, and the Chartist Movement (B), which advocated the implementation of democratic processes, reflected the liberal sentiment of that society.

176. **(B)** The Association Act and the repudiation of the Concordat of 1801 were related to the Dreyfus Affair (B), in which the Church supported the military and the political Right. The Boulanger Crisis (A) and the Panama Scandal (C) were internal threats to the Third Republic. The War in Sight Crisis of 1875 (D) with Germany did not result in a conflict. The Paris Commune (E) was an attempt to establish a socialist regime.

177. **(C)** The only nation in this list to fit this data for the years shown is the Soviet Union, which during the 1930s was rapidly industrializing under Joseph Stalin's Five-Year Plans. The graph shows little pig iron production before 1920 and a steep rise in production after 1930. The fall in cattle production during some years reflects the Communist government's perennial problems with farm production; it also reflects the chaos of Stalin's forced reorganization of Soviet agriculture into collective farms.

178. **(E)** The chart clearly shows the increase in cattle production from 1923 to 1928, and then its decrease from 1928 to 1933. The chart also shows that there is no inverse law of production operating on pig iron and cattle (D); for example, pig iron and cattle both increased dramatically from 1934 to 1936. And the chart clearly shows that the Great Depression alone could not have caused production declines (A), since pig iron production increased by 250% from 1928 to 1934. The other conclusions require additional information that the chart does not provide. Unlike Germany and France, Russia really had no industrial infrastructure to be destroyed during World War I (C), although Russia suffered larger losses in human life. And the huge increase in pig iron production was part of an industrial program (B), not an instrument of foreign policy.

179. **(D)** The 1920s were a mixture of both conservative and liberal trends. On the liberal side, women were granted the right to vote with the ratification in 1920 of the 19th Amendment to the Constitution. Both fashion and morality (A) took a liberal turn with hemlines going up, the braless look in vogue, and sexuality taking center stage in American movies and life. With new forms of credit and advertising, combined with increases in wages and productivity, consumerism became the new American ethic and many Americans borrowed money as never before to finance their newfound materialistic dreams (C). On the conservative side, Prohibition was enacted with the passage of the 18th Amendment in 1919 (B). Its enforcement began on a large scale in 1920, opening the door for bootlegging and the rise of

organized crime in America. The Ku Klux Klan (E), using new advertising techniques to market itself, reached a peak membership of 5 million people in 1925, before sex scandals, corruption, poor leadership, and public revulsion at Klan activities discredited its power base and broke it as a major political force. Through the mid-1920s, however, the Klan was a force to be feared and accommodated, and Klan activities had a very intimidating effect on local and regional politics in the South, Midwest, and mid-Atlantic regions of the country. The only choice not characteristic of the 1920s is massive union power and growth (D). While union power had begun to grow and take hold in some areas during the Progressivist period before World War I, it was eclipsed by the probusiness economic growth philosophies of Harding, Coolidge, Hoover, and the Republicans. Progressivist reforms were rolled back throughout the 1920s, negating many of the gains made in regulating businesses and securing labor rights at the federal level. Massive union power and growth would not return to the fore until the enactment of Franklin Roosevelt's "New Deal" in the late 1930s and early 1940s, when a combination of New Deal legislation, frustrated and angry workers, discredited management, and a reviving economy forced businesses to accept unions and negotiate with them more fairly.

180. **(B)** During the late 1940s, the United Nations urged its members to remove their diplomats from Spain (B). Franco's Fascist regime in Spain was to be isolated, in the hope that it would collapse. In 1951, the United States adopted a more benevolent policy toward Spain because of its perceived needs in the Cold War against the Soviet Union.

181. **(E)** Boccaccio's *Decameron* (A), Chaucer's *Canterbury Tales* (B), Thomas More's *Utopia* (C), and Erasmus's *Praise of Folly* (D) advanced themes which were clearly anticlerical. They were representative of the humanistic works of the day in which the misdeeds and abuses of the clergy were a popular theme. Thomas à Kempis's *The Imitation of Christ* (E) was a prayer book designed for meditation; it was approved by the Church.

182. **(E)** The English Chartist Movement was a radical political group, largely composed of workers and laborers, who agitated for political reform. Their list of demands, the "People's Charter," called for a secret ballot (I); universal male suffrage (II); equal electoral districts (III), which meant redistricting; annual Parliaments (IV); and salary payments for members of Parliament (V). With the exception of annual Parliaments, all of these reforms were implemented prior to the First World War. Both the Liberal and Conservative parties expressed support for some of the Chartist principles in the Reform Bills of 1867, 1884, and 1885.

183. **(A)** Harry Truman led the United States through one of the most difficult periods in its history. Despite the overwhelming victory in World War II that left the United States as the dominant economic and military power in the world, America faced a host of challenges to which there were no clear-cut solutions.

Truman's no-nonsense style, although sometimes effective, often lacked the subtlety necessary to deal with these problems. Organized labor (B) found itself at odds with Truman's antilabor stance throughout 1946 and 1947. When unions went on strike after World War II ended, Truman opposed the strikes and, combined with anti-union sentiment in Congress, effectively forced labor to back down. Even though labor, as a whole, supported Truman in the 1948 presidential election, it did so only because union leaders knew they would receive even less support from a Republican administration. Northern liberals (C), who generally supported the union move-ment, disagreed with Truman's labor policies as well as his fervent anti-Communist policies, which many felt had made American-Soviet problems worse than they had to be. Southern Democrats (D) resented Truman's efforts for price controls and his continued attempts to maintain the large role of the federal government created by the New Deal and World War II. They favored a smaller federal government that would return power to the state level. They also resented his support for civil rights as laid out in his "Fair Deal" proposals of the 1948 presidential election. The only support Truman received from Southern Democrats stemmed from their hostility toward every Republican dating back to the post–Civil War Reconstruction. Any Democrat, even Truman, was considered preferable to any Republican. Industry leaders often disliked Truman's policies because although he had taken antilabor stands on many issues, he did not go as far as they would have liked, and industrial leaders knew they would get more support from a Republican administration. Ur-ban ethnic groups (A), while not in agreement with Truman's policies, were more likely to support them than any of the other groups listed. Many came from coun-tries that were now under Soviet control and openly supported Truman's contain-ment doctrine. They also agreed with Truman's call for a higher minimum wage and increased aid to education, both of which would increase their own opportunities for economic advancement. Since many of the unions were dominated by white males, Truman's antiunion positions were not opposed by most urban ethnic groups. Also, since the New Deal had benefited many ethnic groups, most supported a continua-tion of New Deal–type reforms and the large federal role that went with it. Many of these groups had received no tangible help from state governments and had no desire to see power returned to the state level.

184. **(D)** Count Saint-Simon (A) advocated socialist concepts during the Restora-tion period in France until his death in 1827, but died before the "Liberal Regime." During the Liberal Regime of Louis Philippe (1830–48), radical economic and social plans were advanced by the Utopian socialists Charles Fourier (B), Louis Blanc (C), who is identified with the National Workshop Program, and Auguste Blanqui (D), and the anarchist journalist Pierre Joseph Proudhon (E), author of *What is Property?*

185. **(B)** The "Fifty Million Bill" was the appropriations bill named after the amount of money requested by McKinley to prepare the United States for war against Spain in 1898. It represented the imperialism that permeated the nation at the time and the sense of inevitability that went with it. Although McKinley (C)

requested the money and signed the bill, he disagreed with the prowar philosophy it represented. He, like Grover Cleveland (A) before him, was a staunch anti-imperialist and did everything he could to avoid war with Spain. He made the $50 million request only after every diplomatic alternative had failed. Woodrow Wilson (E) also shared this anti-imperialist philosophy. Although Wilson's administration often engaged in imperialistic activity in Central America, Wilson publicly renounced the "Big Stick" philosophy and "Dollar Diplomacy," and used military intervention only when he felt it was necessary to maintain order. While Taft (D) was more openly imperialistic, his "Dollar Diplomacy" philosophy focused on the use of money rather than military force to control Central America. While Taft did use the military when he felt it was necessary, he preferred diplomacy and economic persuasion whenever possible. Teddy Roosevelt's (B) "Big Stick" philosophy is the most similar to that represented by the Fifty Million Bill. He saw the United States as the policeman of the Americas and was much more openly imperialistic and much more willing to use force as a first rather than a last resort.

186. **(A)** Italian Renaissance art has been most appropriately described as neoclassicism in which the traditional characteristics of harmony and symmetry were valued (A). Italian Renaissance art was not a revolt against the classical style (B), the triumph of symbolism (E), a romantic idealism predicated upon notions of secular fantasy (D), nor characterized by the spectacular and the deliberately nonsymmetrical (C).

187. **(C)** While historians have debated this over the years, the bulk of the archaeological evidence and eyewitness testimony indicates that Custer's men did not panic; they attempted to form skirmish lines and mounted an organized defense. Their defeat resulted from the overwhelming numbers of Sioux attacking them on open ground where there was little defensive cover to protect them from the onslaught. Custer did disobey orders by attacking the Sioux encampment before reinforcements arrived (D). The original plan called for Custer and Terry to attack in concert, not for Custer's force to attack the main encampment by themselves. The 700 men in Custer's regiment were not nearly enough to defeat the 2,000 to 3,000 warriors estimated to have been in the camp at the time. In addition, Custer divided his men into three separate forces in an effort to surround the Sioux camp and attack it from several directions at once. Unfortunately, this left each force unable to support the other two forces if the Sioux fought back (A). Custer feared the Sioux would run at the first sight of a large force of soldiers, which is what they had done in most previous encounters. When his scouts informed him, inaccurately, that the Sioux had spotted his command, he hurried his attack, convinced that the Sioux would run away rather than fight. When he attacked, he found himself committed against a much larger encampment than he had envisioned, and his men were now hopelessly out of position to complete the attack (B). The latest archaeological digs at the battle site indicate that the Sioux were much better armed than anyone had previously realized, including the army or Custer (E). Many of them had repeating rifles which could fire more rapidly and were more reliable than the rifles issued to

the cavalrymen. When Custer led his 211 men into the Little Big Horn, he attacked a much larger and better-armed force than he anticipated, and he did so in a manner that left him isolated from the remaining two-thirds of his regiment and from other reinforcements who were still miles away. Despite what appears to have been an attempt at defense by his tiny command, they were probably wiped out in little more than thirty minutes of heavy fighting.

188. **(B)** Construed as an intellectual threat to the Church, early 16th century humanism maintained that the true source of authority within the Church was scripture (B). That position challenged the need for the Church as a continuing source of authority. Within the Church itself, the conciliar movement argued that the episcopal order of the Roman Catholic church should be altered (A) to challenge papal supremacy (E). The issue of the "New Science" (D) did not emerge until the next century. While there was considerable criticism of the Church and its failure to assist the poor (C), that did not constitute an intellectual threat to the Church.

189. **(C)** Edward Albee, who rose to prominence with *Who's Afraid of Virginia Woolf* (1962), became a master of post–World War II absurdist theater. The other playwrights were more influenced by pre–World War II currents of thought, and their works, like Albee's, derived their energy from a distaste for commercial theater and an interest in prevalent intellectual currents. The works of both O'Neill (E)—perhaps the most important of these playwrights—and Rice (B) showed the influence of Expressionism, Naturalism, and the contemporary currents in psychology. The works of Clifford Odets (D) showed the influence of experimental theater and the American leftism of the thirties. Anderson (A) fused such forms as the verse drama and the musical comedy satire with a modern sensibility.

190. **(D)** The infamous "three-fifths" rule (IV) was largely a concession to the South during the framing of the Constitution, and had to do with Congressional apportionment, not voting rights; slaves could not vote during colonial days, either. The concept of voting rights in colonial America largely resembled the British concept of basing voting rights on land ownership (III). The Land requirement—usually that the land must earn 40 shillings per annum—was easily met by most landowning males (I). Women were barred by statute from voting in only four colonies (V), but very few extant records show women actually voting at all. Voting rights often also formed along religious lines as well (II).

GRE History – Test 1
ANSWER SHEET

1. Ⓐ Ⓑ Ⓒ Ⓓ Ⓔ us	37. Ⓐ Ⓑ Ⓒ Ⓓ Ⓔ E	73. Ⓐ Ⓑ Ⓒ Ⓓ Ⓔ E
2. Ⓐ Ⓑ Ⓒ Ⓓ Ⓔ E	38. Ⓐ Ⓑ Ⓒ Ⓓ Ⓔ us	74. Ⓐ Ⓑ Ⓒ Ⓓ Ⓔ us
3. Ⓐ Ⓑ Ⓒ Ⓓ Ⓔ E	39. Ⓐ Ⓑ Ⓒ Ⓓ Ⓔ E	75. Ⓐ Ⓑ Ⓒ Ⓓ Ⓔ us
4. Ⓐ Ⓑ Ⓒ Ⓓ Ⓔ E	40. Ⓐ Ⓑ Ⓒ Ⓓ Ⓔ E	76. Ⓐ Ⓑ Ⓒ Ⓓ Ⓔ E
5. Ⓐ Ⓑ Ⓒ Ⓓ Ⓔ us	41. Ⓐ Ⓑ Ⓒ Ⓓ Ⓔ E	77. Ⓐ Ⓑ Ⓒ Ⓓ Ⓔ E
6. Ⓐ Ⓑ Ⓒ Ⓓ Ⓔ us	42. Ⓐ Ⓑ Ⓒ Ⓓ Ⓔ us	78. Ⓐ Ⓑ Ⓒ Ⓓ Ⓔ E
7. Ⓐ Ⓑ Ⓒ Ⓓ Ⓔ E	43. Ⓐ Ⓑ Ⓒ Ⓓ Ⓔ us	79. Ⓐ Ⓑ Ⓒ Ⓓ Ⓔ E
8. Ⓐ Ⓑ Ⓒ Ⓓ Ⓔ E	44. Ⓐ Ⓑ Ⓒ Ⓓ Ⓔ us	80. Ⓐ Ⓑ Ⓒ Ⓓ Ⓔ us
9. Ⓐ Ⓑ Ⓒ Ⓓ Ⓔ E	45. Ⓐ Ⓑ Ⓒ Ⓓ Ⓔ E	81. Ⓐ Ⓑ Ⓒ Ⓓ Ⓔ E
10. Ⓐ Ⓑ Ⓒ Ⓓ Ⓔ E	46. Ⓐ Ⓑ Ⓒ Ⓓ Ⓔ E	82. Ⓐ Ⓑ Ⓒ Ⓓ Ⓔ E
11. Ⓐ Ⓑ Ⓒ Ⓓ Ⓔ us	47. Ⓐ Ⓑ Ⓒ Ⓓ Ⓔ E	83. Ⓐ Ⓑ Ⓒ Ⓓ Ⓔ us
12. Ⓐ Ⓑ Ⓒ Ⓓ Ⓔ us	48. Ⓐ Ⓑ Ⓒ Ⓓ Ⓔ E	84. Ⓐ Ⓑ Ⓒ Ⓓ Ⓔ E
13. Ⓐ Ⓑ Ⓒ Ⓓ Ⓔ E	49. Ⓐ Ⓑ Ⓒ Ⓓ Ⓔ us	85. Ⓐ Ⓑ Ⓒ Ⓓ Ⓔ E
14. Ⓐ Ⓑ Ⓒ Ⓓ Ⓔ E	50. Ⓐ Ⓑ Ⓒ Ⓓ Ⓔ us	86. Ⓐ Ⓑ Ⓒ Ⓓ Ⓔ E
15. Ⓐ Ⓑ Ⓒ Ⓓ Ⓔ E	51. Ⓐ Ⓑ Ⓒ Ⓓ Ⓔ E	87. Ⓐ Ⓑ Ⓒ Ⓓ Ⓔ us
16. Ⓐ Ⓑ Ⓒ Ⓓ Ⓔ E	52. Ⓐ Ⓑ Ⓒ Ⓓ Ⓔ E	88. Ⓐ Ⓑ Ⓒ Ⓓ Ⓔ us
17. Ⓐ Ⓑ Ⓒ Ⓓ Ⓔ us	53. Ⓐ Ⓑ Ⓒ Ⓓ Ⓔ E	89. Ⓐ Ⓑ Ⓒ Ⓓ Ⓔ E
18. Ⓐ Ⓑ Ⓒ Ⓓ Ⓔ us	54. Ⓐ Ⓑ Ⓒ Ⓓ Ⓔ E	90. Ⓐ Ⓑ Ⓒ Ⓓ Ⓔ E
19. Ⓐ Ⓑ Ⓒ Ⓓ Ⓔ E	55. Ⓐ Ⓑ Ⓒ Ⓓ Ⓔ E	91. Ⓐ Ⓑ Ⓒ Ⓓ Ⓔ E
20. Ⓐ Ⓑ Ⓒ Ⓓ Ⓔ E	56. Ⓐ Ⓑ Ⓒ Ⓓ Ⓔ us	92. Ⓐ Ⓑ Ⓒ Ⓓ Ⓔ us
21. Ⓐ Ⓑ Ⓒ Ⓓ Ⓔ E	57. Ⓐ Ⓑ Ⓒ Ⓓ Ⓔ E	93. Ⓐ Ⓑ Ⓒ Ⓓ Ⓔ us
22. Ⓐ Ⓑ Ⓒ Ⓓ Ⓔ E	58. Ⓐ Ⓑ Ⓒ Ⓓ Ⓔ E	94. Ⓐ Ⓑ Ⓒ Ⓓ Ⓔ E
23. Ⓐ Ⓑ Ⓒ Ⓓ Ⓔ us	59. Ⓐ Ⓑ Ⓒ Ⓓ Ⓔ E	95. Ⓐ Ⓑ Ⓒ Ⓓ Ⓔ E
24. Ⓐ Ⓑ Ⓒ Ⓓ Ⓔ us	60. Ⓐ Ⓑ Ⓒ Ⓓ Ⓔ us	96. Ⓐ Ⓑ Ⓒ Ⓓ Ⓔ E
25. Ⓐ Ⓑ Ⓒ Ⓓ Ⓔ us	61. Ⓐ Ⓑ Ⓒ Ⓓ Ⓔ us	97. Ⓐ Ⓑ Ⓒ Ⓓ Ⓔ us
26. Ⓐ Ⓑ Ⓒ Ⓓ Ⓔ E	62. Ⓐ Ⓑ Ⓒ Ⓓ Ⓔ E	98. Ⓐ Ⓑ Ⓒ Ⓓ Ⓔ us
27. Ⓐ Ⓑ Ⓒ Ⓓ Ⓔ E	63. Ⓐ Ⓑ Ⓒ Ⓓ Ⓔ E	99. Ⓐ Ⓑ Ⓒ Ⓓ Ⓔ E
28. Ⓐ Ⓑ Ⓒ Ⓓ Ⓔ E	64. Ⓐ Ⓑ Ⓒ Ⓓ Ⓔ E	100. Ⓐ Ⓑ Ⓒ Ⓓ Ⓔ E
29. Ⓐ Ⓑ Ⓒ Ⓓ Ⓔ E	65. Ⓐ Ⓑ Ⓒ Ⓓ Ⓔ us	101. Ⓐ Ⓑ Ⓒ Ⓓ Ⓔ E
30. Ⓐ Ⓑ Ⓒ Ⓓ Ⓔ us	66. Ⓐ Ⓑ Ⓒ Ⓓ Ⓔ E	102. Ⓐ Ⓑ Ⓒ Ⓓ Ⓔ us
31. Ⓐ Ⓑ Ⓒ Ⓓ Ⓔ us	67. Ⓐ Ⓑ Ⓒ Ⓓ Ⓔ E	103. Ⓐ Ⓑ Ⓒ Ⓓ Ⓔ us
32. Ⓐ Ⓑ Ⓒ Ⓓ Ⓔ E	68. Ⓐ Ⓑ Ⓒ Ⓓ Ⓔ E	104. Ⓐ Ⓑ Ⓒ Ⓓ Ⓔ E
33. Ⓐ Ⓑ Ⓒ Ⓓ Ⓔ E	69. Ⓐ Ⓑ Ⓒ Ⓓ Ⓔ us	105. Ⓐ Ⓑ Ⓒ Ⓓ Ⓔ E
34. Ⓐ Ⓑ Ⓒ Ⓓ Ⓔ E	70. Ⓐ Ⓑ Ⓒ Ⓓ Ⓔ us	106. Ⓐ Ⓑ Ⓒ Ⓓ Ⓔ us
35. Ⓐ Ⓑ Ⓒ Ⓓ Ⓔ us	71. Ⓐ Ⓑ Ⓒ Ⓓ Ⓔ E	107. Ⓐ Ⓑ Ⓒ Ⓓ Ⓔ us
36. Ⓐ Ⓑ Ⓒ Ⓓ Ⓔ E	72. Ⓐ Ⓑ Ⓒ Ⓓ Ⓔ E	108. Ⓐ Ⓑ Ⓒ Ⓓ Ⓔ us

E = European History question   US = US History question

109. Ⓐ Ⓑ Ⓒ Ⓓ Ⓔ E	136. Ⓐ Ⓑ Ⓒ Ⓓ Ⓔ E	164. Ⓐ Ⓑ Ⓒ Ⓓ Ⓔ E
110. Ⓐ Ⓑ Ⓒ Ⓓ Ⓔ E	137. Ⓐ Ⓑ Ⓒ Ⓓ Ⓔ E	165. Ⓐ Ⓑ Ⓒ Ⓓ Ⓔ US
111. Ⓐ Ⓑ Ⓒ Ⓓ Ⓔ E	138. Ⓐ Ⓑ Ⓒ Ⓓ Ⓔ E	166. Ⓐ Ⓑ Ⓒ Ⓓ Ⓔ US
112. Ⓐ Ⓑ Ⓒ Ⓓ Ⓔ US	139. Ⓐ Ⓑ Ⓒ Ⓓ Ⓔ US	167. Ⓐ Ⓑ Ⓒ Ⓓ Ⓔ US
113. Ⓐ Ⓑ Ⓒ Ⓓ Ⓔ US	140. Ⓐ Ⓑ Ⓒ Ⓓ Ⓔ E	168. Ⓐ Ⓑ Ⓒ Ⓓ Ⓔ US
114. Ⓐ Ⓑ Ⓒ Ⓓ Ⓔ E	141. Ⓐ Ⓑ Ⓒ Ⓓ Ⓔ E	169. Ⓐ Ⓑ Ⓒ Ⓓ Ⓔ E
115. Ⓐ Ⓑ Ⓒ Ⓓ Ⓔ E	142. Ⓐ Ⓑ Ⓒ Ⓓ Ⓔ E	170. Ⓐ Ⓑ Ⓒ Ⓓ Ⓔ US
116. Ⓐ Ⓑ Ⓒ Ⓓ Ⓔ E	143. Ⓐ Ⓑ Ⓒ Ⓓ Ⓔ US	171. Ⓐ Ⓑ Ⓒ Ⓓ Ⓔ US
117. Ⓐ Ⓑ Ⓒ Ⓓ Ⓔ E	144. Ⓐ Ⓑ Ⓒ Ⓓ Ⓔ US	172. Ⓐ Ⓑ Ⓒ Ⓓ Ⓔ US
118. Ⓐ Ⓑ Ⓒ Ⓓ Ⓔ US	145. Ⓐ Ⓑ Ⓒ Ⓓ Ⓔ E	173. Ⓐ Ⓑ Ⓒ Ⓓ Ⓔ E
119. Ⓐ Ⓑ Ⓒ Ⓓ Ⓔ US	146. Ⓐ Ⓑ Ⓒ Ⓓ Ⓔ E	174. Ⓐ Ⓑ Ⓒ Ⓓ Ⓔ US
120. Ⓐ Ⓑ Ⓒ Ⓓ Ⓔ E	147. Ⓐ Ⓑ Ⓒ Ⓓ Ⓔ E	175. Ⓐ Ⓑ Ⓒ Ⓓ Ⓔ US
121. Ⓐ Ⓑ Ⓒ Ⓓ Ⓔ E	148. Ⓐ Ⓑ Ⓒ Ⓓ Ⓔ E	176. Ⓐ Ⓑ Ⓒ Ⓓ Ⓔ E
122. Ⓐ Ⓑ Ⓒ Ⓓ Ⓔ E	149. Ⓐ Ⓑ Ⓒ Ⓓ Ⓔ US	177. Ⓐ Ⓑ Ⓒ Ⓓ Ⓔ E
123. Ⓐ Ⓑ Ⓒ Ⓓ Ⓔ E	150. Ⓐ Ⓑ Ⓒ Ⓓ Ⓔ US	178. Ⓐ Ⓑ Ⓒ Ⓓ Ⓔ US
124. Ⓐ Ⓑ Ⓒ Ⓓ Ⓔ US	151. Ⓐ Ⓑ Ⓒ Ⓓ Ⓔ E	179. Ⓐ Ⓑ Ⓒ Ⓓ Ⓔ US
125. Ⓐ Ⓑ Ⓒ Ⓓ Ⓔ US	152. Ⓐ Ⓑ Ⓒ Ⓓ Ⓔ E	180. Ⓐ Ⓑ Ⓒ Ⓓ Ⓔ US
126. Ⓐ Ⓑ Ⓒ Ⓓ Ⓔ US	153. Ⓐ Ⓑ Ⓒ Ⓓ Ⓔ US	181. Ⓐ Ⓑ Ⓒ Ⓓ Ⓔ E
127. Ⓐ Ⓑ Ⓒ Ⓓ Ⓔ US	154. Ⓐ Ⓑ Ⓒ Ⓓ Ⓔ US	182. Ⓐ Ⓑ Ⓒ Ⓓ Ⓔ E
128. Ⓐ Ⓑ Ⓒ Ⓓ Ⓔ E	155. Ⓐ Ⓑ Ⓒ Ⓓ Ⓔ E	183. Ⓐ Ⓑ Ⓒ Ⓓ Ⓔ US
129. Ⓐ Ⓑ Ⓒ Ⓓ Ⓔ E	156. Ⓐ Ⓑ Ⓒ Ⓓ Ⓔ E	184. Ⓐ Ⓑ Ⓒ Ⓓ Ⓔ US
130. Ⓐ Ⓑ Ⓒ Ⓓ Ⓔ E	157. Ⓐ Ⓑ Ⓒ Ⓓ Ⓔ US	185. Ⓐ Ⓑ Ⓒ Ⓓ Ⓔ US
131. Ⓐ Ⓑ Ⓒ Ⓓ Ⓔ E	158. Ⓐ Ⓑ Ⓒ Ⓓ Ⓔ US	186. Ⓐ Ⓑ Ⓒ Ⓓ Ⓔ E
132. Ⓐ Ⓑ Ⓒ Ⓓ Ⓔ US	159. Ⓐ Ⓑ Ⓒ Ⓓ Ⓔ E	187. Ⓐ Ⓑ Ⓒ Ⓓ Ⓔ E
133. Ⓐ Ⓑ Ⓒ Ⓓ Ⓔ US	160. Ⓐ Ⓑ Ⓒ Ⓓ Ⓔ E	188. Ⓐ Ⓑ Ⓒ Ⓓ Ⓔ E
134. Ⓐ Ⓑ Ⓒ Ⓓ Ⓔ US	161. Ⓐ Ⓑ Ⓒ Ⓓ Ⓔ US	189. Ⓐ Ⓑ Ⓒ Ⓓ Ⓔ US
135. Ⓐ Ⓑ Ⓒ Ⓓ Ⓔ E	162. Ⓐ Ⓑ Ⓒ Ⓓ Ⓔ US	190. Ⓐ Ⓑ Ⓒ Ⓓ Ⓔ US
	163. Ⓐ Ⓑ Ⓒ Ⓓ Ⓔ US	

GRE History – Test 2
ANSWER SHEET

1. Ⓐ Ⓑ Ⓒ Ⓓ Ⓔ US	37. Ⓐ Ⓑ Ⓒ Ⓓ Ⓔ E	73. Ⓐ Ⓑ Ⓒ Ⓓ Ⓔ E
2. Ⓐ Ⓑ Ⓒ Ⓓ Ⓔ E	38. Ⓐ Ⓑ Ⓒ Ⓓ Ⓔ US	74. Ⓐ Ⓑ Ⓒ Ⓓ Ⓔ E
3. Ⓐ Ⓑ Ⓒ Ⓓ Ⓔ E	39. Ⓐ Ⓑ Ⓒ Ⓓ Ⓔ US	75. Ⓐ Ⓑ Ⓒ Ⓓ Ⓔ E
4. Ⓐ Ⓑ Ⓒ Ⓓ Ⓔ US	40. Ⓐ Ⓑ Ⓒ Ⓓ Ⓔ E	76. Ⓐ Ⓑ Ⓒ Ⓓ Ⓔ US
5. Ⓐ Ⓑ Ⓒ Ⓓ Ⓔ US	41. Ⓐ Ⓑ Ⓒ Ⓓ Ⓔ US	77. Ⓐ Ⓑ Ⓒ Ⓓ Ⓔ US
6. Ⓐ Ⓑ Ⓒ Ⓓ Ⓔ E	42. Ⓐ Ⓑ Ⓒ Ⓓ Ⓔ US	78. Ⓐ Ⓑ Ⓒ Ⓓ Ⓔ US
7. Ⓐ Ⓑ Ⓒ Ⓓ Ⓔ E	43. Ⓐ Ⓑ Ⓒ Ⓓ Ⓔ US	79. Ⓐ Ⓑ Ⓒ Ⓓ Ⓔ E
8. Ⓐ Ⓑ Ⓒ Ⓓ Ⓔ E	44. Ⓐ Ⓑ Ⓒ Ⓓ Ⓔ E	80. Ⓐ Ⓑ Ⓒ Ⓓ Ⓔ E
9. Ⓐ Ⓑ Ⓒ Ⓓ Ⓔ US	45. Ⓐ Ⓑ Ⓒ Ⓓ Ⓔ US	81. Ⓐ Ⓑ Ⓒ Ⓓ Ⓔ E
10. Ⓐ Ⓑ Ⓒ Ⓓ Ⓔ US	46. Ⓐ Ⓑ Ⓒ Ⓓ Ⓔ E	82. Ⓐ Ⓑ Ⓒ Ⓓ Ⓔ E
11. Ⓐ Ⓑ Ⓒ Ⓓ Ⓔ E	47. Ⓐ Ⓑ Ⓒ Ⓓ Ⓔ E	83. Ⓐ Ⓑ Ⓒ Ⓓ Ⓔ US
12. Ⓐ Ⓑ Ⓒ Ⓓ Ⓔ E	48. Ⓐ Ⓑ Ⓒ Ⓓ Ⓔ E	84. Ⓐ Ⓑ Ⓒ Ⓓ Ⓔ E
13. Ⓐ Ⓑ Ⓒ Ⓓ Ⓔ E	49. Ⓐ Ⓑ Ⓒ Ⓓ Ⓔ US	85. Ⓐ Ⓑ Ⓒ Ⓓ Ⓔ E
14. Ⓐ Ⓑ Ⓒ Ⓓ Ⓔ US	50. Ⓐ Ⓑ Ⓒ Ⓓ Ⓔ US	86. Ⓐ Ⓑ Ⓒ Ⓓ Ⓔ US
15. Ⓐ Ⓑ Ⓒ Ⓓ Ⓔ US	51. Ⓐ Ⓑ Ⓒ Ⓓ Ⓔ E	87. Ⓐ Ⓑ Ⓒ Ⓓ Ⓔ US
16. Ⓐ Ⓑ Ⓒ Ⓓ Ⓔ US	52. Ⓐ Ⓑ Ⓒ Ⓓ Ⓔ US	88. Ⓐ Ⓑ Ⓒ Ⓓ Ⓔ E
17. Ⓐ Ⓑ Ⓒ Ⓓ Ⓔ E	53. Ⓐ Ⓑ Ⓒ Ⓓ Ⓔ E	89. Ⓐ Ⓑ Ⓒ Ⓓ Ⓔ E
18. Ⓐ Ⓑ Ⓒ Ⓓ Ⓔ E	54. Ⓐ Ⓑ Ⓒ Ⓓ Ⓔ E	90. Ⓐ Ⓑ Ⓒ Ⓓ Ⓔ US
19. Ⓐ Ⓑ Ⓒ Ⓓ Ⓔ E	55. Ⓐ Ⓑ Ⓒ Ⓓ Ⓔ US	91. Ⓐ Ⓑ Ⓒ Ⓓ Ⓔ E
20. Ⓐ Ⓑ Ⓒ Ⓓ Ⓔ E	56. Ⓐ Ⓑ Ⓒ Ⓓ Ⓔ E	92. Ⓐ Ⓑ Ⓒ Ⓓ Ⓔ E
21. Ⓐ Ⓑ Ⓒ Ⓓ Ⓔ US	57. Ⓐ Ⓑ Ⓒ Ⓓ Ⓔ E	93. Ⓐ Ⓑ Ⓒ Ⓓ Ⓔ US
22. Ⓐ Ⓑ Ⓒ Ⓓ Ⓔ US	58. Ⓐ Ⓑ Ⓒ Ⓓ Ⓔ US	94. Ⓐ Ⓑ Ⓒ Ⓓ Ⓔ US
23. Ⓐ Ⓑ Ⓒ Ⓓ Ⓔ E	59. Ⓐ Ⓑ Ⓒ Ⓓ Ⓔ US	95. Ⓐ Ⓑ Ⓒ Ⓓ Ⓔ E
24. Ⓐ Ⓑ Ⓒ Ⓓ Ⓔ E	60. Ⓐ Ⓑ Ⓒ Ⓓ Ⓔ E	96. Ⓐ Ⓑ Ⓒ Ⓓ Ⓔ E
25. Ⓐ Ⓑ Ⓒ Ⓓ Ⓔ US	61. Ⓐ Ⓑ Ⓒ Ⓓ Ⓔ E	97. Ⓐ Ⓑ Ⓒ Ⓓ Ⓔ E
26. Ⓐ Ⓑ Ⓒ Ⓓ Ⓔ E	62. Ⓐ Ⓑ Ⓒ Ⓓ Ⓔ E	98. Ⓐ Ⓑ Ⓒ Ⓓ Ⓔ E
27. Ⓐ Ⓑ Ⓒ Ⓓ Ⓔ E	63. Ⓐ Ⓑ Ⓒ Ⓓ Ⓔ US	99. Ⓐ Ⓑ Ⓒ Ⓓ Ⓔ US
28. Ⓐ Ⓑ Ⓒ Ⓓ Ⓔ US	64. Ⓐ Ⓑ Ⓒ Ⓓ Ⓔ E	100. Ⓐ Ⓑ Ⓒ Ⓓ Ⓔ E
29. Ⓐ Ⓑ Ⓒ Ⓓ Ⓔ US	65. Ⓐ Ⓑ Ⓒ Ⓓ Ⓔ E	101. Ⓐ Ⓑ Ⓒ Ⓓ Ⓔ E
30. Ⓐ Ⓑ Ⓒ Ⓓ Ⓔ E	66. Ⓐ Ⓑ Ⓒ Ⓓ Ⓔ E	102. Ⓐ Ⓑ Ⓒ Ⓓ Ⓔ E
31. Ⓐ Ⓑ Ⓒ Ⓓ Ⓔ E	67. Ⓐ Ⓑ Ⓒ Ⓓ Ⓔ E	103. Ⓐ Ⓑ Ⓒ Ⓓ Ⓔ US
32. Ⓐ Ⓑ Ⓒ Ⓓ Ⓔ US	68. Ⓐ Ⓑ Ⓒ Ⓓ Ⓔ US	104. Ⓐ Ⓑ Ⓒ Ⓓ Ⓔ E
33. Ⓐ Ⓑ Ⓒ Ⓓ Ⓔ E	69. Ⓐ Ⓑ Ⓒ Ⓓ Ⓔ E	105. Ⓐ Ⓑ Ⓒ Ⓓ Ⓔ E
34. Ⓐ Ⓑ Ⓒ Ⓓ Ⓔ E	70. Ⓐ Ⓑ Ⓒ Ⓓ Ⓔ E	106. Ⓐ Ⓑ Ⓒ Ⓓ Ⓔ US
35. Ⓐ Ⓑ Ⓒ Ⓓ Ⓔ US	71. Ⓐ Ⓑ Ⓒ Ⓓ Ⓔ US	107. Ⓐ Ⓑ Ⓒ Ⓓ Ⓔ E
36. Ⓐ Ⓑ Ⓒ Ⓓ Ⓔ E	72. Ⓐ Ⓑ Ⓒ Ⓓ Ⓔ US	108. Ⓐ Ⓑ Ⓒ Ⓓ Ⓔ E

E = European History question   US = US History question

109. Ⓐ Ⓑ Ⓒ Ⓓ Ⓔ US	136. Ⓐ Ⓑ Ⓒ Ⓓ Ⓔ E	164. Ⓐ Ⓑ Ⓒ Ⓓ Ⓔ E
110. Ⓐ Ⓑ Ⓒ Ⓓ Ⓔ US	137. Ⓐ Ⓑ Ⓒ Ⓓ Ⓔ E	165. Ⓐ Ⓑ Ⓒ Ⓓ Ⓔ E
111. Ⓐ Ⓑ Ⓒ Ⓓ Ⓔ US	138. Ⓐ Ⓑ Ⓒ Ⓓ Ⓔ US	166. Ⓐ Ⓑ Ⓒ Ⓓ Ⓔ E
112. Ⓐ Ⓑ Ⓒ Ⓓ Ⓔ US	139. Ⓐ Ⓑ Ⓒ Ⓓ Ⓔ US	167. Ⓐ Ⓑ Ⓒ Ⓓ Ⓔ E
113. Ⓐ Ⓑ Ⓒ Ⓓ Ⓔ E	140. Ⓐ Ⓑ Ⓒ Ⓓ Ⓔ E	168. Ⓐ Ⓑ Ⓒ Ⓓ Ⓔ US
114. Ⓐ Ⓑ Ⓒ Ⓓ Ⓔ E	141. Ⓐ Ⓑ Ⓒ Ⓓ Ⓔ E	169. Ⓐ Ⓑ Ⓒ Ⓓ Ⓔ E
115. Ⓐ Ⓑ Ⓒ Ⓓ Ⓔ E	142. Ⓐ Ⓑ Ⓒ Ⓓ Ⓔ E	170. Ⓐ Ⓑ Ⓒ Ⓓ Ⓔ E
116. Ⓐ Ⓑ Ⓒ Ⓓ Ⓔ US	143. Ⓐ Ⓑ Ⓒ Ⓓ Ⓔ E	171. Ⓐ Ⓑ Ⓒ Ⓓ Ⓔ E
117. Ⓐ Ⓑ Ⓒ Ⓓ Ⓔ US	144. Ⓐ Ⓑ Ⓒ Ⓓ Ⓔ US	172. Ⓐ Ⓑ Ⓒ Ⓓ Ⓔ E
118. Ⓐ Ⓑ Ⓒ Ⓓ Ⓔ E	145. Ⓐ Ⓑ Ⓒ Ⓓ Ⓔ E	173. Ⓐ Ⓑ Ⓒ Ⓓ Ⓔ E
119. Ⓐ Ⓑ Ⓒ Ⓓ Ⓔ E	146. Ⓐ Ⓑ Ⓒ Ⓓ Ⓔ E	174. Ⓐ Ⓑ Ⓒ Ⓓ Ⓔ US
120. Ⓐ Ⓑ Ⓒ Ⓓ Ⓔ E	147. Ⓐ Ⓑ Ⓒ Ⓓ Ⓔ E	175. Ⓐ Ⓑ Ⓒ Ⓓ Ⓔ E
121. Ⓐ Ⓑ Ⓒ Ⓓ Ⓔ E	148. Ⓐ Ⓑ Ⓒ Ⓓ Ⓔ US	176. Ⓐ Ⓑ Ⓒ Ⓓ Ⓔ E
122. Ⓐ Ⓑ Ⓒ Ⓓ Ⓔ US	149. Ⓐ Ⓑ Ⓒ Ⓓ Ⓔ E	177. Ⓐ Ⓑ Ⓒ Ⓓ Ⓔ E
123. Ⓐ Ⓑ Ⓒ Ⓓ Ⓔ US	150. Ⓐ Ⓑ Ⓒ Ⓓ Ⓔ E	178. Ⓐ Ⓑ Ⓒ Ⓓ Ⓔ E
124. Ⓐ Ⓑ Ⓒ Ⓓ Ⓔ E	151. Ⓐ Ⓑ Ⓒ Ⓓ Ⓔ E	179. Ⓐ Ⓑ Ⓒ Ⓓ Ⓔ E
125. Ⓐ Ⓑ Ⓒ Ⓓ Ⓔ E	152. Ⓐ Ⓑ Ⓒ Ⓓ Ⓔ US	180. Ⓐ Ⓑ Ⓒ Ⓓ Ⓔ US
126. Ⓐ Ⓑ Ⓒ Ⓓ Ⓔ E	153. Ⓐ Ⓑ Ⓒ Ⓓ Ⓔ E	181. Ⓐ Ⓑ Ⓒ Ⓓ Ⓔ E
127. Ⓐ Ⓑ Ⓒ Ⓓ Ⓔ US	154. Ⓐ Ⓑ Ⓒ Ⓓ Ⓔ E	182. Ⓐ Ⓑ Ⓒ Ⓓ Ⓔ E
128. Ⓐ Ⓑ Ⓒ Ⓓ Ⓔ US	155. Ⓐ Ⓑ Ⓒ Ⓓ Ⓔ E	183. Ⓐ Ⓑ Ⓒ Ⓓ Ⓔ E
129. Ⓐ Ⓑ Ⓒ Ⓓ Ⓔ US	156. Ⓐ Ⓑ Ⓒ Ⓓ Ⓔ US	184. Ⓐ Ⓑ Ⓒ Ⓓ Ⓔ E
130. Ⓐ Ⓑ Ⓒ Ⓓ Ⓔ E	157. Ⓐ Ⓑ Ⓒ Ⓓ Ⓔ US	185. Ⓐ Ⓑ Ⓒ Ⓓ Ⓔ US
131. Ⓐ Ⓑ Ⓒ Ⓓ Ⓔ E	158. Ⓐ Ⓑ Ⓒ Ⓓ Ⓔ E	186. Ⓐ Ⓑ Ⓒ Ⓓ Ⓔ E
132. Ⓐ Ⓑ Ⓒ Ⓓ Ⓔ E	159. Ⓐ Ⓑ Ⓒ Ⓓ Ⓔ E	187. Ⓐ Ⓑ Ⓒ Ⓓ Ⓔ E
133. Ⓐ Ⓑ Ⓒ Ⓓ Ⓔ US	160. Ⓐ Ⓑ Ⓒ Ⓓ Ⓔ E	188. Ⓐ Ⓑ Ⓒ Ⓓ Ⓔ E
134. Ⓐ Ⓑ Ⓒ Ⓓ Ⓔ US	161. Ⓐ Ⓑ Ⓒ Ⓓ Ⓔ E	189. Ⓐ Ⓑ Ⓒ Ⓓ Ⓔ E
135. Ⓐ Ⓑ Ⓒ Ⓓ Ⓔ E	162. Ⓐ Ⓑ Ⓒ Ⓓ Ⓔ E	190. Ⓐ Ⓑ Ⓒ Ⓓ Ⓔ E
	163. Ⓐ Ⓑ Ⓒ Ⓓ Ⓔ US	

GRE History – Test 3
ANSWER SHEET

1. (A) (B) (C) (D) (E) E	37. (A) (B) (C) (D) (E) E	73. (A) (B) (C) (D) (E) US
2. (A) (B) (C) (D) (E) E	38. (A) (B) (C) (D) (E) E	74. (A) (B) (C) (D) (E) US
3. (A) (B) (C) (D) (E) E	39. (A) (B) (C) (D) (E) US	75. (A) (B) (C) (D) (E) US
4. (A) (B) (C) (D) (E) US	40. (A) (B) (C) (D) (E) E	76. (A) (B) (C) (D) (E) E
5. (A) (B) (C) (D) (E) E	41. (A) (B) (C) (D) (E) US	77. (A) (B) (C) (D) (E) E
6. (A) (B) (C) (D) (E) E	42. (A) (B) (C) (D) (E) US	78. (A) (B) (C) (D) (E) E
7. (A) (B) (C) (D) (E) E	43. (A) (B) (C) (D) (E) US	79. (A) (B) (C) (D) (E) E
8. (A) (B) (C) (D) (E) E	44. (A) (B) (C) (D) (E) E	80. (A) (B) (C) (D) (E) US
9. (A) (B) (C) (D) (E) US	45. (A) (B) (C) (D) (E) E	81. (A) (B) (C) (D) (E) E
10. (A) (B) (C) (D) (E) E	46. (A) (B) (C) (D) (E) E	82. (A) (B) (C) (D) (E) E
11. (A) (B) (C) (D) (E) US	47. (A) (B) (C) (D) (E) E	83. (A) (B) (C) (D) (E) E
12. (A) (B) (C) (D) (E) US	48. (A) (B) (C) (D) (E) US	84. (A) (B) (C) (D) (E) E
13. (A) (B) (C) (D) (E) E	49. (A) (B) (C) (D) (E) E	85. (A) (B) (C) (D) (E) US
14. (A) (B) (C) (D) (E) E	50. (A) (B) (C) (D) (E) E	86. (A) (B) (C) (D) (E) US
15. (A) (B) (C) (D) (E) US	51. (A) (B) (C) (D) (E) US	87. (A) (B) (C) (D) (E) E
16. (A) (B) (C) (D) (E) US	52. (A) (B) (C) (D) (E) E	88. (A) (B) (C) (D) (E) E
17. (A) (B) (C) (D) (E) US	53. (A) (B) (C) (D) (E) US	89. (A) (B) (C) (D) (E) E
18. (A) (B) (C) (D) (E) E	54. (A) (B) (C) (D) (E) US	90. (A) (B) (C) (D) (E) E
19. (A) (B) (C) (D) (E) E	55. (A) (B) (C) (D) (E) US	91. (A) (B) (C) (D) (E) US
20. (A) (B) (C) (D) (E) E	56. (A) (B) (C) (D) (E) E	92. (A) (B) (C) (D) (E) E
21. (A) (B) (C) (D) (E) E	57. (A) (B) (C) (D) (E) E	93. (A) (B) (C) (D) (E) US
22. (A) (B) (C) (D) (E) US	58. (A) (B) (C) (D) (E) US	94. (A) (B) (C) (D) (E) US
23. (A) (B) (C) (D) (E) E	59. (A) (B) (C) (D) (E) E	95. (A) (B) (C) (D) (E) E
24. (A) (B) (C) (D) (E) E	60. (A) (B) (C) (D) (E) E	96. (A) (B) (C) (D) (E) E
25. (A) (B) (C) (D) (E) E	61. (A) (B) (C) (D) (E) E	97. (A) (B) (C) (D) (E) E
26. (A) (B) (C) (D) (E) US	62. (A) (B) (C) (D) (E) US	98. (A) (B) (C) (D) (E) E
27. (A) (B) (C) (D) (E) US	63. (A) (B) (C) (D) (E) US	99. (A) (B) (C) (D) (E) US
28. (A) (B) (C) (D) (E) E	64. (A) (B) (C) (D) (E) E	100. (A) (B) (C) (D) (E) E
29. (A) (B) (C) (D) (E) US	65. (A) (B) (C) (D) (E) E	101. (A) (B) (C) (D) (E) E
30. (A) (B) (C) (D) (E) US	66. (A) (B) (C) (D) (E) E	102. (A) (B) (C) (D) (E) E
31. (A) (B) (C) (D) (E) E	67. (A) (B) (C) (D) (E) US	103. (A) (B) (C) (D) (E) E
32. (A) (B) (C) (D) (E) E	68. (A) (B) (C) (D) (E) E	104. (A) (B) (C) (D) (E) US
33. (A) (B) (C) (D) (E) E	69. (A) (B) (C) (D) (E) E	105. (A) (B) (C) (D) (E) E
34. (A) (B) (C) (D) (E) E	70. (A) (B) (C) (D) (E) US	106. (A) (B) (C) (D) (E) US
35. (A) (B) (C) (D) (E) US	71. (A) (B) (C) (D) (E) US	107. (A) (B) (C) (D) (E) US
36. (A) (B) (C) (D) (E) E	72. (A) (B) (C) (D) (E) E	108. (A) (B) (C) (D) (E) US

E = European History question   US = US History question

109. Ⓐ Ⓑ Ⓒ Ⓓ Ⓔ E	136. Ⓐ Ⓑ Ⓒ Ⓓ Ⓔ E	164. Ⓐ Ⓑ Ⓒ Ⓓ Ⓔ E
110. Ⓐ Ⓑ Ⓒ Ⓓ Ⓔ E	137. Ⓐ Ⓑ Ⓒ Ⓓ Ⓔ E	165. Ⓐ Ⓑ Ⓒ Ⓓ Ⓔ E
111. Ⓐ Ⓑ Ⓒ Ⓓ Ⓔ E	138. Ⓐ Ⓑ Ⓒ Ⓓ Ⓔ E	166. Ⓐ Ⓑ Ⓒ Ⓓ Ⓔ US
112. Ⓐ Ⓑ Ⓒ Ⓓ Ⓔ E	139. Ⓐ Ⓑ Ⓒ Ⓓ Ⓔ US	167. Ⓐ Ⓑ Ⓒ Ⓓ Ⓔ US
113. Ⓐ Ⓑ Ⓒ Ⓓ Ⓔ US	140. Ⓐ Ⓑ Ⓒ Ⓓ Ⓔ E	168. Ⓐ Ⓑ Ⓒ Ⓓ Ⓔ E
114. Ⓐ Ⓑ Ⓒ Ⓓ Ⓔ US	141. Ⓐ Ⓑ Ⓒ Ⓓ Ⓔ US	169. Ⓐ Ⓑ Ⓒ Ⓓ Ⓔ US
115. Ⓐ Ⓑ Ⓒ Ⓓ Ⓔ US	142. Ⓐ Ⓑ Ⓒ Ⓓ Ⓔ US	170. Ⓐ Ⓑ Ⓒ Ⓓ Ⓔ E
116. Ⓐ Ⓑ Ⓒ Ⓓ Ⓔ E	143. Ⓐ Ⓑ Ⓒ Ⓓ Ⓔ E	171. Ⓐ Ⓑ Ⓒ Ⓓ Ⓔ E
117. Ⓐ Ⓑ Ⓒ Ⓓ Ⓔ E	144. Ⓐ Ⓑ Ⓒ Ⓓ Ⓔ US	172. Ⓐ Ⓑ Ⓒ Ⓓ Ⓔ E
118. Ⓐ Ⓑ Ⓒ Ⓓ Ⓔ US	145. Ⓐ Ⓑ Ⓒ Ⓓ Ⓔ US	173. Ⓐ Ⓑ Ⓒ Ⓓ Ⓔ US
119. Ⓐ Ⓑ Ⓒ Ⓓ Ⓔ US	146. Ⓐ Ⓑ Ⓒ Ⓓ Ⓔ E	174. Ⓐ Ⓑ Ⓒ Ⓓ Ⓔ US
120. Ⓐ Ⓑ Ⓒ Ⓓ Ⓔ E	147. Ⓐ Ⓑ Ⓒ Ⓓ Ⓔ US	175. Ⓐ Ⓑ Ⓒ Ⓓ Ⓔ E
121. Ⓐ Ⓑ Ⓒ Ⓓ Ⓔ E	148. Ⓐ Ⓑ Ⓒ Ⓓ Ⓔ E	176. Ⓐ Ⓑ Ⓒ Ⓓ Ⓔ E
122. Ⓐ Ⓑ Ⓒ Ⓓ Ⓔ E	149. Ⓐ Ⓑ Ⓒ Ⓓ Ⓔ E	177. Ⓐ Ⓑ Ⓒ Ⓓ Ⓔ E
123. Ⓐ Ⓑ Ⓒ Ⓓ Ⓔ US	150. Ⓐ Ⓑ Ⓒ Ⓓ Ⓔ E	178. Ⓐ Ⓑ Ⓒ Ⓓ Ⓔ E
124. Ⓐ Ⓑ Ⓒ Ⓓ Ⓔ E	151. Ⓐ Ⓑ Ⓒ Ⓓ Ⓔ E	179. Ⓐ Ⓑ Ⓒ Ⓓ Ⓔ US
125. Ⓐ Ⓑ Ⓒ Ⓓ Ⓔ US	152. Ⓐ Ⓑ Ⓒ Ⓓ Ⓔ E	180. Ⓐ Ⓑ Ⓒ Ⓓ Ⓔ E
126. Ⓐ Ⓑ Ⓒ Ⓓ Ⓔ E	153. Ⓐ Ⓑ Ⓒ Ⓓ Ⓔ US	181. Ⓐ Ⓑ Ⓒ Ⓓ Ⓔ E
127. Ⓐ Ⓑ Ⓒ Ⓓ Ⓔ US	154. Ⓐ Ⓑ Ⓒ Ⓓ Ⓔ US	182. Ⓐ Ⓑ Ⓒ Ⓓ Ⓔ E
128. Ⓐ Ⓑ Ⓒ Ⓓ Ⓔ US	155. Ⓐ Ⓑ Ⓒ Ⓓ Ⓔ US	183. Ⓐ Ⓑ Ⓒ Ⓓ Ⓔ US
129. Ⓐ Ⓑ Ⓒ Ⓓ Ⓔ US	156. Ⓐ Ⓑ Ⓒ Ⓓ Ⓔ E	184. Ⓐ Ⓑ Ⓒ Ⓓ Ⓔ E
130. Ⓐ Ⓑ Ⓒ Ⓓ Ⓔ E	157. Ⓐ Ⓑ Ⓒ Ⓓ Ⓔ US	185. Ⓐ Ⓑ Ⓒ Ⓓ Ⓔ US
131. Ⓐ Ⓑ Ⓒ Ⓓ Ⓔ E	158. Ⓐ Ⓑ Ⓒ Ⓓ Ⓔ E	186. Ⓐ Ⓑ Ⓒ Ⓓ Ⓔ E
132. Ⓐ Ⓑ Ⓒ Ⓓ Ⓔ US	159. Ⓐ Ⓑ Ⓒ Ⓓ Ⓔ E	187. Ⓐ Ⓑ Ⓒ Ⓓ Ⓔ US
133. Ⓐ Ⓑ Ⓒ Ⓓ Ⓔ E	160. Ⓐ Ⓑ Ⓒ Ⓓ Ⓔ E	188. Ⓐ Ⓑ Ⓒ Ⓓ Ⓔ E
134. Ⓐ Ⓑ Ⓒ Ⓓ Ⓔ E	161. Ⓐ Ⓑ Ⓒ Ⓓ Ⓔ US	189. Ⓐ Ⓑ Ⓒ Ⓓ Ⓔ US
135. Ⓐ Ⓑ Ⓒ Ⓓ Ⓔ US	162. Ⓐ Ⓑ Ⓒ Ⓓ Ⓔ E	190. Ⓐ Ⓑ Ⓒ Ⓓ Ⓔ US
	163. Ⓐ Ⓑ Ⓒ Ⓓ Ⓔ US	